Intersectionality and Women's Access to Justice in Africa

Gender and Sexuality in Africa and the Diaspora

***Series Editors*:** Besi Brillian Muhonja (James Madison University) and Babacar M'Baye (Kent State University)

Gender and Sexuality in Africa and the Diaspora publishes innovative interdisciplinary research on intersections of gender, sexuality, and other political, social, economic, cultural, and geographic identity markers. The series has particular interest in groundbreaking scholarship on herstories/histories, elements and politics of gender and sexuality that center critical African and African Diaspora thought and philosophies within global contemporary theoretical debates across the disciplines.

Recent Titles in the Series:

Intersectionality and Women's Access to Justice in Africa edited by J. Jarpa Dawuni
Gender and Sexuality in Kenyan Societies: Centering the Human and the Humane in Critical Studies edited by Besi Brillian Muhonja and Babacar M'Baye
Gender and Sexuality in Ghanaian Societies edited by Martha Donkor and Amoaba Gooden
Cabo Verdean Women Writing Remembrance, Resistance, and Revolution: Kriolas Poderozas edited by Terza A. Silva Lima-Neves and Aminah Fernandes Pilgrim
Gender and Education in Kenya edited by Esther Mukewa Lisanza
Women and the Nigeria-Biafra War: Reframing Gender and Conflict in Africa edited by Gloria Chuku and Sussie Okoro
Gender and Sexuality in Senegalese Societies edited by Babacar M'Baye and Besi Brillian Muhonja
Child Rape in Ghana: Lifting the Veil by Martha Donkor

Intersectionality and Women's Access to Justice in Africa

Edited by
J. Jarpa Dawuni

Foreword by
Julia Sebutinde

LEXINGTON BOOKS
Lanham • Boulder • New York • London

Published by Lexington Books
An imprint of The Rowman & Littlefield Publishing Group, Inc.
4501 Forbes Boulevard, Suite 200, Lanham, Maryland 20706
www.rowman.com

86-90 Paul Street, London EC2A 4NE

British Library Cataloguing in Publication Information Available

Library of Congress Cataloging-in-Publication Data

Names: Dawuni, J. Jarpa, editor. | Sebutinde, Julia, 1954- writer for foreword.
Title: Intersectionality and women's access to justice in Africa / edited by J. Jarpa Dawuni ; foreword by Julia Sebutinde.
Description: Lanham : Lexington Books, [2022] | Series: Gender and sexuality in Africa and the diaspora | Includes bibliographical references and index. | Summary: "This book examines women's access to justice in both traditional and statutory courts through an intersectional lens. It analyzes the lived experiences of women and their access to justice by situating the courtroom as both a spatial and a temporal arena for seeking justice (as litigants) and for seeking access to the bench (as judges)"— Provided by publisher.
Identifiers: LCCN 2022034594 (print) | LCCN 2022034595 (ebook) | ISBN 9781793632678 (cloth) | ISBN 9781793632685 (ebook)
Subjects: LCSH: Women—Legal status, laws, etc.—Africa. | Sex discrimination in justice administration—Africa. | Intersectionality (Sociology)
Classification: LCC KQC145.W64 I58 2022 (print) | LCC KQC145.W64 (ebook) | DDC 342.608/78—dc23/eng/20220924
LC record available at https://lccn.loc.gov/2022034594
LC ebook record available at https://lccn.loc.gov/2022034595

This book is dedicated to the memories of my grandmother Ayishetu Maayi Ngala, my mother Mercy Lardi Ngala, and my aunt Alima Ngala. Thank you for teaching me the values of feminism.

&

To all the women who fight for justice, equity, and fairness.
To the rural women whose voices are often not
heard above the loud noises of injustice.
To the women judges who hold their ground
against all odds and challenges.

Contents

Foreword xi

Acknowledgments xv

Introduction 1

1 Layered Intersectionality and Framing Feminist Legal Discourse on Access to Justice for Women 3
J. Jarpa Dawuni

PART I: WOMEN AND ACCESS TO THE BENCH 27

2 Status of Women Judges in Algeria: Achievements and Pathways for the Future 29
Samia Bourouba

3 Opening the Door for Women in the Cape Verdean Judiciary 51
Vera Duarte

4 Women Judges in Ethiopia 69
Maame Efua Addadzi-Koom and Biruh Gemeda Gage

5 Battle for Women in the Egyptian Judiciary: Reality, Laws, and Aspirations or a Dream Come True? 95
Omnia Taher Gadalla

6 Making Gains for Women's Rights: Using Gender Quotas to Achieve Gender Equality in the Composition of the Supreme Court of Kenya 117
Annerita Murungi and Agnes Meroka-Mutua

7 "Your Whole Life Is an Interview to Get to the Bench": Gender and Judicial Appointments in Malawi 139
Rachel Ellett

8 Gender Transformation of the Judiciary in South Africa 161
Baratang Constance Mocumie

9 A Critical Assessment of the Status of Women Judicial Officers in Uganda 189
Josephine Ndagire

PART II: WOMEN AND ACCESS TO THE COURTROOM 213

10 Women's Property Rights and Discriminatory Land Tenure Systems in Ghana: The Adjudicative Role of Courts 215
Michael Addaney

11 The Making and Unmaking of Gender: Reflections on Questions of Gender and the Judiciary in Namibia 241
Kennedy Kariseb

12 Women and Environmental Justice Issues in Nigeria: An Evaluation 259
Eghosa Ekhator and Pedi Obani

13 Contribution of the Judiciary to the Advancement and Protection of Women's Matrimonial and Inheritance Rights in Rwanda 285
Odette Uwineza and Marie-Rose Turamwishimiye

PART III: WOMEN AND ACCESS TO TRADITIONAL JUSTICE 309

14 Gender and Customary Justice among the Podoko of the Mandara Mountains of the Far North Region of Cameroon 311
Jeremie Diye

15 Juxtaposing the Efficacy of Testacy and Intestacy to Inheritance Rights: For Rukuba Widows and Children under Nigeria's Plural Legal System 333
Rebecca Emiene Badejogbin and Vicki Lawal

16 Transforming Traditional Justice through Gender Diversification: Comparing Two South African Communities 353
Sindiso Mnisi Weeks

Conclusion and Recommendations 379

17 Intersectionality, Access to Justice, and Women's Experiences: Policy Recommendations 381
J. Jarpa Dawuni and Stephen Muthoka Mutie

Index 399

About the Contributors 417

Foreword

Access to justice means different things to different people. To some it is a question of appropriate laws and rules of procedures applied fairly to all members of society regardless of gender or social standing, while to others it entails the affordability of legal processes. To others yet, access to justice may entail gender-sensitive approaches to the law with a view to overcoming long-standing discriminatory biases, rules, and practices that hinder a particular gender's access to justice. International human rights law recognizes access to justice both as a basic human right and as a means of protecting the rights of other human beings. At an international level, that right is grounded in the 2030 Agenda for Sustainable Development and is embodied in Sustainable Development Goal 16 which, inter alia, promises to guarantee access to justice for all. Access to justice has been defined by the UNDP as "the ability of people to seek and obtain a remedy through formal or informal institutions of justice, in conformity with human rights standards."

Discriminatory justice systems deny women and their families legal protection and effective remedies, often leaving the victims feeling that the justice system is a preserve of a privileged few and not a bastion for the vulnerable. In order to end the gender inequalities that prevent women from accessing justice, it is critical that the institutions charged with the responsibility to administer justice are fair, affordable, effective, and accountable and that women are included and visible in the delivery of justice. Inclusivity requires, for example, that discriminatory laws, practices, and cultural and religious beliefs founded on the perception of women as legal minors who cannot fully enjoy the same rights as men are changed. Even where fair laws are in place, they must be enforced fully and without gender bias. Limited representation of women in the justice sector and women's limited knowledge of their rights are further barriers that prevent women from fully and effectively accessing justice. Only by understanding these barriers and their impact on the everyday lives of women can we truly begin to develop partnerships and find solutions toward guaranteeing this universal right of access to justice for all.

Despite a wealth of domestic legislation, constitutional provisions, and international treaties that guarantee equal access to justice, women, and African women in particular, continue to experience hurdles or setbacks to the full realization of their accessibility to justice. Whether as judges or litigants in the courtroom, African women continue to face multiple and interlocking systems of marginalization in the justice system. The examples cited in this book from across the African continent, including from Algeria, Ethiopia, Nigeria, Cameroon, Malawi, Kenya, Uganda, Ethiopia, Rwanda, Namibia, South Africa, and Cape Verde, clearly demonstrate that despite the best efforts to address gender imbalances in accessibility to justice, there are still wide gaps that need to be bridged in many of these countries.

Intersectionality and Women's Access to Justice in Africa is a collection of chapters that examine some of the factors that adversely affect women's equal access to the courtroom and/or hinder their realization of meaningful legal redress. At face value, it is easy to assume that the ability for litigants to access justice and to effectively seek and obtain a remedy in a competent court of law or tribunal is an equal opportunity open to all persons, regardless of such factors as gender or socioeconomic standing. A detailed study of the legal systems, institutional norms, judicial practices, and policies, however, reveals that nothing could be further from the truth. In what is described as "layered intersectionality," the chapters in *Intersectionality and Women's Access to Justice in Africa* skillfully demonstrate the intersecting challenges women of different identities across the African continent (as litigants or judges) face in their quest for justice. The chapters also examine the interplay between the power and gender dynamics in the courtroom, taking into account such factors as race, ethnicity, and religious and sociocultural norms.

The novelty of this book is found in how it examines women's access to justice not only in terms of the formal legal systems and judicial practices applicable in various African countries, but also in terms of the impact of the various customary or traditional justice systems appertaining in many African communities. The book highlights some of the inherent gender biases and challenges that often intersect with other variables, especially in the areas of land and property ownership, matrimonial rights, and inheritance, to further marginalize women's accessibility to justice.

Drawing on my own career spanning over 40 years as an advocate and judge at national and international levels, I can say without any fear of contradiction that the higher up the legal/ judicial ladder one climbs, the greater, more varied, and subtler the gender and institutional challenges one encounters. Moreover, as the first African woman judge to be elected to serve on the International Court of Justice (the principal judicial organ of the United Nations) and only the fourth woman judge to ever serve on that court in over seventy-five years of its existence, I identify with many of the narratives represented in the various chapters of this book.

The recommendations for reform contained in the last chapter of *Intersectionality and Women's Access to Justice in Africa* should attract the keen interest of government agencies, civil society, domestic and international courts, and funding agencies that seek to make their justice systems more inclusive and to bolster women's access to justice. In what is described as the "feminization of the judiciary" the authors offer reforms that include creating or cultivating a gender-sensitive institutional culture that involves women judges and decision-makers at all levels; creating a justice system that offers equal opportunities, responsibilities, and power to women as decision-makers; and through the training of decision-makers (men and women) in gender-sensitive jurisprudence. Other reforms envisaged include removal of the educational and professional barriers that impede women and girls from accessing the legal profession or the bench; factors that hinder their promotion and appointment to leadership positions in the justice system; as well as introducing policy and laws that proscribe religious, customary, or sociocultural practices that discriminate against women or hinder their access to the courtroom as litigants.

Finally, I agree with the conclusion of the authors that if genuine gains are to be realized in promoting women's access to justice, all stakeholders must ensure that existing laws on women's rights are interpreted and applied in conformity with international human rights standards. There is no doubt that considerable strides have been made globally in the promotion of peaceful and inclusive societies for sustainable development; the provision of access to justice for all; and in building effective, accountable institutions. On the African continent, however, much remains to be done to realize these progressive aspirations. *Intersectionality and Women's Access to Justice in Africa* is a must read that is guaranteed to help all stakeholders understand and better target the barriers that prevent women from accessing justice. When women are included in the decision-making process that affects their rights and when justice systems are fair, representative, fully responsive, and accountable, then and only then will genuine inroads be made in poverty reduction, sustainable peace, and development in their communities.

Dr. Julia Sebutinde
Judge, International Court of Justice, The Hague, Netherlands
Former Judge, Special Court for Sierra Leone
Former Judge, High Court of Uganda

Acknowledgments

From August 9 to 12, 2019, a group of 22 scholars met at the University of Ghana, Legon, for a three-day workshop on *Gender and Judging in Pluralistic Societies: A Comparative Assessment of Access to Justice for Women across Africa*. The main goal of the workshop was to understand the ways in which law, culture, history, ethnicity, and religion intersect with gender and the impact of such intersections on women's access to justice across Africa.

The workshop was sponsored by Point Sud Center for Research on Local Knowledge and German Research Foundation (DFG) and organized in partnership with the University of Ghana *Institute of African Studies*. Additional funding for this project was provided by the German Agency for International Development (GIZ) who supported the production of the book. Over the three-day workshop, the scholars visited the courts and had the chance to sit in and observe a woman judge in a case. After the court hearing, the judge met with the scholars to discuss the type of cases that come to her courtroom and the challenges women litigants in particular face. Given that some of the participants were lawyers, they had the opportunity to share what happens in courtrooms in their countries. For the scholars who were not lawyers, it was illuminating to be in the courtroom and to watch justice in action.

This book would not have been possible without the funding for the workshop provided by the DFG for which I am grateful. I acknowledge the management skills of Dr. Marko Scholze who coordinated all matters relating to the workshop. I also give thanks to my co-organizers of the workshop, Dr. Aram Ziai, University of Kassel, Germany; Dr. Akosua Adomako Ampofo at the Institute of African Studies, Accra, Ghana; and Dr. Lydia Nkansah at the Faculty of Law, Kwame Nkrumah University of Science and Technology, Kumasi, Ghana. Special thanks to my coordinating assistants Atchere Asuah-Kwasi, Mawusi Kudu, and Mawunya Kudu who each played instrumental roles in helping to coordinate the activities of the workshop. I extend my gratitude to all the staff at Yiri Lodge, at the University of Ghana for their professionalism in ensuring that we had a smooth stay during the workshop.

To all the workshop participants who traveled to Accra, Ghana, thanks for making the three days an intellectually stimulating, informative, fun, and rewarding exercise. Special thanks to all the contributors in this book for enduring the triple blind review processes and keeping to the task.

I am eternally grateful to my family whose steadfast love and support for my constant academic travels, long hours of research, and endless days of reviewing the chapters that together make up this book. You are the light that keeps me on this path of knowledge production, and I flourish because of your support, love, care, and encouragement. I do what I do because you make it possible.

For all who read this book, I hope you find it not only intellectually stimulating, but that it offers you guideposts for activism and that you are driven to make change in ensuring an expansion of opportunities for access to justice for women across Africa.

Introduction

Chapter 1

Layered Intersectionality and Framing Feminist Legal Discourse on Access to Justice for Women

J. Jarpa Dawuni

INTRODUCTION

Women's access to equal and quality justice is an ongoing challenge. Providing equitable access to justice for women is an aspiration for development practitioners, promoters of the rule of law, and human rights and women's rights activists. Academic scholarship on the topic of access to justice tends to view access to justice for women through the lens of women as victims or of women as litigants in court. While feminist scholarship on gender and judging discusses women's access to the bench, it has not often been framed as an issue of access to justice for women seeking opportunities to join the bench. What this book does is to center the experiences of women by examining the two sides of the courtroom in one book—by exploring women's access to the courtroom as judges and women's access to the courtroom as litigants.

The book draws on the definition of access to justice from the United Nations Development Program (UNDP): "the ability of people to seek and obtain a remedy through formal or informal institutions of justice, and in conformity with human rights standards" (UNDP, 2005, p. 5). There is an implied gender neutrality in the use of the word "people" in this definition; however, a deeper exploration of the opportunities and challenges faced by women vis-à-vis men shows that women continue to face challenges attributable mainly to their gender.

Access to justice, broadly defined, raises the interconnected questions of who gets to the courtroom and what institutional mechanisms determine their experiences? These questions are the central framework used in this book, which seeks to explore the boundaries of the courtroom as a place for women as subjects (*judges*) and women as objects (*litigants*). I conceptualize *subjects* as the individuals responsible for the application and interpretation of the law—in this case women judges. By objects, the conceptualization of which refers to the individuals who come to the courts in search of justice—in this case women litigants. Whether their status is of subject or object will alter the challenges, power hierarchies, and hurdles women face in the process of accessing justice in the courtroom.

To achieve the goal of exploring access to justice for women, the book adopts a dichotomous variable by examining women as insiders within the courtroom (judges) and women as outsiders to the courtroom (litigants). As this chapter and the other chapters in this book will show, irrespective of their positionality as insiders or outsiders, women still have intersecting challenges they must navigate in accessing formal or informal arenas of justice. In this book, by applying a non-essentialist framing of "women," I acknowledge that women are positioned at various distinct levels of power and privilege; thus, while it might be easy to conclude that women judges are higher up the power hierarchy than women who are coming to the courts to seek justice, a deeper analysis and disaggregation of their experiences shows the interlocking and overlapping challenges each group—and each individual within the group—faces in their attempts to gain access to the courtroom. What this book does is to bring the two distinct bodies of literature into conversation with one another, by examining women's varied experiences in their attempts to gain access to the courtroom in pursuit of justice. For women judges, access to the courtroom takes the form of access to the bench as a judge; access to promotion; and access to being heard as equals before their colleagues, litigants, and court clerks (Dawuni & Masengu, 2019; Dawuni, 2016). For women as litigants, access to the courtroom often takes the form of seeking remedies for the perceived legal wrongs done to them.

In this chapter, I apply a dichotomous conceptualization of the courtroom as both a spatial and an institutional arena where different actors seek justice. In the first conceptualization, I argue that judges' pursuit of justice manifests in their responsibility for enforcing justice, whereas litigants' pursuit of justice often entails seeking remedies for a perceived wrong (in the case of a plaintiff) or defending a perceived wrongdoing (in the case of a defendant). The traditional understanding of the courtroom does not include the factor of how women as judges also seek to assess the courtroom as an arena where they work—a place where access to justice begins with the entry requirements to becoming a judge. The chapters on Algeria, Cape Verde, Ethiopia, South Africa, and Uganda show the different accessibility challenges to becoming judges that women face. While the opportunity structures may have widened for some, as demonstrated in Ndagire's chapter on Uganda and Meroka and Murungi's chapter on Kenya, women are not fully incorporated in the judiciary at equal levels to men, as Addadzi-Koom and Gage demonstrate in the case of Ethiopia, and as Mocumie argues in the case of South Africa.

The second conceptualization of the courtroom focuses on women as litigants. In this sense, the courtroom is presented as a physical space where parties to a case converge to seek justice. I extend the courtroom to include arenas that fall outside the statutory courts—in this case the courtroom also includes traditional justice systems where litigants seek redress for perceived wrongs. The courtroom as a physical space and the different power and gender dynamics are explored in chapters in parts II and III of the book.

To fully understand the impact of gender on women's positionality within the gender and judging discourse, scholars must examine the separate, yet similar challenges women face either as *actors* (*judges*) or *subjects* (*litigants*) within the courts. Applying such a dichotomous approach will enhance our understanding of the similarities and differences between and within the non-essentialized categorization of women, and the pathways that determine their access to the courts. Access to justice often entails access to the courtroom, and while the pathways may seem narrower for some women than others—due to the multiple layers of disenfranchisement discussed in the paradigm of intersectionality—women's access to the courts as judges also presents various layered and overlapping challenges that are explored in some of the chapters.

CONTEXTUAL FRAMING: WHY INTERSECTIONALITY?

The concept of intersectionality has garnered a wealth of literature within feminist discourse. Broadly defined, intersectionality acknowledges the existence of multiple and interlocking identities that determine the experiences and outcomes of individuals in society (Collins, 1993; Collins, 2000; Crenshaw, 1989; Harris, 1989). Intersectionality as a theoretical concept developed out of the works of Black feminist scholars (Collins & Bilge, 2016) and gained prominence through the defining work of socio-legal feminist scholar Kimberlé Crenshaw (1989) in her seminal piece on "Demarginalizing the intersection of race and sex: A black feminist critique of antidiscrimination doctrine, feminist theory and antiracist politics," which highlighted how the interlocking of race and sex adversely affects Black women seeking legal redress in court. Crenshaw's (1989) exposition on how intersectional identities limited women's access to justice in the court of law is instructive for this book given its focus on intersectional biases and given how social and legal structures affect women's access to justice.

Intersectionality has not been without its critics. Chang and Culp (2000) question what exactly constitutes the intersections we have to examine and how many of these intersections exist at any given time. To address anti-essentialism in intersectionality, McCall (2005) provides three complexities for analytically evaluating the lived realities of women as a general category. First, *anticategorical complexity* "is based on a methodology that deconstructs analytical categories" (p. 1773). The second approach, *intercategorical complexity*, "requires that scholars provisionally adopt existing analytical categories to document relationships of inequality *among* social groups and changing configurations of inequality along multiple and conflicting dimensions" (p. 1773, emphasis by the author). The third approach, *intracategorical complexity*, "acknowledges the stable and even durable relationships that social categories represent at any given point in time, though it also maintains a critical stance toward categories" (p. 1774).

It is the intercategorical complexity that this book adopts, by highlighting the relations of inequality that exist *among* women as a social group seeking access to justice through the courts. Thus, a woman's social standing as a judge, relative to that of a rural uneducated woman, does not prevent the former from facing her own set of gendered social axes of oppression in her attempts to navigate the professional, institutional, and personal boundaries she occupies and operates within. The "changing configurations of inequality along multiple and conflicting dimensions" (McCall, 2005, p. 1773) become apparent when one juxtaposes the challenges the two groups of women face independent of each person's standing in society. Consequently, the relative privilege of an educated woman judge does not always shield her from the multiple and intersecting dimensions of exclusion she may experience due to gender, culture, ethnicity, class, religion, and other identities or categories she embodies.

Intersectionality has morphed from theory to praxis, from its initial location within U.S. feminist critical theory discourse, to being applied in multiple contexts around the world (Lewis, 2013; Vrushali, 2013). Consequently, examining intersectionality as a method of study in interrogating multiple, interlocking, layered, or additive categories of identities makes it applicable to studying subjects outside the U.S. context (Anthias, 2013; Lewis, 2013; MacKinnon, 2013).

Given the historical development and centrality of race in intersectional analyses, most women across African countries may not fit neatly into the intersection of gender and race when analyzed solely within their temporal and geographic context. Within Africa, studies on race and gender are mostly applicable in the South African context, where race, gender, class, age, and other identities intersect to produce different outcomes for women in the judiciary (Masengu, 2016; Albertyn & Bonthuys, 2016), women at the bar

(Chitapi, 2018; Klaaren, 2020), or women in the academy (Mabokela & Mawila, 2004; Prah, 2017). Other scholars applying an intersectional lens within the African context include Moore and Himonga (2017), who examine how racist institutional structures in existing laws combine with gender and women's weak positionality in customary marriages to rob them of their right of access to justice in matrimonial cases under customary law.

Beyond the South African context, where race features more prominently, across other parts of the African continent, the closest approximation to race would be ethnic identity. For instance, in most communities across Africa, the inherent socially constructed power structures of ethnic identity privilege some ethnic groups over others (Rabinowitz, 2020; Shetler, 2015). I am by no means equating the disastrous nature of racism with ethnicity, but I am attempting to draw a parallel to how institutionalized ethnic norms that find expression in customary laws can combine with dominant discourse and practices on gender that find expression as sexism to produce a double or triple matrix of domination for women within the African context.

FEMINIST DECOLONIALITY

The bifurcation of feminism between the "West" versus the "Rest" has led to tensions within the global feminist movement (Carastathis, 2016; Mohanty et al., 1991; Nesiah, 2003; Tamale, 2020; Wing, 2000). Global feminist solidarity has been fragmented along multiple lines due to the reproduction of privilege and inherent power structures of feminists located in the global north or the "West" (Carastathis, 2008). Consequently, global south feminists have mobilized their intellectual capacity to resist the multiple layers of oppression through the adoption of a decolonial feminist stance in their research and activism (Mohanty, 2013; Nesiah, 1993; Tamale, 2020).

The intersectional framework of the experiences of African women must be applied through the prism of coloniality and decoloniality. The daily lived experiences of most women across Africa do not occur at the intersection of race; thus, an analysis of race as an intersectional framing may be limited in scope, when applied to their intersectional experiences. Notwithstanding the place of race as far removed, a deeper analysis reveals that women across Africa are still affected by race from the impact of hegemonic, imperialistic global systems and structures that reinforce their marginalization domestically. These historical continuities of imperial exclusions have combined with neocolonial capitalist systems to create new legal orders that have ripped African women of their agency, what Lugones (2010) aptly calls "racialized, capitalist gender oppression" (p. 747). A contextualized framing of intersectionality within the African context must be viewed through a decolonial lens, to better situate the experiences of women across the continent of Africa.

The decolonial feminist lens applied to this study is informed by the work of many African feminist scholars who have addressed the issues of gender construction within the African context as a colonial enterprise (Apusigah, 2009; Cole et al., 2007; Dosekun, 2020; Mama, 2020; Zeleza, 2005). These scholars do not argue that gender did not exist in Africa. Rather, analyzed individually and collectively, these bodies of scholarship seek to situate the ways in which the lived experiences of African women are informed by the multidimensionality of their precolonial, colonial, postcolonial, and neocolonial experiences. These continuities and ever-changing dynamics of the multilayered ways of being are constantly informed by neocolonial globalization praxis and power structures.

Aptly captured by Tamale and Oloka-Onyango (1995), the impact of colonial racism and continuing global hegemonic exploitation cannot be divorced from the daily realities of the oppressed in neo-colonized spaces. In *Decolonization and Afro-feminism*, Tamale (2020) further calls for a centering of the African feminist experience through a scholar-activist stance that filters the African woman's experience through the global hegemonic structures that continue to marginalize Black people. Tamale's (2020) examination of legal pluralism and the need to decolonize customary law, religious relativism, and family gender justice call for constructivist pathways for understanding, unpacking, and repacking what gender justice ought to be for women across Africa.

Gender justice cannot be achieved across Africa without an ontological emphasis on traditional justice systems, which continue to be an important avenue for most citizens seeking justice across the continent. In her study of Kenya, Uganda, and Tanzania, Nyamu-Musembi (2002) notes the important distinction between state-sponsored traditional courts and community-based courts operating autonomously from the government. The state-sponsored courts tend to have more resources than the community-based courts, while the community-based courts may have stricter enforcement of customary practices that do not inure to the benefit of women. Weeks's chapter on South Africa falls into the first group of state-sponsored courts; Diye's chapter on Cameroon and Badejogbin and Lawal's chapter on Nigeria fall into the second category of community-based courts. Despite the state's involvement in some customary justice systems, the lack of funding by the state and an overreliance on external donors tend to make these two arenas especially restrictive for women, who often have limited resources to seek legal help. With gender-sensitivity training not extended to the customary systems, these arenas remain parochial, and gender biases are reinforced and passed on through judgments or settlements that come before the chiefs. Even in statutory courts, gender biases persist, thereby narrowing the opportunity structures for women (Nyamu-Musembi, 2002). These gender biases in the application of laws are discussed in the chapter by Uwineza and Turamwishimiye on women's access to matrimonial property in Rwanda and in Addaney's chapter on women and access to land in Ghana.

EXPANDING INTERSECTIONALITY BEYOND BORDERS

As discussed before, intersectionality as theory (Crenshaw, 1989; Cho et al., 2013; Nesiah, 2003) and as method (MacKinnon, 2013) has traveled beyond the borders of U.S. Black feminist circles. Given the prominence of intersectionality as a buzzword in feminist discourse, this chapter examines the extent to which this theory applies to the experiences of Black women outside the U.S. context.

By focusing on two categories of women—women as judges and women as litigants (in statutory courts and in traditional courts)—what this book does is to break away from the essentialist portrayal of women as a monolithic group within specific categories. For women in each of these categories, and within each of these categories, there are intersecting layers of simultaneous privilege and discrimination that they may experience.

Certainly, we cannot conclude that all the women are privileged because of their professional status. While they all have the opportunity to be judges, in pursuit of this opportunity, different women face different challenges, whether informed by race, ethnicity, class, or religion. Women seeking justice in the traditional court structures may come up against laws and legal and judicial structures that limit their ability to receive justice. Lastly, for women seeking justice in the traditional courts, as shown in the chapters on Nigeria, Cameroon, and South Africa, there are multiple layers of culture-laden challenges that intersect with gender and other variables to further marginalize their ability to receive justice (Gouws, 2017). Given these complex and variegated ways in which women face gender-based realities, this book agrees with the assertion by Nash (2008) that "in painting black women, for example, as wholly oppressed and marginalized, intersectional theory cannot attend to variations within black women's experiences that afford some black women greater privilege, autonomy, and freedom" (p. 12).

Intersectionality as theory, method, and praxis has been explored by scholars within the African context. A 2017 special issue of the *Agenda* journal examined the applicability of the concept of intersectionality with the goal of addressing "questions of how to do intersectional research; how intersectionality is lived and subjectively experienced; how intersectionality might inform our understanding of practices of resistance; how context—place and history—informs the identities at stake; how social status, such as marital status and profession, might be important identity categories in African contexts, independent of class; and how to expand an intersectional approach beyond social relations, to include intersections of social power with material resources such as water" (Meer & Müller, 2017).

To produce a nuanced analysis of the variations within women's experiences, this chapter conceptualizes intersectionality within the legal arena in African contexts by focusing on five key indicators/variables that overlap and intersect with the social category of gender. I theorize a new model of intersectionality within the African context, which I call layered intersectionality. Layered intersectionality adopts an institutionalist approach in furthering our understanding of how institutional norms and practices are informed by social norms and practices and manifest in the limited and sometimes contested opportunities for women seeking access to justice and access to the courtroom. I theorize layered intersectionality, not as distinct from intersectionality as we know it, but rather as an approach that allows us

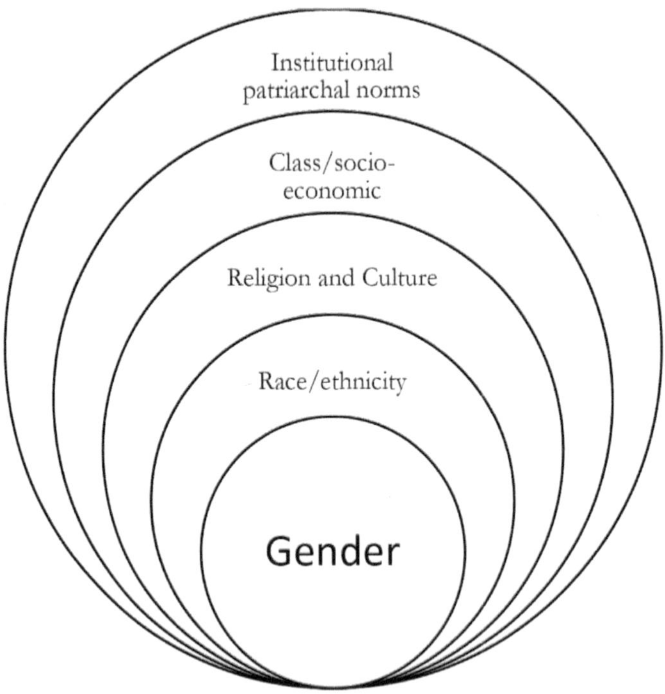

Figure 1.1 Layered Intersectionality.* *Source*: Created by author. *This figure is an original representation of the idea by the author.

to see that one does not have to stand at the intersection of multiple oppressions. One's experience of oppression can be layered. Layered oppressions imply that a person experiences the outcomes of oppression indirectly, rather than directly. The guise of privilege (as a judge) does not shield a woman from experiencing discrimination in her own courtroom, within the judicial institutions she works in, and through the societal rules that inform her daily existence. The five variables are presented in figure 1.1 and are not listed in any order of importance or centrality.

GENDER

Gender as a social construct is at the nucleus of every woman's daily existence. As presented in the figure above, the different layers of a person's position in society can either expand or restrict the extent to which their lived experiences are determined by their gender. Within the African context, gender has not always had a defining role in determining people's relative position in society. As Oyewumi (1997) posits in the case of the Yoruba, age plays an important role in social construction, and a woman's gendered positionality and authority may change as she advances in age. The genesis of gender as a social construct is well noted in the feminist literature. Narrowly conceptualized, the traditional definition of gender has been reduced to a binary—what constitutes female or the feminine, and what constitutes male or the masculine. The distinct characteristics, expectations, and privilege accorded to each of these two binary definitions have led to the subordination of the female gender. In essence, the word gender has become synonymous with women, female, or the feminine. Feminist response to the bifurcation of gender as either male or female has been examined in research and advocacy, with calls for recognizing the broad spectrum of gender identities and the attendant politics of representation (Crocco, 2001; Mohammed, 2020).

In this book, while recognizing the broad spectrum of gender identities, I consider one set of gender identity—woman or female. I explore how gender as constituted within this social category affects different categories of women differently. Drawing on the corpus of intersectional theory, I argue that the gender issues captured by the two dichotomous themes discussed in this book—women as judges and women as litigants—present at one end, some commonality of experiences, but at the other end, differences in experiences when combined with other identity markers such as ethnicity, class, and socioeconomic standing. The gendered experiences of women require an intercategorical analysis that allows for observations of the nuances within the lived experiences of women as units of analyses (McCall, 2005).

Drawing on the works of African feminist scholars (Achebe, 2020; Amadiume, 1987; Oyewumi, 2003), I problematize gender as a fluid classification which allows women to move between societal boundaries once they acquire other social identities. This gender fluidity does not necessarily relate to sex, but to the social constructions of gendered expectations which are linked to the perceived power one has, whether due to education, economic standing, marriage, religious affinity, or other factors. Thus, for women who are educated and choose to become judges, their pathways to mobility within the social class structure are easier than for women without such educational opportunities, exemplified by the relatively weak positionality of those who often seek justice through traditional court systems. On the other hand, for example, a woman without formal education but who is a businesswoman or a religious leader may have a privileged gender positionality, sometimes free of social gendered expectations, but other times not free from those expectations.

RACE/ETHNICITY/GEOGRAPHIC LOCATION

Intersectionality recognizes the discussion of the racialized experiences of women as not singular, but rather interlocking with other social boundaries to reproduce, reinforce, and reify the subordination of Black women (Collins & Bilge, 2016; Crenshaw, 1989). On the face of it, it may be argued that intersectionality in its pure form may not be suitable for studying the experiences of women outside of the U.S. or the global north context. However, intersectionality has been used to frame global issues such as environmental justice, women's reproductive rights, and women and digital media (Collins & Bilge, 2016). The social construction of race has been weaponized to divide the world into categories of the "haves" versus the "have-nots," the "developing" versus "developed," the "global north" versus the "global south." The deconstruction of race is therefore essential to an understanding of how it positions different people along different global hierarchies and power structures within the racialized hegemonic global systems.

Given that sub-Saharan Africa is comparatively racially homogenous, race may not be a strong variable as used within the discourse on intersectionality. Ethnicity comes closest to race, where ethnicity is used as a social construct to distinguish people, often with gendered implications (Shetler, 2015). Similarly to the racialization of human existence, the ethnicization of human existence can have different and overlapping power structures which, when combined with other social boundaries, can adversely affect women.

Racial politics comes into play mostly within the South African context, where the history of apartheid created deep racial divides that impacted access to legal education, access to judicial clerkships, and access to training to become a judge (Andrews, 2022; Albertyn & Bonthuys, 2016). Weeks's chapter in this book explores the role of women as conduits of justice in customary justice systems and the inherent challenges they face. Mocumie's chapter examines women and access to the courts as judges, highlighting the continuities of intersecting challenges women of different identities face.

CLASS AND SOCIOECONOMIC STANDING

According to Marxist feminists, class is a primary variable in the subordination of women in society (Ballan, 1976; Jarrett, 2015). For this strand of feminism, the social production of labor within a capitalist, patriarchal system determines the location and agency of women, far more so than their gender does. When viewed within this framework, the socioeconomic standing of women determines their class. Whether viewed through the lens of Marxist feminism or pure liberal capitalist economics, lower socioeconomic standing does have an adverse effect on the protection of rights and on the ability of the victimized to access justice in the courtroom. When comparing the two categories of women in this book—women as judges and women as litigants—it may immediately appear that women as actors within the law have better socioeconomic and class standing than do women as litigants. Operating within a class system that views women as generally subordinate to men means that women as judges are not free from gender-based discrimination, although their relative positionality may be better than that of indigent women who come to the courts to seek justice.

For instance, as described in Bourouba's chapter on Algeria, even though women make up close to 40% of the Algerian judiciary, women still do not have access to leadership positions within the judiciary. Equally, Ellett's exploration of the calculations women make in their choice to either join the bench or stay at the bar as lawyers shows that they are also informed by the class structure that women judges in the judiciary face—the perception that they are less qualified to be appointed as judges. The same is true of Uganda: Ndagire juxtaposes the symbolic progress women have made within the judiciary against the challenges they continue to face in breaking the glass ceiling of leadership. The strategic choices and calculations women have to make about whether to join the bench or not, and the challenges they experience on the bench, are partly predicated on a class structure that privileges men as the "knowledgeable" or "leadership material" class (Masengu, 2022). This "class" of who is considered qualified is based not on merit, but rather on a system that privileges the male or masculine as the norm. For women who fall outside the category of judges, the intersectional challenges are heightened, as they must struggle against class, low socioeconomic standing, gender, and other cultural norms that limit their access to the courtroom to seek justice.

RELIGIOUS AND CULTURAL NORMS

Culture and religion are mutually reinforcing frames of reference, often informing the social construction of gender in different societies. Sonnveld and Lindbekk's (2017) work on women judges in the Middle East and North Africa highlights the role of religion in determining women's access to the bench as judges and also women's access to the courts in pursuit of justice. In Tunisia, Klibi (2016) argues that the successful secularization of the state by the Constitution of 2014 partly explains the expanded opportunity structures for women to access the bench as judges. In her chapter in this book, Gadalla provides a picture of the struggles and activism of women as they seek access to justice in realizing their vision of becoming judges in Egypt.

Despite the pluralistic legal systems characteristic of most countries in Africa, in countries with a strong Islamic presence, women appear to lag in numerical representation on the bench. This is true for countries in the Sahel region of Africa, as well as other Muslim dominant countries such as Senegal, Somalia, and Sudan. While data inaccessibility makes it a challenge to adequately quantify the number of women vis-à-vis men, available data as of 2019 indicate that there are only two women judges in Somalia (UNECA, 2019). Religion has been used to prevent women from serving on some courts. In Nigeria, women are not allowed to be judges in the Federal Sharia Court. Similarly, in Kenya, women are not allowed to be judges in the Kadhi courts. In Senegal, women have made little progress as judges, with less than 30% representation of women on the bench, even though women have risen to top judicial leadership positions (Dawuni, 2020).

With regard to women's access to the courts in pursuit of justice as litigants, religion has played a defining role in determining the laws that exist in these countries. Colonial importation of legal systems has left traces of Christianity and Islam in the formulation of customary laws (Ndulo, 2011). Thus, where judges follow strict adherence to the law, with little room for judicial imagination and creativity in the interpretation of laws, women stand to be victimized given that most customary and religious laws do not favor women (Mamdani, 1996; Shomade, 2022). Subsequently, the confluence of religion and culture on the experiences of women's access to justice creates a state of multiple jeopardies when combined with other interlocking challenges women encounter in their daily existence.

PERSISTENT INSTITUTIONAL PATRIARCHAL CULTURES, NORMS, AND PRACTICES

Persistent patriarchal cultures and norms affect women's access to the courts in a multitude of ways, and I briefly touch on two. First, women's access to the court as judges is still contested in some jurisdictions. While expanded educational opportunities have widened the pathways to law schools, in some countries, the pathway to the judiciary remains narrow. As discussed before, recruitment policies continue to privilege men as judges in religious courts in Egypt, Nigeria, Kenya, and Somalia. In South Africa, institutional racism and the apartheid system privileged White men over others, and racism combined with patriarchy to privilege Black men and White women over Black women (Albertyn & Bonthuys, 2016; Masengu, 2016). Notwithstanding the commendable trend of women's rise to top judicial leadership positions across the continent (Dawuni & Kang, 2015), in many other courts and jurisdictions, the pathways to judicial leadership for women remain narrow and sticky (Aura-Odhiambo, 2018; Dawuni, 2022). Women continue to push against the ghosts of institutional patriarchal cultures born out of the formation of the legal profession as a male occupation. In Nigeria, Uzebu-Imarhiagbe (2020) notes that the relative ease of women joining the judiciary has not been met with parity on the bench. The gendered nature of workplace practices and institutional cultures within the profession at the bar and the bench are enduring institutional challenges.

Second, women's access to the courts as litigants remains narrow. Women's ability to access the courts is a rule of law issue when existing laws in customary and statutory courts do not favor the promotion and enforcement of women's rights. Access to justice for women is limited; this is a human rights issue when justice sector institutions are not responsive to legally empowering the rights of women through the interpretation of laws that would help advance their rights. The chapters in this book touch on these two critical points.

ORGANIZATION OF THE BOOK

Writing a book that spans the continent of Africa is not an easy task given the heterogeneity of languages, cultures, legal systems, religions, and class systems, to name a few. To avoid the essentialist nature of some research that uses two or three case studies as representative of the vast continent, this book attempts to cover a diverse range of countries, with different legal histories and legal traditions and spanning the five regions of the continent. Table 1.1 shows the diversity in coverage.

Table 1.1 Geographic Diversity of the Book

East	*West*	*North*	*South*	*Central*
Kenya	Nigeria	Algeria	South Africa	Cameroon
Uganda	Ghana	Egypt	Malawi	
Rwanda	Cape Verde		Namibia	
Ethiopia				

Source: Created by author.

Table 1.2 Legal Tradition

Common Law	*Civil Law*	*Hybrid*	*Pluralistic*
Kenya	Algeria	South Africa	All countries, at varying levels that include some customary law and/or sharia law
Uganda	Cape Verde	Namibia	
Rwanda	*Cameroon		
Ghana	Ethiopia		
Malawi	Egypt		
*Cameroon			

Source: Created by author.
*Cameroon has a dual legal system that uses common law in the north and the southern parts of the western region of the country, while civil law is prevalent in the francophone zones covering roughly eight regions of the country.

Given that legal pluralistic societies draw heavily from their former colonial oppressors, the form of imposition of the foreign legal system, the duration of colonization, and the penetration of the colonial administration in the country determine the extent and impact of the crystalized pluralistic outcome (Shomade, 2022). While almost all countries on the continent can be characterized as having a pluralistic legal system, table 1.2 shows the main legal systems operating in the countries covered in the book.

STRUCTURE OF THE BOOK

Table 1.3 presents the three thematic areas covered in the book. The first part consists of chapters that examine women's access to the court as judges, by exploring the pathways, processes, and experiences of women on the bench. The second part examines women's access to justice as litigants through an exploration of the laws and judicial practices that affect the meaningful realization of their rights. The third part examines how the confluence of legal pluralism and gender affect and determine women's access to justice within traditional justice systems. When brought together, these three parts highlight different, yet intersecting, variables. Together, the chapters show that when gender is held constant, the outcomes on women's access to the courts and access to justice remain limited and contested.

Table 1.3 Themes Covered by the Book

Issue	*Country Chapters*
Women and access to the bench	Algeria, Cape Verde, Kenya, Malawi, Uganda, South Africa, Egypt
Women and access to the courtroom (statutory justice)	Ghana, South Africa, Nigeria, Rwanda, Namibia
Women and access to traditional justice systems	Cameroon, Nigeria, South Africa

Source: Created by author.

PART I: WOMEN AND ACCESS TO THE BENCH

Bourouba's chapter explores the development of women's access to the courts as judges in Algeria. Tracing the constitutional and legal framework, and the structure of the judicial system, she used empirical methods to analyze the results of interviews with women judges to understand their lived experiences as judges within an evolving political context from the independence era to the time of writing. While teasing out some of the success in getting more women on the bench, Bourouba hints at the challenges women face in accessing leadership positions within the Algerian judiciary.

Gadalla's chapter on Egypt examines the long battle to women's representation on the Egyptian bench. Tracing the advocacy efforts by HerHonorSettingTheBar, she lays out the multiple strategies including litigation, which have been used to demand women's equal representation on the bench. Though some gains have been made, there is still a long way to go to achieve parity in the Egyptian judiciary.

Ellett's analysis of women judges in Malawi points to the intersection of class, gender, and sociocultural norms that have combined to position women as outsiders in the courtroom. By examining the formal and informal processes for selection to the bench, Ellett highlights the effect of structural and discriminatory professional norms, women's weaker political support networks, and sociocultural factors as key constraints to women's access to the bench. To address the pipeline challenges, the chapter provides recommendations for targeted policy changes to improve the legal educational pipeline, changes to the appointment processes, and expansion in the formal and informal support structures for women to advance within the profession.

Meroka and Murungi's chapter on Kenya explores the extent to which institutional norms and policies such as constitutional provisions provide pathways for women's access to the courtroom as judges. The authors note that though the 2010 Constitution and the "two-thirds" gender principle as provided in Article 27(8) have had a positive impact on the number of women in the lower courts, the same has not happened in the Supreme Court, despite the appointment of the first woman chief justice. Given this context, the intersectional nature of power hierarchies produces less optimal outcomes for women's representation in higher courts. The authors extend their argument to examine how the symbolic underrepresentation of women on the Supreme Court may be affecting the substantive underrepresentation of women's rights cases in the jurisprudence of the court. This chapter highlights how, due to their intersectional nature, intercategorical differences are simultaneously reinforcing the marginalization of women's access to courts—both as judges and as litigants in the type of gender jurisprudence delivered by the court.

In Ethiopia, women account for 30% of the federal judicial bench, and the judiciary is headed by a woman as president and chief justice. The development of women's access to the judiciary in Ethiopia has not received scholarly attention, despite the importance of the country in the history of Africa's resistance to colonial rule. Addadzi-Koom and Gage present the first synopsis and empirical analysis of women in the Ethiopian judiciary. Tracing the institutional legal developments in the country, and using a mix of survey and interviews, the authors argue that despite the appointment of a woman chief justice, women's access to the bench as judges has not been an easy journey. The chapter examines the intersectional nature of gender, class, religion, and sociocultural norms that limit the opportunity structures for women's access to the courts as judges.

Ndagire's chapter on Uganda provides a potent analysis of the position of women in the Ugandan judiciary. Using a historical institutionalist approach, the chapter traces the development of gender norms from the social and political context as a basis for the high representation of women in the judiciary. Ndagire argues that the symbolic representation of women has led to women judges pioneering gender-sensitive approaches to the law, by challenging long-standing discriminatory biases, rules, and practices. While this symbolic representation is thus impressive, women continue to face challenges in accessing leadership positions within the court hierarchy, with only one woman having served as deputy chief justice to date, despite the high qualifications of women on the bench. The chapter explores the factors that influence both the recruitment and promotion of judicial officers, as well as appointment to leadership positions.

Two chapters in this section are the firsthand personal narratives of women judges in two courts, in different parts of the continent. Given the importance of legal narratives as a core methodology in intersectional theory (Harris, 1989; Collins, 2000), the two chapters provide a strong contribution to the book through a discursive approach to storytelling. The chapter on Cape Verde by Vera Duarte traces the trajectory of women in the Cape Verdean judiciary from her time on the bench as the first woman judge. Duarte situates the lives and experiences of women on the bench through legal storytelling and historical analysis to build a foundation for future studies of women in the Cape Verdean legal and judicial systems. As Duarte argues, "understanding my life, the political developments in my country and my professional journey are critical to understanding the current situation of women in the Cape Verdean judiciary."

Mocumie's chapter on South Africa builds on the legal narrative technique, offering a personal reflection of her 30-year journey from the magistracy to the Supreme Court of Appeal. The chapter provides a lucid discussion on the intersectional nature of gender, race, and professional hierarchy in determining where women find themselves within the judiciary. The chapter potently highlights how age (judicial seniority) and gender insensitivity within the bench can intersect to silence women judges.

PART II: WOMEN AND ACCESS TO THE COURTROOM

The set of chapters in the second part of the book examine women's access to the court as litigants and investigate when and how women can seek redress in courts, and what the outcomes are. Drawing on various theoretical frameworks, the chapters in this section converge on the role of the pluralistic nature of legal systems across Africa and the ways in which such systems, when combined with other intersecting and overlapping experiences, affect women, often with less desirable outcomes.

Ekhator and Obani's chapter on Nigeria explores an important issue that lies at the intersection of gender, environmental justice, and access to justice in the courtroom. They argue that while the exploitation of oil and gas has affected people living in those communities, women, especially rural women, have been adversely affected due to their reduced access to food, water, energy, and basic livelihoods. Compounded by poverty and other socioeconomic challenges, women's access to meaningful legal redress for their challenges in the Nigerian courts is limited. By exploring the effectiveness of women-led protests and recent judicial developments that indicate the prospects for improving women's access to justice, the authors argue that women in the Niger Delta could adopt litigation, including foreign or cross-border litigation, as one of their formal strategies to improve access to environmental justice.

Addaney's chapter on Ghana explores women's access to land. The chapter examines the intersection of gender, ethnicity, and prevailing patriarchal customs on women's access to land. Taking a human rights-based approach, the chapter examines customary law in land governance and the adjudicating role of the courts in striking a balance in protecting women's right to property in Ghana. The chapter finds that customary laws governing land tenure and property rights in Ghana are discriminatory and do not comply with acceptable international standards and practices on women's property rights. It also reveals that there has been some progress toward equity in ownership and access to property by women through judicial efforts that have transformed customary practice.

Kariseb's exploration of the question of gender in the Namibian judiciary presents a positive prognosis of the development of gender and access to justice for women litigants. Kariseb examines the intersection of legal pluralism and cultural relativism in slowing down the promotion of women's rights. Using various case reflections, the chapter analyzes the interpretation given to cases with gendered implications for women by the superior courts of Namibia. The chapter highlights how the courts' interpretation of gender positively influenced rights protection for women and argues that Namibia's relatively gender-responsive legislative framework, coupled with judicial awareness of the historical exploitation of women in Namibia—particularly under colonialism and apartheid—serves as a catalyst for promoting a gender-sensitive judiciary.

Uwineza and Turamwishimiye's chapter on Rwanda engages in a historical mapping of the exclusion of women from access to matrimonial and inheritance rights. They observe that since 1999, notwithstanding constitutional guarantees of equality, nondiscrimination, and the right to property, the courts continued to apply discriminatory norms that excluded women from realizing their matrimonial and inheritance rights. Thus, while the laws were reformed, gender insensitive judicial interpretation of the laws by some judges has limited women's access to the full realization of their rights. It would take the passage of successive gender-neutral laws, such as laws governing matrimonial regimes and successions (1999), land (2005), and persons and family (2016) for the Supreme Court to affirm and justify the legitimacy of women's property rights. The chapter brings to the fore the importance of intercategorical differences, as women in informal marriages were not allowed to access matrimonial rights until the passage of the gender-based violence law in 2009. Despite these developments, the chapter also hints at some persisting inconsistencies within the laws that continue to limit women's full realization of their matrimonial and succession rights in the courts.

PART III: WOMEN AND ACCESS TO TRADITIONAL JUSTICE

The three chapters in the third and final section of the book drill down into the impact of traditional legal systems on women's access to justice. The chapters in this section explore the ways in which traditional courts continue to play important roles as the arenas where most litigants across Africa seek justice

(Mukhopadhyay & Quintero, 2008; Moore & Himonga, 2017). Together, the chapters illuminate how the intersecting impact of gender, religion, cultures, and patriarchal norms and socioeconomic standing combine to narrow the entry points for women's access to traditional justice systems.

Weeks's chapter on South Africa both describes women's access to traditional courts as "judges" and explains what such traditional gender participatory arrangements can mean for women's access to justice in traditional settings. The chapter's argument is framed within the Traditional Leadership and Governance Framework Act (2003), which requires gender diversity in the composition of traditional courts. Comparing two traditional settings—one where women participate in the traditional courts, and another where they do not—the chapter explores the significance and impact that gender diversification can have on transforming traditional justice by examining women's "voice" and delivery of justice in and through women's participation in these forums. Using a decolonial feminist theoretical approach, the chapter engages with the impact of colonialism on these institutions, which have come to be dominated by a patriarchal identity and masculinist ideals that intersect with other identities to diminish women's voice and agency.

Badejogbin and Lawal explore the challenges for women and children in accessing their right to inheritance among the Rukuba people of Nigeria. By analyzing the laws that regulate inheritance in testate and intestate succession, the authors identify statutory and customary laws that act as a double jeopardy against women and children. By highlighting the challenges inherent in pluralistic legal societies, the chapter draws attention to the intersections of gender, customs, class, and patriarchal norms that limit women's access to traditional justice. The authors explore how national laws may be used to address these gaps.

Diye's chapter on customary justice among the Podoko people of the Mandara Mountains in Cameroon explores how traditional justice mechanisms seek to protect the rights of accused persons. The chapter examines the roles women play in the delivery of justice as actors and juxtaposes these roles with women's roles as subjects seeking justice for offenses perpetrated against them. The chapter raises and attempts to answer questions on women's access to customary or traditional justice.

DRAWING THE CURTAIN: CONTRIBUTIONS AND RECOMMENDATIONS

As mentioned at the outset, the goal of this book has been to examine the presence of women as actors (judges) vis-à-vis women as subjects (litigants). By using an intersectional framing of the issues that both categories of women face in their pursuit of access to the courtroom, this book problematizes the justice arena as a site of gendered contestation where, even though the intersectional identities of women are reflected differently, the commonality of their experiences is rooted in the gendered framing of institutional mechanisms and processes.

A set of chapters in this book show that women's pursuit as actors in the court (as judges) is neither smooth nor linear. Once the pathways are open, mobility within the judicial ranks can be limited, and as the case of Egypt shows, very restricted. For women litigants, on the other hand, the pathways are even narrower, when combined with the layers of discriminatory gendered hierarchies discussed in individual chapters. These gendered hierarchies remain dynamic and fluid, and women can move up within these hierarchical structures. However, as demonstrated by Weeks's chapter on South Africa and Diye's chapter on Cameroon, despite the role of women in justice delivery in traditional systems, their powers are still limited by patriarchal norms.

This book contributes to the burgeoning literature on gender and judging by presenting some new case studies on women and access to the bench. Building on the country cases covered in *Gender and Judging in Africa: From Obscurity to Parity?* (Bauer & Dawuni, 2016) and *Gender, Judging and the Courts in Africa: Selected Studies* (Dawuni, 2022), the new case studies presented here include Algeria, Ethiopia, Uganda, Malawi, and Cape Verde.

The major contribution of this book lies in the use of intersectional and decolonial frameworks to analyze the lived experiences of women and their access to justice by situating the courtroom as both a spatial and a temporal arena for seeking justice (as litigants) and for seeking access to the bench (as judges). Invariably, I argue that though women access the courts for different reasons (either as judges or litigants), there are patterns of mutually reinforcing discriminatory practices that each group shares with the other based on shared gender identities. Given that gender identities are fluid, women experience different levels of discrimination depending on which of their layered identities are at play at a given point in time. The last chapter of the book provides policy recommendations for the various actors engaged in addressing issues of gender and access to justice.

REFERENCES

Achebe, N. (2020). *Female monarchs and merchant queens in Africa.* Ohio University Press.

Albertyn, C., & Bonthuys, E. (2016). South Africa: A transformative constitution and a representative judiciary. In G. Bauer & J. Dawuni (Eds.), *Gender and the judiciary in Africa: From obscurity to parity?* (pp. 49–66). Routledge.

Amadiume, I. (1987). *Male daughters, female husbands: Gender and sex in an African society*. Zed Books.
Andrews, P. (2022). Pursuing gender equality through the courts: The role of South Africa's women judges. In J. Dawuni (Ed.), *Gender, judging and the courts in Africa: Selected studies* (pp. 189–208). Routledge.
Anthias, F. (2013). Intersectional what? Social divisions, intersectionality and levels of analysis. *Ethnicities*, *13*(1), 3–19.
Apusigah, A. A. (2009). Is gender yet another colonial project? A critique of Oyeronke Oyewumi's proposal. *QUEST: An African Journal of Philosophy/Revue Africaine de Philosophie*, *XX*, 23–44.
Aura-Odhiambo, R. (2018). Gender equality: Integration of women in the judiciary in Kenya. In W. Kabira, P. Mbote, N. Kabira, & A. Meroka (Eds.), *Changing the mainstream: Celebrating women's resilience* (pp. 93–122). University of Nairobi Press.
Ballan, D. (1976). *Feminism and Marxism*. World View Publishers.
Bauer, G., & Dawuni, J. (2016). *Gender and judging in Africa: From obscurity to parity?* Routledge.
Carastathis, A. (2008). The invisibility of privilege: A critique of intersectional models of identity. *Les Ateliers de l'Ethique*, *3*(2), 23–38.
Carastathis, A. (2013). Identity categories as potential Coalitions. *Signs: Journal of Women in Culture and Society*, *38*(4), 941–965.
Carastathis, A. (2016). Intersectionality and decolonial feminism. In *Intersectionality: Origins, contestations, horizons* (pp. 199–232). University of Nebraska Press. https://doi.org/10.2307/j.ctt1fzhfz8.11.
Chang, R. S., & Culp, J. M. (2002). After intersectionality. *University of Missouri—Kansas City Law Review*, *71*(4), 485–492.
Chitapi, R. (2018). Women in law: Navigating the tensions of gender bias and intersectionality at the Cape and Johannesburg Societies of Advocates (the Bar). *Agenda*, *32*(2), 43–52.
Cho, S., Crenshaw, K. W., & McCall, L. (2013). Toward a field of intersectionality studies: Theory, applications, and praxis. *Signs: Intersectionality: Theorizing Power, Empowering Theory*, *38*(4), 785–810. https://www.jstor.org/stable/10.1086/669608.
Cole, C., Manuh, T., & Miescher, S. (2007). *Africa after gender?* Indiana University Press.
Collins, P. H. (1993). Black feminist thought in the matrix of domination. In C. C. Lemert (Ed.), *Social theory: The multicultural and classic readings* (pp. 615–625). Westview Press.
Collins, P. H. (2000). *Black feminist thought: Knowledge, consciousness, and the politics of empowerment*. Routledge.
Collins, P. H., & Bilge, S. (2016). *Intersectionality: Key concepts*. Polity Press.
Crenshaw, K. (1989). Demarginalizing the intersection of race and sex: A black feminist critique of antidiscrimination doctrine, feminist theory and antiracist politics. *University of Chicago Legal Forum*, *1*(8), 139–167.
Crocco, M. S. (2001). The missing discourse on gender and sexuality in the social studies. *Theory into Practice*, *40*, 65–71.

Dawuni, J. (2016). To "Mother" or not to "Mother": The representative roles of women judges in Ghana. *Journal of African Law*, *60*(3), 419–440.

Dawuni, J. (2020). Women in judiciaries across Africa. In O. Yacob-Haliso & T. Falola (Eds.), *The Palgrave handbook of African women's studies* (pp. 353–374). Palgrave Macmillan.

Dawuni, J. (Ed.). (2022). *Gender, judging and the courts in Africa: Selected studies*. Routledge.

Dawuni, J., & Kang, A. (2015). Her ladyship chief justice: The rise of female leaders in the judiciary in Africa. *Africa Today*, 62, 45. https://doi.org/10.2979/africatoday.62.2.45.

Dawuni, J., & Masengu, T. (2019). Judicial service commissions in Nigeria and Zambia. In S. Sterett & L. Walker (Eds.), *Research handbook on law and courts* (pp. 213–230). Edward Elgar Publishing.

Dosekun, S. (2020). African feminisms. In O. Yacob-Haliso & T. Falola (Eds.), *The Palgrave handbook of African women's studies* (pp. 48–61). Palgrave Macmillan.

Gouws, A. (2017). Feminist intersectionality and the matrix of domination in South Africa. *Agenda*, *31*(1), 19–27.

Harris, A. (1989). Race and essentialism in feminist legal theory. *Stanford Law Review*, *42*, 581–616.

Jarrett, K. (2015). *Feminism, labour and digital media*. Routledge.

Klaaren, J. (2020). South Africa: A profession in transformation. In R. Abel et al. (Eds.), *Lawyers in 21st-century societies: Vol. 1: National reports* (pp. 535–546). Bloomsbury.

Klibi, S. (2016). Tunisia: A new constitution and more women judges. In G. Bauer & J. Dawuni (Eds.), *Gender and the judiciary in Africa: From obscurity to parity?* (pp. 80–92). Routledge.

Lewis, G. (2013). Unsafe travel: Experiencing intersectionality and feminist displacements. *Signs*, *38*(4), 869–892.

Lugones, M. (2010). Toward a decolonial feminism. *Hypatia*, *25*(4), 742–759.

Mabokela, R. O., & Mawila, K. F. N. (2004). The impact of race, gender, and culture in South African higher education. *Comparative Education Review*, *48*(4), 396–416.

MacKinnon, C. A. (2013). Intersectionality as method: A note. *Signs*, *38*(4), 1019–1030.

Mama, A. (2020). 'We will not be pacified': From freedom fighters to feminists. *European Journal of Women's Studies*, *27*(4), 362–380. https://doi.org/10.1177/1350506820953459.

Mamdani, M. (1996). *Citizen and subject: Africa and the legacy of late colonialism*. Princeton University Press.

Masengu, T. (2016). It's a man's world: Barriers to gender transformation in the South African judiciary: Perspectives from women advocates and attorneys. *International Journal of the Legal Profession*, *23*(4), 305–319.

Masengu, T. (2022). One sauce for the goose, another for the gander: Zambian women judges and perceptions of illegitimacy. In J. Dawuni (Ed.), *Gender, judging and the courts in Africa: Selected studies* (pp. 209–230). Routledge.

McCall, L. (2005). The complexity of intersectionality. *Signs*, *30*(3), 1771–1800.

Mohammed, W. F. (2020). Deconstructing homosexuality in Ghana. In S. N. Nyeck (Ed.), *Routledge handbook of queer African studies* (pp. 167–181). Routledge.
Mohanty, C. T. (2013). Transnational feminist crossings: On neoliberalism and radical critique. *Signs*, *38*(4), 967–991.
Mohanty, C., Russo, A., & Torres, L. (Eds.). (1991). *Third world women and the politics of feminism*. Bloomington: Indiana University Press.
Moore, E., & Himonga, C. (2017). Centering the intersection of race, class, and gender when a customary marriage ends. *Agenda*, *31*(1), 104–115.
Mukhopadhyay, M., & Quintero, S. (2008). Gender and access to justice in sub-Saharan Africa. Report of the conference held in Johannesburg, South Africa. Amsterdam: KIT and CALS. Available at https://www.kit.nl/wp-content/uploads/2018/08/1530_Gender-and-access-to-justice_Conference-report-2008.pdf. Accessed January 20, 2021.
Meer, T., & Müller, A. (2017). Considering intersectionality in Africa. *Agenda, 31*(1), 3–4. https://doi.org/10.1080/10130950.2017.1363583.
Nash, J. C. (2008). Re-thinking intersectionality. *Feminist Review*, *89*, 1–15.
Ndulo, M. (2011). African customary law, customs and women's rights. *Indiana Journal of Global Legal Studies*, *18*(1), 87–120.
Nesiah, V. (1993). Toward a feminist internationality: A critique of U.S. feminist legal scholarship. *Harvard Women's Law Journal*, *16*, 189–210.
Nesiah, V. (2003). The ground beneath her feet: "Third World" feminisms. *Journal of International Women's Studies*, *4*(3), 30–38.
Nyamu-Musembi, C. (2002). Are local norms and practices fences or pathways? The example of women's property rights. In A. An-Na'im (Ed.), *Cultural transformation and human rights in Africa*. Zed Books.
Oyewumi, O. (1997). *The invention of women. Making an African sense of western gender discourses*. University of Minnesota Press.
Oyewumi, O. (Ed.). (2003). *African women and feminism: Reflecting on the politics of sisterhood*. Africa World Press.
Prah, E. (2017). Stratifications of blackness: Meditations on the intersect of gender, race and age. *Agenda*, *31*(1), 71–77.
Rabinowitz, B. (2020). Ethnicity and power in Sub-Saharan Africa: Do colonial institutions still matter? *Comparative Politics*, *52*(3), 405–437.
Shetler, J. B. (2015). *Gendering ethnicity in African women's lives*. University of Wisconsin Press.
Shomade, S. (2022). *Colonial legacies and the rule of law in Africa: Ghana, Kenya, Nigeria, South Africa, and Zimbabwe*. Routledge Press.
Sonneveld, N., & Lindbekk, M. (2017). *Women judges in the Muslim world: A comparative study of discourse and practice*. Brill.
Tamale, S. (2020). *Decolonization and Afro-feminism*. Daraja Press.
Tamale, S., & Oloka-Onyango, J. (1995). The personal is political, or why women's rights are indeed human rights: An African perspective on international feminism. *Human Rights Quarterly*, *17*(4), 691–731.
United Nations Development Program (UNDP). (2005). Programming for justice: Access for all – A practitioner's guide to a human rights-based approach to access

to justice. Available at https://www.un.org/ruleoflaw/files/Justice_Guides_ProgrammingForJustice-AccessForAll.pdf. Accessed January 16, 2022.

United Nations Economic and Social Commission for Western Asia (UNECA). (2019). Women in the judiciary in the Arab states: Removing barriers, increasing numbers. Available at https://archive.unescwa.org/publications/women-judiciary-arab-states. Accessed February 16, 2022.

Uzebu-Imarhiagbe, E. (2020). Women in the Nigerian judiciary: Considerable headway or organised progress? *International Journal of the Legal Profession*, *27*, 175–188.

Vrushali, P. (2013). From patriarchy to intersectionality: A transnational feminist assessment of how far we've really come. *Signs*, *38*(4), 847–867.

Wing, A. (Ed.). (2000). *Global critical race: An international reader*. New York University Press.

Zeleza, P. T. (2005). Gender biases in African historiography. In O. Oyěwùmí (Ed.), *African gender studies: A reader* (pp. 207–232). Palgrave Macmillan.

Part I

WOMEN AND ACCESS TO THE BENCH

Chapter 2

Status of Women Judges in Algeria

Achievements and Pathways for the Future

Samia Bourouba

INTRODUCTION

After its independence, Algeria undertook the major operation of institutional resetting. It faced huge difficulties, due to the lack of qualified staff, as its population was young and the number of educated Algerians was far from enough to fill the empty spaces left by the French. Women contributed to the war for liberation equally as men and were expected to contribute similarly in the public and political life of building the new institutions of a state whose people have undergone attempts to erase their identity and the debasement of 132 years under colonial occupation. The Constituent Assembly, created after the independence in 1962, had eight women among its 196 members (4.08%). The first legislature (the National Assembly, established in 1964) was composed of 138 members—including only two women deputies (1.44%). As for executive power, the first female minister was appointed in 1982, as a secretary of state for social affairs. In political life, the participation of women was very weak during the reign of the Front de Liberation Nationale, and the opening of the political field in 1989 brought about only one woman head of a political party. Since then, the situation has not changed much as of October 2019, there have only been four women heads of political parties.

With the low historical and current participation of women in public life, it is important to measure the progress of the representation of women in the judiciary, 57 years after Algeria's independence. What was the situation in 1962, where women magistrates were almost absent? How has parity been achieved in 2019 through several trajectories and temporal phases? What challenges remain to be addressed? To answer these questions, this chapter proceeds in the following manner: the first part is dedicated to the historical background of the legal system, the second part discusses the court structure and organization, the third part focuses on gender and representation, the fourth part engages in qualitative analyses of the experiences of women magistrates, and the fifth part examines challenges and obstacles hindering women magistrates' access to senior positions. The conclusion part provides a projection on the steps that have yet to be taken to complete the gender parity that has been achieved in the number of judges in 2019 and which remains to be strengthened in the different levels of the courts.

Interviews with 15 female magistrates were conducted during November and December 2019. The magistrates were from both judicial and administrative courts, this included two female judges in the Supreme Court, two in the Council of State, two in the appeal courts, and nine in first degree courts. The interviewee judges belong to different generations and have known the periods before and after the reforms. The years on the bench range from 5 to 29 years. The interviews fed into the fourth part of this chapter and made it possible to measure the evolution of women judges in senior positions and to understand the constraints.

HISTORICAL BACKGROUND: THE FALLOUT OF COLONIZATION AND THE RELIGIOUS AND CULTURAL HERITAGE

Algeria adopted a position of positivism that makes positive law the first in the hierarchy of norms and confers Sharia to a minor role. Since the first Algerian Constitution in 1963, then the successive constitutions of 1976, 1989, and 1996 (the Constitution which is currently in force) Sharia is not considered a source of law, unlike some constitutions from comparable Arab countries (Egypt, Mauritania, Saudi Arabia among others). Consequently, the main purpose of the basic principles ruling the state is the sovereignty of the people. However, the formulation of Islam as the religion of the state is found in the four constitutions adopted since independence. Arab states refer to Islam in their constitutions in four main levels: in the preamble, when identifying state religion, the compliance of legislation to religious principles, and for conditions to elect the head of state (some Arab constitutions make religion a condition of the scope of some rights and freedoms, others incorporate traditional religious institutions into the constitutional provisions, such as the corporal punishment as cited in the Koran). These constitutions can be classified into two categories: the first, which appears in the constitutions of the majority of Maghreb states, considers Islam the religion of the state; the second, in the constitutions of many Middle East states, makes Sharia a source of law (Hoffner, 2013). Constitutions of the first category are Algeria, Jordan, Mauritania, Morocco, and Tunisia. Constitutions of the second category are

Bahrain, Comoros, Egypt, Iraq, Kuwait, Libya, Oman, Palestine, Qatar, Saudi Arabia, Somalia, Sudan, Syria, United Arab Emirates, and Yemen. Very few Arab constitutions do not refer to religion (this is the case in Djibouti and Lebanon which are multi-faith states).

Algeria belongs to the first category, as it considers Islam the religion of the state. This formulation was used for the first time in Arab state constitutions in 1950 and has no consequence on the organization of power and institutions which model the more or less absolute separation of state and religion. This reference tends to legitimize the regime and leads to the administration of religion by the state. The Algerian Constitution, by this formulation, doesn't make Sharia a source of law, which can be considered a triumph of modernity and separation of religion and state. But Sharia is not totally ruled out of the legal order, and two legal documents refer to Sharia expressly: the civil code and the family code.

The civil code, adopted in 1975, mentions the sources of law hierarchically in Article 1 and stipulates that "in the absence of any legal disposition, and the judge pronounces himself according to the principle of Islamic law." The family code (adopted late in 1984) contains a similar provision in Article 222, which states that in the absence of a provision in this law, reference is made to the provisions of Sharia law. Despite the fact that Sharia is not elevated as a source of law by the Constitution, many scholars and judges make an interpretation of the stipulation "Islam is the religion of state," especially when they refer to matters relating to personal status, they don't accord another text a place above Sharia law.

Women's rights have evolved and been strengthened throughout the successive constitutions, influenced by dominant ideologies of each era. The principle of equality between men and women and nondiscrimination on the basis of sex was consecrated in the first Algerian Constitution, in a unique provision, Article 12 of the 1963 Constitution states: all citizens of both sexes have the same rights and the same duties. The 1976 Constitution made more specifications, stipulating that the Constitution guaranteed all civil, economic, social, and cultural rights for Algerian women. The 1989 Constitution did not just proclaim the principle of equality and nondiscrimination, but added an obligation weighing on the institutions to eliminate obstacles that hinder women's development and their effective participation in all fields. An important step was taken in 2008 with the amendment of the constitution of 1996 Constitution, Article 31b is added with stipulation that the "state works for promoting the political rights of women by increasing their chances of access to representation in elected assemblies."

Organic law 12-03, adopted on January 12, 2012, aims to increase the chances of women's representation in elected assemblies. This law came to implement this constitutional consecration by the adoption of measures binding political parties and obliging them to make a quota when preparing the electoral list.

Organic law 12-03 was greeted by politicians, civil society organizations, and above all by the women themselves, who considered their participation in the public life had not reflected their real weight in the society, after their sacrifices in the fight against terrorism. They believed their sacrifices during the war of national revolution had not been rewarded, and they were often marginalized.

During the Ottoman reign, the judicial system was organized into two main orders: Islamic courts and rabbinical courts (composed of three rabbis). Islamic courts were divided into civil courts and criminal courts and were made up of one judge (cadi), and two judges in Algiers, representing two Sunni schools: Maliki (Moors, the Algerian Arab population, and other Muslims) and Hanafi (for the Turkish population). The justice was considered as delegated by the Dey (governor) to specialized persons—cadis—who were mostly recruited among doctors of law, according to their morals and their competence (Bontems, 1976, pp. 71–73). The Ibadite population was not granted autonomous courts (even though the majority of the Algerian Muslim population is ruled by the Maliki rite, it is important to mention that a part of population belongs to the Ibadite school) (Sambron, 2005, pp. 123–142). During the French occupation, the 1834 decree relating to general command and the high administration of French possessions in the north of Africa regulated the first judicial organization under colonization, with ordinary courts, and the 1842 decree declared the decline of rabbinical courts.

The Muslim courts were reestablished by the decree of October 1, 1854, and they were exclusively employed in civilian and commercial disputes between Muslims. The whole of Algeria was gradually divided into 326 judicial districts called *mahakmas*, and 19 appeal courts called *medjles* were created. These were composed of four judges (cadi), with the establishment of a council of Muslim jurisprudence composed of nine members. It is noteworthy that after this autonomous phase, the decrees of 1859 and 1866 made these courts dependent on the French courts. Although the Muslim courts during the period 1842-1870 can be considered autonomous, the cadis were named by the governor in respect of conditions related to their age and degrees (Bontems, 1976, pp. 385–396; Collot, 1987, pp. 187–188).

Since the 1849 decree, administrative tribunals were created separately, composed of departmental councils and administrative courts. A new phase was started in 1870 and lasted until 1962, at which time the Algerian judicial organization was modeled on that of France. French courts are organized on the basis of specialization, the double degree of jurisdiction, and the unity of the civil and criminal tribunals, parallel Muslim courts were reduced.

COURT STRUCTURE AND ORGANIZATION: REFLECTION OF SOVEREIGNTY

The judicial system adopted by Algeria after independence was influenced on a large scale by the French judicial organization. Despite the innumerable problems which assailed the new Republic, it was necessary to provide the country with new institutions, to respond to the needs of the situation, and to the aspirations of the people (De Bana, 1964, p. 98). It was necessary to reestablish justice throughout the country and deal mainly with the departure of French magistrates. In order to achieve what some scholars called the *decolonization of justice* (Mathetes, 1966, p. 111), Algeria adopted the first law on judicial organization in July 1965, ordinance N° 65-278, which entered into force in 1966. This law was adopted to address the unification of jurisdictions and to bring the judge closer to the litigant, especially in some counties. During 1965–1966, there were nearly 420 Algerian judges, of which 45 graduated with law degrees (Mathetes, 1966, p. 113). The majority of these were more qualified in Koranic law than modern Algerian law, and so a reskilling was necessary. The Ministry of Justice organized training sessions and published books and legal bulletins in order to standardize and strengthen the legal training intended for all judicial personnel, including judges. A reskilling center was created in 1972 (by Decree N° 72203) to provide practical training for newly recruited magistrates and further training for active magistrates, and transformed in 1987 (by Decree N° 87208) to a National Institute for the Judiciary.

The judicial map in Algeria developed in many steps. The Parliament adopted law 62-157 on December 31, 1962, on renewal until further notice of the legislation in force on December 31, 1962, which allowed the courts to apply French laws, except those which are in contradiction with national sovereignty, with the purpose of avoiding a legal vacuum. This consequently led to the extended presence of four administrative courts established during colonization and the annulment of the link with the Council of State in France.[1] An analysis of many laws adopted after independence shows that Algeria adopted a unified judicial system, dedicated through the abrogation of administrative courts inherited from colonization, and their attributions were transferred to the courts of appeal, by law n° 65-278, which reformed the organization of the judiciary in 1965.

The 1965 reform transformed the administrative courts by integrating them as the administrative chambers of appeal courts in three districts; this launched the unified judiciary system period which lasted 31 years (until 1996). The judicial system stemming from the 1965 reform was reflected in judicial courts composed of a single judge[2] with the Supreme Court (created on June 18, 1963, by law n° 63-218 and established on March 7, 1964) at the top and composed of four chambers.

Currently, there are 293 ordinary tribunals, 48 appeal courts, and the Supreme Court which was organized after 1963 by law 89-22, with eight chambers, until abrogation of law 89-22 by Organic law 11-12 in 2011. With the introduction of new provisions, and the reduction of the Supreme Court chambers to seven, the administrative chamber was cancelled after the creation of the administrative tribunals.

The administrative tribunals were created separately in the 1996 Constitution, which contained provisions dedicated to the Council of State, the highest court in the administrative courts structure. The organic law of 1998 specified its composition and jurisdiction. Administrative courts are the first degree courts in the administrative justice, and the law issued in 1998 regulated their composition. Only 42 courts of 48 planned were created by 2019. See figure 2.1.

After the adoption of the dual judicial system, composed of judicial tribunals and administrative tribunals, a Tribunal of Conflict was created by an organic law in 1998 to settle the jurisdiction conflicts between judicial courts and administrative courts.

The High Council of Magistracy is governed now by the Organic law 04-12 of 2004. It is the disciplinary institution of judges, headed by the president of the Republic and composed of elected judges and personalities appointed by the president of the Republic;[3] it is not considered a tribunal in the proper sense of the word, but rather an institution in charge of appointment, transfer, and promotion of judges. The presence of female members—especially judges—started slowly, and has developed since, with the creation of administrative courts which allowed female judges to be elected in the council. Since 2004, two female judges (out of 12) have since been elected by their peers. The female presence in this council is mainly due to the nomination of female members in the designated quota of the president of the Republic. Seven women are members of this institution (out of 22), including two judges, who are also members of the administrative courts.

The third constitution of Algeria created a Constitutional Council in 1989, but the first constitution of 1963 planned its creation. In the first setup of this council, it did not include any female members, and the first woman member was nominated in January 1999. The constitutional amendment of 2016 raised the number of members from 9 to 12, and three women are members of this current composition. They were nominated by the former president of the Republic Abdelaziz Bouteflika as stated by the Constitution, and reflected his policy to promote the participation of women in the public life and for them to hold high positions of authority. In his speech at the opening of the judicial year, the outgoing president of Republic Bouteflika stressed "the need to continue the effort to promote the place of the Algerian woman in our society and make their roles even more effective by removing obstacles to allow her

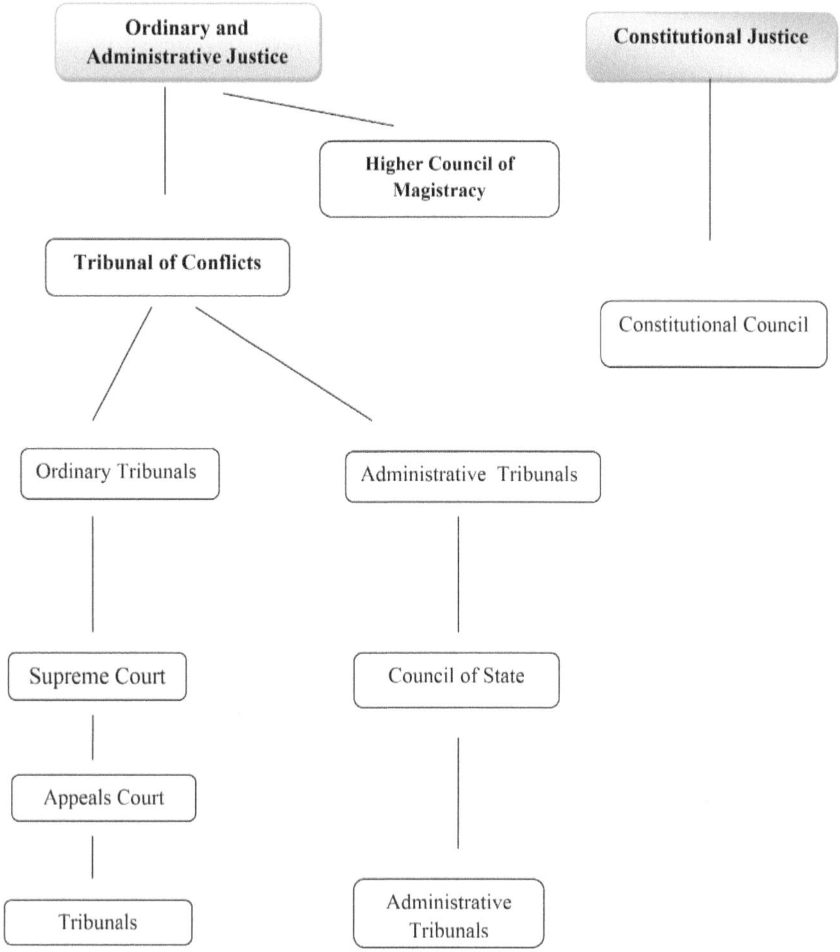

Figure 2.1 Structure of the Algerian Judiciary. *Source*: Created by author with data from Constitution of 1996, Organic law 05-11 on judicial organization.

to make an even greater contribution, just like her Algerian brother in all sectors."[4] In the last appointments the former president of Republic made in July 2018, there are 3 female members among 12.

A National Institute of Magistracy (renamed Higher School of Magistracy in 2005) was created in 1990 by Executive Decree 90-139 as a specialized institution in charge of magistrate training. Graduating candidates from law schools can attend the institute after they successfully complete the entrance examination. The student judges have a three-year training, shared between courses and practical stage in the courts; at the end of their training they fill out a *Fiche de voeux* (a request form, completed by the magistrate students at the end of their training to formulate their choice of assignment) and are assigned to their posts, respecting their classification in order of merit (see Organic law 04-12 on the status of the judiciary). They are appointed as trainee magistrates for one year and are established after advice from the High Council of Magistracy. In the context of reforming the training, it will be extended to four years instead of the current three.

GENDER AND REPRESENTATION: A STEPWISE INCREASE

The recruitment of judges since independence has gone through several stages. A few months after independence, many decrees were adopted to delegate lawyers, clerks, chief interpreters, graduates from the Higher Islamic Studies Institute, and professors at the faculty of law into the functions of judges, to address the new situation of a lack of judges. Belmihoub Selma Nadia (Nee Zemirli) had the opportunity when she was nominated as children's judge by Decree No. 62-45, adopted on November 22, 1962 (Gazette n° 906, 1962, p. 72), and she was probably the only female judge in 1962. The youngest female judge, Nadia Hammadi, 21 years old, was appointed to the Supreme Court in 1964 (Keswani, 2002, p. 134).[5] A judicial section was created within the Ecole Nationale d'Administration in 1965, which took charge of the training of 22 promotions to the judiciary. The presence of female students started from the 1971–1975 promotion with a low number (2 female students among 12). Subsequent to that, some promotions witnessed the absence of female students, and the number never went past five female students in the judicial section[6] and that remained the case until 1990.

The first promotions from 1990 to 2004, recruited by the National Institute of Magistracy, have noticed a low presence of female students. The first one in 1990 consisted of 197 magistrate students, and 44 of them were female (22%), but gradually their number increased. In the 50th promotion (2004–2007), 137 among 289 students were female (46%), and in the 90th promotion (2009–2012) there was equality between female (145) and male (144) students, with 50% for the first time. The last promotion (those who finished training in 2017) was composed of 232 magistrate students, 128 of which were female (55%), the rate for the first time going above parity (Internal Higher School of Magistracy statistics, Direction of Initial Training, n.d.).

There is a trend of gender equity of the judiciary by the increase in the number of women training in the Higher School of Magistracy as mentioned before, but also by the presence of more women judges in courts. This can be explained by the evolution of the Algerian social and economic situation, due mainly to increased opportunities for women to access legal studies and work.[7] According to the existing scholarship on the issue of gender in Algeria, the university remains, for the majority of women, the primary place for their success in society. Once graduated in law, many women opt for the judicial competition and succeed; their number has not stopped increasing for years to achieve parity (Allia, 2005; Belmihoub, 2016; Cheriet, 2009, 2010; Keswani, 2002; Lalami, 2008; Marzouki, 2010; Vandevelde-Dailliere, 1979). This is a worldwide trend noticed both in legal education and legal profession (Menkel-Meadow, 1986; Michelson, 2013). If this gender equity is an opportunity to transform the perception of a traditionally male-dominated profession, it is still slow to materialize in some other Arab countries, where women still face obstacles to reaching the position of judge, mainly due to religious considerations (Sonneveld, 2017, pp. 5–6; Lindbekk, 2017, p. 286, Hamad, 2016).[8]

The number of women judges in Algeria witnessed a slow evolution since independence, with very low numbers after independence, but saw gradual growth, especially from the end of the 1990s. Examination of the official Gazette shows that there are grounds for distinguishing three main stages during the period of 1962–1997. From 1962 to 1971, no more than three women were appointed as judges per year, from 1972 to 1994 their numbers increased slightly, and from 2000 it begun to exceed that of male magistrates. The access of women to higher education and their choice of a judicial career remains the main factor of this increasingly marked presence. Despite the increase in the number of women being called as judges, the presence of female judges in senior leadership positions is still low—partly the result of the persistence of negative cultural attitudes that have an impact on women's access to senior position.[9]

In 1998, among 2,324 practicing judges, 547 were women (23.53%); their distribution shows that their presence is low in the Supreme Court, and more importantly in tribunals (United Nations, 1998, p. 18). In 2004, 922 judges were women (32%), among a total of 2,811, distributed mainly in tribunals and less in the Supreme Court. In 2009, out of a total of 3,582 magistrates, 1,318 were women. In 2010, 1,318 judges were female magistrates out of 3,582 (36.82%), two are presidents of appeal courts (out of 48) and seven are presidents of tribunals.

In 2019, there were 6,326 magistrates: 2,854 of them are female judges which gives a percentage of 45.2%, an almost complete parity[10] (the number of judges since independence grew by a factor of 15 times from original figure [from 420 judges in 1966 to 6,326 in 2019]). Two are female presidents of appeal courts,[11] a small number occupy the position of presidents of tribunals, and the parity noticed in the total figure tends to fade when looking closely at the higher positions occupied by female judges. The distribution of female judges in senior positions in 2019 can be seen in figure 2.2.

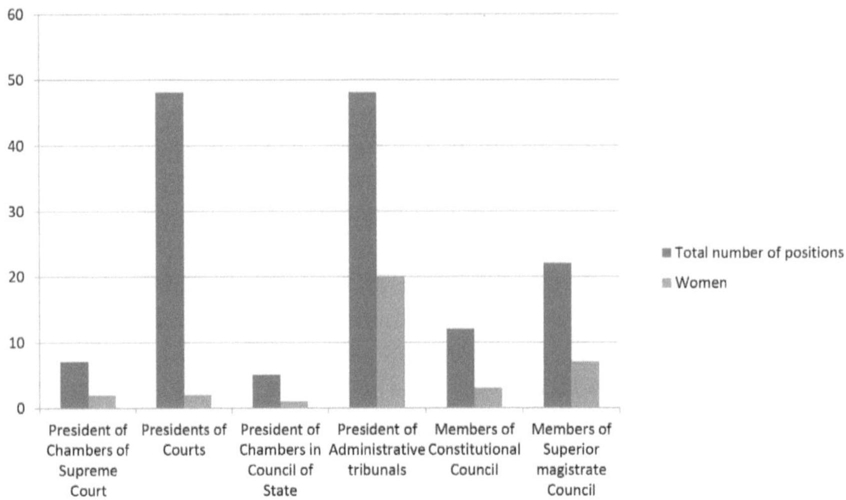

Figure 2.2 Percentage of Women Judges in Senior Positions or Members of Councils in 2019. (The data used are quoted on page 37 above). *Source*: Created by author with data from Judiciary of Algeria.

The gender parity discussed before reflects the majority of trained female magistrates at the higher school of magistracy, who join the courts after their three years' initial training, and which strengthens the feminization of the judiciary. Women are present in the different courts of the dual judiciary system but in less senior positions. These positions allow the female magistrates to reconcile their family and professional life and to make professional sacrifices for their families.

For the judicial courts, women are designated as counselor judges in first degree courts and appeal court, and Supreme Court, but a woman has never been positioned as president of the Supreme Court, mainly due to the generation effect (Dawuni & Kang, 2015). The overrepresentation of men in the top hierarchy can be partially explained by the generation effect which relies on the most senior judge appointed as the president of the court. Due to career advancement by seniority, we find a growing feminization in the new generation of judges and if this trend continues, the generational effect will turn to the advantage of women—but this may be a long wait. The generational effect can consequently be seen as a *glass ceiling* which limits women's access to senior management positions.[12]

A contrary trend is noticed in the administrative courts, where the president of the Council of State from 2001 is a female judge. When established in 1998, the Council of State was headed by a male judge, and since then all successive presidents have been women. In 1998, 16 of the 34 judges in the Council of State are women. The explanation can be found in the will of the political power to establish parity between the two high courts in the judicial system and to compensate the underrepresentation of female judges in the Supreme Court. The policy of promoting more female judges, initiated by the former president of the Republic A. Bouteflika, and to overcome their underrepresentation in the ordinary courts, contributed to this growth and has been facilitated by the creation of administrative courts and the appointment of female judges as their president since 1998.

The appointment of female magistrates to the prosecution has been very low. We find the designation of the first deputy attorney general of tribunal in 1978 (Gazette n 39, 1978, p. 662). The first female prosecutor-in-chief of an appeals court, Djamila Zigha, was appointed in 2014, opening up hope for more appointments to this post. Attorney general positions have been occupied almost exclusively by male magistrates, although female magistrates are being appointed in increasing number.

In the last judicial reshuffle made on August 7, 2019, the interim head of state Abdelkader Bensalah removed 35 presidents of appeal courts (72%). One female judge was appointed as president, which brings their number to two female judges as presidents of Appeals Court out of 48 (4.16%). There was a reshuffle in the prosecution which affected 132 general prosecutors, and no female judges were appointed to this position, which means that there are currently no female judges in this position in the 48 appeal courts.[13] The virtual absence of female judges in the body of prosecutors is mainly due to the perception of this as a profession for men, but also reflects a question of preferences and family constraints for women judges (Hamad, 2016; Klibi, 2016; Sonneveld, 2017; Lindbekk, 2017).

The gradual feminization of the judiciary in Algeria is shared with some other professions and appears to follow the trend in postcolonial states. It is perceived as a major achievement in developing countries like Algeria, which seek to give opportunities to all components of the society in the growth of the nation (Dawuni & Masengu, 2019; Bauer & Dawuni, 2016; Kamau, 2013).

The representation of female judges in senior positions differs according to whether they are in judicial or administrative courts. While they are well represented in the administrative courts (and these are recent creations), the most conclusive analysis is that concerning the judicial courts—even though female judges have only been present in these courts for a few years—their access to certain posts remains limited. Since a few years ago, female judges who have worked at different jurisdictional levels are appointed to specific positions, like the president of the National Council of Human Rights, and the National Delegate for Children (new institutions created in the latest constitutional amendment of 2016).[14]

One can assert that the goal is still far from being achieved, but it is important that the journey has started, and the pace is increasing the presence of women in the judiciary. In the long run, these women will find a place in the higher judiciary positions. Female judges are themselves conscious of the importance of reaching such positions, convinced of their real contribution to the justice mission in general, and the implementation of human rights standards in particular.

WOMEN AND THE JUDICIARY: EXPERIENCE OF FEMALE JUDGES

There is no doubt that the analysis of the status and role of women in the Algerian judicial system refers to taking up the challenge of considering the place given to women in socialization processes, for the construction of the modern nation-state in Algeria, and not as a linear process of consensual integration into fixed institutions (Cheriet, 2010, p. 17). While it is necessary to trace the evolution of the place of female judges in this global context, it is not possible to trace the evolution of female judges without referring to those concerned, their experiences, and their feelings through the course of their career. This chapter uses qualitative interviews as a source of information and in order to contextualize their experiences.[15] These interviews allow me to note and draw conclusions from reality.[16] The results confirm the various analyses provided through this chapter.

The women interviewed joined the judiciary either through the judicial section of the Ecole Nationale d'Administration or by success in the competition of the Higher School of Magistracy, a choice and a dream that they fulfilled with determination, and of which they are proud. "It has been my dream since high school, I aspired to bring justice to society in general, to women in particular and to my mother who did not have the chance to join school during the colonization period" said Judge 1. For the most experienced judges 1, 2, 3, and 4, they were almost unanimous in showing that joining the judiciary was a dream that many have fulfilled to ensure their long absence due to the very small number of educated women before and a few years after independence, "I, like many women chose the office of magistrate by conviction in a period when very few women attended this training compared to men," said Judge 4. They gradually climbed the ladder from judge to presidents of tribunals, presidents of chambers in courts, and advisers at the Supreme Court and the Council of State. Promotions are made by the hierarchy, based on needs, as required by law and sometimes on the proposal of the direct supervisor, and done on the basis of competence for both sexes, and for Judge 2, "My skill and dedication to my work opened the doors for promotions from the first degree court to the Supreme Court."

As discussed earlier, the laws adopted after independence have increasingly allowed women to become magistrates and to benefit from promotions. Some of those interviewed, who joined the judiciary during the 1980s, claimed that the very low number of female judges during the first years will continue to increase with the education and success of women, Judge 3 confirmed that "women's access to education has allowed many to choose the judiciary, which is considered as a noble profession, it's a question of profile and vocation."

Women judges who exercised their profession during the period of terrorism in the 1990s have defied all threats against them by extremists, who wanted to ban them from work, uttering death threats against them. They decided to exercise their noble profession by braving these risks, moving to their workplace despite the risks and the attacks perpetrated against women. They were supported by their male colleagues against this widespread threat, themselves threatened by this religious extremism. Judge 1 noted that "joining courts during the black decade was a challenge for female judges to ensure justice despite the conjuncture, when several institutions were almost at a standstill." Judges 5, 6, and 9 equally noted that the courage of the pioneer women judges paved the way for success for the generations that followed, "the challenge taken up by the woman magistrate is a reflection of the fight of the Algerian woman against terror and injustice" (Judge 6). This is to say that the fight of the Algerian woman remained intact in the most difficult moments of the country as discussed in the interviews mentioned before.

Apart from this period of instability, which was an exception, the magistrates who joined the profession earlier in the 1980s noted that the environment of the exercise of their work has changed a lot, whether for their entourage of judges or the perception of the litigants, who in certain remote regions of the country were not inclined to see female magistrates judging their cases. If at the start of their appointments to positions of responsibility there were sometimes sensitivities on the part of some of their male colleagues,

"this dissipated when they practiced their profession with dedication and excelled, and they ended up being accepted" (Judge 4).

The function of a judge, especially in senior positions, has the effect of increasing the tasks of female judges and adding to their responsibilities, especially if they are married and have children. Female judges say they make an effort to strike a balance between their professional responsibilities and family obligations, "especially when they have sick children in their care, their responsibilities multiply" (Judge 5). Despite these obligations, they succeeded in taking up the challenge and climbing the ladder to access positions of responsibility; for Judge 11, "it is an achievement of which women are proud of, for a profession they have chosen, and in which they feel self-realization," and for Judge 13, "all my satisfaction is to be able to achieve this professional family balance."

The women interviewed believe the presence of female magistrates contributes to better justice, as they bring their own experiences as mothers and family leaders with dependent children to their work. They can ensure a flexible interpretation of the law, not to infringe it but to accompany its application with a touch of equity and humanity. According to Judge 10, "Women judges are more humane in divorce cases as they measure suffering for divorced women and their children", and according to Judge 8, "Justice rendered is more humanized." Their convinced choice for the magistracy is supported by their sacrifices and their continuous work, "they read a lot, and do continuous research despite the load of files to be processed" said Judge 14, "and perfect themselves all the time to give their best" according to Judge 10.

However, this strong presence of female magistrates must aim to promote competence, that's why for Judge 3 "collegial work with their male colleagues remains beneficial in several respects to ensure good justice, they complement each other and are not mutually exclusive."

Unanimously, the future for the female judge in Algeria is promising, because they experienced the evolution of their situation and managed to assert themselves through their skills and dedication, but some of them are a little skeptical, as Judge 9 who considers that "the enjoyment of political rights remain a determining factor for a positive outlook," and Judge 12 who asserts that "strengthening the independence of the judiciary will participate in a more assertive place for female judges." Finally, "the strong presence of women in the judiciary must constitute a precious asset compared to other Arab and Muslim countries, some of which do not allow women to access this function" said Judge 15. After having reached parity in 2019, these women hope that other colleagues will access senior positions. The achievements must be maintained.

Female judges concerned about their career development took the opportunity to express their support for reforms initiated by Abdelaziz Bouteflika, the former president. To this end Fettouma Rebbouh, a judge in the Office of the Minister of Justice, declared on the occasion of the celebration of the International Women's Day, in March 8, 2018:

> Reforms allow promotion of woman in justice sector on the criterion of competence. These appointments reflect the desire to set up mechanisms and bases for equality and parity through the designation of women in decision-making positions, which will promote its role in development. (Benrahal, 2018)

OBSTACLES AND CHALLENGES: CHANGES STILL TO BE MADE

The legal background that provides an equal position to women and men developed and strengthened since the 1996 Constitution is still insufficient, because women face obstacles to access political life in general and the judicial function in particular. Achievements have been made for female magistrates who were in the minority after independence and who managed to position themselves in the judiciary, but in less senior positions. The period of terrorism in the 1990s, called the Black Decade as mentioned before, was a big test for female judges, who were under threat by terrorists. Yet, the women judges interviewed indicated that these threats did not dissuade many of them from performing their duties, and these threats no longer deter some of them dealing with terrorism cases. Female judges also contributed in the trials of major corruption cases in the mid-2000s. They also served as presidents of tribunals and investigating judges, some of them were compared to internationally renowned judges such as Carla Del Ponte, the general prosecutor of the International Criminal Tribunal for the former Yugoslavia.

Despite the fact that the law offers access to women for all functions in the same way as men, stereotypes and social barriers still exist.[17] Female judges exist in an environment made by men and for men, and whatever their skills, experiences, and integrity, they never had the chance to become the first president of the Supreme Court and even less, general prosecutor in the highest court. Promotions remain exclusively for men, and women have never been solicited; the constraints related to the post of prosecutor and which require a presence at any time cannot be invoked by appointers as a reason for not appointing women. Choosing the profession of the judiciary means that they fully assume its constraints.

It is not the laws or the skills that prevent the promotion of female judges into such positions of responsibility, but rather, a change of mentality is imperative on both sides, to challenge the traditional views of the socially accepted jobs for women and the fight to introduce a new gender relationship in the postcolonial era. The weight of traditions and societal perceptions of women's roles, added to the interpretation of Sharia in the state and its place in legal sources, combine to create a hindrance to women's full actualization of their roles and functions as judges.

In some comparative systems—such as France, which is the closest system to Algeria—the fear is that the feminization of the judiciary could have a negative effect on the progress of justice cases, that female judges will be accused of partiality in family matters, and that justice will be rendered by women for women (Bessière, Gollac, & Mille, 2016, Cohen, 2018). A great deal more is left to be done to change these perceptions and that could include a study of the cases and jurisprudence by women and men judges to see if there are discernable gender patterns.

CONCLUSION AND RECOMMENDATIONS: A MIXED APPRAISAL

Many barriers stand in the way of women as they try to access senior positions in the judiciary, despite the feminization of the field in Algeria, and even if the texts give them a place equal to that of their male colleagues. Female judges themselves see their roles as serving to open the doors that are still closed for other women.

New challenges facing the judiciary call for implementation of laws that are more technical. Political leaders, during the revolution and after independence, expressed a strong will for making women equal contributors in the development of an independent Algeria. The political will was announced in very strong terms in the Tripoli program—quality between woman and man must be in the facts. In 2019, facts are here to prove that the path of equality has actually been taken and the presence of women judges is here to stay.

The entry of women judges into the judiciary is not only a quantitative question but also a qualitative one, as it reflects an inclusive policy. The constitutional revision announced in January 2020 by the new president Abdelmadjid Tebboune could reinforce the access of female judges to senior positions and the achievement of gender parity in accordance with the constitutional principle of equality. This chapter has filled a gap in the existing body of knowledge on gender and judging by providing a foundation for the study of gender and judging in Algeria. Beyond the symbolic representation of women judges which this chapter has focused on, future studies can look at the substantive representation of women—namely, what other impacts have come about as a result of the feminization of the Algerian judiciary. Such assessments could include changes in jurisprudence and other institutional changes within the judiciary as a whole.

NOTES

1. An agreement between temporary Algerian authorities and France was concluded on August 28, 1962, and a provision disbarred cases concerning Algeria or local Algerian authorities or public enterprises under Algerian authority, and same solution for affairs in concern with France before administrative courts in Algeria.

2. This reform came in substitution of 3 appeal courts and 17 high courts and 120 district courts existing during colonization. Mathetes (1967, pp. 112–113).

3. This council is composed of the justice ministry as deputy chairman, the first president of the Supreme Court, the attorney general of the Supreme Court, 10

magistrates elected by their peers, and six personalities chosen by the president of the Republic due to their competence. Detailed information can be consulted in law n° 04-12 (September 6, 2004) (Alg.).

4. (Speech of the outgoing President at the opening of the judicial year 2008–2009, Algiers, Thursday, October 29, 2008), cited in A. Bouteflika, Discours et messages, Decembre Janvier 2009, Anep, Alger, 2010.

5. She was a graduate in law. In the magistracy of this time, law graduates who accessed the judiciary were required to at least 21 years of age and 35 at the most.

6. We can find one female student in five promotions (9th, 10th, 11th, 17th, and 19th), two in three promotions (8th, 18th, and 21th), three in two promotions (13th and 23th), four in three promotions (14th, 15th, and 20th), five in one promotion (16th), and no female students in eight promotions (2nd, 3rd, 4th, 5th, 6th, 7th, 12th, and 22nd). Information is available in the website of the Ecole Nationale d'Administration: http://www.ena.dz/index.php/en/archives-des-diplomes-de-l-ena.

7. For more details, see Josiane Chiabrero: L'enseignement superieur feminin en Algerie depuis l'independence, *Cahiers de la Mediterrannee*, (8), 1, 1974, 39.

8. Many scholarship can be consulted on the feminization of justice in general and in Algeria in particular.

9. This reality was explained in the initial report of Algeria before Comittee on the Elimination of Discrimination against Women. It is a fact that changing mentalities and combating stereotypes is the most difficult task in any society, and a long time is needed to make changes in the society.

10. Discourse of the minister of justice pronounced at the opportunity of the International Women's Day on March 8, 2019.

11. Zoubida Daoud and Houria Zilabdi.

12. Céline Bessiere, Sybille Golac, Muriel Mille, Féminisation de la magistrature: quel est le problème?, La découverte, *Travail, genre et sociétés*, *2*(36), 2016, 175–180, available on https://www.cairn.info/revue-travail-genre-et-societes-2016-2-page-175.htm.

13. El Moudjahid, August 10, 2019.

14. On the international scale, a female judge issued from the administrative jurisdictions was elected as judge in the African Court on Human and People's Rights in March 2017.

15. Interviewees identities are withheld in accordance with their request to protect their identities.

16. A special thanks to magistrates who agreed to dedicate the time for these interviews despite their heavy professional obligations.

17. Women in the judiciary in the Arab state. Removing barriers, increasing numbers. ESCWA, SPDL, UNOHCHR, ICJ, 2019, p. 42.

REFERENCES

Ali, S. (2000). *Gender and Human Rights in Islam and International Law: Equal before Allah, Unequal Before Man?* (1st edition). The Hague; Boston: Springer.

Allia, K. (2005). Femmes diplômées et secteurs d'activité en Algérie. *Cahiers du CREAD* (74), 61–72.

Apap, G. (1997). Etre magistrat en Algérie. Extraits d'interviews réalisées auprès de magistrats ayant exercé leurs fonctions en Algérie—Google Search. *Le Genre Humain, Le Seuil*, (32), 121–134.

Belmihoub, M. C., Friedrich-Ebert-Stiftung, & Büro Algier. (2016). *Etude exploratoire sur l'acces des femmes au marche du travail en Algérie.*

Benachour, Y. (2009). Statut de la femme et Etat de droit au Maghreb. In Y. Benachour, J.-R. Henry, R. Mehdi, & Institut de recherches et d'études sur le monde arabe et musulman (Eds.), *Le débat juridique au Maghreb: De l'étatisme à l'État de droit: Études en l'honneur de Ahmed Mahiou* (pp. 237–241). Paris: Éditions Publisud-Iremam.

Bessière, C., Gollac, S., & Mille, M. (2016). Féminisation de la magistrature: Quel est le problème ? *Travail, Genre et Sociétés*, *36*, 175. https://doi.org/10.3917/tgs.036.0175

Boigeol, A. (1996). Les femmes et les Cours. La difficile mise en œuvre de l'égalité des sexes dans l'accès à la magistrature. *Genèses. Sciences sociales et histoire*, *22*(1), 107–129, 40 pp. https://doi.org/10.3406/genes.1996.1372.

Bontems, C. (1976). *Manuel des institutions Algeriennes: De la domination turque a l'independance*. Paris: Editions Cujas.

Bouteflika, A. (2010). *Discours et messages*. Alger: Anep.

Cheriet, B. (2009). Le genre et la citoyenneté comme « troc » dans l'Algérie postcoloniale. *Diogene*, *225*(1), 89–100.

Cheriet, B. (2010). Femmes, droit de la famille et système judiciaire dans les Etats du Maghreb: Le cas algérien. In S.-Z. Souria, C. Boutheina, R. Fouzia, B. Khalid, & A. Monia (Eds.), *Femmes, droit de la famille et système judiciaire en Algérie, au Maroc et en Tunisie*. UNESCO Publishing.

Chiabrero, J. (1974). L'enseignement supérieur féminin en Algérie depuis l'independance. *Cahiers de la Mediterrannée*, (8), 1, 35–44. https://doi.org/10.3406/camed.1974.1398.

Cohen, M. (2018). Judicial Diversity in France: The Unspoken and the Unspeakable. *Journal of the American Bar Foundation*, *43*(4), 1542–1573. https://onlinelibrary.wiley.com/doi/abs/10.1111/lsi.12331

Collot, C. (1987). *Les institutions de l'Algérie durant la période coloniale (1830–1962)*. Paris; Alger: Edition du CNRS; Office des publications universitaires.

Constitution of the People's Democratic Republic of Algeria, 1963.

Constitution of the People's Democratic Republic of Algeria, 1976, as amended, 1979.

Constitution of the People's Democratic Republic of Algeria, 1976, as amended, 2002, 2008, and 2016.

Constitution of the People's Democratic Republic of Algeria, 1989.

Cuniberti, G. (2007). *Grands systèmes de droit contemporains*. Paris: LGDJ.

Dawuni, J., & Kang, A. (2015). Her Ladyship Chief Justice: The Rise of Female Leaders in the Judiciary in Africa. *Africa Today*, Bloomington, *62*(2), 45–69.

Dawuni, J., & Masengu, T. (2019). Process and Progress: Women and Judicial Appointments to the Bench in Nigeria and Zambia. In W. Sterret & W. Lee (Eds.), *Law and Courts*. Edward Elgar Research Handbook.

De Bana, K. (1964). *Les principes du droit public algérien et institutions politiques, Initiation à la science du droit*. Alger: Etudes Africaines.

Decree N° 62-45 (November 22, 1962) (Alg.).
Decree N° 72-203 (1972) (Alg.).
Decree N° 87-208 (1987) (Alg.).
Decree 1834 (August 10, 1834) (Fr.).
Decree 1842 (September 26, 1842) (Fr.).
Decree 1854 (October 1, 1854) (Fr.).
Decree (1859) (Fr.).
Decree 1866 (March 17, 1866).
Discourse of the Algerian Minister of Justice at the opportunity of international day of women, March 8, 2019.
El Moudjahid, August 10, 2019.
Executive Decree No. 90-139 (May 19, 1990).
Femme et marché du travail, rapport, CNES, 25e session plénière, April 2005, 215 p.
Hamad, M. (2016). Egypt. The Lingering Battle for Female Judgeship. In G. Bauer & J. Dawuni (Eds.), *Gender and the Judiciary. From Obscurity to Parity?* (pp. 16–320). New York: Routledge Publishers.
Hoffner, A.-B. (2013, February 1). L'islam dans les Constitutions des pays du monde musulman. *La Croix*. Retrieved from https://www.la-croix.com/Religion/Spiritualite/L-islam-dans-les-Constitutions-des-pays-du-monde-musulman-_NG_-2013-02-01-906436.
https://www.mjustice.dz/fr/mapdzfr/.
Kamau, W. (2013). Women Judges and Magistrates in Kenya: Challenges, Opportunities and Contributions. In U. Schultz & G. Shaw (Eds.), *Gender and Judging* (pp. 167–190). Oxford: Hart Publishing.
Keswani, M.-J. (2002). The Evolution of the Role of Women in Algeria (1830–1992): Between Rhetoric and Reality (Doctoral, Durham University). Retrieved from http://etheses.dur.ac.uk/1725/.
Klibi, S. (2016). Tunisia: A New Constitution and More Women Judges. In G. Bauer & J. Dawuni (Eds.), *Gender and the Judiciary. From Obscurity to Parity?* (pp. 80–92). New York: Routledge Publishers.
Lalami, F. (2008). L'enjeu du statut des femmes durant la période coloniale en Algerie. Editions Antipodes. *Nouvelles Questions Féministes*, *27*(2), 16–27.
Law n° 62-157 (December 31, 1962) (Alg.) Law no. 63-218 (June 18, 1963) (Alg.).
Law n° 04-12 (September 6, 2004) (Alg.) https://www.cairn.info/revue-nouvelles-questions-feministes-2008-3-page-16.htm.
Legeais, R. (2016). *Grands systèmes de droit contemporains: Approche comparative*. Paris: LEXISNEXIS.
Lindbekk, M. (2017). Women Judges in Egypt: Discourse and Practice. In N. Sonneveld & M. Lindbekk (Eds.), *Women Judges in the Muslim World* (pp. 284–316). Leiden: Brill. Retrieved from https://brill.com/view/book/edcoll/9789004342200/B9789004342200_012.xml.
Mahiou, A. (2012). Les séquences du changement juridique en Algérie. Cinquante ans de droit (1962–2012). Insaniyat / إنسانيات. *Revue algérienne d'anthropologie et de sciences sociales* (57–58), 73–89. https://doi .org /10 .4000 /insaniyat .13689.

Mahiou, A. (2017). Les droits de l'homme dans les constitutions algériennes (1963–2016). In Pedone (Ed.), *Mélanges en l'honneur du professeur E. Decaux* (pp. 675–688). Retrieved from https://hal-amu.archives-ouvertes.fr/hal-01831780.

Marzouki, N. (2010). Algeria. In S. Kelly & J. Breslin (Eds.), *Women's Rights in the Middle East and North Africa: Progress Amid Resistance*. Freedom House.

Mathétés, O. (1967). La réforme judiciaire algérienne, Annuaire de l'Afrique du Nord, Centre national de la recherche scientifique. Centre de recherches sur l'Afrique méditerraneéenne (CRAM) (éds.) (pp. 111–119). Paris: Editions du CNRS.

Menkel-Meadow, C. (1987). *The Comparative Sociology of Women Lawyers: The "Feminization" of the Legal Profession.* Retrieved from https://escholarship.org/uc/item/9x36g2xv.

Michelson, E. (2013). Women in the Legal Profession, 1970–2010: A Study of the Global Supply of Lawyers. *Indiana Journal of the Legal Global Studies*, *20*(2), 1071–1137.

Moghadam, V. (n.d.). *Women, Law, and Judicial Decision-Making in the Middle East and North Africa: Toward Gender Justice*. 19.

Mohsen-Finan, K. (2008). L'évolution du statut de la femme dans les pays du Maghreb. *Note de l'Ifri*, 12.

Oussedik, F. (2011). Postcolonie et rapports de genre en Algérie. *Tumultes*, *37*(2), 81–98.

Organic law 04-12 (September 6, 2004) (Alg.).

Organic law 05-11 (July 17, 2005) (Alg.).

Organic law 11-12 (July 28, 2011) (Alg.).

Organic law no. 12-03 (January 12, 2012) (Alg.).

Prud'homme, P. (2014). Baudouin Dupret, La charia. Des sources à la pratique, un concept pluriel. *Lectures*. Retrieved from http://journals.openedition.org/lectures/14497.

Ruiz, V. (n.d.). The Role of Women Judges and a Gender Perspective in Ensuring Judicial Independence and Integrity. Retrieved April 8, 2020, from UNODC: The Doha Declaration website: //www.unodc.org.

Saïdi, K. (2006). La réforme du droit algérien de la famille: Pérennité et rénovation. *Revue internationale de droit comparé*, *58*(1), 119–152. https://doi.org/10.3406/ridc.2006.19414

Sambron, D. (2005). L'évolution du statut juridique de la femme musulmane à l'époque coloniale. *Histoire de la justice*, *16*(1), 123–142.

Schultz, U., & Shaw, G. (Eds.). (2013). *Gender and Judging*. Oxford; Portland, Oregon: Hart Publishing.

Sonneveld, N. (2017). Women's Access to Legal Education and Their Appointment to the Judiciary: The Dutch, Egyptian and Indonesian Cases Compared. In N. Sonneveld & M. Lindbekk (Eds.), *Women Judges in the Muslim World* (pp. 51–98). Leiden: Brill. Retrieved from https://brill.com/view/book/edcoll/9789004342200/B9789004342200_012.xml.

Sud Horizons. Benrahal, Neila. 2018. Les magistrates engagées pour l'application des reformes.

United Nations, Committee on the Elimination of Discrimination against Women, Initial Reports of State Parties, Algeria, September 1, 1998, CEDAW/C/DZA/1.

Vandevelde-Dailliere, H. (1980). *Femmes Algeriennes à travers la condition féminine dans le constantinois depuis l'indépendance*. Alger: Office des Pubs. Universitaires.

Wilson, B. (2005). Will Women Judges Really Make a Difference?: The Fourth Annual Barbara Betcherman Memorial Lecture. *Family Court Review*, *30*(1), 13–25. https://doi.org/10.1111/j.174-1617.1992.tb01265.x.

Women in the Judiciary in the Arab States. Removing Barriers, Increasing Numbers, ESCWA, SPDL, UNOHCHR, ICJ, 2019 (E/ESCWA/ECW/2019/2).

Chapter 3

Opening the Door for Women in the Cape Verdean Judiciary

Vera Duarte

INTRODUCTION

This reflective piece uses legal narrative to situate the lives and experiences of women in the law. I will use legal storytelling and historical analysis to build a foundation upon which future studies of women in the Cape Verdean legal and judicial systems can be built. Understanding my life, the political developments in my country and my professional journey are critical to understanding the current situation of women in the Cape Verdean judiciary.

TRACING MY PERSONAL JOURNEY TO THE LAW

I was born and raised in the cosmopolitan port city of Mindelo, São Vicente, in the Cape Verde archipelago off the West African coast. Ancestors on my maternal side came from a Sephardic Jewish couple—Moses Benrós and Mesaltob Cohen—who, in 1856, left Tangier, Morocco, passed through Gibraltar, and settled in Cape Verde with their three sons—Aaron, Abraham, and Isaac—in the second half of the nineteenth century. Isaac Benrós, who raised a family and died in 1905 in Santo Antão, Cape Verde, was my mother's grandfather and my great-grandfather. My ancestors on the paternal side came from the African continent and were brought to the archipelago as slaves. I do not know which ethnicity they belonged to, due to the family breakdown that accompanied enslavement, but they most likely were of Wolof, Papel, or Balanta origin.

Like most Cape Verdeans, I am the fruit of a long process of crossbreeding that took place between these groups, along with Europeans from Portugal and elsewhere. We are a globally mestizo people. My father, Domingos

António Duarte (São Nicolau, 1918–São Vicente, 1989), was a great woodworker who, through commitment and hard work, became a successful trader of farm crops. He was a perfect example of a self-made man. He liked to farm and was a great artist, and an accomplished pianist and 12-string guitar player.

My mother, Eufémia Filipa Benrós de Melo Duarte (Santo Antão, 1928—São Vicente 2018), had planned to become a nurse but soon married and her children became her reason for living. She was of good families, although with few possessions, and lived on the imminently rural island of Santo Antão. Her father cultivated a taste for reading in his nine children, and evenings were filled with him reading to them, typically novels by Victor Hugo and other classic authors. All of his children, including the girls, studied at least until the fourth grade of primary education, which was unheard of in the first half of the twentieth century, when women had no access to schooling. They grew up in a cultured, yet modest environment.

The nine children that my father had, the last five being the result of marriage with my mother, went to primary and secondary school. Five attended college. We were six girls and three boys, but access to everything was the same for everyone, because both my father and mother were open-minded people and raised their children on a philosophy of equality. I was always the best student and loved reading.

During my childhood, paddling and whipping were still used to "educate" children, but I was extremely fortunate to never have been subjected to my parents' whips or teachers' spankings. I was small and terribly afraid of being beaten and think that's why I always tried to be a good daughter and student. I remember as if it were today, the day my fourth-grade teacher asked what we wanted to be when we grew up, and at the age of 10, I was the only student who raised her hand to answer. Without hesitation, I declared: "a lawyer!"

Years later, I wondered why I had said that and understood that the answer most likely came to me because my parents were always saying, "She is going to be a lawyer" because I really liked to ask questions. Toward the end of high school, when I had to choose which area of study to pursue, I chose the section that gave access to law courses. However, Gil Eanes High School that year couldn't offer that section because of an insufficient number of candidates.

To stay in São Vicente, it would have been normal for me to change course to another path with access to history, psychology, or sociology, instead of law. But I was stubborn in my choice, and my parents sent me to boarding school in Lisbon, Portugal, from 1968 to 1970, so that I could study law.

I then started at the Faculty of Law of the University of Lisbon. It was all I wanted! I've always been very rooted in the causes of justice. Marginalization and perceptions of inferiority of women, de facto and de jure, always bothered me. I saw in law school, until then only available to men, a real way of challenging the status quo and providing me with the necessary means to work on issues related to justice for women: the right to equal rights and opportunities. I always thought of the law as a form of struggle for rights.

CAPE VERDE'S INDEPENDENCE AND LEGISLATIVE REFORM

In 1974, while in my fourth year of law school, the Carnation Revolution (also known as the Cravos Revolution) took place in Portugal. The April 25, 1974, bloodless military coup overthrew the Estado Novo regime and would bring democracy to Portugal and independence to its then "overseas provinces" of Angola, Cape Verde, Guinea-Bissau, Mozambique, and Sao Tome.

Like most Cape Verdean students in Lisbon, I immediately interrupted the course and returned to Cape Verde to work on reconstruction of my country. Although in the first year I was a teacher of politics and Portuguese at Ludgero Lima High School, the following year I was invited to work at the Legislation and Documentation Studies Office of the Ministry of Justice in Praia, which had been established in the capital of Cape Verde. There began my professional career as a lawyer.

National Reconstruction was the name given to the initial phase of Cape Verde as an independent country, following the proclamation of independence on July 5, 1975, by the National People's Assembly, the Max Legislative Body. The first fundamental law the country adopted was the Cape Verdean Political Organization Act (better known as the Law on the State Political Organization or LOPE). In a mere 22 articles, this law declared Cape Verde as an independent and sovereign state, instituted the organs of power, and abrogated all norms that were contrary to the principles and objectives of the African Party of Guinea and Cape Verde Independence (Partido Africano para a Independência da Guiné e Cabo Verde in Portguese [PAIGC]), which led the struggle for national liberation under Immortal Amílcar Cabral.

Article 22 of the LOPE stated: "The Portuguese Legislation in force on this date temporarily maintains its validity in all that is not contrary to national sovereignty, the present Law, the other Laws of the Republic and the principles and objectives of the PAIGC." Profound reforms to the legal system inherited from colonialism began to be introduced, in the light of the LOPE and through the Ministry of Justice headed by the distinguished jurist Dr. David Hopffer Almada and the Office of Studies, Legislation and Documentation (GELD) guided by late jurist Dr. César Fernandes.

Our legal system was the same as Portugal's legal system, which was modeled on the French Civil Code system. It is noteworthy that the Cape Verde archipelago was uninhabited upon the arrival of navigators in the service of the *El Rei* of Portugal, and a Creole mestizo society was formed, resulting from the settlement made with Portuguese and other Europeans and free and enslaved Africans from the main continent. Thus, a traditional African justice system has never been formed. So unlike most other African legal systems, we did not experience the duality of the judicial system, with a traditional justice governed by customs and an official justice governed by colonial legislation.

Also the Indigenous Statute—which defined the rights and duties of the natives of other Portuguese colonies, including Angola, Mozambique, and Guinea-Bissau, during the colonial period—was not applied in Cape Verde. The Cape Verdean legal and judicial system was always shaped by the Portuguese system, as we were part of Portuguese territory and sovereignty.

Desiring change, soon after the declaration of independence, the judicial structure inherited from colonialism was reorganized in new ways "more in line with the realities of our land and the interests of our People," as emphasized in the preamble of Decree-Law 33/75 of October 16, which created the new judicial organization for the country. This decree established many major innovations. The judicial territory of the Republic of Cape Verde was divided into two regions, Barlavento and Sotavento, and these two subregions were subdivided into zones. During this time, we witnessed the greatest revolution in the Cape Verdean judiciary—the creation of Zone Courts. These courts were intended to provide a justice of proximity, and in them functioned elected judges—either three or five—who were supposed to prosecute petty civil cases and crimes—cases that disturbed social peace and overwhelmed the courts that are commonly referred to as "civil and criminal trifles."

In areas where there were five judges, two had to be women; if there were three, one had to be a woman, which immediately confirmed the change in attitude toward women's participation in the public domain.[1] Initially, judges were residents of the territorial district encompassed by the Zone Court, had no legal background, and usually were illiterate people or educated only through fourth grade.

I participated fully in the extraordinary experience of helping to prepare the laws that established the creation and functioning of the courts, in establishing the courts themselves, and in holding seminars to instruct judges about their judicial functions. I traveled at least twice across all the islands of the archipelago, first boosting the holding of the public assemblies that elected judges, then giving them seminars. This absolutely unique process gave rise to *A Popular Justice in Cape Verde*,[2] a reference book by Portuguese sociologist Boaventura de Sousa Santos, who accompanied us on this adventure.

With the advent of multiparty democracy and the victory of the Movement for Democracy Party (MpD) in 1991, the government of the Second Republic abolished the Zone Courts. These courts were considered politicized because at least one of the judges had to be a militant in the PAIGC party, which had gained independence and was in power. The 1977 Zone Courts Guide effectively recommended that at least one of the judges should be a member of the Zone Political Committee "so that there can always be a close link between popular court activity and party guidelines."

I feel solutions could have been found within the Zone Courts, by depoliticizing their composition and completely judicializing their performance. Their elimination left a void that led to the overburdening of the courts of trial, and the government is finally seeking to mitigate this gap by establishing small claims courts.

CONSTITUTIONAL EVOLUTION OF CAPE VERDE

I offer an overview of the evolution of the constitutional history by first presenting the major developments. The constitutional laws in Cape Verde, all of the National People's Assembly, were as follows:

1. LOPE, Political Organization Law of the State of Cape Verde, July 5, 1975
2. Political Constitution of the Republic of Cape Verde, September 5, 1980
3. Constitutional law no. 1/III, December 17, 1988
4. Constitutional law no. 2/III, September 29, 1990
5. Constitution of the Republic of Cape Verde, August 5, 1992

Our first Constitution was created in 1980. Through this Magna law, a one-party regime was institutionalized and PAIGC was defined in Article 1 as the leading force of society. Years later, the great breach would come to pass with constitutional law no. 2/III/90 that repealed Article 4º of the Constitution and institutionalized the precipice of pluralism. Following January 1991 legislative elections, which gave the MpD victory, a new constitution was promulgated in 1992, establishing Cape Verde as a democratic state. This new constitution gave broad rights, freedoms, and guarantees to citizens; established the fundamental rights of the citizen, established a system of government of balance of power between the various organs of sovereignty; and enshrined a strong and independent judiciary.

Today, over 46 years after independence, for a population of half a million people, Cape Verde has a total of 25 courts—the Supreme Court of Justice, two Courts of Appeal, and 22 District Courts. Small claims courts were introduced into our judicial organization but have not yet been established.

ATTEMPTS TO PROMOTE WOMEN'S RIGHTS IN CAPE VERDE

In the first years after independence and following judicial reform—bearing in mind that the LOPE proclaimed the equality of all before the law—the Cape Verdean government, through the Ministry of Justice where I worked, began to change laws that regulate the legal situation of people. All provisions of both civil and criminal law that enshrined discriminatory norms on grounds of gender or other identity were gradually being amended or repealed. I will only refer to the laws in which I participated directly.

By Decree-Law 69/76 of July 3, 1976, we assigned equal rights to both spouses within a marriage, eliminating the denomination of head of household assigned to the male spouse and giving equal status to both spouses. We created the legally recognized de facto union figure, giving legal rights of marriage to de facto unions between men and women which indicated stability in the union lasting more than three years. We legislated divorce by mutual agreement and litigation, allowing it to be treated as a solution rather than as a sanction for effectively broken marriages. We gave divorce legal treatment to the termination of the legally recognizable de facto union that lasted more than three years.

With Decree-Law 84/76 of September 25, 1976, we abolished the discriminatory and stigmatizing denomination of legitimate and illegitimate children, as born out of wedlock between their parents. We sought to eliminate or diminish the figure of the incognito father by allowing the woman, at the time of registration of the unaccompanied child to declare the name of the alleged father, and the conservatory to proceed to officially verify the declared paternity. If confirmed, this would be on the child's record. If not confirmed, a paternity investigation by the Public Prosecution Service as Curator of Minors would take place. This was not only for the child's name to have both parents on the register, but also for future possible maintenance actions, if either parent did not voluntarily comply with the obligation to provide maintenance to the minor child.

All of these amendments were later incorporated and deepened by Decree-Law 58/81 of June 20, 1981, which approved a new Family Code and repealed all material contained in Book IV of the Civil Code in force on July 5, 1975 (the Portuguese Civil Code). The new Family Code established the following general and fundamental principles:

1. Secularization of marriage
2. Monogamy
3. Family stability
4. Equal rights and duties between men and women

5. Equality of children before the law
6. Child Protection
7. Protection of maternity
8. Protection of needy people

Years later, Book IV of the Civil Code was rebuilt, maintaining the innovations provided by later legislation that enshrined equal rights between men and women and other progressive norms. To complete the picture of the fundamental legislative changes in which I was privileged to have participated, it is worth mentioning two pieces of legislation that enormously impacted women's lives: the law of nationality and the law of voluntary termination of pregnancy.

Decree-Law 71/76 of July 24, 1976, established absolute equality between men and women in the acquisition and loss of Cape Verdean nationality, departing from the general principle that it is the wife who must acquire the nationality of her husband.

Law 9/3/86 of December 31, 1986, of the National People's Assembly, allowed for abortion in the following terms:

1. Termination of pregnancy is not punishable when performed with the consent of the pregnant woman, within the first 12 weeks of pregnancy, in a hospital, under medical care and under regulated terms.
2. Termination of pregnancy during any gestation period is not punishable by law, provided that it takes place under the other conditions set forth in the preceding paragraph when:
   a) Continued pregnancy results in a serious risk of death to the woman or danger of serious and permanent injury to her physical and mental health.
   b) It is intended to prevent probable transmission to the fetus of a serious hereditary or contagious disease.
   c) It is intended to prevent the unborn child from suffering serious physical defects or mental disorders.

This law was highly controversial because it triggered immense displeasure in the ruling Catholic Church in the country. The church severely penalized the political party then in power, which lost the following elections in 1991. But the law survived and continues to this day, being the first law of voluntary termination of pregnancy (IVG) in the Community of Portuguese Speaking Countries.

SERVING IN THE JUDICIARY IN CAPE VERDE AND HUMAN RIGHTS INSTITUTIONS

In 1977, I went back to Lisbon to complete the law course I had interrupted in 1974. When I returned to Cape Verde in 1978, I resumed work as a legal adviser to the general secretary of the government that supported then Prime Minister Commander Pedro Pires. But soon after, I was appointed an attorney of the Republic.

With my appointment as a prosecutor in 1978 for the first time since the proclamation of national independence, the state of Cape Verde had a woman in the judiciary. I was also the first woman magistrate in the Portuguese-speaking African Countries (PALOP). This was only possible because of the revocation by virtue of the constitutional provision prohibiting discrimination between men and women of the colonial era legal prohibition of women from participating in certain professions such as the judiciary and diplomacy.

This was a unique moment in my life and professional career because, in addition to everything that a public prosecutor does—prosecuting, representing the state, and defending the rights of citizens—I was able to materialize many of the values that moved me, including:

1. Fiercely combatting violence against women and children
2. Guaranteeing legal actions against parents who abandoned their children
3. Determine the paternity of a child born out of wedlock

In addition to working in the proceedings, I have always sought out-of-court settlement of disputes, encouraging people to seek resolution before filing a lawsuit.

My personal achievements as the first woman prosecutor in the Cape Verdean judiciary were noted internationally. I was interviewed by several newspapers, including the *Washington Post* in the United States and *The Observer* in the United Kingdom. I was referenced in editions of the World Who's Who of Women 1984 (p. 194); the International Register of Profiles, Edition VIII, 1985 (p. 259); and the World Who's Who of Women 1986, Eighth Edition (p. 188), among others. All of these publications greatly emphasized the fact that I attended law school and was the first Cape Verdean magistrate.

In 1979, I was invited to join the delegation of Prime Minister Pedro Pires to attend the VI Summit of Non-Aligned Countries in Havana, Cuba. I had the incredible experience of meeting and talking with most of the leaders of Africa, Asia, and Latin America, many of which are no longer with us, including Mozambique military commander Samora Machel, Palestine Liberation Organization chairman Yasser Arafat, Ghana president Jerry Rawlings, Grenada prime minister Maurice Bishop, and Cuba prime minister Fidel Castro. A few other women participated. It is worth noting that the Non-Aligned Movement—whose fundamental pillar is solidarity in peoples—began in the 1960s with the Bandung Conference in Indonesia, in 1963.

I was invited to visit the judicial institutions of the United States in 1981, and in the company of jurists from other African countries, we visited judicial institutions from various American states. We had a memorable meeting with U.S. Supreme Court Justice Sandra Day O'Connor, herself the first woman on the Supreme Court of the United States of America.

After being a public prosecutor in the two main judicial regions of the country, Praia and Mindelo, I went to train at the Center for Judicial Studies in Lisbon, an institution specialized in the training of magistrates, as there was no Cape Verdean magistrate training institution. I was the first woman to attend and there still is no judicial training institution in Cape Verde at the time of this writing. When I returned and after working in some departments of the Ministry of Justice, there was another moment of achievement in the Cape Verdean judicial system, when in 1992 I was appointed to a two-year term, by presidential decree, as judge counsel to the Supreme Court (STJ). For the first time, the highest judicial body in the country included a woman who joined four other men to serve on the five-justice bench.

I was reelected as supreme counsel judge by the Superior Council of the Judiciary, for a new term, now five years. Other women followed in the judiciary, notably Dr. Teresa Évora, who joined the judiciary in 1987 as the first female Judge of Instancia at the Tribunal da Praia and was elected to the Supreme Court in 1998. Judge Fatima Colonel was elected to the STJ in 1993 and has served as president of the STJ since 2015. At that time, the Supreme Court had generalist competence, and all judge counselors were to judge civil, criminal, administrative, constitutional, and electoral matters.

The visibility that these positions brought me and the activism I have always been involved with for human rights got me invitations to various international functions. In 1993, I was elected by the Organization of African Unity (OAU), the current African Union (AU), as the first woman to be a member of the African Commission on Human and Peoples' Rights (ACHPR) in the assembly held in Cairo, Egypt, and I became vice chair of the commission. The African Commission is a quasi-judicial body charged with the promotion and protection of human rights across the continent, interpreting the African Charter on Human and Peoples' Rights, and analyzing individual allegations of violations of the African Charter. The commission is composed of African experts nominated by the state parties, 11 of whom are elected with terms of six years.

The African Charter, also known as the Banjul Charter, is a regional human rights instrument approved by the OAU Assembly in 1981 and entered into force on October 21, 1986, which was proclaimed African Day of Human Rights. Under it, the African Commission was established in 1987 and is based in Banjul, the Gambia. In 1995, I was invited to join the International Commission of Jurists (ICJ), a body that fights for the rule of law around the world and which includes lawyers and judges of all nationalities. The ICJ is an international nongovernmental organization created in 1952, the year of my birth, that is based in Geneva, Switzerland, and works to develop national and international standards of human rights and the rule of law.

Also, that year, I was invited to join the Lisbon-based North-South Center of the Council of Europe, which fights to promote human rights, democracy, and the rule of law, contributing to North-South dialogue and global interdependence, having joined its executive committee representing the south. I was also a member of the International Federation of Women in Legal Careers, the African Federation of Women in Legal Careers, and other regional African organizations, all linked to women and law.

As a member of these organizations, I had permanent ongoing dialogues with regional human rights organizations in Africa, Europe, and America. I would like to recall with great reverence the late Isaac Nguema, president of the African Commission, and Judge Petiti of the European Court of Human Rights, who have always welcomed me with great affection and guided me in the intricacies of human rights organizations.

As a result of this activity, I was awarded the Council of Europe's North-South Human Rights Prize of Lisbon, and I approached major human rights defenders around the world, including the late French lawyer Stéphane Hessel, Peter Gabriel, Simone Veil, Kofi Annan, Bob Geldof, Frene Ginwala, Lula da Silva, Margarite Barankitse, Mario Soares, Graça Machel, Mary Robinson, Emma Bonino, and Abderrahman Youssoufi, all North-South Human Rights awardees.

The greatest joy and pride in this participation was my work in drafting the Additional Protocol to the African Charter on Human and Peoples' Rights on the Rights of Women in Africa (Maputo Protocol), a legal instrument that prohibits ancestral rights-violating practices of women, such as female genital mutilation and widow inheritance.

I must confess that this is my most gratifying memory of my participation in the ACHPR. Although I had many important moments in the commission, especially when I joined in 1993 and was able to speak with the immortal Nelson Mandela, in a memorable meeting with the president of the Republic of Cape Verde, the late Dr. António Mascarenhas Monteiro, whose adviser I was. It was also unforgettable to commemorate the 10th anniversary of the establishment of the commission in the Republic of Mauritius with distinguished secretary general of the OAU Dr. Salim Ahmed Salim, who became a great friend.

As African commissioner, I proposed to the ACHPR the holding of a seminar on women's rights, which took place March 8–9, 1995, in Lomé, Togo. I chaired this event, which gave me the extraordinary opportunity to propose the creation of the legal instrument that would later become the Maputo Protocol. The contributions of Senegalese Dr. Adama Dieng and Nigerian Dr. Tokumbo Ige in this regard were also very important.

I was privileged to participate in the writing of the document that led to the Maputo Protocol as part of the working group formed and chaired by Ghanaian commissioner Vitor Dankwa. I visited several African heads of state as part of a delegation to raise awareness of the need to adopt the document. The adoption of the Maputo Protocol happened at the second ordinary session of the AU conference in Maputo, Mozambique, on July 11, 2003. The protocol entered into force on November 25, 2005, a date that is significant in the United Nations system as the start of the 16 days of activism against gender-based violence.

I also made advocacy campaigns with Dr. Maria das Dores Gomes, for ratification by Cape Verde of the protocol on the establishment of the International Criminal Court and participated in various initiatives aimed at disseminating the most relevant regional and international legal instruments for the promotion and protection of women's human rights.

I also participated in the drafting of reports to the Commission on Human Rights. In particular, I went to Geneva to present our country's report to the Convention Against All Forms of Racial Discrimination and to the Women's Status Committee in New York, addressing African women.

Years later, as chairperson of the National Commission for Human Rights and Citizenship (CNDHC), I traveled once again to all the islands that make up the country of Cape Verde to collect subsidies for the elaboration of the first National Action Plan for Human Rights and Citizenship, which would be adopted in 2003, and in which we emphasized women's rights, including:

1. Promoting gender equality and equity in the labor market by taking necessary legal and administrative measures to prevent and punish discrimination against women and sexual harassment.
2. Promoting a true culture of gender equity by including gender perspective in national development policies and disseminating in all municipalities.

When I was president of the CNDHC, my team recommended to the government that cross-sectional studies on human rights be added to the Cape Verdean school curriculum. By curious coincidence, I was then appointed Minister of Education and Higher Education in 2008 and was able to introduce the Citizenship Education curriculum. Later I would be invited, along with my colleague and future prime minister of Cape Verde Dr. José Maria Neves and other African guests, to connect with leaders in the United States for a month. Because of my activism, each time presidential elections are held in Cape Verde, I am invited to present my candidacy, which I have never done. At their invitations, I joined the Honor Committees of the presidential nominations of Commander Pedro Pires, Dr. Aristides Lima, and Dr. Jorge Fonseca.

REFLECTIONS ON MY SERVICE

First and foremost is the satisfaction of having been able to do something for the sake of women and humanity. More concretely, I would like to note the situation of women in the judiciary in Cape Verde. Data from the judiciary of Cape Verde indicate that as of May 2022, the gender composition of the judiciary is as follows: 26 women (37.5%) and 44 men (62.5%). For the public prosecutor's office, there are 25 women (38.5%) and 40 men (61.5%). In the practice of law, women are adequately represented, and the presidency of the bar has been held for several years by women, including Dr. Lígia Fonseca, Dr. Leida Santos, and Dr. Sofia Lima. Of note is the entry of women to the Judiciary Police (a police organization responsible for criminal investigation that is dedicated to the fight against organized crime, drug trafficking, and economic and financial crime), and some have already reached leadership positions. Dr. Jacqueline Semedo is the deputy national director.

We are thus achieving parity in the judiciary that we have not achieved in other sectors. Women judges and prosecutors of the Republic are in all levels of the judicial hierarchy, and for several years, the STJ has been chaired by a woman, Dr. Fatima Colonel.

In order to assess progress, it is necessary to examine comparative data from the National Institute of Statistics, for 2017, concerning the presence of women in other sectors. These statistics show that women still have a long way to go in public offices:

These numbers speak for themselves and reveal to society the disparity between the judiciary and other sectors. I can see that the fight against violence that we have always defended is a national priority today, and increasingly progressive laws seek to reduce this scourge. The president of the Republic, Dr. Jorge Carlos Fonseca, is ambassador of this cause. However, much remains to be done for meaningful progress.

There has also been an increase in childcare and protection, both in terms of the promotion and protection of children's rights, and the expansion of

Table 3.1 Gender Representation in Public Offices

Office	*Female (%)*	*Male (%)*
Parliament	23.6	76.4
Municipal deputies	29	71
Mayor	0	100
Women leaders in business	35	65
Leaders of civil society organizations	11.1	88.9
Ministers of state	25	75

Source: Created by author with data from National Institute of Statistics, 2017.

childcare networks to the most vulnerable. It should be emphasized that my career has always focused on the judicial and quasi-judicial processes; the popularization and dissemination of the approved laws; and in the holding of numerous conferences, seminars, and other meetings at national and international levels on the most diverse subjects related to women's rights and human rights.

Unfortunately, I cannot rely on sex-disaggregated statistical data on the decisions of judges and prosecutors in such sensitive areas as paternity investigation, child support, gender-based violence, or even contentious divorce as the data do not exist. To my knowledge, no study has yet been conducted with statistical data comparing the performance of female magistrates with the performance of male magistrates in such gender-related cases. But it is a widespread perception that women's access to the judiciary as magistrates has made all magistrates pay greater attention to these sensitive issues of women's lives.

The right of women to access the bench as judges is constitutionally established. The individual merit in the administration of good justice is, of course, independent of gender, since women do not suffer from any *capitis diminutio* and must therefore have access to all professions on equal terms.

The experience of women in the judiciary in Cape Verde has been truly successful, and the fact that we have almost reached parity is proof of the exercise of our personal choice and right to equal employment. We believe this is the path to pursue. The gains have been substantive. But I must point out that the participation of female magistrates in courts outside the country, such as in other regional and international courts, is not yet well known.

A few exceptions include Dr. Raquel Medina, who has been invited to participate in election observation missions in other African countries. I was also invited to lead the delegation of the then OAU to presidential elections in Santomé, but for reasons of force majeure I could not accept it. However, I have even gone on international missions from the United Nations such as Côte d'Ivoire to verify the violation of human rights by President Gbagbo's regime and to Angola also to verify human rights violations by the regime of President Eduardo dos Santos. Not to mention that during my tenure at the ACHPR I had jurisdiction over Portuguese-speaking African Countries. Another exception is Drª Januária Costa, who served as a judge of the Economic Community of West African States Court of Justice in Abuja, Nigeria (ECOWAS Court of Justice).

There is also a long way to go before women's participation in all sectors approaches their participation in the judiciary. Just to illustrate, as I write this in July 2019, the presentation of the Parity Bill should take place at the National Assembly. However, it is with a sense of frustration that we found that it was removed from the agenda of this session and should only be rescheduled for October 2019. Despite this setback, I believe women deputies supported by civil society will stay focused, and the project will be scheduled again. Statistics show that female representation in Parliament grows by 3.9% every five years and at this rate we would not reach parity until 2081.

CONSIDERATIONS ON THE IMPACT OF WOMEN'S ENTRY INTO THE JUDICIARY

Being the "first woman" in any profession or situation is not easy. Of course, I have at times been the target of discriminatory behavior and condescending comments because I am a woman in a territory still considered to belong to only men or operating on masculine institutional standards. But such behaviors never really bothered me because I was determined from a young age that I would never be a victim, neither of fate, nor of society, nor of circumstances, nor of people. Much less a victim of machismo, racism, or classism.

I do not deny that conditions at the outset were favorable to me. I was born in a family with a father who gave me a bright future and a mother who encouraged me. They had the financial means that allowed me to study what I wanted. I can say that I was shielded from possible feelings of inferiority both because I was a woman and I was African.

I have always encountered throughout my life, my studies, and my professional career, colleagues or others who somehow, sometimes try to downgrade me, sometimes try to mock me with less credible comments about a woman's presence or position in society and in professional settings. Generally, I would say that the global women's emancipation movement, my training in law, and my personal agency, inherited from my mother's spirit of rebellion and non-subordination, all helped me get to where I am.

Undeniably, there were times when I felt hurt by the behavior of others but never weakened. I have always studied hard, successfully completed courses, and dedicated myself wholeheartedly to my profession. With my heart and soul, I have also successfully dedicated myself to family life, allowing me to clearly demonstrate the compatibility of family life with a professional career. In 1977, I married Dr. Jose Maria dos Reis Martins. Our two children are Nuno Miguel Duarte Martins and José Miguel Duarte Martins. I divorced in 1994, and in 1999 married my current husband, António Filipe Lobo de Pina, an engineer. So far I have four granddaughters and other family members around me that give me a lot of happiness.

Over the years, it has always been possible to maintain human rights activism as my second skin. Whether in my country or internationally, I have always had an active voice in favor of human rights and law, especially of women and children. To be as exhaustive as possible, I must add that a vocation for writing has always accompanied me and has been what has kept me busy since I retired in 2010.

Nowadays, my main activity focuses on writing and giving lectures. With 11 books published—poetry, fiction, essay, and chronicles—many of them have as their fundamental theme the condition of women and are greatly impacted by my work in the judiciary and the constant challenge to human rights.[3] The themes of violence against women and child sexual abuse are always present in my writing. This activity has been crowned with some distinctions and awards that greatly encourage me. I would like to highlight the Tchicaya Tam'si 2001 African Poetry Prize, which profoundly impressed me. I was the first woman to receive such a distinction.

LOOKING INTO THE FUTURE

I have always believed that there is a dialectical relationship between the emancipation of women and women in law. From an early age, I realized that a legal woman could greatly help in her own process of emancipation and empowerment.

As violence against women was one of the first causes that informed my activism, I believe it was one of the unconscious factors that led me to choose law school and then the judiciary as a professional career. My parents had always said that I was very challenging and would certainly be a lawyer. At the age of 10, I declared that I wanted to be a lawyer. At 15, I left my family to study at a boarding school in Portugal, which gave me access to law school. A half century later, if I went back to the beginning, I would do the same. Why? Because I felt that the course fulfilled my main expectations by giving me weapons that have allowed me throughout my life to fight for justice, people's rights, and women's *rights*, which has always been my fundamental ambition.

Forty years after being the first woman in the judiciary, today we have an almost equal judiciary in the country. Twenty years after being the first woman on the ACHPR, today there are countless women who have joined the committee. Almost 25 years after being the first woman to win the North-South Human Rights Award, today, countless women have earned this award. In 2005, the Additional Protocol to the African Charter on Women's Rights that I had the honor to propose came into force and has played an important role in criminalizing traditional practices that violate women's human rights. We believe that the better known and applied, the better the situation of African women.

Cape Verde had the first Joint Government, which I was fortunate to integrate, and today other Portuguese-speaking countries are joining this achievement. In a process that began with the proclamation of independence in 1975, the country is increasingly adopting civil and criminal legislation in line with gender equality, with the fight against gender-based violence a national priority.

Women's empowerment and parity are actively pursued by the Cape Verdean nation, in line with the UN Sustainable Development Goals. Today the participation of Cape Verdean women in the judiciary is almost at parity with the male presence if we consider the judiciary in its totality. The Bar Association, with broad female participation, has been chaired by women for many years. Assistant judicial staff, including bailiffs, technicians, and advisers, are also mostly female.

While we are sure of the fundamental role that women's presence in the judiciary plays in the process of gender equality and equity, we understand that achieving such goals requires competition from a variety of other factors and sectors, further compounded by limited national resources and weak political will. Women's human rights are an integral and indivisible part of universal human rights and encompass all rights of civilians. Its promotion and protection belong to everyone, especially to governments and the international community.

The fight against poverty that affects large sections of humanity, especially women, and prevents them from fully enjoying their rights is something that challenges the cause of human rights and therefore challenges us. Today, it is through poetry, fiction, essays, and other forms of written intervention that I fight for my ideals.

But human rights and law will always be my second skin and I can only close this narrative with the presentation of my most recent initiative in this area. It is a call to the United Nations to create an international legal instrument to limit individual wealth, bearing in mind that poverty most severely affects women and children. I had the opportunity to personally deliver this appeal to UN secretary general Dr. António Guterres and under secretary general Dr. Adama Dieng on May 5, 2018, in New York, where I was attending the commemorations of the Portuguese Language and Communities Day. The text is sufficiently enlightening that I conclude by thanking all those who influenced me, those who accompanied me, and those I had the honor to influence. Here is the proposal:

> Appeal to the United Nations for the adoption of an International Convention (or Declaration) establishing limitations on the individual possession of wealth.
>
> Noting with deep disgust that 1% of the population holds 80% of the world's wealth and the 26 richest men in the world have as much wealth as the 3.6 billion people who make up half the planet; Noting with infinite sadness that 1/4 of the world's population lives below the poverty level; Firmly believing that the humanity of this 21st century cannot and must not live with such indecency and immorality; I propose to urge the United Nations to adopt an International

Convention (or Declaration) establishing limitations on the individual possession of wealth. The remnants would revert to the neediest. If this idea interests you, take ownership, expand, disseminate and reach the United Nations!

NOTES

1. The 1977 "Guide to Zone Courts" recommended that at least two of the judges in the Zone Council of Justice be women.
2. De Sousa Santos, B. (2015). *A Popular Justice in Cape Verde*. Almdedinas Editions. The book was presented by Dr. Vera Duarte in Praia in May 2015.
3. Duarte, V. (1993). *Amanhã A Madrugada*. Lisboa, Vega.

REFERENCES

Duarte, V. (2001). *O Arquipélago da Paixão*. Praia, Artiletra.
Duarte, V. (2004). *A Candidata*. Sonangol.
Duarte, V. (2005). *Preces E súplicas Ou Os Cânticos da desesperança*. Instituto Piaget.
Duarte, V. (2007). *Construindo a utopia: Temas E conferências sobre direitos humanos*. V. Duarte.
Duarte, V. (2013). *A palavra e os dias: Crônicas*. Nandyala.
Duarte, V. (2017). *A Matriarca: Uma estória de mestiçagens*. Pedro Cardoso Livraria.
Duarte, V. (2018a). *A reinvenção do Mar Antologia poética*. Rosa de Porcelana.
Duarte, V. (2018b). *De risos & Lágrimas*. Pedro Cardoso Livraria.
Duarte, V., & Duarte, S. (2019). *Cabo Verde, Um roteiro sentimental: Viajando Pelas Ilhas da Sodad, do Sol e da Morabeza*. Mudjer Edições.
Duarte, V., & Lopes Leão. (2010). *Ejercicios poéticos Exercícios poéticos*. Gobierno de Canarias.

Laws, Decrees, and Treaties

Book IV of the Civil Code in force on July 5, 1975 (the Portuguese Civil Code).
Constitutional law no. 1/III, December 17, 1988.
Constitutional law no. 2/III, September 29, 1990.
Constitution of the Republic of Cape Verde, August 5, 1992.
Decree-Law 69/76 of July 3, 1976.
Decree-Law 84/76 of September 25, 1976.
Decree-Law 58/81 of June 20, 1981.
Decree-Law 71/76 of July 24, 1976.
Law 9/3/86 of December 31, 1986.
LOPE, Political Organization Law of the State of Cape Verde, July 5, 1975.
Political Constitution of the Republic of Cape Verde, September 5, 1980.
Protocol to the African Charter on Human and Peoples' Rights on the Rights of Women in Africa (Maputo Protocol), 2005.

Chapter 4

Women Judges in Ethiopia

Maame Efua Addadzi-Koom
and Biruh Gemeda Gage

INTRODUCTION

Ethiopia's first woman chief justice, Meaza Ashenafi, was appointed in November 2018 (Sisay, 2018).[1] The appointment of this pioneer woman in law as the president of the Federal Supreme Court could mark a turnaround for women's presence in and contribution to Ethiopia's judiciary. Within a year of her appointment as the chief justice, six women judges were appointed to the Supreme Court (Gage, 2020). It is too early to tell if her appointment has made a significant or lasting improvement to women's representation within the federal judiciary but there is a promising feminization of the judiciary through the continued increase in women's appointments to the bench and through her agenda, which strongly features gender issues. While she is in charge of the federal judiciary, Meaza also envisions establishing an association for women judges that will strengthen and sustain women's presence in the judiciary.

Over the past few years, scholarship on gender and judging in Africa has been emerging, creating a classic cottage industry for African legal academics (Bauer & Dawuni, 2016). Several authors have documented various literature on gender and judging in a number of African countries, including Ghana, South Africa, Rwanda, Egypt, Nigeria, Tunisia, Tanzania, Kenya, Zambia, and Benin (Addadzi-Koom & Nkansah, 2021; Bauer & Dawuni, 2016; Dawuni, 2016a, 2020, 2021; Dawuni & Kang, 2015; Masengu, 2016, 2020).

To our knowledge, there has not been any published research on gender and judging in Ethiopia; thus, this chapter will be the first. The chapter has two main aims: first, to investigate how the judicial appointment process impacts gender representation in the federal courts; and second, to investigate the experiences of women judges in Ethiopia's judiciary—their contribution and challenges. To achieve this end, we have made women's voices the pivot of the investigation. Therefore, we rely mainly on the open-ended survey responses of 12 women judges at the federal courts, with judicial experience ranging from 8 to 15 years, to produce the narratives in this chapter. Respondents identities remained anonymous throughout the survey to protect their identities. We also use data from other documentary sources, such as legislation, books, scholarly articles, and official websites. As the first study on gender and judging in Ethiopia, the survey was primarily exploratory, and we attempt to position the findings and recommendations within the wider emerging literature in the African context. This chapter also adds to the existing scholarship by setting up an agenda for further and future studies on gender, judging, and representation in Ethiopia's judiciary.

The discussions in this chapter draw on two main theories: the critical mass and difference theories. The critical mass theory, applied to gender and minority research in the social sciences, suggests that minority groups can have marked impact once they form a critical mass (Dahlerup, 2006b; Grey, 2006). The theory has been used in recent years to evaluate women's representation on the bench and its impact on judicial outcomes in Africa (Albertyn & Bonthuys, 2016; Dawuni, 2016b; Yoon, 2016). In gender and judging research, critical mass theory posits that having sufficient proportions of women represented on the bench, a minimum of 30%, will feminize the bench, decrease the overarching masculine predispositions in the judiciary, and potentially yield positive judicial outcomes for women (Albertyn & Bonthuys, 2016). Closely linked to the critical mass theory is the idea that *critical acts* and *critical actors* are equally necessary to drive qualitative change into a new level (Childs & Krook, 2006; Dahlerup, 2006b).

In this chapter, the critical mass theory and its corollaries are used to explain how and to what extent the representation of women as judges in Ethiopia affects women's rights. Our argument is that the critical mass theory is instrumental in ensuring not only that a critical mass of women judges influences women's rights but also that societal perceptions about women on the bench change. We make a case for the need for more critical acts by the critical mass of women judges. We also argue for critical actors in leadership at the bench to advance a gender-friendly workplace culture in the judiciary, gender-sensitive policy changes (substantive representation), and even more women's presence in the judiciary (descriptive representation).

The difference theory, on the other hand, emphasizes the difference that women judges bring to the bench particularly through their processes and decisions. Difference theorists argue that the presence of women judges is necessary to influence the outcome of gender-specific cases including matrimonial and gender-based violence cases (Cowan, 2013; Gilligan,

1982; Kenney, 2013). A number of case studies testing the validity of the difference theory have been inconclusive and render the theory empirically questionable. (Coontz, 2000; Dawuni, 2021; Malleson, 2003). Thus, there is no uniform response to the question of whether women judges make a difference in judicial decision-making. This chapter therefore provides empirical evidence to supplement existing case studies on the difference theory from an Ethiopian perspective. We argue, based on the survey data, that women judges in Ethiopia have made a difference (though minuscule) in judicial processes and outcomes and have the potential to do more given the appropriate conditions.

The chapter is organized into five sections, in addition to the introduction and conclusion. The first section, the historical overview, describes the general characteristics of the legal traditions practiced in Ethiopia, which largely follows the civil law system, and comments on the larger debate on whether some legal traditions (civil and common law systems) are better than others at promoting gender representation. The court structure and the gendered representation of women within the rank and file of the courts are outlined in the second section. The third section discusses the process of appointment to the bench, reviewing the constitutional provisions and other relevant laws. It also includes a brief discussion, based on the survey findings, of how the appointment process impacts gender representation and diversity. In the fourth section, we draw on the larger framework of critical mass and difference theories to discuss the perceptions about and actual practices of how women judges seek to promote women's rights. The challenges and obstacles women judges face and how they address them are in the fifth section.

HISTORICAL OVERVIEW

Ethiopia is an ancient country with a history of statehood spanning well over 3,000 years (Gudina, 2011). Hence, the country has developed its own legal traditions that differ from one internal region to another but are distinct from those in the rest of the world. Modern Ethiopia, with a modern system of government, was established a little over 150 years ago, but its codified set of laws with modern courts emerged only in the 1950s (Zewde, 2001). Until recently, the country observed a wholly customary and extremely fragmented law with either a religious or a sacred character. For instance, one of the earliest written laws was the nomocanon "Fetha Nagast," or the Law of Kings, which was drafted in Egypt in the thirteenth century and translated from Arabic into the Ge'ez language in the sixteenth century. Ethiopia's first modern and written constitution was enacted in 1931 by the then emperor Haile Selassie I (Ministry of Capacity Building, 2005).

The modern Ethiopian legal system largely follows the continental (civil law) system, where law is promulgated by the legislature, although the system also has common law elements (Ministry of Capacity Building, 2005). The continental legal system has a mixture of modern (secular), customary, and religious rules that coexist and operate in parallel. Research is needed to determine whether decisions rendered by the courts had any contribution in terms of lending principles by way of precedents during the period of law reform and codification in 1960s. As J. Vanderlinden (1966) states, "in all periods of Ethiopian legal history, our information concerning case law is very limited." However, what does exist is the *Digest of old Ethiopian Judgments*, prepared in 1952 for the purposes of drafting and codifying the 1960 Civil Code of Ethiopia (Woldemelak, 2005). This digest, which is made up of three volumes of old hand-written judgments starting from ancient times (as the Ca Veut of the English translation states), contains 7,296 summaries of civil judgments, proving that Ethiopian legal system was somewhat developed before the codification and modernization process started in the late 1950s (Woldemelak, 2005).

As mentioned before, Ethiopia's legal system has incorporated some features from the common law system as well, like giving precedence to the rulings of the Cassation Bench of the Federal Supreme Court. As Article 4 of the Federal Courts re-amendment Proclamation no. 454 of 2005 states, the Supreme Court cassation division is empowered to render a decision that is binding on federal as well as regional courts at all levels as long as the decision is rendered by at least five judges. Therefore, court judgments are now a source of law in Ethiopia.

Another feature of the Ethiopian legal system is its pluralism. Article 34(5) of the 1995 Constitution recognizes the validity and applicability of non-state laws such as religious and customary laws in some social fields (including personal and family law), making legal pluralism an important manifestation of federalism and a means to accommodate the rights of various multicultural groups in the country. Here, it should be noted that the Constitution establishes a federal system of government (the Federal Democratic Republic of Ethiopia—FDRE) with parliamentary democracy as stipulated under Article 45. Hence, regional states have their own constitution and laws that are enacted by the regional councils in areas or on topics reserved for them by the federal constitution. They also set up their own judiciary. The diversity of the population—more than 85 distinct ethnic groups and several religious groups, including Orthodox Christianity, Protestantism, Islam, Catholicism, Judaism, and indigenous religious beliefs—is one of the main reasons that legal pluralism and a federal system of government are necessary in Ethiopia. The scope of this chapter is, however, limited to the federal judiciary and laws.

In Ethiopia, the judiciary, or more specifically the Supreme Court, has not been granted the power to interpret the Constitution. Instead, the House of the Federation (HoF), the upper chamber of Parliament, composed of representatives of nations and nationalities (ethnic groups), has the ultimate power to interpret the Constitution if and when a constitutional dispute arises (1995 Constitution, Arts 53–62). Some legal scholars argue that because the highest judicial organ has been denied the power to undertake a constitutional review and that task has been granted to the HoF, a political entity, Ethiopia's constitutional review system cannot effectively protect human rights (Abebe, 2012). The Supreme Court's lack of ultimate power to interpret the Constitution, however, does not mean that it plays no role in interpreting the Constitution. Apart from applying the Constitution in everyday cases, Article 63/2 provides for the chief justice (president of the Supreme Court) to play an important role in determining which cases or questions need to be escalated to the HoF for interpretation. The chief justice of the Federal Supreme Court also heads the Council of Constitutional Inquiry, a body made up of prominent legal experts that examines constitutional issues and submits its findings with authoritative legal advice to the HoF before the latter makes its decision on constitutional issues.

In Ethiopia's legal system, the judiciary applies three types of legislature-enacted laws: proclamations, regulations, and directives. Proclamations are beneath the FDRE Constitution in hierarchy but are above regulations and directives, which are the second and third ranking legislations, respectively. There are also international agreements, which become part of the Ethiopian legal system when they are signed by the government and ratified by the Parliament. The *Negarit Gazeta* is Ethiopia's official legislative and executive (administrative) law reporter, in which all proclamations and regulations are printed in chronological order. The first issue appeared on March 30, 1942, and it has been published regularly, in Amharic and English, ever since.

The foregoing overview is relevant because in comparing the gender balance among judges in the judiciary, it is important to consider the unique features of the legal system in question. In civil law systems, women can usually be recruited to the judiciary directly from law schools, before they face possible career disruptions and family commitments, while in common law systems women often face statutory requirements of at least five to seven years post-qualification experience to qualify for the bench, by which time they may have been slowed down by other career and familial obligations (Galligan & others, 2017). As described earlier, Ethiopia follows the civil law system for the most part, with a few traces of common law traditions. The appointment process for judges is clearly written down in law and so may encourage a greater representation of women in the judiciary. In fact, a mechanism was implemented that allows fresh law school graduates to be fast-tracked into becoming judges at the lower federal courts, after receiving some training (Article 11 of the Amended Federal Judicial Administration Council Establishment Proclamation No. 684/2010). This fast-tracking system has significantly increased the number of women judges in federal courts because it provided an opportunity for high achievers from all law schools in the country to directly join the judiciary and it actively supported female law graduates through affirmative action. The current, and first woman, chief justice, Meaza Ashenafi, was herself a beneficiary of this system when she was first appointed as a judge (EBC, 2018).

However, much still needs to be done to achieve a fair representation of women in the judiciary, especially in the regional states. This trend of having a higher proportion of women in the higher (federal) courts than in the lower (regional) courts in Ethiopia represents what Dawuni (2016c) labeled as the paradox of stagnation, where the growth of women at the lower courts stagnates. Dawuni (2016c) hypothesized, based on a similar trend of women's representation on the bench in Ghana, that the paradox of stagnation will be offset when more women trickle up to the higher courts and more women are recruited into the judiciary. We believe this hypothesis to be true for Ethiopia as well, as will be seen later in this chapter.

COURT STRUCTURE AND REPRESENTATION OF WOMEN

The structure of the overall Ethiopian judiciary is laid out in Chapter 9 of the FDRE Constitution, which describes the arrangement of the courts at the federal and the state levels. Article 79(1) of the Constitution establishes an independent dual judicial system: the federal courts and the state courts, each with their own structures and administrations. Hence, judicial power, at federal and state level, is vested in the courts. According to Article 78(2) of the 1995 Constitution, supreme federal judicial authority is vested in the Federal Supreme Court, which sits in Addis Ababa, but the House of People's Representatives can decide, by a two-third-majority vote, to establish subsidiary federal courts across different regions of the nation whenever there is a need. Accordingly, federal high courts have been established in the five regional states of Afar, Benishangul-Gumuz, Gambela, Somali, and SNNPR (now including the new Sidama Region) (Proclamation No. 322/2003). The seats of federal courts are Addis Ababa and Dire Dawa City Administration, but they may choose to seat themselves at any place within the country if deemed necessary for the efficient rendering of justice (Article 30 of Proclamation No. 1234/2021).

Another unique feature of the 1995 Constitution is that, in addition to those "regular" courts, it recognizes Religious Courts and Customary Courts which had a de facto existence long before the current judiciary was established. For instance, the Sharia courts were officially recognized for the first time in the 1940s (Abdo, 2020), but federal Sharia courts were made a part of the federal judicial system only after the enactment of the Federal Courts of Sharia Consolidation Proclamation no. 188/1999. Sharia courts are established alongside the structures of regular federal courts (the Sharia First Instance Court, High Court, and Supreme Court levels) and exercise judicial authority mostly on marital matters (personal law) falling under Sharia law. However, this study does not look at the representation of women in Ethiopian Sharia courts.

Similarly, those customary courts that were already functioning when the current constitution came into force in 1995 were given recognition by the law and continue to exist. There are also other administrative tribunals at the federal level that are established by law under the executive to do the work of the judiciary on administrative matters like tax, trade competition, consumer protection, labor, and civil servants' disputes with their employing government offices. Of course, the decisions of all federal Sharia and administrative courts are subject to a review by the Federal Supreme Court.

The city administration of Addis Ababa, the capital of Ethiopia, has its own establishment charter that provides for municipal courts and Social Courts. Social Courts also exist in some other regional states even though they are not specifically mentioned in the FDRE Constitution (Ministry of Capacity Building, 2005). The City Charter creates only two levels of City Courts that exercise municipal jurisdiction: the First Instance and Appellate Courts. This means that there is no Supreme Court in the municipal system, although a cassation bench is included within the Appellate Court. Cassation review of the Appellate Court decisions can be brought before the Federal Supreme Court, which also decides jurisdictional conflicts between the city and federal courts (Wondirad, 2013). The Addis Ababa City Courts have jurisdiction over civil and petty offense cases happening within the city.

Federal judicial authority is structured into three levels of federal courts based on their competency. Based on this arrangement, we have the Federal Supreme Court, which is the highest federal judicial organ; the Federal High Court; and the Federal First Instance Court. State judicial power, which is similarly vested in state courts, is also structured into state supreme, high, and first instance courts. These courts exercise judicial authority within state jurisdiction and the jurisdiction of federal courts as delegated by the federal constitution. Federal judicial power in relation to matters falling under the jurisdiction of federal high courts and first instance courts is delegated to state supreme and high courts, respectively. The Federal Supreme Court has a Cassation Division which has the power to review and overturn decisions of lower federal courts and the State Supreme Court that are deemed to have contained fundamental errors of law. According to Article 10 of proclamation no. 1234/2021, such judicial decisions by the cassation bench on the interpretation of laws are binding on all federal and state courts from the date the decision is rendered. According to Articles 11–15, 25, and 29 of the Federal Courts Proclamation No. 1234/2021, each federal court may have a civil, criminal, and other divisions. Under every division, each court (bench) will have a presiding judge and two other judges. Federal Courts, as entities, are supervised and managed by court presidents, who double as judges and administrators with responsibilities and obligations to the president of the Supreme Court (Wondirad, 2013).

Figure 4.1 provides a graphic representation of the judicial structure in Ethiopia. Please note here that the cassation bench is just a special bench within the Supreme Court and that no judge is directly or specifically appointed as a judge to a cassation. However, since it has the powerful task of reviewing legal errors made by all other courts, including on final decisions made by the Supreme Court, it is shown separately in the figure.

Representation of Women in Federal Courts

The representation of women in the judiciary has recently shown a significant increase following government efforts to improve the balance, including the appointment of the first woman chief justice in Ethiopia (Sisay, 2018). Tables 4.1–4.3 show the gender distribution of judges at the three levels of federal

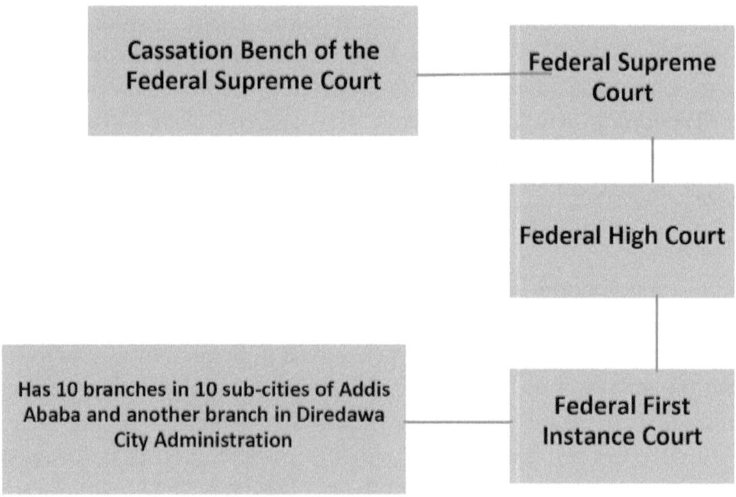

Figure 4.1 Structure of Federal Courts in Ethiopia. *Source*: Created by author with data from Constitution of the Federal Democratic Republic of Ethiopia, Articles 80 and 81 Federal Courts Proclamation No. 1234/2021, Chapter 3.

Table 4.1 Gender Distribution of Judges at the Federal Supreme Court, Obtained from the Human Resource Department of the Federal Judicial Administration Council, February 2022

Gender	*Number*	*Percentage*
Female	13	29.5
Male	31	70.5
Total	44	100

Source: Created by author with data from Federal Judicial Administration Council, January 2022.

Table 4.2 Gender Distribution of Judges at the Federal High Court

Gender	*Number*	*Percentage*
Female	32	22.3
Male	112	77.7
Total	149	100

Source: Created by author with data from Federal Judicial Administration Council, January 2022.

Table 4.3 Gender Distribution of Judges at the Federal First Instance Court

Gender	*Number*	*Percentage*
Female	74	34.2
Male	133	65.8
Total	187	100

Source: Created by author with data from Federal Judicial Administration Council, January 2022.

courts as of January 2022. The data was acquired from the Federal Judicial Administration Council, which oversees the nomination, appointment, and management of all federal judges.

The data in tables 4.1–4.3 shows that at the federal level the number of women decreases as we progress from the lower federal level court (the First Instance Court) through to the higher federal level court (Federal Supreme Court). This statistic reinforces the trickle-up hypothesis that the judiciary is feminized as women naturally and automatically ascend the ladder of promotion (Dawuni, 2016a; Malleson, 2003). This trend at the federal level contrasts with the overall distribution of women in the judiciary: the number of women judges at the regional level is less than at the federal level, a fact that discredits the trickle-up approach to feminizing the judiciary but rather supports Dawuni's (2016c) paradox of stagnation.

Taking 30% as the minimum required for a critical mass to be achieved, the data presented in tables 4.1–4.3 also reveal that only at the Federal First Instance Court can the percentage of women judges (34.2%) be said to form a critical mass according to the critical mass theoretical framework. There is, however, a promising chance of attaining a critical mass of women judges at the Federal High Court and Supreme Court levels in the near future. Then again, when the presence of women at the three federal level courts is considered as a whole, they form a critical mass, with 30.1% of all federal level judges being women. Further discussion on the impact of this critical mass of women can be found in the fifth section of this chapter.

APPOINTMENTS AND REPRESENTATION

The Constitution enshrines a broad range of cardinal principles regarding the judiciary. One such cardinal principle is the independence of the judiciary, which entails both the institutional independence of the courts and the personal autonomy of judges (1995 Constitution, Art. 78(1)). The Constitution guarantees the institutional independence of the judiciary under Article 79(2), which states that "courts of any level shall be free from any interference or influence of any governmental body, government official or from any other source." Sub-article 6 of the same article directs the Federal Supreme Court to draw up and administer the budget of federal courts when the House of Peoples' Representatives approves it.

With regard to the individual independence of judges, Article 79(3) states that "judges shall exercise their functions in full independence and shall be directed solely by the law." Article 79(4) further states that no judge may be removed from their duties before they reach the retirement age of 60 years (Proclamation No. 684/2010, Article 12[1]) except for violation of disciplinary rules or gross incompetence or grave illness as determined by an independent Judicial Administration Council (JAC).[2] Additionally, the JAC's decision to remove a judge on the aforementioned grounds must be approved by the House of Peoples' Representatives or the concerned State Council (when the judge works in a state court) by a majority vote. These strict conditions for removal of judges give judges the confidence to decide on cases without fear of repercussions from their superiors, the executive, or other external persons. The president and vice president of the Federal Supreme Court are appointed by the House of Peoples' Representatives based on the recommendation (direct nomination) by the FDRE prime minister (1995 Constitution, Art. 81). All other federal judges are appointed by the House of Peoples' Representatives after having been selected by the Federal JAC, which then submits their names to the prime minister, who in turn submits them to the house. A similar process is followed in appointing judges for regional (state) courts.

The flow chart in figure 4.2 shows the steps of the appointment process in a simplified form.

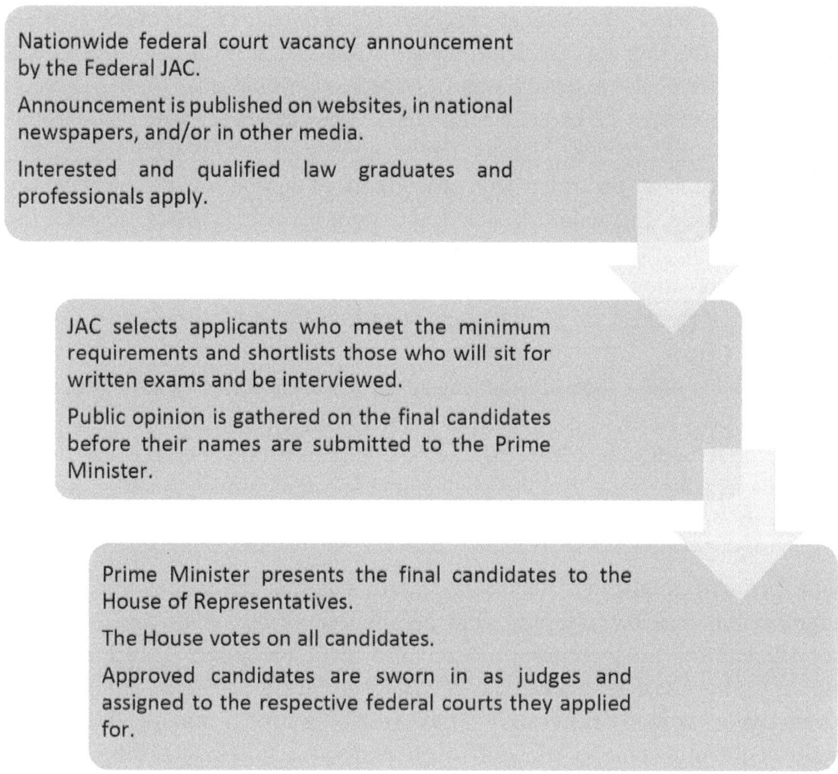

Figure 4.2 Three-step Appointment Process for Regional (State) Court Judges. *Source*: Created by author with data from Constitution of the Federal Democratic Republic of Ethiopia, Article 81. Federal Judicial Administration Proclamation No. 1233/2021, Chapter 3, Articles 20–33.

As the body that administers all issues of appointments, promotions, discipline, and other conditions of employment for federal judges, JAC is expected to make the necessary efforts to ensure representations of women (Amended Proclamation No. 684/2010). To improve the representation of women in federal courts, JAC applies affirmative action when selecting nominees from the pool of legal professionals who apply. This affirmative action is constitutionally backed under Article 35(3) of the Constitution:

> The historical legacy of inequality and discrimination suffered by women in Ethiopia taken into account, women, in order to remedy this legacy, are entitled to affirmative measures. The purpose of such measures shall be to provide special attention to women so as to enable them compete and participate on the basis of equality with men in political, social and economic life as well as in public and private institutions.

Given the absence of existing research on how the appointment process outlined above impacts gender representation and diversity in the federal courts in Ethiopia, the survey was intended to provide data on the subject. Respondents were asked whether they faced any challenges with the appointment process as women. Neither the responses of the women judges nor an examination of the rules and procedures of appointment revealed any significant issue that would hinder the appointment of women. In fact, the recruitment process, through affirmative action, encourages women to apply for judicial positions.

A judge at the Federal First Instance Court disclosed:

> Personally, I didn't face any challenges. All the legal process and procedures were met during my appointment. Plus, there is an affirmative action (support for women candidates) during the selection process. For instance, if a male and female candidate score the same point during selection, women candidates tend to be preferred.

That women applicants faced no gender-based challenges during the appointment process, coupled with affirmative action, may possibly have contributed to the increase in number of women judges in Ethiopia in recent years. As of January 2022, 30.1% of judges at the three federal level courts were women (Federal Judicial Administration Council, 2022). The increased representation of women on the bench notwithstanding, gender parity in the judiciary remains a remote goal. What then could be the cause of the current underrepresentation of women judges in federal courts? In answering this question a number of factors need to be considered: the history of the judiciary and its legal traditions, past discriminatory practices, and the various challenges women faced and still face in completing their education.

The present reality of gender disparity at the bench is also the legacy of flawed cultural norms, male-dominated systems, and discriminatory practices that have negatively affected women's participation. For instance, affirmative action only began to be implemented after the 1995 Constitution was enacted, and it took a while for the implementation to yield the statistics we see today. The appointment process also includes an ethnic group quota system that may limit some women applicants. As one respondent lamented:

> The biggest challenge for me was the application of quotas for different ethnic groups to be appointed as a judge. The fact that different nationalities had to be represented in the courts [judicial positions] sometimes limits those qualified candidates from holding the position.

Fewer females than their male counterparts join universities in Ethiopia, and this is even more apparent in law schools. One respondent explained that a prevailing educational policy prioritizing the sciences over the arts was another contributory factor: "the education policy of the country (which uses 70/30 per cent quota for natural sciences and social science studies) when allocating students to the university is limiting the number of students who get to the law school." Thus, few women will graduate from law school, which in turn means there is an even smaller pool of women legal professionals to choose judges from. In the words of a Federal High Court judge:

> The biggest challenge in my opinion [is] to reach high school and complete high school with good grades so that girls can study law in university. Only top students can get to law schools, especially the good ones like AAU [Addis Ababa University]. Finishing law schools has some challenges as well like financial problems, harassment from some professors and students,. . . etc.

This chain of events directly reflect the underrepresentation of women in the federal and state courts. Having discussed the current state of gender and representation on the bench in Ethiopia, its promoters, and drawbacks, we now turn our focus to how women judges have contributed to the judiciary.

WOMEN'S CONTRIBUTIONS TO THE JUDICIARY

In this section, we offer some insights into the actual practices and perceptions of how women at the bench in Ethiopia contribute to the judiciary and promote women's rights. We attempt to answer two questions here: Will an increase in the number of women judges make a difference? And, do women judges bring something different to the administration of justice and promotion of women's rights? The discussion is guided by the critical mass and difference theories and presents evidence from the survey data.

Women's Presence on the Bench: A Substantive Representation?

As to whether an increase in the number of women judges will make a difference in the judiciary, proponents of the critical mass theory are of the view that it will. They proffer that a higher number of women at the bench, a critical mass of about 30%, will significantly promote women's rights and challenge patriarchal rules and interpretations (substantive representation) (Albertyn & Bonthuys, 2016; Dahlerup, 2006a). However, the survey respondents were divided on this inquiry; while some felt that an increase in the number of women at the bench will promote women's rights, others did not feel so strongly about it. For example, in one judge's view, "Yes! Having more women is vital in assuring women's rights are respected," but another was a bit hesitant, stating that "I cannot say for sure it will make such difference as I have no information to that but on such [gender] issues women judges could have a better understanding & interpretation than men judges though."

A majority of the judges, however, favored the claims of critical mass theorists. As it stands now, with about 30.1% of judges at the federal level courts in Ethiopia being women, a proportion that meets the critical mass threshold, there is no strong evidence that the increased number of women judges have made a manifest impact on the judiciary's promotion and understanding of women's rights. It is yet to be known whether the increased number of women judges has generated gender-sensitive judicial outcomes in Ethiopia. The views expressed by the respondents were at best anecdotal and will require additional in-depth and large-scale research to ascertain the veracity or otherwise of the critical mass theory as it pertains to gender-equitable judicial outcomes in Ethiopia.

Change in Workplace Culture and Descriptive Representation

There are other dimensions of change that a critical mass of women in the judiciary may engender: change in the judicial workplace culture and the acceleration of women's numerical representation on the bench (descriptive representation) (Dahlerup, 2006a). Concerning change in workplace culture, critical mass theory posits that when the critical mass target is achieved at all levels (federal and regional), Ethiopia's judiciary may become more women friendly in its environment and infrastructure. With a critical mass at the federal level of Ethiopia's judiciary, our survey data does not fully confirm this claim: there were some complaints by respondents about the work environment not being friendly for women, such as unsuitable restrooms. Details of such complaints are discussed in the sixth section.

The justification for the claim that a critical mass of women judges would further increase, or accelerate, women's numerical representation is that by the time a critical mass target is achieved, long-standing prejudices against women's ability to function as judges will have been substantially disintegrated and replaced with new parity norms. Again, the veracity of this claim has not manifested entirely in Ethiopia, since biased social perceptions against women judges persist. The fifth section, describing the challenges and obstacles women judges face, expands on these biases.

Judicial Legitimacy and Symbolic Representation

Despite the limitations of the critical mass claims in Ethiopia, women's presence on the bench remains crucial for advancing the judiciary's legitimacy in the eyes of court users and the public at large. As one respondent affirmed:

> Yes, especially for cases related to rape, family (divorce) and the like, women interpret the law in a different way. We can easily understand the problems and concerns of the women victims. I noticed that child victims of sexual violence feel safer and explain more when they testify in front of a female judge.

Another woman judge believed that the presence of women at the bench "will bring about positive change." Again, having women judges provides a symbolic representation of a diversified judiciary that could draw in more women. A respondent mentioned becoming a judge because of representation: "when I was a student in law school, I closely knew a woman who was a judge and whom I saw as a role model. I wanted to become a judge after her."

Diversity in Judicial Processes and Decisions

Even though the survey data does not establish a strong connection between the number of women judges in Ethiopia and its impact on gender-equitable judicial outcomes, which would buttress the critical mass theory, we argue that the data makes a good case for the difference theory. Central to the difference theory is the change women judges bring to judicial processes and decisions. The theory justifies women's place on the bench on the grounds that women judge cases differently from men and so will be more sensitive, especially in dealing with gender-specific cases. The difference theory does not emphasize *difference due to an increase in the number of women* as much as the critical mass theory does; rather, it emphasizes *difference because women's viewpoint on issues is different from men.*

A respondent confirming that women judges bring something different to the bench said:

> There is something different that women bring to the bench especially on a rape & other GBV cases. We can relate [to] some of those issues like female body parts, menstrual cycle, pregnancy . . . which we easily understand. Men usually don't want to be assigned to rape benches in my experience. Victims are also shy to tell their stories to male judges.

Some respondents, however, were quick to add that not much difference was visible in cases less related to gender: "It depends on the type of the case. In family cases or sexual harassment cases, women judges can bring something different than their male counterparts. But, in other cases like commercial cases, I don't see a difference."

Gender Sensitivity at the Bench

Just as critics of the difference theory caution against gender essentialism—conflating women judges with feminism or gender sensitivity—as a possible consequence of the theory (Andrews, 2021; Malleson, 2003), a Federal High Court judge made a similar note. She stated that women judges do make a difference but "not because they are women per se. Everyone brings different experiences and perspectives to the bench. Even the experience and perspective of women from different background[s] is different."

In their personal capacities, some of the judges mentioned being more sensitive to gender-related issues as their way of making a difference at the bench. One Federal High Court judge said, "I try to understand the perspective of women that are brought to the court. I am more compassionate I think than men judges." A judge at the Federal First Instance Court explained, "When the cases relate to divorce or rape, I tend to be more sympathetic to the issues of women and follow the case until its execution."

Improved Work Ethics and Societal Perceptions

Aside from the promotion of women's rights, some judges indicated that they made a difference through their work ethics, with the intention of breaking down some long-standing practices within the judiciary and stereotypes about women's ability to function effectively as judges. Women judges mentioned arriving punctually at work without fail and being more committed to their work at the bench and disposing more cases than their male counterparts.

Also, the societal perception that women are less susceptible to corruption was found to be another way through which the presence of women at the bench makes a difference, in that having more women judges will portray the judiciary as an incorruptible institution.

Women at the Bench: A Difference Made?

Overall, we argue, based on the survey responses, that women judges in Ethiopia are indeed making a difference, in their own small way and more in line with the tenets of the difference theory than those of the critical mass theory. We also share in the arguments of scholars who assert that critical acts and actors will more likely make a significant difference in Ethiopia than will critical mass. Our critical actor/act-oriented argument is that having women as critical actors, such as in leadership within the judiciary and engaging in critical judicial acts, will affect the gender-equitable changes and gender diversity desired in the judiciary. For example, having Chief Justice Meaza Ashenafi as a critical actor undertaking critical acts within the judiciary will do more to advance the gender diversity and equity on the bench than merely having a critical mass of women judges.

Some statements by the respondents reflected the reality of the critical actor/act claims on the ground: "I believe there will [be] an increasing number of female judges (especially with the appointment of a female chief justice) and education of more women in universities," one said. Another stated:

> The appointment of the first woman chief justice has already opened new possibilities for women judges. It has smashed the assumption that women can't achieve that position. With the appointment of more judges to the federal and regional courts hopefully in the future, I see a brighter future for women in law practice.

The discussion in this section has highlighted some of the ways women's presence on the bench has impacted Ethiopia's judiciary, as found in the survey and drawing from the critical mass and difference theories. To an extent, women judges in Ethiopia have contributed to the judiciary's gender sensitivity, enhanced women's symbolic representation, and transformed societal perception of corruption in the judiciary, among other changes. However, their contributions are not without barriers. Therefore, we now turn to look at the challenges and obstacles that women judges face that hinder their continued contribution to the judiciary and their personal progression in performing their judicial functions.

CHALLENGES AND OBSTACLES

The survey elicited from the respondents the unique challenges they face as women judges. This section discusses their responses.

Balancing Family, Work, and Social Life

Family–work–social life balance was a commonly cited challenge. Most of the respondents mentioned that they had to take work home with them due to the "high load of cases," which made it impossible to limit their working hours. A judge indicated working for up to 16 hours on some days. Another reported working 130–150 cases in a month while at the family bench. Regularly bringing work home takes a toll on the family and social life of women judges, who are often the primary caregivers at home.

The interview responses revealed that the struggle to balance family and work life was shared by women judges who had family support and those that did not. "I get a lot of help from my husband and family. But sometimes, I sacrifice my personal time/life for the work as there is a high load of cases," a respondent stated. Another, without family support, disclosed: "It is very difficult as I don't have support from my husband or other family members. My husband is a lawyer too and it is difficult to raise children while working as a judge in high court where there is high case load."

Despite this difficulty balancing, some respondents spoke about having strategies to deal with the problem, such as not taking on more cases than they can handle and allotting time for each task based on their experience over the years. Others were managing the problem without a clear strategy.

Biased Societal Perceptions

Another major challenge that emerged was the biased societal perception of women judges' abilities and attitudes. "Some clients don't want to be served by female judges because they think that we lack competence," a judge pointed out. Another mentioned, "sometimes the lack of trust by the public. There's a wrong perception regarding the capacity of women judges in understanding the case." Others believe that women judges are too harsh, less flexible, and indifferent. Thus, the typical Ethiopian woman judge has to work twice as hard as a man judge to be deemed as capable of performing her judicial roles.

Aside from the socially defined gender roles that inform these biased perceptions, religious disposition also plays a role. One respondent speaking on the contributory role of religion said, "some Muslim men don't want to stand in front of a female judge because of religious issues."

The findings also revealed that these prejudiced perceptions of women judges were less prevalent among the urban population as compared to the rural inhabitants. In the view of a Federal High Court judge, "the social perception is good in Addis Ababa because people are more educated here and there are many women judges. But I can imagine it is more difficult in other rural areas." To address some of these perception challenges and change the existing social perceptions, respondents recommended increasing the numbers of women judges and women in leadership within the judiciary. In their individual capacities, some judges have adopted stringent work ethics, such as being punctual, resisting external influences, and disposing of more cases than their male counterparts to assuage the negative biases.

Unconscious Bias as an Exclusionary Mechanism

The survey also revealed that there were some vestiges of the biased communal perception of women judges within the practices of the judiciary. For instance, respondents had observed that certain types of cases were more often assigned to women than to men and vice versa. A respondent reported:

> Certain cases reserved for women. The relationship between judges is ok[ay] but when it comes to higher officials (management), they tend to assign women to certain cases only. For example, on commercial matters, male judges tend to be assigned more.

It was recommended that women judges be given more time and opportunity to handle all types of cases, so they build their capacity.

Intersectional Identity of Women Judges

Some respondents also expressed that they experienced additional layers of challenge apart from being women. Age, ethnicity, and maternity were identified as factors that created intersectional burdens for some women judges. When asked about the unique challenges women judges face, the respondent with the least working experience—eight years at the bench—said, "there are different attitudes towards female judges, but most are not favorable towards us. This is especially bad towards young female judges." On ethnicity as an additional challenge, one respondent explained:

> The biggest challenge for me was the application of quotas for different ethnic groups to be appointed as a judge. The fact that different nationalities had to be represented in the courts (judicial positions) sometimes limits those qualified candidates from holding the position.

This assertion may be debatable and needs further investigation. In fact, dissecting women's representation in the judiciary along ethnic lines could yield interesting results and also help in identifying the groups that are most disadvantaged in terms of representation, but that is not the objective of this chapter. However, it is important to mention here that when examining the relevant laws, we did not find any legally prescribed or reserved quotas for different ethnic groups (nations, nationalities, and people, as the 1995 FDRE Constitution refers to them). What exists is an obligation for the federal government to make sure that all ethnic groups are represented in the federal government, including in government agencies, the judiciary, and the military. For instance, the Federal Civil Servants Proclamation no. 1064/2017 states, under Article 50, that the placement of personnel in a government institution shall take into account fair representation of nations, nationalities, and peoples. Those nations, nationalities, and peoples that have less representation within a government institution shall be given the advantage of affirmative action in recruitment, promotion, transfer, redeployment, education, and training. Articles 35(3) and 39(3) of the 1995 Constitution also give the right of equitable representation in state and federal governments to women and ethnic groups, respectively.

Commenting on obstacles emerging from maternity another respondent said, "Some emanate from nature (biological features that only women experience like going through pregnancy while working and giving birth)." Thus, while some challenges were shared by most women judges, some faced additional challenges that could be debilitating.

Gendered Consequences of Work Environment and Ethics, Housing, and Transport

There were also seemingly general restraints that had gendered effects. For example, the inadequacies of the work environment, workplace ethics, poor housing, and transport for all judges presented distinctive difficulties for women judges. A judge at the Federal First Instance Court explained:

> The other challenge is that the work environment in the court is not completely safe for women especially when we decide on some controversial or big cases. Plus, we don't have a housing and transport service from the government, so the job is riskier for female judges. You might meet the families of the people that you convicted outside the courtroom. The court building itself is not work friendly, especially if female judges are pregnant or have some disability. But we're still required to meet the minimum number of cases to see just like the male judges.

Throwing more light on infrastructural inadequacies, a Federal High Court judge mentioned that most of the court buildings "lack a suitable toilet for female judges." The responses also revealed that the female members of the judiciary—the citadel of justice—were not immune from gender discrimination and harassment. In the words of one respondent, "gender bias and few times harassment" also characterized her working environment.

Diverse Lived Experiences of Women Judges: A Final Word

Although the challenges discussed here are common to women judges, we do not hold them out as the collective experience of women at the bench in

Ethiopia. We are mindful of the diverse and individual lived experiences of women judges who may not share in the obstacles cited here, and the survey data reflects this reality. For example, one respondent indicated that she did not face any peculiar challenges as a woman judge. "No issues at all. We respect each other," she said. Another responding to our inquiry about any restraints on work–life balance remarked, "I haven't yet faced any problem balancing my work and personal life so far." Five respondents also mentioned having a collegial working environment that minimized any challenges they might have had.

The responses also showed that some of the challenges were waning. For instance, there has recently been an improved perception of women judges' abilities, especially in urban Ethiopia, due to increased representation and the appointment of the first woman chief justice. There were also favorable perceptions, such as of women being less susceptible to corruption. These diverse realities notwithstanding, the unique challenges of women judges remain and clearly it will take more than symbolic representation and a critical mass of women at the bench to forestall them.

CONCLUSION

This chapter had two main aims: to examine the impact of the judicial appointment process on gender representation in the federal courts and to investigate women judges' experiences in Ethiopia. The discussions relied principally on survey data from women judges and were anchored in the critical mass and difference theories. We demonstrated that affirmative action was ingrained in the appointment process for judges, backed by law. We also came to the conclusion that due to the strict legal procedures guiding recruitment of judges, in addition to the affirmative action measures, women were not hindered in any significant way during the appointment process. This fact notwithstanding, it was established that women were still underrepresented in the judiciary due to factors such as past discriminatory practices and other educational challenges.

Based on the findings, five main recommendations for increasing gender representation and diversity in Ethiopia's judiciary are proposed.

1. The first is to actively recruit women into the judiciary, with particular focus on the state courts.
2. The second is to embark on a campaign to get more girls to enter law school. As aptly captured by one respondent, "Get more women into law schools and the rest will take care of itself."
3. The third is educating more girls and women to pursue a judicial career and to demystify the myths surrounding women in the judicial space.

"Educate more women, encourage them to study law and show them that being a judge is not as difficult for women as it is said to be or as they [have] heard of," one judge offered. A similar sentiment was shared by another respondent thus: "Educating (informing) girls studying law about the life and work of a judge can help reduce their fear of the job and encourage them to take it as a career. Girls in school assume that the job is too difficult for a woman."

4. The fourth recommendation is to further simplify the recruitment process for women applicants as part of the affirmative measures already in place. In the view of one woman judge, "making less procedures as to selection [and] appointment with regard to judgeship process for female candidates as compared to that of men candidates" will encourage even more women to apply.
5. Finally, empowering existing women judges in executing their duties will be a symbolic act that could potentially draw in more women. "The most important thing I think is to empower the existing judges, facilitate their growth and incentivize them. If that's done [if existing female judges are satisfied], more women will be attracted to the field," one respondent suggested.

Challenges unique to women judges in the performance of their duties were also identified, including the struggle to balance family, work, and social life; prejudiced social perceptions about the abilities of women judges; and an unfriendly working environment. Despite these challenges, women judges in Ethiopia continue to contribute to the judiciary through their conscious gender-sensitivity approach to cases, impeccable work ethics, and symbolic representation.

We also made a case for impact beyond a critical mass of women judges in Ethiopia, arguing for critical actors and acts—of which the appointment of the first woman chief justice is one, and a first step in the right direction. Gender diversity and equity in Ethiopia's judiciary looks promising although there is still a long way to go. There remain challenges and gaps that require more research to unearth and address. We believe the findings in this chapter have set the scene for future research initiatives and interventions related to gender and judging in Ethiopia.

NOTES

1. See more on Meaza's life and accomplishments at Meaza Ashenafi: first woman chief justice, available at https://www.africanwomeninlaw.com/african-women-in-law/Meaza-Ashenafi.

2. The Federal JAC is a body established to undertake and facilitate the whole process of appointment, administration (placement, transfer, salary, allowance, medical benefits, and promotion), evaluation, and removal of federal judges, except the president and vice president of the Federal Supreme Court, who are directly nominated and presented to the House of Peoples' Representatives for appointment by the prime minister (Proclamation No. 684/2010, Art 6[1]). The JAC is made up of the president of the Federal Supreme Court (as chairman), vice president of the Federal Supreme Court, presidents of the Federal High and First Instance Court, three members of the Parliament, the attorney general, one senior federal judge, one lawyer, one academician, and one distinguished citizen selected by the council. This diverse 12-member council is expected to strengthen its independence.

REFERENCES

Abdo, M. (2020). Federal Sharia Courts in Addis Ababa: Their administration and the application of law in the light of recent developments. In S. Epple & G. Assefa (Eds.), *Legal pluralism in Ethiopia* (pp. 139–162). Transcript.Open. https://doi.org/10.14361/9783839450215-008.

Abebe, A. K. (2012). The potential role of constitutional review in the realisation of human rights in Ethiopia. *University of Pretoria*. https://repository.up.ac.za/bitstream/handle/2263/23887/Complete.pdf?sequence=10&isAllowed=y.

Addadzi-Koom, M. E., & Nkansah, L. A. (2021). Women at the bench: Does it make a difference? Assessing the impact of women judges in addressing gender-based issues in Ghana. In *Oñati Socio-Legal Series Forthcoming: Gender and Judging in the Middle East and Africa*. https://doi.org/10.35295/OSLS.IISL/0000-0000-0000-1175.

Albertyn, C., & Bonthuys, E. (2016). South Africa: A transformative constitution and a representative judiciary. In G. Bauer & J. Dawuni (Eds.), *Gender and the Judiciary in Africa: From Obscurity to Parity?* (pp. 49–66). Routledge.

Andrews, P. (2021). Pursuing gender equality through the courts: The role of South Africa's women judges. In J. Dawuni (Ed.), *Gender, Judging and the Courts in Africa: Selected Studies* (pp. 189–208). Routledge.

Bauer, G., & Dawuni, J. (Eds.). (2016). *Gender and the Judiciary in Africa: From Obscurity to Parity?* Routledge.

Childs, S., & Krook, M. L. (2006). Should feminists give up on critical mass? A contingent yes. *Politics & Gender*, *2*, 522–530.

Constitution of the Federal Democratic Republic of Ethiopia (Proclamation no. 1/1995).

Coontz, P. (2000). Gender and judicial decisions: Do female judges decide cases differently than male judges? *Gender Issues, 18*, 59–73. https://doi.org/10.1007/s12147-001-0024-7.

Cowan, R. (2013). Do women in the judiciary make a difference? In U. Schultz & G. Shaw (Eds.), *Gender and Judging* (pp. 26–37). Hart.

Dahlerup, D. (2006a). The critical mass theory in public and scholarly debates. In R. Campbell & S. Childs (Eds.), *Deeds and Words: Gendering Politics after Joni Lovenduski* (pp. 137–163). ECPR Press.

Dahlerup, D. (2006b). The story of the theory of critical mass. *Politics & Gender*, *2*, 511–522.

Dawuni, J. (2016a). Gender and the judiciary in Africa: An introduction. In G. Bauer & J. Dawuni (Eds.), *Gender and the Judiciary in Africa: From Obscurity to Parity?* (pp. 1–15). Routledge.

Dawuni, J. (2016b). To "mother" or not to "mother": The representative roles of women judges in Ghana. *Journal of African Law*, *60*(3), 419–440. https://doi.org./10.1017/S0021855316000115.

Dawuni, J. (2016c). Ghana: The paradox of judicial. In G. Bauer & J. Dawuni (Eds.), *Gender and the Judiciary in Africa: From Obscurity to Parity?* (pp. 120–136). Routledge.

Dawuni, J. (2020). Women in judiciaries across Africa. In O. Yacob-Haliso & T. Falola (Eds.), *The Palgrave Handbook of African Women's Studies* (pp. 1–22). Palgrave Macmillan. https://doi.org/10.1007/978-3-319-77030-7_75-1.

Dawuni, J. (Ed.). (2021). *Gender, Judging and the Courts in Africa: Selected Studies*. Routledge. https://doi.org/10.4324/9780429327865.

Dawuni, J., & Kang, A. (2015). Her ladyship the chief justice: The rise of female leaders in the judiciary of Africa. *Africa Today, 62*(2), 45–69. https://doi.org/10.2979/africatoday.62.2.45.

EBC Ethiopian Broadcasting Corporate. (2018). 'ኑሮ እና ቢዝነስ, ከወ/ሮ መአዛ አሸናፊ ጋር የተደረገ ቆይታ', ኑሮ እና ቢዝነስ. *Life and Business*. Retrieved from https://www.youtube.com/watch?v=IrojpH_IBLU.

Federal Courts (Amendment) Proclamation no. 254/2001.

Federal Courts (Amendment) Proclamation no. 321/2003.

Federal Courts Proclamation (Re-amendment) Proclamation no. 454/2005.

Federal Courts Proclamation No. 1234/2021.

Federal Courts Proclamation 25/1996, as amended by Federal Courts Proclamation 138/1998.

Federal Courts of Sharia Consolidation Proclamation no. 188/1999.

Federal High Court Establishment Proclamation no. 322/2003.

Federal Judicial Administration Council Establishment Proclamation no. 684/2010.

Gage, B. G. (2020). Meaza Ashenafi: First woman chief justice. Institute for African Women in Law. https://www.africanwomeninlaw.com/african-women-in-law/Meaza-Ashenafi.

Galligan, Y., Haupfleisch, R., Irvine, L., Korolkova, K., Natter, M., Schultz, U., & Wheeler, S. (2017). *Mapping the Representation of Women and Men in Legal Professions across the EU*. European Parliament. https://www.europarl.europa.eu/RegData/etudes/STUD/2017/596804/IPOL_STU(2017)596804_EN.pdf.

Gilligan, C. (1982). *In a Different Voice*. Harvard University Press.

Grey, S. (2006). Numbers and beyond: The relevance of critical mass in gender research. *Politics & Gender*, *2*, 492–502.

Gudina, M. (2011). *Ethiopia: From Autocracy to Revolutionary Democracy, 1960s–2011*. Merera Gudina.

Kenney, S. J. (2013). *Gender and Justice: Why Women in the Judiciary Really Matter*. Routledge.

Malleson, K. (2003). Justifying gender equality on the bench: Why difference won't do. *Feminist Legal Studies*, *11*(1), 1–24. https://doi.org/10.1023/A:1023231006909.

Masengu, T. (2016). It's a man's world: Barriers to gender transformation in the South African judiciary. Perspectives from women advocates and attorneys. *International Journal of the Legal Profession*, *23*, 305–319. https://doi.org/10.1080/09695958.2016.1179639.

Masengu, T. (2020). The judicial service commission and the appointment of women: More to it than meets the eye. *International Journal of the Legal Profession,* 27(2), 1–21. https://doi.org/10.1080/09695958.2019.1622547.

Ministry of Capacity Building and Center for International Legal Cooperation. (2005). *Comprehensive Justice System Reform Program: Baseline Study Report.*

Sisay, A. (2018, November 1). Ethiopia appoints first woman supreme court president. *The East African.* https://www.theeastafrican.co.ke/tea/news/rest-of-africa/ethiopia-appoints-first-woman-supreme-court-president-1405628.

Vanderlinden, J. (1966). An introduction to the sources of Ethiopian law from the 13th to the 20th century. *Journal of Ethiopian Law*, *3*(1), 227–302.

Woldemelak, W. (2005). *Perspectives on the Ethiopian Legal System.* Addis Ababa, Ethiopia: W. Woldemelak.

Wondirad, A. (2013). *An Overview of the Ethiopian Legal System.* Nzacl Yearbook 19. Victoria University of Wellington.

Yoon, M. Y. (2016). Tanzania: Women judges as agents of judicial education. In G. Bauer & J. Dawuni (Eds.), *Gender and the Judiciary in Africa: From Obscurity to Parity?* (pp. 93–107). Routledge.

Zewde, B. (2001). *A History of Modern Ethiopia, 1855–1991.* Ohio University Press.

Chapter 5

Battle for Women in the Egyptian Judiciary

Reality, Laws, and Aspirations or a Dream Come True?

Omnia Taher Gadalla

Female empowerment, gender equality, and ending all forms of discrimination against women are core objectives of both the UN Sustainable Development Goals (SDG's 2030) and African Union Agenda 2063. Every African country adopted the text of the latter in 2013 and committed itself to implementing these goals and tailored its vision for the next 50 years to acknowledge the importance of these issues. The 1995 Beijing declaration stated that achieving

> equality between women and men is a matter of human rights and a condition for social justice and is also a necessary and fundamental prerequisite for equality, development, and peace. A transformed partnership based on equality between women and men is a condition for people-centered sustainable development. (The United Nations, 1995)

However, achieving these goals has been and still is threatened by stereotypes and misconceptions that have been inculcated into people's minds. One of the stereotypes that still prevents women—especially Africans—from reaching their real and full potential is the underestimation of women's capability to hold positions in the judiciary. Even though many African countries allow women to sit on the bench in all capacities, up to and including presiding over the Supreme Court, the situation is different in Egypt. The Egyptian judiciary has a long history of banning female law graduates—even the highest-ranked graduates—from applying for judicial positions. Rather, it disqualifies women applicants and legalizes discrimination against their representation on the bench. In 2008, when women were granted an exception and permitted to apply, they were all subsequently disqualified. This discrimination has continued despite numerous international conventions that Egypt has ratified and incorporated into its constitution.

Recently, after years of discrimination, a number of female law graduates in Egypt have broken their long silence and filed cases claiming their right to join the bench as equals with their male colleagues. This open defiance of an unjust system has contributed to creating a new paradigm, reviving the hopes of Egyptian women in general and female law graduates in particular. Civil society and feminists have been encouraged to resume the legal fight for equality and stand in solidarity after many decades of failure. Nevertheless, these attempts at establishing equality have tended to collide with the same stereotypes, more or less, that women in different countries have encountered since the last century. Egyptian women have undergone harsh times in the struggle to claim their fundamental rights, of which they have been deprived both directly by the judiciary and indirectly by the government and the wider community. Nevertheless, tenacious feminine opposition, pushed by political will, finally achieved victory in 2022, allowing females to apply for the judiciary directly for the first time since its establishment a century ago.

Having Egyptian women on the bench is not simply a question of providing them with a particular job opportunity with privileges; rather, it is an issue of human rights and dignity, both of which were violated by unjustified discrimination against 49% of the population. "Representation of women in the judiciary is key to ensuring that the courtroom accurately represents its citizens, addresses their concerns and provides them with sound decisions" (Evans, 2019).

This chapter presents a comprehensive overview of the issue, covering different perspectives. The first section focuses on the presence of Egyptian women in the legal field in general and the judiciary in particular, with an overview of the Egyptian judiciary and court structure. The second section presents documented cases where the appointment of Egyptian women as judges was rejected. The third section reviews the national and international legal rules that support Egyptian women's right to sit on the bench. The fourth section presents the author's own experience via the challenges she has faced over the past eight years since 2014. A list of recommendations will be found in the conclusion.

BACKGROUND ON EGYPTIAN WOMEN'S PRESENCE IN THE LEGAL FIELD IN GENERAL AND THE JUDICIARY IN PARTICULAR

Egyptian women have been members of the legal profession since the 1930s. In 1933, Naima Al-Ayoubi was the first female student to complete a bachelor's degree in the Faculty of Law at an Egyptian university. She applied to the Egyptian Bar as the first female lawyer before the National Courts, when the profession was dominated by men.[1] Further, Munira Thabit was the first woman to enroll in the French Law School of Cairo in 1924 and the first to earn a *license en Droit*, which enabled her to be registered as the first Arab lawyer and to practice law before the Egyptian Mixed Court (Moustafa, 2015). Furthermore, Egyptian women held the positions of law school dean, law professors, ministers, diplomats, and members of Parliament, and participated in drafting laws for decades. They also served as legal counsels and heads of legal departments in national and international organizations and corporations. At present, Egyptian women represent around half of the students in the Faculties of Law and are acquiring top ranks with high grades. Egyptian women preceded others in the Arab and African region—and some European countries—in obtaining their rights to political participation. In addition, Egypt has traditionally been a pioneer of development in the region and has a history of feminist politics dating from 1923, when Hoda Sha'arawi helped found the Egyptian Feminist Union.

In contrast, the representation of Egyptian women in the judiciary is shockingly low. Despite the fact that the Egyptian legal framework did not prevent women from being appointed to the judiciary, the number of women judges kept Egypt at the bottom of the list. Until January 2022, female law graduates were banned from applying to the judiciary and Egyptian women judges constituted 0.7% (Abdulaal, 2018) (153 women judges among more than 22,000 male judges). Moreover, they did not join the bench in the same ordinary fashion as their male counterparts; rather, they were selected from members already appointed to the Administrative Prosecution Authority and the Egyptian State Lawsuits Authority.

JUDICIAL HISTORY IN EGYPT

Egypt is an African and Arab country; its modern judicial system can be traced back to 1875, when the Mixed Courts were established and modeled on the French legal system. During that time, Egypt was an Ottoman province applying the principle of extraterritoriality, where European laws were applied to Europeans residing in Egypt. A few years later, in 1883, the National Courts were established with jurisdiction over all legal disputes among Egyptians. After that, the Mixed Courts were shut down by Royal decree in 1948.

Egypt adopts the Civil Law system, whereby judges are appointed, not elected. The judiciary is a dual system consisting of the Ordinary Judiciary established in 1883 and the Administrative Judiciary (State Council). The Egyptian Court system is a multitiered system, where the Ordinary Court consists of the Courts of First Instance, the Courts of Appeal, and the Court of Cassation (sits at the apex of the ordinary judiciary, established in 1931). The Administrative Courts, meanwhile, consist of the Administrative Courts, the Administrative Judiciary Courts, and the Supreme Administrative Court (sits at the apex of the administrative judiciary, established in 1955).

Hence, Egyptian law graduates who want to join the judiciary can apply to one of the following entities/institutions once an announcement has been made. Table 5.1 represents the courts and judicial structure in Egypt:

(a) The State Council (Administrative Judiciary), established in 1946 (to which females were prevented from applying until January 27, 2022):

Its role is to adjudicate disputes involving government actions and omissions, personnel, and disciplinary actions involving government employees and administrative contracts. There are also departments for opinions and legislation, which advise public entities on diverse aspects of public law, such as administrative contracts, tenders, and ministerial decrees. The State Council is represented by the Special Board, which consists of the seven most senior judges, including the Head of the State Council, while the General Assembly consists of the judges of the State Council, excluding the junior judges. There is also the Division Commission that consists of judges: it prepares case documents and drafts an advisory legal opinion recommending what it views as the correct application of the law to cases under review by the court.

(b) Public Prosecution (to which females were prevented from applying until January 31, 2022):

The Public Prosecution has two major functions: (a) to file criminal actions when acting as public prosecutors before a criminal court, and (b) to have the right to initiate actions even if the plaintiff has relinquished his/her right to do so. Public prosecutors also investigate crimes,

Table 5.1 The Judicial System and Court Structure

Supreme Constitutional Court (SCC)	
The Ordinary Judiciary comprises:	*The Administrative Judiciary (State Council) comprises:*
Court of Cassation	Supreme Administrative Court
Court of Appeal	Administrative Judiciary Courts
Court of First Instance (Primary Courts/ Summary courts)	Administrative Courts
Judges starting at: The Public Prosecution	Judges starting at: The Division Commission of the State Council
Ordinary courts are administered by the Supreme Judicial Council	The State Council is administered by the Special Board of the State Council

Source: Created by author.

visit crime scenes, question the accused, and order the imprisonment of the accused. Joining the Public Prosecution is the path to becoming a judge in the Ordinary Courts. Nevertheless, some members of the Public Prosecution remain and achieve promotion within the latter, potentially qualifying for the post of Head of the Public Prosecution.

(c) Administrative Prosecution Authority ("APA"), established in 1954 (females have allowed to apply since 1954):

Its role is to investigate violations of professional duties and financial and administrative irregularities involving government entities and their personnel, and to prepare disciplinary actions before the State Council. Women now account for 43% (Al-Shorouk Newspaper, 2017).

(d) Egyptian State Lawsuits Authority ("ESLA"), established in 1874 (females have been allowed to apply since 1978):

Its role is to represent the state before national and international courts and arbitration tribunals. It also has the power to plead on behalf of the state. Women now account for 13% within this entity (Qaraa', 2017). Despite the latter two being legally classified as independent judicial entities, they do not perform the true judicial function of settling disputes.

Egypt also has a Supreme Constitutional Court ("SCC"), established in 1969, which has exclusive jurisdiction to decide on matters regarding the constitutionality of laws and regulations as well as negative and positive conflict of jurisdiction. Finally, Egypt has a separate Military Judiciary and Prosecution—which neither appoint women nor allow them to apply—affiliated to the Armed Forces. This Military Judiciary has a separate application process for male law graduates that differs from the recruitment process to join the Armed Forces themselves.

EGYPTIAN WOMEN IN THE JUDICIARY: HISTORICAL BACKGROUND

Since the 1940s, Egyptian women have been claiming their right to hold judicial positions. The judiciary has consistently and unfairly rejected female applicants' challenges to administrative decisions which disqualified them from being judges. Before being rejected, each of these female applicants went through different levels of administrative procedures. This consequently reflects a setback in the process of applying for judicial positions and a flagrant practice of discrimination against female graduates.

The early cases showed that women were allowed to apply and go through the same evaluation procedures as their male counterparts and were disqualified at the final stage based on gender. Yet, in more recent cases—including the author's—women were even denied the right to apply for the judiciary in the first place. They were not even allowed the right to submit their applications and be evaluated, as a matter of procedural justice. The trend developed from women being "still unable to apply due to social factors" to their being "not eligible by nature," which was very alarming and caused serious social and constitutional ramifications.[2]

It is worth mentioning the old and modern Islamic scholarly view about women as judges, as we shall see it being relied upon by the courts in the following cases. Egypt's Dar Al-Ifta, the supreme authority responsible for issuing religious edicts, approved of women being appointed as judges. It issued various fatwas (religious edicts) in 2002, 2006, and 2008, making it clear that there is no primary text (in the Quran or the Sunnah) that prohibits women from assuming judicial posts. In a fatwa issued in October 18, 2013, the Grand Mufti, Dr. Shawki Allam, issued the latest fatwa stating that women are allowed to hold the office of judge according to the opinion of Hanafi school and Zahri jurists and al-Tabari (Ali, 2013). On the other hand, older Islamic doctrines of the Shafiite, Malikite, and Hanbalite schools prohibit females from sitting as judges. Al-Ahnaf accepted female judges in the civil and commercial judiciary, but not the criminal judiciary. Al-Zaherya and El-Tabary opined that females are eligible to sit as judges in general.[3] Yet, the grounds on which these prohibiting opinions rest no longer exist and accordingly have no place. Judgments exist as long as their underlying reasons exist and vice versa.

Generally speaking, Egypt follows the Hanafi school of jurisprudence in matters of Sharia, which doesn't allow women to be criminal judges. However, Egypt appointed its first female criminal judge in 2009 and legislated myriad laws that fail to accord with Hanafi jurisprudence. This clearly proves that Islam is not the main issue in this respect (as always alleged) and makes it evident that the opposing voices "base their argument only on the fact that most of the schools of jurisprudence prohibited women from holding the rank of a judge without referring to a text explicitly prohibiting this from the Quran or Sunna" (Elsayed, 2007: 145).

Returning to the feminist struggle, the first case of this kind was filed in 1949 by Ms. Aisha Rateb against the State Council after rejecting her application to be appointed as a judge (Khalil, 2003),[4] after she had successfully gone through the application procedures and interview and passed the exam. Her case was an unprecedented step in the history of the Egyptian judiciary, because the reasoning cited in the judgment based the rejection of females' applications on the discretionary power of the authorities to decide the eligibility of women to occupy such positions. The judgment declined to consider this as discrimination against her or abuse of power. The decision was adopted despite its violating the Egyptian Constitution, which grants men and women equal rights.[5]

Shortly after this, another woman filed a case after she applied in 1950 to the State Lawsuits Administration—renamed later to ESLA—and was rejected due to her gender. When she challenged this decision before the court, her case was rejected. The judgment stated that the grounds for rejecting females' application were not Egyptian law or Sharia law, but rather the culture and customs of Egyptian society. Although it accepted the principle of equality between men and women, it once again relied on the discretionary power of the authorities to decide the eligibility of women to occupy such positions based on the social and cultural context, which it refused to consider as an abuse of power.

The judgment went further, stating that

> it should not be concluded from this that the administration [ESLA] has established a general absolute rule that women do not qualify, at any time, to occupy positions in the judiciary, the Public Prosecution, and State Lawsuits Administration. Such an absolute rule shall not be accepted in light of the aforementioned. Moreover, it is not acceptable to argue otherwise, based on the noble Islamic sharia, since there are no provisions in the Islamic jurisprudence "Fiqh" prohibiting Muslim woman from occupying the judiciary if she is eligible for it.[6]

Few decades later, in 1978, Ms. Hanem Mohamed's attempt to apply to the State Council was rejected, and she challenged this decision. On June 12, 1979, Challenge No. 63, judicial year 20, the Supreme Administrative Court surprisingly stated that "traditions are no longer the basis of rejecting women as judges since its development in recognition of women's right in the judiciary." Yet it rejected the challenge, referring to Article 2 of the 1971 Constitution—stating that Islamic Sharia is a base and source for the law (Ghazi, 2013).[7] Shockingly, the judgment constituted a step back in the understanding of Islamic Sharia by the judiciary and based its rejection on one of three Islamic schools of "Fiqh," while religious arguments were provided for the first time to justify the view that women do not qualify to be judges. The judgment went further by asserting the discretionary power of the State Council to adopt the opinion it deems suitable without thereby abusing its power. The judgment also argued that the law on the State Council neither includes a rule obliging the council to appoint women judges, nor a rule providing that women must be treated as equal to men in occupying such positions. The judgments of the administrative courts regarding the issue "laid down a rule which was evidently used as a judicial precedent. It is therefore surprising that very little academic analysis, writings and jurisprudential reviews have been conducted with respect to these important decisions" (Elsayed, 2007: 139).

A few years later, Ms. Fatma Lashin, a lawyer, applied to enroll in the Public Prosecution in 1992 and was rejected due to her gender. Consequently, she filed case No. 80, judicial year 67 in the Court of Cassation. The judgment was issued in 2005 rejecting the appointment of females to the Public Prosecution (Nasrawi, 1998).

The turning point and the real major external pressure occurred in 2001, when the UN Committee on the Elimination of Discrimination against Women issued a crucial report which shed light globally on the total absence of Egyptian women in the judiciary. At that time the report was a real driving force for the government to adopt a slightly different approach toward female Egyptian judges, so as to gain a better image worldwide. It stated:

> The Committee expresses its concern that stereotypical attitudes about the roles of women and men in the family and society are reflected in the low level of representation of women in decision making at all levels and in all areas. The Committee expresses its concern in particular that, although there is no law that prohibits the appointment of women as judges, no woman has ever been so appointed.[8]

In 2003, after decades of feminist advocacy, Egyptian women celebrated the first ever female judge appointed to the SCC, Tahani Al-Gebali—a lawyer (no longer in the court) appointed by unprecedented presidential decree, who served in the court between 2003 and 2013.

Unfortunately, Tahani Al-Gebali's appointment was not that promising, since it was not followed by the creation of a new generation of female judges and prosecutors who could be appointed and promoted on their merit, just like their male colleagues. The government failed in the real test when the new round of applications of judges and prosecutors began and women's applications were rejected, confirming that gender was the reason, despite Tahani Al-Gebali's seat on the SCC bench (Khalil, 2003).

Later, in 2007, 31 women judges were appointed,[9] followed by further appointments in 2008; and 26 women judges were selected in 2015 from the already appointed members of APA and ESLA to work as judges in the first instance and appeal courts. That places the number of women judges by October 2021 at 66 women judges. It was apparent that these appointments were merely a way to appease national and international demands for the introduction of women into Egypt's judiciary, but did not reflect real effective equality and empowerment.

However, Egypt's project of slowly adding women to the judiciary suffered a setback. In August 2009, the State Council's Special Board, charged among other tasks with vetting new appointments to the Administrative Judiciary, announced that it would accept applications from women on August 24, 2009. Following that, women applied to serve as judges to the State Council and were interviewed. This prompted the State Council's General Assembly to request an emergency meeting on February 15, 2010, where 88% of the judges voted against females' appointment to the State Council. Despite clearly contradicting the Constitution, the General Assembly affirmed that the structure and organization of the State Council, including the appointment of new members, fell within their own exclusive competence; they disregarded the interview process, asserting that their decisions were binding.

Following this conflict, and the contradictory decisions made by the Special Board and General Assembly of the State Council, Minister of Justice Mamdouh Marei on February 18, 2010, requested an Advisory Opinion of the SCC regarding the interpretation of Article 73 and Article 83 of the State Council Law and their application to the appointment criteria for the State Council.

The conflict escalated on February 22, 2010, when Judge Mohamed Al-Husseini, head of the Egyptian State Council at the time, overturned the General Assembly's decision and proceeded with the interviewing process, stating that his stance was supported by the Constitution and that his decision took precedence over any other decisions in this regard. He was severely criticized by fellow judges, and some filed cases to remove him from his position (Abdoun, 2010).

Egypt's SCC on March 14, 2010, ruled against the February 15 vote. It also emphasized the equality of all citizens and stated that the criteria were clear and could not be interpreted by the State Council to exclude women. Moreover, the SCC also stated that the latest amendment of the State Council Law by law no. 136 of the year 1984 made the Special Board of the State Council competent to appoint the new judges, while the General Assembly has no role in such appointments. The SCC admitted that the General Assembly has the power to promulgate the internal regulation of the State Council; however, such regulation cannot supersede what is regulated by law. The General Assembly convened again, and the majority of Special Board members who had previously supported appointing women as judges reversed their decision. Thus, the interviewing process was put on hold, and consequently, women were never appointed to serve in the State Council (Al-Wahaidy, 2017) until October 2021, despite the SCC's obligatory opinion. Mayada Fahmi, one of the female law graduates (class of 2008) who was interviewed but ultimately excluded from the appointed list, filed a case at the State Council, but to no avail (Lindbekk, 2017).

It is worth mentioning that although Egypt has now 153 women judges working in the ordinary courts, they are not equal in their status and appointments compared to male judges since they "were directly appointed as judges, without having had the opportunity to gain prior experience, for example, working as public prosecutors before being a judge. Obtaining prior experience as a prosecutor is considered an important element in the preparation of any judge in the ordinary courts. Writers like Khalil (2003) criticized the approach" (Elsayed, 2007: 136). This is affirmed by Judge Samar who remarked that "at the start of her work as a judge she felt afraid because she was inexperienced, and that the Minister of Justice at the time had told the recently appointed female judges that they would be subjected to more critical scrutiny than their male colleagues. The newly-appointed female judges were subjected to considerable pressure to perform, as they self-reflected, "we had a lot to prove for ourselves and the next generation" (Lindbekk, 2017: 296).

What is more, Egypt was ranked 134th of 153 countries in the Global Gender Gap 2020 (World Economic Forum, 2020). The appointment of 66 women judges (until that year) changed nothing, as it had been in 109th place out of 115 in 2006 prior to their appointment. In addition, the World Justice Project ranks Egypt 125th out of 128 in the Rule of Law index 2020 (World Economic Forum, 2020). Appointing women judges in the normal way would definitely affect these results, as it would decrease the gender gap while simultaneously providing more qualified judges to sit on the bench working hand in hand with their male colleagues, setting aside any differences, and challenging social norms to implement the rule of law.

Considering the above historical context, it appears that "the judicial decisions were based on social norms, reflected in the judge's personal preferences rather than based on the applicable laws, which mandated equality for women" (Elsayed, 2007: 139). This not only glaringly affects the impartiality and independence of the judiciary and the rule of law but also distorts women's self-perception of their capabilities and sense of citizenship, as I witnessed myself as a lecturer in a female-only law school (Gadalla, 2020). Further, we can explicitly say that until October 2021 no woman had entered the State Council, Public Prosecution, or Court of Cassation since these bodies' establishment (which remains the case for the Court of Cassation to date), and only two were selected to the Supreme Constitution Court. Taking into consideration the aforementioned percentages of women judges, it is clear that Egyptian women are woefully underrepresented among judges, which has broad implications for the democratic legitimacy, equality of representation, and fairness of the justice system. It is also a flagrant proof that society is lagging behind the law.

NATIONAL AND INTERNATIONAL LEGAL RULES THAT SUPPORT WOMEN SITTING ON THE BENCH

The right of Egyptian women to sit as judges is strongly entrenched and supported by national laws and international conventions.[10] Nationally, on

January 18, 2014, Egypt adopted a new constitution which grants women the right to be appointed to all the Judicial Authorities, stressing the state's responsibility to "guarantee women's right of holding public and senior management offices in the State and their appointment in judicial bodies and authorities without discrimination."[11] It also criminalizes discrimination, stressing the state's responsibility to "take necessary measures for eliminating all forms of discrimination, and the Law shall regulate creating an anti-discrimination independent commission for this purpose."[12] Further, it affirms the right of equal opportunities and equality[13] and declares that appointment to public positions is merit based.[14]

Yet, despite all these constitutional articles, the judiciary's opposition to right holders and the overthrow of the Constitution has remained the dominant feature of the scene whether under the Constitution of 1923, 1971, 2012, or the current Constitution of 2014.

On the international level, Egypt signed and ratified the UN Convention on the Elimination of All Forms of Discrimination Against Women 1979,[15] which stipulates that

> parties shall take all appropriate measures to eliminate discrimination against women in the field of employment in order to ensure, on a basis of equality of men and women, the same rights, . . . in particular: (b) the right to the same employment opportunities, including the application of the same criteria for selection in matters of employment. (c) The right to free choice of profession and employment, the right to promotion, job security and all benefits and conditions of service.[16]

Yet, even with the existence of such crystal clear national and international articles, there was no guaranteed right of Egyptian female law graduates to become judges until 2022. As I witnessed myself and described in the following lines, the application of these legal rules and principles had not been taken into effect.

A RIGHT IS NEVER LOST AS LONG AS SOMEONE STRIVES TO CLAIM IT: REFLECTIONS ON PERSONAL EXPERIENCE—HER HONOR SETTING THE BAR

I graduated from the Faculty of Law and Sharia at Al-Azhar University, class of 2013,[17] with the grade of excellent and distinct honor, and ranked second among the graduating class. My story started on January 30, 2014—soon after Egypt adopted the new constitution—when I went to submit my application, just as my male colleagues did, for a judicial position as announced by the State Council. The officials utterly refused to accept my application, stating explicitly "judicial positions are for males only." I tried to discuss it with them and claim my rights, which are supported by explicit constitutional articles, but with no avail. Consequently, I submitted a complaint to the head of the State Council, but nothing changed. As a result, no option was left but to file a case in the hope of obtaining my rights. Since then, I started the *#HerHonorSettingTheBar*,[18] an initiative that worked on supporting other graduates who were banned from applying to the judiciary and also suffered discrimination.[19]

The first case (No. 30105/2014) was to challenge the negative administrative decision by which I was prevented from submitting my documents for holding a judicial position. While the first case was before the courts, Presidential Decree No. 356 was issued on September 8, 2015, by which my male colleagues were appointed to judicial positions. Therefore, I had to submit a complaint followed by filing the second case (No. 20222/January 2016) to challenge that decree in regard to the exclusion of qualified female law graduates.

One of the first challenges was that the State Council was the competent judicial body and my opponent at the same time. I submitted my case at the State Council against the State Council, as I had no other entity to resort to (an unconstitutional situation). Simultaneously, I was deprived of access to the different judicial degrees and my case was transferred directly to the last degree (Supreme Administrative Court). Hence, when a negative judgment was issued, I couldn't challenge it since it was binding and final.

Later, the Division Commission Department in the State Council issued reports (a consultative opinion to the court, which is mostly adopted by the court) on the two cases. These reports prioritized the discretionary power of the State Council over international conventions and the Constitution. They also repeated the same unjust reasons and excuses for what they deemed appropriate standards justifying rejecting the appointment of women judges. Moreover, the report denied my plea that the council's rejection of my application was an act of discrimination and recommended entirely dismissing the case; it stated that "the State Council has the right to select the applicants it sees fit and the Constitution did not specify any conditions it needs to abide by."

Regarding the first case, in April 2017 a judgment was issued declaring "the inadmissibility of the case" due to the absence of an administrative decision. It nonetheless stated in the reasoning that "the challenge is to an administrative decision." It also mentioned that "the call for applications to hold the judicial position is addressed to male law graduates exclusively." The judgment was issued in a hearing without notifying my lawyer or me of the date of the hearing, and consequently rejected my right to hold a judicial position. The Supreme Administrative Court in the judgment, and the Division

Commission's report, quoted from the aforementioned early judgments and contradicted its own precedents, which established that being qualified is the first objective criterion for joining the bench and appointing the most qualified applicants is the direct way to reinforce justice. This criterion seems applicable for males only.

With regard to the second case, on February 24, 2018, I challenged the unconstitutionality of the current situation of the case as well as some articles of the State Council Law and its Internal Regulation. I asked to transfer my case to the SCC to review and issue a judgment. Another challenge arose in achieving such a problematic transfer, since the State Council has discretionary power to decide whether my transfer request would be accepted or not. Nonetheless, I pleaded personally before the court; the presiding judge tested my knowledge of the law and the pleas invoked in the memorandum. The unconstitutionality pleas were as follows:

First, the unconstitutionality of Article 73 of the State Council Law and Article 186/2 of its Internal Regulation where they failed to stipulate women's right to be appointed and prohibit discrimination against women, as those articles violate Articles 11, 53, and 186[20] of the Constitution, citing the SCC judgment in 2007 stating:

> In case the ordinary or regulatory legislator fails to mention, regulate or protect a constitutional right, this cannot provide a way to escape from the harsh consequences of violating the Constitution. On the contrary, this shall be a serious ground to plead the unconstitutionality of such provisions, not because of what it stipulates, but because of what it fails to stipulate, whether intentionally or not. Based on that, the Constitutional Court repeatedly ruled the unconstitutionality of legal and regulatory provisions based on grounds related to the failure of the legislator to include provisions that grant the full enactment of constitutional rules. Accordingly, if the legislator, be it ordinary or regulatory, failed to regulate rights properly, by, intentionally or unintentionally, failing to regulate an aspect of legal provisions, that would be deemed a violation of the constitutional protection of such right and accordingly a violation of the Constitution. This is conditional upon such failure of the legislator reaching the extent that the regulation of such right will not be complete unless they are stipulated.

Second, the unconstitutionality of Article 186-2 of the Internal Regulation of the State Council that obliged the State Council to abide by General Assembly decisions and prohibited the State Council from deciding contrary thereto.

Third, the unconstitutionality of the General Assembly's decision issued on February 15, 2010, which deprives women of their constitutional right to be appointed to the State Council despite its violation of Articles 9, 11, 14,

53, and 186 of the Constitution and by which I along with other graduates were deprived of our right to apply and go through the required procedures and attend an interview related to such appointment.

Prior to the fourth session of the hearing on October 8, 2018, the State Council organized a conference where an EU delegate asked the Head of the State Council about the absence of women judges in the State Council. He replied, "The appointment of female judges is just a matter of time as we don't have proper logistics yet for women judges. Isn't it enough having seven women ministers?" (Napoleon, 2018).

On October 13, 2018, the said statements were presented before the court, which shows an intentional delay of constitutional rights which is equivalent to the denial of these rights and justice as well as a violation of the Constitution. The case was adjourned again to December 22, 2018, to submit a supplementary memorandum on the matter in addition to the unconstitutionality of the declared justifications for banning women from sitting as judges. Those justifications are unacceptable and contradict the Women's Empowerment National Strategy 2017, which includes having 25% women judges, as well as the country's 2030 vision and the African Agenda 2063. The case has been postponed several times in a row since then. Justice delayed is justice denied.

On November 3, 2018, the SCC issued its judgment regarding Article 104 of the State Council Law, which gives the Supreme Administrative Court the original competence to decide on the State Council members' challenges in cases related to their appointment (after being interviewed), promotion, and other related issues. The article was found to be unconstitutional, since it deprives them of the degrees of judiciary. Unfortunately, my case was incorrectly classified under this category by the State Council. My challenge was initially to an administrative decision, since I was banned from even applying, and this differs from the category of State Council members' cases. Nevertheless, this judgment affected my case as it was transferred from the Supreme Administrative Court to the Administrative Judiciary Court to be reviewed again from the very beginning. That transfer happened while I was waiting to get my case transferred to the SCC. This indeed prolonged the duration of litigation and violated my right to due process; however, it gave me a second chance to challenge the judgment before the Supreme Administrative Court when it was rejected in October 2020, with no hearing session set to date.

In parallel with the judicial path, from 2014 I started to contact and coordinate with the Egyptian National Council for Women (NCW), UN Women Egypt, Parliament members, feminist and human rights institutions, journalists, and media to shed light on the case and to gain support. Regarding the NCW, on January 30, 2014, I met Mrs. Mervat Al-Tallawy, head of the

NCW at the time, and submitted a complaint describing the situation and what we have been through regarding the rejection of females' applications. Consequently, she addressed a letter to the State Council, requesting the appointment of women as judges and saying this is a constitutional right. The council's response was to threaten a lawsuit against the NCW for "insulting and interfering in the judiciary's [internal] affairs." It totally ignored the constitutionality aspect of appointing women as judges. I submitted another complaint on January 28, 2016, when Dr. Maya Morsy presided over the NCW. I met her, Judge Amal Ammar, and Judge Sanaa Khalil, members of NCW's Legislative Committee, and was told that "NCW is working on the case with the presidency to avoid any conflict with the judiciary as happened before." There was also a proposal to secure intervention by NGOs to support the case legally; I followed up many times, but eventually, nothing was done.

I went to the UN Women Egypt office and discussed the issue with one of its officials in the Anti-Discrimination and Violence Unit, who told me "we can only work through national channels and we are currently working on this issue in cooperation with the NCW and Public Prosecution and we are getting positive responses." This is strange in view of the fact that the Public Prosecution itself still bans women from applying as of the time of writing.

Contact with many members of Parliament encouraged a few to take action. In December 2017, a Draft Law on the appointment of women to the judiciary, intended to eliminate long-standing discrimination and demanding gender equality in judicial positions, was introduced by Parliament member Nadia Henry (Farid, 2018) with an explanatory memo written by myself. The bill was then referred to the Legislative and Constitutional Affairs Committee. It states that all judicial entities should be committed to appointing women in accordance with the same criteria on which men are selected and that any laws and regulations to the contrary shall be revoked.[21]

After I reached out to Parliament member Dina Abdel Aziz, on October 16, 2017, she requested an explanation from the Minister of Justice, Mohamed Hossam Abdel-Rahim, regarding this discrimination and the reasons behind the violation of the Constitution by the State Council.[22] In April 2018, the minister of justice responded to the request, saying that he had contacted the State Council regarding the appointment of women judges, and stating that, although he is a member of the executive authority, he has no authority over it. The minister justified his response by referring to the superficial argument that the Constitution was not explicit in obliging the judicial authorities to appoint women, and the question might require a constitutional amendment.[23]

As a result of the above, discussions on women's rights to access the judiciary were intense in the Parliament in January 2018. Later, the press published the statement by Dr. Aly Abd El-A'al, head of the Parliament, that "women's appointment as judges in the Egyptian State Council will happen very soon" (Essam, 2018). Further, in November 2016, the Parliament was discussing the Anti-Discrimination Commission Law which is mentioned in Article 53 of the Constitution and was supposed to be issued, but unfortunately, as yet has not been (Fares, 2016).

In addition to the national efforts engaging directly with key stakeholders, I contacted many NGOs, human rights organizations, and feminist institutions. I also tried to shed light on the case through attending and speaking in many symposiums and conferences in different cities in the Republic, focusing on different aspects of the issue and its social, legal, and judicial impact on the whole community, not just women. Moreover, I tried to raise awareness about the case by contacting law professors in other universities and law students, attending conferences to raise the issue and putting it on the agenda of the concerned officials, and writing articles about it. Despite this activism, the lack of interest, partly due to the fear of political repercussions, was evident—some law schools, even nongovernmental institutions, refused to hold symposiums about the case, trying to avoid anything that might be considered political and controversial. Further, the court's decisions to spread the hearings over a long time have diminished the ability to rally public support and keep the public engaged.

In addition, since 2014, I have submitted 350 complaints by registered mail to the Egyptian president with copies to the first lady, the prime minister, the minister of justice, the Parliament's president, the head of the Supreme Council of Judiciary, the head of the State Council, the head of the Human Rights Committee in the Parliament, the head of the National Council of Human Rights, and the head of the NCW and many Parliament members.

Finally, the cause that Her Honor Setting The Bar fought for over the past eight years has been accomplished. Its endeavors have been crowned by a tangible result and have finally ended one form of discrimination in the Egyptian community, about a century after the establishment of the Egyptian judiciary.

On March 8, 2021, Egyptian president Abd El-Fattah El-Sisi' directed the minister of justice to include women judges in the Public Prosecution and the State Council.[24] Accordingly, in October 2021, 11 women judges from among the 66 women judges in the ordinary courts were transferred to the Public Prosecution and another 98 women judges were transferred from the APA and ESLA to the State Council. That places the total number of women judges at 153 across Egypt to date (The National Council for Women, 2017). However, the most important fact was that discrimination remained and female law graduates were still banned from applying to the judiciary.

Afterward, due to the criticism that was directed at the practice of repeated ad hoc appointments instead of opening the doors to female law graduates to apply equally, instead of applying the provisions of the Constitution, on January 27 and 31, 2022, the State Council and the Public Prosecution opened the gates for the female law graduates to apply—for the first time in history in the case of the latter, and only the second time in that of the former. This revolutionary step promises more and more empowerment for the coming generations and development for the judiciary as well.

Such a step has been taken after eight years of litigation and campaigning, attempting to obtain constitutionally fundamental human rights, which were unfortunately violated and severely breached. This was a violation of the right to justice, the right to official appointment based on an objective criterion, and the right to equal opportunities.

CONCLUSION AND RECOMMENDATIONS

Egyptian women judges' representation in the judiciary has been a historical challenge despite all the national and international norms that assert and guarantee this right to women. Many attempts were made to overcome the illegal and inhumane status to which women were thus relegated, which ultimately yielded positive results in 2022. While women celebrate this achievement, at the same time, it raised the question: Why did it take so long for this milestone to be achieved?

To overcome similar challenges and be able to achieve the African 2063 agenda and the UN SDGs, Egypt must adopt a clear vision combined with a practical step-by-step agenda on how to empower women in all fields, and especially in the judiciary. Among numerous possible solutions, Egypt could, for example:

(i) Give effect to Article 53 of the Constitution, which criminally penalizes any discrimination based on gender and immediately prosecutes those who exercise such discrimination. Furthermore, by establishing the "Anti-Discrimination Commission" with vast powers and the ability to issue decisions that are binding even upon state authorities.

(ii) Design courses on gender issues and rights, particularly for judges and key officials who are part of the decision-making process regarding such issues, and make this course part of the obligatory six-month training for newly appointed judges. Furthermore, create frameworks and disciplinary procedures to tackle gender-related issues and abide by international guidelines. Benefiting from the Global Judicial Integrity Network's experience in this regard would be a great help. This incorporates "gender-related issues into its new judicial conduct training package, which is currently being piloted in over 40 countries . . . also the drafting of an issue paper on gender-related issues to serve as an international standard for judiciaries" (Evans, M, 2019).

(iii) Host conferences and judicial exchange programs aiming at teaching Egyptian judges about the successful experience of other countries that appointed women judges.
(iv) Start a consolidated gender-awareness campaign aiming to raise public awareness of gender issues and women's empowerment. This could include a general part directed to the public, in addition to more customized sub-campaigns and trainings given to particular professions. It could also include the revision of all education curricula to remove all stereotyping of women and their roles in society and insert inspiring examples of successful women.
(v) Create a committee in the Parliament with the mission of reviewing all laws and regulations that either allow discrimination against women or fail to stipulate necessary guarantees of fair treatment for women. Such a committee is to report to the Parliament and the—potential—Anti-Discrimination Commission and should make definite recommendations to the Parliament regarding how it should amend the laws to be nondiscriminatory; it should also have precise follow-up strategies to measure the effectiveness of such amendments and whether there should be more amendments to ensure such protection.

To conclude, appointing women judges in Egypt has been, and remains, a very vital cause and a successful step toward women's empowerment. Still, without structural reform to protect this step and guarantee fair representation, promotion, and nomination to regional and international positions, this step will risk being only a limited exception that will not lead to achieving the goals Egypt is aiming for by adopting the UN SDGs and the African Union Agenda 2063. Her Honor Setting The Bar has always had hopes that Egyptian women will come out victorious, occupy judicial positions, and eventually put an end to all forms of discrimination. This goal was attained not only as a result of steps by an individual, but our cumulative steps that all made a positive difference toward it, thereby lending support to the assertion that "a right is never lost, as long as someone strives to claim it."

NOTES

1. Ms. Al-Ayoubi enrolled in the university in 1929. While some—mistakenly—assert that Mofida Abd El-Rahman was the first lawyer, the credit actually goes to Naima El-Ayoubi. Moufida Abdel Rahman (1914–2002). The Lady Lawyer. (2004). *Al-Ahram Weekly On-Line*. http://weekly.ahram.org.eg/Archive/2004/672/chrncls.htm.

2. "Progress towards Parity: The Representation of Women in the Judiciary" Article published by the UNODC – Global Judicial Integrity Network – April 2021. A joint article with Prof. Jarpa Dawuni, professor of Political Science at Howard University, Washington, DC, and founder of Institute of African Women in Law. https://www.unodc.org/dohadeclaration/en/news/2021/04/progress-towards-parity-the-representation-of-women-in-the-judiciary.html.

3. Egypt's Dar AlIftaa (2012, December 3). *Egypt's Mufti affirms that women are allowed under Islamic Jurisprudence to be judges and hold high positions* [post]. Facebook. https://www.facebook.com/EgyptDarAlIfta/posts/538114389551681.

4. Rateb was an international law professor at the Cairo University Law School and served as Egypt's second female minister of social affairs and the country's first female ambassador. She died in 2013.

5. The Decision rendered on case No. 33 for the fourth judicial year. The Administrative Judiciary Court, the Second Circuit. 1952, February 20.

6. The Decision rendered on case No. 243 for the sixth judicial year. The Administrative Judiciary Court, the First Circuit. 1953, December 22.

7. This regression was based on social trends in Egypt at the time of President Al-Sadat, which expanded the role of Islamic Sharia Law and Islamic groups, which was concurrent and closely associated with the Saudi Islamic *Sahwa* "awakening" movement. The official manifestation of this trend was the setting of the principles of Islamic Sharia as the sole source of the legislation by the amendment to Article 2 of the Constitution citing the Principles of Islamic Sharia as "the main source of legislation" rather than "**a** main source" of legislation.

8. The United Nations Committee on the Elimination of Discrimination against Women- (2001, January 15–February 02). *Concluding comments of the Committee on the Elimination of Discrimination against Women: Egypt.* https://www.un.org/womenwatch/daw//cedaw/cdrom_cedaw/EN/files/cedaw25years/content/english/CONCLUDING_COMMENTS_ENGLISH/Egypt/Egypt%20-%20CO-3%20&%20CO-4-5.pdf. P. 5, Para 340.

9. By March 2007, the SJC had received applications from 124 female applicants.

10. The same principles were enshrined in the Universal Declaration of Human Rights 1948, UN Convention on the Political Rights of Women 1953, UN International Covenant on Civil and Political Rights 1966, UN Declaration on the Elimination of Discrimination against Women 1967, African Charter on Human and People's Rights 1981, Universal Islamic Declaration of Human Rights 1981, Montreal Universal Declaration on the Independence of Justice 1983, UN Basic Principles on the Independence of the Judiciary 1985, Cairo Declaration on Human Rights in Islam 1990, Arab Charter on Human Rights 2004 by the Arab League and Cairo Declaration of Arab Woman 2014 by the Arab League, Arab Woman Organization.

It is worth mentioning that conventions ratified by Egypt are deemed to be national law and shall prevail if they contradict national law, according to Article 151 of the Egyptian Constitution.

11. Article 11.

12. Article 53.

13. Article 9.

14. Article 14.

15. Egypt's ratification was on September 1981. The Decree of the Minister of Foreign affairs No. 111 for the year 1981, as published on December 17, 1981, publishing the Treaty and declaring the date of its entry into force.

16. Article 11.

17. It teaches Egyptian law compared to Sharia. It adds richness to the study and comprehensive perspectives as well.

It is the second oldest Islamic University in the world, where females and males have separate faculties.

18. Her Honor Setting The Bar (n.d.). *Home* [Facebook page]. https://www.facebook.com/%D8%A7%D9%84%D9%85%D9%86%D8%B5%D8%A9-%D8%AD%D9%82%D9%87%D8%A7-Her-Honor-Setting-The-Bar-277991102857130/?modal=admin_todo_tour.

19. To know more about the Initiative and its activities, please see Gadalla, O. (2020, April 3). Egyptian women judges: Setting the bar for gender equality. *Institute for African Women in Law*. https://www.africanwomeninlaw.com/post/the-egyptian-woman-judge-setting-the-bar-for-gender-equality.

And the UNESCO, the American University of Beirut and the Asfari Institute for Civil Society project video. https://www.facebook.com/1076934306/posts/10222728411613709/?d=n.

20. Which stipulates, "Judges are independent, cannot be dismissed, are subject to no other authority but the law, and are equal in rights and duties. The conditions and procedures for their appointment, secondment, delegation, and retirement are regulated by the law."

21. The first article of the draft law places an obligation on all judicial bodies to appoint women to judicial offices and ensure that the conditions of their appointment are consistent with those that are applicable to men. In its second article, the draft law nullifies any law that infringes on the obligation set forth in Article 1.

Article 3 of the draft law invalidates any procedures concerning the appointment of judges if such procedures do not comply with Article 1 of the draft law.

Benarbia, S. (2018, January 22). Egypt: adopts the draft law on the appointment of women to the judiciary. International Commission of Jurists. https://www.icj.org/egypt-adopt-draft-law-on-the-appointment-of-women-to-the-judiciary/.

22. Parliament member submitted a question to the minister of justice requests appointing women as judges in the State Council (n.d). Parlmany News.

23. The argument was mainly advanced verbally by the State Council that the wording of the Constitution says that the state "grants/guarantees" the right of women to be appointed in judicial bodies and institutions and that the word grant does not have a binding effect of the judicial bodies, thus, there must be a constitutional amendment to change the wording to "oblige," which is incorrect legally. Even if it's controversial, the articles of the conventions are very obvious and we are bound by them.

Aly, N. (2018, April 23). Minister of Justice: Appointing women judges in the State Council needs Constitution amendment. *Al Youm Al Sabe' electronic newspaper*.

24. This indeed has serious consequences and triggers legitimate concerns about the integrity, impartiality, and independence of the judicial authority and the intervention of the executive authority on the judicial authority and the constitutional principle of the separation of powers. Most importantly, why the judiciary itself did not apply the Constitution as it is supposed to be instead of being forced to apply it.

REFERENCES

Abdoun, S. (2010, February 23). Judges contest decision to bar female judges from state council. *The Daily Newspaper Egypt*. https://wwww.dailynewssegypt.com/2010/02/23/judges-contest-decision-to-bar-female-judges-from-state-council/.

Abdulaal, M. (2018). Top judicial positions include 16 Egyptian female judges. *Egyptian Streets*. https://egyptianstreets.com/2018/08/09/top-judicial-positions-include-16-egyptian-female-judges/.

Abu Ghazi, E. (2013, March 15). Permeant constitution 1971 which didn't last. *Al-Shorouk Newspaper*. http://www.shorouknews.com/columns/view.aspx?cdate=15032013&id=830bfab1-fd9c-4b39-9dbf-804ede54602b.

Ali, L. (2013, October 18). Via video . . . The Mufti affirms that it is permitted for women to become judges and hold high positions in the state. *Al Youm Al Sabe' Electronic Newspaper*.

Al-Shorouk Newspaper. (2017). Statistics: Percentage of female consulars in the APA is 43% in 2015. *Al-Shorouk Newspaper*. https://www.shorouknews.com/news/view.aspx?cdate=07032017&id=ae68d01f-281c-4926-b326-d9d223307653.

Al-Wahaidy, F. (2017, November 14). MPs call for equal gender representation in the judicial system. *Egypt Today*. http://www.egypttoday.com/Article/2/32508/MPs-call-for-equal-gender-representation-in-judicial-system.

Elsayed, A. (2007). Female judges in Egypt. *Yearbook of Islamic and Middle Eastern Law Online*, *13*(1), 135–149. https://doi.org/10.1163/22112987-91000168.

Essam, G. (2018, January 28). The head of the parliament: Egypt will witness appointing women judges in the state council very soon. *Al-Ahram Newspaper*. http://gate.ahram.org.eg/News/1807988.aspx.

Evans, M. (2019, September 13). Why the gender of your judge matters. *Apolitical*. https://apolitical.co/solution_article/why-the-gender-of-your-judge-matters/.

Fares, M. (2016, November 13). The draft of (Anti-Discrimination Commission) law before being discussed. *Al Youm Al Sabe' electronic newspaper*.

Farid, S. (2018, February 21). Analysis: Is there a place for women within Egypt's judiciary?. *Al Arabiya News*. https://english.alarabiya.net/en/features/2018/02/21/Is-there-a-place-for-Egyptian-women-within-judicial-positions-.html.

Gadalla, O. (2020, October 2). Her honor setting the bar: Fighting for equality in Egypt's judiciary. *Tahrir Institute for Middle East Policy*. https://timep.org/commentary/analysis/her-honor-setting-the-bar-fighting-for-equality-in-egypts-judiciary/.

http://www.ahram.org.eg/NewsPrint/241552.aspx.

Khalil, A. (2003, September 23). Egypt's first female judge may remain 'the only'. *Women News*. https://womensenews.org/2003/09/egypts-first-female-judge-may-remain-the-only/.

Lindbekk, M. (2017). Women judges in Egypt: Discourse and practice. In N. Sonneveld & M. Lindbekk (Eds.), *Women judges in the Muslim world: A comparative study of discourse and practice* (pp. 285–317). Brill. https://doi.org/10.1163/9789004342200.

Moustafa, R. (2015). Munira Thabet, first Egyptian lady to obtain *license en Droit*. *Rosaelyoussef*. https://www.rosaelyoussef.com/162700/%d9%85%d9%86%d9%8a%d8%b1%d8%a9-%d8%ab%d8%a7%d8%a8%d8%aa-%d8%b9%d9%85%d9%8a%d8%af%d8%a9-%d8%a7%d9%84%d8%b5%d8%ad%d9%81%d9%8a%d8%a7%d8%aa.

Napoleon, M. (2018, October 8). The head of the state council replies the EU delegate "appointing women judges is a matter of time." *Al-Shorouk Newspaper*. https://www.shorouknews.com/news/view.aspx?cdate=08102018&id=fa7b9576-7b1d-4715-84cd-391d60f3a9a0.

Nasrawi, S. (1998, July 14). Woman pursues Egyptian judgeship. *Associated Press*. Retrieved April 21, 2020, from https://www.apnews.com/7f46e49d0e327a4c32a3b1ec2e31968c.

Qaraa', I. (2017, March 31). Egyptian state lawsuits authority: The authority was a pioneer in celebrating Egyptian Women. *Al-Masry El-youm Newspaper*. https://www.almasryalyoum.com/news/details/1110574.

The National Council for Women. (2017). *The national strategy for the empowerment of Egyptian women 2030: Vision and pillars*. http://ncw.gov.eg/wp-content/uploads/2018/02/final-version-national-strategy-for-the-empowerment-of-egyptian-women-2030.pdf.

The United Nations. (1995). *Beijing declaration and platform for action*. https://www.un.org/en/events/pastevents/pdfs/Beijing_Declaration_and_Platform_for_Action.pdf.

World Economic Forum. (2020). *Gender gap report*. https://www.weforum.org/reports/gender-gap-2020-report-100-years-pay-equality.

Chapter 6

Making Gains for Women's Rights

Using Gender Quotas to Achieve Gender Equality in the Composition of the Supreme Court of Kenya

Annerita Murungi and Agnes Meroka-Mutua

INTRODUCTION

While significant progress has been made in achieving gender equality in the judiciary in Kenya, this is not the case for the Supreme Court of Kenya (SCOK) (Vladini & Shortell, 2016). Until 2021, when a woman was appointed as the chief justice and president of SCOK, only two of seven court positions had ever been held by women. This historic milestone also marked the first time since the promulgation of the Constitution of Kenya (CoK) in 2010 that the two-thirds gender rule in the composition of the Supreme Court was fulfilled. Even so, it has been a struggle to have this constitutional promise fulfilled, as will be discussed in this chapter. Even when women have been appointed as judges based on merit, the conditions under which they work have remained by social and gender norms largely patriarchal, thus making it difficult for them to perform effectively in their roles. This chapter argues that in order to maintain gains made in achieving the two-thirds gender rule, policy frameworks still need to be put into place. Gender equality in this sense is not simply about having the requisite number of female judges in office; it also is about having working spaces that are gender sensitive. This is important because we shall see in this chapter that historically, women have shunned top leadership positions for fear that society will see them as not conforming to social and gender norms that preserve leadership positions for men.

The struggle to have women included in the apex court is not unique to Kenya. In India, only of the Supreme Court's 29 judges is a woman, and since its establishment in 1950, only five women have ever been appointed as judges of the court (Gosh et al., 2018). In the United Kingdom, it was not until 2017 that the first woman was appointed as president of the Supreme Court (Dearden, 2017). However, there are also positive examples, where at least one-third of the judges of the Supreme Court are women. In the United States and Canada, three of the nine judges of their Supreme Courts are now women (Aoláin, 2015). In countries such as Benin, Niger, Rwanda, Ghana, Nigeria, and Sierra Leone, two women have served as presidents of their highest courts (Dawuni & Kang, 2015). Thus, while there may be challenges in ensuring gender representation in Supreme Courts around the world, it is still possible to do so.

Gender equality in the courts is vital because women bring a gender perspective in decision-making, thus enhancing the rights of women (Hunter, 2015). Further, women's representation enhances the legitimacy of the judiciary because the judiciary is seen as providing equal opportunity to both men and women (Hunter, 2015). However, the idea of ensuring gender equality in the courts is not readily supported (Suk, 2013). Some scholars argue that the appointment of judges to the Supreme Court should be based on merit first and foremost, and gender should just be one of the many factors that the appointive body has to take into consideration (Suk, 2013). In South Africa, for example, while the Constitution recognizes the need for gender equality in public appointments, Dawuni and Kang (2015) indicate that in practice, gender considerations are subordinate to merit and racial considerations undermining the number of women in the Supreme Court.

The argument in this chapter is twofold: first, the inclusion of more women in the Supreme Court will enhance the protection of women's rights in Kenya. Second, gender equality in the Supreme Court may be achieved through the use of gender quotas. This chapter is structured into four main parts. The introduction has provided the background and highlighted the gender equality gap that exists in the SCOK. The second section theoretically grounds the work by discussing the relevance of gender quotas in promoting gender equality in the judiciary. The third section discusses the importance of having female judges in the Supreme Court and specific ways in which female judges have contributed to the enhancement of women's rights in Kenya, and it also highlights the struggle that female judges face in discharging their duties. The third section demonstrates that gender inequality goes beyond the numbers of female judges in the Supreme Court. It highlights that gender inequality is also evident in how female judges are perceived by society, and that working conditions within the judiciary also have a negative impact on female judges. The fourth section discusses how gender equality has been achieved in the lower courts by having in place specific policy interventions. The fourth section also outlines the need for policy interventions with regard to the Supreme Court because although the court is now compliant with the two-thirds gender rule, there are still no clear policy guidelines that require the Judicial Service Commission to ensure that the two-thirds rule is met and maintained. Without such policy guidelines, there is an ever-present danger that the current gender composition may not be maintained. This section explains how gender quotas may be used to achieve gender equality in Kenya's Supreme Court. The fourth section further highlights the challenges that the SCOK has had in the past had in making progressive decisions about implementation of the two-thirds gender rule and argues that this might be attributed to the gender composition of the court.

GENDER QUOTAS AS A VEHICLE FOR ACHIEVING GENDER EQUALITY IN THE SCOK

Quotas refer to the requirement that individuals are recruited, taking into consideration traditionally excluded groups such as women, racial and ethnic minorities, and persons with disabilities. Gender quotas ensure that a certain number of the underrepresented gender are recruited into public office. There are three types of gender quotas: reserved seats, legal candidates' quotas, and voluntary political party quotas (Ochiel, 2016). The Constitution or a statute can legally mandate gender quotas or they can be instituted voluntarily. In Kenya, Article 27(8) of the Constitution provides for the use of gender quotas in appointive and elective bodies. The debate for and against the use of gender quotas in increasing women representation in leadership positions has centered on the tension between selection by gender and selection by merit (Phillips, 1995, pp. 85–114). Proponents of gender quotas view them as a temporary measure for increasing women's representation until a level playing field between women and men is reached (UN Women, 2014). Critics, such as Anisa Somani (2013), argue that judicial appointments in the Supreme Court should be based solely on merit without taking into consideration other factors like gender. However, merit looks to academic and professional qualifications, and work experience, but not necessarily to lived experience. Concerning gender matters, lived experience as a woman plays a significant role in shaping one's understanding of the cases she determines.

Geoffery Bindman and Karon Monaghan (2014) argue that the concept of merit in the appointment of Supreme Court judges is ill-defined. They demonstrate that the creation of a diverse judiciary in itself should be regarded as an element of merit. Obstacles such as the culture of exclusivity, which stereotypes "the judge as a white male barrister" (Bindman and Monaghan, 2014, p. 6), whether real or imagined, impede potential candidates from underrepresented groups. There is the need to have diversity in the pool of candidates to enhance training and mentoring, and to improve opportunities for qualified people from diverse backgrounds. In this regard, quotas are necessary for the realization of the representation of the underrepresented "other."

Melody Valdini and Christopher Shortell (2016) admit that there exists a cross-national variation when it comes to the presence of women in the highest courts. The two conducted a study in 50 democracies to assess women's representation in the constitutional courts. They argue that the selection mechanism used determines women's presence. Their finding is that where selectors are sheltered from electoral accountability, they are less likely to select women as judges because they do not benefit from credit claiming; and where selectors are exposed and can claim credit, the unique traits and visibility generate an incentive to appoint women. It is for this reason that these scholars refute the argument that gender quotas are vital for enhancing women's representation and instead argue that the selection method is critical. They focus on the impact of the method, culture, and availability of qualified women judges on women representation in the Supreme Court. They argue that the highest courts have unique traits and visibility; hence the appointment of women will be handled differently than in lower courts.

Scholars like Elsje Bonthuys (2013), Rachael Johnson (2014), and Ruth Cowan (2006) argue that the appointment of women in the courts of South Africa is gender biased despite constitutional provisions on gender equality and gender quotas. Cowan (2006) notes that the provision of gender quotas in the South African Constitution has not enhanced women's representation, a situation that is mirrored in Kenya. Factors that affect the inclusion of women in the judiciary include continued patriarchy and sexism by the gatekeepers, the presumption that women are not qualified, gender equality being considered subordinate to racial equality, and underrepresentation of women in the bar (Cowan, 2006). Consequently, Cowan (2006) argues that the appointing authority is a gatekeeper positioned at the door of the courts, and if not committed to gender parity, will act as an impediment to the appointment of women. This points out the need to ensure that the composition of the appointing authority is gender sensitive.

In her study of women's appointment as judges, Shirley Abrahamson (1984) explores four questions that women appointed to the highest court are often asked. These include: Were you appointed because you are a woman?; Do you think you were appointed as the token woman on the bench?; Do you view yourself as representing women in court?; and Do you think women would make a difference in the administration of justice?" (Abrahamson, 1984, p. 91). The implication here is that society's perception is that a woman cannot make it on merit, and while gender quotas can enhance women's representation, such stereotypes, if not addressed, will hinder the success of gender quotas (Abrahamson, 1984).

Nancy Arrington et al. (2017) contend that the need to have more women serving in higher courts is because the presence of women may influence the law—that diversity on the court provides it with legitimacy, and legitimacy affects the way courts develop jurisprudence. The authors indicate that the underrepresentation of women in apex courts is as a result of "deeply complicated socio-cultural norms, including limited availability pools that follow from gendered appointments to lower courts, elite networks that fail to identify qualified candidates and culturally structured role perceptions that make a prestigious judicial career simply easier for men to pursue" (Arrington et al., 2017, p. 5). Gender quotas cannot be effective unless such impediments are addressed.

Dawuni and Kang (2015) argue that the legal system, selection method, commitment of gatekeepers, and regional representation are likely to influence the number of women in top positions in the judiciary and this explains why some African countries have had female judicial leaders. On the question of whether the use of gender quotas positively impacts the appointment of female judges, they argue that this is not always necessarily the case (Dawuni & Kang, 2015). In countries such as Kenya and South Africa, where gender quotas are used, women have not been appointed to top positions in the judiciary, until recently in 2021 when the first female chief justice was appointed in Kenya, 58 years after independence. In the same breath, in countries such as Ghana, where there are no gender quotas, women have been appointed to such positions (Dawuni & Kang, 2015).

The use of quotas necessarily addresses not just the question of numbers, but also the issue of creating favorable working conditions that enable female judges to effectively perform their duties. As we shall see in the next section, gender inequality in Kenya's Supreme Court must be addressed, both at the level of inclusion of female judges and at the level of creating a gender-sensitive work environment once female judges are appointed. At the same time, societal perceptions and institutional working conditions that negatively impact the way female judges work also must be addressed. Gender quotas are a vehicle through which gender equality at both these levels can be achieved.

DISPENSING GENDER JUSTICE: THE ROLE AND LIMITATIONS OF FEMALE JUDGES

The role female judges play in enhancing women's rights cannot be overemphasized. Rosemary Hunter (2006) has argued that women's representation in the judiciary is not merely about tokenism but rather that female judges increase the democratic legitimacy of the courts and symbolize equal opportunity for both men and women in the legal profession (Hunter, 2015). Besides, female judges bring gender perspectives in the determination of cases (Hunter, 2015). Monica Podgorny (2012) argues that there is a need to have gender equality at the Supreme Court in order to remove gender bias in legal reasoning.

It should, however, be noted that gender is not the only factor that might lead to progressive jurisprudence being developed by the courts in gender-related matters. Constitutional provisions that require judges to promote gender equality also play a significant role, as happened in the case of the *In the Matter of the Principle of Gender Representation in the National Assembly and the Senate*, 2012. The Kenyan people aware of the historical gender inequalities made no mistake during the Constitution making and hence a provision was included in the CoK, 2010 to the effect that not more than two-thirds of the members of elective public bodies shall be of the same gender. It was for this reason that the then attorney general of the Republic of Kenya moved the Supreme Court's jurisdiction on advisory opinion as to whether that provision under Article 81(b) as read with other articles of the Constitution that promote gender equality requires progressive realization of the enforcement of the one-third gender rule or requires the same to be implemented during the general elections which were scheduled for March 4, 2013.

The then chief justice, the Hon. Willy Mutunga, held the sole dissenting opinion that the two-thirds gender rule should be implemented during the 2013 general elections, which were the first general elections under the new Constitution, promulgated in 2010. The other judges held that the two-thirds gender rule should be progressively realized, leading to a situation whereby the constitutional rule was not implemented during the 2013 elections. Kenya is still struggling to attain the two-thirds gender rule and Parliament has not yet taken any legislative measures to begin the progressive realization of the rule as directed by the Supreme Court. Arguably, it is the progressive constitutional provisions on gender equality that guided the CJ to dissent.

In addition to progressive constitutional provisions, the gender of judicial officers is also important in influencing the decisions that judges make. Here, we consider some decisions passed by female judges in Kenya that have promoted women's rights and inspired confidence in women to approach the courts for justice.

In *L.N.W. v. Attorney-General & 3 Others, 2016*, Lady Justice Mumbi Ngugi held that all children born out of wedlock should have the right and/or liberty to have the names of their fathers entered on their birth certificates. In this case, the petitioner, a single mother of a child born outside marriage, sought guidance from the court concerning the rights of children born outside wedlock and the circumstances under which the name of the biological father should be inserted in the birth certificate of the child.

Ngugi also decided the case of *Mary Wanjuhi Muigai v. The Attorney General & Another, 2015*, where she ruled in the applicant's favor that Section 6 of the Marriage Act No. 4 of 2014 must be read as including all marriages celebrated under all religious faiths duly recognized and registered in Kenya. She further said that the practice of polygamy and registration of polygamous marriages without the consent of the previous wife or wives is inconsistent with the equality provisions of the Constitution.

In the case of *In the Matter of JOO v. The Attorney General & 6 Others, 2018*, Lady Justice Abida Ali Aroni found in favor of the applicant and faulted Bungoma County Hospital, the Bungoma County government, and the Cabinet Secretary of Health for violating the applicant's human rights under both Kenya's Constitution and international law when the applicant, who was then pregnant, sought medical assistance from the hospital during her delivery in 2013. The applicant claimed to have suffered physical and verbal abuse by hospital employees. The judge concluded that the applicant's rights to health and dignity had been infringed on and threatened and found that the county government neglected or failed to ensure that health care facilities provide quality maternal health care services.

Lady Justice Teresia Matheka in the High Court case of *Re Estate of Francis Mwangi Mbaria (Deceased), 2018* held that the deceased's daughters qualified as his dependents and therefore ought to be considered for inheritance from his estate.

In *Eunita Anyango Geko & Another v. Philip Obungu Orinda, 2013*, High Court Judge, Lady Justice Ruth Sitati, ruled that the applicant was married to the deceased in Migori, Kenya, in a polygamous woman-to-woman marriage in accordance with Suba Customary Laws, and the 11 children born out of the union were therefore the children of the deceased and entitled to inherit her estate.

On the other hand, the lack of gender equality in the composition of courts could have a negative impact on cases on women's rights. Agnes Meroka-Mutua (2018) demonstrates that in several cases relating to gender equality that went to the SCOK, the court failed to pass decisions that would enhance the implementation of women's rights. But in cases relating to human rights generally, the court made very progressive decisions.

So far, we have seen that female judges make a difference, and they play a crucial role in promoting women's rights through judicial decision-making. However, societal structures continue to block women from joining the bench. Ruth Aura-Odhiambo (2018) argues that earlier, and for a long time, most women were discouraged from undertaking certain courses that were deemed to be masculine, and law was among these courses. This explains the absence of women in the early years of the judiciary, as well as their low numbers currently, at the apex of these key professions and more significantly, the attitude that women cannot take up top leadership positions within male-dominated professions; this, however, is changing after the promulgation of the 2010 CoK (Aura-Odhiambo, 2018).

The reluctance by women to take up top positions in the judiciary is evident in the appointment of judges to the SCOK. In 2016, for the post of CJ, out of 14 applicants, only two were women; by contrast, for the post of deputy chief justice, 14 out of 15 applicants were women (Standard Team, 2016). In 2021, only 3 of the 10 shortlisted candidates were women. Yet the qualifications for appointment to the position of DCJ are the same as those for the position of the CJ, as provided for under Article 166(3) of the Constitution. Sally Jane Kenney (2016) explains that female candidates preferred the DCJ position to the CJ one because of the kind of malice that tends to surface during judicial selection processes, when women tender their interest for top positions.

During 2016 interviews for the position of the DCJ, one female candidate was asked by the Judicial Service Commission whether there was a perception that the DCJ position was reserved for women and why she had applied for this position (Citizen TV, 2016). Her response was that one "can only climb a tree from the bottom" (Citizen TV, 2016). She also said there "is a feeling out there that this commission (referring to the JSC) is male-dominated" (Citizen TV, 2016).

Hostility from other judges, lawyers, and litigants is another reason hindering the professional performance of female judges, and as a result of such hostility, female judges are more likely to face disciplinary action as compared to male judges (Kenney, 2013). In Kenya, this is apparent. Three female judges of the SCOK have faced disciplinary action and been treated in a harsh manner when compared with the way in which male judges of the same court have been treated. For instance, in 2019 SCOK, one of the male judges of the SCOK was accused of threatening one of his security guards with a gun (Ombati, 2019). The alleged offense was reported to the police, but the matter was later settled between the parties, and no charges were brought against the judge (Ombati, 2019). The judge remains in office, with little attention paid to this incident.

When compared to two specific incidents involving female judges, it is clear that female judges are treated more harshly by society and also are easily disciplined. The first incident is the removal of former deputy chief justice Nancy Baraza from office in 2012, following allegations that she pinched the nose of a security guard. A disciplinary hearing generated a lot of media attention that painted Baraza in a bad light and dented her reputation (Malanda, 2012). Indeed, it can be argued that the negative media attention the matter received contributed to her eventual removal from office. The second incident relates to accusations of corruption leveled against Deputy Chief Justice Philomena Mwilu (Musau, 2019). In newspaper reports, Mwilu stated that she had been ridiculed on social media and shamed with a public arrest (Wasuna & Misiko, 2018).

In another case, *Lady Justice Kalpana H. Rawal & 2 others v. Judicial Service Commission & 6 Others, 2016*, the issue concerned the retirement age of judges. Earlier constitutional provisions allowed judges to retire at age 74, but under the new constitutional dispensation, Article 167(1) requires judges to retire at 70. Rawal was appointed under the provisions that set the retirement age at 74. However, she was promoted to the office of DCJ under the new provisions so there was uncertainty concerning her retirement age. When she turned 70, the JSC initiated the process of replacing her, and it was deemed that she had retired. She sought court orders to stop the recruitment process, pending the determination of her retirement age. She argued that the court had granted similar orders as those she sought to a male judge of the same court to stop his replacement, pending the determination of his retirement age. She requested that similar orders be extended to her, but she was not granted the orders, in very blatant differential treatment (Kamau, 2015).

All three women who have held the position of DCJ have been embattled, and their cases have been publicized widely in a manner that humiliated them and limited the extent to which they were able to effectively discharge their duties. While women have worked hard so as to be meritoriously appointed as judges, societal perceptions of women continue to hinder the way women can perform their duties. Further, women are easily removed from office as compared to men. Therefore, it is not sufficient that conditions are created to ensure the inclusion of women, as has been done under Kenya's constitutional provisions on the one-third gender representation rule. That is only a starting point. Conditions under which women work and prevailing patriarchal norms also must be addressed to ensure that women remain in office once appointed.

It is notable that immediately after assuming office, Chief Justice Martha Koome, who is also the president of the Supreme Court, was already facing resistance, which began even at the time of her shortlisting (Okoth, 2021). The president of the Law Society of Kenya (LSK) objected to her shortlisting, questioning her suitability for the position. Upon her recommendation as the JSC nominee and her name being submitted to the president for approval, again the LSK president called into question the hasty way in which her name was sent to the president and further, he called into question the legality of the process. He petitioned the JSC to release their performance matrix and scorecards of all interviewed candidates. Further, he alleged that the process of scoring for each candidate and voting needed to be verified and that a candidate (male) had his scores altered by the commissioners (Okoth, 2021). After taking oath of office, Justice Koome initiated the process of negotiations to have the 41 judges appointed and the president approved the nominations of 34 of 41 judges of the High Court and Court of Appeal. The president had withheld the approval of the judges for two years for reasons he did not disclose. However, six of the judges were not approved, and this created serious questions and anxiety because the president has no constitutional mandate to refuse to approve judges who have been nominated for appointment by the JSC (Njeru, 2021).

Koome therefore started her term at a time when the judiciary and executive had serious differences. The president's speech during Madaraka Day celebrations on June 1, 2021, a day when Kenya celebrates the gaining of political independence from Britain, indicated that there was indeed a sense that the judicial arm was seen as impeding the will of the people of Kenya and slowing down progress, particularly following the nullification of the presidential elections in 2017 by the Supreme Court, then headed by retired CJ David Maraga and also following the declaration that the Building Bridges Initiative (BBI) as unconstitutional by the High Court. Notably, two of the judges who presided over the BBI case were appointed as Court of Appeal judges and they were among the six whose nomination the president did not approve. Thus, Koome faces an uphill task, where patriarchal structures may work together with an already difficult relationship between the judiciary and the executive. There is therefore an impetus to create a gender-sensitive working environment within the judiciary.

TOWARD GENDER EQUALITY IN KENYA'S SUPREME COURT: THE USE OF QUOTAS TO ENSURE WOMEN'S INCLUSION IN THE SUPREME COURT

While significant progress has been made in achieving gender equality in representation within Kenya's judiciary, as is reflected by the composition of all other courts (Judicial Service Commission, 2017), until 2021, the exception was the Supreme Court. Gender equality provisions in the appointment of judges were put in place to address the low numbers of women in the judiciary under the old constitutional regime. The Taskforce on Judicial Reforms (2010) found that women were underrepresented in the justice sector, and although there were sufficient numbers of female magistrates and paralegals in higher levels of the judiciary, there were fewer women and specifically, no woman had ever served as CJ. There were no female Court of Appeal judges and no female Kadhis (judicial officers of the Islamic Courts) (Taskforce on Judicial Reforms, 2010).

Patricia Mbote and Migai Aketch (2011, p. 113) note that "indeed women were underrepresented in the higher echelons of the judiciary and predominate in the lower cadres." The Taskforce on Judicial Reforms thus recommended that the JSC ensure gender parity at all levels in the judiciary as stipulated in the CoK. In selecting judges, the JSC is guided by the principle of gender equality under Article 172(2) (b) of the CoK while taking into account merit. Further, Section 3 of the Judicial Service Act (JSA) requires the JSC and judiciary to enhance gender equity and protection of human rights. Section 14(1) of the Schedule of JSA further requires the JSC after the conclusion of interviews to deliberate and nominate the most qualified applicants, taking into account gender, regional, ethnic, and other diversities. The JSC plays a critical role in the selection and appointment of judges, and its commitment to enhancing gender equality is essential.

When the CoK was promulgated in 2010, the JSC embarked on implementing judicial reforms under the new constitutional dispensation to enhance public confidence in the justice sector (The Judiciary, 2017). One reform was the appointment of judges and magistrates in a manner that takes into account constitutional principles on equality and inclusivity (Gainer, 2015). In its 2015/2016 annual report, the JSC indicated that it complied with the two-third gender principle as 61% of the judges in superior courts were male, while 39% were female (JSC, 2017). Women accounted for 32% in the Court of Appeal, 43% in the High Court, 38% in the Environment and Land Court, and 23% in the Employment and Labour Relations Court, while men accounted for 68%, 57%, 62%, and 67%, respectively. At the subordinate level, the gender gap between men and women was very small. Male magistrates accounted for 50.4%, while female magistrates accounted for 49.6%. Distribution by gender was more women than men in the Chief Magistrates Court (54%), Resident Magistrates Court (61%), and Senior Principal Magistrates Court (54%) (Judicial Service Commission, 2017).

Until 2021, the gender composition of SCOK stood at 29% women and 71% men, contrary to the constitutional requirement that not more than two-thirds of the members of an appointive or elective body shall be of the same gender. The question of whether the JSC is complying with the two-thirds gender principle in the appointment of judges to the Supreme Court was litigated in two important cases. The first is the *Federation of Women Lawyers of Kenya (FIDA) & Others v. Attorney General & another, 2011(FIDA Case)*, where FIDA argued that the JSC had failed to take into consideration the "correct arithmetic of the Constitutional requirements of gender equality." In rejecting the petition, the court held that the JSC had conducted the shortlisting, the interviews, and the recommendations of the SCOK judges in accordance with the Constitution, and Part V and Section 30 of the JSA 2011. The court held that judicial appointments should be based on merit first and not on the concept of equality alone. The court stated that "we reckon that judicial appointments should be based on merit, non-discrimination and they must reflect the diversity of our people, but in this case, we have no evidence that the JSC, in the exercise of its functions under Article 172 of the Constitution as read together with the JSC Act, failed to comply with Article 27." The court further asked the petitioners to keep their "feminine missiles to their launch pads" until the state puts in place legislative and other measures to implement the two-third gender rule in appointive positions.

The second case is *National Gender & Equality Commission & Another v. Judicial Service Commission & 2 Others, 2017, (NGEC Case)*, where the petitioners argued that a woman should have been nominated to fill the void left by a retiring SCOK justice instead of a man, as this would have brought the number of women in the court to three. The respondents argued that the implementation of the two-thirds gender principle had already been addressed in the FIDA case and asked the court to be guided by that decision. The petitioners relied on the decision in the case of *Marilyn Muthoni Kamaru & 2 Others v. Attorney General & Another, 2016*, and argued that in appointive positions, gender equality can still be achieved in the absence of implementing legislation. The court agreed with the petitioners that indeed it is easier to achieve gender parity in appointive positions in the absence of implementing legislation since all that is required are "policies and affirmative action based on goodwill." However, the court still dismissed the petition and held that the JSC did not breach the provisions of the Constitution or the Judicial Service Commission Act when recommending a male candidate for appointment as judge of the Supreme Court, neither did the JSC breach the two-thirds gender principle as contemplated by the CoK. The court at Paragraph 41 held thus:

> It is difficult to fault the first Respondent for recommending the interested party for appointment to the Supreme Court, making the number of men five. It would have been ideal to recommend a woman for appointment, but that is not to say an ideal situation is the same as a clear breach of the Constitution or the law on the two-thirds gender [principle]. Even if one applied a mathematical formula to the question at hand, the result would invariably have been the same, that two-thirds is 5 while one-third is 2. The number of judges being uneven, the figure can only be approximate and not exact.

In these two cases, the court indicated that appointment of judges to the SCOK is first to be based on merit, with gender equality considered among other factors. While in the earlier case of *In the Matter of the Principle of Gender Representation in the National Assembly and the Senate, 2012*, the court asked Parliament to enact implementing legislation for the two-thirds gender rule; in the *NGEC case*, the court recognized that attaining gender equality in appointive positions does not require legislation but goodwill. Yet it still went ahead and recommended that the JSC put in place policy measures, thus demonstrating the need for basic written provisions to guide the process of implementing constitutional provisions on gender equality.

With regard to the issue of merit, it is important to point out that in Kenya, to be appointed as a judge of the SCOK, a candidate must meet requirements stipulated under Article 166 of the Constitution, which include holding a law degree; being an advocate of the High Court of Kenya; having 15 years' experience either as a distinguished academic, legal practitioner, or such experience in any other relevant legal field. All of the women shortlisted for the position of judge of the SCOK met these basic minimum criteria and therefore merited the appointments. Consequently, and in accordance with the constitutional provisions, gender could have been used as an inclusion/exclusion criterion. The *FIDA* and *NGEC* cases show that the SCOK has failed to promote the inclusion of female judges in the SCOK. The evidence that the JSC has been able to comply with the two-thirds gender principle in other judiciary positions clearly shows that the same can apply in the SCOK, and there exists a significantly large pool of qualified women judges.

The gender composition of the SCOK matters greatly because, as a court of last resort, it plays a critical role in the development of jurisprudence. Arguably, the SCOK's gender composition has contributed to the court's failure to protect the constitutional two-thirds gender rule. In the *FIDA case*, the SCOK made light of the use of affirmative action and held that the selection of judges must be based first and foremost on merit. The danger is that under the principle of stare decisis (or legal precedent), which is anchored under Article 163(7) of the CoK, all the courts of Kenya, other than the SCOK, are bound by the decisions of the SCOK, meaning that the court might have effectively undermined affirmative action as provided for under the Constitution.

These varying perspectives on the use and effectiveness of gender quotas inform our argument on how gender quotas may be used. First, the Supreme Court already held in the *NGEC case* that the JSC can begin to implement the constitutional two-thirds gender rule in the absence of legislation that specifically mandates and provides it with the blueprint to do so. However, such proactive implementation of this rule in the absence of enabling legislation should be an interim measure and should not do away with the need for legislation. Steps taken by the JSC to implement the rule in the absence of enabling legislation should also lead to the development of best practices to be used as the basis for legislation. Thus, the specific type of quotas that should be used should be provided for under statute and should be agreed upon through a proper consultative process.

Second, the application of the principle of intersectionality, which emphasizes the need to consider between gender and other axes of inequality such as ethnicity, religion, or disability, will be useful in ensuring that the JSC applies constitutional requirements on equality. It has been challenging to find a formula for implementing the constitutional provisions on gender equality because there are only seven positions for judge of the SCOK, and the law requires the JSC to take into consideration various factors in addition to merit, such as regional balancing, ethnicity, and social diversity. The JSC should apply the principle of intersectionality to solve this challenge. This means that the JSC should particularly encourage women from vulnerable groups and marginalized communities to apply for the position of judge of the SCOK. Those who meet the minimum criteria should have gender and any other axis of vulnerability or marginality considered as an inclusion criterion when making recommendations for appointment. Kenya can learn lessons from Rwanda, where this approach of encouraging more female candidates to apply has been effectively used (Bauer & Dawuni, 2016).

Third, the JSC should move away from its current approach to gender equality in the SCOK, where it has failed to apply the constitutional provisions and then seeks to explain the failure (fail and explain approach). Instead, the JSC should use the approach of taking all reasonable measures to implement the constitutional provisions, and if it still does not meet the requirements on gender equality, it must provide a satisfactory explanation as to why it did not before it can proceed to make recommendations for appointments (comply and explain approach).

Fourth, the JSC, in collaboration with other stakeholders such as civil society and professional bodies such as the LSK, should work toward putting in place policy mechanisms and affirmative action programs. For instance, the JSC should consider a prequalification list to ensure that where low numbers of qualified women apply for the position of a judge of the SCOK, the commission readvertises specifically to target more applications from qualified women. After taking such actions and still not finding adequate numbers of qualified female candidates, the JSC could provide a reasonable explanation for failing to recommend the appointment of female judges.

CONCLUSION

The JSC does not need to wait for Parliament to enact legislation in order to achieve the two-thirds gender rule. Articles 27(6), (8), 81(b), and 100 of the CoK compel the JSC to comply the two-thirds gender rule. It is our observation that the SCOK, being the court of last resort and custodian of the Constitution, has failed to ensure implementation of this constitutional rule, and this might be attributed to the gender composition of the court. We have argued here that female judges do indeed play a crucial role in developing progressive jurisprudence in gender-related matters. Had the composition of this court been gender sensitive, jurisprudence on the two-thirds gender rule would have been developed in a more progressive manner.

It is now ten years since the Supreme Court Advisory Opinion, *In the Matter of the Principle of Gender Representation in the National Assembly and the Senate, 2012*, where the court held that the two-thirds gender rule should be realized progressively and further recommended enacting legislation to aid in its implementation. The recommended legislation has still not passed. While the JSC appointed a female chief justice in 2021, it did so without any policy guidelines to ensure that the two-thirds gender rule is met and maintained in the appointment of judges of the SCOK. This remains a risk because as in the absence of such guidelines, there are no safety measures to ensure that progress is maintained. Even more importantly, there is a need to have policy guidelines that will promote a gender-sensitive work environment for female judges because, as we have seen, female judges continue to experience difficulties while in office that are largely informed by gender norms.

With the absence of this legislation, we propose an amendment to Section 30 of the Judicial Service Commission Act as read together with the First Schedule to the Act, to include a provision that out of the seven names recommended to the president for appointment to the Supreme Court, not more than four shall be of the same gender; and in the event that the JSC fails to comply with this provision, the president shall reject the list of names recommended for appointment. Similarly, we propose an amendment to Article 172(2) (b) of the CoK to require that a minimum of at least three members of the constitutional seven appointed as judges of the Supreme Court be male or female. In addition, we propose that the JSC should put in place guidelines to promote a positive work environment for female judges. As we have seen, women who do make it into office as judges often face a hostile work environment, and this undermines their effectiveness. Thus, gender quotas in this context play a three-pronged role: the first is the attainment of the constitutional provisions on the inclusivity of female judges; the second is the promotion of a positive work environment; and the final one is the development of progressive jurisprudence on gender-related matters, which ultimately will lead to the realization of women's rights in Kenya.

REFERENCES

Abella, R. S. (1987). *The Dynamic Nature of Equality* (S. Martin & K. Mahoney, Eds.). Carswell.

Abrahamson, S. S. (1989). The Woman has Robes: The Four Questions. *Golden Gate University Law Review, 14*(3), 489–503.

Adams, K., & Byrnes, A. (Eds.). (2000). *Gender Equality and the Judiciary: Using International Human Rights Standards to Promote the Human Rights of Women and the Girl Child at the National Level.* Commonwealth Secretariat.

Aoláin, F. (2015). More Women – But Which Women? A Reply to Stéphanie Hennette Vauchez. *European Journal of International Law, 26*(1), 229–236.

Baraza, N. (2008). Lost Between Rhetoric and Reality: What Role for the Law and Human Rights in Redressing Gender Inequality. *Kenya Law Reports, 2*, 1–6.

Bauer, G., & Dawuni, J. (Eds.). (2016). *Gender and the Judiciary in Africa: From Obscurity to Parity.* Routledge.

Bennett, C. (2014). A Gender Agenda: The Effectiveness of Quota Systems in Increasing Women's Meaningful Participation in Politics. *Australian Institute of International Affairs*, 1–6.

Biegon, J. (Ed.). (2016). *Gender Equality and Political Processes in Kenya: Challenges and Prospects.* Strathmore University Press.

Bindman, G., & Monaghan, K. (2014). *Judicial Diversity: Accelerating Change.* Report of the Judicial Appointments Commission.

Bohnet, I. (2016). *What Works: Gender Equality by Design.* Harvard University Press.

Bonthuys, E. (2013). Gender and the Chief Justice: Principle or Pretext? *Journal of South African Studies, 39*(1), 59–76.

Brown, W. (2004). Tolerance and/or Equality? The "Jewish Question" and the "Woman Question." *Journal of Feminist Cultural Studies, 15*(2), 1–31.

Bryson, V. (1999). *Feminist Debates: Issues of Theory and Political Practice.* Macmillan.

Clark, M. (2015). Gender Quotas: A Path to Women's Empowerment? *Vanderbilt Undergraduate Research Journal, 10*, 1–8.

Coalition on Violence against Women. (2005). *Judicial Attitudes of the Kenyan Bench on Sexual Violence Cases: A Digest.* COVAW.

Constitution of Kenya Review Commission. (2005). *The Final Report of the Constitutional of Kenya Review Commission.* CKRC.

Cornell, R. W. (2005). Change Among the Gatekeepers: Men, Masculinities and Gender Equality in the Global Arena. *Journal of the University of Chicago Press, 30*(3), 1801–1825.

Council of Europe. (2016). *European Judicial Systems: Efficiency and Quality of Justice.* CEPEJ Studies No. 23 Council of Europe.

Cowan, R. (2006). Women's Representation on the Courts in the Republic of South Africa. *University of Maryland Law Journal of Race, Religion, Gender and Class, 6*(2), 291–318.

Dahlerup, D. (2006). *Women, Quotas and Politics.* Taylor & Francis.

Darhour, H., & Dahlerup, D. (2013). Sustainable Representation of Women Through Gender Quotas: A Decade's Experience in Morocco. *Women's Studies International Forum, 41*, 132–142.

Dawuni, J. (2018). Breaking the Veil of Masculinity? Women in Ghana's Legal Academy. In U. Schultz et al. (Eds.), *Gender and Careers in the Legal Academy.* Hart Publishing.

Dawuni, J., & Kang, A. (2015). Her Ladyship Chief Justice: The Rise of Female Leaders in the Judiciary in Africa. *Africa Today*, *62*(2), 44–69.

Dearden, L. (2017, July 17). Baroness Hale of Richmond becomes First Woman Appointed as UK's Most Senior Judge. *Independent*. http://www.independent.co.uk/news/uk/home-news/baroness-hale-of-richmond-first-woman-appointed-britains-supreme-court-president-most-senior-judge-a7852661.html.

Devins, N. (1988). Gender Justice and Critics. *California Law Review*, *76*, 1377–1406.

Dickson, B. (2015). Activism and Restraint within the UK Supreme Court. *European Journal of Current Legal Issues*, *12*, 1–23.

Durham, C. M. (1989). Gender Equality in the Courts: Women's Work is Never Done. *Fordham Law Review*, *57*, 981–983.

Eunita Anyango Geko & another v. Philip Obungu Orinda [2014] eKLR, Miscellaneous Civil Application 1 of 2013.

Federation of Women Lawyers Kenya (FIDA-K) & 5 Others v. Attorney General & Another [2011] eKLR, Petition 102 of 2011.

FIDA Kenya. (2012). *Women's Land and Property Rights in Kenya*. FIDA Training Handbook.

Franceschet, S., Krook, M. L., & Piscopo, J. M. (2012). *The Impact of Gender Quotas*. Oxford University Press.

Gainer, M. (2015). *Transforming the Courts: Judicial Sector Reforms in Kenya, 2011–2015*. Trustees of Princeton University, 1–21.

Gibson-Morgan, E. (2015). Gender Equality in the Judiciary in England and France: Making it a Living Reality. *Revue Miroirs*, *2*. http://www.revuemiroirs.fr/links/femmes/volume2/article7.pdf.

Gopal, G., & Salim, M. (Eds.). (1998). *Gender and Law: Eastern Africa Speaks*. World Bank.

Griffith, J. A. G. (1977). *The Politics of the Judiciary*. Manchester University Press.

Halka, E. (1996). Madam Justice Bertha Wilson: A Different Voice in the Supreme Court of Canada. *Alberta Law Review*, *35*(1), 242–265.

Hawkins, R., & Martin, R. (1995). Democracy, Judging and Bertha Wilson. *McGill Law Journal*, *41*, 1–58.

Hunter, R. (2006). *The High Price of Success: The Backlash against Women Judges in Australia* (S. McIntyre & E. Sheeshy, Eds.). Ottawa University Press, 281–301.

Hunter, R. (2015). More than Just a Different Face: Judicial Diversity and Decision Making. *Journal of Current Legal Problems*, *68*, 119–141.

In the Matter of the Principle of Gender Representation in the National Assembly and the Senate [2012] eKLR, Advisory Opinion No. 2 of 2012.

Inglehart, R., & Norris, P. (2003). *Rising Tide: Gender Equality & Cultural Change around the World*. Harvard University Press.

J O O (also known as J M) v. Attorney General & 6 Others [2018] eKLR, Petition 5 of 2014.

Johnson, R. E. (2014). Women as a Sign of the New: Appointments to South Africa's Constitutional Court Since 1994. *Journal of Politics and Gender*, *10*(4), 595–621.

Judicial Service Commission. (2017). *Annual Report and Financial Statements: 2015–2016*. Judicial Service Commission.

JUSTICE. (2017). *Increasing Judicial Diversity*. https://files.justice.org.uk/wp-content/uploads/2017/04/06170655/JUSTICE-Increasing-judicial-diversity-report-2017-web.pdf.

Kabira, W. M., & Kimani, E. N. (2012). The Historical Journey of Women's Leadership in Kenya. *Journal of Emerging Trends in Educational Research and Policy Studies, 3*(6), 842–849.

Kaimenyi, C., Kinyi, E., & Chege, M. S. (2013). An Analysis of Affirmative Action: The Two-Thirds Gender Rule in Kenya. *International Journal of Business, Humanities and Technology, 3*(6), 1–97.

Kalpana H. Rawal & 2 Others v. Judicial Service Commission & 3 Others [2016] eKLR, Civil Application No. 11 & 12 of 2016.

Kamau, M. (2015, September 25). Deputy CJ Kalpana Rawal's Bid to Stop Recruitment of Successor Flops. *Standard Digital*. https://www.standardmedia.co.ke/article/2000177375/deputy-cj-kalpana-rawal-s-bid-to-stop-recruitment-of-successor-flops.

Kamau, W. (2013). *Women Judges and Magistrates in Kenya: Challenges, Opportunities and Contributions* (U. Schultz & G. Shaw, Eds.). Oxford Hart Publishers.

Kenney, S. J. (2013). *Gender and Justice: Why Women in the Judiciary Matter*. Routledge.

Kenney, S., & KWJA. (2016, August 8). *Report on the KWJA Session with Professor S Kenney*. KWJA. http://kwja.org/document/breaking-the-glass-ceiling-report-on-the-kwja-session-with-prof-s-kenney/.

Kichana, P. (Ed.). (2005). *Judiciary Watch Report: Judicial Reform in Kenya*. Kenya Section of the International Commission of Jurist.

Kindiki, K. (2007). *Reinforcing Judicial and Legal Institutions: Kenyan and Regional Perspectives*. Kenya Section of the International Commission of Jurists.

Kombo, B., Sow, R., & Mohamed, F. J. (2013). *Journey to Equality: 10 Years of the Protocol on the Rights of Women in Africa*. Equality Now.

Krook, M. L. (2016). Contesting Gender Quotas: Dynamics of Resistance. *Journal of Politics, Groups and Identities, 4*(2), 268–283.

L.N.W v. Attorney General & 3 others [2016] eKLR, Petition No. 484 of 2014.

Malleson, K. (2014, May 23). The Case for Gender Quotas for Appointments to the Supreme Court. http://ukscblog.com/case-gender-quotas-appointments-supreme-court/.

Maribe, J. (2016, September 27). *Judges Fatuma Sichale, Hannah Okwengu Interviewed by JSC*. Citizen Digital. https://citizentv.co.ke/news/judges-fatuma-sichale-hannah-okwengu-interviewed-by-jsc-143079/.

Marilyn Muthoni Kamuru & 2 Others v. Attorney General & Another [2016] eKLR, Petition 566 of 2012.

Mary Wanjuhi Muigai v. Attorney General & Another [2015] eKLR, Petition 237 of 2014.

Mbote, P. K. (2013). *Fallacies of Equality and Inequality: Multiple Exclusions in Law and Legal Discourses*. University of Nairobi, 1–48.

Mbote, P. K., & Aketch, M. (2011). *Kenya: Justice Sector and the Rule of Law*. Open Society Foundations.

McCormick, P., & Job, T. (1993). Do Women Judges Make a Difference? An Analysis by Appeal Court Data. *Canadian Journal of Law and Society*, *8*, 135–148.

Meier, P., & Lombardo, E. (2013). Gender Quotas, Gender Mainstreaming and Gender Relations in Politics. *Journal of Political Science*, *65*(1), 46–62.

Men Engage Alliance, UN Women & UNFPA. (2014). *Men, Masculinities and Changing Power: A Discussion Paper on Engaging Men on Gender Equality from Beijing 1995 to 2015*. UNFPA. https://www.unfpa.org/sites/default/files/resource-pdf/Men-Masculinities-and-Changing-Power-MenEngage-2014.pdf.

Meroka-Mutua, A. (2018). *Public Interest Litigation and Women's Rights in Kenya: The Double Edged Sword* (P. K. Mbote, W. M. Kabira, N. Kabira, & A. Meroka, Eds.). University of Nairobi.

Monopoli, P. A. (2007). Gender and Justice: Parity and the United Supreme Court. *Georgetown Journal of Gender and the Law*, *8*, 43–65.

Musau, N. (2019, July 7). Mwilu: I Have Never Been This Scared, But I'm Going Nowhere. *Standard Digital*. https://www.standardmedia.co.ke/article/2001332866/mwilu-i-ve-never-been-this-scared.

Mutunga, W. (2014). *The 2010 Constitution of Kenya and its Interpretation: Reflections from the Supreme Court Decisions*. University of Fort Hare, 1–21.

Mwaura, P. (2012, January 20). Baraza has Helped to Revive the Art of Nose Pinching. *Daily Nation*. https://www.nation.co.ke/oped/opinion/Baraza-has-helped-to-revive-the-art-of--nose-pinching/440808-1310982-879k9xz/index.html.

National Gender & Equality Commission & another v. Judicial Service Commission & 2 Others [2017] eKLR, Petition 446 & 456 of 2016 (Consolidated).

National Gender and Equality Commission. (2016). *Status of Equality and Inclusion in Kenya*. National Gender and Equality Commission. https://www.ngeckenya.org/Downloads/Status%20of%20Equality%20and%20Inclusion%20in%20Kenya.pdf" https://www.ngeckenya.org/Downloads/Status%20of%20Equality%20and%20Inclusion%20in%20Kenya.pdf.

Njeru, B. (2021, June 4). 34 Judges Appointed by President Uhuru to Take Oath. *The Standard*. https://www.standardmedia.co.ke/national/article/2001414810/34-judges-appointed-by-uhuru-take-oath.

Nyamori, M. (2019, May 16). Baraza Recalls Ouster, Says Some Judges have Done Worse. *Standard Digital*. https://www.standardmedia.co.ke/article/2001325669/baraza-fired-for-pinching-guard-as-others-go-scot-free.

Nzomo, M. (1997). Kenyan Women in Politics and Public Decision Making. In G. Mikell (Ed.), *African Feminism: The Politics of Survival in Sub-Saharan Africa*. University of Pennsylvania Press.

O'Brien, D. Z., & Rickne, J. (2016). Gender Quotas and Women's Political Leadership. *American Political Science Review*, *110*(1), 112–126.

Ochiel, D. (2016). *Unpacking the Gender Rule and the Supreme Court Advisory Opinion of December 2012: Quotas Options for the Representation of Women in Kenya*. Heinrich Böll Stiftung, East and Horn of Africa and the African Women's Studies Center at the University of Nairobi, 1–12.

Odhiambo, A. R. (2018). Gender Equality: Integration of Women in the Judiciary in Kenya. In P. K. Mbote, W. M. Kabira, N. Kabira, & A. Meroka (Eds.), *Changing the Mainstream: Celebrating Women's Resilience*. Nairobi: University of Nairobi.

Okoth, B. (2021, April 27). JSC Picks Court of Appeal Judge Martha Koome for Chief Justice Position. *The Standard*. https://www.standardmedia.co.ke/author/brian-okoth.

Ombati, C. (2019, April 7). Guard Withdraws Gun Complaint against Judge. *Standard Digital*. https://www.standardmedia.co.ke/article/2001319902/guard-withdraws-gun-complaint-against-justice-ibrahim.

One UN on Gender in Kenya. (2015, December 12). *Kenyan Judiciary Pushing the Wheel of Justice in Gender Equality: HeForShe*. https://www.genderinkenya.org/news/kenyan-judiciary-pushing-the-wheel-of-justice-in-gender-equality-heforshe/.

Parliament, Republic of Kenya. (1997, April 23). *Parliamentary Hansard*. Parliament.

Philips, A. (1998). *The Politics of Presence*. Oxford University Press.

Piscopo, J. M. (2015). States as Gender Equality Activists: The Evolution of Quota Laws in Latin America. *Latin American Politics and Society*, *15*(7), 27–49.

Podgorny, M. (2012). *Gender-Equal Representation on the Supreme Court Bench: Adding the Missing Perspective to Judging*. Paper presented at the 5th Annual Canadian Law Students Conference at the University of Windsor, Faculty of Law, 1–32.

Rackley, E. (2014). *Women, Judging and the Judiciary: From Difference to Diversity*. Routledge.

Re Estate of Francis Mwangi Mbaria (Deceased) [2018] eKLR, Succession Cause 1238 of 2012.

Ridgeway, C. L. (2001). Gender, Status, and Leadership. *Journal of Social Issues*, *57*, 637–655.

Somani, A. A. (2013). The Use of Gender Quotas in America: Are Voluntary Party Quotas the Way to Go? *William & Mary Law Review*, *54*(4), 1451–1488.

Standard Team, (2016, July 8). List of Applicants for CJ, Deputy CJ and Supreme Court Judges. *Standard Digital*. https://www.standardmedia.co.ke/article/2000207975/list-of-applicants-for-cj-deputy-cj-and-supreme-court-judges.

Suk, J. C. (2013). Gender Quotas After the End of Men. *Boston University Law Review*, *93*, 1123–1140.

Taskforce on Judicial Reforms. (2010). *Final Report of the Taskforce on Judicial Reforms*. http://kenyalaw.org/kl/fileadmin/pdfdownloads/Final_Report_of_the_Task_Force_on_Judicial_Reforms.pdf.

The Judiciary, Republic of Kenya. (2013). *State of the Judiciary and Administration of Justice Annual Report 2012–2013*. https://www.yumpu.com/en/document/read/49829153/report-state-of-the-judiciary-and-the-administration-of-justice-annual-report-2012-2013.

The Judiciary, Republic of Kenya. (2017). *Sustaining Judiciary Transformation: A Service Delivery Agenda 2017–2021*. http://kenyalaw.org/kl/fileadmin/pdfdownloads/Strategic_BluePrint.pdf.

UNDP. (2012). *Gender Equality and Women's Empowerment in Public Administration: Uganda Case Study*. file:///C:/Users/user/Downloads/UgandaFinal%20-%20HiRes.pdf.

UN Women. (2014, March 11). *Women in Politics Map 2014 Statement by John Hendra*. http://www.unwomen.org/en/news/stories/2014/3/women-in-politics-map-2014.

Valdini, M. E., & Shortell, C. (2016). Women Representation in Highest Court: A Comparative Analysis of the Appointment of Female Justices. *Sage Journals*, *69*(4), 865–876.

Wasuna, B., & Misiko, H. (2018, August 28). Deputy Chief Justice Philomena Mwilu Arrested. *Daily Nation*. https://www.nation.co.ke/news/Deputy-Chief-Justice-Philomena-Mwilu-arrested/1056-4732484-m59wxbz/index.html.

Wilson, B. (1990). Will Women Judges Really Make a Difference? *Osgoode Hall Law Journal*, *20*, 507–522.

Yankwich, L. R. (1975). *The Art of Being a Judge* (G. R. Winters, Ed.). The American Judicature Society.

Chapter 7

"Your Whole Life Is an Interview to Get to the Bench"

Gender and Judicial Appointments in Malawi

Rachel Ellett

INTRODUCTION

Efforts to expand recruitment of women to the bench are occurring at a time when we witness the increased judicialization of politics.[1] When key political disputes come to the courts, this increases scrutiny of individual judges and intensifies the overall institutional insecurity of the courts. First, this chapter suggests that these phenomena are potential deterrent for all judicial candidates, including potential women appointees. Because of a high level of public scrutiny, job insecurity, poor benefits, and political pressure, the highest levels of the judiciary may not be a desirable career path for successful lawyers—for either men or women. Moreover, given that women often face other structural obstacles to advancement and tend to possess weaker political support networks, judicial appointments may be particularly unattractive. Second, while the number of women law school graduates worldwide has increased, in some countries, including Malawi, the pipeline of women law graduates and lawyers is uneven or stalled. On average, despite an overall significant increase in women appointed to the highest levels of the judiciary in sub-Saharan Africa (Dawuni & Bauer, 2016), in most countries there is a long way to go before women reach parity with men in the judiciary's upper echelons. And, according to the 2019 SADC Gender Barometer, there is tremendous variation within sub-Saharan Africa. Some countries exceed parity (Zambia 54%), and others remain stubbornly low (Madagascar 12%),[2] and the year-to-year swings in percentage can move dramatically up and down.

In 2021, women judges comprised 30% of judges in Malawi's top courts. There was a significant jump in women's representation at both the High Court and Supreme Court of Appeal between 2002 and 2006 and again between 2011 and 2015. In 2013, there was a dramatic jump to 27%, when six women judges—including the first female chief justice—were appointed by Malawi's first women president Joyce Banda. A slight percentage drop between 2009 and 2011 is due to the expansion of the High Court bench, without a concomitant increase in female appointees. In late 2020, the High Court expanded from 26 to 36. Of the 36, 13 are women (Registrar of the Judiciary of Malawi). As for the magistrate's courts, data from the 2010 National Justice Baseline Survey indicated that 30% of the magistrates were women (2006–2010). However, official court data from January 2021 (Registrar of the Judiciary of Malawi) lists only 18% of magistrates as women, or 13 out of 72.

This chapter posits that to understand the gendered dynamics of judicial appointments in Malawi, we need to look at both women lawyers who go to the bench and those who do not. To be sure, structural gendered constraints that restrict the pipeline of women judges in Malawi are significant. This begins in school and goes through to early legal careers. However, taking a cue from Fox and Lawless's work (2004, 2010, 2011) on why women choose not to enter politics, this chapter focuses on Malawi's women lawyers who have *chosen not* to enter the upper echelons of the bench. Over the last several years, I have interviewed many accomplished and successful women lawyers and law professors. When asked why they have not joined the bench, they indicate that the institution is too politicized and underperforming, they cannot exercise true independence, that the salaries are low, and that the lifestyle is not compatible with family life. This 'choice' narrative augments and potentially complicates—although does not necessarily eclipse—existing theories of women's advancement in the judiciary. These include: the marginalization of women through formal structures (Arrington et al., 2021; Bratton & Spill, 2002; Dawuni & Masengu, 2019; Iyer, 2013; Kenney, 2018), reduced pipelines of women lawyers, and the constraints of oppressive social and professional systemic constraints (Masengu, 2016, 2021; Slotnick et al., 2017). This chapter offers evidence that elite women lawyers in Malawi are rational actors—actors who maximize their self-interest and future potential career opportunities within complex structural constraints.

In 2016, I conducted 11 interviews, ranging in length from 30 minutes to 2 hours, with a combination of High Court and Supreme Court judges, members of the Malawi Law Society, and private practice lawyers and private company secretaries. Several of the interviews were repeat informants from fieldwork conducted in 2007 and 2013. To maintain confidentiality in a small community of legal elites, the interviewees are not named. Between

2019 and 2020, I exchanged further written correspondence with one of the interviewees.

The chapter proceeds as follows: First, literature on the formal and informal structures of judicial appointments is connected with theories of women's representation on the bench. Second, this theoretical framework is contextualized by considering the judicialization of politics, the politicization of appointments, and an intensification of media coverage. Third, this chapter offers an in-depth analysis of Malawi, moving from an assessment of the formal and informal structural obstacles for women candidates, to an examination of 'choice' within intersecting discriminatory constraints and how that might impact women's self-assessment of their qualifications.

THEORIZING OBSTACLES TO GENDER PARITY ON THE BENCH

Structure

Globally, the supply of qualified female judicial candidates has increased over time as the number of women law graduates increases.[3] Law school acceptance and graduation rates as a barrier to expansion of women on the bench are diminishing. For example, in Kenyan law schools, the ratio of females to males is almost 50:50, with some schools exceeding 50% for women. A steady or increasing pipeline of lawyers is critical to sustained representation on the bench, and it appears that Malawi is being left behind. In Africa's early post-independence years, there was a paucity of qualified candidates for appointment at all levels of the bench (Ellett, 2013; Kamau, 2013). The pool of potential judicial candidates has increased since 1990 because of the expansion of the private legal sector, but internal promotion still dominates the advancement process. Historically in commonwealth Africa, judges were treated as bureaucrats within the Ministry of Justice. Slow advancement through the hierarchical ranks of the judiciary or the Ministry of Justice was the norm.

Moving from the pipeline to recruitment, selection mechanisms for judges are a set of process-oriented rules and relationships between appointment bodies. The judiciary and the political environment operating through a series of dynamic institutional interactions (Garoupa & Ginsburg, 2009, 2011) unfold through two stages: nomination of candidates and the appointments stage (Arrington et al., 2021). How these processes interact with informal norms and which particular configuration of rules best promotes diversity has provoked scholarly debate. Take, for example, the difference between appointment versus election systems. Bratton and Spill (2002) find that transparent appointment systems are more likely to diversify the bench (such as South

Africa and Canada); yet Iyer (2013) finds only a short-lived uptick in the United Kingdom after an appointment commission was established. Escobar-Lemmon et al. (2021) conclude that selectors who are electorally accountable are not more likely to appoint the first woman to the bench, whereas Valdini and Shortell (2016) find the opposite. In contrast, others *did* find that the method of selection positively influences gender diversity (Williams & Thomas, 2008). Dawuni and Masengu (2019: 227) argue that judicial appointment bodies in Nigeria and Zambia positively impact opportunities for qualified women applicants when they "strictly adhere to the guidelines."

No single selection system offers a perfect scenario for diversifying the judiciary (Kenney, 2018: 212; Malleson, 2006, 2009). To clarify, shifting away from personal connections toward qualifications is helpful for women (Kenney, 2013; Malleson, 2009), but we should reframe it as a necessary, though not sufficient condition. Moreover, shifting to a merit system invariably increases the level of complexity and number of actors. In Kenya, for example, the new Judicial Service Commission (JSC) is expansive and diverse: the chief justice (chairperson), three judges, the attorney general, two lawyers, a member of the public service commission, and two members of the public (Sec. 171(1) Kenya Constitution). Specific attention is given to the question of gender equality through the public interview process and while gender equality has improved under this system (Kamau, 2013), it is also a more complex process that potentially opens more points of political interference or patronage.

Capturing the judicial appointment process as dynamic with multiple actors, rather than a static set of rules, allows us to uncover the roles played by supporting actors. As Michelson (2013: 1102) has argued, "[s]ignificant levels of lawyer feminization are exceedingly rare without significant bar expansion." Having a woman of influence on the JSC or in the position of chief justice, or a supportive bar association can be significant force in appointing women judges (Kenney, 2009; Kamau, 2013) or conversely, in blocking them (Barmes & Malleson, 2011). For example, Aloysie Cyanzayire was president of the Rwanda Supreme Court from 2003 to 2013 and was also chairperson of the high council of the judiciary—roles that allowed her to support recruitment of women into the judiciary (Kamatali, 2015: 148). Extending outward to international organizations, Escobar-Lemmon et al. (2021) outline how links between the legal profession and international women's nongovernmental organizations enhance gender diversity on the bench. For example, in Kenya, Kamau (2013) details how a lawsuit filed by women's rights organization FIDA-Kenya challenging the failure of the JSC to submit equal names of men and women to the president,[4] while ultimately unsuccessful, later resulted in an almost equal number of women and men nominated (Kamau, 2013). Indeed, broader meaningful political commitment to realizing regional and international statutes on gender parity (Escobar-Lemmon et al. 2021) also represents a significant factor in prioritizing female judicial appointments. Kamatali (2015: 148) adopts the term "insider-outsider collaboration" to refer to small networks of women lawyers who know and support each other. Where there are key women in positions of power relative to judicial appointments, there is a favorable national policy encouraging women to enter public service, and where there are supportive networks of women lawyers; we should expect to see an increase in female appointees.

Most prospective women judges in the world face the prospect of operating in a "hostile masculine environment" (Feenan, 2009). Women judicial candidates deal with the double bind of societal discrimination and the hostilities of a male-dominated legal profession. The profession, often conservative in nature, can act as a gatekeeper to judicial appointments (Barmes & Malleson, 2011). Mirroring Malleson's (2006) findings from the United Kingdom on the preference for barristers over solicitors, Masengu (2016) notes how the significant role of the bifurcated legal profession (advocates and attorneys) and the conservative bar association has blocked advancement of women into the higher levels of the judiciary in South Africa. The bar and the legal profession writ large use discriminatory perceptions of women's abilities and an uneven distribution of work duties to explicitly and repeatedly block women (Masengu, 2016). Across the commonwealth, the seniority principle still exists, where judges put forth the most senior member for promotion. This helps promote collegiality but may not help women. As Dawuni and Kang (2015: 59) notes, the effects of the seniority principle depend on secondary factors: "Where few women are judges, with fewer years of experience, it may work to women's disadvantage, but where women have the same number of years of service as their male counterparts, it may work in their favor." Cultures of professional discrimination or unwritten norms, such as the seniority principle, become entangled in the structural constraints (from candidate identification to nomination and vetting).

Choice

The common argument on why women don't 'choose' to push for public office is 'lack of ambition' (Fulton et al., 2006; Jenson & Martinek, 2009). Yet, in their study of political candidate recruitment, Fox and Lawless (2012: 20) found the central reason to be: "[w]omen perceive an electoral environment that is biased against them. [. . .] And the fact that women remain the primary caretakers of the home and children adds a high degree of complexity to the decision to run office." In sum, women are less likely than similarly situated men to consider running for office, less likely to receive encouragement to run for office, and less likely to believe they are qualified to seek office (Fox & Lawless, 2010). While we cannot automatically translate this to judicial candidates, Jenson and Martinek (2009: 387) found that "since moving up on the bench involves a political appointment, perhaps those that are most judicially ambitious recognize that they must also be politically ambitious to succeed."

In sub-Saharan Africa, hostilities of the legal profession toward the appointment of women are well documented (see, for example, Dawuni & Bauer, 2016; Dawuni & Masengu, 2019; Masengu, 2022). As Kamau (2013) outlines, Kenyan women judges are less accepted by the public and work in challenging physical environments—challenges compounded by insensitive transfer policies that force many women to place their children in boarding schools. This is a problem also seen in the United Kingdom, where High Court judges may travel for long periods on circuit (Malleson, 2006). By contrast, at lower levels of the judiciary, women may enter government service rather than private practice because it provides them with regular work hours, despite poorer remuneration, as Uzebu-Imarhiagbe (2020) found in the case of Nigeria. In Nigeria, robust representation of women at the lower levels of the courts helped generate better representation at the High Court level when it became fairly established to tunnel 90% of appointments to the High Court through these lower-court channels.

Thus, the decision-making of potential judicial candidates is rooted in myriad perceptions of appointment processes and the tangible benefits and working conditions of judges. Furthermore, as courts become increasingly drawn into tense political disputes, they may be democratic heroes one day, and then violently shut down the next by insecure political elites (Ellett, 2019). The judicialization of politics in Africa's hybrid regimes necessitates a more dynamic and perhaps more challenging public role for judges both on and off the bench (Ellett, 2019; VonDoepp, 2018). As captured by Prempeh (2006):

> What may be inappropriate conduct for a judge in a politically competitive, mature democracy with a rights-assertive public may not be improper or problematic in a less-than-open political system [. . .] judges might risk even greater social irrelevance if they remain wedded to a passive conception of the judicial role. (p. 602)

High-level political cases increase the visibility of High Court judges. And in many instances, the more assertive the decision-making, the more targeted the judge becomes. Visible examples include the fate of presidential elections being handed to the courts or high-level corruption cases. Courts have ruled on presidential elections in Kenya, Liberia, Ghana, Malawi, Namibia, Sierra Leone, Uganda, Zambia, and Côte d'Ivoire, to name a few (see Azu, 2013). Judges face interference in many ways (VonDoepp & Ellett, 2013), and rules on appointments to the courts, judicial budgets, and judges' security of tenure do not always effectively insulate the courts. Some improvements have been made over time. For example, such concerns were reflected in measures taken to enhance judicial autonomy in Kenya's 2010 Constitution (see VonDoepp, 2018). Over time, the process has become more dynamic, more competitive and, consequently, more controversial. As Kenney (2018: 219) notes in the case of Kenya, judges have been caught up in a great deal of turnover and controversy and women in particular have been subjected to a harsh double standard. In short, to enter the judiciary is to step into a volatile political arena, and consequently, as judges' decisions become more politically high stakes, so does the appointment process. As Masengu (2020) finds in Zambia, despite formal improvements in the JSC, women face politics during interviews, male-dominated patronage networks, and partiality in recruitment processes—all of which serve to maintain executive dominance in judicial appointments.

Finally, in regard to public scrutiny, the proliferation and democratization of the media has amplified public scrutiny and interest in judicial appointments. The media plays an important role in propagating and proliferating gender stereotypes. In addition, social media is a forum where even greater reputational damage can be done, with little ability of women candidates to control the narrative. The intense politicized nature of the coverage of appointments is overlaid by gender bias. For example, Escobar-Lemmon et al. (2016: 271) found that "female justices are often covered as women—and by extension, news coverage is different for men and women. The male appointee simply becomes another justice, whereas the female appointee retains the additional badge (and baggage) of the 'woman on the court.'" The lives and biographies of judicial candidates are now available for all to see in online searches. In South Africa, for example, the politics of judicial appointments are particularly intense, in an environment where the makeup of the judiciary is seen as a proxy for how far the country has come since the end of apartheid (Albertyn & Bonthuys, 2016). And while integration of the majority racial group has progressed well, appointment of women still lags (Masengu, 2016).

APPOINTMENT OF WOMEN JUDGES IN MALAWI

A) Formal and Informal Structures

Historical Context—After independence in 1964, Malawi was slow to indigenize the judiciary. As authoritarianism advanced, judges were considered to be civil servants, and thus were liable to be dismissed at any time. This was formalized in 1985, when a presidential decree allowed President

Hastings Kamuzu Banda to remove judges without parliamentary approval (Constitutional Amendment, Act. No. 11 1985, Sec. 64, No. 3.c.). With the exception of Anastasia Msosa, who was appointed in the last two years of Banda's regime (1964–1994), there were no women judges in the upper levels of the judiciary and at the time of transition to multipartyism in 1994, judges already sitting in the higher echelons of the court were left in place (Ellett, 2013). Msosa was the first woman appointed to the High Court (1992) and the Supreme Court of Appeal (1997); she was the first head of the Malawi Electoral Commission (1993–1997 and 2005–2012) and the first woman appointed chief justice (2013–2015).[5] Malawi also had Africa's second female president, Joyce Banda, who served for two years (2012–2014). Table 7.1 shows the percentages of women judges at the High Court and Court of Appeal between 2002 and 2021.

The worst interference in the multiparty period was the attempted impeachment of three judges in 2001, which was seen as a direct response to the judiciary's failure to bolster President Bakili Muluzi's third-term bid. Parliamentarians voted to impeach three High Court judges (for "incompetence" or "misbehavior") after each made rulings in separate cases perceived to be politically biased or which challenged the government. Ultimately, charges against the three were dropped by the president under pressure from international donors. A 2002 International Bar Association fact-finding mission concluded that despite efforts to remain independent, there was "active

Table 7.1 Percentage of Women Judges in Malawi 2002–2021[1]

Year	*% Women Judges*
2002	9
2006	20
2007	19
2008	17
2009	17
2010	15
2011	13
2012	19
2013	27
2015	33
2018	30
2019	25
2020	25
2021	30

Source: Created by author with data from various sources.

[1]2002 data from Malawi Strategic Country Gender Assessment (SCGA) 2002; 2006–2010 data from the 2010 National Justice Baseline Survey; 2013 data collected by author from Malawi High Court Registrar in 2014; 2015–2019 data from the SADC Gender Barometer; 2020 data from the WOJAM, via email correspondence February 4, 2020; formal list of all judges and magistrates in Malawi from High Court Registrar January 2021. Also consulted—Chavula (2016) and Ntaba (2015).

political subversion of judicial independence" (IBA, 2002: 41). These punctuated incidents give credence to the narrative that the High Court is a politicized space for lawyers to choose to enter, combined with Malawi's long history of appointing from within the judicial hierarchy, that is, from the magistracy to the high court.

Unreliable Pipeline—Pipeline arguments are critical to understanding gender parity on the bench, and the pipeline starts with primary and secondary school. For example, the Malawi School Certificate Education examination reported an overall pass rate of 41% in 2020 (35% for females), a drop from 50% in 2019 (43% female) and 63% in 2018.[6] While longitudinal data on percentage of female graduates at the University of Malawi was not readily available, analysis of a single-year (2018) list of admitted students reveals striking variation between programs and departments. Female students are reaching parity or even surpassing male students in the humanities and school of education. But they are still unrepresented in science, technology, engineering, and mathematics subjects.[7] The law faculty has produced an uneven supply of women LLB graduates, with little improvement over the last 30 years.[8] At Chancellor College (historically the only law school in Malawi), the number of women law graduates has averaged 27% from 1995 to 2021.[9] The pattern of LLB women graduates fluctuates: in 1996, it was 31%; in 2021, it was 19%. Outreach efforts, dispelling myths, and encouraging more girls to apply to law school—deliberate efforts by the law faculty to balance gender—are underway.[10]

Another narrowing of the pipeline occurs when LLB graduates take their Malawi Law Examinations (bar exams). For example, in 2016, 5 out of 27 candidates passed the bar exam, and three of those were women.[11] Under the 2018 Legal Education and Legal Practitioners Act (No. 13), the Council for Legal Education will oversee the Malawi Institute of Legal Education, which trains lawyers who want to practice law. This includes noncitizens and those who gained their LLBs outside of Malawi. In addition, legal education can now be offered by other institutions of higher education beyond Chancellor College.[12] This liberalization of legal education in Malawi will likely expand the overall pipeline of qualified lawyers in the country, too.

Formal Appointment Body and Qualifications—Turning now to the formal provisions of judicial appointment, under the 1994 Constitution, the formal body charged with providing a recommendation on appointments to the president is the JSC. The chief justice is appointed by the president and approved by the legislature. The president also appoints members of the commission.[13] The formal system has improved since the early 1990s, through the introduction of public advertisements for openings in the judiciary. These advertisements do not indicate that women are strongly encouraged to apply.[14]

There is no provision on gender balance within the JSC, but the new Gender Equality Act (2014) may impact the composition of this body. An advocate for women on the commission is potentially an important factor in championing women candidates (see Kamatali, 2016; Kamau, 2013). To date, two women magistrates have sat on the commission and Chief Justice Msosa chaired the commission between 2013 and 2015. In recent public comments, alluding to possible expansion of the JSC, former chief justice Andrew Nyirenda commented that "[t]he JSC is not ideal, it is the judiciary talking to itself."[15]

Beyond the Constitution,[16] there is a robust framework of national (Gender Equality Act, 2013), regional (Maputo Protocol), and international (CEDAW) laws promoting the inclusion of women in public life. Under the Gender Equality Act No. 3 of 2013, "[a]n appointing or recruiting authority in the public service shall appoint no less that forty percent (40%) and no more than sixty percent (60%) of either sex in any department in the public service" (Sec. 11-(1)). This has potential implications for both the makeup of the JSC and the judiciary itself. If followed correctly, the formal institutional framework for judicial appointments in Malawi would push the JSC toward improving gender equity (see Dawuni & Masengu, 2019).

Under Sec. 12-(1) of the Gender Equality Act, when an appointing authority doesn't comply with the 40% minimum rule, "the court shall, on application by the aggrieved person, make an order against the appointing or recruiting authority to ensure compliance." This opens the door to possible litigation in the event that there is a potential woman candidate who believes she was overlooked. While the cases of Kenya or South Africa demonstrate that more robust and transparent appointment processes are helpful in achieving gender equity, they are not a panacea (Albertyn & Bonthuys, 2016; Kamau, 2013) and may intensify the politicization of the process. Informal sexist structures of power are woven into the processes of appointment and are pernicious. Following, I consider evidence of the effect of these ongoing discriminatory norms and biases.

Qualifications, Promotion, and Appointment—Historically, Malawi has drawn judges from within the internal judicial hierarchy and promoted them on the basis of seniority. This is not a formal statutory rule, rather a historical norm. It is speculative whether the system of seniority for promotion in the Malawian judiciary is helpful to women. First, it should be noted here that the seniority principle may have been helpful in the appointment of Malawi's first woman chief justice, Anastasia Msosa. It was an easy appointment for Joyce Banda because Msosa was the most senior judge in the system. The Courts Act specifically provides that the chief justice shall be the most senior judge and Parliament basically rubber stamps it.[17] In Msosa's case, 117 out of 118 MPs voted to ratify her appointment. So, on one hand, hierarchy depoliticizes the process, but on the other it could potentially narrow the pipeline (see Dawuni & Kang, 2015). As one interviewee notes:

> The judiciary since I've joined has been a career judiciary where you expect someone who has worked in the system to be better. People [outside] were never interested [. . .] because of remuneration. Since the new constitution they found it interesting. But this has also to do with transparency. [. . .] [I]n the past they wouldn't advertise the position of judge. Some people didn't know that there was a vacancy. It was head hunting. Where the Chief Justice would say, let me go approach so and so.[18]

The most recent female judicial appointees have worked their way through the judicial hierarchy or through the Ministry of Justice, typically either chief magistrate or registrar. Two recent female appointees came from outside the judiciary and the Ministry of Justice (although they have at some time in their careers served there).[19] Women remain underrepresented at the magistrates' level in Malawi—18% in 2021 (Registrar of the Judiciary of Malawi). Trends toward appointment of private practice lawyers or corporate lawyers could be helpful in increasing women appointees because it automatically expands the pool (Malleson, 2006). Membership in the Malawi Law Society has doubled over the past decade from around 317 in 2012 to around 600 in 2021.[20] Only two women have been appointed to the apex Supreme Court of Appeal. Under Sec. 112(1) of the Malawi Constitution, qualified appointees must be a lawyer currently qualified to practice or a "judge of a court." This reduces the pool of potential female appointees, compared to Uganda, South Africa, and Kenya, all of which do not restrict to practice and may appoint from academics or corporate lawyers, for example.[21]

Influence of the Chief Justice—The question of under-recruitment is complex. For example, one interview informant suggested that they had not been approached yet, but if she wanted to move to the judiciary she "[w]ould go to them [the JSC]." It is hard to draw causal connections here, but on balance it seems that the hierarchical, top-down culture works against the appointment of women. As one observer noted, "I think traditionally, judiciary works like the military. If they pass you over, there must be a reason for a pass over so that everyone knows that these are the issues and I know why I am not fit to be a judge." Indeed, the overall impression is that decision-making on the JSC is heavily shaped by the chief justice and criteria for selection are opaque. Another interview informant reflected, "[I] was a member and what used to happen—I might be wrong [. . .] whenever there was a vacancy at that time, the Chief Justice would consult the senior members of the judiciary."[22]

This account reflects the "tap on the shoulder" phenomenon of appointments as described by Malleson (2009) and Masengu (2016). Interviewees both inside and outside the judiciary highlight the informal and politicized nature of appointments. For example,

> I was approached by some of the judges saying we'd like you to join us. My name had been on the table for some time. But because it would appear at that time the people who were recommended were only from some other region, I'm from the X region.[23]

Another argued more explicitly, "Judges are appointed based on the political authority of the day. [. . .] Of course the JSC provides advice to the President but the one who appoints the judges is the President."[24] Historical controversies around regionalism and judicial appointments in Malawi represent a potential obstacle to the appointment of women. Malawi's political parties and voting patterns have historically aligned with one of the three ethnic regions—North, Central, and Southern (Ellett, 2013; VonDoepp, 2005). And if there is some regional balancing in judicial appointments, it will de facto limit the pool of potential women candidates. Historically, concerns regarding region and ethnicity have eclipsed gender in the appointment of judges in Malawi. While there are echoes here of race eclipsing gender in the context of South Africa (Albertyn & Bonthuys, 2016; Masengu, 2016), in Malawi it is a secondary rather than primary obstacle to the expansion of women on the court. More broadly, it illustrates the high level of politicization in judicial appointments and a diminution of the pool of women candidates.

This chapter has not addressed the literature on whether women are the best promoters of women. However, in the case of Malawi, there was a major dividend of female appointees when Banda was president.[25] From a strategic perspective, Valdini and Shortell (2016: 865) found that "when the selectors are exposed and can claim credit, [. . .] the unique traits and visibility of the highest court generate an incentive to appoint women." Literature on whether gender bias is more prevalent in men versus women is mixed. Amanda Clayton (2015) found that Malawian women voters may hold stronger cultural views or norms around gender roles. Banda's popularity at home quickly waned as she presided over a period of unprecedented corruption. Public disgust reached its apotheosis over Banda's handling of the so-called 'Cashgate scandal' (Zimmerman, 2015). Yet, she continued to be lauded internationally as Africa's second woman president. This disconnect between internal audiences and external (international or regional) audiences in judicial appointments may lend support to strategic theories of appointment (Valdini & Shortell, 2016). While several interviewees clearly stated that Banda was explicitly and deliberately promoting the advancement of women, this needs to move from anecdote to broader comparative research.

Finally, turning to allies supporting women appointees (Kamatali, 2015; Kamau, 2013; Kenney, 2009): the Women Lawyers Association of Malawi and the Women Judges Association of Malawi (WOJAM) are both vibrant and active professional bodies. Some regard them as potentially more independent than the Malawi Law Society. They tend to focus on less political or confrontational issues in their work (advocacy on gender-based violence, access to justice for women) and don't publicly work toward the appointment of women. But the networking, mentoring, and support structures that emerge are important—this widens the pool of potential appointees. As one lawyer noted:

> We have an active Women's Lawyers Association. They are helpful to your career. Networking with other women—in the corporate world we help each other with problems—we talk and get together. All the lawyers in my section are women. I try to groom them to the level I am at.[26]

In 2017, the International Association of Women Judges intervened after the death of Supreme Court justice Mbendera, to request that the president appoint a woman. The president responded by saying no Supreme Court justice had died and citing the women who had been appointed to offices other than the judiciary (the electoral commission, the clerk of Parliament, four female ambassadors).[27] One woman judge highlighted the significance of the Law Society suggesting that without the backing of the society it may be challenging to get to the highest levels of the bench: "I did receive support from the Law Society for my appointment. The opportunity to be seen and heard outside the system is critical. Networking is critical, as is mentoring. Your whole life is your interview to get onto the bench."[28] While the pool of potential women candidates and appointees is too small to draw robust conclusions, one interviewee suggested she wasn't aware of a woman candidate receiving negative pushback from the MLS.[29] This complicates the findings of Barmes and Malleson (2011), Masengu (2016), and Slotnick (2017) on law societies as gatekeepers to women advancing within the judiciary.

B) Choice Intersects with Structure: Why Women Choose Not to Join the Bench

Operating in a judicialized political environment is not a gendered experience per se. However, it is the case that a judicialized environment *in combination* with burdensome social expectations and professional discriminatory practices operates in a way that potentially serves a gatekeeping function for women. As Justice Twea of the Supreme Court of Appeal in Malawi noted in quoting Lord Woolf: "a Judge is public property." High visibility, compounded by poor salary and benefits, and a lack of control over internal transfers represent substantive disincentives. Salary levels for judges in the commonwealth are often insufficient. This weakens the appointment pipeline of senior lawyers willing to accept a significant drop in income relative to their current or potential private practice earnings (Van Zyl Smit, 2015: 70). Furthermore, corruption or perceptions of corruption are pervasive, and political pressure can be immense. The 2020 constitutional court judgment overturning the 2019 presidential election results in Malawi has only heightened this political scrutiny and pressure.[30]

In addition to the general challenges of working under high public scrutiny, women in Malawi face conservative traditional expectations regarding the roles of women in public life (women are seen as keepers of culture) and a hostile culture within the male-dominated legal profession. Despite many welcome political changes, including a woman president and chief justice, "[M]uch of the traditional role of women still prevails in Malawi. She is the caretaker; her role is largely limited to the private domain" (Amundsen & Kayuni, 2016: 1). In their study of the 2014 presidential elections in Malawi, Kayuni and Kondwani (2016: 3) found that negative discourse against female candidate Joyce Banda was heavily gendered and underscored the "unnatural presence" of women in public positions of power, shaped by powerful religious and traditional forces: "[U]n-natural, un-cultural, and un-Christian: Banda's power is illegitimate."

Clayton, Robinson et al. (2020: 620) found that while Malawians didn't discriminate against women political candidates in a generalized sense, there were "societal barriers in place that prohibited the emergence of viable women candidates (those who are married with young children) and by a campaign environment that is particularly negative for women." In short, "women candidates overwhelmingly identified a toxic political climate in which sexist rumormongering perpetuated by their political competitors negatively affected voters' opinions about them specifically" (Clayton, Robinson et al. 2020: 619). This kind of gender denigration negatively affects candidate reputation. While judges in Malawi are not elected, as Jensen and Martinek (2009) note, high-level judicial posts are political and contentious. While judicial candidates are not explicitly publicly campaigning, once they signal their interest in higher-level judicial appointments, they activate a system of latent biases. Women candidates must network within the legal profession to advance their careers, and that same high-level networking can be used against them, by questioning their so-called moral fitness for high office.

The elite women lawyers I interviewed were eminently qualified and senior enough to be sitting in the upper echelons of the judiciary. They were described by one observer as some of the "best legal minds in Malawi." Some graduated top of their class from the University of Malawi (in some cases as the only woman graduate). From there, negative experiences in private practice ultimately pushed lawyer interviewees into the corporate legal field. Over the last 20 years, as the Malawian economy has grown and the private sector has expanded, more opportunities have emerged in large banks, insurance companies, and private corporations. Corporate law offers stable pay, international exposure, school fees paid, company car, stable work hours, and less public exposure (Author interviews, 2016). The career paths of these elite Malawian women lawyers progressed in the following manner:

1. All went straight from law school at[31] Chancellor College to the Ministry of Justice, some in the prosecutor's office and some in legal aid.
2. Within one to two years, all went into private practice.
3. Within one to four years of private practice, all left litigation to move to corporate law (as company secretaries who perform legal functions for the corporate organization as lawyers).

Each woman indicated that they have deliberately and strategically chosen a career path outside of the judiciary. Why? The opacity of the appointment process and contentious politics are cited as a deterrent. One interviewee stated: "Because of cultural stereotypes, men are threatened by women candidates. Men see the appointment of women judges as a zero-sum game. Look at the comments page after women are appointed."[32] It is evident why these ambitious women would not stay in the initial low-level government jobs, but why were they not encouraged to continue a career in private practice? According to a senior member of the Malawi Law Society:

> [the] challenges of managing a law firm, connections, skills, lack of security, school bills—that is not desirable for women. With a corporate job you get school fees, pensions, a car as part of the package. In Malawi litigation, what you put in does not correspond with the money you get. It is barely enough to survive.

Interviewees did not assess themselves as less qualified compared to equally situated male candidates, notwithstanding "[p]erceptions in the judiciary that you should have experience at the bar." Their choice is hitting an informal institutional structural obstacle—a preference for "many years of advocacy in the higher courts" (Malleson, 2006: 139). In addition to the lack of incentives and the financial risks of staying in private practice, women reported a hostile working environment at larger firms: "Family issues are why I took this job—stress—this is more comfortable. 'Growing up' I experienced intimidation from senior male lawyers."[33] Another informant noted that overall, while they "liked private practice (litigation)," pressure related to "billable hours, pressure to get clients" and ultimately "(At) [Firm X]—they wanted to hire me as a senior partner but said they didn't want women to go on maternity leave."[34] In 2016, there were only two women-run law firms, it was previously three.

The informal dynamics of law firms present obstacles to women's advancement—"men continue to do business in a certain way, women can't do it without stigma."[35] Pointing to the significance of popular perceptions of lawyers, one interviewee notes: "In five to 10 years I may join private practice—would set up my own firm. But I don't really like doing litigation—the public don't trust us." "Cultural set-up doesn't help—we cannot be aggressive. No space to entertain clients or have a drink. The law profession is a men's profession."[36] In other words, to 'act like a man' for professional purposes was to risk personal reputation. There is a constant tension at work here between performing two different roles that are on the surface incompatible: "[d]espite all this professional success. I am still asked to go and cook at funerals, weddings and engagements. I have to be two different people: Office 'me' and Mother/Wife/Church goer/neighbor."[37] And the high level of public exposure associated with the judiciary brings professional and personal/family reputational risks.

Rather than holding negative self-perceptions, several interviewees were instead dismissive of the performance of the judiciary. For example, "I have considered the judiciary [. . .] it is a fallback position." Or as another pointedly noted: "I have seen gaps that are there in the judiciary. Judgments are shallow." Or: "I miss going to court. But the judiciary has integrity issues, issues of appointment. They need to clean up a lot." Once on the bench, it appears that women are less likely to chair crucial committees or divisions, less likely to be selected for career-changing cases.[38] Finally, several informants noted that there is less control over postings in the judiciary and there is the possibility of transfer within the judiciary, and this is problematic for women who have more direct responsibilities at home.

CONCLUSION

This chapter reviews the myriad challenges that women in Malawi face as they rise to the highest levels of the judiciary. Structural barriers are omnipresent in various forms: (1) formal structural systems—educational/professional pipelines plus opaque appointment procedures—are a drag on recruitment and appointment, particularly when combined with (2) intersecting informal systems of professional and sociocultural discrimination and (3) prominent roles for both allies and gatekeepers.

In addition to the uneven and narrow pipeline of women law graduates and lawyers, the level of public scrutiny, job insecurity, and political pressure, the judiciary may not be an attractive career path for successful private practice lawyers—for either men *or* women. But with the addition of structural and sociocultural obstacles for women, High Court judgeships may be a particularly risky or undesirable proposition. Simply put, in an environment of hostile politics and historically weak protections for judicial independence, judges need informal support structures. Evidence from Malawi suggests that such support structures are weaker for women than men. When asked why they are not on the bench, senior women lawyers in Malawi respond that it is rarely that they have not been asked, but rather it's that the institution is too politicized and underperforming. Judges cannot exercise true independence, salaries are low, and the lifestyle is not compatible with family life. These are all rational, strategic decisions, not because the women lawyers feel 'less qualified' than their male counterparts.

The case of Malawi affirms existing theories about formal appointment rules and women on the bench: narrow qualification standards, promotions from within the judiciary, weak transparency and poor remuneration, when combined with discriminatory norms are problematic. Moreover, the restrictive makeup of the JSC on average disadvantages women more, given the double-bind of weaker political support networks and strong sociocultural discriminatory attitudes. Reform of Malawi's formal selection mechanisms is a necessary, though not a sufficient step toward equal representation.

The candidate pipeline in Malawi is narrowed in two stages: educational barriers and then legal professional barriers. Potential women candidates are lost at secondary school and at law school. Law graduates remaining then face challenges passing the bar exam, may become unqualified for judicial office by choosing corporate law as a pathway, or, if they enter the magistracy, the barriers for promotion remain substantial. Informants uniformly note that within the legal profession writ large, male gatekeepers block women's promotion and advancement.

Looking forward, more research needs to be conducted on the role of support networks and allies for potential women appointees and for women who sit on the bench. Here Kamatali's (2015: 148) conceptualization of "insider-outsider collaboration" is helpful. Where small networks of women lawyers know and support each other, where there are key women in positions of power relative to judicial appointments, and there is a favorable national policy encouraging women to enter public service, we tend to see more women appointed. These three conditions were reflected in the temporary bump in female appointees in 2012–2013 in Malawi. Finally, more research needs to be conducted on the proportion of women in JSCs and the legislature and on the advocacy potential of women lawyer and judges associations, both international and domestic.

NOTES

1. The judicialization of politics typically occurs where courts are used to address core policy or political disputes (Hirschl, 2008).

2. Southern Africa Development Community Gender Barometer 2019. Downloaded from https://genderlinks.org.za/wp-content/uploads/2019/08/StateOfWomenSADC2019rev2.pdf Nyamweda, T., & Morna, C. (2019). *State of Women in SADC 2019 Report*. Gender Links Johannesburg, South Africa.

3. In the United States, women law graduates have made up close to 50% of graduates in the last 20 years, and in the last couple of years have surpassed male graduates. Yet, women's upward mobility and persistence in the legal profession is still recognized as a problem. In the United States, women constitute only 30% of non-equity partners and 20% of equity partners. Source: https://www.americanbar.org/content/dam/aba/administrative/office_president/womeninlawsummit_harvard_finalreport.pdf.

4. *Federation of Women Lawyers (Fida-Kenya) & 3 others v. Attorney General & 2 others* [2016] eKLR http://kenyalaw.org/caselaw/cases/view/118523/.

5. "Justice Anastasia Msosa: The woman who has been it all in the Judiciary," *The Nation*, February 20, 2019. https://mwnation.com/justice-anastasia-msosa-the-woman-who-has-been-it-all-in-the-judiciary/.

6. "Malawi Registers Lowest MSCR Pass Rate in 10 yrs," by Noel Mkwalia *Kulinji.com*, January 4, 2021, https://kulinji.com/article/news/2021/malawi-registers-lowest-msce-pass-rate-10-yrs#:~:text=The%20Malawi%20National%20Examinations%20Board,Malawi%20introduced%20a%20new%20syllabus.

7. "2018 University of Malawi Selection List Out: Check Names Here," *Malawian Watchdog*, March 17, 2018, http://www.malawianwatchdog.com/featured/breaking-news-2018-university-of-malawi-selection-list-out-check-names-here/.

8. Author correspondence, Respondent B, 2015.

9. Author correspondence, Respondent B, 2015 and 2021.

10. "St Michaels Girls Students Urged to Pursue a Career in Law," *University of Malawi News Site*, November 25, 2016—https://flaw.cc.ac.mw/news/st-michaels-girls-students-urged-to-pursue-a-career-in-law-25-11-2016 and "LLB3 Students Inspires students at St. Monica Secondary School," *University of Malawi News Site*, November 10, 2016, https://flaw.cc.ac.mw/news/llb3-students-inspires-students-at-st-monica-secondary-school-10-11-2016.

11. "Five Out of 57 Pass Lawyers Bar Exam," by Suzgo Khunga, *The Nation*, January 20, 2016, https://www.mwnation.com/five-out-of-57-pass-lawyers-bar-exam/.

12. "Malawi Revises Criteria of Admitting Lawyers: Bill to Deal with Embezzlement of Client's Funds," by Wanga Gwede, *Nyasa Times*, December 8, 2017, https://www.nyasatimes.com/malawi-revises-criteria-admitting-lawyers-bill-deal-cases-embezzlement-clients-funds/ and see 2018 Act here https://malawilii.org/mw/legislation/act/2018/31.

13. Sec. 117 Constitution of Malawi.

14. Author correspondence, Respondent B, September 2020.

15. Opening comments at the Southern African Litigation Centre (SALC) Workshop on Judicial Independence in Southern Africa, Malawi, January 2016.

16. Institutions to promote women's participation in public life are enshrined in the 1995 Constitution, which states that gender equality is to be attained through the full participation of women in all spheres of Malawian society, on the basis of equality with men (Chapter 3.13., i and ii). The Constitution further prohibits discrimination on the grounds of sex, along with such other factors as race, color, language, religion, political or other opinion, nationality, ethnic or social origin, disability, property, birth, or other status (Chapter 4.20., i).

17. Author interview, Senior Judge, via email, February 2020.

18. Author interview, Respondent A, Johannesburg, SA, July 2013.

19. Author interview, Senior Judge, via email, February 2020.

20. http://malawilawsociety.net/lawyers.pdf (2012) downloaded April 2013; and see also "Malawi Law Society Wants Improved Legal System," *The Nation*, May, 24, 2021 https://www.mwnation.com/malawi-law-society-wants-improved-legal-system/?fbclid=IwAR0r-kHaNFijr6ntGuEPiLT0z7EqRSyGi0h5jVBCrtujGsHcHTvvJa-uso0 downloaded May 2021.

21. Author correspondence with Respondent B, September 2020.

22. Author interview, Respondent D, Blantyre, Malawi, July 2013.

23. Author interview, Respondent G, Blantyre, Malawi, July 2013.

24. Author interview, Respondent K, Blantyre, Malawi, July 2013.

25. Note however that Joyce Banda only completed the process for the first three female judges she appointed, the nominations originated under President Bingu just before he died. (Author interview, Senior Judge, via email, February 2020).

26. Author interview, Respondent V. Blantyre, Malawi, January 2016.

27. Letter provided by Senior Judge via email, February 2020.

28. Author interview, Respondent X. Blantyre, Malawi, January 2016.

29. Author interview, Senior Judge, via email, February 2020.

30. https://www.theguardian.com/world/2020/feb/03/malawi-court-annuls-2019-election-results-calls-new-ballot.

31. A company secretary is essentially the chief administrative officer of a corporation. Holders of this position are experienced lawyers.

32. Author interview, Respondent X, Blantyre Malawi, January 2016.

33. Author interview, Respondent S, Blantyre, Malawi. January 2016.

34. Author Interview, Respondent U, Blantyre, Malawi. January 2016.

35. Author interview, Respondent T, Blantyre, Malawi. January 2016.

36. Author interview, Respondent V, Blantyre, Malawi, January 2016.

37. Author interview, Respondent W, Blantyre, Malawi, January 2016.

38. Author correspondence, Respondent B, September 2020.

REFERENCES

Albertyn, C., & Bonthuys, E. (2016). South Africa: A Transformative Constitution and a Representative Judiciary. In *Gender and the Judiciary in Africa: From Obscurity to Parity?* (Eds. J. Dawuni and G. Bauer). New York: Routledge.

Amundsen, I., & Kayuni, H. (2016). Women and Politics in Malawi: An Introduction. In *Women and Politics in Malawi* (Eds. Inge Amundsen and Happy Kayuni). Bergen, Norway: Chr. Michelsen Institute (CMI).

Arrington, N., Bass, L., Glynn, A., Staton, J., Delgado, B., & Lindberg, S. (2021). Constitutional Reform and the Gender Diversification of Peak Courts. *American Political Science Review, 115*(3), 851–868.

Azu, M. (2013). The Role of the Judiciary in Strengthening Democratic Governance in Africa: An Examination of the Resolution of Recent Presidential Election Disputes in Ghana and Kenya (LLM Diss. Faculty of Law. Addis Ababa University, Ethiopia).

Barmes, L., & Malleson, K. (2011). The Legal Profession as Gatekeeper to the Judiciary: Design Faults in Measures to Enhance Diversity. *The Modern Law Review, 74*(2), 245–271.

Bratton, K., & Spill, R. (2002). Moving up the Judicial Ladder: The Nomination of State Supreme Court Justice to the Federal Courts. *American Politics Research, 32*(2), 198–218.

Chavula, E. (2016). A Critical Analysis of Women Participation in the Law Reform Process: A Case of the Law Commission in Malawi. MA Dissertation submitted in partial fulfillment for the MA in Women's Law at the Southern and Eastern African Regional Centre for Women's Law, University of Zimbabwe.

Clayton, A. (2015). Women's Political Engagement under Quota-mandated Female Representation: Evidence from a Randomized Policy Experiment. *Comparative Political Studies, 48*, 333–369.

Dawuni, J., & Bauer, G. (eds.). (2016). *Gender and the Judiciary in Africa: From Obscurity to Parity?* New York: Routledge.

Dawuni, J., & Kang, A. (2015). Her Ladyship Chief Justice: The Rise of Female Leaders in the Judiciary in Africa. *Africa Today, 62*(2), 45–69.

Dawuni, J., & Masengu, T. (2019). Judicial Service Commissions in Nigeria and Zambia. In *Research Handbook on Law and Courts* (Eds. S. Sterrett and L. Demetrius Walker). Cheltenham, UK and Northampton, US: Edward Elgar.

Ellett, R. (2013). *Pathways to Judicial Power in Transitional States*. New York and London: Routledge.

———. (2019). Judicial Power. In *Routledge Handbook of Democratization in Africa* (Eds. G. Lynch and P. VonDoepp). London and New York: Routledge.

Escobar-Lemmon, M., Hoekstra, V., Kang, A., & Kittilson, M. (2016). Just the Facts? Media Coverage of Female and Male High Court Appointees in Five Democracies. *Politics & Gender, 12*(2), 254–274.

Escobar-Lemmon, M., Hoekstra, V., Kang, A., & Kittilson, M. (2021). Breaking the Judicial Glass Ceiling: The Appointment of Women to High Courts Worldwide. *Journal of Politics, 83*(3), 662–674.

Fox, R., & Lawless, J. (2004). Entering the Arena? Gender and the Decision to Run for Office. *American Journal of Political Science, 48*(2), 264–280.

———. (2010). If Only They'd Ask: Gender, Recruitment, and Political Ambition. *The Journal of Politics, 72*(2), 310–326.

———. (2011). Gendered Perceptions and Political Candidacies: A Central Barrier to Women's Equality in Electoral Politics. *American Journal of Political Science, 55*(1), 59–73.

Fulton, S., Maestas, C., Maisel, S., & Stone, W. (2006). The Sense of a Woman: Gender, Ambition, and the Decision to Run for Congress. *Political Research Quarterly, 59*(2), 235–248.

Garoupa, N., & Ginsburg, T. (2009). Guarding the Guardians: Judicial Councils and Judicial Independence. *American Journal of Comparative Law, 57*(1), 103–104.

Hirschl, R. (2008). The Judicialization of Mega-Politics and the Rise of Political Courts. *Annual Review of Political Science, 11*(1), 93–118.

International Bar Association. (2002). *IBAHRI Fact-Finding Mission to Malawi.* Downloaded from https://www.ibanet.org/Article/NewDetail.aspx?ArticleUid=4c736e88-2983-47ea-9f50-3f204368c25b.

International Development Law Organization. (2020). *Women's Professional Participation in Kenya's Justice Sector: Barriers and Pathways.* Downloaded from https://www.idlo.int/sites/default/files/pdfs/publications/idlo-kenya-womens-professional-participation-low-res_march2020.pdf.

Iyer, S. (2013). The Fleeting Benefits of Appointments Commissions for Judicial Gender Equity. *Commonwealth & Comparative Politics, 51*(1), 97–121.

Jensen, J., & Martinek, W. (2009). The Effects of Race and Gender on the Judicial Ambitions of State Trial Court Judges. *Political Research Quarterly, 62*(2), 379–392.

Kamatali, J. M. (2015). Rwanda: Balancing Gender Quotas and an Independent Judiciary. In *Gender and the Judiciary in Africa: From Obscurity to Parity?* (Eds. G. Bauer and J. Dawuni). New York: Routledge, pp. 33–48.

Kamau, W. (2013). Women Judges and Magistrates in Kenya: Challenges, Opportunities, and Contributions. In *Gender and Judging* (Eds. U. Schultz and G. Shaw). Oxford: Hart Publishing.

Kayuni, H., & Kondwani, F. (2016). The Gatekeepers: Political Participation of Women in Malawi. *CMI Brief, 15*(12). Downloaded from https://www.cmi.no/publications/file/5929-gatekeepers-political-participation-women-malawi.pdf.

Kenney, S. (2009). *Which Judicial Selection Systems Generate the Most Women Judges? Lessons from the United States.* Available at SSRN: https://ssrn.com/abstract=3324661.

———. (2013). *Gender and Judging.* New York: Routledge Press.

———. (2018). Measuring Women's Judicial Empowerment as Part of Political Empowerment. In *Measuring Women's Political Empowerment across the Globe: Strategies, Challenges and Future Research* (Eds. A. C. Alexander, C. Bolzendahl, and F. Jalalzai). Palgrave Macmillan.

Malleson, K. (2006). Rethinking the Merit Principle in Judicial Selection. *Journal of Law and Society, 1*(33), 126–140.

———. (2009). Diversity in the Judiciary: The Case for Positive Action. *Journal of Law and Society, 36*(3), 376–402.

Masengu, T. (2016). It's a Man's World: Barriers to Gender Transformation in the South African Judiciary. Perspectives from Women Advocates and Attorneys. *International Journal of the Legal Profession, 23*(3), 305–319.

———. (2020). The Judicial Service Commission and the Appointment of Women: More to it Than Meets the Eye. *International Journal of the Legal Profession, 27*(2), 161–174.

———. (2022). One Sauce for the Goose, Another for the Gander: Zambian Women Judges and Perceptions of Illegitimacy. In *Gender, Judging and the Courts in Africa: Selected Studies* (Ed. J. Dawuni). New York: Routledge, pp. 209–230.

Michelson, E. (2013). Women in the Legal Profession, 1970–2010: A Study of the Global Supply of Lawyers. *Indiana Journal of Global Legal Studies*, *20*(2), 18.

Ntaba, Z. (2015). *Where are the Women in the Legal Profession?* Presentation at SADC Lawyers Association AGM, 2015 (Slides on file with author).

Nyamweda, T., & Morna, C. (2019). *State of Women in SADC 2019 Report.* Gender Links Johannesburg, South Africa.

Schultz, U., & Masengu, T. (2020). Women and Judicial Appointments. *International Journal of the Legal Profession*, *27*(2), 113–117.

Slotnick, E., Schiavoni, S., & Goldman, S. (2017). Obama's Judicial Legacy: The Final Chapter. *Journal of Law and Courts,* *2*(5), 363–422.

Uzebu-Imarhiagbe, E. (2020). Women in the Nigerian Judiciary: Considerable Headway or Organized Progress? *International Journal of the Legal Profession,* *2*(27), 175–188.

Valdini, M., & Shortell, C. (2016). Women's Representation in the Highest Court: A Comparative Analysis of the Appointment of Female Justices. *Political Research Quarterly*, *69*(4), 865–876.

Van Zyl Smit, J. (2015). *The Appointment, Tenure and Removal of Judges under Commonwealth Principles: A Compendium and Analysis of Best Practice* [Report of Research Undertaken by Bingham Center for Rule of Law]. British Institute of International and Comparative Law.

VonDoepp, P. (2005). The Problem of Judicial Control in Africa's NeoPatrimonial Democracies: Malawi and Zambia. *Political Science Quarterly, 120*(2), 275–301.

———. (2018). The Judiciary: Courts, Judges and the Rule of Law. In *Institutions and Democracy in Africa: How the Rules of the Game Shape Political Developments* (Ed. N. Cheeseman). Cambridge and New York: Cambridge University Press, pp. 304–326.

Vondoepp, P., & Ellett, R. (2011). Reworking Strategic Models of Executive-Judicial Relations: Insights from New African Democracies. *Comparative Politics, 43*(2), 147–165.

Williams, M., & Thames, F. (2008). Women's Representation on High Courts in Advanced Industrialized Countries. *Politics & Gender, 4*(3), 451–471.

Zimmerman, B. (2015). Voter Response to Scandal: Cashgate. In *The Malawi 2014 Tripartite Elections: Is Democracy Maturing* (Eds. N. Patel and M. Wahman). Lilongwe: National Initiative for Civic Education, pp. 215–235.

Chapter 8

Gender Transformation of the Judiciary in South Africa

Baratang Constance Mocumie

INTRODUCTION

In this chapter, I attempt to address an elusive aspect of transformation of the judiciary: gender transformation. I use the word "elusive" because although there is a long tradition of espousing gender equality in South Africa since the dawn of democracy in 1994—based on inter alia gender equality—gender equality has yet to be fully realized. In 1994, there were eight White male judges, two White female judges, three African male judges, one Indian male judge, and no African women judges. Gender transformation has started to gain momentum only in the last seven to eight years. Unlike in the United Kingdom, the United States, and Canada, where gender diversity has been under discussion for more than two decades, in South Africa, discussions were previously focused more intensively on racial diversity (Bonthuys, 2015). Gender is obscured, lacking any in-depth interrogation. Yet it is one of the two requirements espoused in section 174 of the 1996 Constitution.

South Africa inherited a judicial and legal profession that was in place before the democratization of the Republic (Van de Vijer, 2006). Members of that profession were almost exclusively White and male. But the makeup of the profession had to be retained for the sake of continuity in the administration of justice and to avoid the loss of skills and experience that these White men had acquired over the years (Van de Vijer, 2006, p. 148). As of January 22, 2020, of the 571 judges in the country, 160 were women of all races.[1] Of the 160 women judges, 73 were African women and 55 were White women; 19 were Indian women and 13 were Colored women. There are currently 26 leadership positions across the country, but only 23 are occupied. Three were vacancies in the Northern Cape, Limpopo, and Mpumalanga for deputy judges president. There were only four women in leadership positions: one president of the Supreme Court of Appeal,[2] one judge president (JP),[3] one deputy judge president (DJP),[4] and one acting president of the Land Claims Court.[5] In short, after more than 20 years of constitutional democracy, women have acquired only 36% of the leadership positions.[6]

The historically slow pace of gender transformation in South Africa is the reason it is necessary to focus on women in the judiciary. Although commendable progress in transformation of the judiciary based on race has been made, more still needs to be done along the lines of gender. I argue that gender equality can be achieved only if and when it is accepted that there are impediments to women's achieving equality in the prevailing conditions and clear guidelines are in place for eradicating those impediments. However, these efforts need to be bolstered by an obvious commitment (political and otherwise) to achieving gender equality on the bench. I hope that this account will contribute constructively to the dialogue on gender transformation in the judiciary.

To consider the gender aspect of transformation in South Africa, the chapter is divided into four sections. In the first section, I introduce a discussion of the meanings of "transformation" and "merit," and I analyze the perceived tension between the two in the South African judiciary. Thereafter, I examine two closely related transformative issues in the judiciary: equitable work allocation (or the lack thereof) and acting judicial appointments. I argue that these two important issues have been detrimental to women who aspire to ascend in the judiciary by presenting systemic and legislative hurdles that impede women's upward movement. I then identify the two main challenges that women experience at a personal level in their quest to be appointed to the higher courts—namely, balancing family life and judicial work, and gendered insensitivity shown by the Judicial Service Commission (JSC) during interviews. The penultimate section is a discussion, drawn from my own experience, of the role that mentorship plays in overcoming these challenges. I conclude by making recommendations to carve a path toward achieving a judiciary that reflects a transformed attitude toward gender.

THE MEANING OF "TRANSFORMATION" AND "MERIT" AND THE PERCEIVED TENSION BETWEEN THE TWO IN THE CONTEXT OF THE SOUTH AFRICAN JUDICIARY

The road leading to a transformed judiciary, especially in respect to women, has not been an easy one. To examine how South Africa has fallen short in this regard, it is necessary to refer to the Constitution. Section 174 of the

Constitution is the provision that governs the appointment of judicial officers. It reads:

(1) Any appropriately qualified woman or man who is a fit and proper person may be appointed as a judicial officer. Any person to be appointed to the Constitutional Court must also be a South African citizen.
(2) The need for the judiciary to reflect broadly the racial and gender composition of South Africa must be considered when judicial officers are appointed.

Section 174(1) has often been referred to as the merit provision, with subsection (2) considered the diversity/transformation provision (Olivier, 2013). The interpretation of these sections has led to a divergence of views and opinions from all quarters of society. In the past, I have observed conflicting attitudes in the JSC interviews. In some interviews of the JSC, the commission has been adamant in stating that the JSC's mandate is to create a diverse bench that is representative of all South Africans. Yet in follow-up interviews, I witnessed an approach that sought expertise in exclusive areas of the law from which the majority of people—in particular women—have historically been excluded.[7] This discrepancy has often led to confusion regarding what the JSC is looking for.

Merit—Section 174 of the Constitution of the Republic of South Africa (1)

The word "merit" has different meanings in different fields that I need not traverse in this chapter. In general, it is how society chooses to construct and apply it that determines what it means (Malleson, 2006). It also varies from one society to another (Malleson, 2006). Margaret Thornton (2007, p. 401) described it as "a claim to excellence, commendation or worth," as an abstract term that has "no meaning without reference to the social context in which it appears." As such, in the context of the South African judiciary and the assessment, selection, and appointment of judges, the requirement of "merit" lacks clarity; it is not a completely objective and universal standard. In general, many assumptions are made about what constitutes "merit" when one candidate is said to have more merit than another. I consider the views of writers in this area, to indicate some of the difficulty the JSC has had in each session when it interviewed candidates for appointment.

For decades, to be appointed a judge in South Africa, one had to be an advocate and, importantly, have attained the status of silk. One of the retired judges of the Supreme Court of Appeal, Fritz Brand, described silk status, which only senior and accomplished advocates are bestowed with, as "the recognition by the President as the head of State, of the esteem in which the recipients of silk are held in their profession because of their integrity and of their experience and excellence in advocacy" (SAFLII, 2013, para. 7). In South Africa's context, as Masengu (2016) noted, the inference is that these attributes, rightly or wrongly, are found in White males as the only ones who exclusively plied their "excellence in advocacy" (Brand cited in SAFLII, 2013, para. 7) in the higher courts, especially the Appellate courts in South Africa.[8] Years later, retired JP Ngoepe of the Gauteng Division affirmed the view that the pool from which judges should be appointed is advocates; putting it in very clear terms, he stated that "the best source of appointments is the advocates' profession" because "inexperienced advocates, academics and attorneys will impoverish the bench as with few exceptions they do not have the necessary competence for the office" (Ngoepe, 2000, p. 27), and because "magistrates do not have the same training and background as advocates in private practice" (p. 50). Another retired judge, Constitutional Judge Johann Kriegler, in his unpublished 2009 lecture "Can Judicial Independence Survive Transformation," expressed the belief that merit has been compromised in recent selections. Kriegler asserted:

> This ethnic/gender balance criterion has become the be-all and end-all when the JSC makes its selections. And if it isn't the be-all and end-all, [at] the very least it has been elevated to the overriding, fundamental requirement. It overrides subsection (1) of section 174, and I believe that that is a breach of the constitutional mandate. The constitutional mandate instructs the Judicial Service Commission in section 174(1) to appoint people that are appropriately qualified. That's a precondition. That's a mandatory requirement. (para. 16)

These are all men in leadership positions who had the power to identify people and recommend their appointment as acting judges and, ultimately, permanent judges. Whether by design or default, they all seemed to prefer an understanding of merit that, in my view, made the judiciary a preserve of elite White and male power. The statistics referred to later in this chapter demonstrate this very preference under their leadership.[9]

How then should "merit" be defined or constituted? Chief Justice Gleeson of the Australian High Court pointed out:

> There is plenty of room for argument about what constitutes "merit" in judicial selection. But if it means nothing else, it must at least include *the capacity to preside over adversarial litigation, conduct the proceedings with reasonable efficiency, and produce a well-reasoned judgment at the end.* (Emphasis by the author; as cited in Thornton, 2007)

Olivier says that the meaning of merit is not fixed but is dependent on several interrelated variables. It does not necessarily have to be derived solely from the functions of the position. Other factors in addition to appropriate legal experience and technical ability can also be considered components of merit, including the considerations contained in section 174(2). In this way, a closer interrelationship, or perhaps even "a blend" between the section 174 requirements, is achieved. According to Olivier (2013, p. 455), "the recent 'criteria' formulated by the JSC . . . [during September 2010] ('the 2010 Guidelines') certainly seem to point towards 'a blending' of merit and diversity."

The uncertainty over the meaning of merit in relation to, and in the context of, transformation has led to different understandings by different analysts, thereby creating tension in the relationship between merit and transformation/diversity. Under the leadership of former chief justice Ngcobo, the Mahomed guidelines were refined and developed to close the gaps between what the two requisites (sections 174(1) and (2)) mean and how they should be interpreted that the JSC found through past interviews. Those much clearer guidelines, currently used and adapted under Chief Justice Mogoeng Mogoeng, were released in 2010. But until then, this contentious space, that is merit vis-à-vis transformation/diversity, has been complicated by the lack of transparency regarding precisely what the selection criteria are for appointment to the bench (both acting and permanent).[10] I must concede that if one looks at foreign jurisdictions, it becomes apparent that this uncertainty is not unique to the South African judiciary. However, from my observation of the JSC in South Africa over the past decade, it is clear that it means that at the very least the applicant should have the appropriate academic qualifications and at most a junior law degree.[11] But what should the applicant possess over and above those formal qualifications? It is this question that is contentious during interviews, even among the commissioners.[12]

In a transforming society with a history of oppression and discrimination based on race and gender, merit should not mean excellence in advocacy only; nor should it refer to only what the historical definition under an apartheid system created as standards of merit, which excluded opportunities for Black South Africans to gain such qualifications and merit (Albertyn & Bonthuys, 2016). Merit should also not refer to academic qualifications and skills in a few areas of commercial law only. There is a fairly well-documented perception, certainly in South Africa, that experience in areas related to commerce (insolvency, banking, competition, marine law) makes one a more qualified and skilled lawyer because these areas are more technical (Masengu, 2016b).[13] For many current legal professionals in South Africa, that preferred experience was gained through privileged access to practicing as an advocate before the advent of the Constitution. Although a few women were allowed to serve as article clerks or to serve pupillage in big firms or under White male counsel, they were in general excluded from opportunities to work in areas of law traditionally viewed as being the purview of men. In this way, women were barred from acquiring the experience perceived as necessary for judicial office.[14]

What it means to be meritorious in South Africa is linked to the history of entrenched racism and to the myth of Black persons being intellectually inferior to White persons, a myth that persists. Worse yet, for Black women, their appointment to the bench is often viewed as being tantamount to a decline in efficiency (Ntlama, 2014). Thus, even when they have proved themselves on the bench and at the bar, Black women continue to face resistance from others, especially White men, because they "do not belong." In a surprising turn of events, even a handful of Black men from the ranks of the Bar and side Bar hold similar views. Rackley (2007) noted that women constantly have to justify their presence on the bench, and this is the reality of women in South Africa too.

Transformation/Diversity Clause—Section 174(2)

Transformation is defined as "a complete reconstruction of the state and society, including a redistribution of power and resources along egalitarian lines" (Albertyn & Goldblatt, 1998, cited in Goldblatt, 2018, p. 41, note 91).

Considering the racialized and patriarchal history of South Africa,

> the need for a broadly representative judiciary is underlined in a society such as ours, which is still deeply divided on racial grounds. This means [having a] judiciary which broadly reflects who we are, and who all of us are, both majorities and minorities. (Budlender, 2005, as cited in Olivier, 2013, p. 451)

Cowen (2010), who has been watching this aspect closely in the judiciary, says discussions about transformation should not be simply about the personnel, but about "their value systems, their approach to justice, their capacity for justice [and] their understanding of the direction of the Constitution" (as cited in Olivier, 2013, p. 452). Gender representation (alongside race) in the judiciary has a distinct and special place by virtue of the provisions of section 174(2), which stand on a different footing than section 9.[15] This provision requires, in mandatory terms, that those responsible for appointing judicial officers must consider "the need for the judiciary to reflect broadly the racial and gender composition of South Africa" (Cowen, 2010, as cited in Olivier, 2013, p. 450). In public discourse, there is an understanding that the judiciary, like all other institutions, needs to be transformed.

However, "there is no clear consensus on the actual meaning and role of representivity, its relationship to the idea of diversity, and their place and effects in transforming the judiciary" (Albertyn, cited in Olivier & Hoexter, 2014, as cited in Olivier, 2013, p. 450). In my view, in the judicial context, among others, transformation requires changes in the way judges are appointed, a change in the demography of judges, and a change in underlying attitudes of the judiciary that would see them embracing the principles of a fundamentally new legal order.

Former judge of the Supreme Court of Appeal Theron, now a justice of the Constitutional Court, spoke on gender equality in the judiciary at a conference for women judges. She highlighted that the appointment of women to the bench has many benefits for society at large; but most importantly, it gives legitimacy to the judiciary and encourages a perception of a judiciary that is impartial and promotes public trust and confidence that justice will be done, which can be seen as the "ultimate justification" for the appointment of women to the bench (Theron, 2011). The promotion of public trust is especially important to people who come from the places where the disputes originated. The president of the Supreme Court, Justice Maya, recently observed that the appointment of women to the bench makes it easier even for women who come from the rural areas or the townships to approach courts, knowing that there are women on the bench—people who can relate to what they have experienced (Maya, 2016).

Masengu (2016a) has also argued that gender diversity can enhance judicial impartiality on the bench and strengthen judicial independence. One premise of her argument is that the presence of women judges who themselves had been outsiders on the bench creates room for the consideration of previously unheard voices and perspectives.[16] This consideration means that there is a likelihood that there will be less bias among judges because they are being challenged by perspectives from other judges who are not like them. Furthermore, this step will lead to what former Constitutional Court judge Kate O'Regan referred to as "the uncovering of prejudices masquerading as common-sense," which is an important part of judicial self-awareness (O'Regan, 2012, p. 1176).

Masengu's and O'Regan's positions are supported by Grossman (2012), who argued that gender transformation is imperative for what she calls "normative legitimacy," where the presence of both sexes on the bench matters because each sex brings a unique perspective to the act of judging. She argued that this is so because men and women approach law or facts differently or influence each other's decisions based on either socially constructed "gender" or biologically predetermined distinctions. Thus, she opined, benches with a disproportionate number of one sex are inherently flawed, because both sexes are required for impartial decisions and results (Grossman, 2012). The importance of diversity to high-quality decision-making is a perspective shared by Olivier (2013), who asserted that

> women judges can bring an alternative dimension to judging, most likely in human rights cases involving discrimination against women or other marginalized groups or individuals or cases of domestic or spousal abuse. In these cases, the perspectives that could be offered by women judges based on their situation within patriarchal societal and institutional structures could prove invaluable. (p. 457)

This is particularly important in the context of group-based decision-making, where women could "potentially offer a deeper appreciation" of challenges faced by marginalized groups, thereby fostering a more "balanced decision-making process which might increase the likelihood of a just, fair and legitimate outcome" (Olivier, 2013, p. 457).

Another justification for gender representation is cited by Clark (2004), who made the point that the appointment of women judges is particularly important because it instructs present and future generations about women's talents, thereby shattering stereotypes and modeling possibilities for women.

My perspective, and that of women judges who were appointed between 2006 and 2008, is that the appointment of women has made a difference, particularly in cases of abuse and gender-based violence against women and children. For example, when women form part of the appeal panels in such cases, inappropriate remarks that used to be made by male colleagues—for example, saying that rape within a family is less reprehensible than rape outside it[17] and that a woman must go to great lengths to escape the clutches of her assailant and rapist to prevent rape[18]—are less common. There is a deeper respect for victims of such gender-based violent crimes.

The Motivation for an Inclusive Interpretation of Section 174(1) and (2)

The Constitution states in its preamble that it was adopted as the supreme law to "heal the divisions of the past" and "to free the potential of each person." Because South Africa is founded on the values of human dignity and non-sexism, the JSC is obliged to recommend women for appointment to achieve transformation and to avoid unfair discrimination against women who aspire to be judges. Compliance with this constitutional obligation is not intended only to increase the numbers of women—it is also about complying with the demand for such transformation by the South African society and several global conventions of which South Africa is a signatory, including the Convention on the Elimination of All Forms of Discrimination Against Women.[19]

De Vos's (2013) observation on the tension between merit and transformation is perhaps more telling and enlightening as an opinion provided by a

White man in South Africa who has studied law at one of the most prestigious universities and holds one of the most prestigious positions in society: that of a professor in law. He says those who are culturally and economically not in the dominant group (or who have not managed the skill to mimic the attributes and attitudes of the culturally and economically dominant group) are often dismissed as "not possessing the requisite 'merit' to be appointed to positions" (para. 4).[20] This narrow approach, he says, is bound to lead to tension between merit and transformation and inevitably to the conclusion that the two are incompatible. I will argue, as Olivier (2013) does, that the two are not incompatible but can coexist in potential candidates for judicial office—a blending of the merit and the diversity requirements (as cited in Masengu, 2016).

Like De Vos (2013), I am convinced that

> in a multicultural society like South Africa, the kind of experience and skills assumed to confer high merit on one candidate for appointment to the bench might very well make such a candidate less suitable for an appointment because it hinders that candidate's ability to dispense justice between ordinary people. (para. 6)

It may also "hinder that particular individual from interpreting and applying the various provisions of the Constitution in a manner that would promote and protect the interests of the vulnerable and marginalized of our society" (para. 8). In De Vos's view, this is because those who have never walked in the shoes of those who appear before them may continue to apply the law as they deem it right, regardless of the litigants' socioeconomic conditions, their cultural background, and their upbringing.

The body in charge of the appointment of judges in South Africa is the JSC, established under section 178 of the Constitution.[21] The JSC interviews judicial candidates, and the president thereafter appoints judges and JPs on the recommendation of the JSC. In these instances, the president relies on the recommendation made by the JSC's vigorous live broadcasted interviews of the judges. Rarely does the president choose not to confirm the appointments recommended by the JSC. The procedure of appointing the chief justice, deputy chief justice, and president of the Supreme Court of Appeal and the deputy president of the Supreme Court of Appeal differs from that of other judges.[22] For these positions, the president nominates one candidate for each and that person is interviewed by the JSC. If the interview was satisfactory, the president appoints the candidates after consulting with the JSC and the leaders of the National Assembly in accordance with section 174(3) of the Constitution.[23] In the case of the ordinary Constitutional Court justices, the JSC must send the president three more names than the number of vacancies, and the president selects appointments from the list after consulting with the chief justice and members of other parties.[24]

These JSC interviews have been the focal point for the confusion concerning the JSC's application of the so-called merit and transformation clauses in section 174. In addition, there has been confusion about what weight should be given to each during the assessment of candidates in the process of making judicial appointments (Olivier, 2013). They have also left an impression that there is no common understanding of the relationship between section 174 (subsections (1) and (2)) among the commissioners themselves.

In this chapter, I am suggesting that there is no tension between merit and transformation. The two traits can both be found in one fit and proper person who aspires to be a judge in South Africa, because a person who is competent or technically experienced enough to discern the legal issues before them for adjudication can also be a person with the necessary decorum, patience, objectivity, and sensitivity to the socioeconomic conditions of South Africa's citizens resulting from the country's painful history of apartheid, racial discrimination, and patriarchy. This person must also necessarily exercise autonomy and independent judgment in law, giving expression to the values underpinning the Constitution.

One inclusive interpretation of the section 174 requirements is represented by the requirement of "potential to grow and develop oneself" that the JSC recognized in its 2010 Guidelines. In coining the notion of having the "potential to grow and develop oneself," the JSC must have considered the challenges that would result from the prevailing notion of "meritorious appointment" and a recognition of the privileged education and lives White male legal practitioners enjoyed, to the exclusion of all other races and genders, in expert areas such as commercial law. The notion was developed under the late chief justice Ismail Mahomed and was carried through by his successors in title, with a clear intent to transform the judiciary. It is my view that the "potential to grow and develop oneself," if given the prominence it deserves, can still play a vital role in ameliorating the perceived tension between merit and transformation. It recognizes that legal practitioners of different backgrounds were never given equal opportunities to become meritorious, but requires applicants to demonstrate potential (merit).[25]

Ironically, it is these previously disadvantaged individuals whose presence on the bench will give the judiciary the aforementioned legitimacy in the eyes of all who appear in the courts (Andrews, 2022). This is especially pertinent for women, who make up the majority of society.[26] If those empowered to appoint judicial officers lose sight of this factor during the selection and assessment process, the judiciary will never be transformed along gender lines at the same pace at which it is being transformed regarding race. To disregard the pool of candidates who have the potential to grow and sharpen their skills over some time on the bench can never be justified,[27] particularly considering that there are systemic barriers that I will refer to hereafter that continue under the leadership of JPs who were also regarded as transformation appointees. However, it would seem that more recently, the factor of "potential to grow and develop one's self" has effectively been equated with whether a person has acted in the judicial position for which they are applying. This demand for applicants to have acted before seems to go against what was initially envisaged to achieve a transformed judiciary. This situation will be discussed further in the subsequent section.

It should be noted that I am not advocating for the appointment of candidates who may be incompetent or incapable simply because they have been disadvantaged. The submission made in this chapter is that the appraisal of a person's competence and ability should be considered in light of South Africa's history, taken together with the person's capabilities as alluded to in the above paragraph and their potential to grow and develop themselves. In the absence of anything else, an appointment based solely on merit (as defined by some) can divest the judiciary of the diversity that it is enjoined to have. An appointment based on traditional notions of merit will, on its own, debase the struggle against apartheid. It will amount to a continuation of the dominance of one race and gender: White men. To disregard competent and eligible women because they have never practiced in those few areas flies in the face of the commitment to equality espoused in section 9 of the Constitution.

To emphasize the point that merit and transformation are not necessarily mutually exclusive, I offer several examples in which women have made themselves available for senior vacancies in the judiciary to positions that they have never acted in before. They are competent professionals who led and served by example; they include women such as President Maya and DJP Patricia Goliath, who are a testament to the fact that acknowledging that someone meets the transformation requirement is not tantamount to saying they do not have merit. These women's presence on the bench and in their respective leadership positions has most certainly not lowered the standards. In my view, the perceived tension that has led to much consternation over whether to appoint an experienced White man rather than a competent woman albeit without such experience as her White male counterpart should never have caused any consternation in the first place.

ACTING APPOINTMENTS

In South Africa, acting judges are appointed to fill temporary vacancies or the unavailability of sitting judges who, every four years, go on long leave, or, in rare instances, are ill. The use of part-time judges is a feature of the English court system. Under that system, [acting] appointments were made to allow candidates to establish their suitability and to manifest their intention of making themselves available themselves for full-time appointments (Andrews, 2022; Harms, 2004). Even after the advent of democracy, there has been what I deem a lack of political will by the responsible ministries[28] and heads of courts to give more women lawyers, including the magistracy, opportunities to act as judges to capacitate them for permanent appointment. This is evidenced by the fact that women account for a very small percentage of acting appointments, a point that will be detailed further below.

More pertinent to note here is that although acting as a judge is not a prerequisite for judicial appointment, it does play a significant role in the process (Rabkin, 2010). The line of questioning often adopted by the JSC indicates that having had an acting appointment before applying for a permanent position is considered important. Even though all the chief justices as chairpersons of the JSC have expressed on several occasions that acting appointment is not a prerequisite for permanent appointment, very few candidates have been appointed permanently without having previously acted in any superior court they applied for. In 2013, the South African Chapter of the International Association of Women Judges (SAC-IAWJ) called for a firm set of criteria to be developed to determine who should serve as acting judges to qualify and be eligible for a permanent appointment when vacancies are available. This was done to ensure that more women can qualify to apply for positions on the bench.[29]

The media and civil society have also begun to question the importance of acting appointments. A 2015 report on the comments of one civil society organization stated, "If one of the most important criteria for becoming a judge was that the individual would have needed to have acted as one, the process of becoming an acting judge too 'is a mystery,' said [Allison] Tilley," who is head of Advocacy and Special Projects at the Open Democracy Advice Center (as quoted in Thamm, 2015, para. 13). The explanation for the lack of criteria is important because it speaks to the frequently heard argument that the pool of women lawyers is just not large enough to provide candidates for judicial appointments. On this point, different views have been expressed by several JPs during the JSC interviews and legal conferences. One such view is that expressed by the JP of Gauteng, Judge Dunstan Mlambo. In a 2014 address to the SAC-IAWJ, he said,

> I surmise that the basis for the call to fast-track gender transformation in the judiciary is that, 20 years into our democracy, we have only one female Head of court, and generally the appointment of women has lagged markedly behind. This is so [even though] women in general, and those who enter legal practice,

are more in number than their male counterparts. This is according to the latest statistics from the Law Society of South Africa.[30]

He acknowledged that the judiciary indeed lagged in achieving gender transformation despite there being more than enough women legal professionals who enter the legal practice. However, as the literature indicates, they often do not remain in the profession, and those who do stay do not progress to the senior level. At that time, it was difficult for Mlambo to identify women from private practice (both attorneys and advocates) who could take up acting opportunities. This was the case particularly because there was a paucity of women who had consistently engaged with high court litigation, whether in argument as advocates or as instructing attorneys. Hence, women who did not have this experience would, in his view, struggle to cope with the kind of matters that might come before them as acting judges, because litigants want judges who will deal with their matters expeditiously and without delay.

It is encouraging to see that, despite the somewhat dire situation described eight years ago, some progress has been made concerning Gauteng acting appointments. To date, Gauteng division can boast of the most diverse acting appointments list. JPs must go out of their way to seek and develop women candidates from different pools, because that is the only way the cycle of exclusion and privilege will be broken. When one looks at the JSC's recommendations for permanent appointments in the last 5–10 years, the candidates recommended for the permanent appointment had acted as judges for some time, if not an uninterrupted period of at least one year. It is noteworthy that those who were appointed without having acted before are in leadership positions—namely, JP Molemela, who was appointed as JP of the Free State (2015); DJP Goliath for the Western Cape (2016); and DJP Mokgohloa for Gauteng (Limpopo) (2016), although she had previously acted in KwaZulu-Natal. The JSC must be commended on these three appointments. This is an indication that there is room for the JSC to take such bold steps if women are to be encouraged and persuaded to make themselves available for such leadership positions.

A glance at the current statistics for acting appointments available from the Department of Justice, as of May 2021,[31] provides further evidence that women are lagging in being given acting appointments. Table 8.1 shows the number of women called up to act in comparison with their male counterparts—in the Constitutional Court, the Supreme Court of Appeal, the Labour Appeal Court, the High Courts, and the Land Claims court.

Between 2012 and 2020, a total of 2,127 acting opportunities were available. On aggregate, women made up only 29% of those chosen for acting opportunities. The statistics show that only the Northern Cape had granted 50% of its acting opportunities to women.[32]

Table 8.1 Acting Appointment Opportunities 2012–2020[1]

Court/Division	*% Female Judges per Division*	*% Male Judges per Division*
Concourt	30	70
SCA	32	68
Northern Cape	44	56
Western Cape	27	73
North West	28	72
Free State	33	67
Gauteng	25	75
KwaZulu-Natal	29	71
Eastern Cape	31	69
Competition Appeal Court	21	79
Labour and Labour Appeal Court	22	78
Land Claims court	26	74

Source: Created by author with data from Department of Justice, as of May 2021.
[1]Acting opportunities denote the number of vacancies that were available to be filled on an acting basis; it is not the total amount of judges who filled those vacancies. Hence, for example, if one judge acted in a court on four occasions, that would be recorded as four acting opportunities.

It is clear from the statistics that far fewer women than men are given acting appointments. If women cannot get positions acting as judges, it makes getting permanent appointment that much more difficult for them. In the current circumstances, the effect is dire; women will never have an "equal opportunity" to be considered for appointment to the higher courts. However, as was already stated before, what compounds the problem is that there is a lack of clarity about the criteria for becoming an acting judge or for how the process works. The deputy chief justice on delegation by the chief justice, the president of the Supreme Court, and JPs have complete discretion in making recommendations to the Minister of Justice and Constitutional Development. In the same vein, and based on the need for transparency and legitimacy in the process, this practice needs to be open, and legal bodies must be given the opportunity to participate in the process along the same lines as when the candidates are nominated for permanent appointment.

In July 2020, the Minister of Justice and Constitutional Development and Correctional Services, Mr. Lamola, developed a document for discussion with heads of court to address the perceived mystery around acting appointments of judges. He proposed, within the broader mandate of transformation of the judiciary, the following as guidelines:

1.1 Candidates considered for appointment as acting judges should be appropriately qualified persons.

1.2 Candidates must be fit and proper persons who are competent and have integrity.
1.3 Candidates must have the potential to be appointed permanently.
1.4 Heads of court may consider the expertise and experience of such candidates. This also applies to candidates recommended for appointment in the specialized courts, regarding the specialized nature of the work of these courts.
1.5 Candidates must have a minimum of 10 years of cumulative experience in one or more of the following areas:
    1.5.1 practicing attorney or practicing advocate;
    1.5.2 magistrate;
    1.5.3 lecturing in law at university and legal advisers in private companies with satisfactory practical experience;
    1.5.4 public law and the administration of justice: provided that public servants shall not be considered for appointment as acting judges.

I am not aware of the collective response of the heads of court to this proposal.[33] According to two JPs I interviewed, these criteria never became legislation. They stated that if they had, their ability to be innovative when a specialized vacancy arose on the bench would have been stifled. It remains to be seen how this step taken by the minister, if accepted by the heads of court, will affect this long-standing prerogative of the heads of court—and whether there will be any increase in the number of women given acting appointments, which should inevitably translate into permanent appointments.

WORK ALLOCATION AS A HURDLE FOR THE UPWARD PROGRESSION OF WOMEN

Work allocation, also known as preparation of the court roll, is the responsibility of the JP of each division in the high courts and specialist courts. In the Supreme Court of Appeal, it is the responsibility of the president and the deputy president. In the Constitutional Court, it is that of the chief justice and the deputy chief justice. In the high courts and the Supreme Court of Appeal, the JPs and the president allocate cases to the judges according to each judge's experience, skills, and expertise in the varying fields of law.

Scholars and commentators have marveled at the continuing lack of gender diversity in all courts and have argued that it results from negative stereotypes portraying women as secretaries or housewives (Levinson & Young, 2010, p. 1). These stereotypes operate, consciously or unconsciously, within decision-makers to subordinate women at the highest levels of the legal profession.

Chitapi's (2015) research at the Cape Bar has also revealed that women are pigeonholed into family law, maintenance, divorce, and matrimonial issues, as these are considered "soft law." One of the advocates interviewed in the research added that the common belief is that the "big boys" playground is commercial work, insolvency, section 471 inquiries into "big insolvencies, and big corporate disputes." Consequently, Chitapi (2015) opined, this is a contributing factor to the reluctance to brief women on commercial law and insolvency matters because these are considered more "complex" areas of law and are also more lucrative. It might be that these perceptions about women and their legal abilities have a knock-on effect, beginning with skewed briefing patterns in favor of men and eventually crystallizing into the work allocated to women once appointed a judge because they are considered not to have experience in those areas specially reserved for men who manned commercial practices in private practice. This turns into JPs allocating commercial cases mostly to White men with that background.

The point here is that heads of courts do not allocate cases in a manner that is mindful of the transformative values and purposes underpinning section 174. In general, as I have observed, work allocation that is based on legal background experience has had particular consequences for legal practitioners from the magistracy for the following reasons: The majority of magistrates have been forced to preside only in criminal matters and family matters, except for a handful who were in private practice, mostly White males. Before 2014, the Regional Courts had jurisdiction only over criminal matters. As a result, when they appeared before the JSC, they felt shortchanged because they lacked experience in commercial matters, which was regarded as an essential weakness. That is why for a long time, despite their decades of experience in criminal work, Regional Court magistrates and District Court magistrates were consistently overlooked for acting appointments in the High Courts.

Even though women make up more than 40% of the magistracy, they tend to be confined to specific courts such as family law and criminal law (Masengu, 2016). This becomes important when the JSC wants to see a wide variety of experiences. Masengu (2016) observed further that if a candidate who appeared before the JSC had been presiding in the family courts only for the past five years, the commissioners would say that such candidate had not presided in commercial matters. So how can such a candidate become a judge? This point is illustrated in one interview for the KwaZulu-Natal High Court Division in 2015. A candidate who is widely respected by fellow magistrates was asked, despite her vast experience spanning 20 years, whether she had presided in civil cases in the High Court. She responded that she had not but had presided over civil cases in the Regional Court. She was asked if she did not think that she should wait until she had acted and presided in civil matters in the high court before availing herself. She did not agree with this proposition and was overlooked for appointment, both in that round and the next. It is reasonable to infer that this was the case simply because she was never assigned any civil matter, even when she acted in the High Court after her interview.[34] My understanding from one of the senior magistrates I spoke to is that this process has changed in most magistrates' court.[35] There is now a rotation system in place in every magistrate court in South Africa that will assist in ensuring that all magistrates do get to act on all matters.

Laudable progress has been made in the allocation of work in the Supreme Court of Appeal since the change of leadership in 2015. Before 2016, there was an obvious preference for certain types of judges. These were mainly regarded as experts in areas such as patents, copyrights, maritime law, intellectual property, tax law, competition law, insolvency/liquidation, a few specialized areas of contract law, and constitutional matters emanating under the administrative justice legislation to form panels of five members. Perhaps cases were allocated as they were because of the view that the courts must maintain high standards; or, in my view, the feeling was that women were not up to the task. However, the practice unwittingly perpetuated the notion that some judges were not good enough to hear and adjudicate certain matters because they were not specialists or experts in certain areas of the law in their practices. This type of allocation deprived litigants of the diversity of members who have been appointed permanently or as acting in the Supreme Court of Appeal. The advantages of such diversity were highlighted earlier in this chapter.

The debilitating effect of this type of allocation that existed in the SCA before 2016 continues in most superior courts on appeal matters. Because of continued gender imbalance in those courts, White male judges who hail from the bar continue to dominate a few specialized areas of the law. Therefore, if heads of court want to contribute to the transformation of the judiciary to reflect the diversity espoused in the Constitution, they must ensure that more women are identified and given the opportunity to act in the superior courts (the High Courts, the specialists' courts, the Supreme Court of Appeal, and the Constitutional Court). This is necessary so that women acquire experience and the requisite skills to adjudicate in those courts whenever called upon to serve on the bench. Their ongoing judicial training must include specialized areas of work. This will then allow the heads of court to bravely allocate work equally to women and to men.

In the SCA, 2018 ushered in a new era of diversity on judicial panels—panels comprising a diverse assembly of women and men with different backgrounds, all equally capable of bringing their perspectives to bear on the appeals before them and of producing judgments that ordinary South Africans can relate to and understand, thereby bringing legitimacy to the bench. For example, a closer examination of the court rolls of the Supreme Court of Appeal since 2018 indicates that there has generally been a conscious shift in the allocation of cases among all justices regardless of gender. Also, for every complicated matter, a fair number of women are on the panels hearing the appeals, in areas in which they were not regarded as experts previously, painting a picture of a mixed panel of those who specialized in those areas and those who did not. This allocation of work in the SCA has taken place visibly and consciously with the clear intention of transferring and sharing skills, which can only lead to a transformed judiciary. Such bold steps, if adopted, will fast-track transformation in the South African judiciary and tilt the scale of judicial transformation toward a gender balance.

FURTHER CHALLENGES WOMEN FACE

Balancing Family Life and Judicial Work

In addition to the above-cited systemic challenges, striking a balance between family life and work on the bench is a hurdle for women that arises from a patriarchal society across the world. This conclusion is informed by insights garnered from some of the JSC interviews and the personal perspective of several women, to whom I have spoken, and those interviewed by the JSC, who are single parents, never married, or previously married but raising young children. Being selected becomes problematic if they apply for a position in another division or a higher court. The fact that they have young children is added to considerations about whether they are fit and proper persons for appointment to the superior courts. The additional question that they always get from commissioners is: Are you willing to uproot your children and relocate with them? It must be borne in mind that when one relocates, there is no support system in the judiciary to facilitate the children's travel to and from school. Ad hoc arrangements have to be made, but they differ from division to division and are regarded as personal favors. This means women in such situations have no chance to stay in chambers late to catch up on work, as their male counterparts do. Alternatively, they must place their children in boarding schools.[36] In some instances, their children cannot cope with being uprooted from their familiar environment. The dilemma of choosing between being a judge and being a mother becomes unbearable, which leads to those competent women not making themselves available for acting and/or permanent appointment to the higher courts (Andrews, 2022; Masengu, 2020).

Gendered Insensitivity at the JSC

The interview of Judge Nozuko Mjali in October 2014 highlighted the gender insensitivity within the JSC. Judge Mjali had sought a transfer from Mthatha High Court to her hometown in Bisho because of criminal charges against her husband that led to her young children being without either parent. During her interview for Bisho High Court, she was subjected to intense questioning about her reasons for seeking a transfer to the court where her home was situated, even though these reasons were well known to the commissioners. Among other things, she mentioned the long travel hours of travel required to get from Bisho to Mthatha. She was also unable to find suitable schools for her children in Mthatha, where she was based, because one of her children is a special needs child. She broke down during her interview, the details of which were widely reported.[37] The interview continued without any adjournment. No questions were asked about her suitability as a judge. As much as there is no provision for an application for transfer or relocation in the JSC Act, the application, in my view, should have been dealt with internally on its merits with the support of the JP concerned and possibly the support of Judge Mjali's colleagues.

MENTORSHIP

Recently, considerably more attention is being given to the benefits of mentorship in the workplace. The literature indicates that mentoring provides support for women professionals to address the personal and organizational challenges that act as barriers to their upward mobility (Kanter, 1977; Noe, 1988; Ragins, 1989; Ragins & Scandura, 1994; Wright & Wright, 1987, as cited in Wallace, 2001, p. 366). Mentorship offers important benefits: It "enhances professional women's sense of social integration at work and reduces their work—family conflict" (Wallace, 2001, pp. 366–367); it also benefits mentees more than non-mentees in terms of certain "career outcomes, such as salary, promotions, performance, and perceptions of reward satisfaction and fairness" (Burke, 1984; Dreher & Ash, 1990; Dreher & Cox, 1996; Fagenson, 1989; Scandura, 1992, 1997; Whitely, Dougherty, & Dreher, 1991, as cited in Wallace, 2001, p. 367). The psychosocial functions of mentoring "include role modeling, counseling, and friendship, which primarily enhance proteges' sense of competence, clarity of identity, and effectiveness" (Kram, 1983, as cited in Wallace, 2001; pp. 366–367).

Former JP of the Northern Cape High Court Division Judge Kgomo, in his unpublished keynote address to the SAC-IAWJ in 2011, emphasized the importance of mentorship.[38] He said that mentoring bridges the gap between permanent appointment to the higher courts and the position occupied before that. He lamented that although mentorship should be regarded as critical in the judiciary, like coaching in the corporate world, it is not given the necessary attention. He stated further that mentorship in the judiciary should be regarded as an investment in legal practitioners from the magistracy, attorneys, and even academia. These represent another potential group of aspirant judges that can replace, as he put it, "so-called vastly experienced White male advocates who profess to possess experience in certain areas of the law." From 2003/2004 until his retirement in 2018, JP Kgomo, as the JP and head of court of the Northern Cape High Court Division, developed and implemented a mentorship program that produced seven female judges in different courts of South Africa. Of the seven women judges in the program, one is now in a leadership position—DJP Patricia Goliath of the Western Cape Division.[39] Two are now justices of the Supreme Court of Appeal: this author and Justice Fikile Mokgohloa, who was formerly in the Limpopo Division.

WHERE TO NOW? PROPOSED SOLUTIONS

In the above discussion, I have demonstrated that unless the barriers identified are dealt with as proposed, the road to achieving gender equality will be long. I have demonstrated that merit and transformation are mutually inclusive. Thus, in the spirit, purport, and values underpinning the Constitution, there should be no tension regarding the interpretation of section 174(1) read with section 174(2). There is a need to transform the judiciary and to achieve equality between women and their male counterparts at all levels of the judiciary. To do so, I propose the following short-term and long-term solutions to the challenges I have set out before.

Short-Term Solutions

Acting Appointments

Heads of court must give women and men equal opportunities to act in the higher courts to correct the imbalance depicted by the statistics referred to before. They must also provide clear guidelines to all interested parties, particularly those practicing law.

Work Allocation

Heads of court must contribute to the transformation of the judiciary to ensure that a rapid reflection of the diversity espoused in the Constitution, section 174, becomes a reality sooner rather than later. All judges should receive training in specialized areas so that the heads of court can allocate work equally to women and men to empower them equally. This allocation of work must be made in alignment with their oath of office: without fear or favor.

Mentorship

Heads of court must make it their responsibility to mentor individuals who are identified not only by them but also by their peers and legal bodies for possible acting and permanent appointment. This identification should be based on transparency and without necessarily adopting the criteria of the JSC for permanent appointment. If strict criteria of permanent appointment are used in the divisions, that may hamstring transformation and the discretion of the heads of court to bring in all who qualify, with particular focus on women.

Long-Term Solutions

Equal, Progressive, and Empowering Training of All Legal Practitioners and Judicial Officers in All Courts

Aspirant judges training of magistrates, attorneys, and the academia under the auspices of the South African Judicial Education Institute focuses mainly on substantive training on criminal law, civil law, and judgment writing with no specific reference to the Constitution in interpreting legislation and other instruments. From my observation, its curriculum is not structured to target more women to be empowered for acting and eventually permanent appointment. Nor does it target women for specialized training to create a bigger pool for future appointments. There is no social context training[40] that creates awareness of all issues that go into judgment writing based on lived experiences and of the impact of those lived experiences on the decisions judicial officers make (Fedler & Olckers, 2001).

The Strategic Plan of the Department of Justice, Justice Vision 2000, continues to be relevant, as it calls for greater representation of women on the bench. Under the leadership of the former minister of justice, Brigitte Mabandla,[41] as part of Vision 2000,[42] a program was developed to fast-track the identification, training, and appointment of women as judges. Over 90% of those who underwent training under the specialized program were appointed judges in the high courts across the country. The benefits of the program's impact on gender transformation are worthy of a separate discussion. Such discussion is outside the ambit of this chapter.

The Composition of the JSC

The legal bodies that sit on the JSC should appoint more women as their representatives to sit on the JSC.[43] Furthermore, when the president is designating four persons to the JSC, he should, on advice of the minister of justice, consider including women who can represent the voice of women in the judiciary or legal profession.[44] Diversity in the JSC is necessary for many reasons. More women can bring different perspectives to the JSC (Masengu, 2020, p. 24); there is symbolic importance in ensuring that a powerful body such as the JSC is gender diverse (Masengu, 2020, p. 152), and the presence of more women can be an antidote to discrimination against women (Kenney as cited in Masengu, 2020, p. 148); and the presence of more women can improve both the reality and people's perceptions of the JSC's impartiality or lack of it (Masengu, 2020).

Engagement and Consultation with NGOs and Legal Bodies

There are several legal bodies in South Africa that participate in the nomination and appointment of the country's judges. These are the SAC-IAWJ, South African Women Lawyers Association, National Association of Democratic Lawyers, and Black Lawyers Association. It is suggested that the JSC should consult in depth with such legal bodies in respect to acting appointment guidelines and any other issues that are pertinent to judicial appointments. Likewise, there should be some consultation with NGOs in the gender space; their perspectives on gendered legal issues should be considered, as should that of Canada generally (Mokgoro, 2010).

Acting Appointment Guidelines

The recent proposal of the minister of justice regarding developing guidelines for acting as judges, discussed before, will go a long way toward dispelling the mystery that shrouds acting appointments. The heads of courts who have consistently taken the lead in promoting the appointment of women should be commended, and those who have been doing poorly should not only be admonished: they must be called to account by the chief justice (as the head of the judiciary and the chairperson of the JSC) for making little effort in striving for equal representation of men and women.

Addressing Women's Challenges

Finally, with regard to women's challenges, I suggest that: First, women must speak up about specific challenges so that they are documented. Second, organizations that have women members should rally around their plight. These organizations should take up these challenges within the proper channels in the judiciary to ensure that there is an effective support system for women in the judiciary. For example, these organizations should call for the availability of facilities in their work environment that can lighten women judges' burden in carrying out their responsibilities on the bench, such as electronic systems (functioning laptops, connection to the virtual library, availability of research staff) at the homes of the judges that will enable them to leave the chambers during the day to continue working from home. More lessons learned from other jurisdictions, such as Canada, show that if there are facilities such as preschool for young children for those judges who still have young children, the parents can share child-rearing responsibilities. Gym facilities will assist in reducing the stress levels that are an inevitable result of the amount of work done in courts, especially appellate courts.

CONCLUSION

The solutions proposed before cannot be achieved without engagement with relevant stakeholders. Ultimately, a question needs to be asked: If the intention of the drafters of section 174(2) was to ensure that the judiciary comprises diverse judges who are technically competent and constitutionally transformed—is this being achieved? If the answer to that question is not an unequivocal yes, then it is not enough to say we have come a long way since 1994 and made great strides in transforming the judiciary. We need to keep striving to ensure that the judiciary is a place where women and men are equally up to the task of dispensing justice without fear, favor, and prejudice, and are given the opportunity to complete that task. This goal cannot be achieved while women continue to face the hurdles described in their judicial journeys. An inclusive interpretation of section 174(1) and (2) will result in a legitimate and diverse judiciary represented equally by competent men and women. This is a constitutional imperative!

NOTES

1. Statistics obtained from the National Office of the Department of Justice, January 2020.

2. President of the Supreme Court of Appeal, Justice MMM Maya, appointed May 22, 2017.

3. JP M. Leeuw (North West High Court division). Former JP M. B. Molemela (Free State High Court division) was appointed to the Supreme Court of Appeal in 2018.

4. DJP Patricia Goliath (Western Cape High Court division). Former DJP Fikile Mokgohloa (Limpopo High Court division) was appointed to the Supreme Court of Appeal in 2019.

5. Acting JP S. Meer (Land Claims Court).

6. Northern Cape, Limpopo, Mpumalanga, and North West Divisions of the High Courts have since January 2020 appointed four women as deputy judges president.

7. Transcripts and videos of the JSC interviews can be found at https://www.judgesmatter.co.za/.

8. Brand draws this inference from the data of statistics on the number of advocates in South Africa in 2015: Of 482 senior counsels nationally, only 16% are PDIs with as few as 32 (a mere 6.6%) being women, and only 11 of these are Black (GCB statistics, April 2015).

9. See Section II Acting Appointments, only with reference to those in leadership positions: former president of the Supreme Court of Appeal Lex Mpati and former JP of the Gauteng High court Division Bernard Ngoepe.

10. This is still the case six years after a complaint by the Democratic Rights and Governance Unit and Sonke Gender Justice regarding gender discrimination in the appointment of judges in acting positions and permanently to the Commission on Gender Equality.

11. Pre 1994, a junior law degree referred to B. Proc and B. Juris. Post 1994, it is LLB.

12. Some commissioners have insisted on appointing only "meritorious candidates."

13. See also Centre for Applied Legal Studies (2014, August), *Transformation of the legal profession*, available at https://www.wits.ac.za/media/wits-university/faculties-and-schools/commercelaw-and-management/research-entities/cals/documents/programmes/gender/Transformation %20of%20the%20Legal%20Profession.pdf; see also R. Chitapi (2015), Women in the Legal Profession in South Africa: Traversing the Tension from the Bar to the Bench [unpublished thesis], available at https://open.uct.ac.za/handle/11427/15211.

14. Ultimately, they would be forced to move on somewhere else, and their principal would claim that they gave them the opportunity and that they shared their experience with them.

15. Section 9 of the Constitution prohibits unfair discrimination on various listed grounds: race, gender, sex, pregnancy, marital status, ethnic or social origin, color, sexual orientation, age, disability, religion, conscience, belief, culture, language, and birth.

16. See, pp. 46–70.

17. For a discussion of the comments of this nature, see *S v. Abrahams* 2002 (1) SACR 116 (SCA) para. 29, available at http://www.justice.gov.za/sca/judgments%5Csca_2001/2000_088.pdf.

18. *S v. Nkomo* 2007 (2) SACR 198 (SCA) at 206–208.

19. Other regional conventions that place obligations on South Africa in this respect include Article 2 and Article 9(2) of the *Protocol to the African Charter on Human and Peoples' Rights on the Rights of Women in Africa* and Article 7 of the SADC's *Protocol on Gender and Development*. See also International Labour

Organisation Constitution and Association Conventions at http://www.ilo.org/dyn/normlex/en/f?p=1000:12001:::NO:::.

20. See also Masengu (2016b) note 17, which is supported by one of the interviewees who said she was asked to change her voice and mannerisms. This is a practical example of the subtle discriminatory conduct against women who don't fit in and are expected to relinquish who they are in order to belong.

21. Regulated by the JSC Act, 1994 (Act No. 9 of 1994): Procedure of Commission, *Government Gazette* No. 7616 Volume 453, March 27, 2003, No. 24596.

22. In terms of section 174(3) of the Constitution of South Africa, 1998, the president, as the head of the national executive, after consulting the SCA and the leaders of parties represented in the National Assembly, appoints the chief justice and deputy chief justice and, after consulting the JSC, appoints the president and the president of the Supreme Court of Appeal.

23. Constitution of the Republic of South Africa 1996.

24. Section 174(4) of the Constitution.

25. This was evident in JSC interviews conducted from 1996. See www.justice.gov.za/reportfiles/1999reports/1999_judicial%20service%20commhtm.

26. Women make up 51% of South Africa's population. See 2017 mid-year population estimates available at http://www.statssa.gov.za/publications/P0302/P03022017.pdf.

27. Much can be said about the pool of females in the legal profession. Suffice to say that South African statistics seem to bear out a similar attrition trend in other jurisdictions—that is, despite female graduates' exceeding male graduates, the number of women in the profession steadily declines. The 2017/2018 Statistics from the Law Society of South Africa indicate that in 2017, female law graduates numbered 2,917, approximately 676 more than male students; yet women make up only 39% of practicing attorneys. As of 2018, only 25% of advocates were women. Perhaps most telling is that in 2018, there were only 50 women silk advocates (the most senior advocate position attainable) of a total of 537 silks, and 396 of them were White men. See "Statistics for Legal Profession 2017/2018," available at https://www.lssa.org.za/wp-content/uploads/2019/11/LSSA-STATS-DOC-2017-18.pdf.

28. Ministry of Constitutional Development and Ministry of Women in the Presidency.

29. SAC-IAWJ Annual conference held at the University of KwaZulu-Natal, August 9–11, 2013.

30. As keynote speaker at the SAC-IAWJ 2012 Annual General Meeting, held at Pretoria University on August 9, 2014.

31. Statistics obtained from the Department of Justice and Constitution and Correctional Services, Judicial Support Unit.

32. The Limpopo and Mpumalanga High Court Divisions have been deliberately left out of the table because they were established only in 2018 and 2019, respectively. The Electoral court has its unique character such that there are only three judges at any given time, and currently those three are men. From its inception, the chairperson has always been a man.

33. As of May 2021.

34. Ms. S. Maphumulo, Regional Court magistrate, interviewed for KwaZulu-Natal division in April 2016. http://www.judgesmatter.co.za/the-jsc/2016/jsc-candidates-2/ms-sitembiso-maphumulo/.

35. Chief Magistrate of Welkom, Ms. A Motlekar.

36. Justice Dambuza lamented this in her JSC interview on April 14, 2015, at the Radisson Blu Le Vendome Hotel, Sea Point.

37. NEWS24, "Judge Tells JSC about husband's arrest for rape," October 8, 2014, by Niren Tolsi, http://www.news24.com/Archives/City-Press/Judge-tells-JSC-about-husbands-arrest-for-rape-20150430; see also *The Con Magazine*: "The New JSC in a Man's World," November 10, 2014, by Kayt Hindle, available at http://www.theconmag.co.za/2014/11/10/the-new-jsc-and-the-patriarchy/.

38. This unpublished keynote speech was delivered at the Annual General Meeting of the SAC-IAWJ, held at the University of Nelson Mandela Metropolitan on August 10, 2011.

39. The Gauteng division also operates a mentorship program, but it differs slightly. The cadets do not sit with the mentors on the bench.

40. Social context training is compared with diversity training in corporate parlance, but the two differ substantively.

41. The first and only woman Minister of Justice and Constitutional Law post, 1994, 2002–2005.

42. Initiated under the tenure of Dr. Penuell Maduna, spearheaded by former director of the Gender Directorate Advocate Joyce Maluleke, now director general in the Office of Women in the Office of the Presidency.

43. Section 178(1) *(e)* & *(f)* of the Constitution of the Republic of South Africa, 1996.

44. Section 178(1) *(j)* of the Constitution of the Republic of South Africa, 1996.

REFERENCES

Albertyn, C., & Bonthuys, E. (2016). South Africa: A transformative constitution and a representative judiciary. In G. Bauer & J. Dawuni (Eds.), *Gender and the Judiciary in Africa: From Obscurity to Parity?* New York: Routledge, 2016, 49–66.

Andrews, P. (2022). Pursuing gender equality through the courts: The role of South Africa's women judges. In J. Dawuni (Ed.), *Gender, Judging and the Courts in Africa: Selected Studies*. New York: Routledge, 189–208.

Bonthuys, E. (2015). Gender and race in South African judicial appointments. *Feminist Legal Studies*, *23*(2), 127–148. https://doi.org/10.1007/s10691-015-9285-5.

Chitapi, R. (2015). Women in the Legal Profession in South Africa: Traversing the Tensions from the Bar to the Bench [Unpublished LLM thesis]. University of Cape Town.

Clark, M. L. (2004). One man's token is another woman's breakthrough: The appointment of the first women federal judges. *Villanova Law Review, 49*(3), 487–548. http://digitalcommons.law.villanova.edu/vlr/vol49/iss3/2.

De Vos, P. (2013, April 11). *The JSC Must Redefine Merit to Advance Judicial Transformation.* Constitutionally Speaking. http://constitutionallyspeaking.co.za/the-jsc-must-redefine-merit-to-advance-judicial-transformation/.

Fedler, J., & Olckers, I. (2001). *Ideological Virgins and Other Myths*. Justice College.

Goldblatt, B. (2018). *Developing the Right to Social Security—A Gender Perspective*. Routledge.

Grossman, N. (2012). Sex on the bench: Do women judges matter to the legitimacy of international courts? *Chicago Journal of International Law*, *12*(2), article 9, 647–682. https://chicagounbound.uchicago.edu/cjil/vol12/iss2/9/.

Harms, L. T. C. (2004, May 21). *Transparency and Accountability in the Judicial Appointment Process*. Paper presented at the 12th Annual International Judicial Conference, Bucharest, Romania. http://www.sabar.co.za/law-journals/2010/august/2010-august-vol023-no2-pp36-38.pdf.

Kriegler, J. (2009, September 2). *Can Judicial Independence Survive Transformation?* Constitutionally Speaking. https://constitutionallyspeaking.co.za/can-judicial-independence-survive-transformation-a-public-lecture-delivered-by-judge-johann-kriegler-at-the-wits-school-of-law/.

Levinson, J. D., & Young, D. (2010). Implicit gender bias in the legal profession. *Duke Journal of Gender Law & Policy, 18*(1). https://scholarship.law.duke.edu/djglp/vol18/iss1/1.

Malleson, K. (2006). Rethinking the merit principle in judicial selection. *Journal of Law and Society, 33*, 126–140. https://doi.org/10.1111/j.1467-6478.2006.00351.x.

Malleson, K., & Russel, P. (Eds.). (2006). *Appointing Judges in an Age of Judicial Power*. University of Toronto Press.

Masengu, T. (2016a). Gender transformation as a means of enhancing perceptions of impartiality on the bench. *South African Law Journal*, *133*(3), 475–490. http://hdl.handle.net/1854/LU-8555847.

Masengu, T. (2016b). It's a man's world: Barriers to gender transformation in the South African judiciary; perspectives from women advocates and attorneys. *International Journal of the Legal Profession, 2*(3), 305–319. https://doi.org/10.1080/09695958.2016.1179639.

Masengu, T. (2020). What lies beneath: The complex nature of appointing women judges in Zambia and South Africa [Unpublished doctoral thesis]. Ghent University and University of Cape Town. http://hdl.handle.net/1854/LU-8664196.

Maya, M. (2016, August 12). *The Role of Women in the Advancement of the Judiciary: Tilting the Scales of Judicial Transformation?* Address delivered at the University of KwaZulu-Natal, Howard College, South Africa.

Mokgoro, Y. (2010). Judicial appointments. *Advocate*, *23*(3). https://www.yumpu.com/en/document/view/10357918/judicial-appointments-by-justice-yvonne-mokgoro-former-judgewho.

Ngoepe, B. M. (2000). Judges' forum: White paper on the judicial system—Memorandum by Pretoria judges. *Advocate, 13*(1), 27–32. https://www.gcbsa.co.za/law-journals/2000/firstterm/2000-firstterm-vol013-no1-pp27-28-and-30-32.pdf.

Ntlama, N. (2014, November 13–16). *The Transformation of the South African Judiciary: A Measure to Weaken its Capacity?* Presentation at New York Law School's workshop Constitutional Rights, Judicial Independence and the Transition to Democracy: Twenty Years of South African Constitutionalism, New York, NY, United States.

Olivier, M. (2013). A perspective on gender transformation in the South African judiciary. *South African Law Journal, 13*(3), 448–464. https://gimmenotes.co.za/wp-content/uploads/2019/01/Olivier-2013-SALJ.pdf.

O'Regan, K. (2012). A pillar of democracy: Reflections on the role and work of the Constitutional Court of South Africa. *Fordham Law Review, 81*, 1169–1186.

Rabkin, F. (2010, April 28). Women need a foot in the judiciary door. *Business Day*. https://www.pressreader.com/south-africa/business-day/20100428/281663956215903.

Rackley, E. (2007). Judicial diversity, the woman judge and fairy tale endings. *Legal Studies, 27*(1), 74–94. https://doi.org/10.1111/j.1748-121X.2006.00039.x.

SAFLII [South African Legal Information Institute]. (2013). *General Council of the Bar and Another v. Mansingh and Others* (417/2012) [2013] ZASCA 9; 2013 (3) SA 294 (SCA); [2013] 2 All SA 542 (SCA). http://www.saflii.org/za/cases/ZASCA/2013/9.html.

Thamm, M. (2015, April 15). Choosing our judges 101: How to rise (or not) through the legal ranks. *Daily Maverick*. https://www.dailymaverick.co.za/article/2015-04-15-choosing-our-judges-101-how-to-rise-or-not-through-the-legal-ranks/.

Theron, L. V. (2011, August 13). *Representation of Women in the Judiciary*. Presentation at a Conference on Gender Equality with Emphasis on Education and Training: Driving an Inclusive Culture, North-West University, Potchefstroom, South Africa.

Thornton, M. (2007). 'Otherness' on the bench: How merit is gendered. *Sydney Law Review, 29*(3), 391–413. https://www.researchgate.net/publication/228194393_Otherness_on_the_Bench_How_Merit_Is_Gendered.

Van de Vijer, L. (2006). *The Judicial Institution in Southern Africa: A Comparative Study of Common Law Jurisdictions*. Siber Ink.

Wallace, J. E. (2001). The benefits of mentoring for female lawyers. *Journal of Vocational Behavior, 58*, 366–391. https://doi.org/10.1006/jvbe.2000.1766.

Chapter 9

A Critical Assessment of the Status of Women Judicial Officers in Uganda

Josephine Ndagire

INTRODUCTION

In 1893, the *Kabaka* (King) of Buganda entered into a treaty with the British on the basis of which the Kingdom of Buganda (known as Uganda at the time) would become a British protectorate in 1894 (Mugambwa, 1989, p. 446). At the time, Buganda Kingdom was one of the several kingdoms and chiefdoms in present-day Uganda. Hence, none of the other cultural groupings had entered a similar agreement by the time Buganda became a protectorate (Mugambwa, 1989, p. 447). In March 1900, the Kingdom of Buganda signed a new agreement with the British—the Uganda Agreement, 1900 (hereinafter, 1900 Buganda Agreement). This agreement solidified the relationship with Buganda Kingdom and served as a precursor for similar agreements with other communities (1900 Tooro Agreement; 1901 Ankole Agreement). It is one of the most consequential agreements between the British and natives, and survived a whole 50 years (Mugambwa, 1989, p. 449). The impact of this agreement is still felt, including issues related to challenges in the land tenure system. The 1900 Buganda Agreement essentially proclaimed the applicability of colonial laws in the entire protectorate, including Buganda Kingdom, thus bestowing a common law heritage from the onset (Haydon, 1960, p. 18; 1900 Buganda Agreement, art. 5). As such, judicial precedent (stare decisis) is central to judicial interpretation (Constitution, art. 132(4)). Uganda's legal system therefore embodies several features of the English legal system. Laws applicable in Uganda include common law, statutory law, doctrines of equity, and customary law. In 1902, the British enacted the Uganda Order in council, which vested all civil and criminal jurisdiction over all persons in the newly established High Court. Native courts retained jurisdiction over customary matters, divorce, and some misdemeanors. To the extent that it was retained, native law existed alongside English law and was restricted to specific contexts and upon passing the "repugnancy test." Uganda has since had a pluralistic legal system.

The African continent witnessed a wave of constitutional reforms in the 1990s. The radical transformation of the continent's political landscape was aimed at ending decades of autocratic rule and unending coups, as well as bolstering economic stability (Wachira, 2018). The collapse of the Soviet Union led to the rise of Western influence in Africa through institutions such as the International Monetary Fund, World Bank, and United States Agency for International Development. Consequently, international financial institutions made demands in policy changes and pushed for privatization, currency devaluation, reduction in size and cost of the public sector, removal of subsidies for public services, and reduction of state intervention in agricultural pricing and marketing. Political change meant democratic reforms that were, in many instances, a prerequisite for economic assistance (Sahr, 1992, pp. 31–33). Several African governments such as the NRM in Uganda recognized the need for full public participation of all citizens in governance and decision-making processes. As a former rebel movement, democratic reforms were crucial not only for obtaining aid/economic assistance but also as a means of obtaining legitimacy in the international community. The NRM therefore adopted women-friendly policies across public sectors (Goetz, 2002, pp. 555–557).

WOMEN IN PUBLIC LIFE

Public life is intrinsically linked to politics. And politics is ruled by cultural and religious beliefs. Historically, political parties organized around ethnicity and religion. The oldest party, for instance, the Democratic Party, was predominantly comprised of *Baganda* (largest ethnic group) and was Roman Catholic. *Baganda* loyalists formed the *Kabaka Yekka* (Only the King) party. The post-independence regimes were thought to have been oblivious to gender discrimination and injustices (Goetz, 2002, p. 552), which led to the exclusion of women from public life (Goetz, 2002, p. 553).

In present times, political parties are largely defined by ideology and less by religious and tribal/ethnic affiliation. Women are a critical constituency, and their participation is highly visible. This drastic shift is largely due to the NRM government, which seized power in 1986. To distinguish itself from previous regimes, the NRM aggressively pursued inclusive policies—from destigmatizing HIV to affirmative action for vulnerable groups. For years, the Constitution of Uganda 1995, promulgated under the NRM government, was lauded as one of the most progressive on the continent (Mukholi, 1995,

p. 261). Its legal framework, specifically, the constitutional guarantees and affirmation of women's rights, opened spaces for dialogue with minority groups (Odoki, 2005, pp. 49–47 and 136–63).

Initially, the NRM suspended party politics, to ostensibly enable merit-based competition for public service, without party backing, in order to broaden opportunities for ordinary Ugandans to participate in government decision-making processes (Goetz, 2002, pp. 553–557). It is against this backdrop that grassroots women groups—mostly made up of professionals—lobbied for the appointment of women to leadership positions. A manifesto by women groups demanded a women's ministry and women's representation at all levels of local government. In a hasty response, the NRM government appointed women to positions in ministries and the Uganda Constitutional Commission (UCC)—a body that was tasked with drafting the 1995 Constitution. Victoria Sekitoleko was appointed minister for agriculture, and Gertrude Njuba became the deputy minister for industries. Miria Matembe and Mary Maitum were appointed to the UCC. Furthermore, a ministry for women was created, and 34 seats were reserved for women in the legislative assembly (Goetz, 2002, pp. 553–557).

Women appointed to the UCC played a critical role by advocating for the incorporation of equality and gender parity clauses in the Constitution (Goetz, 2002, pp. 556). The new Constitution crystallized the regime's commitment to women's rights. Articles 32 and 33 accord women full and equal rights with men. Affirmative action in favor of marginalized groups, including women, youth, persons living with disabilities, and other vulnerable groups, was enshrined in Article 32 of the Constitution to address historical inequalities in the pre- and postcolonial era. These provisions acknowledge historical injustices and seek ways of redress through affirmative action and prohibit laws, customs, and traditions that are prejudicial to the welfare and dignity of women. These provisions formed the basis upon which women entered public spaces as equal players.

However, the NRM exploited the emancipation process and the new women's movement to consolidate power by turning women into a power base allied to the regime (Tamale, 1999). In political spaces, women were handed slots in the legislative body and reciprocated with support (Tamale, 1999; Ahikire, 2004), which continues to this day. More telling, the NRM at times opposed measures that challenged discriminatory cultural practices relating to marriage and property. For instance, the regime has not supported the Domestic Relations Bill, which offers adequate protections for women in domestic relations. While its history stems back to 1964, it was introduced in 2003. It took about two years to reach the Parliamentary and Legal Affairs Committee, and despite the NRM holding majority seats since taking power, it still has not been passed. Women had to organize in other ways—primarily, by negotiating and building alliances with men to push legislation through (Tamale, 1999), or through public interest litigation (*Uganda Association of Women Lawyers and Others v. Attorney General*, 2004).

Starting in the 1990s, the number of the women in the judiciary increased. Today, they comprise 44% of judicial officers. However, as a historically patriarchal institution, and one in which men still form a majority, female judicial officers are not accorded the same opportunities. For the most part, women judges, specifically, remain in the background and seem more like support actors.

COURT STRUCTURE IN UGANDA

The government exercises other powers through the executive and the judiciary, headed by the chief justice. The chief justice is deputized by the deputy chief justice—a member of the Court of Appeal, which doubles as the Constitutional Court. In that regard, they head of both courts (Const. art 136(1)). The principal judge heads the High Court to which they are also a member (Const. art 141(1)). The chief justice may delegate some of his responsibilities to the deputy chief justice or the principal judge. Together, the three constitute the leadership of the judiciary, followed by justices of the Supreme Court, justices of the Court of Appeal/Constitutional Court, and judges of the High Court. The seniority of individual judges is determined by the period spent on the bench, and where applicable (for instance, where justices/judges have spent an equal amount of time on the bench), age is taken into account. The older judge is deemed more senior (Judicature Act, Sec. 2).

Uganda is divided into magisterial areas (Magistrates Courts Act, sec. 2). These have a Chief Magistrates Court as well as Grade I and Grade II Magistrates Courts (Magistrates Courts Act, sec. 161). A chief magistrate heads the Chief Magistrates Court in his/her magisterial area. The court has jurisdiction over criminal cases where the maximum penalty is a life sentence and civil cases not exceeding 50 million Uganda Shillings in value (approximately US$13,585). Appeals to the Chief Magistrates Courts lie from the Grade I Magistrates Court. Uganda also has a Family and Children Court in every district.

Local Council Courts are the first courts of instance. They are mostly composed of men, with women elected to the position of secretary of women affairs. These courts operate at the village level and are vested with jurisdiction over simple criminal and civil matters, including debts; contracts; assault; conversion; damage to property; trespass; disputes in respect of land held under customary tenure; disputes concerning marriage, marital status, separation, divorce, and parentage of children; and disputes relating to identity of a customary heir and customary bailment (Local Council Courts Act, sec. 10).[1]

APPOINTMENT PROCESSES

Article 128 of the Constitution guarantees judicial independence. This provision notwithstanding, Articles 142 and 144 of the Constitution bestow upon the president extensive appointment and removal powers. As such, the executive maintains tight control over the judiciary, which is somewhat nuanced in the nomination and appointment process. Article 147(2) of the Constitution established the Judicial Service Commission (JSC), whose primary mandate is to appoint and discipline judicial officers. The commission comprises nine

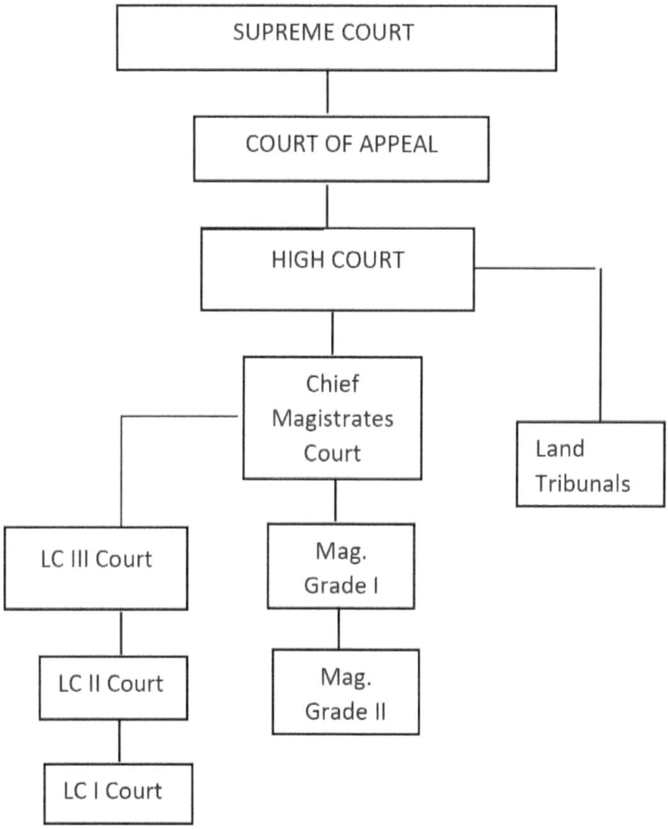

Figure 9.1 Court Structure in Uganda. *Source*: Created by author with data from Articles 129 and 243 Constitution of the Republic of Uganda, 1995; Sec. 161 Magistrates Courts Act and Sec. 10, Local Council Courts Act.

members appointed by the president. It is headed by a chairperson and deputy chairperson who must be qualified to serve on the Supreme Court. Other members include two nominees of the Uganda Law Society, two members of the public nominated by the president, a Public Service Commission nominee, the attorney general, a Supreme Court justice, a Court of Appeal justice, and judges of the High Court.

The specific mandate of the JSC is laid out in Article 147 of the Constitution. Among other functions, the commission advises the president on the appointment of justices of the Supreme Court, Court of Appeal/Constitutional Court, judges of the High Court, the chief registrar, and other court registrars. The president nominates judicial officers from a list of nominees provided by the commission. From the list, the president nominates judges, and the names are then sent to the Parliament for approval. Once Parliament approves the president's nominees, he appoints them as judges. In reality, President Yoweri Museveni's government has enjoyed an overwhelming majority in Parliament since it took power in 1986.

The commission directly appoints magistrates and registrars following advertisement of vacancies and interviews. In the recent past, however, the commission started advertising vacancies in courts of record, including the position of chief justice.

On the whole, judicial officers enjoy security of tenure. This notwithstanding, Article 144 of the Constitution outlines circumstances under which a judicial officer may be removed from office. Yet again, the procedure to remove a judicial officer vests a lot of power in the executive: the president must appoint a tribunal to investigate allegations against the judges before removing them from office.

AFFIRMATIVE MEASURES AND GENDER REPRESENTATION

Affirmative action is a set of policies intended to address historical injustices, usually, against minority populations or other disadvantaged groups, such as, women. Globally, states have adopted affirmative action measures as a means of fulfilling international obligations, specifically, the advancement of gender equality (Busby, 2006, pp. 42–58; Crosby et al., 2013, p. 488; Clayton & Crosby, 1992, pp. 12–13; Rabe, 2001, p. 254). In Uganda, affirmative action measures are credited for increasing the number of women on the bench. As of August 2022, there was a total of 548 judicial officers, 266 (48.8%) female and 272 (51.1%) male (The Judiciary, 2022).

Overall, women are well represented in the judiciary. Over the past three decades, Uganda has witnessed a rise in the number of female judges. The

Table 9.1 Judicial Composition

Category	*Female*	*Male*	*Total*
Justices and Judges	43 (45.2%)	52 (54.7%)	95
Registrars	21 (57.4%)	23 (42.5%)	54
Magistrates	192 (48.4%)	204 (51.5%)	396
Total	266 (48.8%)	272 (51.1%)	548

Source: Created by author with data from The Judiciary: Republic of Uganda (2022).
Note: Female judicial officers currently comprise 266 (48.8%) of the total number of judicial officers (The Judiciary, Republic of Uganda, 2022).

International Bar Association commended honorable lady justices Mukasa Kikonyogo, Lillian Tibatemwa Ekirikubinza, Julia Sebutinde, Faith Essy Mwondha, and Solomy Balungi Bossa for annulling unconstitutional practices (Mukiibi & Kafeero, 2019), spearheading the fight against corruption in public service (Musamali, 2002; Daily Monitor, 2012), and promoting women's rights (*Muwanga v. Kintu*, 1997; International Bar Association, pp. 26–30). The aforementioned lady justices are also celebrated as 'firsts' in various positions at home and abroad.

Justice Mukasa Kikonyogo, for instance, served as the first female magistrate Grade 1 in 1971 and first female chief magistrate in 1973. She was later appointed as the first female High Court judge in 1986. In 1997, Justice Kikonyogo was the first and only female to become deputy chief justice of Uganda (Mushoborozi, 2018). Justice Tibatemwa-Ekirikubinza sits on the Supreme Court and was the first woman to earn a PhD in Law in Uganda and the East Africa region. She was also the first female professor of law in the East African region and the first female deputy vice chancellor of Makerere University (New Vision, 2018). In 2018, she was elected to the International Commission of Jurists for a five-year term (Thembo, 2018) and to the Court of Appeal in Seychelles in 2019 (Daily Monitor, 2019). Her contemporary, Justice Sebutinde, serves at the International Court of Justice and is celebrated as the first African woman to sit at the court. Justice Sebutinde also served as a presiding judge at the Hague-based United Nations Special Court for Sierra Leone in the trial against former Liberian president Charles Taylor (Butagira, 2016). In 2018, Justice Bossa was elected to the International Criminal Court (The Independent, 2017).

CONTRIBUTIONS OF WOMEN JUDGES

Women judges generally adopt a gender-sensitive approach to the law (Sherry, 1986, p. 165; Schroeder, 2002, p. 255; Hale & Hunter, 2008, p. 237; Martin, 1993, p. 166; Escobar et al., 2021, p. 5). Women judges have consistently taken the experiences of women into consideration when judging and thus interpreted the law in a manner that increases access to justice for women (Dawuni, 2016). Globally, justices Navi Pillay, Elizabeth Odio Benito, Cecilia Medina, and Theresa Doherty are acclaimed for their roles in progressively interpreting legislation on gender violence (International Development Law Organization, 2018, p. 16).

There is wide consensus that affirmative measures should not be an attempt to merely increase the demographic composition of judiciaries, but rather, bring on board women with capacity, talent, ability, and competence (Masengu, 2016, p. 10; Malleson, 2006, p. 131). Worldwide, influential women judges have proved that progressive policies and activism toward increasing women's participation in the judiciary and decision-making processes are not merely an antidote to gender paucity, but a stride that yields better justice outcomes.

In Uganda, women judges have made notable contributions in the areas of gender equality, sexual offenses, unconstitutional practices, and corruption. Justice Bossa has, for instance, demonstrated progressive and independent thinking over the years. In 1997, she adopted a broad interpretation of "spousal contribution to marital property." As presiding judge in *Muwanga v. Kintu*, High Court Divorce Appeal No. 135 of 1997, she ruled that contributions to marital property could be indirect. She found that a wife indirectly contributed to household expenses through day-to-day chores and as such was entitled to an equal share of property. More than a decade later, the Supreme Court cited the case and adopted her interpretation in *Julius Rwabinumi v. Hope Bahimbisomwe*, Civil Appeal No. 30 of 2009. The lead judgment was written by Justice Esther Kisaakye of the Supreme Court. In a country where the majority of women are uneducated housewives, this judgment attached value to the work of women in the home.

While serving as a judge at the High Court, Justice Lydia Mugambe's ruling in *CEHURD, Mubangizi Michael & Musimenta Jennifer v. Executive Director of Mulago National Referral Hospital & Attorney General*, Civil Suit No. 212 of 2013, was acclaimed for setting precedent in negligence and maternal health (Musoke, 2017). Justice Mugambe found for the plaintiffs, whose newly born baby was stolen from hospital premises after birth. Her judgment was particularly recognized for holding the state accountable in failing to protect women against circumstances that render them vulnerable (Musoke, 2017). Justice Mugambe currently holds the position of inspector general of government. For years, the courts in Uganda applied the cautionary rule in sexual offenses (a judge had to warn himself of the dangers of convicting an accused person in the absence of corroborating evidence). While a few judges, including Justice Timothy Lugayizi, were critical of the rule and declined to apply it (*Uganda v. Peter Matovu*, 2001), in 2015, the Supreme Court upheld the judgment of Justice Elizabeth Musoke, who had convicted an accused person without applying the cautionary rule (*Ntambala Fred v.*

Uganda, 2015). In her judgment, Justice Ekirikubinza noted that the rule is not "legally justifiable," and that since women were the majority of victims in sexual offenses, the rule was discriminatory, as it adversely affected them. She concluded:

> I would therefore find it right to proceed under Article 132 (4) of the Constitution to depart from this Court's previous decisions cited in this judgment where the cautionary rule was held to be a requirement in sexual assault prosecutions.

This judgment overturned decades of injustice and prejudice against female victims of sexual offenses. The rule was based on the idea that victims of sexual offenses tend to be untruthful and malicious.

Justice Faith Mwondha rose to fame while serving as inspector general of government from 2005 to 2009 (New Vision, 2018). She ordered the arrest of former health ministers Maj. General Jim Muhwezi and Captain Mike Mukula, who were charged with misappropriating an amount of UGX 1.6 billion (approximately US$424,800) of the Global Alliance for Vaccines and Immunization Fund, donated to Uganda for treatment of children infected with HIV/AIDS, malaria, and tuberculosis. Captain Mukula was sentenced to four years in prison by the Anti-Corruption Court (Angumya, 2013). Justice Mwondha further uncovered embezzlement of UGX 8 billion (approximately US$2,124,400) at the National Social Security Fund (NSSF) by Bakoru Bakoko, former Gender, Labor and Social Development minister and other NSSF officials (Angumya, 2013).

Women have made substantive contributions to social justice. Sally J. Kenny notes that women judges typically find for the plaintiff in sex discrimination cases (Kenny, 2013, p. 3). However, such an observation should not be attributed to male and female stereotypes. Kenny (2012, p. 1526) elucidates:

> Feminist consciousness is a political achievement and not an inevitable result of being female or living a life as a woman. So too should we understand that the creation of a group of judges, men and women, who bring a gender lens to judging, is an organizational accomplishment and not an automatic result when a certain number of women judges join a court.

With respect to aptitude, key characteristics of judging include independence and audacity (Adams, 1927; Vernon, 1933). Eminent common law jurist, Lord Thompson Denning, in one of his dissents on the Court of Appeal of England, suggested a binary classification of judges, the *timorous souls*—fearful of new cause of actions and the *bold spirits*—embracing any cause of action if justice so required (*Candler v. Crane*, 1951). According to Denning, progressive development of the law required judicial creativity and the courage of bold spirits (Kirby, 1986, p. 103). Justices Bossa, Musoke, Ekirikubinza, and others demonstrated bold and uncompromising qualities that are not specific to any one gender.

A CLOSER LOOK AT THE STATUS OF WOMEN JUDGES

Achieving equal representation on the bench is a commendable and critical first step. Substantive representation, however, demands that women are accorded equal opportunities, in terms of special appointments—say, to head commissions of inquiry, promotion from one level to another, and appointment to key leadership positions. Leadership, specifically, is a telling indicator of women's progress on the bench (Kenney, 2018, p. 209; Dawuni, 2015, p. 15). This section takes a critical look at the judiciary to determine whether women are meaningfully represented. The assessment goes beyond the artificial metrics of representation and asks whether women progress and hold leadership positions in the judiciary.

Across the African continent and in countries that possess distinct legal systems (common law, civil law, and mixed systems), there has been an increase of women in leadership positions in the judiciary. Women have served as presidents of the highest court in Burundi, Gabon, Guinea-Bissau, Malawi, Ghana, Nigeria, Benin, Lesotho, Sierra Leone, Senegal, and Rwanda—some serving as few as six years and others more than 28 years (Dawuni & Kang, 2015, p. 50). This notwithstanding, there are also countries on the continent where women have not been accorded leadership opportunities.

Tokenism is the idea of appointing members of minority groups to positions where they have been historically excluded to appear inclusive and progressive. Token appointments focus more on the numbers and optics and less on merit. There have been claims of tokenism in Uganda, specifically, in respect of women's representation in Parliament (Tamale, 1997). Token representatives are therefore not necessarily the most qualified candidates and may or may not compete favorably with their male counterparts or cause the change expected of them. Tamale argues that in Uganda's Parliament, token women in fact influenced the House and caused change by building alliances with men (Tamale, 1997).

It cannot be stated with certainty that female judicial officers are token appointees, or that tokenism is responsible for their stagnation in the judiciary. It is, however, a fact that the NRM government has pursued an aggressive gender parity policy across public sectors and has made some questionable appointments. Women have become a key constituency to the regime's survival, making tokenism in the judiciary plausible. Be that as it may, there are indeed several qualified women both within the judiciary and elsewhere that qualify for promotions and leadership positions.

The candidates' suitability and qualifications, aside, there are other factors, particularly, political affiliation. It could be the case that since women joined public service much later, they are less senior than equally qualified men. And if a male judge belongs to the ruling party, chances are that they will be elevated or promoted. The role of politics in judicial appointments has called into question the legitimacy of the appointments process, and has in turn, eroded public trust and confidence in the judiciary (International Commission of Jurist, 2014, p. 2; Lieven, 2017, p. 19; United Nations, 2019, p. 55).

Whereas women form about 44% of judicial officers, indeed boasting impressive numbers across the bench (50% on the Supreme Court), their representation in leadership positions within higher courts of the judiciary—High Court, Court of Appeal, and the Supreme Court—is dismal. The judiciary has been majorly headed by men since its establishment by the Uganda Order-in-Council in 1902. NRM government has made five chief justice appointments since it took power in 1986. No woman has ever been appointed. The position of chief justice is currently held by Hon. Justice Alfonse Owiny-Dollo who is deputized by the Hon. Richard Buteera, head of the Court of Appeal. The Hon. Dr. Flavian Zeija is the principal judge and head of the High Court. The trio forms the leadership of the judiciary. Women have only held leadership positions at the lower bench. Her Worship Sarah Langa heads magistrates' courts. She is the first woman to hold the position substantively, having replaced Her Worship Flavia Senoga Anglin, who held the position in acting capacity.

Uganda has had one female deputy chief justice, Justice Laeticia Mukasa-Kikonyogo (2001–2010), but no woman has been appointed principal judge. In High Court, men head all divisions. Of the seven divisions three are headed by male judges, deputized by women, while four are male dominated.

The exclusion of women from leadership positions raises questions of some form of segregation. Horizontal segregation is demonstrated where people perform distinct jobs as a result of gender inequality and societal attitudes. In this kind of arrangement women take on stereotypically female jobs in low paying sectors (Wirth, 2001, pp. 10–13). On the other hand, vertical segregation is directed to the hierarchical structure of organizations within specific professions. In essence, men hold more responsible, challenging, and skilled jobs. Vertical segregation generally corresponds to the theory of the glass ceiling which consists of attributes of appreciation such as pay, status, control, and authority (Wirth, 2001, pp. 10–13). With all senior positions—held by male judicial officers, there is clearly vertical segregation in the appointment and promotion practices of the judiciary.

Table 9.2 Heads and Deputies of Various High Court Divisions

High Court Divisions	*Heads*	*Deputies*
Criminal division	Hon. Justice Michael Elubu	Hon. Justice Asiimwe Tadeo
Civil division	Hon. Justice Sekaana Musa	Hon. Justice Emmanuel Baguma
Land division	Hon. Justice Keitirima John Eudes	Hon. Justice Henry Kawesa Isabirye
International Crimes division	Hon. Justice Kutosi Wangutusi	Hon. Lady Justice Jane F.B Kiggundu
Anticorruption division	Hon. Justice Lawrence Gidudu	Hon. Lady Justice Margaret Tibulya
Commercial division	Hon. Justice Stephen Mubiru	Hon. Justice Duncan Gaswaga
Family division	Hon. Justice David Matovu	Hon. Lady Justice Ketrah Kitarisibwa Katunguka

Source: Created by author with data from The Judiciary: Republic of Uganda, 2022.
Note: The official records of the judiciary show that female judicial officers do not substantively lead divisions of the High Court (The Judiciary, Republic of Uganda, 2022).

In their assessment of factors that may influence the rise of women to leadership positions in the judiciary, Dawuni and Kang (2015) examine different legal systems. According to their study, judges in common law countries have more prestige, as a result of their discretionary powers to create precedent, while those in civil legal systems merely apply the letter to the law (Dawuni & Kang, 2015, p. 56). Similarly, Malleson (2006, p. 132) argues that where the position of chief justice is considered high compared to that of a president of the Constitutional Court, relinquishing that position to a woman is likely contentious. Malleson (2003, p. 177) also argues that women, who ascend to upper ranks of the judiciary in common law countries, usually end up as "sole women trail blazers." This assessment is particularly true when tested in Uganda in respect to Justice Kikonyongo and the position of deputy chief justice, although it may not resonate in other countries (Dawuni, 2020, p. 12; Dawuni & Kang, 2015).

The character of judiciaries in Africa is disparate, and some judiciaries have indeed made significant progress in increasing the number of women on higher courts (Dawuni, 2020, p. 8). It is likely that the more women join the judiciary, the higher the likelihood of more women in senior or leadership positions (Bauer & Dawuni, 2016).

As mentioned earlier, Article 142 of the Constitution vests the power of appointment and approval of all judicial officers serving at the Supreme Court, Court of Appeal/Constitutional Court, and the High Court in the president, who acts on recommendation of the JSC and with the approval of Parliament (Const. art. 142). Inevitably, the appointment of judicial officers is a politicized process. The result is that lawyers affiliated to the NRM party are more likely to be appointed as judges. The phrase "cadre judges" is commonly used in the legal fraternity to refer to judicial officers whose appointment is based more on loyalty to the NRM than merit (Okudo, 2016). In 2016, Rtd Hon. Justice Wilson Tsekooko, former justice of the Supreme Court, decried the rise of cadre judges and the dire consequences on judicial independence and integrity (Okudo, 2016).

It is therefore obvious that appointments are not solely based on merit. It is no coincidence, for instance, that both the current and former chief justices are former cabinet ministers and NRM members of Parliament. Predictably, former chief justice Bart Katureebe gained a reputation of ruling in favor of the president and NRM government in politically sensitive cases (*Rtd Col. Dr. Kizza Besigye v. Electoral Commission & Yoweri Kaguta Museveni*, 2007; *Amama Mbabazi v. Museveni & Ors*, 2016). In a 2018 petition challenging the constitutionality and legality of the removal of the age limit for presidential candidates to allow the incumbent to run for another term, Justice Katureebe was among the narrow majority who decided in favor of the move. Interestingly, the new chief justice, Alfonse Owiny-Dollo, was President Museveni's legal counsel in the 2006 presidential election petition challenging the president's victory (Amamukirori, 2017) and has held several political appointments in the past.

Uganda Judicial Officers Association has expressed dissatisfaction with the appointment process of judicial officers over the years. In January 2016, the president of the association called for transparency in the nomination and appointment process. He further recommended that promotions should follow "Performance Efficiency Audits." In October 2006, the association expressed concern over the appointment of politicians to the bench, indicating at the time that over 95% of judicial appointments since 1997 were political.

It is not uncommon for high-performing judges to be sidelined due to their independent mindedness. Justice Bossa has, for instance, suffered major career setbacks despite having a solid academic and professional record. She has about 23 years of experience in legal practice, having served at the High Court since 1998, until her appointment to the Court of Appeal in 2013. While she was one of the few qualified judges to serve on the Constitutional Court/Court of Appeal, her ascendance was slower than many of her juniors with hardly a comparable record of achievement. Prior to her appointment at the International Criminal Court, Justice Bossa wrote to the Judicial Services Commission, claiming she had been unfairly sidelined for the position of deputy chief justice and had on several attempts failed to secure a promotion to the Supreme Court (Kiyonga, 2017). Her progressive approach has pushed her to the sidelines of an increasingly politicized and partisan judiciary. This fact is widely known in the public and acknowledged in the judiciary. President Museveni has on several occasions castigated "activist judges" and labeled them as saboteurs (International Bar Association, p. 23; Van De Vijver, p. 221).

Justice Bossa was part of a panel at the Constitutional Court that annulled the Anti-Homosexuality Act in 2014, on grounds that it was not passed in accordance with the law, that is, the required legislative quorum (Wekesa, 2014). The president had assented to the bill following months of a highly publicized and polarizing debate that gained the attention of the international community. The bill had a penalty of life imprisonment for engaging in homosexual acts (Karimi & Thompson, 2015). At the time, Justice Bossa was married to the former vice president and stalwart member of the Uganda People's Congress—an opposition political party (Nantume, 2018).

Following appointments to the Supreme Court in 2015, several observers in public and legal circles expressed disappointment over those that were eventually appointed. Prof. Frederick Ssempebwa, a representative of the Uganda Law Society at the JSC, noted that the commission had nominated Justices Bossa, Frederick Egonda-Ntende, and Remmy Kasule to the Supreme Court on several occasions in vain (Kakaire & Kiyonga, 2015). In similar fashion, a judicial officer who preferred anonymity observed that it was "strange that the three justices were not appointed, despite their proven track record as outstanding jurists" (Kakaire & Kiyonga, 2015). A senior judge who also preferred anonymity during an interview with the Citizen Newspaper publication spoke of how justices Bossa, Kasule, and Egonda-Ntende were not only rejected for promotions on several occasions but also sidelined from politically sensitive cases, due to their "activism"—a disguised reference to their independence (Okudo, 2018).

The United Kingdom has a reputation for strictly adhering to the principle of merit in judicial selections and appointments. Proponents for the principle of merit generally apply a "maximalist approach," which seeks to appoint the best candidate for the job regardless of any other considerations (Malleson, 2006, p. 128). The maximalist approach is also applied to positions that require performance of varied and complex duties and instances where the quality of candidates is high (Malleson, 2006, p. 129). The United Kingdom's commitment to the maximalist approach in judicial appointments is rationalized by the roles and functions of judges, which require a high degree of quality in performance and independence (Malleson, 2006, pp. 132–133). It is worth noting, however, that women may be disadvantaged by this approach because of the number of years they are likely to spend out of active practice, for various reasons, including having and raising children (Malleson 2006).

Following the maximalist approach, the JSC has over the years nominated highly qualified women justices for leadership positions in the judiciary. In

2017, five female justices, namely: Ekirikubinza, Stella Arach Amoko, Esther Kisaakye, Irene Mulyagonja, and Hellen Obura, were nominated for the position of deputy chief justice.

At the time, there were only two male nominees, including current chief justice Alfonse Owiny-Dollo, who was appointed deputy chief justice. A deputy chief justice should either be justice of the Supreme Court or Court of Appeal or possess no less than 15 years of experience in legal practice before a court of unlimited jurisdiction in civil and criminal matters (Const. art. 143(1)). At the time of the nominations, Justice Ekirikubinza had served as a judge of the Supreme Court and the Court of Appeal for five years (Mushoborozi, 2018) while Justice Kisaakye had served as a judge of the Supreme Court for eight years (Butagira & Wandera, 2019). Both justices hold doctorates in law and were well published as scholars, having been appointed to the judiciary from academia. Justice Mulyagonja had served on the bench for five years as a High Court judge (Butagira & Wandera, 2019) and practiced for 15 years (Daily Monitor, 2016). Justice Amoko was justice of the Supreme Court and previously had practiced in the Attorney General's chamber for 18 years. She had also been a High Court judge for 13 years and deputy principal judge of the First Instance Division of the East African Court of Justice for seven years.

Justice Owiny-Dollo, on the other hand, had juggled legal practice with a career in politics. He was called to the bar in 1988 and was a member of Parliament between 1996 and 2001. From 2006 to 2008, he worked as legal counsel for Riek Machar, the inaugural vice president for Southern Sudan. Owiny-Dollo was appointed to the High Court in 2008 and later to the Court of Appeal in 2015 (Wekesa, 2014). He also served as minister of state for Foreign Affairs for two years and minister of state in charge of Northern Uganda Reconstruction Program (Wekesa, 2014). All the nominated women were highly qualified. Justices Amoko and Mulyagonja were exceptional candidates and more qualified than the eventual appointee, by all measures.

As mentioned earlier, the Court of Appeal doubles as the Constitutional Court, which is mandated to interpret the Constitution. The court hears cases on accountability and democratic governance and gives meaning to "Human Rights and Freedoms" in Chapter IV of the Constitution. While Deputy Chief Justice Owiny-Dollo is an accomplished jurist, he previously held several political appointments and was an active member of the ruling party that he represented in Parliament. Prior to joining the High Court, Deputy Chief Justice Dollo was President Museveni's legal counsel in a petition disputing the results of the presidential election in 2006 (Wekesa, 2014). Against that backdrop, his appointment at the time lends credence to the argument that political affiliation is a silent and decisive factor.

BOLSTERING WOMEN'S ADVANCEMENT ON THE BENCH

The number of women on the bench and where they are situated within the judiciary is due to a number of factors, including the appointments process (Dawuni, 2020, p. 9) and the legal system (Dawuni & Kang, 2015). It appears that internal selection processes in the judiciary are more likely to yield more female judicial officers in leadership positions than external processes (Dawuni & Kang, 2015). In countries where an independent body selects, interviews, and makes recommendations on who can be appointed, the composition of the body is critical (Dawuni, 2015). The appointing body is more likely to appoint female judicial officers if its constitution is representative (Dawuni & Kang, 2015).

This observation is particularly true in the case of Uganda. The JSC has over the years had more female commissioners and has had a woman at the helm. For instance, out of nine members who constitute the composition of the commission, five are currently women, including Justice Faith Mwonda (deputy chairperson), Rosemary Nyakikongoro and Christine Amongin Aporu (public representatives), Norah Matovu Winyi, and Ruth Sebantindira who represent the Uganda Law Society (Daily Monitor, 2020). The JSC has consistently recruited women and nominated them for leadership positions and promotions.

It has been argued that judicial appointing bodies tend to reflect societal gender biases and, in some instances, may hinder the elevation of women to senior positions (Dawuni & Masengu, 2019). In Uganda's case, the JSC has shortlisted women for key positions on numerous occasions. The recruitment and nomination process is, however, subject to some form of vetting or interference by the executive, manipulation by special interest groups (say, political parties), and individuals (Dawuni & Masengu, 2019). These actors—gatekeepers—could stifle or aid the advancement of women on the bench (Dawuni & Kang, 2015; Dawuni, 2020, p. 10). This could perhaps explain why candidates (including women) who are perceived as hostile or apolitical are not appointed by the president despite being nominated by the JSC.

Experiences elsewhere are instructive on how some of these hurdles may be navigated. Efforts toward gender parity in the United States were majorly advanced by individual women and women groups (Kenney, 2012). Women's groups advocated for the appointment of a woman to replace U.S. Supreme Court associate justice William O. Douglas during President Gerald Ford's administration and protested the composition of the president's advisers on the matter, as being all men and mostly opponents of the Equal Rights Amendment (Kenney, 2012, p. 1514).

During President Jimmy Carter's administration, the Washington Women's Network comprising over 1200 members publicized open positions in the judiciary, lobbied for suitable candidates, pressured senators to appoint women to nominating commissions and testified before the Senate Judiciary Committee about the slow pace of appointing women to judicial positions.

There is need for the National Association of Women Judges Uganda (NAWJU) and Uganda Women's Network (UWONET) to work collectively toward redefining women's places within the judiciary to cause change in respect to leadership positions. NAWJU is a 27-year-old association with over 80 jurists at the forefront of advocating for women's rights and access to the legal system within the judiciary (The Judiciary, 2020), while UWONET is a network with a membership of 20 women's rights organizations that actively advocates for gender parity and empowerment nationally. This happens in three thematic areas, including women's governance and leadership. Women's networks in Uganda, particularly the NAWJU in partnership with UWONET, should play a more active lobbying role for female judicial officers who are nominated to positions of leadership. Women are a political constituency and could easily secure leadership, if well organized.

Adherence to strict requirements by the appointing bodies generally could increase the number of female judicial officers in the judiciary (Dawuni & Masengu, 2019), and arguably, the number of female judicial officers in leadership positions. However, female judicial officers must strive to occupy leadership positions, by being competitive and prepared for such opportunities (Masengu, 2016).

Interestingly, in Zambia, women perform better than men in both the interviews and the postgraduate qualifications (Dawuni & Masengu, 2019). In Uganda, the JSC advertises vacant positions although the interviewing process is shrouded in secrecy. Furthermore, the JSC shortlists suitable candidates for any given position within higher courts—the critical decision lies with the president who chooses the appointee (for courts of record) from the list. And while Parliament must confirm the appointments, the ruling party has an overwhelming majority, currently at 336 of 529 seats. There even have been instances where the president has ignored candidates recommended by the JSC.

CONCLUSION

There has been a shift in the status of women in post-independence Uganda. The NRM strategy over the past three decades deliberately aimed to allow women space in public life witnessed an increase in the number of women in public life. Policies such as affirmative action have increased women's access to education and enabled them to obtain qualification necessary for public life. In politics, the Constitution introduced gender quotas—each district must have a woman representative. Overall, women hold about 30% of parliamentary seats. This figure is replicated in business, law, health, agriculture, and all other sectors. Women have become an active bloc that continues to support the NRM government.

Women constitute 44% of judicial officers. At the Supreme Court, women hold half of the seats. Women are also well represented on the Court of Appeal/Constitutional Court and the High Court. A critical assessment, however, reveals that women have been locked out of leadership positions on the bench. Currently, none of the seven divisions of the High Court is headed by a woman. Men also hold top leadership positions—chief justice, deputy chief justice, and principal judge. No woman has ever been appointed chief justice or principal judge, and only one woman has held the position of deputy chief justice.

The absence of women in leadership positions is not due to a lack of qualified and experienced women. The judiciary has several qualified women for leadership. Indeed, the JSC has on numerous occasions nominated women. External factors seem responsible for the exclusion of women, and among these, is perhaps a tendency to be apolitical on one hand, and critical and progressive on the other. Going by the trends, the NRM government seems more comfortable with judicial officers who are openly supportive of the regime. Firstly, the vast majority of past and current chief/deputy chief justices have been involved with the NRM party in some capacity. Secondly, since women joined the bench much later, it is highly likely that there are always qualified men with more years of experience than men.

It is therefore important for women to organize and be more intentional about taking up leadership in the judiciary. Networks such as UWONET and NAWJU should ensure that women are meaningfully represented on the bench. NAWJU should take a more active role; the association is almost exclusively focused on building the capacity of female judicial officers. The association should organize from within by positioning its members for key positions and lobbying for gender parity in judicial leadership.

NOTE

1. Article 129(1)(d) provides for the establishment of subordinate courts by Parliament.

REFERENCES

Adams, H. F. (1927). The Good Judge of Personality. *Journal of Abnormal and Social Psychology, 22*(2), 172–181. https://psycnet.apa.org/doi/10.1037/h0075237.

Ahikire, J. (2004). Towards Women's Effective Participation in Electoral Process: A Review of the Ugandan Experience. *Feminist Africa*, 8–26.

Amama Mbabazi v. Museveni &Ors (Presidential Election Petition No.1 of 2016) [2016] UGSC.

Amamukirori, B. (2017). Justice Owinyi Dollo to be sworn in today as deputy Chief Justice. *New Vision.* Retrieved from https://www.newvision.co.ug/new_vision/news/1462701/justice-Owiny-Dollo-sworn-deputy-chief-justice.

Angumya, E. (2013). Mukula guilty of embezzling Gavi funds. *The Observer*. Retrieved from https://observer.ug/component/content/article?id=23224:mukula-guilty-of-embezzling-gavi-funds.

Bauer, G. & Dawuni, J. (2016). *Gender and the Judiciary in Africa. From Obscurity to Parity*. Routledge.

Busby, N. (2006). Affirmative Action in Women's Employment: Lessons from Canada. *Journal of Law and Society, 33*(1), 42–58. https://dx.doi.org/10.1111/j.1467-6478.2006.00346.x.

Butagira, T. (2016). Justice Sebutinde speaks on new world court job. *Daily Monitor*. Retrieved from https://www.monitor.co.ug/News/National/-/688334/1289640/-/bg3qr9z/-/.

Butagira, T., & Wandera, A. (2019). Uganda Supreme Court gets new judges. *Daily Monitor*. Retrieved from https://www.monitor.co.ug/News/Education/688336-714346-kdcwrv/index.html.

Candler v. Crane, Christmas and Co. [1951] 2 K. B.

Clayton, S., & Crosby, F. (1992). *Justice, Gender and Affirmative Action: Critical Perspective of Women and Gender*. University of Michigan Press.

Crosby, F. J., Sabitini, L., & Aizawa, M. (2013). Affirmative action and Gender Equality. In: Ryan, M. & Branscombe, N. (eds). *The sage hand book of gender and psychology*. Sage Publication Ltd.

Daily Monitor. (2012). Celebrating women of influence-Justice Julia Sebutinde: The face of anti-corruption. Retrieved from https://www.monitor.co.ug/SpecialReports/ugandaat50/Justice-Julia-Sebutinde--The-face-of-anti-corruption/1370466-1418290-m0wgt8/index.html.

Daily Monitor. (2016). Irene Mulyagonja: My long journey to the IGG office. Retrieved from https://www.monitor.co.ug/Magazines/Full-Woman/Irene-Mulyagonja---My-long-journey-to-the-IGG-office/689842-3254598-dms77w/index.html.

Daily Monitor. (2019). Justice Tibatemwa joins Seychelles Court of Appeal. Retrieved from http://www.judiciary.go.ug/data/smenu/93/Judicial%20Structure.html.

Daily Monitor. (2020). Museveni appoints Justice Buteera to the Judicial Services Commission. Retrieved from https://www.monitor.co.ug/uganda/news/national/museveni-appoints-justice-buteera-to-judicial-service-commission-1908734.

Dawuni, J. (2015). Gender and the Judiciary in Africa: An introduction. In: Bauer, G. & Dawuni, J. (eds). *Gender and the judiciary in Africa: From obscurity to parity?* Routledge.

———. (2015) Ghana: The Paradox of Judicial Stagnation. In: Bauer, G. & Dawuni, J. (eds). *Gender and the judiciary in Africa: From obscurity to parity?* Routledge. http://works.bepress.com/josephine-dawuni/15/.

Dawuni, J., & Kang, A. (2015). Her ladyship chief justice: The rise of female leaders in the judiciary in Africa, *Africa Today, 62*(2), 45–69. https://doi.org/10.2979/africatoday.62.2.45.

Dawuni, J., & Kuenyehia, A. (2019). International Courts and the African Woman Judge: Unveiled Narratives. *Feminist Legal Studies,* 27, 357–360. https://doi.org/10.1007/s10691-019-09402-5.

Dawuni, J., & Masengu, T. (2020). Process and Progress: Women and Judicial Appointments to the Bench in Nigeria and Zambia. *Law and Courts* http://works.bepress.com/josephine-dawuni/8/.

Dupper, O., & Sankaran, K. (2014). *Affirmative Action: A view from the Global South.* SUN PReSS.

Escobar, M. C., Hoekstra, V. J., Kang, A., & Kittilson, M. (2021). Breaking the judicial glass ceiling: The appointment of women to high courts world-wide. *Journal of Politics, 83*(2), 662–674. https://doi.org/10.1086/710017.

Goetz, A. (2002). No Short Cuts to Power: Constraints on Women's Political Effectiveness in Uganda. *Journal of Modern African Studies, 40*(4), 549–575. https://doi.org/10.1017/S0022278X02004032.

Hale, B., & Hunter, R. (2008). A Conversation with Baroness Hale. *Feminist Legal Studies, 16* (2), 237–248. https://doi.org/10.1007/s10691-008-9090-5.

International Bar Association. (2007). Judicial independence undermined: A report on Uganda. *An International Bar Association Human Rights Institute Report.*

International Commission of Jurists. (2014). Women and the Judiciary. Geneva Forum Series No.1. *International Commission of Jurists.* www.icj.org.

———. (2016). Egypt's Judiciary: A tool of Repression. Lack of Effective Guarantees of Independence and Accountability. *International Commission of Jurists.* https://www.refworld.org/docid/586e71ea4.html.

International Development Law Organisation. (2018). Women Delivering Justice: Contributions, Barriers, Pathways. *International Development Law Organization Publications.* https://www.idlo.int/publications/women-delivering-justice-contributions-barriers-pathways.

Kakaire, S., & Kiyonga, D. (2015). Museveni's choice of judges for promotion raises questions. *The Observer.* Retrieved from https://observer.ug/news-headlines/39903-museveni-s-choice-of-judges-for-promotion-raises-questions.

Karimi, F., & Thompson, N. (2015). Uganda's president signs anti-gay bill into law. *CNN.* Retrieved from http://edition.cnn.com/2014/02/24/world/africa/uganda-anti-gay-bill/index.html.

Kenney, S. J. (2002). Breaking the Silence: Gender Mainstreaming and the Composition of the European Court of Justice, *Feminist Legal Studies, 10,* 258–270. https://doi.org/10.1023/A:1021227929264.

———. (2012). Choosing Judges: A Bumpy Road to Women's Equality and a Long Way to Go. *Michigan State Law Review, 2012*, 1499. https://ssrn.com/abstract=3324682.

———. (2013). *Gender and Justice: Why women in the Judiciary Really Matter*. Routledge.

———. (2018). Measuring Women's Judicial Empowerment as Part of Political Empowerment. In: Alexander, A., Bolzendahl, C., & Jalalzai, F. (eds). *Measuring Women's Political Empowerment across the Globe: Gender and Politics*. (pp. 207–227). Palgrave Macmillian. https://doi.org/10.1007/978-3-319-64006-8_10.

Kirby, M. D. (1986). Lord Denning: An Antipodean Appreciation. *Denning Law Journal, 1*(1). https://doi.org/10.5750/dlj.v1i1.153.

Kiyonga, D. (2017), Justice Bossa hits out at the JSC for denying her Kavuma's job. *The Observer*. Retrieved from https://observer.ug/news/headlines/54226-justice-bossa-hits-out-at-jsc-for-denying-her-kavuma-s-job.

Lieven, N. (2017). Increasing Judicial Diversity. *JUSTICE*. www.justice.org.uk.

Local Council Courts Act. (2006). https://www.ugandalaws.com/principal-legislation/local-council-courts-act-2006.

Magistrates Court Act. Chapter 16, Laws of Uganda. https://ulii.org/akn/ug/act/1998/10/eng%402020-02-14.

Malleson, K. (2006). Rethinking the Merit Principle in Judicial Selection. *Journal of Law and Society, 33*(1), 126–140. https://doi.org/10.1111/j.1467-6478.2006.00351.x.

———. (2003). Prospects for parity: the positions of women in the judiciary in England and Wales. In: Shaw, G., & Schultz, U. (eds.) *Women in the world's legal profession. Onati international series in law & society* (pp. 175–190). Hart Publishing. http://www.waterstones.com/waterstonesweb/advanced.

Martin, E. (1993). The Representative Role of Women Judges. *Judicature, 77(*3), 166–172. www.ojp.gov.

Masengu, T. (2016). It's a Man's World: Barriers of Gender Transformation in the South African Judiciary: Perspectives from Women Advocates and Attorneys. *International Journal of the Legal Profession,* 1–15. https://doi.org/10.1080/09695958.2016.1179639.

———. (2016). Gender transformation as a means of enhancing perceptions of impartiality on the bench. *South African Law Journal, 133*(3), 475–490. http://hdl.handle.net/1854/LU-8555847.

———. (2017). The Vulnerability of Judges in Contemporary Africa: Alarming Trends. *Indiana University Press, 63*(4), 3–19. https://doi.org/10.2979/africatoday.63.4.01.

Mugambwa, J. (1989). A 'Protected State' in the Uganda Protectorate? Re-Examination of Buganda's Colonial Legal Status. *African Journal of International and Comparative Law, 1*(3), 446–465. http://researchrepository.murdoch.edu.au/id/eprint/15694.

Mukholi, D. (1995). *A complete guide to Uganda's Fourth Constitution: History, politics and the law*. Fountain Publishers.

Mukiibi, E. & Kafeero, S. (2019). Judges who have ruled against Museveni. *Daily Monitor*. Retrieved from https://mobile.monitor.co.ug/News/Judges-Museveni

-Amama-Mbabazi--Oder-Mwangusya/2466686-5079758-format-xhtml-h0vx6h/index.html.

Musamali, G. (2002). Faith Mwondha the tough IGG. *New Vision*. Retrieved from https://www.newvision.co.ug/new_vision/news/1164584/faith-mwondha-tough-igg.

Musoke, J. (2017). Justice Mugambe's ruling on lost baby offered mothers ray of hope. *Daily Monitor*. Retrieved from https://www.monitor.co.ug/uganda/oped/commentary/justice-mugambe-s-ruling-on-lost-baby-offered-mothers-ray-of-hope-1706834.

Mushoborozi, T. (2018). Celebrating women who broke the gender Barrier. *Daily Monitor*. Retrieved from https://www.monitor.co.ug/artsculture/Reviews/Celebrating-women-who-broke-the-gender-barrier/691232-5012112-o7logmz/index.html.

Mutibwa, P. (1992). *Uganda since independence: A story of unfulfilled hopes*. Africa World Press.

Muwanga v. Kintu, High Court Divorce Appeal No. 135 of 1997.

Nantume, G. (2018). Justice Bbosa at a glance. *Daily Monitor*. Retrieved from https://www.monitor.co.ug/Magazines/Full-Woman/Justice-Bossa-glance/689842-4289612-vi85mfz/index.html.

New Vision. (2018). Justice Lillian Tibatemwa elected to commission of jurists. Retrieved from https://www.newvision.co.ug/new_vision/news/1472007/justice-lillian-tibatemwa-elected-international-court.

Ntambala Fred v. Uganda, Criminal Appeal No. 34 of 2015.

Odoki, J. (2005). *The Search for a National Consensus: the Making of the 1995 Uganda Constitution*. Fountain Publishers.

Okudo, I. (2016). Cadre judges killing court image-Justice Tsekooko. *Daily Monitor*. Retrieved from https://www.monitor.co.ug/News/National/Cadre-judges-killing-court-image-Justice-Tsekooko/688334-3182116-9c2qp8z/index.html.

———. (2018). Uganda's age limit ruling: A thin line between politics and law, *The Citizen*. Retrieved from https://www.thecitizen.co.tz/magazine/politicalreforms/1843776-4692034-f1myrf/index.html.

Phillip, E. V. (1933). Some Characteristics of the Good Judge of Personality. *The Journal of Social Psychology, 4*(1), 42–57. https://doi.org/10.1080/00224545.1933.9921556.

Rabe, J. (2001). *Equality, Affirmative Action and Justice*. Books on Demand.

Rtd Col. Dr. Kizza Besigye v Electoral Commission & Yoweri Kaguta Museveni (Election Petition No. 1 of 2006) [2007] UGSC 24.

Sahr, J. K. (1992). *Democratization in Africa: African views, African voices*. Washington, DC: The National Academies Press. https://doi.org/10.17226/2041.

Sherry, S. (1986). The Gender of Judges. *Law and Equality: A Journal of Theory and Practice 4*(1). University of Minnesota Libraries Publishing https://scholarship.law.umn.edu/lawineq/vol4/iss1/13.

Schroeder, M. (2002). Judging with a Difference. *Yale Journal of Law and Feminism, 14*(2). https://digitalcommons.law.yale.edu/yjlf/vol14/iss2/7.

Tamale, S. (1999). *When Hens Begin to Crow. Gender and Parliamentary Politics in Uganda*. Routledge.

The Constitution of the Republic of Uganda. (1995). https://statehouse.go.ug/sites/default/files/attachments/Constitution_1995.pdf.

Thembo, J. (2018). Lady Justice Prof. Tibatemwa elected to the ICJ. *Insider*. Retrieved from https://theinsider.ug/index.php/2018/03/02/lady-justice-prof-tibatemwa-elected-to-the-icj/.

The Independent. (2017). Uganda's justice Solomy Balungi Bossa elected ICC judge. https://www.independent.co.ug/ugandas-justice-solomy-balungi-bossa-elected-icc-judge/.

The Judiciary. (2020). Republic of Uganda; National Association of Women Judges-Uganda. https://judiciary.go.ug/data/smenu/84/National%20Association%20of%20Women%20Judges.html.

The Judiciary. (2020). Republic of Uganda. Judicial officers http://www.judiciary.go.ug/data/smenu/91/Judicial.

United Nations. (2019). *Achieving Gender Equality, Women's Empowerment and Strengthening Development Cooperation: Dialogues at the Economic and Social Council*. United Nations Publications.

Uganda v. Peter Matovu, Criminal Case No. 146/2001.

Uganda Association of Women Lawyers and Others v. Attorney-General, Const. Petition No. 2 of 2003, [2004] UGCC 1.

Van De Vijver, L. (ed). (2006). *The judicial institution in Southern Africa: A comparative study of common law jurisdictions*. University of Cape Town. Siber Inc Publishers.

Wachira, M. (2018). Africa's constitutional democracies: The case of a dissolving picture. *The East African*. Retrieved from https://www.theeastafrican.co.ke/tea/news/rest-of-africa/africa-s-constitutional-democracies-the-case-of-a-dissolving-picture-13858.

Wekesa, A. (2014). We have received public backlash for annulling the anti-gay law. *Daily Monitor*. Retrieved from https://www.monitor.co.ug/News/National/We-have-received-public-backlash-for-annulling-antigay-law/688334-2469726-jxprxhz/index.html.

Wirth, L., & International Labour Office. (2001). *Breaking through the glass ceiling: Women in management*. Geneva: International Labor Office. https://www.ilo.org/public/libdoc/ilo/2001/101B09_102_engl.pdf.

Part II

WOMEN AND ACCESS TO THE COURTROOM

Chapter 10

Women's Property Rights and Discriminatory Land Tenure Systems in Ghana

The Adjudicative Role of Courts

Michael Addaney

INTRODUCTION

The right to property is a fundamental pillar of all democratic societies and may encompass any "vested interest" (Alias and Daud, 2006: 326). However, access to land is possibly the fundamental thrust of all property rights and is important for developing countries, where land makes up three-quarters of wealth (De Soto, 2000; USAID, 2005; Deininger, 2003). For many people, access to land is essential for attaining a dignified life (Gelbspan and Thea 2013). Gilbert (2013: 116) asserts that land rights serve as a catalyst for economic growth, social development, and poverty alleviation, making it a crucial issue for "social justice and equality." For instance, access to land constitutes the basis of access to food, housing, and development, and the lack of access creates vulnerability and economic insecurity for many people (Commission on Human Rights, 2002, 2005). Despite the importance of land in the lives of many people, UN Habitat (2008) estimated that half of the world's rural population faces insecure property rights in land and about a quarter of the world's people are landless, making insecure land titles and landlessness major contributory factors in poverty and food insecurity around the world. The situation is exacerbated by sociocultural factors in Africa (Knight, 2020) that make access to land a human rights issue.

Despite the significance of the right to land, in Ghana, land is generally governed by customary law (Agyeman-Budu, 2017) and thus, the prevailing patriarchal customs of many ethnic and tribal groups in Ghana have disadvantaged women when it comes to the ownership of and access to land (Addaney et al. 2022). Article 36(8) of the 1992 Constitution of Ghana provides that

> the State shall recognise that ownership and possession of land carry a social obligation to serve the larger community and, in particular, the State shall recognise that the managers of public, stool, skin and family lands are fiduciaries charged with the obligation to discharge their functions for the benefit respectively of the people of Ghana, of the stool, skin, or family concerned and are accountable as fiduciaries in this regard.

This implies that the Constitution guarantees the right to property for all and further recognizes the role of customary law in land governance since land is primarily owned by customary institutions. The pivotal role of customary law in land governance and the need for the courts to strike a balance with protection of women's right to property are essential for ensuring inclusive and equitable ownership and access to productive resources. The use of customary law by traditional courts and the Lands Commission has often left a trail of unsolved problems, such as unpaid compensation to women, absence of consultation with land-owning women, and compulsory transfer of land from women to men to the dissatisfaction of the original owners (see Agyeman-Budu, 2017).

This chapter uses a doctrinal method and insights from the human rights-based approach to development to evaluate relevant literature and case law on women, customary law, land rights, and related issues. Human rights obligations have the potential to inform and strengthen international and national legal response to inequalities within land governance regimes (Nyarko, 2019). The human rights-based approach is theoretically and substantively grounded on international human rights norms and principles, which are operationally directed toward the promotion, protection, and fulfillment of human rights (Office of the High Commissioner for Human Rights, 2015). This approach is underpinned by the notion that policies, programs, and plans are to be anchored in a system of rights and corresponding obligations established by law (Office of the High Commissioner for Human Rights, 2014: 16). Thus, it analyzes obligations, inequalities, and vulnerabilities to redress discriminatory practices and unjust distributions of power that impede progress and undercut human rights (Orellana, 2012). The literature was obtained from existing scholarly works, policy documents, and reports from global, national, and local levels. The analysis focused on peer-reviewed articles, books, and reports on women, customary law, and land rights in Ghana using Google Scholar, WorldCat and Google search, SAGE Journals online, JSTOR, and CAB International.

This study also made use of legal and policy documents and reports, such as judicial decisions and quasi-judicial reports. National and local level literature review focused on women and gendered land tenure systems and legislation obtained from national and decentralized institutions such as the Lands Commission. All literature was streamlined and integrated to provide a framework for analyzing women, customary law, land rights, and the refereeing role of the courts in Ghana. This chapter discusses the theoretical and conceptual grounding of women's access to property, situating it in the land tenure and customary rights paradigm, then appraises the international and regional human rights framework on women's right to property. It next evaluates the role of Ghanaian courts in striking a balance between customary law and human rights to safeguard women's property right and finally offers conclusions and recommendations.

WOMEN, LAND TENURE SYSTEMS, AND ACCESS TO PROPERTY IN GHANA: THEORETICAL AND CONCEPTUAL ANALYSIS

The concept of "tenure" is a social construct that expresses the relationship between individuals and groups of individuals by which rights and obligations concerning control and use of land are defined (Nyarko, 2019). The system of landholding (land tenure) has evolved over the years concerning land as a natural resource, its use, and development. Land tenure involves the various laws, rules, and obligations governing the holding and/or ownership of rights and interest in land (Nyinevi, 2017). It also can refer to the way in which rights to land are obtained and distributed. Land tenure in Ghana is generally communal in nature, with land collectively owned by an extended family, clan, or community of ancestrally related people with the control or administration of the land vested in the leader or his appointee. This has determined the nature of land administration over the years. All land in Ghana is governed by customary laws, notably those related to transfer of title (Nyarko, 2019). The customary system has been the most robust system in practice, estimated to hold 80–90% of all underdeveloped land in Ghana, though with varying tenure management systems (Kassanga and Kotey, 2001).

Land tenure security continues to pose a challenge to actual and potential users. Tenure security is an important issue contributing to changes in tenure regimes in Ghana. Two factors crystalize the problem of tenure insecurity, namely, the right of ownership under a particular tenure system, and inequitable distribution or sharing of land under certain tenure system. There have been efforts by governments and subnational institutions to make the tenure system a mechanism for realizing gender equity, poverty reduction, efficiency, and sustainable resources (UNDP, 2005; Toulmin, 2000; Cotula, Toulmin and Quan, 2006). For instance, international development agendas such as the expired Millennium Development Goals and the current Sustainable Development Goals contain targets on ensuring equitable ownership and access to land and other productive resources (e.g., SDG 5 Target 5A). Target 5A provides for equal rights to economic resources, property ownership, and financial services.

According to the UN, this target obliges governments to undertake reforms to give women equal rights to economic resources, as well as access to ownership and control over land and other forms of property, financial services, inheritance, and natural resources, in accordance with national laws (UN SDG Tracker, 2016). The Ghana Shared Growth and Development Agenda II (2014–2017) underscored the relevance of ensuring inclusive access to and ownership of land (National Development Planning Commission of Ghana, 2015). However, using land tenure as a tool for achieving these goals is not easy because of the complexities of traditional land tenure that require multidimensional solutions tailored to respond to cultural, political, and economic demands at various levels (Cotula, 2007). These complications have led to some reforms in Ghana whereby the government seeks to replace the customary tenure system with an equitable and responsive system to enhance tenure security to foster inclusive economic growth, encourage sustainable development, and reduce poverty (Toulmin and Quan, 2000; Cotula, 2007; World Bank, 2005). Achieving an equitable land tenure system requires addressing gender inequalities and discrimination embedded in customary land norms and practices (Addadzi-Koom and Nkansah, 2021). Cotula et al. (2006:2) argue that:

> Securing equitable land rights requires developing and implementing policy, legal and practical tools that are appropriate for different groups and circumstances and that pay special attention to specific land tenure needs for poorer and more vulnerable groups; supporting democratic land institutions and land administration systems that are decentralized and problem centered, and that makes links with existing indigenous and customary mechanisms for managing land; improving access to effective systems of land dispute resolution, including courts, alternative dispute resolution and customary procedures.

The prevailing right to land (property) and sociocultural norms adversely affects women's ownership of and access to land. This manifests through various existing stereotypes such as the confinement of women to food production while men dominate cash crop production.

Land ownership and the customary land tenure system are very important in Ghana, and the chiefs and their people will strongly oppose any sweeping attempt to intervene (Mends and Meijere, 2006). This not notwithstanding, the new Land Act of 2020 (Act 1036) requires all stools, skin, clan, or family that own land to establish a Customary Land Secretariat.[1] Land ownership in Ghana can broadly be divided into three main categories: customary ownership, state ownership, and split (partnership between the state and the customary owners) (Nyarko, 2019). Bebelleh (2009: 23) conceptualizes customary land ownership as follows:

> Where the right to use or to dispose of use-rights over land rest neither on the exercise of brute force, nor on the evidence of rights guaranteed by government statute, but on the fact that they are recognised as legitimate by the community, the rules governing the acquisition and transmission of these rights being usually explicitly and generally known, though not normally recorded in writing.

Thus, the issue of land and its ownership is linked with customs, systems, and values of that community, which grounds the social, political, and religious beliefs of the people. Land tenure is also theorized as the system of landholding that has evolved from peculiar political and economic circumstances, cultural norms, and religious norms. It includes rules, regulations, and institutional structures, both customary and enacted legislation which influences the holding and appropriation of land and its resources for socioeconomic reasons (Ubink, 2018). Land tenure differs from community to community and spells out the land-use system of a particular community or society. Institutional arrangements under which a person gains access to land largely determine, among other things, how long they can still use a piece of land, their rights over fruits of their labor, and their ability to undertake long-term improvements on land (Toulmin and Quan, 2000). Land tenure therefore plays an important role in the livelihood of people and a society's political, social, and economic structures.

There are various types and forms of land rights (Nyarko, 2019). These varieties help us to understand relationships between land rights and tenure security. To analyze these relationships between the existing tenure situation in an area and the applied methods of tenure regularization, the scale is redesigned as a breadth of tenure (Asperen, 2007). The scale is based on freehold, traditionally a Western concept that implies the absolute right to control, manage, use, and dispose of a piece of property (ECA, 2009). Statutory tenure systems are established by national governments. Generally, uniform rules and regulations are implemented by a central authority and a standard, codified registration system is used, in which ownership rights usually are ascribed to the person or persons whose name is on the title, deed, or registry, and sales and transfers can be executed with any willing buyer (Brooklings, 2011). Rules governing acquisition and transmission of those rights are usually explicit and generally known, though not normally recorded in writing. One of the main characteristics of customary tenure is the reciprocal relationship between membership of the family, tribe, or clan and access to land (Anaafo, 2015; Platteau, 2002). In general, any member of the group can return to their village and is entitled to use a piece of land, independent of the period of absence. Another characteristic is that community heads allocate unappropriated land (Ubink, 2018). In customary systems tenure rights are ostensibly controlled and allocated according to traditional practice (Brooklings, 2011).

The dominant land tenure system in Ghana is the customary system, in which the land ownership is vested in a collective (family, lineage, or clan) while the individual enjoys unrestricted rights of usage (Mends and Meijere, 2006). The head of such a collective is regarded as a symbol of the residuary, reversionary, and ultimate ownership of all land held by this community. The current system is characterized by the coexistence of different modes of supply originating at different stages of development. This complex mosaic can be traced to history, colonial legacy, and current economic pressures and opportunities, as well as natural and ecological characteristics. Mends and Meijere (2006) understand colonialism as adding to this complex tenure tradition and that after independence, most countries nationalized most of their land, including tracts of customary land in the name of social justice, equitable access to land, and prevention of speculation—making the imposition of a regime of state ownership of all lands in many African countries. However, Ghana still has indigenous tenure. Concerning customary landholding, the administration of stool lands is not without the extensive government regulation even though they are vested in the hands of the stool or kin. Article 267 of the 1992 Constitution[2] enshrines:

> A grant to a non-member of the land owning stool/skin requires the concurrence of the Lands Commission. All revenue in respect of stool/skin lands whether in the nature of capital or periodic payments including rents, royalties, etc. must be paid to the office of Administration of Stool Lands; and no freeholds can be granted of such lands, including customary freeholds.

This implies that the customary land tenure system is based on the belief that "land belongs to a vast family of which many are dead, few are living and countless numbers are still unborn" (Mends and Meijere, 2006). Apusigah (2006:5) argues for the use of "land rights" instead of "land ownership." According to Apusigah (2006), in customary jurisprudence, nobody can claim ownership rights. Everybody can claim access and control rights, including women and men who may have allodial and/or usufructory rights. Land ownership can at best be termed allodialship[3] and/or usufruction.

Therefore, landholding, rather than ownership, will be a more appropriate description in that context, as land property rights are classified into bundles of rights encompassing use, investment, exclusion, and transfer rights with and without permission from chiefs, family heads, community organization, and outside authorities (Nyarko, 2019; Quisumbing and Otsuka, 2001). Ownership rights are usually ascribed to the person or persons whose name is on the title although transfer can be done for a buyer of the land. The allodial and/or usufruction type of system entered Ghana through colonialism, where colonial masters implemented their rules and views pertaining to land rights (Nyarko, 2019).

Customary land tenure encompasses various land tenure system rather than a single tenure system under which land is owned either communally or individually. Quisumbing and Otsuka (2001) argue that there is a shift from communal to individualized tenure on the distribution of land in societies where the social order is moving from a strictly matrilineal system to an egalitarian system, in which sons and daughters inherit land from their parents with little or no gender bias. According to them, two forms of inheritance exist—ancestral and earned. Ancestral property is always inherited by women and passed on from mother to their daughters, while the earned property is relatively flexible and can be passed on to either gender (Quisumbing and Otsuka, 2001). Under communalization of land, property is not owned by a single person or family but rather the whole community. People outside the community cannot claim ownership, but those within can claim ownership of the land. Under communal ownership, uncultivated forest and woodland are owned by the community, where the chief or leader of the community controls the land (Quisumbing and Otsuka, 2001). This then moved from community owned to family owned, where cultivated lands were traditionally held by individual households and also by the extended family heads. Land held by the extended family is owned by the family, and members have access to it. As a result of population pressure, the growing profitability of agroforestry and expansion of tree-crop farming, there has been a gradual shift from the communally owned to individualized ownership over time where individuals own land privately (Bebelleh, 2009; Quisumbing et al., 2000). Individual land ownership is considered to be more secured, as it offers secured rights (Quisumbing and Otsuka, 2001).

Gender and kinship relations play a central role in the way land rights and production relations are determined (Bebelleh, 2009). Customary land tenure systems generally have clearly defined control over resources, which are gender segregated based on traditional norms that operate in such a way as to limit the land rights of women (Runger, 2006; Whitehead and Tsikata, 2003; Food and Agriculture Organization [FAO], 2006). Awumbilla (2002: 45) shows that women's access to ownership and control of productive resources is "to a large extent determined by kinship system headed by men in the families, customary laws, norms and practices that give them control over land, the allocation of land and other resources owned by the family." However, women contribute significantly to land development, such as agricultural production, and are the worst victims of poverty across Ghana because of the poor land tenure system (UNDP Human Development Report, 2019; FAO, 2006). FAO (2003: 09) underscores the need for land tenure policy frameworks that explicitly address gender inclusiveness in accessing land. Without this, women may be excluded from the benefits of land administration, management, and development schemes. This is reinforced by the prevailing norms in which land rights tend to be held by men or kinship groups controlled by men, with women having access mainly through a male relative, usually a father or husband. Even under this arrangement, women are customarily obliged to hand over proceeds of any farm sales to a male and have little say over how those earnings are used (Kimani, 2008).

Concerning the connection between women, land tenure, and property rights in Ghana, several factors limit women's property rights. For instance, poverty among women limits them from accessing land due to the complexities and cost of legal procedures involved, as well as lack of awareness of legal provisions on land acquisition (Bebelleh, 2009). As a result, most women are incapable of taking steps to assert their land rights and are in a position of considerable insecurity. In traditional settings, women generally tend to have lesser opportunity of complying with such formal processes because of their limited access to information and lack of financial resources (Addaney et al., 2022). The restricted access of women to formal structures for land management has been attributed to their higher rates of illiteracy, language barriers, and societal perceptions on the role of women regarding matters involving property (Addaney et al., 2022; Bebelleh, 2008). These challenges are exacerbated by a highly patriarchal inheritance system and tenurial arrangement that negatively influence women's land rights, access, ownership, and land uses (Bebelleh, 2006), as women usually acquire land through inheritance as wives, daughters, or sisters.

There are two systems of inheritance in Ghana: patrilineal (inheriting through the father's lineage) and matrilineal (inheriting through the mother's lineage). The inheritance system is generally skewed against women and girls in favor of men and boys (Bebelleh, 2008; Ameyaw and De Vries, 2021). Men often inherit family property as heads of family and leaders and thus have primary rights of inheritance of land and property, while women and girls have user rights mediated through their relationship to men.

On spousal property, the prevailing law developed by the courts is grounded on a broad constitutional provision that requires equitable distribution of property. For instance, Article 22 of the Constitution provides that:

> (1) A spouse shall not be deprived of a reasonable provision out of the estate of a spouse whether or not the spouse died having made a will. (2) Parliament shall, as soon as practicable after the coming into force of this Constitution, enact legislation regulating the property rights of spouses. (3) With a view to achieving the full realization of the rights referred to in clause (2) of this article—(a) spouses shall have equal access to property jointly acquired during marriage; (b) assets which are jointly acquired during marriage shall be distributed equitably between the spouses upon dissolution of the marriage.

The constitutional provision guarantees equitable right to property of all spouses, including women, whether due to death of the other spouse or divorce. However, the inability of Parliament to enact legislation as provided in this provision has worsened the challenges, impeding the effective implementation of women's property rights in Ghana. Generally, under Ghanaian customary law, a woman has the right to own property in her own name, and marriage has little to no effect on this exclusive proprietary right (Addadzi-Koom and Nkansah, 2021). A woman can therefore acquire property in her name before and after marriage since the theory of community property in marriage is foreign to Ghanaian customary law. Kuenyehia and Ofei-Aboagye (1998) argue that each spouse retains all property acquired through their individual efforts in their names.

Under Ghanaian customary law, the right of a woman to own self-acquired property in her name in marriage is only hindered when the woman and her husband jointly contribute for the maintenance of their household. Self-acquired property continues to remain the absolute property of the woman when her marriage ends, either through divorce or death of her spouse (Addadzi-Koom and Nkansah, 2021). However, recent cases show that judges are relying on their own culturally shaped notions of fairness, and standards of progressive thinking to ensure parity in tandem with the 1992 Constitution of Ghana which provides a seemingly more just standard for the distribution of marital property (Mensa-Bonsu and Mensa-Bonsu, 2021). The 1992 Constitution has therefore influenced the making of generally better judicial outcomes for wives and widows. For instance, in some cases, the court has decided that the wife was entitled to a share of the matrimonial estate ranging from one-third to half of the matrimonial estate (Mensa-Bonsu and Mensa-Bonsu, 2021, 45). It should, however, be acknowledged that in all those cases, the judges held that the wife had made a substantial and monetary contribution to the acquisition of the property. As would be discussed in subsequent sections, there has been progress toward the recognition of wives' marital property rights regardless of monetary contribution, or indeed, any input. However, the decisions have not always been consistent as expected.

CUSTOMARY LAW AND WOMEN'S RIGHT TO PROPERTY: INTERNATIONAL AND REGIONAL HUMAN RIGHTS DIMENSIONS

This section discusses customary law and women's rights to property in relation to international and regional law and assesses whether Ghana's law on right to landed property conforms to those international standards. Ghana has signed and ratified several international and regional treaties that impose legal obligations on the country. However, the legal effect and impact of some of these treaties is uncertain as Ghana, a dualistic state,[4] has in the past consistently failed to "domesticate" such treaties (Nyarko, 2019; 1992 Constitution of Ghana, Article 75). The right to property can be traced to the Universal Declaration of Human Rights (UDHR), which is the cornerstone of contemporary international human rights law (Schabas, 2013). Article 17 of the UDHR (1948) provides that "everyone has the right to own property alone as well as in association with others" and that "no one shall be arbitrarily deprived of his property." This provision thus recognizes the fundamental nature of the right to property and prohibits other factors that may interfere with the enjoyment of the right. Article 17 protects both individual and collective property ownership rights but has been criticized for its vagueness, especially in failing to provide guidance on the normative content and scope of the right and the types of property rights that may be owned (Sprankling, 2012: 461). Despite its ambiguity, Article 17 has played a significant role in affirming the right to property and has become the standard by which the United Nations General Assembly has repeatedly called on states to respect the right to property.[5] The antidiscrimination stance of the UDHR on property ownership implies that discriminatory sociocultural practices and norms that prohibit certain groups from owning property should be outlawed.

The right to property was omitted from the International Covenant on Civil and Political Rights (ICCPR) and the International Covenant on Economic, Social and Cultural Rights (ICESCR) due to disagreements between the negotiating states about the extent that states could restrict the right (van Banning, 2002; Schabas 1991; Krause, 2001). However, this omission has been addressed through the explicit protection of the right to property in some group-specific treaties preceding the covenants. For instance, the Convention on the Elimination of All Forms of Discrimination Against Women in Article 16(1)(h) provides as follows:

> (1) States Parties shall take all appropriate measures to eliminate discrimination against women in all matters relating to marriage and family relations

> and in particular shall ensure, on a basis of equality of men and women: . . . (h) The same rights for both spouses in respect of the ownership, acquisition, enjoyment and disposition of property, whether free of charge or for a valuable consideration.

In this regard, Article 26 of the ICCPR provides a free-standing right to nondiscrimination of all forms, including enjoying the right to property, even though the right to property is not specifically guaranteed in the ICCPR. Aside from conventional human rights law, there is compelling evidence to support a conclusion that the right to property has assumed a rule of customary international law. State practice is almost unanimous on the recognition of the right to property, as evidenced by the inclusion of the right to property in the constitutions and legislation of 95% of the 193 UN member states (Sprankling, 2012). Shortcomings of the right to property under the international human rights regime have been remedied by regional human rights systems, including the African human rights system.

Most regional human rights systems recognize the right to property and encompass the right to procedural fairness in matters relating to the right to property.[6] Under the African human rights system that is applicable to Ghana, Article 18(3) of the African Charter makes provision for the elimination of discrimination against women and children: "The State shall ensure the elimination of every discrimination against women and also ensure the protection of the rights of women and the child as stipulated in international declarations and conventions." The right to property is protected under Article 14 of the African Charter as follows:

> The right to property shall be guaranteed. It may only be encroached upon in the interest of public need or in the general interest of the community and in accordance with the provisions of appropriate laws.

Subsequent instruments, such as the Protocol to the African Charter on Human and Peoples' Rights on the Rights of Women in Africa (Maputo Protocol), also protect the right of women to own property (Article 6[j]). Article 21 of the protocol further provided for the right to inheritance and enumerates that:

> (1) A widow shall have the right to an equitable share in the inheritance of the property of her husband. A widow shall have the right to continue to live in the matrimonial house. In case of remarriage, she shall retain this right if the house belongs to her or she has inherited it. (2) Women and men shall have the right to inherit, in equitable shares, their parents' properties.

The Maputo Protocol also provides for the right to land as one of the key elements of the right to food security (Article 15[a]). It further requires states to guarantee all women the right to property as an essential component of the right to sustainable development (Article 19[c]). Unlike Protocol No. 1 to the European Convention on Human Rights and American Convention on Human Rights, the ACHPR does not provide details of the right holders (whether individuals, groups, or legal persons), nor the normative content of the right. It merely commits states to guarantee the right to property (Ouguergouz, 2003). The inclusion of the right to property in the ACHPR has been criticized by Oloka-Onyango (1995: 49) as being of questionable facility in the African context, given the varied tenure systems in African societies and the fear that the right to property ultimately advantages customary, communal, or patriarchal interests.

Additionally, the African Commission on Human and Peoples' Rights (African Commission) has provided some clarity on the nature of the right through several soft-law instruments. For example, the *Principles and Guidelines on Economic, Social and Cultural Rights in the African Charter* adopted by the African Commission in 2011 provides that the right to property protects the rights of both individuals and groups to the acquisition and peaceful enjoyment of property. It provides that the right to property protects the communal ownership of land and other natural resources and places an obligation on states to ensure security of tenure and to prevent interference by third parties as well as state agents (African Commission, 2011). The *State Party Reporting Guidelines for Economic, Social and Cultural Rights in the African Charter* adopted by the African Commission in the same year mirrors these requirements and emphasizes the obligations of states to report on legislative and practical measures taken to ensure the enjoyment of the right to property on a nondiscriminatory basis (African Commission, 2011). Ghana has not explicitly domesticated most of the international and regional human rights instruments it has ratified, including the African Charter and Maputo Protocol. The vacuum left by the omission of the right to property in the ICCPR and the ICESCR has led to the development of many soft-law instruments aimed at addressing property rights in land and providing guidelines to be adhered to when the right is interfered with.[7]

This section shows how factors such as cultural and social norms and poverty have played out in perpetuating prevailing inequalities in women's right to land and property in Ghana and underscored the emerging and important role of courts in this scheme of events. It sets the stage for the next section, which critically analyzes case law and other emerging legislative developments addressing the challenges resulting from inequitable land governance.

EXISTING LAWS ON WOMEN'S PROPERTY RIGHTS IN GHANA

Similar to other African countries, Ghana operates a pluralist land tenure system consisting of state-sanctioned land titles and land held under customary law as discussed before. Both systems are recognized by the 1992 Constitution (Constitution of Ghana, Articles 36(8) and 257). About 80% of land in Ghana is held under customary systems (Ubink and Quan, 2008). The remaining 20% is held by government and individual freehold owners (Akrofi and Whittal, 2013). Customary law in Ghana is relative to specific tribes, ethnicities, and communities and is generally unwritten. Land governance in Ghana is plagued with a lot of constraints, including insecurity of tenure, inadequate land policy and gendered inequalities, and related problems with acquiring the right to land. The prevailing challenges are mostly due to the legal framework for land administration (Agyeman-Budu, 2017). For instance, the legal regime for land administration consists of constitutional provisions, policy instruments, statutory enactments, judicial decisions, common law principles, and customary laws and practices that have been enacted and developed over the years to regulate land rights. The courts also have ruled on customary law issues, resulting in a body of legal precedents for some land-related customs.

Until recently, there were some 166 laws regulating land administration that established 13 different mandates for different agencies (Nyarko, 2019; Agyeman-Budu, 2017; Quaye, 2006). This sometimes leads to conflicts between various judicial decisions from courts of coordinate jurisdiction whose judgments are of equal legal force (Daily Graphic, 2021). There also were inconsistencies between legislative provisions and the 1992 Constitution, creating confusion and increased incidents of land litigation as various parties contest the import and practical consequences of the varied interpretations of land laws in Ghana. The new Land Act of 2020 (Act 1036, section 282) therefore marks a watershed for land administration in the country, by revising, consolidating, and harmonizing the laws on land to ensure sustainable land administration and effective land tenure and to provide for related matters.

The 1992 Constitution (of Ghana) in Article 18(1) expressly provides for the right of everyone to own property "alone or in association with others." However, the right to property may be interfered with in accordance with laws that are "necessary in a free and democratic society" for the public safety, the economic well-being of the state, and the protection of the rights of others. The extent to which these customary land rights are protected under Ghanaian law and how that affects women's right to property as well as the intervening role of the court are examined in the next section. The legal framework governing property rights in Ghana includes the 1992 Constitution of Ghana, legislation, and other policies.[8] Chapter 5 of the 1992

Constitution covers fundamental human rights and freedoms. In terms of women's property rights, Article 22 of the Constitution captioned, "Property Rights of Spouses," provides that:

> (1) A spouse shall not be deprived of a reasonable provision out of the estate of a spouse whether or not the spouse died having made a will. (2) Parliament shall, as soon as practicable after the coming into force of this Constitution, enact legislation regulating the property rights of spouses. (3) With a view to achieving the full realization of the rights referred to in clause (2) of this article—(a) spouses shall have equal access to property jointly acquired during marriage; (b) assets which are jointly acquired during marriage shall be distributed equitably between the spouses upon dissolution of the marriage.

This provision is important for a number of reasons. First, it provides generally for the property rights of all spouses, including women—whether as a result of the death of the other spouse or upon the dissolution of marriage. Second, and most importantly, the legislature is obliged to pass legislation that regulates the property rights of spouses. Finally, it is quite clear from the wording of Article 22(2) that the framers of the Constitution must have envisaged the prolonged delay that was to beset the enactment of the law regulating the property rights of spouses. This is evidenced from the use of the words "*as soon as practicable* in clause (2) of article 22."[9] The failure of Parliament to enact this legislation to date has allowed the existing gendered ownership and access to land in some ethnic groups in the country to persist and thus weakens the effective implementation of women's property rights in Ghana. Although not yet in force, the Property Rights of Spouses Bill holds promise to comprehensively deal with the subject. For instance, Article 22(3) requires spouses to have equal access to property jointly acquired during marriage and for matrimonial property to be equitably distributed between the spouses upon termination of the marriage.

The Matrimonial Causes Act of 1971 (Act 367) is meant "to provide for matrimonial causes and for other matters connected therewith." In terms of the property rights of women upon a divorce or dissolution of marriage, sections 19 and 20 of Act 367 are relevant. Section 19 states that:

> The Court may, whenever it thinks just and equitable, award maintenance pending suit or financial provision to either party to the marriage, but no order for maintenance pending suit or financial provision shall be made until the court has considered the standard of living of the parties and their circumstances.

Similarly, section 20 provides as follows:

> (1) The Court may order either party to the marriage to pay to the other party such sum of money or convey to the other party such movable or immovable

property as settlement of property rights or in lieu thereof or as part of financial provision as the court thinks just and equitable. (2) Payments and conveyances under this section may be ordered to be made in gross or by instalments.

These provisions ensure that both women and men, especially women, are taken care of financially and property wise in the event of a dissolution of marriage. This is because it is an irrefutable fact that women for decades have been discriminated against, especially customarily, upon the dissolution of marriage or death of their husbands. The law was therefore intended as a corrective measure for this unjust state of affairs. Aside from monetary compensation, the court can order property (both movable and immovable) to be transferred to one party as part of financial settlement. These provisions leave no doubt that women's property rights in Ghana are designed to be protected and safeguarded during and after divorce proceedings.

Customary Law, the Courts, and Advancing Women's Property Rights in Ghana

The dynamics of the law governing property rights in Ghana and associated customs make courts the last hope for women. Consequently, the legal codification of customary law and human rights is arguably a sure means of enforcing their protection. The case of *Quartey v. Martey* was arguably the starting point for the "oppression" of women in terms of their property rights in post-independent Ghana (1959 GLR: 377). The case involved the plaintiff (wife of the deceased), who sued her deceased husband's family, claiming among other things, a share of her deceased husband's property as she had assisted the late husband financially during his lifetime and had given active assistance to him in all the jobs he did. The court, presided over by the late Justice Ollenu, held as follows:

> By customary law it is a domestic responsibility of a man's wife and children to assist him in the carrying out of the duties of his station in life, for instance, farming or business. The proceeds of this joint effort of a man and his wife and/or children, and any property which the man acquires with such proceeds are by customary law the individual property of the man. It is not the joint property of the man and the wife and/or children. The right of the wife and the children is a right to maintenance and support from the husband and father. . . . I must hold that, in the absence of strong evidence to the contrary, any property a man acquires with the assistance or joint effort of his wife, is the individual property of the husband and not joint property of the husband and the wife. (377)

This implied that women were essentially not eligible to inherit property from the estate of their deceased husbands even if they contributed in their acquisition. Thus, this rule, espoused by the court, was for many years the standard that prevailed in terms of the property rights of women—especially those married under customary law. However, in 1971, there was a glimmer of hope when the Matrimonial Causes Act (Act 367) was enacted.

Section 20(1) of the act led to the courts moving toward the development of the principle of "substantial contribution" as the primary determinant of the property rights of women upon the breakdown of a marriage, be it customary or otherwise. Subsequently in the case of *Abebrese v. Kaah*, Sarkodee J in distinguishing the present case from *Quartey v. Martey* held that

> the rule of customary law that property acquired by a husband with the assistance of his wife and children became the property of the husband alone took its root from the fundamental principle of customary law that the wife and children were dependent upon the husband. That was not the case here. (46)

These decisions by the courts demonstrate that a woman's contribution should be in excess of the assistance contemplated by customary law in order to be entitled as joint owner of the property. The doctrine of "substantial contribution" produced mixed results as the courts were clearly seen to be moving away from the *Quartey v. Martey* epoch, where women could not even have a share of matrimonial property. Consequently, in *Yeboah v. Yeboah*, the high court essentially overruled the decision in *Quartey v. Martey* by holding that no rule of customary law prevented joint ownership of property by spouses. The court thus took account of the wife's indirect contributions in the form of time and effort (such as supervising the construction of the house) toward the acquisition of the house. The court held that although it was difficult to quantify such contributions in monetary terms, a woman's combined direct and indirect contribution entitled her to an equal share of the house with the husband. In *Mensah v. Mensah*, the applicant sought a share of the property on the basis that she had contributed equally in economic terms to the acquisition of property through her earnings at their stores (SCGLR, 1998: 350). The Supreme Court in applying the "equality is equity" principle underpinning Article 22 of the Constitution held that

> the principle that property jointly acquired during marriage becomes joint property of the parties applies and such property should be shared equally on divorce; because the ordinary incidents of commerce has no application in marital relations between husband and wife who jointly acquired property during marriage. (350)

The court clearly favored the equal sharing of joint property in circumstances where it is established that both parties contributed directly or indirectly toward the acquisition of the property. Akrofi and Whittal (2013: 280) argue that if it was established that the parties jointly contributed (financially) to the property acquisition, the property should be shared equally because the courts would not reduce the marital relationship to a commercial arrangement and reduce the sharing of joint marital property to mathematical calculations.

The case of *Gladys Mensah v. Stephen Mensah* (SCGLR, 2012: 391) further broadened the scope of the substantial equality principle when the court reinterpreted the doctrine and outlined some of its fundamental parts. The court held that

> this Court is of the considered view that the Petitioner's contribution even as a housewife, in maintaining the house and creating a congenial atmosphere for the respondent to create the economic empire he has built are enough to earn for her an equal share in the marital properties on offer for distribution upon the decree of divorce. From the evidence on the record, this court will not permit the respondent to use the petitioner as a donkey and after offering useful and valuable service dump her without any regard for her rights as a human being. (391)

The decision by the court in this case guaranteed that women's property rights deriving from marriage become grounded and protected in the law. The fact that the court boldly asserted that domestic chores, however menial or unquantifiable they may be, entitled women to an equitable share in marital property was a step in the right direction toward actual equality in women's ownership and access to land and other properties during divorce or death of partner. Unfortunately, this victory was somewhat short-lived, for the court subsequently produced another decision that some scholars, such as Quaye (2006), deemed as a step backward for the protection of women's property rights in Ghana. In the case of *Quartson v. Quartson*, it was held that the decision in *Gladys Mensah v. Stephen Mensah* was not to be misconstrued. The court warned that its earlier decision was "not to be taken as a blanket ruling which affords spouses unwarranted access to property they were not entitled to." Contrary to this, the court expected all cases to be decided on their merits thereof. Fortunately, the Supreme Court in *Arthur v. Arthur* "redeemed" itself. The case involved a couple who had been married for about a decade. The petitioner alleged that during their stay in France, where the respondent was a professional footballer, he had prevented her from taking up gainful employment, as she was required to essentially drive him as well as their children everywhere. As a result of this arrangement, she alleged that they agreed that his earnings and any property acquired during the subsistence of the marriage were their joint property. The court reaffirmed its belief in the "equality is equity" principle. Its recent decision in *Adjei v. Adjei* (2021) also underscored the equality is equity principle. For instance, the court held that

> any property that is acquired during the subsistence of a marriage, be it customary or under the English or Mohammedan Ordinance, is presumed to have been jointly acquired by the couple and upon divorce, should be shared between them on the equality is equity principle. (10)

The approach of the courts affirms the position of international human rights law that favors equality and equitable ownership of, access to, control over, and usufructory rights to land and property.

It is apparent that irrespective of any quantifiable "substantial contribution," the presumption in Ghanaian law now seems to be that all marital property acquired during the subsistence of marriage are prima facie deemed to be joint property that ought to be shared equally upon dissolution of marriage, unless proven otherwise. These transformations in women's ownership and access to matrimonial property are largely influenced by the gendered and kinship relations that are fundamental in determining land rights and production relations (Bebelleh, 2009). As underscored by scholars (e.g., Runger, 2006; Whitehead and Tsikata, 2003; FAO, 2006), customary land tenure systems generally have a clearly defined control over resources that are gender segregated based on traditional norms that operate to limit the land rights of women as compared to men. Therefore, the contradictory decisions in *Quartson v. Quartson* and *Gladys Mensah v. Stephen Mensah* notwithstanding, they address deep-rooted practices in Ghanaian land tenure and property rights systems that were highly discriminatory against women. For instance, Awumbilla (2002: 45) argued that women's access to ownership and control of productive resources are "to a large extent determined by the kinship system headed by men in the families, customary laws, norms and practices that give them control over land, the allocation of land and other resources owned by the family." This observation by Awumbilla (2002) clearly reveals the progressiveness of the courts' decisions in addressing the inherent discrimination against women in land and property ownership and access under customary law. Developments in jurisprudence and legislation toward substantive equality of property rights are noteworthy due to the significant contribution of women to land development and are themselves the worst victims of poverty across Ghana due to the poor land tenure system (HDR, 2019; Nyarko, 2019). In light of literature discussed, the judicial decisions on spousal property rights have positively impacted women's property rights. It should be noted though that the majority of Ghanaian women are still not able to seek justice in the courts in land and property-related matters due to poverty, distance to courts, prolong duration of land-based litigations, and lack of access to relevant information on legal aid. Consequently, most women end up seeking justice in land and property-related matters in traditional courts operated by traditional leaders at various levels. Decisions from these traditional courts are difficult to access and thus obtaining empirical data to assess their effectiveness in addressing challenges women face in accessing property rights is beyond the scope of this chapter due to mobility and financial constraints.

CONCLUSION

This chapter's analysis revealed that customary laws governing land tenure and property rights in Ghana are progressive, being interpreted by the courts to comply with acceptable international standards and practices regarding the fulfillment and implementation of women's property rights. This development demonstrates movement toward equality in ownership and access to property by women through the efforts of the courts. However, in order to further advance the progress being made, Ghana's Parliament must pass the Property Rights of Spouses Bill without further delay. Passing the bill into law would put the courts in a better position to guide the law's development and address the needs of an ever-changing society. Admittedly, legislation on its own does not solve problems, but it would nonetheless be useful in ensuring that Ghana complies with acceptable international standards and practices regarding the fulfillment and implementation of women's property rights. The practical impact of the bill would be to first and foremost domesticate Ghana's international and regional legal obligations in relation to women's property rights as discussed. This would set structures for the enforcement of women's property rights devoid of ambiguities. A process of codification of customary law in Ghana generally and customary property rights in particular must also be accelerated to clarify the issue of property rights due to the different regimes that exist in the country. Finally, the state and civil society should engage in public education to create awareness about women's rights, and particularly property rights, of Ghanaian women to make society receptive to and accommodating of the right of women to own and access property in Ghana.

NOTES

1. Article 295(1) of the 1992 Constitution defines stool lands as "any land, or interests in or right over any land controlled by a stool, skin, the head of a particular community or the captain of a company, for the benefit of the subjects of that stool or

the members of that particular community or company." See Land Act of 2020 (Act 1036) sections 14–17.

2. See other relevant laws such as the Land Act 1036 and the Officer of the Administration of Stool Lands Act, 1994 Act 481.

3. The allodial title of every piece of land is held in common by the members of a community with the chief (tendana) being the custodian of such land. It is the ultimate authority in land matters. Chiefs in northern Ghana sit on animal skins as the symbol of their power while those in the south sit on stools. See Yaro, J.A. "Re-inventing traditional land tenure in the era of land commoditization: some consequences in peri-urban northern Ghana," *Geografiska Annaler: Series B, Human Geography* (2012) 94(4): 351–368.

4. In a dualist legal system, international law stands apart from national law, and to have any effect on rights and obligations at the national level, international law must be domesticated through legislative process.

5. See, for instance, GA Res. 41/132, UN Doc. A/RES/41/132 (December 4, 1986); GA Res. 43/123, UN Doc.A/RES/43/123 (December 8, 1988); GA Res. 45/98, UN Doc. A/RES/45/98 (December 14, 1990).

6. See generally, Article 1, Protocol No. 1 to the European Convention on Human Rights (ECHR); Article xxiii, American Declaration of the Rights and Duties of Man; Article 21, American Convention on Human Rights (ACHR); Article 14, African Charter on Human and Peoples' Rights (ACHPR); Article 31, Arab Charter Human Rights.

7. Notably most international financial institutions, including the World Bank, the IMF, the African Development Bank, and the Asian Development Bank, have policies or guidelines on compulsory land acquisition and resettlement.

8. Examples, State Lands Act of 1962 (Act 125); State Lands Regulations of 1962 (LI 230); State Property and Contracts Act 1960 (CA 6); *Administration of Lands Act of 1962 (Act 123)*; *Minerals and Mining Act 2006 (Act 703)*; Minerals and Mining (Compensation and Resettlement) Regulations, LI 2175 (2012); National Land Policy of 1999, and so on.

9. This is not an excuse for Parliament's failure to pass the bill into law. Section 4 of this chapter reviews the draft Property Rights of Spouses Bill.

REFERENCES

Abebe, S. G. (2012). The need to alleviate the human rights implications of large-scale land acquisitions in Sub-Saharan Africa. *Goettingen Journal of International Law* 4: 873–90.

Abebreseh v. Kaah. (1976) 2 GLR 46.

Addadzi-Koom, M. E., and Nkansah L. A. (2020). Women at the bench: Does it make a difference? Assessing the impact of women judges in addressing gender-based issues in Ghana. Oñati Socio-Legal Series: Gender and Judging in the Middle East and Africa, Available at https://doi.org/10.35295/OSLS.IISL/0000-0000-0000-1175.

Addaney, M., Akudugu, J. A., Asibey, M. O., Akaateba, M. A., Kuusaana, E. D. (2022). Changing land tenure regimes and women's access to secure land for cocoa cultivation in rural Ghana. Land Use Policy 120, 106292.

African (Banjul) Charter on Human and Peoples' Rights OAU Doc. CAB/LEG/67/3 rev. 5 (1981).

African Commission. (2008). Report of the promotion visit to the Republic of Ghana.

African Commission. (2011). *Principles and Guidelines on Economic, Social and Cultural Rights in the African Charter on Human and Peoples' Rights* (24 October), Principles 51–55.

African Commission. (2011) *State Party Reporting Guidelines for Economic, Social and Cultural Rights in the African Charter on Human and Peoples' Rights* (24 October), Guideline 7(A).

Agyeman-Budu, K. (2017). The pursuit of actual equality: Women's matrimonial property rights in Ghana since independence. In: Addaney, M., and Nyarko, M.G. (eds) *Ghana at 60: Governance and human rights in twenty-first century Africa*. Pretoria University Law Press.

Akrofi, E. O. and Whittal, J. (2013). Compulsory acquisition and urban land delivery in customary areas. *South African Journal of Geomatics* 2(4): 280–295.

Alias, A. and Daud, N. (2006). Payment of adequate compensation for land acquisition in Malaysia. *Pacific Rim Property Research Journal* 12(3): 326–349.

Ameyaw, P. D. and de Vries, W. T. (2021), Toward smart land management, land acquisition and the associated challenges in Ghana. A look into a blockchain digital land registry for prospects. *Land* 10: 239.

Anaafo, D. (2015). "Land reforms and land rights change: A case study of land stressed groups in the Nkoranza South Municipality, Ghana," *Land Use Policy* 42: 538–546.

Anseeuw, W., Wily, L. A., Cotula, L., and Taylor, M. (2012). *Land Rights and the Rush for Land: Findings of the Global Commercial Pressures on Land Research Project*. International Land Coalition.

Apusigah, A. A. (2006). Women and Land in the Upper East Region: Analysis on Access, Rights and Security of Land Tenure. (Unpublished Paper).

Bebelleh, F. D. (2009). Land Tenure Security for the Rural Poor and Marginalised Under Ghana's Land Administration Project (LAP). A Master's Thesis Proposal. University For Development Studies, Tamale, Ghana.

Broni, S. (2005). Cleaning the Ghanaian Forest: Theories and Practices of Acquisition, Transfer, and Utilisation of Farming Titles in the Sefwi-Akan Areas. Accra, Ghana: Institution of African Studies, Accra: Legon.

Brooklings, B. (2011). Why Land Tenure Matters for IDPs: Lessons from Sub-Saharan Africa. Washington, DC: Brookings Institution.

Commission on Human Rights. (2002). *Report of the Special Rapporteur on the Right to Food, Jean Ziegler*, UN Doc. A/57/356 (27 August) (Ziegler Report).

Commission on Human Rights. (2005). *Report of the Special Rapporteur on Adequate Housing as a Component of the Right to an Adequate Standard of Living, Miloon Kothari*, UN Doc.E/CN4/2005/48 (3 March).

Cotula L., Toulmin C., and Quan J. (2006). Better land access for the rural poor: Lessons from experience and challenges ahead. IIED, FAO.

Cotula, L. (2007). *Changes in Customary Land Tenure System in Africa*. London: IIED.

Cotula, L. (2009). '*Property Rights, Negotiating Power and Foreign Investment: An International and Comparative Law Study of Africa*' unpublished PhD thesis, University of Edinburgh.

de Soto, H. (2000). *The Mystery of Capital: Why Capitalism Triumphs in the West and Fails Everywhere Else*. New York: Basic Books.

Deininger, K. (2003). *Land Policies for Growth and Poverty Reduction*. Washington, DC: World Bank.

Econmomic Commission for Africa. (2009). *Land Tenure System and their Impacts on Food Security and Sustainable Development in Africa*. Ethiopia: Addis Ababa.

FAO. (2012). Voluntary Guidelines on the Responsible Governance of Tenure of Land, Fisheries and Forests in the Context of National Food Security (Voluntary Guidelines).

FAO. (2003). *Gender and Access to Land*. Italy, Rome: FAO Land Tenure Series 4.

FAO. (2006). *Land Tenure Alternative Conflict Management*. Italy, Rome: FAO Land Tenure Manual 2.

Gelbspan, P. and Thea, F. G. V. (2013). *Land in the Struggle for Social Justice: Social Movement Strategies to Secure Human Rights*. Available at http://www.terradedireitos.org.br (accessed 16 July 2020).

Gilbert, J. (2013). Land rights as human rights: the case for a specific right to land. *SUR International Journal on Human Rights* 10(18): 115–134.

Government of Ghana. (1992). The 1992 Constitution of the Republic of Ghana.

IFAD. (2014). *Voluntary Guidelines on the Responsible Governance of Tenure of Land, Fishes and Forests: Implications for IFAD*. https://www.ifad.org/documents/38714170/40264252/Voluntary+Guidelines+on+the+Responsible+Governance+of+Tenure+of+Land%2C+Fisheries+and+Forests+-+Implic.pdf/221ace72-7493-46d3-a9e7-983b3a8e79e0?t=1555415975000 (accessed 2 January 2021).

International Covenant on Civil and Political Rights (ICCPR) 19 December 1966, 999 UNTS 171.

International Covenant on Economic, Social and Cultural Rights (ICESCR) 16 December 1966, 993 UNTS 3.

International Land Coalition. (2003). *Towards a Common Platform on Access to Land: The Catalyst to Reduce Rural Poverty and the Incentive for Sustainable Natural Resource Management* (2003). Available at http://www.landcoalition.org/sites/default/files/legacy/legacypdf/CPe.pdf?q=pdf/CPe.pdf (accessed 2 January 2021).

Kassanga, K. R. and Kotey, A. N. (2001). *Land Management in Ghana: Building on Tradition and Modernity*. London: International Institute for Environment and Development.

Kevane, M. (2004). *Women and Development in Africa: How Gender Works*. Boulder, CO: Lynne Rienner Publishers.

Kimani, M. (2008). *Women Struggle to Secure Land Rights*. New York: United Nations Publications.

Knight, R. S. (2010). *Statutory Recognition of Customary Land Rights in Africa: An Investigation into Best Practices for Law Making and Implementation*. Rome: FAO, FAO Legislative Study. Available at http://www.fao.org/3/a-i1945e.pdf (accessed 10 April 2022).

Knudsen, M. N. and Folds, N. (2011). "Land distribution and acquisition practices in Ghana's cocoa frontier: the impact of a state-regulated marketing system," *Land Use Policy* 28: 378.

Krause, C. (2001). "The right to property". In: Eide, A., Krause, C., and Rosas, A. (eds) *Economic, Social and Cultural Rights: A Text Book*. Cham: Springer.

Kuenyehia, A. and Ofei-Aboagye, E., 1998. Family law in Ghana and its implications for women. In: Kuenyehia, A. (ed) *Women and law in West Africa: Situational analysis of some key issues affecting women*. Legon: Women and Law in West Africa, pp. 23–61.

Mares, R. (2012). Corporate responsibility and compliance with the law: a case study of land, dispossession, and aftermath at Newmont's Ahafo Project in Ghana. *Business and Society Review* 117: 233–280.

Mends, T. M. & De Meijere, J. (2006). A Study of the Institution of the Customary Land Tenure System in the Supply of Property Rights for Urban Development: An example of Accra, Ghana. Available at https://www.fig.net/resources/proceedings/fig_proceedings/accra/papers/ts03/ts03_01_mends_demeijere.pdf (accessed 10 April 2022).

Mensa-Bonsu, M. Y. and Mensa-Bonsu, M. A. S. (2021). To win both the battle and the war Judicial determination of property rights of spouses in Ghana. In: Dawuni, J.J. (ed) *Gender, Judging and the Courts in Africa*. New York: Routledge, pp. 40–56.

Mensah v. Mensah (1998–1999) SCGLR 350.

Michael Gyan Nyarko, M. G. (2019). The Right to Property and Compulsory Land Acquisition in Ghana: A Human Rights Perspective. *African Journal of International and Comparative Law* 27(1): 100–125.

Minority Rights Group International, (2015). *Moving Towards a Right to Land: The Committee on Economic, Social and Cultural Rights' Treatment of Land Rights as Human Rights*. Available at https://www.escr-net.org/resources/moving-towards-right-land-committee-economic-social-and-cultural-rights-treatment-land#:~:text=Rights%20in%20Conflict-,Moving%20towards%20a%20Right%20to%20Land%3A%20The%20Committee%20on%20Economic,on%20thematic%20issues%20such%20as (accessed 10 April 2022).

Nyarko, M. G. (2016). The impact of the African Charter and the Maputo Protocol in Ghana'. In: Ayeni, V.O. (ed) *The impact of the African Charter and the Maputo Protocol in selected African states*. Pretoria: Pretoria University Law Press.

Nyinevi, C. Y. (2017). Challenges to judicial enforcement of socio-economic rights in Africa: Comparative lessons from Ghana and South Africa. In: Addaney, M. and Nyarko, M. G. (eds) *Ghana at 60: Governance and Human Rights in Twenty-First Century Africa*. Pretoria: Pretoria University Law Press.

OHCHR/UN Women, (2013). "Realizing Women's Rights to Land and Other Productive Resources," HR/PUB/13/04.

OHCHR's Submission. Understanding Human Rights and Climate Change, to the 21st Conference of Parties to the UNFCCC (27 November 2015).

Oloka-Onyango, J. (1995). Beyond the rhetoric: reinvigorating the struggle for economic and social rights in Africa. *California Western International Law Journal* 26(1): 1–74.

Orellana, M. A. (2012). The human rights-based approach: a field of action for human rights education. In: Bokulić, S., and Taneja, P. (eds) *Human Rights-Based Approaches to Development Education: A Toolkit for Activists in New EU Member States*. London: Minority Rights Group International.

Ouguergouz, F. (2003). *The African Charter on Human and Peoples' Rights: A Comprehensive Agenda for Human Dignity and Sustainable Democracy in Africa*. Brill Nijhoff.

Parliament of Ghana. (1971). Matrimonial Causes Act of 1971 (Act 367).

Parliament of Ghana. (2020). Land Act of 2020 (Act 1036).

Parliament of Ghana. Property Rights of Spouses Bill of Ghana.

Platteau, J. P. (2002). "The Gradual Erosion of the Social Security Function of Customary Land Tenure Arrangements of Lineage-Based Societies." United Nations University/World Institute for Development Economics Research, Discussion Paper 2002/26.

Protocol to the African Charter on Human and Peoples' Rights on the Rights of Women in Africa 7783 Treaty 0027 (2003).

Quartey v. Martey & Another (1959) GLR 377.

Quartson v. Quartson (2012) 2 SCGLR 1078.

Quaye, B. A. (2006). *Towards an Appropriate Framework for the Effective Utilization/ Management of Geoinformation: A Case Study of Ghana*. TS 82 – e-Governance – Developments. Available at https://www.fig.net/resources/proceedings/fig_proceedings/fig2006/papers/ts82/ts82_05_quaye_0397.pdf (accessed 10 April 2022).

Quisumbing, R. A. and Otsuka, K. (2001). Land Inheritance and Schooling in Matrilineal Societies: Evidence from Sumatra. Capri Working Paper No. 14.

Quisumbing, R. A. et al. (2001). *Land, Trees and Women. Evolution of Land Tenure Institutions in Western Ghana and Sumatra*. Washington, DC: International Food Policy Research Institution.

Republic of Ghana. (1992). *The 1992 Fourth Republican Constitution*. Accra, Ghana: Assembly Press.

Runger, M. (2006). *Governance, Land Rights and Access to Land in Ghana: A Development Perspective on Gender Equity. A Paper Presented at the 5th FIG Regional Conference on the Theme*. Ghana, Accra: Promoting Land Administration and Good Governance.

Schabas, W. A. (1991). The omission of the right to property in the international covenants. *Hague Yearbook of International Law* 4: 135–170.

Schabas, W. A. (2013). *The Universal Declaration of Human Rights: The Travaux Préparatoires, Volume 1, October 1946 to November 1947*. Cambridge: Cambridge University Press.

Sprankling, J. G. (2012). The emergence of international property law. *North Carolina Law Review* 90: 461.

Toulmin, C. (2007). *Securing Land and Property Rights in Sub-Saharan Africa: The Role of Institutions, International Institutional Reform and Development.* International Institute for Environment and Development.

Toulmin, C. and Quan, J. (2000). Evolving Land Rights, Tenure and Policy in sub-Saharan Africa: 31–49.

Tsikata, D. and Yaro, J. (2011). Land Market Liberalization and Transnational Commercial Land Deals in Ghana Since the 1990s. In: *Paper Presented at the International Conference on Global Land Grabbing*. Brighton, UK.

Ubink, J. (2018). Customary Legal Empowerment in Namibia and Ghana? Lessons about Access, Power and Participation in Non-state Justice Systems. *Development and Change* 49(4): 930–950.

Ubink, J. M. and Quan, J. F. (2008). How to combine tradition and modernity? Regulating customary land management in Ghana. *Land Use Policy* 25: 198.

Ubink, J. M., and Amanor, K. (Eds.), (2008). *Contesting Land and Custom in Ghana: State, Chief and the Citizen.* Amsterdam: Amsterdam University Press.

Ubink, J. M., Hoekema, A. J., Assies, W. J. (Eds.), (2009). *Legalizing Land Rights: Local Practices, State Policies and Tenure Security in Africa.* Asia, Latin America: Leiden University Press.

UN Office of the High Commissioner for Human Rights. (2014). *Summary of Discussion of Human Rights Council Panel Discussion on the Relationship Between Climate Change and Human Rights held on 15 June 2009 at Palais des Nations in Geneva, Switzerland.* 16, para 103.

UN-HABITAT. (2008). *Secure Land Rights for All.* Nairobi: UN-Habitat.

United Nations Development Programme (UNDP). (2019), *Human Development Report 2019: Beyond Income, Beyond Averages, Beyond Today: Inequalities in Human Development in the 21st Century.* 179. Available at http://hdr.undp.org/sites/default/files/hdr2019.pdf (accessed 28 January 2021).

Van Asperen, P. C. M. (2007). *Effects of Multiple Land Tenure Regimes on Tenure Security: African Cases. Leiden: 2nd European Conference on African Studies.*

van Banning, T. R. G. (2002). *The Human Right to Property.* Cambridge: Intersentia.

Whitehead A. and Tsikata D. (2003). Policy discourses on women's land right in Sub-Saharan Africa, *Journal of Agrarian Change*, 3(1/2), pp 67–112.

World Bank, (2020). *Women, Business and the Law.* Washington, DC: The World Bank.

Yeboah v. Yeboah (1974) 2 GLR 114.

Arthur v. Arthur (2013) Civil Appeal No. J4/19/2013.

Adjei v. Adjei (2021) Civil Appeal No. J4/06/2021.

Daily Graphic. "Education on new Land Act critical," 10 May 2021. Available at https://www.graphic.com.gh/daily-graphic-editorials/education-on-new-land-act-critical.html.

Chapter 11

The Making and Unmaking of Gender

Reflections on Questions of Gender and the Judiciary in Namibia

Kennedy Kariseb

INTRODUCTION

Over the years, scholars are increasingly beginning to explore the interaction between courts and gender, especially as it relates to women (Resnik, 1996; Halilovic & Sarajero, 2014; Bauer & Dawuni, 2016; Dawuni & Kuenyehia, 2018). This is no surprise, given the historical marginalization of gender as a variable for analysis by courts globally. Notwithstanding the increasing interest in questions of gender by courts, gender as a variable of reflection and analysis remains extremely charged, particularly for African courts, including Namibia's, with plural legal systems informed predominantly by cultural relativism (Ruppel & Ruppel-Schlichting, 2011). The tension largely results from an expanded connotation of gender, seeking to include sexuality and sexual minority rights (Butler, 1999). Traditionally, gender was defined as the "socially constructed identities, attributes and roles for women and men and society's social and cultural meaning for these biological differences resulting in hierarchical relationships between women and men and in the distribution of power and rights favouring men and disadvantaging women" (CEDAW, 2010). Gender, in this context, serves as a matrix of reflection and analysis in which the roles of men and women in society are studied more deeply and reconstructed in order to unravel underlying biases.

In reference to ". . . making and unmaking of gender . . ." in this chapter, gender is seen and understood here as a variable, more so as a means to explain actions, practices, or outcomes. Put differently, the use of the term "gender" as a point of reference for analysis seeks to explain for the regression or progression, and the differentiated impact gender makes in explaining particular actions or practices within Namibian society that affect women. Gender is more than mere biological anatomy, at least for the purposes and context within which it is used in this chapter. This is because gender, as Jill Steans (1998: 139) rightly once articulated, is a matrix that raises questions of power relations, "specifically, power relations between those who decide who or what is 'relevant' and what is deemed to be 'not relevant.'"

Gender has always been a defining aspect of many African societies. This is for the most part true because African societies have appraised cultural relativism as central to their identity and existence (Shivji, 2007; Ngwena, 2018). Often the argument has been made that cultural relativism has been used to shy away from a progressive realization and appreciation of the shortcomings affecting Africa, including in aspects such as development and women's rights (Cobbah; 1987). The undeniable reality remains that African societies were deeply patriarchal and thus premised on a male view of both state and society (Msuya, 2019). Consequently, many cultural practices and male hegemony often affected women negatively (Msuya, 2019). With the rise of women's rights movements in the twenty-first century, gender became a salient issue and was heightened in the case of Africa when women's contributions to the political resistance against colonialism and imperialism were beginning to be acknowledged (Nzomo, 1992; Bradford, 1996). The courts have been important apparatus in the realization and changing attitudes toward women's rights in Africa, Namibia being no exception.

This chapter reflects on this ongoing role of the courts in shaping an equitably gendered society. "Equitably gendered" in this context means a society in which socially defined and assigned roles (and identities) of men and women are fairly balanced to ensure complementarity and coexistence so that both sexes have a meaningful place and status in society. This has been the case for Namibia's superior courts, which, since the attainment of independence in 1990, have been faced with perplex questions relating to gender and the law.

This chapter orients around one central question: Why has a judicial system that has predominantly been the province of male judges appreciably taken judicial notice of women's rights in Namibia? Mindful of the preemptive nature of this broad question, this chapter is rooted in an analysis of Namibian cases where questions of gender were raised to illustrate the appreciable and relatively increasing judicial notice of questions of gender, particularly as it relates to women in Namibia. To this end, this chapter aims to chart a research agenda on gender and the judiciary in Namibia, one hinted on understanding the contrasting reality and relatively positive impact of a patriarchal judicial system on the advancement of women's rights.

The chapter first briefly sets out a methodological and theoretical framework. In the second section, a reflection of four Supreme Court decisions is made to illustrate the relatively gender response nature of the courts as far as women's rights are concerned. These cases' reflections include a discussion of the role of the judiciary in issues related to gender. The fourth section concludes the chapter.

METHODOLOGICAL, CONCEPTUAL, AND THEORETICAL FRAMEWORK

This chapter applies a doctrinal approach based on case reflections and socio-legal reasoning. The emphasis is on analyzing judicial pronouncements of four selected Namibian cases: *Myburgh v. Commercial Bank of Namibia* [2000] NR 255 (SC) (December 8, 2000); *Agnes Kahimbi Kashela v. Katima Mulilo Town Council and Others* [2018] NASC 409 (SC) (November 16, 2018); *Government of the Republic of Namibia v. LM and Others* (SA-2012/49) [2014] NASC 19 (SC) (November 3, 2014)); and the decision in *S v. Katamba* [1999] NASC 7 (SC) (December 7, 1999).

These cases are used as methodological matrixes to illustrate the appreciable manner in which Namibian courts have dealt with questions of gender that affect women's rights. These are not the only cases with gendered implications decided by the Namibian superior courts. While no cases with deep-seated gendered implications are traceable pre-independence—largely because before independence, Namibian courts were merely an extension of the superior courts of South Africa and therefore barred access to courts to a vast majority of the populace (Amoo: 2008)—there were several postindependence decisions that set precedent on gender-related issues. The four cases described in this chapter are the leading ones, in that they set judicial precedent. Their significance and selection also are rooted in the fact that they are all decisions by the highest court of appeal, the Supreme Court of Namibia. While the chapter uses and applies the concept of gender, the focus is on women. This is not to suggest that "gender" is a synonym for women as some scholars have warned in the past (Carver; 1996). On the contrary, the advanced focus on women generally is premised on the fact that gender manifestations have had disproportionate impacts on Namibian women, predominantly for historical reasons (Hubbard, 2010).

A legal-anthropological approach to the study would have been more ideal. Legal anthropology has sought to apply its framework to issues at the intersections of law and culture, including human rights and legal pluralism, as is the case in this study. Within the history of legal anthropology, there have been various methods of data gathering adopted, ranging from literature review of traveler/missionary accounts to consulting informants and lengthy participant observation. Regarding law, in anthropology's characteristically self-conscious manner, the comparative analysis inherent to legal anthropology has been speculated upon and most famously debated by Paul Bohannan and Max Gluckman. The discourse highlights one of the primary differences between British and American anthropology regarding fieldwork approaches and concerns the imposition of Western terminology as ethnological categories of differing societies (see Bohannan, P. 1957. Justice and Judgement among the Tiv. International African Institute).

Gender, both theoretically and practically, understandably forms a central theme of feminist studies. It is gender that manifests the vulnerabilities that women and other groups face. No wonder gender has become an essential facet of feminist analysis, especially from a legal perspective, as such feminist theoretical scholarship gives us an understanding, which is often not the case with pure legal analysis, that the "law reflects social relations, especially the unequal power relations between men and women, with an aspiration to change these inequalities" (van Marle & Albertyn, 2007:5). Inequalities that gender reflections manifest are a clear indication of the vulnerabilities women encounter. Women and other vulnerable groups need the protection of law. Such vulnerability is visible in both state and society. Many times, based purely on their gender, women are the subjects of suppression and exploitation (Dekeseredy, 2020; Malhotra, 2004). The judiciary, as the custodian of laws and legal practice, has an important role to play in responding and remedying the vulnerabilities that women and other vulnerable groups encounter.

Generations of feminist studies have set out in finer detail the disproportionate effects of law, culture, religion, and other forces on women and other vulnerable groups. To this end, feminist theories have advanced the discourse of women and to a lesser extent other identities, in rich and diverse ways. However, all these theoretical advances boil down to challenging the inequalities meted against women and to a lesser extent other groups and identities. One contemporary theory in which the cause of women, especially in light of violence against women (VAW), has been advanced is the "vulnerability theory." This theory has found rooting in the work of American family law scholar and feminist Martha Fineman (Fineman, 2008; Fineman, 2010).

A starting point of Fineman's theoretical discourse on vulnerability is that vulnerability is in itself an inherent part of human conditioning (Fineman: 2008). This is because an integral part of our embodiment as humans carry with it the possibility of misfortune, whether it be by natural causes like drought and famine or by inflicted means through harm, or injury to self, whether through violence, torture at the hands of state agents, or private actors. Unlike Western liberal thoughts on equality, including those of John Locke who posits that all humans are born free and equal (Ian Shapiro 2003), the vulnerability theory begins from the premise that all humans are born vulnerable and that vulnerability comes naturally through "our embodiment which carries with it the imminent or ever present possibility of harm, injury or misfortune" (Fineman, 2010:267).

Such vulnerability can occur through several means and processes, whether intentionally or naturally inflicted. This inherent and common experience of vulnerability forms the basis for any claim that the state must be responsive to such vulnerability because states are endowed with a primary responsibility to promote, protect, and fulfill fundamental human rights. Thus the state, in terms of this theory, is "set to actively assume broad societal responsibility in regard to ensuring equality for citizens and others to whom it owes some obligation" (Fineman, 2010: 256). There is, however, a realization that such responses, whether it is from the state, society, or any process or institution, would always be limited because of the persistent, universal and inherent character of human vulnerability. While society cannot completely erase the vulnerabilities we face, it can to a considerable extent mediate the magnitude of such vulnerability through various mechanisms and processes.

Fineman's vulnerability analysis may also be useful because, in her own words, "understanding the significance, universality, and constancy of vulnerability mandates that politics, ethics, and law be fashioned around complete, comprehensive visions of the human experience if they are to meet the needs of real-life subjects" (Fineman, 2008:10). Though offering an alternative means of advancing the cause of women, especially in the context of VAW, the vulnerability thesis has its fair share of shortcomings. For starters, it is molded "as a stealthily disguised human rights discourse, fashioned for an American audience" (Fineman, 2008:255). This means that the theory remains limited, though not exclusive, in its applicability and expansion to a non-American audience. This could be problematic because the neoliberalized and individualistic conceptions underlying the American society or the Western world for that matter do not gracefully resonate with the more culturally and community-oriented African conceptions of human rights. Traditionally, the characterization of women as vulnerable subjects has not always been appreciated (Knowles, 1996). Often the argument is made that such characterization perpetuates the very same stigmatization it seeks to counter. Put differently, vulnerability is said to label women as weak victims and fragile and thus not worthy of their autonomy (Knowles, 1996). This argument is true to some degree. Vulnerability has the actual or potential implication of denigrating women and other vulnerable groups into victimhood and dependency, but the counterargument of the potential of framing the gendered experiences of women within a vulnerability lens should not also be undermined. A vulnerability analysis has the potential, as Fineman (2008:9) rightly suggests, in "describing a universal, inevitable, enduring aspect of the human condition" that compels a response from state and society. It has this potential because its constant and universal nature enables it to delineate a counter obligation on the part of the state to ensure resilience from inherent (and at times intentionally afflicted) harm. In this regard and "thus reconsidered, the concept of vulnerability can act as a heuristic device, pulling us back to examine hidden assumptions and biases that shaped its original social and cultural meanings" (Fineman, 2008:9).

Notwithstanding the shortcomings mentioned before, the vulnerability analysis remains a useful framework concerning questions of gender, particularly as it relates to women. It provides us a medium through which to view the gendered experiences of women, particularly as it relates to VAW. As Fineman (2008:13) writes, "one promising theoretical potential of making vulnerability central in an analysis of equality is that attention to the situation of the vulnerable individual leads us to redirect focus onto the societal institutions that are created in response to individual vulnerability." Experiences of exploitation, such as gender-based violence (GBV), show not only the implications of gender for women and other vulnerable groups but moreover the ever-present possibility of the vulnerability to violence in all possible forms, based solely on gender.

The ever-present vulnerability that women face is caused by many factors. Gender stereotyping, like determinants such as culture, religion, and the law, is a tool used both in the past and to a lesser extent present, to acerbate the vulnerability of women. This is because gender stereotyping and more especially its purported exploitation of women and other identities has, for a long time and in some cultures, been regarded as accepted. The private dichotomy that reflects the life of women serves as a catalyst for the relegation of women and their susceptibility to abuse, exploitation, and GBV. Our case reflection in this chapter should be seen within this framework of gender as a discourse on vulnerability more so the fact that women are subjects of vulnerability that need the protection of the state. The judiciary as an organ of the state has a role to play and has done so in many respects, as discussed and shown in this chapter.

THE JUDICIARY AND GENDER IN NAMIBIA

In Namibia, one of the last colonies in Africa, gender—especially in the struggle for women's rights—was diametrically linked to the struggle against colonial exploitation and apartheid (Katjavivi, 1988; Emmett, 1999). Struggles against these repressive regimes were not only a response to the political context then prevailing, but also were an immediate reaction to racial, ethnic, and gender segregation. Namibian women were much neglected by colonial regimes, especially European Christianity under the then-prevailing mission work and the racist policies of the South African nationalist government, blended by imitated and distorted Western culture and civilization (Katjavivi, 1988; Du Pisani, 1986). For example, even though Black women appeared in the forefront of mission activities during colonial periods, their status remained secondary to men. Black women had to endure a double jeopardy. Even though women were prominent in the work of the missionaries, educational possibilities, or even active roles in the ecclesiastic and diaconal ministries, were almost impossible purely based on grounds of gender (Totemeyer, 2010; Buys & Nambala, 2003). The situation was even worse under the South African racist regime, as Black emancipation—and even more so Black women's emancipation—in political organs and decision-making processes was a far-fetched reverie. Exploitation on the grounds of gender was a reality for many women under colonial regimes, as was the case in most parts of Africa and beyond (Nzomo, 1992). Neglect of women remained unaltered even after the attainment of independence, resulting in grave disparities between men and women in both state and society. Several legal responses, as discussed below, were made by the government of the day to address some gender inequalities brought about by historical segregation. In addition to these reforms, courts began to play a leading role in (re-)shaping an equitably gendered society where women could have a meaningful role and space, both in state and society.

The legal interventions that were made are enormous. In the context of women's rights, more so their emancipation, the Constitution has been relatively robust in the protection it affords to women (Ruppel, 2008). Beginning with its preamble, the Constitution recognizes the "inherent dignity" and "equal and inalienable rights of all members of the human family" regardless of inter alia "sex." Article 10, which is the equality clause, speaks to the plight of women in Namibia. It is a two-pronged provision, firstly recognizing the equality of all persons, male or female, before the law; and secondly, prohibiting any discrimination on the grounds of "sex, race, colour, ethnic origin, religion, creed or social or economic status."[1]

Besides the formal recognition of equality between the sexes, the Constitution also introduces affirmative action measures aimed at redressing social, economic, or educational imbalances, reflective of the diverse racial and sex classes in the country. Article 23(2) and (3) empowers the government through Parliament to enact legislation, providing directly or indirectly for the advancement of persons within Namibia who have been socially, economically, or educationally disadvantaged by past discriminatory laws or practices. In doing so, the government must be mindful, in terms of subarticle (3) of Article 23, of the "fact that women in Namibia have traditionally suffered special discrimination and that they need to be encouraged and enabled to play a full, equal and effective role in the political, social, economic and cultural life of the nation."

The affirmative action provision in Article 23 should be read in conjunction with the principles of state directives in Article 95(a) of the Constitution, which directs the central government, inter alia, to "actively promote and maintain the welfare of the people by adopting policies aimed at amongst others the enactment of legislation to ensure equality of opportunity for women, to enable them to participate fully in all spheres of society." Although of mere moral persuasion, Article 95(a) to a considerable extent gives a clear guideline to the state's policy of positive discrimination aimed at rendering a comparative advantage to women over men, given the historical global realities that left the female species exploited and politically marginalized. However, the nonjusticiable nature of Article 95(a) of the Constitution may account for the overt reality that to date, affirmative action measures have not been legally moored. Consequently, the political empowerment of women in decision-making organs, particularly at the parliamentary level, depends on the whims and dictates of political parties, without any legislative security. Although political parties, such as the ruling South West Africa People's Organization, has on a *voluntary* basis introduced a 50/50 proportional representation list since early 2015, which enhanced the number of women in Parliament whether that will remain status quo is still to be seen.

There have also been several statutory laws passed to advance the course of women in Namibia. Typical examples include the Married Persons Equality Act, 1996 (providing inter alia for the abolition of marital power of men, the amendment of the matrimonial property law of marriages in community property, domicile of married women, and domicile and guardianship of minor children); Combating of Domestic Violence Act, 2003 (providing for matters relating to domestic violence offenses, including issuing of protection orders in domestic violence matters); Combating of Rape Act, 2000 (criminalizing the act of rape and abolishing the cautionary rule in rape cases); Affirmative Action (Employment) Act, 1998 (categorizing women as a group that needs advancement through affirmative action measures); and Social Security Act, 1994 (establishing a system of benefits for dependent mothers and children, among others).

Another notable means through which legislation has been used to empower women is through legislative affirmative action measures. Legislative affirmative action measures broadly refer to the legislative reservation of seats and/or quotas for women. These measures have been mostly manifested in legislation establishing parastatals and other state-owned enterprises, organs, and institutions. For example, the Sports Act of 2003, Communal Land Reform Act of 2002, Traditional Authorities Act of 2002, and the Electoral Act of 2014 all require a certain number of women to be appointed to their leadership structures and organs. Namibia also ratified and implemented the provisions of the Protocol to the African Charter on the Rights of Women in Africa (Maputo Protocol) and the Convention on the Elimination of All Forms of Discrimination Against Women (CEDAW) in September 2004 and November 1992, respectively.

Besides these aforestated developments, the realization of women's rights has not been automatic. This is because there always have been disparities between the provisions of law and the lived realities of women. In a hybrid legal system like Namibia (Ruppel & Winter, 2011), blended between a Western inherited common law and indigenous customary law system, there are often inconsistencies between customary law and official state laws (Hinz, 2008). A large part of the Namibian population, especially women, relates and identifies with their customary laws and communities. These customary laws often have detrimental effects on their rights, especially in areas such as education, succession, and land and property rights (Ambunda & De Klerk, 2008; Hinz, 2008). As rightly stated by Lotta Ambunda and Stephanie De Klerk in their study on women and custom in Namibia, in most cultural communities of Namibia, gender plays a major role in the assignment of roles and responsibilities. Women's role has been demarcated as one of domesticity, while the public sphere of the economy and political space is for men (Ambunda & De Klerk, 2008). The effect of some of the customary laws and practices has been that women have for the most part been relegated to a private sphere of domestic roles and often unpaid labor.

Despite this grating confluence of the law and the lived realities of women, it is imperative to note that the complexity of women's rights protection in Namibia is undoubtedly marked with progressivity and avant-garde interpretations and applications of constitutional and statutory provisions by the courts. This is evident from the numerous cases courts often have to deal with relating to women.

Several case reflections may be useful in illustrating the appreciable approach the courts have taken regarding questions of gender. For starters, since the attainment of independence, Namibian courts have been confronted with questions with vast legal implications for the protection of the rights of women. Take, for instance, the Namibian Supreme Court's liberating decision in *Myburgh v. Commercial Bank of Namibia*.[2] In this decision, the court was tasked with pronouncing itself on the viability of women regarded as minors for litigation in an era of constitutional democracy. The common law rule under question purported that women, as far as the common estate in a matrimonial home was concerned, remained minors for as long as the marriage subsisted, with the effect that even where the husband became insane, the wife did not acquire contractual capacity and had to either allow her husband's curator to administer the joint estate or apply to court for authorization to administer her own property as though her husband were an absent person.

This placement of the common law was found to be in conflict with cardinal constitutional provisions of the Namibian Constitution. The Supreme Court found that the consideration of women as minors for litigation purposes was a discriminatory practice based on one of the prohibited grounds: sex. In construing the differentiation that informed the discrimination against women, the court alluded that where such discrimination is based on stereotyping by reducing them to minors who cannot act independently, there is no doubt that it impairs the dignity of women as a class or individually. In essence, such differentiation turned a blind eye on the fact that in many marriages in community of property, the intelligence, training, qualifications, natural ability, or aptitude of the woman may render women a far better administrator of the common estate than the husband. The court found that the rules of common law that regarded women as minors for litigation detracted from the provisions of the Constitution and that they ceased to exist when Namibia gained independence on March 21, 1990. This bold and succinct adjudication of the Supreme Court in extirpating the acute disabilities that women married in community of property faced was heavily influenced by the constitutional and statutory protection allotted to women in Namibia.

One of the key responses that have emanated from the Namibian courts in the protection of women can be deduced from its jurisprudence on gender-based VAW and girls. Abominable and ever-exacerbating GBV cases in Namibia have been marked with lengthy and exemplary sentences across a plethora of judgments in Namibian courts. This austere, proactive and progressive deterrence of crimes against women is no longer an abstract theoretical or academic enquiry but rather a reality within both the superior and lower courts of Namibia. In most gendered violence cases, the courts have meted harsh, long-term sentences as deterrence (see local Namibian cases such as *S v. Bothile* [2007] 1 NR 137, *S v. Angula* [2017] NAHCNLD 98, and *S v. Diergaardt* [2019] NAHCMD 454) and in some exceptional cases life imprisonment (*S v. Amseb* [2019] NAHCMD 57). The estimable judicial architecture on VAW and domestic violence cases in Namibia can easily be seen as an inclination of the Namibian courts to embrace modest judicial activism.

Another significant judicial yardstick in relation to women's rights protection in Namibia is the positive developments now visible in sexual offense cases, such as rape. These can largely be attributed to the courts' judicial activism in abolishing the common law "cautionary rule," which requires judges to exercise caution before adopting uncorroborated evidence of certain witnesses on the grounds that such evidence may potentially be unreliable. The rule is most prevalent in sexual offense cases where complainants are often women and girls with no supporting witnesses. The challenge with this rule is that it appeared to have no rational basis and catalyst gender stereotyping; hence the call for its reform in Namibia (Hatchard, 1993). Instead, it demeaned women, contributed to secondary victimization, and contributed greatly to the non-reporting of cases (Adler, 1987; Birch, 1990).

In response to the setbacks emanating from the cautionary rule, an important reassessment was made. This reassessment was primarily meted by the courts through judicial activism. In 1999, the Supreme Court in *S v. Katamba* abolished this rule, with O'Linn AJA advancing his criticism by noting that

> the so-called cautionary rule has no other purpose than to discriminate against women complainants. This rule thus probably is contrary to art 10 of the Namibian Constitution which provides for the equality of all persons before the law regardless of sex. To sum up, the cautionary rule evolved in cases of rape has no rational basis for its existence and should therefore not form part of our law and is probably contrary to the provisions of the Namibian Constitution.

The court was of the opinion that the cautionary rule in sexual cases was perceived by many, in addition to women's rights activists and the victims themselves, as a rule in practice, which places an additional burden on victims (women) in sexual violence cases. The court said it was incumbent on courts to reconcile themselves to their constitutional duty to protect the fundamental rights of victims, and in this regard, they are also required to consider and give some weight to the contemporary norms, views, and opinions of Namibian society.

The Supreme Court's decision in *Agnes Kahimbi Kashela v. Katima Mulilo Town Council and Others* [2018] NASC 409 (November 16, 2018) is another case in point that shows sensitivity to the historical marginalization of women in Namibian society. Its importance lies rooted in the conflict between formal law and customary law and its implications on the rights of women. The legal question dealt with in this case was: What right(s), if any, does an occupier of communal land have when the land which she occupies under customary land tenure is transferred by the government to a local authority? The petitioner in this case, Agnes Kashela, was the daughter of Andrias Kashela, who had acquired customary land rights to occupy the piece of land in the *Mafwe* traditional community. Upon the death of her father in 2001, Ms. Kashela acquired land rights previously held by her father. A difficulty arose when the communal land she occupied became state land, and part of the land she occupied was expropriated and allocated to other occupants, resulting in the devolution of her right to occupancy in terms of customary land tenure. The petitioner challenged this devolution, first in the High Court, where the court dismissed her petition, and later in the Supreme Court, where it was upheld.

According to the High Court, once land ceased to be communal in terms of section 15(2) of the Communal Land Reform Act 5 of 2002 read with section 3 of the Local Authorities Act 23 of 1992, the effect was that the transferee local authority becomes the owner thereof and the land ceases to be communal land. Put differently, once the land ceased to be communal land and became town land, all customary land tenure rights subsisting in the land cease to exist. In support of that conclusion, the court relied on Article 100 of the Namibian Constitution, which decrees that all land belongs to the state, unless it is otherwise lawfully owned.

The Supreme Court diverted from this reasoning and gave a purposive interpretation of Article 100 of the Constitution, taking into account the socioeconomic reality of inequality in the country rooted in its apartheid past. The court marked the "contra-distinction to the system of laws that protected rights in and over land owned mainly by whites, in respect of the land on which the majority of the population lived, and the absence of a coherent system of laws and rules that protected the rights of the people who lived on it." Such was the backdrop, according to the court, against which the claims that Ms. Kashela and those similarly situated should be treated, given that they would lose whatever already limited rights they might have had in communal land upon that land becoming state land and, subsequently, municipal or town land.

When at independence, the state became the lawful owner of the lands on which the majority of Black people lived, immediately a tension arose: the legitimate state interest to develop those areas through the establishment of infrastructure and planned development by local authorities, and availing land on which affected local communities would continue to live and provide for themselves. The notion that one was more important than the other, according to the court, is difficult to reconcile with the Namibian state's duty to look after the well-being of its marginalized communities and to restore their lost dignity. The court found Ms. Kashela acquired a right of exclusive use and occupation of the land in dispute upon the passing of her father and that the right survived and attached to the land even after its proclamation as town land.

In another case, a largely criticized decision for failing to advance the jurisprudence and campaign against forced sterilization of women living with HIV on the basis of their status, in *LM & Others v. Government of the Republic of Namibia* (I 1603/2008 I 3518/2008 I 3007/2008) [2012] NAHC 211 (July 30, 2012), the Namibian Supreme Court can be credited for progressing the bodily autonomy of women, more specially their right to an informed and duly consented sterilization procedure. Although the applicants in this case, HIV positive women, were not able to establish unfair discrimination in that they were sterilized on the basis of their HIV status, the court nonetheless found that purported consent to their sterilization had been coerced, as they had not been told the contents of the consent forms they signed. The court found that this infringed their constitutional rights to life, liberty, dignity, and to found a family, as well as various common law and personality rights, as it diminished their marital prospects and ability to bear children; impacted their bodily and psychological integrity; and caused shock, pain and suffering, and emotional anguish.

Considering the relatively progressive and affirmative outcome of the above cases, the question that remains is what determinants, if any, have contributed to the gender-responsive nature of the Namibian superior courts in women's rights cases. This is an extremely complex question given the generally charged nature questions of gender pose for courts (Resnik, 1993). It is further complicated by growing evidence that the gender of judges often has impacts on the (gender) outcomes of judicial decisions (Dawuni, 2020; Dawuni; 2016; Rackley, 2013; Kenney, 2013). More importantly, this question is particularly acute if one pays close attention to the relatively patriarchal nature of the Namibian judiciary. Since the advent of independence, which marked the genesis of the "new judicial system," the makeup of the Namibian judiciary has remained essentially male. The first female judicial appointments to the courts only appeared around about the mid-1990s, with the appointment of Zimbabwean barrister and judge Mavis Gibson (born Gumede) as a judge of the Namibian High Court main division. Although Justice Gibson occasionally served as an acting judge of appeal in the Namibian Supreme Court, the Apex Court never had a female permanent judge. Of late however, retired female South Africa Constitutional Court judges have occasionally been appointed in acting capacities to serve in this court. It is worth noting that Namibia has never had a female chief justice or judge president. As of 2020, there still were no women among the five permanently appointed Supreme Court justices, and only 7 among the 20 permanently appointed High Court judges are female (which is 7 women out of 25 superior court judges overall, or 35%). That the majority of women judges remain concentrated in lower courts is also emblematic in Namibia (Dawuni, 2016; Cohen, 2018). The magistracy, which consists of justices in lower courts, have consistently had a much more even gender balance, with women comprising 50% of Namibia's 93 magistrates as of May 2017 (47 males and 46 females) (LAC, 2017).

If, as highlighted before, the Namibian judiciary has been male dominated, the question remains: Why then has a judicial system that has predominantly been the province of male judges taken judicial notice of women's rights? While there is no direct and monolithic explanation for the generally gender-receptive nature of the Namibian courts, two determinants loom large as reasonably acceptable explanations. Firstly, Namibia's gender-responsive legislative framework, which took root right from the orthodox days of independence, has served as an incentive for a rights framework that is responsive to women. The numerous legislative instruments referred to in this chapter are evidence of this effect. Some of the most notable instruments worth referencing are Article 10 and 95(a) of the Namibian Constitution, the Affirmative Action (Employment) Act 29 of 1998; Married Persons Equality Act 1 of 1996; Combating of Rape Act 8 of 2000; Combating of Domestic Violence Act 4 of 2003; and the Combating of Trafficking in Persons Act 1 of 2018. Arguably, these legislative instruments, with some of the most protective and promising provisions on women's rights, have had a "chilling effect" on the Namibian judiciary in advancing the rights of women.

Secondly, there generally has been consciousness of the historical marginalization of women in Namibia. This awareness has largely been linked to the country's political history of racial and sexist segregation of the Black majority by the nationalist apartheid regime that governed the country for nearly eight decades. It is for this reason that the Namibian courts have remained mindful of geopolitical and partisan determinants that informed pre-independent Namibia. The vulnerability of women and their marginalization is one such determinant. It therefore is not surprising that the judiciary in Namibia, although male dominated, has been at the forefront of metamorphosing Namibia into an economically, politically, and socially—including on grounds of gender—a positively responsive country. The Supreme Court's decision in the *Kashela* decision discussed before is an illustrious example of the stern reference to the political past of Namibia as a determinant playing a decisive role in gender-related cases.

CONCLUSION

Since the traditional conceptualization of gender as a lens of analysis has been clouded by notable criticisms that it is complex, acutely layered, and at times delineated across the biological differences of the two sexes (Fausto-Sterling, 2012), a more flexible approach to the concept of gender may be warranted. Courts have an important role to play in this regard. In Namibia, gender concerns have particularly been telling across the historic struggle for women's rights as it has been diametrically linked to the struggle against colonial exploitation and apartheid. However, the attainment of Namibia's independence in 1990 brought about a much-needed regime change to reflect the present illustrious making of the law in women's rights and related cases.

The constitutional protection of women, the complementary nature of statutory enactments, and the imposition of lengthy exemplary sentences in cases of domestic VAW are indicators of progress. Furthermore, the abolishment of the cautionary rule and broader judicial precedence in both the superior and lower courts of Namibia are signs of the progressivity of women's rights protection in Namibia. Progress made so far concerning women's rights is commendable and should be sustained. Namibia can be regarded as a promising example of the positive long-term impacts and effects of a gender-responsive legislative framework that can assist courts in advancing women's rights. The Namibian judicial system that remains gender responsive, especially as it relates to women despite being a male-dominated regime, gives the impression that a fertile gender legislative framework could be a safeguard against gender biases in jurisdictions where women's voices are lacking in judicial systems.

NOTES

1. Article 10 (1) of the Namibian Constitution.
2. 2000 NR 255 (SC).

REFERENCES

Adler, Z. (1987). *Rape on Trial*. London/New York: Routledge.

Ah-King, M. (ed.). (2013). *Challenging Popular Myths of Sex, Gender and Biology*. Uppsala: Springer International Publishing.

Ambunda, L., & de Klerk, S. (2008). "Women and Custom in Namibia: A Research Overview" in Ruppel, O. C. (ed.) *Women and Custom in Namibia: Cultural Practices versus Gender Equality*. Windhoek: Macmillan Publishers.

Amoo, S. K. (2008). *An Introduction to Namibian Law: Cases and Materials*. Windhoek: Macmillan Publishers.

Banda, F., & MacKinnon, C. (2006). "Sex, Gender and International Law." *Proceedings of the Annual Meeting of the American Society of International Law*, vol. 100, 243–248.

Birch, D. J. (1990). "Corroboration in Criminal Trial: A Review of the Proposal of the Law Commission Working Paper." *Crim LR*, 667–679.

Bradford, H. (1996). "Women, Gender and Colonialism: Rethinking the History of the British Cape Colony and Its Frontier Zones, c. 1806–70." *Journal of African History*, vol. 37 (3), 351–370.

Buss, D., & Manjii, A. (2005). *International Law: Modern Feminist Approaches*. Oxford: Hart Publishing.

Butler, J. (2002). *Gender Trouble: Feminism and the Subversion of Identity*. Oxford: Routledge.

Buys, G. L., & Nambala, S. (2003). *History of the Church in Namibia, 1805–1990: An Introduction*. Windhoek: Gamsberg Publishing.

Carver, T. (1996). *Gender Is Not a Synonym for Women*. Boulder, CO: Lynne Rienner Publishers.

Chairperson of the Immigration Selection Board v. Frank & Another [2001] NASC 1 (SC).

Charlesworth, H., Charton, S., & Chinkin, C. (2000). *The Boundaries of International Law: A Feminist Analysis*. Manchester: Manchester University Press.

Charlesworth, H., Chinkin, C., & Wright, S. (1991). "Feminist Approaches to International Law." *American Journal of International Law*, vol. 85 (4), 613–635.

Cobbah, J. (1987). "African Values and the Human Rights Debate: An African Perspective." *Human Rights Quarterly*, vol. 9 (3), 309–331.

Cohen, M. (2018). "Judicial Diversity in France: The Unspoken and Unspeakable." *Law and Social Inquiry*, vol. 43 (4), 1542–1573.

Combating of Domestic Violence Act 4 of 2003.

Combating of Rape Act 8 of 2000.

Communal Land Reform Act 5 of 2002.

Convention on the Elimination of All Forms of Discrimination Against Women (1979).

Dawuni, J. (2016). "Ghana: The Paradox of Judicial Stagnation" in Bauer, G. & Dawuni, J. (eds.) *Gender and the Judiciary in Africa: From Obscurity to Parity?*, New York: Routledge, 120–136.

Dawuni, J. (2020). "Women in Judiciaries Across Africa" in Yacob-Haliso, O. & Falola, T. (eds.) *The Palgrave Handbook of African Women Studies*. Palgrave Macmillan.

Dawuni, J., & Bauer, G. (eds.). (2016). *Gender and the Judiciary in Africa: From Obscurity to Parity?* New York: Routledge.

Dawuni, J., & Kuenyehia, A. (eds.). (2018). *International Courts and the African Woman Judge: Unveiled Narratives*. New York: Routledge.

de Beauvoir, S. (1978) (Trans. & ed. H. M. Parsley). *The Second Sex*. London: Jonathan Cape.

Dekeseredy, W. (2020). *Women Abuse in Rural Places*. Oxfordshire: Routledge.

Du Pisani, A. (1986). *SWA/Namibia: The Politics of Continuity and Change*. Johannesburg: Jonathan Ball.

Electoral Act 5 of 2014.

Emmett, T. (1999). *Popular Resistance and the Roots of Nationalism in Namibia, 1955–1966*. Basel: Schlettwein Publishers.

Fausto-Sterling, A. (2012). *Sex/Gender: Biology in a Social World*. London/New York: Routledge.

Fineman, M. A. (2010). "The Vulnerable Subject and the Responsive State." *Emory Law Journal*, vol. 60 (1), 251–267.

Fineman, M. A. (2008). "The Vulnerable Subject: Anchoring Equality in the Human Condition." *Yale Journal of Law and Feminism*, vol. 20 (1), 1–24.

Freeman, M., Chinkin, C., & Rudolf, B. (2012). *The UN Convention on the Elimination of All Forms of Discrimination Against Women: A Commentary*. Oxford: Oxford University Press.

Halilovic, M., & Sarajero, H. H. (eds.). (2014). *Gender and the Judiciary: Selected Findings and Recommendations on the Implications of Gender within the Judiciary of Bosnia and Herzegovina*. DCAF Publishers.

Hatchard, J. (1993). "Abolishing the Cautionary Rule in Sexual Cases in Namibia." *Journal of African Law*, vol. 73 (1), 97–100.

Hinz, M. O. (2008). "Strengthening Women's Rights: The Need to Address the Gap Between Customary and Statutory Law in Namibia" in Ruppel, O. C. (ed.) *Women and Custom in Namibia: Cultural Practices Versus Gender Equality*. Windhoek: Macmillan Publishers.

Hubbard, D. (2007). "Gender and Sexuality: The Law Reform Landscape" in LaFont, S. & Hubbard, D. (eds.) *Unravelling Taboos: Gender and Sexuality in Namibia*. Windhoek: Legal Assistance Centre.

Hubbard, D. (2010). "The Paradigm of Equality in the Namibian Constitution: Concept, Contours and Concerns" in Bösl, A., Horn, N. & du Pisani, A. (eds.) *Constitutional Democracy in Namibia: A Critical Analysis After Two Decades*. Windhoek: Konrad Adenauer Stiftung.

Katjavivi, P. H. (1988). *A History of Resistance in Namibia*. Oxford: James Curry Publisher.

Kenney, S. (2013). *Gender and Justice. Why Women in the Judiciary Really Matter*. New York: Routledge.

Knowles, C. (1996). *Family Boundaries: The Invention of Normality and Dangerousness*. Toronto: University of Toronto Press.

Legal Assistance Centre. (2017). *Namibia Gender Analysis*. Windhoek: LAC Publications.

Locke, J. (2003). *Two Treaties of Government* (trans. by Ian Shapiro (ed.)). Yale: Yale University Press.

Malhotra, M. (2004). *Dimensions of Women Exploitation*. Delhi: Isha Books.

Married Persons Equality Act 1 of 1996.

Msuya, N. (2019). "Concept of Culture Relativism and Women's Rights in Sub-Saharan Africa." *Journal of Asian and African Studies*, vol. 54 (8), 1145–1158.

Myburgh v. Commercial Bank of Namibia [2000] NR 255 (SC).

Namibian Constitution, 1990.

Ngwena, C. (2018). *What is Africanness? Contesting Nativism in Race, Culture and Sexualities*. Pretoria: Pretoria University Law Press.

Nkiwane, V. (2011). "Men, Gender and Law: Investigating the Links Between Masculinity, Gender and Power" in Tsanga, A. & Stewart, J. (eds.) *Women and Law: Innovative Approaches to Teaching, Research and Analysis*. Harare: Weaver Press.

Nzomo, M. (1992). "Women and Democratization Struggles in Africa" in Butler, J. & Scott, J. W. (eds.) *Feminists Theorize the Political*. London: Routledge, 131–141.

Protocol to the African Charter on the Rights of Women in Africa (2004).

Rackley, E. (2013). *Women, Judging and the Judiciary: From Difference to Diversity*. Cavendish: Routledge.

Resnik, J. (1993). "Gender Bias: From Classes to Courts." *Stanford Law Review*, vol. 45 (1), 2195–2210.

Resnik, J. (1996). "Asking about Gender in Courts." *Signs*, vol. 21 (4), 952–990.

Ruppel, O. C. (ed.). (2008). *Women and Custom in Namibia: Cultural Practice versus Gender Inequality?* Windhoek: Macmillan Publishers.

Ruppel, O. C., & Ruppel-Schlichting, K. (2011). "Legal and Judicial Pluralism in Namibia and Beyond: A Modern Approach to African Legal Architecture?" *Journal of Legal Pluralism and Unofficial Law*, vol. 43 (2), 33–63.

Ruppel, O. C., & Winter, G. (eds.). (2011). *Justice from Within: Legal Pluralism in Africa and beyond*. Hamburg: Verlag Dr Kovac.

S v. Amseb [2019] NAHCMD 57.

S v. Angula [2017] NAHCNLD 98.

S v. Bothile [2007] 1 NR 137.

S v. D & Another [1992] 1 SACR 143 (Nm).

S v. Diergaardt [2019] NAHCMD 454.

S v. Jackson [1998] 1 SACR 470 (SCA).

S v. Katamba [1999] NASC 7 (SC).

Shivji, I. G. (2007). *The Concept of Human Rights in Africa*. Oxford: African Books Collective.

Silvester, J. (2015). *Re-Viewing Resistance in Namibian History*. Windhoek: University of Namibia Press.

Slaughter, A. (2009). *A New World Order*. Princeton: Princeton University Press.

Sports Act 13 of 2003.

Steans, J. (1998). *Gender and International Relations: An Introduction*. New Jersey: Rutgers University Press.

Talavera, P. (2007). "Past and Present Practices: Sexual Developments in Namibia" in LaFont, S. & Hubbard, D. (eds.) *Unravelling Taboos: Gender and Sexuality in Namibia*. Windhoek: Legal Assistance Centre.

Totemeyer, G. (2010). *Church and State in Namibia: The Politics of Reconciliation*. Freiburg: Arnold Bergstraesser Institute.

Traditional Authorities Act 25 of 2000.

UN Committee on the Elimination of Discrimination Against Women (CEDAW). (1979). *General Recommendation No. 28 on the Core Obligations of States Parties Under Article* 2 of the Convention on the Elimination of All Forms of Discrimination Against Women United Nations. UN Publication.

van Marle, K., & Bonthuys, E. (2007). "Feminist Theories and Concepts" in Bonthuys, E. & Albertyn, A. (eds.) *Gender, Law and Justice*. Cape Town: Juta & Co, 5–25.

Chapter 12

Women and Environmental Justice Issues in Nigeria

An Evaluation

Eghosa Ekhator and Pedi Obani

INTRODUCTION

Global frameworks such as human rights and Sustainable Development Goals (SDGs) reflect internationally agreed-upon minimum standards for human development outcomes in a way that suggests universality of human needs and priorities. Nonetheless, details of what constitutes a just outcome differ both within and across diverse groups of people, depending on individual and collective values, worldviews, identities, perceptions, and experiences with institutions and other people, across temporal and spatial divides. Similarly, environmental justice has varied meanings, strategies of access, and implications in various contexts (Allen, Fanucchi, McCormick and Zierold, 2019).

Although access to justice, especially environmental justice, continues to be a challenge for "many vulnerable and marginalised groups, women particularly encounter serious barriers to access to justice in society" (Durojaye et al., 2020: p. 224). The experiences of women and their involvement in environment justice can be context specific and influenced by other factors, such as colonialism, political-economic structure, and patriarchy among others (MacGregor, 2021). This is reflected in the Niger Delta, where women who live in rural areas are poorer and bear most of the brunt of environmental injustices arising from oil multinational corporations (MNCs) operations (because they live closer to the oil exploration sites).

Some scholars argue that the contributions of women to the environmental justice paradigm have been relegated to the background in mainstream scholarship on environmental justice (Gaard, 2018; MacGregor, 2021). Even though there has been a plethora of academic publications on women in the

Niger Delta, there is a paucity of research on the gender aspects of environmental justice in Nigeria, especially from a legal perspective.

This chapter focuses on the use of protests and the potential of reliance on litigation in improving access to environmental justice for women, particularly in the rural parts of the Niger Delta region, where there are significant environmental impacts from the operations of the oil and gas industry. The methodology adopted for the chapter is of a doctrinal nature that relies on the analysis of relevant legislation, scholarly publications, and case reports through an environmental justice lens, with emphasis on gender aspects. As defined by the Pearce Committee (1987 in Hutchinson and Duncan, 2012: p. 101) in their report on legal research in Australia, doctrinal research is "research which provides a systematic exposition of the rules governing a particular legal category, analyses the relationship between rules, explains areas of difficulty and, perhaps, predicts future developments." This is distinguishable from other forms of legal research, including reform-oriented research which focuses on the evaluation of existing laws and makes recommendations for review, as required; theoretical research which explores the conceptual underpinnings of legal principles and rules; fundamental research which expounds on "law as a social phenomenon" (Hutchinson and Duncan, 2012: p. 102); and socio-legal research which entails an interdisciplinary analysis of law also involving sociological theory (Banakar and Travers, 2005).

Doctrinal legal research builds on law's intuitive legal research tradition (Hutchinson and Duncan, 2012). It entails the interpretation of primary sources of law, including statutes and cases, to highlight or formulate rules and principles that are relevant for understanding legal processes (Banakar and Travers, 2005). Doctrinal legal research is therefore essentially preoccupied with understanding the legal rules and principles relevant for any given legal question as a basis for normative analysis. This is especially appropriate for our research which is focused on understanding the legal underpinnings for a gender-sensitive analysis of environmental justice in Nigeria. This provides a strong methodological basis for the recommendations for improving women's access to environmental justice, based on the existing laws and environmental justice and women's rights cases from regional courts and quasi-judicial systems and other jurisdictions.

The choice of doctrinal legal research methodology therefore informed the data collection process and analysis (of statutes, judicial decisions, and scholarly literature) for this chapter. The chapter consists of five sections. The first section presents a conceptual framework that focuses on links between gender and environmental justice. The second section analyzes the outcomes of women-led protests in the Niger Delta as a strategy for improving women's access to environmental justice. The third section explores the potential of litigation as an alternative strategy for addressing the limits of protests and promoting a gender-sensitive conceptualization of environmental justice through the decisions of domestic, subregional, and regional courts, and courts in foreign jurisdictions. The fourth section highlights recent domestic judicial and legislative developments impacting prospects for improving women's access to environmental justice. The final section is the conclusion.

CONCEPTUALIZING THE GENDER ASPECTS OF ENVIRONMENTAL JUSTICE

The history of environmental justice doctrine and movement is traced to the United States, where it served as a counterpoint to the discontent for racist government policies in the 1960s and 1970s (Ekhator, 2017). A plethora of studies highlight the inordinate burden of differential environmental harms on minorities (Bullard and Johnson 2002; Holifield, Chakraborty and Walker, 2018). Hence, environmental justice "is the first paradigm to link environment and race, class, gender and social justice in an explicit framework" (Taylor, 2000: p. 542). The dimensions of environmental justice broadly consist of the distribution of costs (distributive justice); compensation for historic inequities and prevention of future occurrences (corrective justice); open, informed, and inclusive decision-making processes (procedural justice); and the intersections between environmental struggles and social and economic justice (Gonzalez, 2013).

Environmental justice doctrine has flourished globally, especially in places with a history of environmental degradation (Ekhator, 2014). The environmental justice paradigm has become a global movement that is no longer limited to the experiences of ethnic minorities in the United States (Sikor and Newell, 2014; Agyeman, 2014; Martinez-Alier et al., 2016). Furthermore, Julian Agyeman (2014: p. 237) argues that "there has been an acceptance among senior figures in the US environmental justice movement that while race is a major factor in US struggles, in other parts of the world a broader set of socio-economic issues are at least as influential."

Different conceptualizations of access to (environmental) justice could be possible, depending on the prevailing circumstances in each country or context. In its narrow conceptualization, access to justice is simply access to the courts, but in its wider meaning it embraces access to the political order and to the benefits arising from social and economic developments in society (Okogbule, 2005; Ugochukwu, 2020). Moreover, public participation and consultation are central to the environmental justice struggle in industrialized countries, whereas in developing countries—especially resource-rich countries—access to or control of natural resources is fundamental to the environmental justice paradigm (Ekhator, 2017). Environmental justice entails considering how the governance architecture of environmental resources affects different individuals and groups, particularly the vulnerable and marginalized, whether changes to/within environmental governance institutions are considered fair by diverse stakeholders, and how human interests can be reconciled with environmental sustainability (Holifield, Chakraborty and Walker, 2018).

Both feminism and environmental justice are linked to women's shared experiences of injustice in different spheres of life (Gaard, 2017). However, the distinct intersections between gender and environmental justice have hardly been explored, except for ecofeminism. Ecofeminist researchers or scholars have played an integral role in informing modern-day scholarship about justice and human-environment interactions (MacGregor in Coolsaet, 2021: p. 234). It has evolved since the 1970s from exploring the linkages between gender, environment, and species, to uncovering the experiences of women of different races and nationalities in connection with patriarchy and the oppression of women linked to environmental degradation (Besthorn and McMillen, 2002). One main crux of ecofeminist perspective is that gender should be "central to the study of environmental justice" (MacGregor, 2021: p. 234). Thus, the understanding or awareness of gender inequalities is germane to the study of environmental justice (MacGregor, 2021).

Nancy Unger (2008: p. 115) contends that women suffer "uniquely from environmental injustices" in different parts of the world. Gender roles determine vulnerability to climate change and other negative environmental externalities, as well as the allocation of and access to environmental goods, with women being often worse off (Onwutuebe, 2019; Hughes, 2021). Other critical gender dimensions of environmental justice include women's exclusion from decision-making on environmental issues (IUCN, 2015), poor consideration of the impact of degrowth and conservation/environmental protection policies on women's livelihoods, and the disproportionate risk of exposure to pollution borne by women because of the siting of polluting industries.

Emphasis on women's vulnerability to climate change and their environmental protection interest could however underemphasize the power differentials that result in this situation across institutions and inadvertently legitimize traditional gender roles that reinforce patriarchy (Bell, 2016). Moreover, the motivations of women in environmental justice movements can be remarkably diverse and include factors beyond vulnerability to climate change (Gomez et al., 2011; Murdock, 2021; Stover and Cable, 2017).

As women are often marginalized from the environmental decision-making process and the environmental injustices impacting them in many parts of the world, they (especially women of color) are at the forefront and sometimes are leaders of environmental activism or action and grassroots (local) environmental movement or change (Murdock, 2021). Similarly, due to women in Africa historically suffering extensive impacts arising from environmental degradation, women also play an integral role in environmental justice movements and the development of environmental conservation practices (Boshoff, 2020). For example, in Kenya, the late Nobel Peace winner Wangari Maathai founded the Green Belt Movement in 1977. The movement (similar to occurrences in other parts of Africa, especially Nigeria, Cameroon, Uganda, and Liberia) was at the forefront of the mobilization of women promoting sustainable livelihoods and environmental justice. Overall, gender aspects of environmental justice buttress the connections between women, environmental justice, access to justice, and African women's resistance movements in the burgeoning global environmental justice paradigm and related scholarship.

WOMEN AND ENVIRONMENTAL JUSTICE IN NIGERIA

The United Nations Environment Programme 2011 report on Ogoniland revealed the shocking levels of oil pollution in Ogoniland in the Niger Delta caused by the operations of Shell Oil Company that are yet to be cleaned up. As one of the most affected groups in Nigeria, women have been actively involved in seeking redress for the negative environmental impacts flowing from operations of oil MNCs in the Niger Delta. The Niger Delta region where oil MNCs maintain significant presence has become a center of incessant violent conflicts with local groups and widespread protests and demonstrations against MNCs accused of exacerbating environmental pollution issues and related health problems (Amnesty, 2020a,b). A recent study demonstrates that children and babies in Nigeria are "twice as likely to die in the first month of life if their mothers were living near the oil spill before falling pregnant" (Hodal in Guardian, 2017; Bruederle and Hodler, 2017). The activities of MNCs in the oil and gas sector have also negatively impacted the economic, social, and physical means of subsistence of women (Babatunde, 2020).

Although access to justice continues to be a challenge for "many vulnerable and marginalised groups, women particularly encounter serious barriers to access to justice in society" (Durojaye et al., 2020: p. 224). Nonetheless, women have been actively involved in seeking redress for the negative impacts flowing from MNC operations in the Niger Delta and have in so doing contributed to improving access to environmental justice in Nigeria by relying on both informal (such as protests and customary processes) and formal (such as litigation) strategies (Turner and Brownhill, 2004).

Women-Led Protests in the Niger Delta and Environmental Justice

Protests by women are not a new phenomenon in Nigeria and have been successful in achieving wider social and political reforms (Obani, 2021). This was evident in women-led protests during the colonial era, including the Aba Women's War in 1929 (in what is now Southeast Nigeria) due to rumors that women were going to be taxed, and the revolt by Abeokuta women in 1948 (Aghedo and Osumah, 2015; Obani, 2021). Post-independence, the Federation of Ogoni Women's Association has been at the forefront of mobilization of women via protests and demonstrations against the negative consequences arising from the operations of Shell and Chevron Corp. in the Niger Delta region (Ikelegbe, 2005; MacGregor, 2021: p. 240).

Women played an active role in peaceful agitations for the development of Ogoniland led by Ken Saro-Wiwa and the Movement for the Survival of the Ogoni People (MOSOP) during the 1990s (Ikelegbe, 2005). Women often led MOSOP demonstrations or protests, marching at the front to bring attention to the nonviolent nature of these demonstrations (Mai-Bornu, 2019). Ogoni women were said to have played an integral role in ensuring that nonviolence became the crux of the Ogoni struggle (Mai-Bornu, 2019; Keys, 2021). Also, Ogoni women's involvement in the struggle led to inclusion of women's issues such as girls' and women's education as important slants of the Ogoni protest (Barikor-Wiwa, 1997; Keys, 2019). It should be noted that MOSOP's nonviolent protests have had a massive impact on Shell's operations in Ogoniland; for more than 25 years, Shell has not operated any of its facilities in Ogoniland due to its rejection by the Ogoni people (Ekhator, 2016). This is notwithstanding that under Nigerian laws, Shell has the right to operate in the region.

Oil companies are not the immediate cause of women's marginalization in the Niger Delta. However, they amplify it in their dealings with oil communities (Renouard and Lado, 2012). The increase in women's engagement in the resource agitation in the Niger Delta has been partly because of the failings in the existing resources governance structure and the appropriation of the incidental benefits to the elites (youth, men, and traditional/community leaders) to the detriment of women (Ikelegbe, 2005; Babatunde, 2018; Babatunde, 2020).

Protests by women are considered as not remarkably successful in the 1990s in the Niger Delta, and many concessions from the oil firms appeared to be token gestures (Ikelegbe, 2005). Charles Ukeje (2004: p. 612) argued that "the demands of the women were essentially 'bread-and-butter' in nature." Also, Evaristus Oshionebo (2009: p. 99) averred that "it is of course debatable whether such aggressive tactics [of the women] have effected substantive changes in the behaviour of TNCs." Furthermore, Munir (2021) argues that scholars should be more nuanced in their analysis of the contribution of women to protests in the Niger Delta.

Overall, women-led protests have had modest but significant impacts on oil MNCs operating in the Niger Delta. For example, some protests and actions led by women have impacted positively on resource governance processes and led some oil and gas firms to establish technical-skills acquisition programs for women's empowerment in the Niger Delta (Ikelegbe, 2005, Munir, 2021). Unsurprisingly, there has been a proliferation of women issues-based groups there (Ikelegbe, 2005). Conversely, some women also have held influential positions in militant groups and played active roles in the insurgency in the region (Ekine, 2008; Oriola, 2012, 2016; Obi and Oriola, 2018). For example, women acted as spies, armed combatants, cooks, spiritual advisers, mediators in kidnapping incidents, and gunrunners among others (Oriola, 2012, 2016).

Given the continued neglect of the Niger Delta by oil MNCs and the Nigerian government, to further ground community protests, some groups became involved in armed militancy and others (especially women) utilized unique ways to protest (Oriola, 2012). Niger Delta women have relied on dramatic strategies in protesting the activities of oil MNCs (Oshionebo, 2009; Okogbule, 2012; Munir, 2021). According to Munir (2020) and Ikelegbe (2005), some strategies used by women included singing and dancing in front of the offices of oil MNCs in the Niger Delta, demonstrating in the nude, and the indigenous concept of "sitting on a man," which, according to Turner and Brownhill (2004), was a tool used by Niger Delta women to physically block the entry of oil workers to oil sites.

In July 2002, women in the Ugborodo community (an oil-producing community in Nigeria's Delta state) took over the premises of Chevron and other oil MNCs and stripped themselves naked. This is a local shaming mechanism and, in some communities, can be used to lay curses on people and objects (Oshionebo, 2009; Okogbule, 2012). As a result of this protest, Chevron/Texaco was forced to declare "a *force majeure* clause in its contracts with its exporters," which led to massive revenue losses (Okogbule, 2012: p. 256). This prompted the company to seek a truce with the women and sign a memorandum of understanding (MOU) with the Ugborodo community (Okogbule, 2012: 256). The MOU included terms beneficial to the larger community, such as upgrading 15 members of the communities who were contract staff to permanent staff status; employment of an individual from each of the five Ugborodo villages every year; building of one house each for traditional rulers of the communities; provision of vital infrastructure, including a community hospital; and payment of monthly allowances to the elderly and establishment of income-generating initiatives (Turner and Brownhill, 2004; Okogbule 2012). Unfortunately, the MOU is yet to be fully implemented by Chevron (Vanguard, 2020).

At the time of writing, protests led by women were still taking place in the Niger Delta. In March 2020, hundreds of women from the Egbema community in Imo state in southeastern Nigeria shut down Sterling Global Oil Company for refusing to pay for funeral arrangements for three members of their community (Onyejiuwa, 2020). Also, in September 2020, women in Ugborodo protested the non-implementation of some MOU provisions and alleged breach of the MOU (Idowu, 2020). It is noteworthy that the MOUs entered between oil MNCs and communities in the Niger Delta are not legally binding contracts, although the Niger Delta communities often consider them to be binding against defaulting oil and gas MNCs (Ekhator, 2016).

Despite various criticisms of the utility of women's protests in the Niger Delta, the protests have also impacted other protests and actions in the country and served as inspiration for similar protests in the other parts of the world (Turner and Brownhill, 2004; Fallon and Moreau, 2016). For example, in 2002, women in California protested naked, and this has become a new anti-war protest tactic. According to Turner and Brownhill (2004: p. 71) (relying on Ivan Gale, 2002), women's protests in the Niger Delta were the inspiration for the women in California and show how this style of protesting has become a global phenomenon.

Furthermore, women-led protests are not limited to Nigeria and are widespread in other parts of Africa, including the Mano River Women's Peace Network of Guinea, Sierra Leone, and Liberia, and the women of Somali who contributed to the Mudug Region Peace Agreement (Keys, 2019). This theme of women-led protests, including naked protests, has been explored by plethora of African feminist writers, including Tamale (2014, 2016), Ahikire et al. (2017), Oyěwùmí (1997, 2016), and Amadiume (1997). Hence, Sylvia Tamale (2016: p. 7) suggests that "in Africa, women have used their bodies to protest extremities; it is usually a weapon of last resort when they find themselves pushed to the edge of the cliff. It is very powerful and always effective in that it draws attention to the issue under dispute. The act of public stripping is even more potent if the women are married and/or mothers."

The limited success of some protests in achieving environmental justice for women in the Niger Delta has resulted in women litigants instituting cases in foreign jurisdictions. The next section highlights the potential of reliance on litigation in improving access to environmental justice of women in Nigeria.

Litigation as an Alternative Strategy for Access to Environmental Justice

There is a plethora of cases in different jurisdictions or countries by Nigerian litigants who allege that they are victims of environmental injustices perpetuated or arising from the activities of oil MNCs in Nigeria (Amnesty International, 2020b). A soaring number of oil and gas pollution-related cases filed both in Nigeria and abroad by, or with the support of, civil society organizations (CSOs) is a sign of rising reliance on litigation (Ako and Ekhator, 2016; Enneking, 2012; Enneking, 2019). For example, *Gbemre v. SPDC* was initiated in a Federal High Court in Nigeria; *Bowoto v. Chevron* and *Wiwa v. Shell* were litigated in the United States; *Akpan v. Shell* was heard at The Hague, Netherlands; and *Bodo Community v. SPDC* was heard in the United Kingdom (Ako and Ekhator, 2016). This section focuses on the gender dimensions of access to justice in the context of oil-related cases filed before domestic courts in Nigeria, subregional and regional courts in Africa, and foreign jurisdictions.

Litigation in Domestic Courts

In the absence of an explicit international framework on regulation of the cross-border activities of MNCs, litigation by domestic courts is one of the strategies that has been relied upon to hold "corporate actors accountable for the adverse human rights and environmental impacts of their activities" (Enneking, 2019: p. 513). Unfortunately, domestic courts in Nigeria have been unable to provide justice or meaningful avenues for providing succor for victims of environmental injustices in the country (Amnesty International, 2020b). Some challenges or obstacles "associated with litigation in Nigeria include limited resources of litigants, delays in the judicial process, the strict requirement of *locus standi proof*, and the overreliance on common law torts such as trespass, negligence and nuisance in suits by litigants (in the absence of an effective framework on oil pollution control or litigation), amongst others" (Ekhator, 2014: p. 68; CEHRD Report, 2015). Another significant barrier is the financial strength of MNCs (Okogbule, 2005; Ekhator, 2014).

Many women in Nigeria who are victims of environmental injustice are poor and unable to afford litigation in many instances (Okafor and Ugochukwu, 2015). This is exemplified in *General Oil Limited v. Oduntan*, wherein Justice Niki Tobi of the Court of Appeal stated that it is widespread knowledge that litigation is an awfully expensive "thing in this country, and the present economic situation has made the position worse. Filing fees have over the years risen. So have fees for counsel" (Okafor and Ugochukwu, 2015: p. 405; Brems and Adekoya, 2010). This is the norm in the Niger Delta, where many communities and litigants, including women, are unable to get justice due to paucity of funding and exorbitant costs of litigation (Frynas, 2001; Munir, 2020).

Notwithstanding the hundreds of cases filed against oil MNCs operating in Nigeria, environmental degradation and environmental injustices associated with operations of MNCs remain rife (CEHRD 2015; Frynas, 2001). Nonetheless, litigation (especially public interest or strategic impact litigation) is one of the most successful strategies used by CSOs, individuals (including women), and communities in Nigeria to influence the regulatory process and activities of MNCs in the oil and gas sector (Ekhator 2014; Ako and Ekhator 2016). For example, Environmental Rights Action, the Nigerian affiliate of Friends of the Earth, has been at the forefront of holding oil MNCs accountable by filing cases in Nigeria and other countries (Greyl et al., 2013). Notwithstanding that litigation as a regulatory strategy is beset by many impediments, public interest litigation could result in the establishment of new precedents and rules and could lead to litigation being pursued on behalf of poor and marginalized individuals, or groups whose voices and concerns might otherwise be drowned out by the legal system (Greyl et al., 2013; Okafor and Ugochukwu, 2014; Ugochukwu, 2020).

In this regard, public interest litigation could be distinguished from strategic litigation per se. Okafor and Ugochukwu (2014: p. 437) assert that "while public interest litigation focuses on the 'interest' being pursued through a lawsuit, strategic litigation is more about the 'impact' expected from a single judicial decision. It is often anticipated that strategic cases will generate an impact that goes well beyond the actual outcome of the individual case." In Nigeria, public interest litigation has been used for a plethora of issues, including women's rights, environmental justice, and the constitutionality of the death penalty (Ugochukwu, 2020; Amechi, 2015).

Most court cases involving women in domestic courts have been mainly focused on issues of women's rights broadly rather than women's access to environmental justice per se or the violations of rights and livelihoods of women in the Niger Delta (Ugochukwu, 2020). There have been hundreds of oil cases in Nigeria; however, they have been mainly instituted by male litigants and local community chiefs due to the patriarchal nature of the Nigerian society and lack of ownership of lands by many women in the country (Munir, 2020). Because of these obstacles, victims of environmental injustices in the Niger Delta, including women, are now accessing courts in foreign jurisdictions instead to secure justice.

Litigation in Subregional and Regional Courts in Africa

Due to the difficulties of accessing environmental justice at the domestic level, women in Nigeria and other parts of Africa have relied on the African

Charter on Human and Peoples' Rights (the African Charter) and the Protocol to the African Charter on Human and Peoples' Rights on the Rights of Women in Africa (the Maputo Protocol) and other international conventions to air their grievances in subregional and regional judiciaries (including quasi-judicial tribunals). These include the African Commission on Human and Peoples' Rights, African Court on Human and Peoples' Rights, and the different subregional judiciaries, such as the Economic Community of West African States (ECOWAS) Community Court of Justice (ECCJ).

The African Charter on Human and Peoples' Rights was domesticated into Nigerian law via the instrumentality of the African Charter on Human and Peoples' Rights (Enforcement and Ratification) Act 1983. In Nigeria, courts have relied on the provisions of the African Charter to invalidate discriminatory practices against women (Arowolo, 2020; Okongwu, 2021). In the case of *Mojekwu v. Ejikeme*, the Nigerian Court of Appeal relied on the provisions of the African Charter and the Convention on the Elimination of All Forms of Discrimination Against Women (CEDAW) to invalidate a customary practice (law) that precluded daughters of a dead man from inheriting his property (Arowolo, 2020)

Also, the African Charter is "often heralded as the first international law instrument to have expressly recognised a generally satisfactory environmental as a human right" (Du Plessis, 2011: p. 36). Article 24 of the African Charter states: "All peoples shall have the right to a generally satisfactory environment favourable to their development." Furthermore, Article 2 of the African Charter, which is the nondiscrimination provision, explicitly prohibits discrimination based on sex, and this provision applies equally to men and women in Africa. However, some scholars have argued that the African Charter has been ineffective in addressing or resolving numerous discriminatory issues that African women encounter in different parts of the continent (Aniekwu, 2009; Okongwu, 2021).

Criticisms over the apparent neglect of women issues in the African Charter led to adoption of the Maputo Protocol in 2003 (Okongwu, 2021; Ezeilo, 2021). The Maputo Protocol is designed to provide further protection for women's rights that are not specifically enshrined under the African Charter or under the CEDAW (Viljoen, 2009). The Maputo Protocol was signed and ratified in Nigeria in 2004 but has yet to be domesticated into Nigerian law. This impedes its applicability in Nigeria. Notwithstanding that many African states have signed and ratified the Maputo Protocol, its application in national, regional, and subregional courts and implementation in some African countries have been problematic (Mwikya, 2020).

While the African Charter provides the right of all peoples to a generally satisfactory environment, provisions on the environment enshrined in the Maputo Protocol are more far-reaching (Chenwi, 2018). For example,

Articles 18 and 19 pledge that all women shall have the right to live in a healthy and sustainable environment and the right to sustainable development (Chenwi, 2018).

There have been few cases dealing with environmental justice issues in the African Commission on Human and Peoples' Rights; however, none has focused on improving access to environmental justice for women (Boshoff, 2020). For example, in *SERAC and CSER v. Nigeria* (popularly known as the *SERAC* case), the African Commission held that the Nigeria government and its agencies were in violation of the African Charter. The African Commission did not exercise jurisdiction over oil MNCs; thus, they were not held culpable for the environmental degradation in the Niger Delta.

In 2012, in the case of *SERAP v. Federal Republic of Nigeria*, the ECOWAS Court of Justice held that the Nigerian government violated Articles 1 and 24 of the African Charter and ordered that the Nigerian government take effective measures within the shortest possible period to restore or remediate the environment of the Niger Delta (Ekhator, 2014; Ekhator, 2020). Notwithstanding that women were not the plaintiffs or litigants in the *SERAP* case, some women's groups in the Niger Delta, such as the Niger Delta Women's Movement for Peace and Development, have claimed that this decision will have positive impacts on women's rights in the region (Omoniye, 2013). Omoniye argues that the *SERAP* decision is an important precedent that upholds the human right to a healthy environment and confirms the human right of the Niger Delta people to live in a pollution-free environment. Unfortunately to date, this decision is yet to be enforced by the Nigerian government.

The ECCJ and the African Court on Human and Peoples' Rights have declared acts of government agencies or laws as violation of the Maputo Protocol in several cases involving women litigants, such as *Dorothy Njemanze & 3 Others v. Nigeria* and *APDF and IHRDA v. the Republic of Mali*, respectively. For the first time in its history, the African Court on Human and Peoples' Rights found a breach of the Maputo Protocol in the *APDF and IHRDA v. the Republic of Mali* (Capone, 2020; O'Connell, 2019; Rachovitsa, 2019). Thus, notwithstanding the strident criticisms of the utility of the African Charter and Maputo Protocol on the protection of women's rights and paucity of cases on environmental justice and women in various domestic, subregional, and regional courts in Africa, it can be contended that the African Charter and Maputo Protocol have had direct and positive impacts on women's rights on the continent (Ekhator, 2019; Ayeni, 2016).

Furthermore, although Nigeria is yet to implement or enforce the ECCJ judgment in *Njemanze*, scholars including Mwikya (2020) and Ojigho (2020) have argued that the decision has had some positive impacts in Nigeria. For example, it has led to improved media awareness (advocacy) of women rights in the country and has enhanced the potential of the ECCJ as a forum that women in Nigeria can use to air their grievances and claims (including environmental justice issues). Besides, CSOs and individuals—especially representatives of local communities in the Niger Delta—have instituted environmental justice cases at the ECCJ on behalf of themselves and Niger Delta communities (Ekhator, 2020). This was reflected in the SERAP case judgment by the ECCJ in 2012. Thus, women litigants from Nigeria can sue the Nigerian government in the ECCJ for environmental injustices arising from the activities of oil MNCs and governmental agencies in the country. However, at the time of writing, cases involving environmental justice and women are yet to be filed at the ECCJ.

On the other hand, in addition to the *Njemanze* case, recent case law on women rights at the ECCJ include *Aminata Diantou Diane v. République du Mali*[1] and *Mary Sunday v. Federal Republic of Nigeria.*[2] These cases, according to Addadzi-Koom (2020: p 165), "have given a voice to the Maputo Protocol towards eliminating human rights violations that have for so long lurked privately and silently amongst women."

Litigation in Foreign Jurisdictions

Many victims of environmental injustice now institute cases in foreign jurisdictions, especially the home states of the MNCs, because they believe they will get justice in those courts (Enneking, 2019). Due to judicial and other institutional impediments in holding oil MNCs culpable for their actions in Nigeria and other developing countries, CSOs have initiated civil actions in foreign jurisdictions, especially in the United States via the Alien Tort Claims Act (ATCA) 1789. The ATCA allows only non-U.S. nationals to sue in U.S. courts for violations or torts under international or U.S. laws (Emeseh et al., 2010; Katuoka and Dailidaitė, 2012). Munir (2020) argues that in environmental litigation, Niger Delta women can take a cue from rural women of the Oriente region of the Ecuadorian Amazon, who instituted lawsuits against Texaco in U.S. courts under the ATCA.

The ATCA jurisprudence on MNCs has been beset by many impediments, as courts in the United States have consistently narrowed the application of the ATCA (Stephens, 2020; Stewart and Wuerth, 2013; Oshionebo, 2009). Indeed, very few cases have been decided on their merits, including *Kiobel v. Royal Dutch Petroleum Co*,[3] which further restricted the remit of the ATCA toward MNCs. In *Kiobel* (this case was instituted by Esther Kiobel on behalf of her husband, who was put to death by hanging by the Nigerian government), the U.S. Supreme Court dismissed the suit against Shell brought by victims of alleged Shell's complicity in state crimes committed against the Ogoni people and held that Shell's connection to the United States was unconvincing (Hitchon, 2013).

The court held that it had no jurisdiction on the matter. This decision was reached despite Shell having business offices in the United States, and hence, the ATCA was held to be inapplicable. In an earlier case, *Wiwa v. Shell*, which also was instituted in the United States, Shell settled out of court with the plaintiff rather than go through the judicial process inherent in the ATCA jurisprudence (Ako and Ekhator, 2016). These cases illustrate how local communities seek to enforce their rights through judicial processes outside Nigeria and provide judicial options to Niger Delta communities and individuals that suffer from environmental injustice accentuated by the activities of oil MNCs in Nigeria.

The Kiobel case is germane to the crux of the argument in this chapter as it illustrates how some women litigants, originally from the Niger Delta who did not get justice in U.S. courts, are now reinstituting their cases as a deliberate strategy in other jurisdictions in the world. Because of difficulties in accessing (environmental) justice in different fora (including Nigeria and under the ATCA in the United States), some widows of Ogoni leaders slain by the Nigerian state subsequently instituted court action in the Netherlands. In 2017, Esther Kiobel and three other widows (Victoria Bera, Blessing Eawo, and Charity Levula) of the Ogoni Nine brought a claim against Shell in the Netherlands, and this case is going through the judicial process in Dutch courts (Amnesty International, 2020b). According to media reports, "[A]t the case's first hearing in February 2019, Esther Kiobel and Victoria Bera gave moving testimonies regarding their late husbands and subsequent struggles for justice. It was the first time either had an opportunity to speak in court" (Amnesty International, 2020b: p. 14). This action by the plaintiffs can be termed feminist or women led because they are the drivers of the process.

PROSPECTS FOR ENHANCING WOMEN'S ACCESS TO ENVIRONMENTAL JUSTICE

Although legal representation may be a barrier to accessing justice, it is possible that, as argued by Ugochukwu (2020: p. 116), "several other substantive and structural factors impede access even before victims can get to the front door of the courts." Arguably, this is the case in the Niger Delta, where women already face state-sanctioned discriminatory practices, such as lack of access to land and the patriarchal nature of the Nigerian society that limits opportunities for seeking redress in the courts. Some challenges associated with litigation in Nigeria include limited resources of litigants, delays in the judicial process, and a strict requirement of locus standi proof (Ekhator, 2014: p. 68; CEHRD Report, 2015). Many women who are victims of environmental injustice are poor and unable to afford litigation without support.

This makes it important to also ensure the monetary compensation of women for environmental injustices and rights violations. Furthermore, notwithstanding the hundreds of cases filed against oil MNCs operating in Nigeria, environmental degradation and environmental injustices associated with the operations of MNCs remain rife (CEHRD, 2015; Frynas, 2001). This further erodes confidence in litigation for environmental justice.

Remarkably, CSOs are playing an important role in supporting local communities in the Niger Delta in accessing environmental justice in foreign jurisdiction. In the case of *Akpan v. Shell*, a civil lawsuit against Shell in the Netherlands based on years of oil pollution allegedly perpetuated by Shell in three villages in the Niger Delta, the collaboration between both local and foreign CSOs and Niger Delta fishermen was essential in successfully holding Shell liable (Greyl et al., 2013).

However, the *locus standi* principle affects the ability of CSOs (and non-governmental organizations—NGOs) to institute action in Nigerian courts (Anozie and Wingate, 2020). Fortunately, there has been recent judicial pronouncement on locus standi for environmental NGOs in instituting legal action on behalf of victims of environmental injustice in Nigeria. In 2018, the Nigerian Supreme Court in the *Centre for Oil Pollution Watch v. Nigerian National Petroleum Corporation* held that environmental NGOs have the locus standi to institute environmental cases in Nigeria, thereby improving access to environmental justice and promoting sustainable development for litigants, victims, and communities in Nigeria (Babalola, 2020). Notwithstanding criticism that it will lead to a floodgate of cases in courts (Olatunbosun and Onu, 2020), this judgment will enable environmental NGOs and CSOs to institute cases, including on behalf of women victims of environmental injustices in Nigeria.

Other recent developments of note regarding prospects for access to justice for women include legislative enactment of some women-friendly laws in Nigeria (Onyemelukwe, 2015; Ekhator, 2019). Enactment of the Violence against Persons (Prohibition) Act in 2015 appears to give a fillip to the view that the Nigerian government is attempting to promote women's rights in the country.

In Uganda, the Ugandan Constitution and some domestic laws such as the National Environment Act of 2019, provides that women should play an active role in environmental management, the Nigerian government could take a cue from these laws when developing similar laws in Nigeria (Kabaseke, 2020). For example, women could be given specific roles in the public participation regime in the oil and gas industry in Nigeria, as well as the compensation process. The reasons for the success of the women-led protests in Nigeria considered in this chapter were partly because the women were involved in negotiating the MOUs between the oil communities and oil MNCs.

Furthermore, there has been little or no case law by subregional and regional judiciaries in Africa explicitly focused on gender aspects of environmental justice. As highlighted earlier in this chapter, one of the few cases at the African Commission that has dealt with environmental protection was the *SERAC* case, which focused on the culpability of the Nigerian government for the environmental degradation in Ogoniland. However, in *SERAC*, there was no discussion of gender impacts of the environmental injustice (Brown and Oder, 2016). The first major decision of the African Court on Human and Peoples' Rights, considering alleged violations of the African Charter provisions on environmental protection, is the *Ogiek* case.[4] The *Ogiek* case is also said to be the African Court's first major judgment on indigenous peoples' rights (Chenwi, 2018). The African Court on Human and Peoples' Rights held that the Kenyan government had violated several articles of the African Charter (Chenwi, 2018; Maluwa, 2020). The decision did not explicitly discuss gender aspects of environmental justice though. Notwithstanding, the ECCJ, however, offers additional prospects for advancing access to environmental justice for women because there is no requirement of exhaustion of local remedies before filing cases at the ECCJ (Ojigho, 2020: p. 19). Also, individuals and NGOs can file cases at the EECJ (Ekhator, 2014). On the other hand, under the African Court on Human and Peoples' Rights, there is a requirement of exhaustion of local remedies before litigants or claimants can institute cases (Ojigho, 2020). Furthermore, under the African Court on Human and Peoples' Rights individuals do not have direct access to the court (Ojigho, 2020; Ekhator, 2014).

Member States need to make declarations recognizing the jurisdiction of the African Court on Human and Peoples' Rights, thereby allowing direct access to individuals in such countries. Nigeria is yet to make such a declaration (Ekhator, 2014). NGOs with observer status before the African Commission and individuals from countries which have made declarations recognizing the jurisdiction of the African Court on Human and Peoples' Rights can also file or institute cases directly (Ekhator, 2014).

Emerging jurisprudence from other jurisdictions also highlights the prospects for advancing access to environmental justice for women through litigation. For example, the Waorani indigenous community in Ecuador won a groundbreaking judgment stopping the government from selling off their land for oil-related activities. This lawsuit was instituted by Nemonte Nenquimo, a woman from the Waorani indigenous community (Global Witness, 2021). Laine Munir (2020) argues that many Niger Delta women are reluctant to institute cases in court; they prefer traditional strategies such as protest or demonstration. This is due in part to the patriarchal nature of environmental justice litigation in Nigeria. However, Niger Delta women can draw from the experiences of women in other parts of the world that have relied on litigation as a direct and additional strategy to improve access to environmental justice.

CONCLUSION

It is imperative to highlight that a definition of access to justice—especially from a Nigerian context—must be all encompassing to include both formal and informal justice mechanisms as well as any other strategies that enhance the ability of marginalized and disadvantaged groups to seek redress or justice for the violation of their rights (Durojaye et al., 2020: p. 226). Addressing the barriers militating against women's access to environmental justice in Nigeria would not only enhance environmental governance in the Niger Delta but also promote the realization of wider SDGs linked to gender equality and environmental sustainability.

Some strategies that are yet to be explored for this purpose include the use of government agencies, such as a legal aid council and human rights commission, to provide free legal advisory services and representation for female litigants as a way of reducing the barriers to justice resulting from the high cost of litigation. Access to the courts is just one aspect of improving women's access to environmental justice. Environmental justice also requires that women victims be adequately compensated for the harms (including related social and economic injustices) they have suffered and requires that strategies be established to prevent recurrence. Moreover, women need to be recognized as critical stakeholders in environmental decision-making and supported to participate meaningfully in open and inclusive public participation processes for environmental governance.

NOTES

1. *Aminata Diantou Diane v. Mali* (2018) ECW/CCJ/JUD/14/18. The claimant in this case was a woman who was a victim of discriminatory practices by the family of her husband after he (the husband) had suffered a stroke. The ECCJ held in her favor and the government of Mali was held culpable for its inability to protect the claimant.
2. *Mary Sunday v. Federal Republic of Nigeria* ECW/CCJ/JUD/11/18. This case is said to be the "first ECCJ decision on domestic violence." Generally, see Addadzi-Koom (2020: p. 157). In this case, the claimant (Mary Sunday) was a victim of domestic abuse perpetuated by her boyfriend. The ECCJ held in her favor.
3. *Kiobel v. Royal Dutch Petroleum Co.*, 133 S.Ct. 1659 (2013). This case further restricted the remit of the ATCA toward MNCs. In the *Kiobel* case, the U.S. Supreme Court dismissed the suit against Shell which was brought by victims of alleged Shell's complicity in state crimes committed against the Ogoni people and held that the

Shell's connection to the United States was unconvincing. This decision was reached notwithstanding that Shell has business offices in the United States and hence, the ATCA was held to be inapplicable.

4. *African Commission on Human and Peoples' Rights v. Kenya*, Application 006/2012, Judgment (African Court on Human and Peoples' Rights, 2017) (Ogiek case or *ACHPR v. Kenya* (Judgment).

REFERENCES

Protocol to the African Charter on Human and Peoples' Rights on the Rights of Women in Africa.

Addadzi-Koom, M. E. (2020). Of the Women's Rights Jurisprudence of the ECOWAS Court: The Role of the Maputo Protocol and the Due Diligence Standard. *Feminist Legal Studies*, *28*(2), 155–178.

African Charter of Human and Peoples' Rights OAU CAB/LEG/67/3 rev. 5, 21 I.L.M. 58 entered into force October 21, 1986. The African Charter is also known as the Banjul Charter.

African Commission on Human and Peoples' Rights v. Kenya, Application 006/2012, Judgment (African Court on Human and Peoples' Rights, 2017) (Ogiek case or *ACHPR v. Kenya* (Judgment)).

African Court on Human and Peoples' Rights, Association pour le Progrès et la DéFense des Droits des Femmes Maliennes (APDF) and the Institute for Human Rights and Development in Africa (IHRDA) v. Mali, Application No. 046/2016, Judgment, May 11, 2018.

Aghedo, I., & Osumah, O. (2015). Insurgency in Nigeria: A comparative study of Niger Delta and Boko Haram uprisings. *Journal of Asian and African Studies*, *50*(2), 208–222.

Ahikire, J., Kanyesigye, J., Nassali, M., Nakayi, R., Katushabe, J., & Pamara, H. (2017). Interrogating large-scale land acquisitions and land governance in Uganda: implications for women's land rights. Uganda Country Report, Centre for Basic Research. Uganda Country Report, Centre for Basic Research.

Agyeman, J. (2014). Global environmental justice or Le droit au monde. *Geoforum*, *54*, 236–238.

Akinsemolu, A. A., & Olukoya, O. A. (2020). The vulnerability of women to climate change in coastal regions of Nigeria: A case of the Ilaje community in Ondo State. *Journal of Cleaner Production*, *246*, 119015.

Ako, R., & Ekhator, E. O. (2016). The civil society and the regulation of the extractive industry in Nigeria. *Journal of Sustainable Development Law and Policy (The)*, *7*(1), 183–203.

Akpan v. Shell C/09/337050 / HA ZA 09-1580.

Allen, S., Fanucchi, M. V., McCormick, L. C., & Zierold, K.M. (2019). The search for environmental justice: the Story of North Birmingham. *International Journal of Environmental Research and Public Health*, *16*(12), 2117.

Amadiume, I. (1997). *Re-inventing Africa: Matriarchy, religion and culture*. Zed Books.

Amechi, E. P. (2015). Strengthening Environmental Public Interest Litigation Through Citizen Suits in Nigeria: Learning from the South African Environmental Jurisprudential Development. *African Journal of International and Comparative Law*, *23*(3), 383–404.

Aminata Diantou Diane v. Mali (2018) ECW/CCJ/JUD/14/18.

Amnesty International. (2020a). Nigeria: No Clean-Up, No Justice: An Evaluation of the implementation of UNEP's Environmental Assessment of Ogoniland, Nine Years on https://www.amnesty.org/en/documents/afr44/2514/2020/en/.

Amnesty International. (2020b). On Trial: Shell in Nigeria: Legal actions against the oil multinational. Nigeria: On trial: Shell in Nigeria: Legal actions against the oil multinational, Amnesty International.

Aniekwu, N. I. (2009). The additional protocol to the African Charter on Human and People's Rights: indications of capacity for African municipal systems. *Law, Democracy & Development*, *13*(2), 22–35.

Anozie, M. C., & Wingate, E.O. (2020). NGO standing in petroleum pollution litigation in Nigeria – Centre for Oil Pollution Watch v Nigerian National Petroleum Corporation. *The Journal of World Energy Law & Business*, *13*(5–6), 490–497.

Arowolo, G. A. (2020). Protecting women from violence through legislation in Nigeria: Need to enforce anti-discrimination laws. *International Journal of Discrimination and the Law*, *20*(4), 245–288.

Ayeni, V. (Ed.) (2016). *The Impact of the African Charter and Maputo Protocol in Selected African States*. Pretoria: Pretoria University Law Press.

Babalola, A. (2020). The Right to a Clean Environment in Nigeria: A Fundamental Right. *Hastings Envt'l LJ, 26*, 3–14.

Babatunde, A.O. (2018). From peaceful to non-peaceful protests: The trajectories of women's movements in the Niger Delta. In C. Obi and T. Oriola (Eds.) *The Unfinished Revolution in Nigeria's Niger Delta*. New York: Routledge (pp. 103–119).

Babatunde, A. O. (2020). Oil pollution and water conflicts in the riverine communities in Nigeria's Niger Delta region: challenges for and elements of problem-solving strategies. *Journal of Contemporary African Studies*, *38*(2), 274–293.

Banakar, R., & Travers, M. (Eds.). (2005). *Theory and Method in Socio-Legal Research*. Oxford: Hart.

Barikor-Wiwa, D. (1997). The Role of Women in the Struggle for Environmental Justice in Ogoni. *Cultural Survival Quarterly*, *21*(3), 46–49.

Bell, K. (2016). Bread and roses: A gender perspective on environmental justice and public health. *International Journal of Environmental Research and Public Health*, *13*(10), 1005.

Besthorn, F. H., & McMillen, D. P. (2002). The oppression of women and nature: Ecofeminism as a framework for an expanded ecological social work. *Families in Society*, *83*(3), 221–232.

Bodo Community v. Shell Petroleum Development Co of Nigeria Ltd [2014] EWHC 1973 (TCC).

Boshoff, E. (2020). Women's Environmental Human Rights in Africa with Reflections on Key Provisions of the Maputo Protocol. In M. Addaney & A. O. Jegede (Eds.) *Human Rights and the Environment under African Union Law* (pp. 107–136). Cham: Palgrave Macmillan.

Bowoto v. Chevron Corp., 621 F.3d 1116, 1120 (9th Cir. 2010).

Brems, E., & Adekoya, C.O. (2010). Human rights enforcement by people living in poverty: access to justice in Nigeria. *Journal of African Law*, 258–282.

Brown, R., & Oder, J. (2016). "The Protection of Women's Economic, Social and Cultural Rights in Africa" In D. M. Chirwa, & L. Chenwi (Eds.) *The Protection of Economic, Social and Cultural Rights in Africa: International, Regional and National Perspectives* (pp. 121–154). New York: Cambridge University Press.

Bruederle, A., & Hodler, R. (2017). The effect of oil spills on infant mortality: Evidence from Nigeria. (September 14, 2017). CESifo Working Paper Series No. 6653 SSRN: https://ssrn.com/abstract=3043605.

Bullard, R. D., & Johnson, G. S. (2000). Environmentalism and public policy: Environmental justice: Grassroots activism and its impact on public policy decision making. *Journal of Social Issues*, *56*(3), 555–578.

Capone, F. (2020). APDH and IHRDA v Mali: recent developments in the jurisprudence of the African Court on Human and Peoples' Rights. *The International Journal of Human Rights*, *24*(5), 580–592.

Centre for Environment, Human Rights and Development (CEHRD). (2015), After Bodo: Effective Remedy & Recourse Options for Victims of Environmental Degradation Related to Oil Extraction in Nigeria, CEHRD—After Bodo.

Centre for Oil Pollution Watch v. Nigerian National Petroleum Corporation [2019] 5 NWLR 518.

Chenwi, L. (2018). "The right to a satisfactory, healthy, and sustainable environment in the African Regional Human Rights System" in Knox, J.H., & Pejan, R. (Eds) *The Human Right to a Healthy Environment*. Cambridge: Cambridge University Press.

Du Plessis, A. (2011). The balance of sustainability interests from the perspective of the African Charter on Human and Peoples' Rights. *The Balancing of Interests in Environmental Law in Africa*, *345*, 35.

Durojaye, E., Mirugi-Mukundi, G., & Adeniyi, O. (2020). Legal empowerment as a tool for engendering access to justice in South Africa. *International Journal of Discrimination and the Law*, *20*(4), 224–244.

Ekhator, E. O. (2014). Improving access to environmental justice under the African Charter on human and peoples' rights: the roles of NGOs in Nigeria. *African Journal of International and Comparative Law*, *22*(1), 63–79.

Ekhator, E. O. (2016). Regulating the activities of oil multinationals in Nigeria: A case for self-regulation. *J. Afr. L.*, *60*, 1.

Ekhator, E. O. (2017). The role of non-governmental organisations in the environmental justice paradigm. *Nnamdi Azikiwe University Journal of International Law and Jurisprudence*, *8*(2), 28–37.

Ekhator, E. O. (2019) Protection and Promotion of Women's Rights in Nigeria: Constraints and Prospects. In M. Addaney (Ed.) *Women and Minority Rights*

Law: African Approaches and Perspectives to Inclusive Development (pp. 17–35). Eleven International Publishing, Netherlands.

Ekhator, E. O. (2020). International Environmental Governance: A case for sub-regional Judiciaries in Africa. In M. Addaney and A. O. Jegede (Eds.) *Human Rights and the Environment under African Union Law* (pp. 209–231). Cham: Palgrave Macmillan.

Ekine, S. (2008). Women's responses to state violence in the Niger Delta. *Feminist Africa, 10*(1), 67–83.

Emeseh, E., Ako, R., Okonmah, P., & Ogechukwu, L. (2010). Corporations, CSR and self regulation: What lessons from the global financial crisis?. *German Law Journal, 11*(2), 230–259.

Enneking, L. F. (2012). *Foreign Direct Liability and Beyond Exploring the Role of Tort Law in Promoting International Corporate Social Responsibility and Accountability*. The Hague: Eleven International Publishing.

Enneking, L. F. (2019). Transnational human rights and environmental litigation: a study of case law relating to shell in Nigeria. In I. Feichtner, M. Krajewski, & R. Roesch (Eds.), *Human Rights in the Extractive Industries* (pp. 511–551). Cham: Springer.

Ezeilo, J. N. (2021). Rethinking women and customary inheritance in Nigeria. *Commonwealth Law Bulletin, 47*(4), 706–718.

Fallon, K. M., & Moreau, J. (2016). Revisiting Repertoire Transition: Women's Nakedness as Potent Protests in Nigeria and Kenya. *Mobilization: An International Quarterly, 21*(3), 323–340.

Frynas, J. G. (2001). Problems of access to courts in Nigeria: results of a survey of legal practitioners. *Social & Legal Studies, 10*(3), 397–419.

Gaard, G. (2018) Feminism and Environmental Justice. In R. Holifield, J. Chakraborty & G. Walker (Eds.), *The Routledge Handbook of Environmental Justice* (pp. 74–88). New York: Routledge.

Gale, I. (2002). "West Marin Women Strip for Peace." Point Reyes Light.

Gbemre v. Shell, Suit No. FHC/B/CS/153/05.

General Oil Limited v. Oduntan, [1990] 7 NWLR (Pt 63) 433.

Glazebrook, T. (2011). Women and climate change: A case-study from northeast Ghana. *Hypatia, 26*(4), 762–782.

Global Witness, (2021). *Women Defying the Climate Crisis: Hear Their Stories*. Global Witness. https://www.globalwitness.org/en/blog/women-defying-climate-crisis-hear-their-stories/.

Gomez, A. M., Shafiei, F., & Johnson, G.S. (2011). Black women's involvement in the environmental justice movement: an analysis of three communities in Atlanta, Georgia. *Race, Gender & Class, 18*(1–2), 189–214.

Gonzalez, C. G. (2013). Environmental Justice and International Environmental Law. In A. Shawkat, J. H. Bhuiyan, T. M. R Chowdhury, and E. J. Techera (Eds.), *Routledge Handbook of International Environmental Law* (pp. 77–97). Abingdon, Oxon: Routledge.

Greyl, L., Ojo, G. U., Certomà, C., Greco, L., & Ogbara, N. (2013). Digging deep the oil world: corporate liability and environmental justice strategies. *EJOLT Report, 9*, 1–73.

Hitchon J, (2013). U.S. Kiobel Decision Bucks 30 Years of Precedent. Inter Press Service News Agency. http://www.ipsnews.net/2013/04/u-s-kiobel-decision-bucks-30-years-of-precedent/.

Holifield R, Chakraborty, J, & Walker, G. (2018) The Worlds of Environmental Justice. In R. Holifield, J. Chakraborty, and G. Walker (Eds.), *The Routledge Handbook of Environmental Justice*. New York: Routledge.

Hughes, K. M. (2021). Climate and Gender Justice in in Sub-Saharan Africa: Emerging Trends Post-Paris 2015. *Wisconsin International Law Journal*, *38*(2), 197–231.

Ikelegbe, A. (2005). Engendering civil society: Oil, women groups and resource conflicts in the Niger Delta region of Nigeria. *Journal of Modern African Studies*, *43*(2), 241–270.

Hutchinson, T., & Duncan, N. (2012). Defining and describing what we do: Doctrinal legal research. *Deakin L. Rev.*, *17*, 83.

IUCN. (2015). Women's participation in global environmental decision making. https://www.wocan.org/sites/default/files/EGI_factsheet_desicion_making_web_sept2015_0.pdf.

Ivan, G. (2002). West Marin Women Strip for Peace. *Point Reyes Light*. https://archive.commondreams.org/scriptfiles/headlines02/1117-02.htm.

Kabaseke, C. (2020). Women's Right to Participation in Environmental Decision-Making in Uganda. In *Human Rights and the Environment under African Union Law* (pp. 287–314). Cham: Palgrave Macmillan.

Kate Hodal. 'Absolutely shocking: Niger Delta oil spills linked with infant deaths' (Guardian Newspaper) 6 November 2017. https://www.theguardian.com/global-development/2017/nov/06/niger-delta-oil-spills-linked-infant-deaths.

Katuoka, S., & Dailidaitė, M. (2012). Responsibility of transnational corporations for human rights violations: deficiencies of international legal background and solutions offered by national and regional legal tools. *Jurisprudencia*, *19*(4), 1301–1316.

Keys, D. D. (2019). *For the Survival of Ogoni People: Women's Contribution to Movement-Building in Nigeria and the United States*. Los Angeles: University of California.

Keys, D. D. (2021). "Here We Are": Ogoni Women's Nonviolent Resistance. *Frontiers: A Journal of Women Studies*, *42*(1), 178–203.

Kiobel v. Royal Dutch Petroleum Co. (2013). 133 S. Ct. 1659.

MacGregor, S. (2021). Gender matters in environmental justice. In B. Coolsaet (Ed.), *Environmental Justice: Key Issues* (pp. 234–248). Abingdon, Oxon: Routledge.

Mai-Bornu, Z. (2019). Oil, conflict, and the dynamics of resource struggle in the Niger Delta: A comparison of the Ogoni and Ijaw movements. *The Extractive Industries and Society*, *6*(4), 1282–1291.

Maluwa, T. (2020). 'Reassessing aspects of the contribution of African States to the Development of International Law through African Regional Multilateral Treaties'. *Michigan Journal of International Law, 41*(2), 327–415.

Martinez-Alier, J. (2014). The environmentalism of the poor. *Geoforum*, *54*, 239–241.

Martinez-Alier, J., Temper, L., Del Bene, D., & Scheidel, A. (2016). Is there a global environmental justice movement? *The Journal of Peasant Studies*, *43*(3), 731–755.

Mary Sunday v. Federal Republic of Nigeria ECW/CCJ/JUD/11/18.

Munir, L. (2020). When local law impedes conflict resolution: Women's Oil Protests in the Niger Delta. *African Conflict and Peacebuilding Review*, *10*(1), 28–49.

Munir, L. (2021). Gender roles in Nigeria's non-violent oil resistance movement. *Canadian Journal of African Studies/Revue Canadienne des études Africaines*, *55*(1), 79–97.

Murdock, E. G. (2021). A history of environmental justice: foundations, narratives, and perspectives. In B. Coolsaet (Ed.). *Environmental Justice: Key Issues* (pp. 6–17). Abingdon, Oxon: Routledge.

Mwikya, K. K. (2020) Litigating the Maputo protocol: An introduction. In K. K. Mwikya, K. Osero-Ageng'o, and E. Waweru (Eds.). *Litigating the Maputo Protocol: A Compendium of Strategies and Approaches for Defending the Rights of Women in Africa* (pp. 1–8). Equality Now. https://www.equalitynow.org/resource/litigating_the_maputo_protocol_2020/.

Obani, P. (2021). *'Soro Soke': Women, Protests, and the Law* [Paper presentation]. Cardiff: Socio-legal Studies Association.

Obi, C., & Oriola, T. B. (Eds.). (2018). *The Unfinished Revolution in Nigeria's Niger Delta: Prospects for Environmental Justice and Peace*. New York: Routledge.

O'Connell, C. (2019). Reconceptualising the first African Women's Protocol case to work for all women. *African Human Rights Law Journal*, *19*(1), 510–533.

Ojigho, O. (2020). 'Litigating gender-based violence and discrimination – The Dorothy Njemanze Case.' In K.K. Mwikya, K. Osero-Ageng'o, and E. Waweru (Eds.). *Litigating the Maputo Protocol: A Compendium of Strategies and Approaches for Defending the Rights of Women in Africa*. Equality Now. https://www.equalitynow.org/resource/litigating_the_maputo_protocol_2020/.

Okafor, O. C., & Ugochukwu, B. (2014). Inventing Legal Combat: Pro-Poor "Struggles" in the Human Rights Jurisprudence of the Nigerian Appellate Courts, 1999–2011. *African Journal of Legal Studies*, *7*(4), 429–456.

Okogbule, N. S. (2005). Access to justice and human rights protection in Nigeria: problems and prospects. *Sur. Revista Internacional de Direitos Humanos*, *2*(3), 100–119.

Okogbule, N. S. (2012). *An Appraisal of the Mutual Impact Between Globalization and Human Rights in Africa* [Doctoral dissertation]. Glasgow: University of Glasgow.

Okongwu, O. C. (2021). Are laws the appropriate solution: The need to adopt non-policy measures in aid of the implementation of sex discrimination laws in Nigeria. *International Journal of Discrimination and the Law*, *21*(1), 26–46.

Olatunbosun, A. & Onu, K. O. N. (2020). The liberalisation of Locus Standi in Environmental cases in Nigeria: An appraisal of the Supreme Court's decision in centre for oil pollution watch v NNPC. *The Gravitas Review of Business & Property Law*, *11*(2), 1–11.

Onwutuebe, C. J. (2019). Patriarchy and women vulnerability to adverse climate change in Nigeria. *Sage Open*, *9*(1), 2158244019825914.

Onyemelukwe, C. (2015). Legislating on violence against women: A critical analysis of Nigeria's recent Violence against Persons (Prohibition) Act. *DePaul J. Women Gender & L.*, *5*, 1–56.

Oriola, T. (2012). The Delta Creeks, women's engagement and Nigeria's oil insurgency. *The British Journal of Criminology*, *52*(3), 534–555.

Oriola, T. (2016). 'I acted like a man': exploring female ex-insurgents' narratives on Nigeria's oil insurgency. *Review of African Political Economy*, *43*(149), 451–469.

Oshionebo, E. (2009). *Regulating Transnational Corporations in Domestic and International Regimes: An African Case Study*. Toronto: University of Toronto Press.

Oyěwùmí, O., (1997). *The invention of women: Making an African sense of western gender discourses*. University of Minnesota Press.

Oyěwùmí, O. (2016). *What Gender is Motherhood? Changing Yoruba Ideals of Power, Procreation, and Identity in the Age of Modernity*. New York: Springer.

Pearce, D. C., Campbell, E., & Harding, D. E. (1987). *Australian Law Schools: A Discipline Assessment for the Commonwealth Tertiary Education Commission: A Summary*. Canberra: Australian Government Pub. Service.

Rachovitsa, A. (2019). On New 'Judicial Animals': The Curious Case of an African Court with Material Jurisdiction of a Global Scope. *Human Rights Law Review*, *19*(2), 255–289.

Renouard, C. & Lado, H. (2012). CSR and inequality in the Niger Delta (Nigeria). *Corporate Governance: The International Journal of Business in Society*, *12*(4), 472–484.

Sikor, T. & Newell, P. (2014). Globalizing environmental justice? *Geoforum*, *54*, 151–157.

Stephens, B. (2020). The rise and fall of the Alien Tort Statute. In *Research Handbook on Human Rights and Business*. Cheltenham: Edward Elgar Publishing.

Stewart, D. P., & Wuerth, I. (2013). Kiobel v. Royal Dutch Petroleum Co.: The Supreme Court and the Alien Tort Statute. *American Journal of International Law*, *107*(3), 601–621.

Stover, K., & Cable, S. (2017). American Women's Environmental Activism. In *The Oxford Handbook of US Women's Social Movement Activism*.

Onyejiuwa, G. (2020). Irate Imo women shut down oil company over unpaid burial rites. Sun Newspaper. https://www.sunnewsonline.com/irate-imo-women-shut-down-oil-company-over-unpaid-burial-rites/.

Idowu, S. (2020). Ugborodo Women sustain siege on Chevron Tank Farms. Thisday Newspaper. https://www.thisdaylive.com/index.php/2020/09/12/ugborodo-women-sustain-siege-on-chevron-tank-farms/.

Senator Adesanya v. The President of Nigeria, 2 NCLR 258 (1981).

SERAC and CSER v. Nigeria (2001) Communication no. 155/96 (African Commission to Human and Peoples' Rights).

SERAP v. Federal Republic of Nigeria, Judgement No. ECW/CCJ/JUD/18/12.

Tamale, S. (2014). Exploring the contours of African sexualities: Religion, law and power. *African Human Rights Law Journal*, *14*(1), 150–177.

Tamale, S. (2016). *'Nudity, protest and the law in Uganda' Inaugural Lecture.* Uganda: Makerere University.

Taylor, D. E. (2000). The rise of the environmental justice paradigm: Injustice framing and the social construction of environmental discourses. *American Behavioral Scientist, 43*(4), 508–580.

Turner, T. E., & Brownhill, L. S. (2004). Why women are at war with Chevron: Nigerian subsistence struggles against the international oil industry. *Journal of Asian and African Studies, 39*(1–2): 63–93.

Ugochukwu, B. (2020). 8 Engendering access to justice in Nigeria. In *Gender, Poverty and Access to Justice: Policy Implementation in Sub-Saharan Africa.* Abingdon, Oxon: Routledge.

Ukeje, C. (2004). From Aba to Ugborodo: gender identity and alternative discourse of social protest among women in the oil delta of Nigeria. *Oxford Development Studies, 32*(4), 605–617.

Unger, N. C. (2008). The role of gender in environmental justice. *Environmental Justice, 1*(3), 115–120.

Usikpedo-Omoniye, C. (2013) Presentation of the Niger Delta Women's Movement for Peace and Development (NDWPD) Presentation of the Niger Delta Women's Movement for Peace and Development Theme: "Promoting transparency and effective engagement of Major Groups and Stakeholders: Developing new models of participation in UNEP." UNEP—UN Environment Programme.

Viljoen, F. (2009). An Introduction to the Protocol to the African Charter on Human and Peoples' Rights on the Rights of Women in Africa. *Wash. & Lee J. Civil Rts. & Soc. Just., 16*, 11–46.

Wiwa v. Royal Dutch Petroleum Co., 226 F 3d 88 (2d Cir. 2000).

Chapter 13

Contribution of the Judiciary to the Advancement and Protection of Women's Matrimonial and Inheritance Rights in Rwanda

Odette Uwineza and Marie-Rose Turamwishimiye

INTRODUCTION

In Rwanda, the battle for women's realization of matrimonial and inheritance rights has been a long journey. As of this writing, Rwandan courts are struggling to translate those rights into reality. Entrenched customary traditions discriminated against women and prevented them from taking advantage of their family's land and assets (Ruhashyankiko, 1984) until 1999. The system that dominated was patriarchal: lineage determined the landholders, and the land was transmitted through male kin, from father to son. This system culminated in women's disinheritance and in the restriction of women's matrimonial rights (Bushayija, 1966). In 1962, equality and nondiscrimination were secured as constitutional rights. However, the absence of gender-neutral implementing laws governing inheritance and matrimonial regimes hampered the courts' enforcement of those rights. The pillar of positive changes has been law no. 22/99/1999—Instituting Part V of the Civil Code Book I and Governing Matrimonial Regimes, Liberalities and Successions—that expressly clarified women's inheritance and matrimonial rights and enabled women to claim such rights before courts of law. By contrast, women in de facto unions have been beyond the scope of this law. However, the protection of their patrimonial rights resulted from case law development. The constant adjustment of laws to achieve effective and efficient protection of women's matrimonial and inheritance rights became a crucial state commitment.

Although different authors (Bayisenge et al., 2015; Bayisenge, 2018; Elisabeth et al., 2010; Pamela et al., 2018) have conducted research on how policies and laws (land policy, land laws, and succession law) have promoted women's land rights and the legal knowledge that women have about such rights in Rwanda, the goal of this chapter is to analyze how women's matrimonial and inheritance rights are translated into reality by courts. In addition, these previous researchers looked primarily at women's land rights. However, women's patrimonial rights do not include only land rights but also other rights that women can have over different properties that may be real assets, including land and personal assets either corporeal (such as cars and ships) or incorporeal (such as shares, dividends, and bank deposits). This chapter therefore aims to describe women's experiences with respect to the judicial advancement of their matrimonial and inheritance rights in Rwanda and challenges they have been facing in the journey toward realizing and securing these rights. This research is very important because having written policies and laws that promote women's matrimonial and inheritance rights is not sufficient. Such policies and laws will play their role or achieve their objectives if they can be properly implemented, and if women can claim such rights and get proper judicial remedies in cases where such rights have been violated.

This research responds to the following questions: How has the Rwandan legal framework contributed to the realization of women's matrimonial and inheritance rights? What is the role of courts with regard to settlement of cases related to women's matrimonial and inheritance rights? How can women's rights be further enhanced? To respond to these questions, in addition to exploring a desk review study, this study drew heavily on case law analysis. The latter is explained as a study of cases conducted to draw essential conclusions about how courts apply certain norms and how they interpret them. It is in fact a process of studying judgments to identify problems in the uniform application of law by the courts and to ascertain the scope of problems that exist in the field of application of certain norms. In this chapter, the process is applied to courts' decisions related to women's matrimonial and inheritance rights that were made in different periods: the period before the adoption of the first law governing matrimonial regimes, liberalities, and succession (1999) and the period after its adoption are studied.

After the introduction, the second section deals with courts' protection of women's matrimonial rights before 1999. The third section focuses on courts' protection of women's matrimonial rights after 1999. The fourth section examines the development of courts' protection of matrimonial rights of women in informal marriages, and the fifth section explores protection of women's inheritance rights.

COURTS' PROTECTION OF WOMEN'S MATRIMONIAL RIGHTS BEFORE 1999

Despite the Constitutions of 1962, 1978, and 1991, which proclaimed individual and collective property rights (Article 23), the right to equality, and the right to nondiscrimination of all citizens (Article 16), along with the equality of a husband and a wife before the law (Article 30), from the precolonial period until 1999, Rwandan traditions prevented women from owning and enjoying land or other property rights in the family (Burnet & RISD, 2003). Despite the existence of the above-mentioned constitutional provisions, women continued to face restrictions with respect to their matrimonial rights from the precolonial period until 1999. Husbands kept exclusive decision-making power in the management of land and other valuable assets of the household (Bushayija, 1966). The situation was worsened by the 1988 Family Law Decree, which reinforced the husband's authority by recognizing him as head of the family (Article 206). This decree resulted in imbalance in spousal marital status because wives could not oppose their husbands' decisions. The nonapplication of constitutional provisions and international law obligations regarding equality and nondiscrimination regarding women's matrimonial rights could be said to result from three causes.

The first is that entrenched traditions, constructed on patriarchal and patrilineal systems, bestowed the privileges of masculinity. Such traditions favored men and sons with regard to land rights and other family resources (Bushayija, 1966). Of note is that the Colonial Charter of October 18, 1908, was extended to Rwanda in 1924; it allowed natives to continue to follow their customs in settling personal and family matters.

The second cause is that land, under customary law, was recognized as an heir's property. Women could have land use rights only through marriage; they could not own the land. Because of the patriarchal system in Rwanda, as in other countries in Africa, husbands and sons had primary land rights, to the detriment and exclusion of women (Odeny, 2013). This was an unfortunate situation for women because land resources constituted the primary valuable assets that the economy of the household relied on (GMO, 2012). Fortunately, the lineage landholding custom was broken up by Organic law no. 08/2005 of July 14, 2005, which determined the modalities of land use and management in Rwanda that gave to the state exclusive control over the land (Article 3) and expressly recognized women's land rights (Article 4).

The third cause was the lack of a specific law regulating the structure of ownership in marriage. This deficiency negatively influenced the realization of women's matrimonial rights, because there was no law that provided details on marriage consequences related to properties, rights, and powers of spouses regarding family properties during and at the end of marriage.

Even though the Decree-law no. 42/1988 of October 27, 1988, instituting the Preliminary Title of Civil Code Book One and governing persons and family regulated rights and obligations of spouses during marriage and consequences of divorce including dissolution of marriage, child custody, and support (Articles 278–286), it left out marriage consequences related to property of the household. Consequently, even after the advent of the 1988 Decree Law, most courts continued to refer to discriminatory customs that denied women's rights to family property during and at the dissolution of marriage. However, in very few cases, some courts used a rights-based approach and allowed women to have and enjoy rights over family property. The following case law analysis indicates the two approaches used by judges.

Denial of Women's Matrimonial Rights by Courts

In different cases decided before 1999, a number of judges did not decide in favor of women in relation to their claims for matrimonial rights, especially at the end of a marriage. Some judges denied such rights completely, while others granted to women an insignificant property with little value compared to the value of the entire family property. For example, in the case *Mukarugendo v. Munyaziboneye* (1987), the wife filed a petition for divorce on the grounds of serious insults, abuse, and maintenance of a concubine. She won the case and obtained divorce on the fault of the husband. In her petition, Mukarugendo claimed for her share from the household's property acquired from the spouses' joint efforts. Unfortunately, the judge considered her claim as not founded and ordered the husband to give her back only the items she had brought with her at the time of the marriage celebration. This was the judge's decision even though the contribution of the wife to the acquisition of the family wealth was undoubted (RISD, Kairaba, & Simmons, 2010).

In the case of *Batamuriza Zaïnabu v. Niyonzima Twalib* (1987), the wife filed for divorce on the grounds that her husband had beaten her. In her petition, she also requested a share of the household property. The wife won the case and got divorced. However, with regard to her claim of a share in the family property, in reference to customary law, the judge decided to give her *impamba* of 150,000 Rwandan francs (RWF). Impamba was a property or a sum of money given to a wife who was leaving her household. It had little value compared to one's contribution to the economy of the household (Kamatali, Uwineza, & Zikamabahari, 2020). This means that the husband retained a large portion of the family property despite the wife's efforts.

In the case *Dusabemariya Illuminata v. Sikubwabo Theodomir* (1993), Sikubwabo (husband) filed a petition for divorce on the ground of serious insults and abuse committed by Dusabemariya (wife) before the Tribunal de Premiere Instance de Gisenyi. The wife was convicted of this offense, and divorce was granted. With regard to property, the court ordered the husband to provide his wife with impamba amounting to 200,000 RWF. The wife felt unhappy with the marriage dissolution and lodged an appeal before the Cour d'Appel de Ruhengeri. The appeal court confirmed the marriage dissolution but canceled the impamba that had been granted to the wife in the first instance. The implication is that receipt of impamba was a fragile and unpredictable customary right. Whether a woman received it depended on the goodwill of the judge.

Sometimes, divorcing women do not claim their matrimonial rights to property, as happened in the case *Uwimana v. Sumbiri* (1992). This behavior would be justified by the customary belief that the property of the family belonged to the husband's lineage and should therefore be transmitted from father to son (RISD & Burnet, 2003).

Courts' Acceptance of Women's Matrimonial Rights with the Use of a Human Rights-Based Approach

In exceptional cases, courts upheld women's matrimonial rights using a human rights-based approach and implementing the constitutional provisions on the rights to equality and nondiscrimination. For example, in *Sebahutu Evariste v. Nikuze Primitive* (1997), the husband claimed for divorce because of the wife's family desertion. At the same time, the wife claimed for divorce on the ground of her husband's adultery. The divorce decision was based on the faults of both spouses. With regard to family property sharing, the judge used a rights-based approach in his ruling. He affirmed the matrimonial rights of the wife and ordered that the family property should be shared equally by the spouses based on Article 16 of the Constitution of 1991, which provides for the right to equality and nondiscrimination.

Nondiscrimination and the equality of wife and husband before the law had been constitutional rights since 1962 and were contained in some ratified international instruments, as was mentioned before. However, even in a case where judges referred to the Constitution, neither judges nor petitioners referred to these rights as had been the case in *Uwimana v. Sumbiri* (1992). Judges were therefore responsible for providing remedies intended to redress women's inequality and discrimination with regard to matrimonial rights, in compliance with the Constitutions and international law. Courts could have constituted an efficient tool to render women's matrimonial rights effective and real, given that the final court's ruling recognizing and enforcing women's patrimonial rights could become binding *erga omnes* (Gender Equality Unit, Supreme Court of Mexico, 2014).

DEVELOPMENTS IN COURTS' PROTECTION OF WOMEN'S MATRIMONIAL RIGHTS AFTER 1999

Since 1999, matrimonial regimes, liberalities, and successions have been governed by a specific law that protects women's matrimonial rights. From 1999 until 2016, they were governed by law no. 22/99 of September 12, 1999. The latter was replaced by law no. 27/2016 of July 8, 2016. These specific laws protect the matrimonial rights of women who are legally married. In Rwanda, the legal marriage recognized is the statutory monogamous marriage celebrated before a public authority. Besides, all people who are legally married are governed by the same statutory law with regard to matrimonial rights either during marriage or at the end of the marriage. This situation is unique to Rwanda; it differs from the situation of legal pluralism that prevails in some East African countries, where different types of marriages, including statutory, customary, and religious marriages, are all legally recognized. In these countries, women's matrimonial rights are different and are governed by different laws applicable to different forms of marriages (Pamela et al., 2018; Lesley, 2014).

Judicial Protection of Women's Matrimonial Rights during Marriage

Law no. 22/1999 (hereinafter referred to as law no. 22/1999) was adopted to govern matrimonial regimes, liberalities, and successions. It constituted a cornerstone in the advancement of protection and enhancement of women's matrimonial rights (GMO, 2012). This law played a paramount role in defining matrimonial structures and in clarifying the rights and management powers of each spouse over the household's property. Thus, the role of the wife in the management of family property has been given paramount consideration depending on the type of the matrimonial structure opted for. Spouses could choose a community property structure, a limited community of acquests, or a separate property structure (Article 2). The attention is paid to the community property structure where the property is jointly owned. By contrast, a separate property structure does not cause any management problem because, in principle, each spouse can manage their personal assets and liabilities autonomously.

Under the community property structure, spouses are treated equally with respect to matrimonial rights, regardless of their individual contributions to the family's economic growth. The wealth of the family is supposed to be a result of the joint efforts of both spouses. Normally, each spouse is reputed to hold undivided equal half interest in the assets and liabilities of the household (Scott, 1979), a condition that takes effect when the marriage has taken place

(Hurry, 1995). In this structure, joint management is a rule, and consent of both spouses is required for the validity of any management act, including the lease, rent, sale, and mortgage of the assets of the community. Thus, after law no. 22/99 was enacted, wives became aware of their matrimonial rights and knew that they could claim them if they were abused. Nearly one-half (48%) of cases linked to law no. 22/1999 were related to abuse of women's matrimonial rights (GMO, 2012), as is analyzed in the following cases.

In the case *Mrs Rwigema Josephine v. ECOBANK RWANDA SA* (2013), Mrs. Rwigema filed a unilateral petition before the Commercial High Court requesting that the court stop the sale of a common house at public auction. That sale was initiated by *ECOBANK RWANDA SA* claiming for the reimbursement of the loan taken out by Mrs. Rwigema's husband, who was pretending to renovate that house. Though Mrs. Rwigema proved that she never signed the mortgage contract, she lost the case, and the court declared her petition not founded. Mrs. Rwigema appealed before the Supreme Court. The latter ruled in her favor and stopped the public auction of the mortgaged house. The Supreme Court's reasoning rested on the absence of the consent of the wife. Additionally, the husband failed to prove that the loan was used to renovate the house in the interest of the household. The court applied Articles 21–22 of law no. 22/199, which required the consent of both spouses for any donation or acknowledgment of rights to the property of the community or the ratification of the transaction by either spouse within six months. This case decided by the Supreme Court created a precedent that has been followed regarding the protection of women's matrimonial rights since 1999.

In the case *Mujawamariya and others v. Bank of Kigali Ltd* (2016), the Supreme Court referred to it to invalidate a mortgage contract signed between Nyagatare Theogene and the Bank of Kigali Ltd. because the contract was concluded without Nyagatare's wife's consent while they were married and in a community property structure. The husband (Nyagatare) died before paying back all of the loan taken from the bank, and the bank wanted to sell the mortgaged house. Because the surviving spouse had never signed the mortgage contract, she claimed for cancelation of the mortgage contract, and her request was granted; this decision contributed to the protection of her matrimonial rights based on law no. 22/99. In Rwanda, the Supreme Court's decisions create precedents, and the Supreme Court has the duty to provide direction regarding how a given debated issue has to be solved judicially. Once it has decided on a case, other courts have to consider it while deciding on similar cases. In this sense, the Supreme Court's decisions regarding protection of women's matrimonial rights in case they have not given consent to some acts related to the management of household's property constituted a sociocultural transformative tool, because judges are required to comply with guidelines set up by the Supreme Court in relation to women's matrimonial rights. In this case, the stare decisis principle contributed to enhancing the wife's management powers in a community property structure.

The consent of either spouse matters as well in cases of alienation of the assets of the community, and this was reinforced in the case of *Habiyakare v. Gahongayire* (2017). The Supreme Court invalidated a sale contract of a family house between Milimo and Habiyakare. It based its ruling on the lack of consent of Milimo's wife while the two were married under the community property structure.

Advancement of Women's Property Rights in Cases of Divorce, Marriage Annulment, Legal Separation, and Marriage Not Followed by Cohabitation

Law no. 22/1999 clarified not only matrimonial rights of spouses during marriage but also their rights at marriage dissolution by divorce. Under community property structures, assets and liabilities might be equally shared between spouses (Article 6), whereas they retain their personal property under a separate property structure. After the adoption of law no. 22/1999, courts developed the best practice of having a section concerning the consequences of divorce on the property of the household in their decisions; these sections granted equal rights to women and men in division of the household property (*Ndizihiwe v. Mukamwezi* (2015); *Nyiramuruta v. Ndayambaje* (2015)).

As mentioned before, law no. 22/1999 was repealed by law no. 32/2016 governing matrimonial structures, donations, and successions. According to this new and current law, divorcing spouses who were married under community property or limited community property structures have the right either to share common property equally or to follow any other sharing method of their choice. Though this last alternative is offered by the law in fault-based divorce, cases analyzed after law no. 32/2016 was passed show that couples opt for equal sharing of assets and liabilities.

Regarding marriage annulment, legal separation, and marriage not followed by cohabitation, there were no legal provisions regulating property rights of spouses. Neither the 1988 Family Law Decree nor law no. 22/99 governing matrimonial structures, liberalities, and successions regulated that matter. Reasonably, courts' decisions related to matrimonial rights of spouses could be unpredictable because of a lack of related clear legal provisions. For instance, in the cases *Uwera M. Louise v. Habyarimana Emanuel* (2010) and *Nyombayire Alexandre v. Nyiracumi Yolanda* (2014), courts accorded marriage annulment but did not decide on the rights of the couples over common property while they were reputed to be under a community property structure. The reasoning behind this ruling might be the need to prevent dishonest brides or grooms from acquiring wealth they did not contribute to.

The court granted annulment in the case *Mukarepubulika F. v. Hakizimana Viateur* (2009), whose subject matter was divorce on the ground of marriage not followed by cohabitation. In addition, the court did not decide on the fate of the property.

The loopholes that led to inconsistencies in courts' decisions related to property in cases of marriage annulment, marriage not followed by cohabitation, and legal separation are covered under the repealing law no. 32/2016 of August 28, 2016, governing persons and family. Pursuant to its Article 195, in case of marriage annulment, putative spouse(s) benefit(s) from the matrimonial structure opted for at the time the marriage was celebrated. This means that the spouses share the property in accordance with their respective matrimonial structure. On the contrary, things remain as they were before the marriage celebration, implying that spouses who did not have good faith, if their marriage is nullified, do not share property according to the matrimonial regime opted for. They go as if no marriage was celebrated. This is not the case for putative spouses (spouses who had good faith in their marriage celebration) who are allowed to share their property in accordance with the matrimonial regime that was opted for.

For marriage not followed by cohabitation, this law expressly considers the condition as one of the grounds for divorce (Article 218, 8) and clearly specifies that in such a case, the matrimonial structure is not enforced (Article 208). There are no matrimonial rights to be exercised.

In the case of legal separation, Article 227 provides that the spouses share provisionally the common assets and liabilities if they were under a community property or a limited community property structure. In a nutshell, after the adoption of law no. 22/99, which was repealed by law no. 27/2016 governing matrimonial structures, courts started upholding and protecting the matrimonial rights of women that women have in accordance with the matrimonial structure opted for by the married couple. Women's rights are accordingly protected either during marriage or at the end of marital relationship.

DEVELOPMENT OF JUDICIAL PROTECTION OF PATRIMONIAL RIGHTS OF WOMEN IN INFORMAL MARRIAGES

Pursuant to Article 20, paragraph 3 of law no. 27/2016, regulated matrimonial structures apply only to spouses who are legally married and become effective after the marriage celebration (Article 19). According to Article 17 of the 2003 Constitution of the Republic of Rwanda revised in 2015, a marital union is recognized only as a civil and monogamous marriage between a man and a woman. Also, Article 166 of law no. 32/2016 requires that such a marriage be celebrated before the public administration. It is tacitly understood that women in informal marriages are outside the scope of law no. 27/2016. The Constitution connects the right to marry with that of founding a family through the provisions of Article 17, paragraph 2, where it stresses that "a right to marry and to found a family is guaranteed by the State." The family referred to here is the nuclear family composed of the mother, the father, and their children. It is important to mention that the nature of the family has been growing over time to include single-parent families, families in de facto unions, and same-sex families in societies that recognize them (Herring, 2009). The concept of "family" is significantly narrowed in Article 17, paragraph 2 of the Constitution mentioned before, and other family types are to some extent stigmatized (Herring, 2009).

Nevertheless, the patrimonial rights of every individual are constitutionally guaranteed irrespective of marital status. The patrimonial rights of women in informal unions are protected by law no. 59/2008 Preventing and Punishing Gender-Based Violence (GBV Law). However, this law puts emphasis on polygamous marriages and calls for protection of a spouse if the other spouse wants to remarry one of their current spouses (Article 39, paragraph 2).

Concerning protection of patrimonial rights of women in informal marriages, courts have made great advances. In the past, women in de facto unions were evicted from the property acquired together with their husbands (Rugege, 2015). Some judges unfairly required that the wife prove her contribution to the acquisition of property, which was sometimes not easy in the absence of documentation (Rugege, 2015). However, the Supreme Court clarified this issue and clearly ruled that people who have lived as a wife and a husband in an informal union would not be required to prove their contributions to the acquisition of property acquired during their informal union. The following paragraphs provide an analysis of court decisions that both did not and did uphold the property rights of women living in informal marriages.

Courts' Decisions That Denied the Patrimonial Rights of Women in Informal Marriages

In the case *Mukankusi Nadia v. Mbyayingabo Issa* (2011), parties cohabited as wife and husband in a de facto union. During their cohabitation, they constructed a house. Later, the husband sold the house without his wife's consent. The wife claimed for invalidation of such sale contract concluded between her husband and Iyamuremye Masudi. Unfortunately, before the court, the wife was asked to prove her contribution to the construction of the house, which she failed to do. The wife lost the case and consequently lost her patrimonial rights over that house. This also happened in *Nyiramutarama Ferdinand v. Kamanutsi Mathieu* (2018). The Intermediate Court of Gasabo made a decision that compromised the protection of the wife's patrimonial rights where Nyiramutarama (the wife) was denied the right to share the assets she had acquired together with her husband during their illegal union. The assets included a car, a motorcycle, and a plot of land. The court's ruling was because she was not able to provide evidence of her contribution to the acquisition of the claimed assets.

Revolutionary Judicial Protection of Patrimonial Rights of Women in Informal Marriages

A revolutionary improvement in the recognition of patrimonial rights of women in informal unions was brought by the landmark case *Gatera Johnson v. Kabarisa Teddy* (2011). Gatera Johnson wanted to remarry and refused to share equally with his ex-wife the property they had acquired during their cohabitation in an informal marriage. He argued that Article 39, paragraph 2 of the 2009 GBV Law mentioned before is unconstitutional because it imposes equal sharing of the properties acquired during cohabitation. He argued that in such a case, a couple living in an informal marriage is treated as a couple married under a community property structure. However, the Supreme Court rejected his argument and decided in favor of the wife, ordering equal sharing of the property that Gatera and Kabarisa had acquired during their cohabitation. The court clarified the issue in its ruling, which was formulated as follows:

> The provision for equal distribution of common assets under article 39 was not solely based on the cohabitation fact. The law does not state that, such a distribution should occur regardless of each party's contribution as would be the case of divorce under community of property regime. Rather article 39 recognises the right of a person who has cohabitated and holds the property commonly owned or acquired together. This has no adverse implication for constitutional provisions on monogamous marriage nor did it legitimize illegal forms of marriage. (Rugege, 2015)

Also in the case *Mutoni Jackline v. Niwenshuti* (2017), the wife (Mutoni) was granted her patrimonial rights over a house acquired during her informal union with Niwenshuti. The latter had a second wife in informal union also. The second wife claimed for sharing of properties they had, including a house that had already been acquired when Niwenshuti was living with Mutoni, and the court ordered such sharing. Mutoni filed a third-party opposition before the court claiming for a reverse of the ruling that ordered equal sharing between Niwenshuti and his second wife; it concerned a house acquired during the informal marriage between Niwenshuti and Mutoni. The court rejected Mutoni's claim, saying that she failed to prove her contribution to the construction of that house. Mutoni lodged an appeal before the High Court of the Republic.

Unfortunately, in its case RCA 0176/14/HC/KIG of February 27, 2015, the High Court confirmed the decision of the Intermediate Court with the same reasoning. Mutoni lodged a second appeal before the Supreme Court, which reversed the previous decision. Referring to the *Gatera Johnson v. Kabarisa Teddy* case mentioned before, the Supreme Court recognized the matrimonial rights of Mutoni over that house and ordered the sharing into three shares following Article 39, paragraph 2 of the 2008 GBV Law. In this case, the Supreme Court emphasized that sharing could rely not on the contribution that each spouse made toward the acquisition or improvement of the assets but rather on the evidence of their cohabitation. Here, the Supreme Court stopped the courts' tendency to request that women prove their contribution to the acquisition of the property while not making the same request of men. That tendency reflected the persistence of the customary consideration of women as people who did not have properties or whose contribution to property acquisition was in doubt.

Again, in the case *Uwiragiye Charles v. Uwamahoro Jeanine*, the Supreme Court confirmed the decision of the High Court of the Republic in the case RCA00239/2016/HC/KIG of September 30, 2016, which ordered equal sharing of the assets acquired by spouses who were living together as wife and husband in an informal union. In that case, the judge specified that spouses in informal marriages who want to separate must share equally the property they acquired together during the period of cohabitation, irrespective of each one's contribution and the origin of the assets. The case clarified that acquisition of either movable or immovable assets during the period of cohabitation is sufficient to justify equal sharing of the property between a wife and a husband. Women are therefore entitled to property rights over assets acquired during cohabitation in informal marriages, as was clarified by the Supreme Court's decisions.

Despite the clarifications made by the Supreme Court, some courts still denied the patrimonial rights of women in de facto unions because of lack of evidence of the women's contribution to property acquisition. This occurred in *Nyiramutarama Ferdinand v. Kamanutsi Mathieu*. The lower court made a decision that compromised the protection of patrimonial rights of women in informal marriages even though the Supreme Court had already set out guidelines when deciding on a similar case, *Uwiragiye Charles v. Uwamahoro Jeanine*.

It is worth noting that in the case RC/INCOST/SPEC 00002/2019/SC of December 4, 2019, the Supreme Court reaffirmed the protection of the patrimonial rights of women in informal marriages and recalled its powers to give direction to courts regarding how to handle particular issues in the interest of the legal protection of women. It also recalled the obligation of lower courts to comply with guidelines set out by the Supreme Court while handling similar cases. In fact, lower courts should follow the stare decisis principle characterizing the doctrine of precedent where decisions of higher courts bind lower courts when they are handling cases with similar legal issues. Waldron (2012) justified the foundation of the stare decisis in imparting justice as follows:

> By commending that judges follow [a] previous decision, *stare decisis* is supposed to make [it] easier for people facing a new situation to predict how [the] court will deal with it: they will deal with it in the way that they have dealt with similar situation[s] in the past.

The situation of the matrimonial rights of women in informal unions not being protected could not occur again if judges from different courts followed the direction given by the Supreme Court on that legal issue. Thus, it is suggested that the Supreme Court's decisions advancing the protection of the matrimonial rights of women in informal marriages be effectively disseminated.

In addition, judges have to know that they are called upon to interpret and apply legal norms and have to abstain from making biased decisions under the influence of historical perceptions and misconceptions about women that result from constructed stereotypes associated with legal status, social economic position, and labor distribution. Under Rwandan customary law, women have been mostly considered as caregivers without autonomy in decision-making and/or as domestic workers whose jobs are unpaid and less important (Bayisenge, 2015), and this perception might have influenced some courts' decisions that denied the patrimonial rights of women in informal unions mentioned in this section. Generally, judges have to refrain from allowing such perceptions to influence their decisions. By denying patrimonial rights to women in informal marriages, judges breach both the supreme law of the country and ratified international human rights instruments that secure women's rights to equality and nondiscrimination and that reaffirm the role of courts and the state in protecting people and making human rights enjoyable. Thus, judges are tasked with upholding human rights, including the property rights of women in informal unions; if they do not do so, traditions and customs incompatible with human rights instruments constitute an infringement of national and international obligations (Stefano, 2001/2002). It is therefore suggested that judges, as members of a particular society, be careful not to be influenced by the cultural values of the society they belong to and to refrain from drawing on their personal experiences when making a ruling.

JUDICIAL PROTECTION OF WOMEN'S INHERITANCE RIGHTS

The Situation before 1999

Exclusion of Women from Inheritance

Generally, before 1999, inheritance was governed by customary law. Rwandan traditions excluded women from inheriting from their parents. This custom was a result of privileged masculinity (Vanhove, 1941) and patrilineal systems that dictated that succession could take place only through male kin (Guyn & Guyenne, 2011; Vanhee, 2014). Women could acquire property through inheritance only when they shared with their male relatives an *ingarigari*. The latter was a property comprising family assets that remained after parents had given the ascending partitions to their male children; it was meant for parents' subsistence. The ascending partition was an act accomplished by parents while they are still alive, by which they share their patrimony between their children or their descendants who acquire full ownership each for the portion devolved to them. This partition shall be regarded as the accomplishment of parents' duties to educate their children and to provide them with a personal patrimony.

Upon the parents' death, ingarigari was shared equally by all children without discrimination. This right was enforced in the case *Mukamuligo Alphonsine v. Rwabahashi François*, where the court ordered that *ingaligali* owned by Mukamuligo's brother must be shared out equally among all the children, male and female alike.

Women's Entitlement to Inheritance Rights through a Human Rights-Based Approach

Despite the customary law that excluded women from succession, in some cases, women were allowed to exercise their inheritance rights through a human rights-based approach. In *Kagwenyonga v. the sons of Rwubusisi* (1956), King Mutara Rudahigwa recognized the equality of all his children with respect to inheritance. The Royal Court decided that Rwubusisi's assets should be shared equally among all his male and female children. It based its decision on human values in an effort to move Rwandan culture and traditions toward justice and equity. Also, in the case *Mukamusoni v. Buyitare*, rendered in 1985, the Court of Appeal denied Mukamusoni's right to inherit equally with her brothers. However, la Cour de *Cassassion* overturned that decision and ordered an equal sharing of the property between Mukamusoni and her brother Buyitare. The court based its decision on the principles of equality and nondiscrimination articulated in Article 16 of the 1978 Constitution. In that decision, la Cour de Cassassion considered customary practices that excluded women from inheritance as gender-discriminatory practices. It then used a human rights-based approach and decided in favor of Mukamusoni.

Again, in the case *Mukagasana Domitile v. Sarushi* (2009), which involved a wife and a husband who died in 1994 without leaving behind any children, the High Court excluded heirs of the family of the wife. The court argued that customary rules allowed succession of heirs only of the deceased husband and excluded heirs of the wife. The High Court ignored the equality and nondiscrimination principles that had been constitutionally guaranteed since 1962 and embodied in different ratified international human rights instruments. Fortunately, the heirs of the deceased wife filed a third-party opposition claiming for equality of rightful heirs of both spouses with regard to inheritance. Thus, in the case *Mukamusoni v. Mukagasana* and others, the High Court decided in favor of the deceased wife's heirs. In its ruling, the court referred to the case of *Mukamusoni v. Buyitare* (1985), discussed earlier, and to the 2003 Constitution to reverse the previous court's ruling. It decided that the wife's family had the right to inherit equal to that of the husband's family. Consequently, each side was entitled to inherit 50% of the entire property.

The Situation after 1999

Since the enactment of law no. 22/1999, women's and girls' rights to property deriving from inheritance have been judicially protected. The law guaranteed equal rights to inheritance for all children, regardless of their sex. In addition, it provided entitlement to bilateral inheritance where the child had the right to inherit from their deceased mother or father (Articles 50 and 60). Consequently, women and female children could get shares in the succession of assets that were inherited exclusively by their brothers (*Mukarubuga Marie v. Munyakinani Jean*) or paternal uncles (Nyiransekeye, 2000), and they had the right to inherit from their brothers and their children (Mukakarara Ancille). However, women's bilateral inheritance generated family conflicts because "some men believe that the law is unjust, and will allow women to benefit from land from two sources: their parents and their husbands" (Musahara, 2006). About 69.4% of inheritance-related cases were filed by women who based their cases on law no. 22/199, which addressed resistance to granting them their inheritance right—resistance influenced by discriminatory customs excluding women from inheritance that were applied for many years. It took some time to evoke a mind-set change in relation to women's inheritance rights (GMO, 2012).

It should be noted that law no. 22/1999 was not retroactive; it did not apply to inheritance from people who died before it was enacted. However, some of the purposes behind its adoption were to enable widows and girl orphans, survivors of the 1994 genocide against the Tutsi, to inherit properties left by their relatives (Polavarapu, 2011), to uphold the constitutional equality and nondiscrimination principles, and to enforce women's inheritance right.

Law no. 22/99 was repealed by law no. 27/2016. This current law also recognizes bilateral inheritance and the equality of all children in relation to inheritance. It additionally regulates the inheritance rights of the surviving spouse. However, putting these rights into practice is impossible in a practical sense, as is discussed below.

Judicial Enforcement of Inheritance Rights of Women as Surviving Spouses

Before August 2016: Lack of the Inheritance Rights of a Surviving Wife

The customary patrilineal system inhibited widowed women from inheriting the assets of their deceased husbands (Berg et al., 2010). Also, pursuant to Rwanda's customary land tenure, widowed women were evicted from the property left by their late husbands (MINITERE, 2004). Upon the death of the husband, the widowed wife could stay in the deceased husband's home and raise children born to the deceased husband on the condition that she gave up her right to remarry (Ruhashyankiko, 1984). In that case, the woman got property usufruct, meaning she could use and enjoy it temporarily, and handed over that property to her sons at their majority age (Polavarapu, 2011). The widowed wife could also opt to move back in with her biological family after the death of her husband. In that context, she could get *imperekeza*—that is, a property having very little value compared with her contribution to the economic development of the household. Also, the widowed wife could marry a brother or any relative of her deceased husband. In that situation, the property she owned with the late husband fell under the control and ownership of the second husband (Kairaba & Simmons, 2010). Consequently, widowed women lived in a constantly precarious situation regarding their property rights resulting from inheritance. They were subject to their biological family or male relatives who were responsible for taking care of them until they remarried (RISD & Burnet, 2003).

Even after 1999, law no. 22/99 did not recognize the inheritance rights of the surviving wife. Consequently, courts denied her the right to take part in the property of the household and upheld traditions that prevented surviving women from inheriting despite their contributions to the growth of the family property. For instance, in *Mukansanga v. Umutoni and Others* (2014), the Supreme Court excluded the surviving spouse from inheriting assets left by the husband. The court's reasoning relied on Rwandan customs that did not entitle women to the right to inherit the property left by their deceased husbands.

The court accorded to the surviving wife only alimony and the administration of the property on behalf of her two minor children. The surviving spouse's disinheritance from the deceased spouse's assets was confirmed in that court's ruling and accepted as such by the surviving spouse (wife). Also, in the case *Mukansoro Monique* (2015), the court ordered that the property left by the late husband be registered under the names of the surviving spouse but granted her powers of managing the property on behalf of the children born from their marriage only. Undoubtedly, the attitude of judges was influenced by customary law and was associated with the absence of express legal provisions regulating the inheritance rights of the surviving spouse in law no. 22/1999.

Since August 2016: Surviving Spouse's Inheritance Rights and Insecurity of Other Rightful Heirs

Law no. 27/2016, which repealed law no. 22/99, provides that the surviving spouse has the right to inherit from their deceased spouse. However, its Article 76, 1 creates some insecurity for other rightful heirs and legatees of spouses married under the community property structure. It provides that in the case of the death of one spouse married under community property, the surviving spouse is entitled to the entire property and fulfills the duty to take care of children born from their marriage. This has led to inconsistencies in courts' decisions regarding enforcing the inheritance rights of the surviving spouse and other rightful heirs. For example, in the case *Mbabanjimana J. B. v. Ntaganzwa Charles* (2017), the Supreme Court validated the contract of sale of a house concluded between a surviving spouse, Mukarushema (the mother of Ntaganzwa), and Mbabanjimana. It refused the claim of Ntaganzwa, another rightful heir, arguing that the law does not require prior approval from other rightful heirs for the surviving spouse to sell a component of the undivided property that was owned by both spouses before the death of one of them. This also happened in *Kajeneza Beatrice v. Bigimba Akinyana Nadege* (2018). A mother of a child born outside of lawful marriage claimed that her son, who had been legally recognized by his deceased father, should inherit. In the first instance and on appeal level, the courts rejected her claim on the ground that the surviving wife had the right to own the entire property upon the death of her husband pursuant to Article 76, 1° because they were married under the community property structure. The courts required the surviving spouse to continue caring for the recognized child.

In fact, Article 76, 1° hampers other rightful heirs' inheritance right. Because the surviving spouse is the one who knows the day-to-day situation of the property, other rightful heirs may end up having less or no property to inherit at the time of the execution of succession. Other rightful heirs need to be protected. They can be, if the surviving spouse is required to act as a possessor of the property and not as the owner (Bernhardt & Burkhart, 2010).

In addition, Article 52, paragraph 3 specifies that for a married couple, the opening of succession occurs upon the death of the surviving spouse or upon that spouse's remarriage. Thus, the execution of succession is not possible while the surviving spouse is still alive and has not remarried. The undivided property falls de facto into the hands of the surviving spouse while there is no legal framework protecting such property, which also contains the share of the deceased spouse that is meant to be inherited by all rightful heirs, including the surviving spouse. Also, the inventory of assets and liabilities occurs at the execution of succession. Thus, inconsistencies that appear in law no. 27/2016 in relation to the inheritance rights of the surviving spouse block not only the realization of those rights by the surviving spouse but also enjoyment of inheritance rights by other coheirs and legatees. It might be useless to acknowledge a right on paper while its exercise is practically impossible.

CONCLUSION

In Rwanda, women were discriminated against and treated unequally to men in relation to matrimonial and inheritance rights until 1999, when the gender-neutral law no. 22/1999 was adopted. Before its adoption, most courts did not uphold women's matrimonial and inheritance rights, as they were applying discriminatory customs and traditions. However, in a few exceptional cases, courts entitled women to claim matrimonial and inheritance rights using a human rights-based approach. In those cases, courts implemented the equality and nondiscrimination principles contained in the Rwandan Constitutions since 1962 and in some ratified international human rights instruments. In fact, in the absence of specific laws, the use of a rights-based approach by courts would have justified the legitimacy of women's matrimonial and inheritance rights within marriage, at the dissolution of a marriage, and in informal marriages.

With the adoption of law no. 22/99, which was repealed by law no. 27/2016, women's matrimonial and inheritance rights were clarified and since then have been enforceable before the courts of law. However, because of the persistence of customary traditions, upholding women's patrimonial rights was a constant battle as women and their attorneys tried to uncouple the law from discriminatory traditions that restricted women from accessing and owning family land and other family resources. More importantly, the Supreme Court played a vital role in enhancing women's patrimonial rights. In some cases, it made some decisions that provided guidance on how issues related to women's patrimonial rights could be handled. The court's decisions helped to prevent any regression vis-à-vis advancement of women's matrimonial and inheritance rights. Today, women can be judicially protected in the event that their matrimonial and inheritance rights are infringed.

REFERENCES

African Charter on Human and Peoples' Rights of 27 June 1980: ratified by Rwanda through the law no. 10/1983 of May 17, 1983.

Annual World Bank Conference on Land and Poverty, Washington, DC.

Bayisenge, J. et al. (2015). Women's land rights in the context of the land tenure reform in Rwanda the experiences of policy implementers. *Journal of Eastern African Studies*, *9*(1), 74–90.

Bayisenge, J. (2015). Women's experiences of land conflicts in the context of land tenure reform in Rwanda. *International Journal of Gender Studies, 3*(1), 118–133.

Bayisenge, J. (2018). From male to joint land ownership: Women's experiences of the land tenure reform programme in Rwanda. *Journal of Agrarian Change*, 18, 588–605.

Berg, N., Horan, H., & Patel, D. (2010). *Women's inheritance and property rights: A vehicle to accelerate progress towards achievement of the Millenium Development Goals* (Paper number 13). International Development Law Organization. https://www.files.ethz.ch/isn/138102/LEWP_Berg.pdf.

Bernhardt, R., & Burkhart, A. (2010). *Real property in a nutshell* (6th ed.). Thomson Reuters.

Burnet, J., & RISD. (2003). *Culture, practice, and law: Women's access to land in Rwanda*. Anthropology Faculty.

Bushayija, S. (1966). *Le mariage coutumier au Rwanda*. Bruxelles: Larcier.

Colonial Charter, of October 18, 1908, extended to Rwanda by the Act of August 21, 1924, on the Government of Rwanda-Urundi.

Constitution of the Republic of Rwanda of 1991.

Constitution of the Republic of Rwanda of December 20, 1978.

Constitution of the Republic of Rwanda of 2003 revised in 2015, *Official Gazette* no. special of December 24, 2015.

Constitution of the Republic of Rwanda of November 24, 1962.

Constitution of the Republic of Rwanda of June 4, 2003, *Official Gazette* no. Special of June 4, 2003.

Convention on the Elimination of All Forms of Discrimination against Women (CEDAW) of December 18, 1979: ratified by Rwanda through the Presidential Order No. 431/16 of November 10, 1980.

Decree-law no. 42/1988 of October 27, 1988, Instituting the Preliminary Title Civil Code Book One governing persons and family.

Elisabeth et al. (2010). Ahead of the game: land tenure reform in Rwanda and the process of securing women's land rights. *Journal of Eastern African Studies*, *4*(1), 131–152.

Gender Equality Unit, Supreme Court of Mexico. (2014, March). *Judicial decision-making with gender-perspective: A protocol making equal rights real.* https://www.unodc.org/res/ji/import/guide/judicial_decision_making_gender_protocol/judicial_decision_making_gender_protocol.pdf.

GMO [Gender Monitoring Office]. (2011, August). *Gender impact assessment of the law no. 22/1999 of 12/11/1999 to supplement book one of Civil Code and institute part five regarding matrimonial regimes, liberalities and successions.* Kigali. http://gmo.gov.rw/fileadmin/user_upload/Researches%20and%20Assessments/Gender_Impact_Assessment_of_the_Law.pdf.

Guyn, F. O. & Guyenne, F. (2011). *Traité de la représentation, du double lien, et de la règle Paterna Paternis, Materna Maternis: Par rapport à toutes les coutûmes de France.* Charleston: Nabu Press.

Herring, J. (2009). *Family law* (4th ed.). UK: Longman. https://web.law.columbia.edu/sites/default/files/microsites/gender-https://www.landesa.org/wp-content/uploads/LandWise-Guide-Womens-land-rights-in-Uganda.pdf.

https://www.scriptiebank.be/sites/default/files/webform/scriptie/Property%20rights%20for%20women%20in%20Rwanda.%20Access%20to%20land%20for%20women%20living%20in%20de%20facto%20unions.%20Scriptie%20Katrijn%20Vanhees.pdf.

International Covenant on Civil and Political Rights of December 19, 1966: ratified by Rwanda through the Presidential Order No. 8/75 of February 12, 1975.

International Covenant on Economic, Social, and Cultural Rights of December 19, 1966: ratified by Rwanda through the Presidential Order No. 8/75 of February 12, 1975.

Kagwenyonga v. the sons of Rwubusisi, Royal Court Rwanda, Judgment of February 2, 1956.

Kamatali, J. M., Uwineza, O., Zikamabahari, J. D. (2020). *Rwandan family law: Matrimonial regimes, donations and successions.* United States Agency for International Development. Cowansville, Quebec, Canada: Les Editions Yvon Blais.

Krause, H. D. (1995). *Family law in a nutshell* (3rd ed.). West Group, University of California.

Law no. 22/1999 of November 12, 1999, to supplement book I of the civil Code and institute part five regarding matrimonial regimes, liberalities, and successions, *Official Gazette* no. 22 of November 13, 1999.

Law no. 27/2016 of July 8, 2016, governing matrimonial regimes, donations, and successions, *Official Gazette* no. 31 of August 1, 2016.

Law no. 32/2016 of August 28, 2016, governing persons and family, *Official Gazette* no. 37 of September 12, 2016.

Law no. 59/2008 on prevention and punishment of gender-based violence in *Official Gazette* no. 14 of April 6, 2009.

Lesley, H. (2014). *Women's land rights in Uganda*, Landesa Center for Women's Land Rights Seattle, USA.

MINITERE [Ministry of Lands, Resettlement and Environment, Government of Rwanda]. (2004). *National land policy*. https://rema.gov.rw/rema_doc/Policies/National_land_policy_english_version_.pdf.

Musahara, H. (2006). *Improving tenure security for the rural poor: Rwanda—Country case study* (LEP Working paper #7). Food and Agriculture Organization of the United Nations. http://www.fao.org/3/k0784e/k0784e00.pdf.

Odeny, M. (2013). *Improving access to land and strengthening women's land rights in Africa*. Paper prepared for presentation at the Annual World Bank Conference on Land and Poverty. The World Bank-Washington DC, April 8–11, 2013.

Pamela, A., Mugisha, R., & Sapsford, R. (2018), Women, land and empowerment in Rwanda. *Journal of International Development*, 30, 1006–1022.

Polavarapu, A. (2011). Procuring meaningful land rights for the women of Rwanda. *Yale Human Rights Development Journal, 14*(1), art. 3. http://digitalcommonns.laws.yale.edu/yhrdlj/vol14/iss1/3.

Protocol to the African Charter on Human and Peoples' Rights on the Rights of Women in Africa: ratified by Rwanda through the Presidential order 11/01 of June 24, 2004.

RA 00967/13.03/84 of April 10, 1985, *Mukamusoni v. Buyitare*.

RC 00350/2017/TB/KCY of January 3, 2018, *Kajeneza Beatrice v. Bigimba Akinyana Nadege*.

RC 0057/09/TB/NGOMA of June 29, 2009, *Mukarepubulika F. v. Hakizimana Viateur*.

RC 0194/09/TB/BSSMANA of January 9, 2010, *Uwera M. Louise v. Habyarimana Emanuel*.

RC 0277/15/TB/NGOMA of May 18, 2015, *Nyiramuruta v. Ndayambaje*.

RC 0373/10/TB/NGOMA of October 25, 2010, *Kayitesi v. Sebagambyi*.

RC 0376/06/TB/BYM of October 24, 2006, *Mukarubuga Marie v. Munakinani Jean, Bitorwa Benoit*.

RC 048/06/BYM of October 6, 2006, Primary Court Byimana Mukakarara Ancille.

RC 0632/13/TGI/NGE of March 31, 2014, *Mutoni v. Niwenshuti*.

RC 0734/12/TB/NGOMA of August 19, 2014, *Nyombayire Alexandre v. Nyiracumi Yolanda*.

RC 10186/86, *Mukarugendo v. Munyaziboneye*, Tribunal de Première instance de Kigali, May 29, 1987.

RC 1019/03/2000 of July 13, 2000, Nyiransekeye.

RC 14115/33, *Uwimana v. Sumbili*, Tribunal de Première instance de Gitarama, October 4, 1992.

RC 19.379/92, *Batamuriza Zainabu v. Niyonzima Twalib*, the tribunal of the first instance of Kigali of May 7, 1993.

RC 20559/R.51/97 of August 29, 1997, Tribunal de Première instance de Ruhengeri, *Nyirabarera v. Ntahontuye*.

RC 26.133/96 Tribunal de Première instance de Kigali, *Munyurwa Faustin v. Kayitakirwa Jeanne*, January 21, 1997.

RC. 18.611/R.46/91 *Ntacyonteze v. Rusiriba*, Tribunal de Première instance de Ruhengeri, April 18, 1992.

RC0009/09/TGI/HYE-RC 0073/010/TGI/HYE *Mukankusi Nadia v. Mbyayingabo Issa*, January 31, 2011.

RC0726/15/TB/KCY of July 31, 2015, Mukansoro Monique.

RC13195/88, *Kayitesi Jeanne v. Nkezabera Jean Marie*, Tribunal de Première instance de Kigali, October 17, 1989.

RCA 00018/2018/TGI/GSBO of September 25, 2018, Intermediate court of Gasabo, *Kajeneza Beatrice v. Bigirimana Nadege.*

RCA 0087/12/HC/KIG of May 10, 2013, *Mukamusoni v. Mukagasana & others.*

RCA 0176/14/HC/KIG of February 27, 2015, *Mutoni v. Niwenshuti and others.*

RCA 0608/10/TGI/MHG April 29, 2011 *Mukamuligo Alphonsine v. Rwabahashi François*, the Intermediate court of Muhanga, April 29, 2011.

RCA 6301/R.14/RC.5686/R.12/KYA of March 12, 1993, Cour d'Appel de Ruhengeri, *Dusabemariya Illuminata v. Sikubwabo Theodomir.*

RCA0162/06/HC/KIG of April 14, 2009, *Mukagasana Domitile v. Sarushi.*

RCAA 0014/15/CS of December 1, 2017, *Mutoni v. Niwenshuti et al.*

RCAA 002/11/CS of April 23, 2014. *Mukansanga v. Umutoni and Others.*

RCAA 0021/15/CS of June 9, 2017, *Mbabanjimana Jean Bosco v. Ntaganzwa Charles.*

RCAA 0134/15/HC/NY of June 30, 2016, High Court of Nyanza, *Ndizihiwe v. Mukamwezi.*

RCAA00043/2016/CS of September 15, 2017, *Uwiragiye Charles v. Uwamahoro Jeanine.*

RCAA0009/14/CS of July 21, 2017, *Habiyakare v. Gahongayire*, Milimo.

RCom. 0001/08/CS of July 24, 2008, *Rwigema Josephine v. ECOBANK Rwanda SA.*

RCOMAA 0008/14/CS, *Mujawamariya and Others v. Bank of Kigali Ltd*, July 22, 2016.

RISD [Rwanda Initiative for Sustainable Development], Kairaba, A., & Simons, J. D. (2011). *Impact of land reform on the land rights and economic poverty reduction of the majority rural especially women who depend on land for their livelihood.* Paper presented at the Annual World Bank Conference on Land and Poverty 2011, Kigali, Rwanda.

RISD, Global Initiative for Economic, Social and Cultural Rights, ActionAid Rwanda. (2017). *Parallel report to the United Nations Committee on the Elimination of Discrimination Against Women, Rwanda, 66th Session.* https://www.ecoi.net/en/file/local/1401753/1930_1497428246_int-cedaw-css-rwa-26607-e.pdf.

RS/INCODT/CIV/0001/13/CS, Muhoza Consolée.

RS/Inconst/Pén.0003/10/CS of January 7, 2011, *Gatera Johnson v. Kabarisa Teddy.*

Rugege, S. (2016). Women and poverty in Rwanda: The respective roles of courts and policy. *African Journal of International and Comparative Law*, 24(4) 476–493.

Ruhashyankiko, N. (1984). Le droit successoral au Rwanda. *Revue Juridique du Rwanda*, *8*(4), 201–209.

Scott, G. (1979). Comparison of the property of aspects of the community property and common law marital property system and their relative compatibility with the current view of the marriage relationship and the rights of women. *Creighton Law Review*, 13(2), 71–119. sexuality/odeny_improving_access_to_land_in_africa.pdf.

Stefano, B. (2001/2001). Gender and law: Women's rights in agriculture. FAO. Legislative study 76, Rev. 1.

Supreme Court, RS/INCONST/SPEC/00002/2019 of December 4, 2019, GLIHD.

Vanhee, K. (2014), *Property rights for women in Rwanda: Access to land for women living in de facto unions*, Master Thesis, Ghent University.

Vanhove, J. (1941). *Essai de droit coutumier du Rwanda.* Brussels: Institut Royal Colonial Belge.

Waldron J. (2012), Stare Decisis and the Rule of Law: A Layered Approach. *Michigan Law Review*, 111(1), 1–32. https://repository.law.umich.edu/cgi/viewcontent.cgi?article=1095&context=mlr.

Part III

WOMEN AND ACCESS TO TRADITIONAL JUSTICE

Chapter 14

Gender and Customary Justice among the Podoko of the Mandara Mountains of the Far North Region of Cameroon

Jeremie Diye

INTRODUCTION

For several decades, violence, clashes, brawls, and complaints have marked the history of humanity. Relationships between individuals and couples are not always peaceful. It is necessary to go back to the past in order to understand how the people of ancient Africa, in general, and those of the Far North of Cameroon, in particular, resolved fights with the aim of restoring or strengthening social cohesion. The regulation of societal life in a well-defined territory requires compliance with a set of rules, laws, and codes established for proper coexistence of the members of that society. This set of codes that allows peaceful coexistence and living together is referred to as "justice." According to the *Nouveau Petit Robert* dictionary, justice can be defined as righteousness, fairness, impartiality, or integrity. In many societies, justice is more of a complex system than a simple, well-defined and circumscribed institution (Fimigué, 2001). Whether among people of the forest, savannah, or mountains, justice in customary institutions is a difficult concept to define because it integrates traditional religion, customs, and morals—elements without which its operationality would not be possible (Adam Abamé et al., 2006: 1). Some authors, when referring to customary justice, use synonyms such as "indigenous justice" and "local law justice."

This chapter focuses on the Podoko, an ethnic mountain group in the Far North region of Cameroon. Podoko society has the family as its basic unit, with a family head exercising authority. Each neighborhood is headed by the head of the lineage, and the clan is headed by a chief who is appointed by the notables. Each Podoko massif[1] has its own chief. However, the existence of autonomous chiefs does not exclude both friendly and conflictual relations between the inhabitants. Daily business in the community is managed by the neighborhood chief and the head of the massif. However, in the absence of the chief, his first wife, *Ness Tengwe Slwandala*, can play this role without limitation of power. Although the head of the massif is the guarantor of justice, this does not prevent the queen mother from performing the same task in his absence. This observation of the gender dynamics in leadership leads to the following questions: What roles do women play in the functioning of customary Podoko justice? How are women found guilty of offenses punished? The chapter proceeds by first examining the conceptual and theoretical framework, then it lays out the methodological framework, and finally examines women and access to justice based on the findings from the fieldwork. The last section sums up the discussion in the conclusion section.

CONCEPTUAL AND THEORETICAL FRAMEWORK

Customary justice refers to the regulatory system practiced before the arrival of Europeans. The qualifier "customary" is used in place of modernity, which refers in popular thought to the Western world. In its institutionalization by colonizers, African justice was known by several names: "customary justice," "indigenous justice," and "local law justice." Upon their arrival, African justice was stamped with the label "customary," as was the entire culture of the continent. This qualifier has a pejorative connotation of an ideological and methodological nature. Ideologically, it connotes seniority, overcoming, and obsolescence. According to colonizers, it was their presence in Africa that marked the beginning of the modernity of this geographical era; hence, the introduction of modern justice. To this end, they preached the disappearance of cultures deemed ancient or customary in favor of so-called modern cultures they brought with them. Thus, customary justice refers to that of the Blacks found in Africa. It refers at the same time to African religious justice, African popular justice, and all the mechanisms of conflict resolution in Africa. Methodologically, African justice is considered "customary" because of the oral tradition that underlies its approach and its transmission from generation to generation (Dekane Emmanuel, 2010).

Customary justice in this chapter refers to the types of justice systems that exist at the local or community level that have not been put in place by the state. It is also a system of justice that generally follows customary law or an uncodified set of rules and behavior, enforced by sanctions and varying over time. Customary justice occupies the majority of court cases in many countries in Africa. It is from this perspective that customary justice systems have evolved considerably in response to colonialism and later independence. Colonialism gave rise to mixed models, where traditional and formal state systems coexisted. Traditional communities, customary law, and traditional justice systems continue to enjoy broad legal recognition in these former colonies (United Nations, Human Rights and High Commission, 2016: 23). I chose to work on customary and gender justice among the Podoko because, in most cases, some customary justice systems are harsh and discriminatory against women.

This chapter draws from feminist theory. Some African feminist scholars have examined the role of women in justice and decision-making (Sheldon, 2017; Achebe, 2011; Parpart et al., 2000; Oyewumi, 2000). Women's contribution to society is not just limited to the home, but extends beyond the domestic sphere. Women are employed in a variety of occupations, work at all levels in the workplace, and contribute enormously to the local as well as national economy. They are actors in the economic sphere, conflict resolution, peace building, and development. Based on this broader vision, women's work is not limited to the home. Women's perspectives and experiences help to challenge the assumption (generated from the male perspective) that women's work is in the home. Theorizing about women's roles should therefore be a flexible and dynamic process (Parpart et al., 2000). In a similar vein, Sheldon in her work on African women's histories argues:

> My first objective was to write a comprehensive narrative of African women's history by bringing together information that is usually scattered and narrowly focused. My second aim was to show that fully understanding the history of the continent requires knowledge of women's contributions to their communities and their accomplishments in their families. (Sheldon, 2017: xi–xii)

Through empirical data collection methods and techniques, the wealth of data on women's power can be observed through a feminist lens. Specifically, Achebe (2005) addresses women's investment of male space, adding to the data already collected by other authors. She demonstrates the presence and importance of local female deities, chiefs, farmers, traders, warriors, and queens in African societies. African feminist concepts are rooted in the nuclear family (Oyewumi, 2002: 3). This social institution constitutes the very basis of feminist theory and is a vehicle for the articulation of feminist values. In addition to feminism, ethical relativism is a lens that has allowed us to better understand how customary justice cannot be static in a world that is constantly changing or evolving, especially in its oral character.

Ethical relativism is the theory that states that morality is relative to the norms of a person's culture. In other words, whether an action is subjective or objective depends on the moral standards of the society in which it is practiced. Relativism is the thought that absolute truth is unattainable and that all claims about the customary resolution of a conflict are linked to the views of those who resolve it (Seungbae, 2014). The justification of relativism comes from the fact that no culture is better than another. The author argues that absolutism no longer explains moral phenomena as relativism does. Therefore, we should choose relativism rather than absolutism. Some absolutists assert that there are universal moral rules. However, what is admitted—for example, in the Podoko society regarding justice—cannot necessarily be the case in any other society of the world. With multiculturalism, the living together of several people belonging to several cultures, norms, prohibitions, and customs is permanently influenced and undergoes constant change.

According to Saint Augustine, the law is of divine origin and the unjust comes from the fall of man in the very beginning of the original sin (Olivier Bertrand ed., 2015). In the same vein, Jean-Jacques Rousseau thinks that justice comes from God and supports the existence of divine despotism, which denies free will, when he writes that what is good and in conformity with order is such by the nature of things and independently of human conventions. All justice comes from God; He alone is the source of it (Rousseau, 2013). To better understand the contours of this chapter, African feminist theory and the theory of relativism help us to anchor the discussion and analysis on the link between subjective law and objective law, when it comes to women's access to justice.

METHODOLOGICAL FRAMEWORK

Our methodology revolves around the types of sources, the mode of collection, and the method of analysis of the collected data. The term 'source' refers to all texts, objects, or facts from which knowledge can be drawn from the past. This includes written sources. We also used alternative sources consisting of oral testimony, observation, and digital documents. Written sources were mainly books, book chapters, journal articles, dissertations, and theses dealing with justice and the history of the mountain people of the Far North of Cameroon or that addressed an aspect of this chapter. This collection is from various documentation and archival centers in Cameroon.

For oral sources, field trips were carried out in the town of Mora and the Podoko villages of Oudjila, Makoulahe, and Kassa. We conducted group and individual interviews to collect testimonies based on a questionnaire developed beforehand. The choice of respondents took into account age, gender, social status, and sector of activity. Notables, princes, wives of the chief, peasants, neighborhood chiefs, patriarchs, and so on were solicited for interviews. The purpose of the interviews was to validate observation results and deepen our understanding. Through an interview guide, each participant was given a chance to express their experience in relation to customary justice, and, in particular, women and customary justice. We opted for a sample of 100 resource people: 63 women and 37 men. We distributed the study population according to their knowledge on the cultural, political, and religious organization of the Podoko people. Interviewee respondents' identities are withheld to protect their identities.

The results show that women are interested in the place of women in customary justice and that few men, on the other hand, are interested and do not find it important that women play a role in customary justice. The interview guide allowed us to learn more about the importance of customary justice and the place women occupy in it. Oral sources also helped us gain a deeper understanding because they constituted a form of knowledge retention in African societies.

The analysis of data collected was done with a thematic and inductive approach. This gave us an opportunity to methodically address facts with a certain degree of depth and complexity by systematically identifying and grouping them by area of interest (theme) and to use a scientific approach that obtains general conclusions from the facts. We were on a quest to let facts decide the conclusion.

SOURCE OF CUSTOMARY LAW AND JUDICIAL ACTORS

One striking aspect of this study is that the institutions of customary Podoko justice are not recorded anywhere. Everything happens according to custom and by the actors of justice: district chiefs, Lawans, mountain chiefs, and queens—notables of the royal court or the patriarchs who are repositories of knowledge.

Custom as the Main Source of Customary Law among the Podoko

Customary justice is practiced by a social group living in the Mandara massifs. The group is the first reference, and the individual has a strong attachment to family and clan structures. The rule of law or custom emanates from the group by consensus, which is then internalized and put into practice. The function of law is to guarantee the status quo by maintaining social peace through adherence to norms, most of the time customarily. When a dispute arises between members of the group, a judge who wants to be, above all, a peacemaker is appointed to settle the issue (Boubacar, 2007).

Custom can be defined as a set of rules established and known by an entire social community and considered by all members as legally binding.

It appears that custom plays an important role given that it constitutes a right created by morals. In fact, at the level of customary justice, the source of the law is custom. This source of law is consolidated by the habit of community members to manage different situations. In each situation, individuals react in the same way, and this habit eventually becomes a customary rule. Unlike the law, custom is not formed by a single act of a legislator (Bwire, 2019; Kariuki, 2015; Ndulo, 2011; Pimentel, 2010). It is gradually and imperceptibly formed by the repetition of similar acts by the social group. Adopted at first by a few, it becomes widespread and then finally accepted by all those among whom the same situations occur again (Kagisye, 2006). In fact, when a rule is used for a long time and becomes part of the habits of the components of society, the judge or the head of the massif imposes it on all the members of the massif. Thus, custom, which is the set of the do's and the don'ts, becomes like a law that must be respected. This is the case of respect for matrimonial and moral rules that concern the entire community. Dekane Emmanuel notes this when he argues that "matrimonial rules highlight the rights and duties (do's and don'ts) that govern marriage [. . .] prohibitions define the perception of incest as a crime" (Dekane, 2010: 54). Prohibitions are not only composed of the offenses of incest but also of adultery, theft, fornication, witchcraft, and so on. Although custom plays a role in strengthening sociability at the village level, it should be considered as a secondary source as it cannot replace or override a written law.

In African societies in general, and among the people of the Mandara Mountains in particular, customary law is more in demand than statutory law. Interview respondents noted that justice among the Podoko people is inspired by customs. It differs from modern justice in that it seeks more amicable settlement and conciliation. The Prince of Udjilla stated that the main objective of customary justice is harmony within the massif.

Among the mountain people of the Far North in general, and the Podoko in particular, custom is the source of customary law insofar as it "defines the principles of reparation for the offenses of witchcraft, divorce, inheritance, adultery, theft, fighting, incest, etc. Psychological, material and corporal punishment in judgments" (Dekane, 2010: 55–56). It is a true source of law. Fines, imprisonment, whips, social marginalization, and exclusion are jurisprudential decisions developed, valued, and perpetuated for the reparation of offenses (Dekane, 2010: 56). Those in charge of enforcement are none other than judicial actors from within the local community.

Judicial Actors

The Podoko people are surrounded by a multitude of judicial actors. Whether at the level of modern or customary justice, people responsible can be quarter heads, heads of massifs, the police, and so on. These actors do not all have the same powers of intervention in the judicial arena. Some work for the promotion of human rights, others are responsible for judging conflict situations, while others are responsible for administration or crime prevention.

In the course of this study, we found through observation that customary justice officials were impartial in the performance of their duties. These are patient, sober people and heads of large families. The neighborhood[2] chief is the intermediary of the mountain chief. In addition to the neighborhood chief, there are some former customary justice auxiliaries and the *Ness Tengwe Slwandala*, alongside the chief of the massif. Interview respondents noted that these judicial actors were patriarchs known for their eloquence, but above all for their knowledge on the disputes that were submitted to them. One respondent indicated that, in decisions concerning justice, the queen, the chief, or even the prince cannot, and has never, judged alone.

Generally, the ruler surrounds himself with different personalities so that together they decide on sanctions and keep their community in a state of peace and prosperity. It is therefore understandable why United Nations-coordinated studies on human rights and customary justice systems in Africa highlight this characteristic in terms of the participation of the chief and even customary justice officials in Africa, stressing that "within traditional justice systems, decisions are made by members of the community—whether it is the chief or deputy chief, the village chief, or an elders' group leading the community—or by a vote of the community in a general assembly" (United Nations, Human Rights and High Commission, 2016: 25).

Women play an important role in maintaining social cohesion on a daily basis. Elderly mothers are actors of justice in the sense that they solve problems through their wisdom and experience, and complainants and wrongdoers accept their advice. Wives of the massif chief are not excluded as they are also actors of customary justice (Sheldon, 2017; Achebe, 2011; Parpart et al., 2000).

Interview respondents indicated that many women are unable to present their concerns at the royal court level or do not want their problems to be presented to the public. To get around this, women seek the intervention of the chief's wife, the *Ness Tengwe Slwandala*. Respondents noted that through her expertise, she manages common problems that are addressed to her. In the presence of the head of the massif in the palace, the queen's powers are limited and her actions are reduced to the management of minor matters. However, in the absence of the leader, she plays the role of the massif leader, and her powers are not limited. It is understandable why she is considered the head of the family and even the head of the village. In the royal family in general, it is the chief's first wife who gives instructions in the chief's absence.

Justice actors, including women, must use all their human qualities to fulfill their mission, which makes them the moral conscience of society.

TYPES OF OFFENSES

Among the problems subject to multiple charges are land disputes or the illegal occupation of part of the fields of others, household disputes, witchcraft, theft, access to water, drunkenness, fighting, and so on. Thus, cases tried by the wife of the head of the Podoko massif are diverse. Offenses that do not fall within her jurisdiction are transferred to the chief.

Social Crimes

The foundations of conflicts among the Podoko are complex and of a social, economic, and cultural nature. No area escapes violence, and the search for solutions to alleviate it is the subject of long discussions. As in the Mandara Mountains, the Podoko massifs are characterized by a large population. Relationships between populations are not always peaceful, as they sometimes result in insults, fights, and violence between individuals and between communities. The most common causes of this are land conflicts, distribution of inheritance, abduction of women, witchcraft, theft, and so on.

Conflicts between members of the same family[3] may involve children of the same father over inheritance or children against their uncles over a piece of land or inheritance, for example. Sometimes trivial at first, incidents between family members can become serious, leading to fights, clashes with knives, and taking revenge. To prevent the atmosphere of fraternity from deteriorating, elders ask these family members to take their problem to the neighborhood chief, the mountain chief, or the queen. Sometimes it is a sister and a brother or two sisters who quarrel over the management of family affairs. The recurrence of this situation can lead to disputes and fights. The same applies to interclan conflicts. There are several reasons that lead to clashes between people. This is the case with the use of wells at the village level in the dry season.

The Mandara Mountains experience high evaporation, and rainfall is rare. This region of Cameroon is characterized by the presence of rocks that do not give room for the drilling of deep wells. This causes easy exhaustion of local water supplies every year, especially during the dry season, when wells near family compounds dry up, and groundwater sources that feed the boreholes equally dry up. Water at the bottom of wells becomes a real source of dispute, not only between neighbors, but sometimes from village to village, especially if the wells are located in the no man's land of a border valley (open access wells). It is around these water points—that is around wells, boreholes, and ponds in the *mayos*—that disputes often break out between villagers because everyone wants to be quickly served but the resource is scarce. Disputes escalate into conflicts. This is what happened in Makoulahe between the Bekoué and Bouda clans among the Podoko. In March 2013, an argument almost turned into a conflict between women in two quarters of the Makoulahe village. The women of Bekoué were accused of drawing water from a well for the construction of houses.[4] Instead of accepting the blame, the Bekoué women responded arrogantly to the Bouda women in the following words: "It is because the women of the Bouda clan were jealous, as there are no beautiful houses in their neighbourhood." The men interviewed expressed concern about this situation, and the Bouda women decided after this exchange of words that no one could get water. As the wells were all located in Bekoué territory, the Bekoué women had to block access to the well. For two days, the women went on strike around the water and Bouda women were unable to get water.

Conflicts over difficulties accessing water can escalate to the raising of swords. Christian Seignobos argues that "a challenge of a few arches can stir up an entire massif. This has always been the sensitive point of the land in that it touches on the past, power and water at the same time" (Seignobos, 1997: 354). Water does not belong to anyone and its use is common. But it sometimes happens that women from other massifs who come to fetch water prevent the women who own the wells from getting their supplies. After a whole day of waiting, arguments and fights follow. Women from the same clan can fight over the use of wells in the village and face many consequences.

In a notshell, access to water, theft, and land boundary disputes are the sources of conflicts which sometimes become tragic at the end in the Mandara Mountains. The same applies to theft and land boundary movements or shifts.

Theft

Cases related to the theft of vegetables (okra, *folere*, *tazba*, *silikia*, etc.) are recurrent, and the perpetrators are mostly women. Border conflicts are frequent in mountain environments because mountains occupy 70% of the total surface area. Agriculture being the main activity of the population, some women spend their time harvesting the produce of others in fields they did not sow. Cases of theft committed by women are numerous and diverse. Sometimes these incidents, which are initially banal among women, can increase and involve families in conflicts.

As the founders of the theory of divine justice argue, the Podoko people firmly believe in the intervention of ancestors in judgments or in the violation of a prohibition. For example, women are prohibited from consuming certain foods, pregnant women from going to sacred places, and so on; otherwise, they may be punished either by sudden death, the appearance of an incurable disease, or by a jumble of misfortunes in the family.

MECHANISMS FOR RESOLVING AND MANAGING VIOLATIONS OF THE *NESS TENGWE SLWANDALA*

Hundreds of abuses observed in classical justice have led the Podokos, and particularly women, to be inspired and rely on a preexisting foundation: customary justice. The procedure for managing or settling infringements is oral, informal, and based on a dialectical method. From the free discussion on fair sharing and good conduct emerge a legal solution. This management, which still interests a significant number of people living on the land, depends on circumstances and offenses.

The *Ness Tengwe Slwandala* Is Always Listening

The resolution of conflicts allows family members to gain experience and strengthen family cohesion. Interview respondents noted that the chief's wife plays a very important role in that there is no question of blaming or indexing the offender, because according to facts, we know who is wrong and who is waiting for compensation. The words she utters then make it possible to repair the rupture of the bond between the protagonists.

One respondent indicated that women who complain that their husbands beat them every time they consume too much of the traditional beer locally called *bilbil* find solutions to their problems with the *Ness Tengwe Slwandala*. In this situation, the *Ness Tengwe Slwandala* acts as a role model and during the conflict management session, she remains calm and attentive throughout the exchanges without interrupting the speech of any party.

The purpose of this listening and speaking is to bring the parties to a consensus in order to find a solution. Interview respondents noted that, for this reason, both parties should not criticize each other's statements, as this can serve as a seed of discontent and rejection of consensus on the part of one party. Thanks to her skills, impartiality, sobriety, and patience in conflict management, the *Ness Tengwe Slwandala* plays an essential role in the social cohesion of the massif.

Fines and Repairs

Fines and repairs consist of a pecuniary penalty which is either a sum of money, or objects or animals that the guilty party is obliged by a decision of the queen or the head of the massif to pay. Part of payment is given to the chieftaincy and to the complainant. District chiefs are responsible for enforcing the fine.

Thieves of field produce, poultry, and livestock, once found guilty, are forced to pay a fine to repair their wrongs. For that, the chief sets the fines. One respondent remembers, when she was still a child, her neighbor, Nabba, had stolen two goats. The offense was not admitted, and after the chief's investigations, it was discovered that it was Nabba who committed the crime. For denying it, the fine was tripled to six goats instead of being doubled to four in relation to what he had stolen. Nabba had to borrow goats to pay this fine. Interview respondents noted that for anyone who stole produce, poultry, or livestock belonging to a massif, they paid twice (double) as much as the stolen property or more depending on the degree of the offense. Once the chief receives these fines, he takes what is due to the chiefdom, and the rest is returned to the complainant. Robbers sometimes may not find the means to pay the levied fine. In this case, they pay it by working in the fields of the chief.

They spend time at the chief's palace looking after a herd of sheep, goats, and oxen, and after a certain period, the culprit returns to his family home. Some women are known in the village for stealing farm produce, domestic animals, ornaments, money, and so on. Once a thief is caught red-handed, a complaint is verbally filed to the queen. In order not to dishonor the thief or the family of the accused person, the queen proceeds by an amicable resolution. For example, one respondent indicated that the thief was asked to bring to the chief's palace twice the amount of the stolen product. This is the case of Tambadi, who allegedly stole okra from her neighbor's farm. One of the women expressed that, "Once I caught her, I asked if she was the one who used to steal from my farm. She answered yes without hesitation. I complained to the leadership and Tambadi was summoned. The latter paid twice as much as she stole."

Generally, the quantity is doubled but sometimes multiplied. You cannot pay back exactly what you stole or borrowed once the problem ends up in the leadership. Before the fine is paid, the complainant and the accused are summoned, and each gives their version of events. When the plaintiff is untruthful, they pay the fine. If there is evidence, the accused takes all the charges. This is not generally the case with the offense of witchcraft, which carries penalties ranging from summons to banning the troublemaker.

Summoning and Banishment

The customary judicial procedure is triggered when a complaint is made. Some issues are confidential and women would not like to bring them up at the council level with the elders. They prefer to pose the problem in the form of a parable or charade in front of the head of the massif. If satisfaction is not found, the complainant sometimes tells the mountain leader that she will greet her sister before leaving. This sister is the chief's first wife. Once in the presence of the chief's wife, the problem is really exposed: an interview respondent noted that "my husband beats me every night when he comes home drunk," "my husband refuses to consummate the marriage for six months now," and "my husband does not take care of me when I am sick. The same applies to our children." To manage such issues discreetly, the head of the massif or the queen summons the person concerned to inform him of the complaint and orders him not to do it again and to pull himself together so that the problem would not be presented to the council of notable. As the Podoko people are a people protective, in most cases, calm returns in the home after the intervention of the queen or the head of the massif.

When a problem persists the head of the massif takes over, assisted by his notables. However, since the creation of customary courts, inter-massif courts, and modern courts, the heads of massifs have not been overstretched to deal with certain crimes. Sometimes, they must notify the competent administrative authorities in the cases of murders, interclan and interethnic conflicts. This is reflected in the UN report: "Many traditional justice systems do not have jurisdiction over serious crimes, but submit them to the police and refer them to formal courts" (United Nations, Human Rights and High Commission, 2016: 22). The heads of mountain ranges play a very important role in the amicable and sustainable management of conflicts. The advantage is that parties in conflict find definite solutions and the risk of repetition is reduced. Business is usually conducted outdoors in the morning. The Podoko customary court is characterized by speed and efficiency.

The crimes of witchcraft were in the past handled by the payment of a fine. The fine was imposed on people who practiced witchcraft and caused disorder in the massif by hiding so as not to be discovered. To identify witches, interview respondents noted that they proceed to an ordeal that consists of putting a product that only the chief's wife and head of the massif and some notables know the source of in the fire, and the guilty person confesses in front of everyone that he is the author of witchcraft practices in the massif.

Interview respondents noted that if no suspects are found, but there is one or many victims of witchcraft practices, the procedure is different; in this case, all women in the neighborhood of the chiefdom are summoned to the palace and interrogated. Once present in the palace, each woman walks to the victim with a little water on her hand to spray on him/her. Once the guilty person is sprayed with the water, the victim writhes in pain to indicate that the woman before him/her is the author of their pain. Until that happens, the procedure continues until the last woman. Once this session is over, the guilty party is instructed to restore the victim. When it is discovered that this is a proven case of witchcraft, there is a fine imposed, and the perpetrator is instructed not to repeat the practice of witchcraft in the massif. In case the fine does not solve the problem, and the guilty party commits another offense, then the ultimate sentence is levied: ostracism, and the troublemaker is then driven out of the village. This decision is made by the chief.

ANALYSIS OF WOMEN AND ACCESS TO JUSTICE

In the Mandara Mountains, crime perpetrators are punished by the custom of each ethnic group.[5] Custom is a source of law among the people of the plains. Long before the coming of the Western civilization in Northern Cameroon, laws were not written but were kept by the great custodians of knowledge who put them into practice during the judgments at the chieftaincy level. These custodians of tradition passed on laws orally to other generations.

Podoko women have easy access to customary justice since they are always well received at either the level of the neighborhood chiefs or that of the chiefs of the massifs. In fact, the first step in resolving a problem is at the level of the neighborhood chief called the *Blama*. When a problem is not resolved there, the case is sent to the chief of the massif.[6] Women complainants or defendants have always been heard by the guarantors of customary justice. The accused is not summoned directly to the chief. Permission is first of all acquired from her husband to summon her. In the case of a young girl, it is the members of her family that are instead summoned. This procedure aims to protect the woman who cannot go alone to the chieftaincy for a matter concerning her.

A woman who complains of being beaten by her husband always wins her case.[7] As there is no prison among the Podoko, either the notables, in agreement with the chief, order the husband to stop mistreating his wife by paying a fine that can vary in cash or in kind, or the husband is called upon to carry out certain tasks in the chiefdom as punishment. These tasks include looking for fodder and water for the chief's livestock and maintaining the crop fields of the chief. The woman is thus placed at the center of work and interests of justice within the chiefdom. It can thus be seen that the law contributes positively to the promotion of women's rights, a person who must be protected by respecting these rights.

Women benefit from a special procedure, especially those who are married compared to men in the enforcement of laws. In general, women and children among the Podoko must return or reimburse stolen goods to the owners if they are found guilty. As we have already noted, the woman cannot respond to a complaint lodged against her for repayment of either a large quantity of stolen beans or millet from the field. It is up to the husband or father of the family to answer the charges and pay the fine. African customary justice focuses on the family, and Muna Ndulo mentions that "human rights norms also proceed on the basis that the protection of the family as a social unit should not be used to justify restrictions on the individual rights of family members" (Ndulo, 2011: 90). Sanctions have a certain standard. They are not written down, but the chiefs of the massifs, neighborhood chiefs, and certain notables, who are custodians of customary law, have a perfect command of the sanctions to be applied for any offenses or faults committed by the population.

The justice system will not ask the wife to pay the fine or to reimburse the stolen goods as it is the man who must pay damages committed by his wife. In this case, the chief will summon the husband or the wife will be asked to inform her husband of an urgent matter concerning him at the chief's palace. In the case where the sanction concerned the performance of community service in the chieftaincy, the husband or the head of the family would take the place of his wife to carry out the tasks reserved for her. It is clear that customary Podoko justice punishes the man more than the woman. If at the time of judgment, the same sanctions were incurred by both men and women, in practice, the application of the laws is not the same, since the man had to serve the sanctions for his wife without the latter suffering any sanction. Thus,

> women are sometimes viewed as an addition to their tribe or clan as opposed to equals in their own right. Hence, once a woman is married, she becomes part of her husband's family and falls under his guardianship. An unmarried woman remains under her father's guardianship and control, so a woman effectively always has a male head over her. (Masengu, 2016: 586)

The ethnic communities of the Mandara Mountains in general and the Podoko community in particular are phallocratic societies. In a phallocratic community, women at first sight play only a secondary role, sometimes overshadowed by their husbands: "Women are exchange values and their possession is an obvious proof of their wealth (. . .) their possession should be evidence of the owner's virility" (Cournut, 2007: 27). Thus, a man who does not possess land, full granaries, wives, and children does not receive the recognition of his virility and therefore does not participate in major decisions that affect the whole village. These archaic values justify the fact that there is no overall good representation of women in customary gender justice. If women are not able to present their views in these traditional justice forums and do so through a chief's wife, elderly women, ward leaders, and their fathers or husbands, this does not mean that they have difficulty accessing customary justice. It is the custom that requires it.

Men sometimes take advantage of this position to abuse women. And yet, when we look closely at women's access to justice, they have never been prejudiced and, as we noted before, they have always been heard with a special ear in the judgment sessions even though they are dominated by the men in society. In contrast to Okoth-Ogendo's work on the disruption of indigenous land tenure systems based on access to land, the phallocratic societies of the Mandara Mountains have a system that they continue to maintain and preserve on the ownership of land or property. Ownership, according to European law, represents the appropriation of rights to use, abuse, and dominate parcels of land (Okoth-Ogendo, 2008).

Among the Podoko, the father of the family is the guarantor of the protection of the family. According to one of the interviewed women,

> even if the children are married and commit crimes, their parents must answer for their actions at the level of the chief if he is alive. This is because there have been several cases where men married with children have sometimes stolen and killed goats that did not belong to them. It was their parents who were summoned to the chieftaincy so that they could pay back the stolen items. As the husband is then the head of the family, when his wife commits an offense, he assumes the consequences.

However, it is important to make an exception. If a woman is accused of witchcraft or adultery, the man cannot answer for these acts. If a woman is accused of practicing witchcraft, her aunts, sisters, cousins—in short, all her women relatives on her mother's side—will go to the chief to claim her innocence, since in Podoko tradition, witchcraft is transmitted from mother[8] to daughter. These women will then say before the notables that they are not related to witches, the proof being that they are all present and do not practice witchcraft. This testimony in favor of one of them has a legal value and implies the immediate cessation of accusations against the accused. Women who support the cause of one of their own play the same role as lawyers in modern justice.

These women, who in principle support the accused, would go back home and tell the chief that they had not sent their sister or daughter to commit the offense of witchcraft. They clear their names and go home. If the woman did not recognize the facts of which she was accused, the ordeal[9] is then applied to find out whether she is guilty or innocent.

All the women interviewed expressed that in the case of adultery, if the husband's complaint is made based on mere suspicion, the complaint is dismissed. If the husband's complaint is accompanied by testimony of one or more persons, the wife and husband are confronted. If the wife confesses the truth, the lover is subject to the penalties of flagrante delicto with the payment of fines. In the case of adultery within a community, the matter is resolved amicably. This restores cohesion between members of the same community. If the woman did not recognize the offense, an oath is taken to determine whether she was right or wrong. If it turned out that she is the guilty party, her husband could keep her because of the children or repudiate her. According to Podoko tradition, continuing to live with an adulterous wife would bring bad luck to all projects undertaken by the wife's boss (her husband).

Land in Mandara Mountain societies in general and among the Podoko in particular is an inheritance. It is a family asset shared between members of the same family or clan. Land also can be obtained by gift or loan—by gift insofar as an individual may have positively marked a patriarch. Land also can be left to offspring. Inheritance of land is transmitted from father to son among the mountain people, "customary practices, such as the levirate—where in the event of the death of the husband, the widow(er) remains in the family as the wife(s) of the deceased's brothers—influence the inheritance capacity of women and their freedom. Due to traditional customs, women do not inherit land" (Osorio et al., 2010). Despite this customary rule, among the mountain people of the Far North of Cameroon, land is the heritage to which anyone can have access, even people who are not part of the village.

Land belonging to the mountain people has a sacred dimension, that is, it is venerated in popular beliefs. Although land belongs to the state and the state has established rules of access to land, restrictions not enshrined in the Constitution or in official texts show another reality at the local level. The parceling out of land has favored the return of migrants to the land, bringing members of the same family into conflict. Land can lose its patrimonial value if the owner has mentioned in his will the distribution of his assets between his male and female children. Modern justice in this case may allow women to inherit land at the village level. However, according to one of our respondents, it is difficult for the latter to exploit the land because "the land at this time is not blessed by the ancestors and cannot be used for agropastoral purposes." The land then loses its patrimonial value. This custom, which discriminates against women, does not date from the colonial era, but from the first ancestors who founded the Podoko villages. It is understandable why land disputes between women and men or other women are almost nonexistent in Podoko.

Chanock (1998) has argued that the mission of the Europeans seemed to be both the liberation of women and the improvement of their living conditions. To support this view, he shows that, in the past, civil law and customary law have failed African women by restricting the rights of women and children. According to Chanock, African customary law is recent and is based on specific economic, institutional, and sociocultural features of colonial rule. Customary law, then, is "invented tradition." Far from embodying the wisdom inherited from ancestors, it is not timeless, nor necessarily ancient, nor does it express a social consensus (Chanock, 1985: 253).

Chanock's analysis of customary law as "invented tradition" is erroneous, Eurocentric, and overly simplistic. Customary justice makes it possible to understand that before the Fulani conquests and colonization, justice in the Mandara Mountains was characterized by respect for customary rules, attendance at chieftaincy courts, and recourse to ordination and divination. As early as 1927, with the decree reorganizing indigenous justice, this judicial system was subjected to the influences of foreign cultures, such as Islam and colonization—colonization thus muzzled custom in modern courts. Colonial administrators created a customary court in each canton to adjudicate disputes. Customary courts are "ethnic courts," meaning justice is dispensed according to customary rules that have been purged of so-called hazardous practices (Saïbou, 2001: 247). The massif chiefs, assisted by administrators, apply their own customs to the parties.

Contact of the chiefs with Westerners has disrupted the application of certain important aspects of the custom. Regulatory powers of the massif chiefs have undergone many changes. Before the Germans and the French came to North Cameroon, traditional chiefs enjoyed autonomy in the management of their massifs. They were free to administer justice without being influenced. However, once Westerners settled in North Cameroon, there was interference by French colonial administrators. From 1916 onward, there was opposition, distrust, and even hostility on the part of the French toward traditional mechanisms of conflict resolution. They imposed the application of their modern form of conflict management.

To extend its influence over the populations of the Mandara Mountains and above all to establish its supremacy, the colonial administrative authority undertook a modernization of traditional judicial structures. Traditional justice began to lose its autonomy in terms of jurisdiction, and the vestibule hut or the shed or the sacred mountain of the ancestors, which served as the supreme jurisdictional body, disappeared in favor of customary courts. It was after studying these resolutions that they realized the effectiveness of the traditional procedure for managing intercommunity relations. In the circumscriptions, this effort to take account of the custom of the guilty parties in judgments was observed. Customary dispute resolution lost its former values in that judgments were supervised by colonial administrators, with chiefs only handling small cases. The most important disputes were referred to the colonial authorities. The impact was felt at several levels:

1. Chiefs were not allowed to organize conflict resolution sessions without the agreement of the French administration.
2. Populations preferred to take their complaints to the French authorities.

The colonial administration influenced the traditional judicial structures through the establishment of modern jurisdictional centers for conflict resolution. Massif chiefs and some patriarchs, once considered important in mediation, were auxiliaries to the courts created by French colonial administrators; this did not change much in terms of the frequency of tensions among the population. However, one of our interview respondents revealed that during this colonial period, women could be heard in the customary courts.

The danger facing customary justice is its abandonment by new generations. The incompatibility of these customary justice mechanisms with Christian and Muslim religions and new judicial procedures for bringing complaints remains the argument that people use to support the abandonment of customary justice. However, modern court structures have an inhumane downside.[10] There is an urgent need to document traditional conflict resolution mechanisms for the new generation as part of the cultural heritage. Preserving and enhancing this tangible and intangible heritage is necessary because it is in danger of being forgotten or disappearing. Also, the guardians of traditions—the priests—are very old and have no disciples to take over. Young people prefer modern justice, but their religion forbids them to use indigenous means of conflict resolution. Every year, knowledge-holders in the highlands and lowland villages die, taking their knowledge with them, which is considered retrograding by the youth, hence this observation:

> This case brings to the fore some of the major challenges faced by African judges in their attempts to interpret, adapt and apply customary law. They have to take into account fundamental changes such as commodification, monetarisation, urbanisation, individualisation, the formation of nuclear families, poverty and unemployment on one hand and the imperatives of modern constitutionalism and the minimum standards imposed by international and regional human rights instruments on the other. It is a challenge accentuated by increasing threats to the existence and survival of customary law because of the growing problem of lack of adequate expertise and sensitivity to the nature and content of the intricate issues often raised in a customary law dispute. (Manga Fombad, 2014: 476)

The state should value customary justice approaches. Efforts are being made, but the changing nature of customary justice makes it difficult to put it down in writing. However, a commission should record these oral laws and seek to reconcile them with modern justice, while promoting and facilitating women's access to justice. Among the Podoko, there is a real desire to give women access to justice with penalties that are not directly inflicted on them. It is important to reflect on the cases of offenses committed by women that Podoko justice considers very serious, such as witchcraft, adultery, and murder.

CONCLUSION

In summary, the main issue in this research was to find out about the role women play in the functioning of customary Podoko justice, and how they were punished when they committed crimes. The chapter thus identified the sources of law at home, emphasizing the main element of custom while identifying the actors within the customary justice system. All cases addressed to the *Ness Tengwe Slwandala* were not very serious offenses because the offenses considered beyond her competence were handled by the head of the massif. Most sanctions were aimed at seeking peace between the protagonists. They thus contributed to the consolidation of social relations, resulting in amicable settlements, fines made substantial within the reach of the offender, and ceremonies of atonement for certain faults are organized. Customary justice focused more on conciliation, reconciliation, and understanding between entities than on seeking to punish the perpetrator of the crime, which strengthened and maintained an environment of peaceful coexistence. However, it is important to note that the domination of the management of customary justice by men does not allow women to have full access to customary justice; hence, there is a need to revise customary laws that discriminate against women in terms of their presence at customary hearings to allow them to exercise their full rights, agency, and voice.

NOTES

1. Each massif is considered as a territorial entity independent of any influence where an ethnic group with a massif chief lives. Each ethnic group is subdivided into multiple villages or massifs and each massif into several clans. A clan is the association of several families with the same ancestor. The family is, therefore, the basic structure of the social organization of the peoples of the Mandara Mountains. The Mandara Mountains or "the citadel mountain" is located in the far north of Cameroon. It is an expression which qualifies many mountains still called massifs with a relief of generally massive form, more or less high, frequently having a mountainous character, and built in geological structures dating from the primary era or from even more distant times.

2. Each mountain had its chief and neighborhood chiefs. Within each concession, the neighborhood chiefs had an appropriate place reserved for the resolution of offences presented to them. Thus, the neighborhood chief brought problems that did not fall within his competence to the level of the chef de massif. Unlike the judgments handed down by the neighborhood chiefs, those handed down by the chief of

massif are final and represent the last instance of customary justice. The sanctions he pronounces are rigorous and the fines are doubled, sometimes tripled.

3. Fights can occur between co-wives. And to resolve this type of conflict, the two wives involved in the problem each bring a chicken. Once the husband eats the chickens, the problem is over. But if the husband cannot manage the problem, the case may be in the leadership.

4. In fact, it is during the dry season that most huts are built. This is because in rainy seasons, it is difficult for the soil to dry quickly and find straw for the roofs.

5. Ethnicity becomes the basis of group unity. Consequently, there is no chief capable of extending his influence over clans that do not fall within his commanding range. Although they speak the same language, share the same land made up of massifs, and share the same traditions or customs, the massifs are autonomous. Each massif has its own chief, which means that ethnicity is not a political unit among mountain peoples. The ethnic group in the Mandara Mountains takes the form of a diversity of independent clans. This character makes the mountain people autonomous and jealous of their freedom.

6. These were rare cases such as witchcraft and murder.

7. It should be noted that sometimes, some women abuse this justice which is favorable to them, insofar as women do falsely accuse their husbands. The penalty for the crime of lying is then severely punished so that it does not happen again.

8. There are no witch doctors among the Podoko, but witches. And men are not affected by the judgments of women accused of witchcraft practices.

9. Human bones or jujube fruits were used to detect the culprit. This practice was abandoned as it was a practice that could take the life of the culprit and destroy his whole family.

10. Electric shocks giving victims pain, convulsions, burns, and scarification. Execution of prisoners, injuries from caning.

REFERENCES

Abamé A., et al. (2006). *Etude comparative de la justice dans le lamidat de Ngaoundere et la chefferie mboum de Nganha (Adamaoua): 1935–1977*. Rapport de Licence en Histoire: Université de Ngaoundéré.

Achebe, N. (2005). *Farmers, Traders, Warriors and Kings. Female Power and Authority in Northern Igboland, 1900–1960*. USA: Portsmouth.

Achebe, N. (2011). *The Female King of Colonial Nigeria: Ahebi Ugbabe*. Bloomington-Indianapolis: Indiana University Press.

Boubacar, D. (2007). *La réforme de la justice et la protection des droits de l'homme en Mauritanie*. Mémoire Master en Affaires internationales: Université du Havre.

Bwire, B. (2019). Integration of African Customary Legal Concepts into Modern Law: Restorative Justice: A Kenyan Example. *Societies*, *9*(1), 17.

Chanock, M. (1985). *Rethinking African Customary Law, Custom and Social Order: The Colonial Experience in Malawi and Zambia*. Cambridge: Cambridge University Press.

Chanock, M. (1998). *Law, Custom and Social Order: The Colonial Experience in Malawi and Zambia*. Portsmouth: Heinemann.
Cournut, J. (2003). *De ce se tem bărbații de femei? (Pourqoui les hommes ont peur des femmes ?)*. Traduction du français par Daniela A. Luca, Bucarest: Maison d'Édition Trois.
Dekane, E. (2010). *Justice traditionnelle chez les Moundang 1927–2006*. Mémoire de Master d'Histoire: Université de Ngaoundéré.
Kagisye, E. (2006). *La résolution des conflits de compétence entre les acteurs de la justice de proximité au Burundi*. Mémoire de DESS: Université du Burundi.
Kariuki, F. (2015). Conflict Resolution by Elders in Africa: Successes, Challenges and Opportunities. *Alternative Dispute Resolution*, *3*(2), 30–53.
Manga Fombad, C. (2014). Gender Equality in African Customary Law: Has the Male Ultimogeniture Rule Any Future in Botswana? *The Journal of Modern African Studies*, *52*, 475–494.
Masengu, T. (2016). Customary Law Inheritance: Lessons Learnt from Ramantele v Mmusi and Others. *African Journal of International and Comparative Law*, *24*(4), 582–603.
Ndulo, M. (2011). African Customary Law, Customs, and Women's Rights. *Indiana Journal of Global Legal Studies*, *18*(1), 87–120.
Okoth-Ogendo, Hwo. (2008). The Nature of Land Rights. In A. Claassens (Ed.), *Land, Power and Custom*. Cape Town: UCT Press.
Olivier, B. (Ed.). (2015). *La cité de Dieu de saint Augustin translated by Raoul de Presles*. Paris: Champion, I, 2, livre IV–V.
Osorio, M., et al. (2010). Base de données Genre et le Droit à la Terre, pratiques de facto d'héritage/de succession. Cameroun. Food and Agriculture Organisation (FAO). http://www.fao.org/gender-landrights-database/country-profiles/listcountries/customarylaw/inheritancesuccessiondefactopracticeschangedinoriginaltranslation/fr/?country_iso3=CMR, site consulté le 19/06/2021.
Oyewumi, O. (2002). Conceptualizing Gender: The Eurocentric Foundations of Feminist Concepts and the Challenge of African Epistemologies. *A Journal of Culture and African Women Studies*. Africa Resource Center. ISSN: 1530–5686, *1*(2), 1–9.
Parpart, J. L., et al. (2000). *Theoretical Perspectives on Gender and Development*. Ottawa: Published by the International Development Research.
Pimentel, D. (2010). Can Indigenous Justice Survive? Legal Pluralism and the Rule of Law. *Harvard International Review*, *32*(2), 32–36.
Rousseau, J.-J. (2013). *Du contrat social*. Paris: Le livre de Poche.
Saïbou, I. (2001). *Conflits et problèmes de sécurité aux abords Sud du lac Tchad (XVIe-XXe siècles): Dimension historique*. Thèse pour le Doctorat/PhD d'Histoire: Université de Yaoundé I.
Seignobos, C. (1997). Maîtrise de l'eau et contrôle de l'érosion, l'exemple Mafa (Nord-Cameroun). In H. Jungraithmayr et al. (Ed.), *L'homme et l'eau dans le bassin du lac Tchad. Séminaire du Réseau Méga-Tchad, J.W. Goethe-Universität, Frankfurt, 13–14 May 1993*. Paris: ORSTOM, 351–365.

Seungbae, P. (2014). Cultural Relativism and the Theory of Relativity. *Filosofija Sociologija, 25*(1), 44–51.

Sheldon, K. (2017). *African Women: Early History to the 21st Century*. Bloomington and Indianapolis: Indiana University Press.

United Nations, Human Rights and High Commission. (2016). *Human Rights and Traditional Justice Systems in Africa*. York and Geneva: United Nations Publication.

Vuattoux, A. (2014). *Gender and judging*, ou le droit à l'épreuve des études de genre. *Tracée, Revue de Sciences humaines, 27*, 123–133.

Chapter 15

Juxtaposing the Efficacy of Testacy and Intestacy to Inheritance Rights

For Rukuba Widows and Children under Nigeria's Plural Legal System

Rebecca Emiene Badejogbin and Vicki Lawal

INTRODUCTION

Testacy describes "a state of leaving a will at one's death" (Garner & Black, 2009).[1] Common law and statutory law regulate statutory wills, while customary law applies to testacy made under customary law which is usually nuncupative (declared orally) in nature (Okanny, 2000). Intestacy,[2] or dying without a will, is regulated by statutory and customary law.[3]

Customary laws in Africa generally vary in different societies, but practices with respect to marriage and the right of inheritance of women are often similar (Cooper, 2008). Under most customary laws in Nigeria, including the applicable customary law of the Rukuba people located about 64 kilometers northwest of Plateau State in north central Nigeria (Blench, 2004), only men and male children may inherit property or land (Waziri, 2007). Women and children have long been regarded as a socially and economically disadvantaged group in Nigeria (Abdulrazaq, 2002), especially with respect to inheritance rights. This situation is exacerbated by the prevalent practice of the Rukuba people in society's most basic structure, the family, where roles are defined for males and females from a very young age to adulthood in line with societal norms (Ayodele, 2014; Muller & Sangree, 1973).

For the Rukuba people, men are regarded as the breadwinners and land-holding practices are conceived in their favor. Being predominantly farmers, farm work is usually performed by both sexes, with men performing the more labor-intensive aspects of the work. Women engage in agricultural activities like farming and petty trading in vegetables, staple foods, and brewing of local beer (Muller & Sangree, 1973), as well as performing their responsibilities as wives and mothers, and keeping the home. By virtue of these roles and practices, men ordinarily end up more economically and socially advantaged, despite the women's crucial contributions toward the enhancement and upkeep of the family. This inequality is conspicuously felt at the death of the "breadwinner." Empirical surveys in the west, north, and south of Nigeria identified disinheritance as a major problem for widows (Ngassa, 2012). This is also applicable to Rukuba widows and children, who are part of a minority tribe in Nigeria and whose experiences, like those of other minority tribes, risk being overlooked.

Social realities have glaringly revealed the disadvantages that ensue for women and children upon the death of a husband and father, respectively (Abdulrazaq, 2002; Ezejiofor, 2011; Ngassa 2012; UNICEF 2001). "Children of widows are . . . among the most disadvantaged . . . often living in conditions of extreme poverty" (UNICEF, 2001, p. 5). A study on children's and women's rights carried out by UNICEF in Nigeria that included the people of Plateau State confirmed that "limited or no property/inheritance rights under customary law, [and] difficulties of enforcing inheritance rights under customary law" are development challenges faced by women, especially in an agrarian economy. In addition, it identified "inadequate legal protection (retrograde) legal provisions, (and) weak enforcement" as challenges confronted by women (UNICEF, 2001, p. 5).

Advocacy for the protection of the rights of women and children in Africa has been ongoing. This can be quite problematic in countries with legal pluralism—where two or more legal systems coexist in the same social field—particularly in the area of inheritance, where women are disadvantaged under customary law. Some African countries are trying to enhance women's positions in inheritance and have taken different approaches (Himonga 2005, 2013; Osman 2019). For instance, in South Africa, a kind of unionization that tries to preserve the "cultural sensibilities" in customary law of intestate succession is adopted while giving room for modifications that incorporate gender equality (Bennett 2011, p. 1049). Nigeria is one such country, and this chapter will assess the viability of these regulations under its plural system.

The Rukuba people (also known as the Inchazi) are situated in the Bassa Local Government Area of Plateau State. Rukuba is one of the more than 40 ethnolinguistic groups in Plateau State, which is the 12th largest of Nigeria's 36 states (Blench, 2004). Its testacy and intestacy laws that provide for the welfare of widows and children from the estate of the deceased husband and father are provided for under applicable statutory and customary law. As one of over 400 ethnolinguistic groups in Nigeria, Rukuba stands the chance of being overlooked in research engagements with respect to the varying rights that apply to Nigerians. The challenges faced by its women and children with respect to inheritance rights are real and pressing. Researching these rights for the purpose of eventually providing solutions is vital.

By focusing on the Rukuba people, this chapter explores statutory provisions and customary laws applicable to them with respect to reasonable provision for sustenance for the wife and child after the demise of the husband and father. It commences with a brief legal framework and background on the Rukuba people, then briefly explains its methodology and analysis of the sources of testacy and intestacy laws for the Rukuba people. The chapter next identifies and examines the spectrum of challenges to determinants of inheritance and makes recommendations for a more viable regulatory system for the protection of the rights of Rukuba widows and children.

LEGAL FRAMEWORK

Generally, legal pluralism operates in Nigeria, as it does in other sub-Saharan African countries based on their colonial experiences and the repercussions that followed colonialism (Moore 1978; Merry 1988; Ige 2015). It also involves the participation of other non-state institutions in wider settings of societal relations (Griffiths, 1986). Nigeria recognizes more than one system of law and is confronted with the challenges associated with legal pluralism, even in its laws on succession. It is on this concept of legal pluralism and its attendant challenges in inheritance that this chapter's research turns. The colonial experience of Nigeria brought about the adoption of common law, doctrines of equity, statutory law (Onyebuchi, 1997),[4] and judicial precedents. These were added to existing diverse customary laws of each ethnic group. In broad terms, "[c]ustomary law derives from social practices that the community concerned accepts as obligatory" (Bennett, 2004). By its nature, it evolves, integrating changing norms in the society. Legal scholarship currently focuses on living customary law, which, according to Gordon Woodman, a professor of African customary law, is customary law that captures developments and adaptations to "current circumstances" (Woodman, 2011, p. 35). Legal pluralists agree that living customary law is not restricted to laws originated or recognized by the state but contains "nonlegal social norms" that regulate social relations and may not necessarily conform to conservative depiction of law (Cotierrel, 2009, p. 71; Erhlich, 2009; Menski, 2006). It is "the law observed by, or rooted in, each ethnic group of Africa regardless of whether it is recognised by the state" (Himonga & Diallo, 2017, p. 7). This chapter leans on this concept. Even though it is acknowledged that diverse customary laws apply to communities, clans, and even families, for the purpose of this chapter, the term customary law in its singular form encompasses the diverse customs applicable to the Rukuba people. The chapter focuses on the welfare of women and children secured by the deceased father and husband in the context of the applicable statutory and customary law.

BRIEF BACKGROUND ON THE RUKUBA PEOPLE

Historical sources suggest that the Rukuba people migrated from Ugba to their present territory around the eighteenth century. They occupy an area of approximately 440 square kilometers situated among small mining camps. The topography of the area is an array of high hills and lowlands. A majority of the residents live in villages among the hills while some have descended to the foothills in search of better opportunities (Encyclopedia; Ashen, 1990). According to Olive Temple, a Scottish explorer of the province of Northern Nigeria and author (1922), the original name for the language is "Ce," but they are now more commonly known as Rukuba, a Hausa term for "people of the rocks," and they are now officially described as such. The original dialect is known as "KuCe" while the people are traditionally known as "BaCe." The tribe is made up of 17 villages within the locality and headed by a local chief known as the "Utu Kiche" (Temple, 1922). Seven paramount villages existed as independent communities but were amalgamated into the district by the British colonial administration in the 1960s. They are surrounded by neighboring tribes of different linguistic subgroups, namely: the Jere, the Buji, the Ribina, and the Amo, with whom they share a close affinity (Blench, 2004).

It is crucial to briefly state the landholding rights of Rukuba women since, to a large extent, they are directly related to their inheritance rights. As in many African traditional societies, before the encroachment of colonialism, women had rights to land as daughters of their fathers and wives although defined within certain limitations (Mtengeti-Migiro, 1991). Land rights were communally owned to ensure sustenance and survival (Nhlapo, 1995). Communities were made up of clans further broken down into families, all under a common ancestor. In some communities, land control was exercised by the head of the family who was male, and proprietary interests were passed down through the male lineage of the fathers in order to maintain the ownership rights of the clans and for noninterference by the male spouses of the daughters, who are usually outsiders (Itua, 2012; Ajigboye and Alabi, 2015). In such communities, the rights of daughters to land were qualified and limited through their father's lineage. A widow had no right of ownership but could possess land allotted to her by her spouse and would lose such possessory rights after the demise of her husband if she had no child or if she remarried (Obi, 1962; Emery, 2006). The widow's limited rights to land were protected under customary law after the departure of her husband, provided she did not remarry from outside her husband's family after his demise, so the land was not lost to another lineage and also that she remain of good behavior (Emery, 2006).

The practice was that the widow was not abandoned but catered for by her husband's family after his demise through a levirate marriage or if she chose to remain unmarried, she could utilize her occupational rights on the land apportioned to her husband for her children's interests (Mtengeti-Migiro, 1991). The customary practice is that a Rukuba widow who chooses to remain in her late husband's house is allowed to keep such landed property only in trust for her sons and is not allowed to sell the land or retain it if she chooses to remarry (Muller & Sangree, 1973). Hence, while under customary law widows and female children do not inherit (family) land, they are protected in a different way. The issue is that male members of the family, in keeping the proprietary interest of the family, have corresponding obligations to cater for the well-being of the women. Unfortunately, the courts, while upholding these proprietary rights of the male, have ignored the obligations that go with it under customary law, therefore leaving women unprotected.

METHODOLOGY

Part of the data for this chapter was derived from the authors' qualitative fieldwork on the Rukuba people in Kihan village in Jebbu Bassa from April 7 to 14, 2014; January 10 to 15, 2021; and February 8 to 14, 2021. The choice of Kihan village was because the researchers' connections gave them access to the field site and to respondents willing to grant interviews. Other data are derived from earlier extensive fieldwork carried out by scholars who researched the Rukuba people (Muller & Sangree, 1973). Additional doctrinal data covering published works and laws also was used for analysis in this chapter.

Research methods within the context of any study provide a systematic outline for linking the data to initial research questions (Yin, 2003). The adopted research methodology for this study is the interview method. The nondisclosure interview was adopted where interviewee/participants/respondents' identities are withheld to protect their identities. Semi-structured interviews were used as the method of data collection. Interviews enable the researcher to explore causation and assess behavioral tendencies (Gorman & Clayton, 2005). Interviews can be conducted in either a structured or unstructured format; they are considered one of the most effective ways of enlisting cooperation from a study population and provide opportunities for a researcher to observe, establish rapport with a respondent, and build up contextual analysis for a study. Interviews are preferable for answering open-ended questions, and the format and wording of the questions often define the structure of the interview. This chapter acknowledges that one of the major problems with interviews is a lack of standardization in the data collection process, which makes it highly vulnerable to interview bias (Burton, 2000; Frankfurt-Nachmias & Nachmias, 1992). Researchers for this chapter tried to avoid this vulnerability by being as objective as possible in the analysis.

Two sets of empirical exercises were conducted. For both interviews, participants volunteered. For the first, the authors were referred to the pastor of a local church that serves the Kihan community. The church has a widow's group and keeps a list of the widows for the purpose of distributing gifts when available and to provide support. The pastor told the group's members about this research and left it to their discretion to decide whether they wanted to participate. Five widows agreed to be interviewed. Culturally, Rukuba women typically would not come forward to grant such interviews and it was therefore a very bold step taken by the ones who participated. This explains the small number of interviewees. The widows ranged in age from 30 to 88—four farmers and one petty trader—and had been widowed for several years.

For the second set of the interviewees or respondents, the authors' contact referred them to some male elders and leaders who were well respected in the community, versed in its culture, and often consulted by community members with respect to its culture and customs. There were five, ranging in age from 46 to 78, whose occupations were a traditional leader, a farmer, a retired teacher, a retired civil servant, and a retired magistrate. Two of the men interviewed were widowers, but that was not the reason for the interview since they were not particularly disadvantaged by reason of their widowhood. The men were interviewed based on their knowledge of the culture on inheritance. Their responses were juxtaposed with those of the women interviewed. The men indicated their reasons for volunteering as being particularly interested in the culture of the Rukuba with respect to inheritance and concerned about the plight of the widows and children after the demise of their husbands and fathers. Outcomes from the interviews support the findings discussed below.

ANALYSIS OF THE SOURCES OF TESTACY AND INTESTACY LAW FOR THE RUKUBA PEOPLE

The practice of testamentary dispositions prevalent in Nigeria reflects one of the consequences of legal pluralism. The challenge for widows and their children, particularly in rural areas, remains daunting. Efforts to create solutions must have the necessary legal environment to thrive. This creates a need to analyze applicable laws.

Statutory Laws

There are statutory and customary laws that regulate testacy and intestacy in Nigeria. Prior to colonization, customary testacy laws applied (Okanny, 2000). During and after colonization, the English common law, local legislations, and the Wills Act[5] (a statute of general application) regulated the statutory wills until the Plateau State Wills Edict applicable in Plateau State was enacted in 1988.[6] This Wills Edict applies to statutory testacy while the applicable customary law applies to customary succession which includes testacy; however, the latter is subject to the repugnancy test. With respect to intestacy, the Administration of (Real Estate) Law[7] and customary law apply where applicable.

Customary Law

The rules that govern wills under statutory law, such as the requirement of writing, do not apply to wills recognized under customary law (Harvey, 1968).[8] The private affairs of the majority of Nigerians are regulated by their respective customary law, with about 80% of dispositions of estates conducted in accordance with customary law (Ezeilo, 2000). Based on the findings of this study, Rukuba customary law permits testacy. The applicable customary law of the Rukuba people regulates the distribution of the deceased estate, which includes a man's testate distribution to his wife or wives and children. Here, the testator usually leaves oral instructions on how his estate should be distributed and managed (Sagay, 2004). Instructions may be in writing if the testator so wishes. For the Rukuba people, under customary law, a testator's testable properties are limited, since they include family and communal property controlled by the head of the family or community, respectively, but are owned by the extended family or community. However, under statutory law, they include "all property to which he is entitled either in law or in equity."[9]

Generally, instructions/declarations of the testator are carried out by the elders in accordance with the testator's customary law (Dadem, 2012). Family members may not hesitate in executing such instructions/declarations but may do so only out of respect for and fear of the dead when they alter the customary rules of succession such as giving more rights of inheritance to his wife and children (Harvey, 1968). However, there have been instances where these dispositions (of maintaining the widow or even where the customary rules of succession were altered) were ignored. Courts have upheld such rights of testamentary disposition under customary law (Osamolu, Oduwole & Oba, 2016). Based on our data, there was an instance in which the directive of a testator that all his property be transferred to the only male child—leaving the widow and three daughters without any inheritance—was respected by the widow's in-laws. The son, however, catered for his mother and sisters. A challenge that must be addressed is when the heir is not the biological son of the widow and abandons her and his half-siblings after carting away the inheritance. Our data revealed instances where the husband's disposition of land made to the widow and her son under customary law was challenged in a polygamous setting. Another verbal disposition leaving the farm to the widow was also not respected by the in-laws. This was reported to the traditional chief, but nothing was done about it.

Customary rules of dispositions may go contrary to constitutional provisions of equality,[10] dignity,[11] and the right to own property,[12] under fundamental human rights and pose a challenge. Although no data is available on how frequently testamentary disposition is utilized in Rukuba customary settings, customary disposition has no doubt featured as the subject of adjudication in the formal courts, including in the cases of *Ayinke v. Ibidunni*[13] and *Nelson v. Nelson*[14] (Badejogbin, 2015). This indicates that there are challenges to the application of applicable laws.

CHALLENGES TO DETERMINANTS OF INHERITANCE

Choice of Marriage

The concept of marriage mentioned here refers to a valid statutory marriage and a valid marriage under the applicable customary law.[15] The nature of the marriage entered into by a widow and her husband is in some instances a determinant of whether she inherits from her husband's estate. Statutory marriage in Nigeria is monogamous, while marriage under customary law is polygamous. The Rukuba family setting is based on marriage, and early marriage is a usual practice (Muller & Sangree, 1973; Muller 1978).[16] The individual choice of law is determined by their choice of marriage.

This choice of law may be absolute or partial. It is absolute only as it relates to intestacy since the choice of marriage will determine whether the provisions of the Marriage Act/Administration of Estate Law will apply or whether it will be solely the customary law of intestacy that is applied.[17] The Marriage Act/Administration of Estate Law would safeguard to an extent the interest of the widow and children while the living customary law of intestacy would otherwise apply, which may expose them to the challenges discussed here. Generally, women may be ignorant of the implication of the choice of marriage entered by them. It is therefore necessary that an awareness program be organized to educate the community, including women, on the implications of the nature of marriage they choose to enter.

Unfortunately, the Plateau State Married Women and Property Edict,[18] which attempts to secure a wife's monetary interests and property rights, is restricted to only women with civil marriages and does not extend to women married under customary law. This clearly contradicts the constitutional provisions that make no restrictions on the right to "acquire and own immovable property anywhere in Nigeria" for all persons,[19] including women who do not have civil marriages.

The choice of law that applies in terms of the inheritance rights of women and children is not absolute under statutory testacy with respect to the Wills Law. This is because the Wills Law subjects the absolute freedom of testamentary disposition of the testator to the applicable customary law. Therefore, as far as statutory testacy is used by the Rukuba testator, certain dispositions must still be subject to the norms of applicable customary law.

The Marriage Ordinance of 1913, which applied in Nigeria, provided that the spouse of a deceased who died intestate inherited his estate. But this Marriage Ordinance was repealed and replaced by subsequent marriage laws over the years (Nwogugu, 2014).[20]

Children, Legitimacy, and Legitimation

In this chapter, a child refers to all biological and adoptive children of the deceased and any other category where the deceased accepts a child as his regardless of the circumstances of the birth. This includes all circumstances where it is proven that the child is a biological child of the deceased. Under common law, any child born outside a valid marriage is an illegitimate child. Under customary law however, legitimacy extends beyond children born within valid customary law marriages to include children "whose fathers have accepted paternity" (Itua, 2012; Commonwealth, 2013). Acknowledgment of paternity by a father could be formal or informal (Sagay, 2004; Commonwealth, 2013).[21] The concepts of legitimacy and legitimation are vital because they determine whether a child is entitled to inherit from the parents. Under common law, a child born outside wedlock and not legitimated by the parents has no right to inheritance (Sagay, 2004).

The statutory meaning of a child also embraces part of what constitutes a child under customary law. For Plateau State in particular, the provision of section 2 of the Wills Edict, which regulates testamentary dispositions and is applicable to the Rukuba people, has an extensive definition of a child. It provides that

> "child" includes a step-child, a child whose paternity has been acknowledged in accordance with any customary law applicable in Nigeria, a child adopted whether before or after the commencement of this Edict in pursuance of an

adoption order made under any statute in Nigeria or in any other country, a child enventresamare, and a child legitimated under any law.[22]

Section 42(2) of the Constitution protects against any form of discrimination based on the circumstances of one's birth. In this light thereof, the clause "a child legitimated under any law" covers all categories seemingly omitted. The categories omitted include a child born outside wedlock whose paternity has not been acknowledged in accordance with any applicable customary law in Nigeria, and a child whose paternity has not been acknowledged at all, whether or not "in accordance with any customary law" but confirmed by DNA testing. Other omissions include a child whose paternity is acknowledged by a customary law applicable outside Nigeria and a child adopted under customary law rules.[23] All these are covered by the Constitution, which supersedes the limitations of the Wills Edict.[24] The seeming restrictions of the right of a Rukuba child subject to testamentary disposition under customary law can be addressed under constitutional provisions.[25] What a widow and child inherit is determined by the rules of testacy and intestacy under applicable laws. With respect to testacy, this is no longer left to the extent of the freedom of testamentary disposition exercised by the testator. This freedom is restricted under both the statutory and Rukuba customary law systems.

Freedom of Testamentary Disposition

The Rukuba testator's freedom of testamentary disposition under the Wills Act was absolute. It was, however, changed by the Plateau State Wills Law in 1988. This freedom, as it currently stands in Plateau State, is subject to the fetters of customary law, religious restrictions, provision for family members and dependents, and the court's discretionary power to make orders that affect the testator's freedom of testamentary disposition (Abayomi, 2004). In Nigeria, customary law, which is viewed as state law based on tacit state recognition in the Constitution and through its institutions (Badejogbin, 2019), is applicable in the manner prescribed by statute—in this case, the Plateau State Wills Law.

Testamentary freedom of a testator under customary law is limited by customary norms of inheritance and this is intertwined with statutory limitations. Under current statutes, the freedom of testamentary disposition for a testator is regulated by the Wills Edict and has two broad restrictions. These are the limitation of customary law and the testator's obligations to family members. These have implications on dispositions to wives and children.[26] The widow and child may apply to court within six months from the grant of probate if the testator did not make financial provisions for them under his will.[27] The Wills Edict of Plateau specifically subjects the testator's freedom of testamentary disposition to his obligations to make adequate provision for his wife and children. Where he fails to do so, it can be a ground for challenging the validity of the will.

Would the subjectivity of the testator's disposition to customary law override the requirement to make financial provision for family where the testator bequeaths his property for the upkeep of his family? Both requirements are contained in the same law, which, in section 3(1), appears to state how a conflict between them should be resolved; that is, all provisions of the edict are subject to customary law restriction. Given customary law's leaning, this may not lead to positive outcomes for the wife and children.

The solution to this dilemma could lie in how each provision fares under constitutional scrutiny. Since the Wills Edict is subject to the Constitution, issues would no doubt be tied to the rights to dignity, equality, right to own property, and gender. The authors' position is that priority be given to that which passes these constitutional tests. Hence, the customary law restriction may fail and thereby give room for the survival of the requirement that adequate financial provision be made for the family.

The argument here is also that customary law restrictions must be interpreted subject to the estate of the deceased being sufficient to reasonably provide for the widow and children of the deceased. In other words, should the courts be inclined to uphold the customary law restriction, the deceased's landed property should go to other male relatives only if the widow and children can be adequately catered for from the remaining estate. This is another dimension to the application of constitutional scrutiny.

A SPECTRUM OF ISSUES, DIFFERENCES, AND RECOMMENDATIONS

The Supreme Court of Nigeria in the case of *Mojekwu v. Iwuchukwu*,[28] refusing to make a finding on the Court of Appeal's[29] assertion of unconstitutionality of a custom that prohibited women from inheriting land, cautioned against a sweeping condemnation of all customs regarding women (Nwabueze, 2010). In notable cases of statutory testate succession, such as *Lawal Osula v. Lawal Osula*[30] and *Uwaifo v. Uwaifo*,[31] concerning the dispositions of property that should go to the first son under customary law, the courts have refrained from applying constitutional standards of equality of both sexes and have rather upheld the customary law rule that bequeaths these properties to the eldest sons. In fairness to the courts, discrimination on grounds of gender was not an issue for determination before the Supreme Court in these cases.

Paradoxically, the provisions of the Administration of Estate Law for some states, including Lagos State and the old Mid-Western States, applicable to a deceased married under the Marriage Act seem to be more in favor of the wife and children than where there is a valid will. This is because the widows and children are the main beneficiaries under the Administration of Estate Law for Lagos and Mid-Western States because the widow inherits one-third of the estate.[32] These are therefore recommended for Plateau State, with modifications that would improve the plight of the widow and child. The reason is that one-third of the estate may be insufficient to cater for the upkeep of the widow and child, and the prescription for adequate financial provision by the testator under the Wills Edict would be more appropriate. The Plateau State Wills Edict has no doubt been a great improvement on the Wills Act as discussed before, despite the encumbrances of both statutory and customary law testacy. The situation is worse under intestacy.

Currently, the Administration of Estate Laws applicable in respective states prescribe how the estate of a deceased person who died intestate should be distributed. Applicable in Plateau State is the Administration (Real Estate)[33] law, which merely qualifies what property of the testator should be administered. This law applies only to the real property of a testator, of which the testator could dispose by will, and is not required to distribute in a manner prescribed under customary law.[34] It provides that the testator's heir-at-law "shall be equally entitled to the grant of a letter of administration with the next of kin."[35] It is, however, silent on the plight of the widow and the child with regard to inheriting from the estate of the deceased. This void is filled by Section 37 of the High Court Civil Procedure Rules, but it merely enables the court to give such directions to protect the interest of the widow and child where they apply, without categorically stating their right for priority consideration in the estate of the deceased. It therefore leaves this to the discretion of the judge.

Other jurisdictions have attempted to address the protection of rights in plural legal systems irrespective of the choice of law of the people. A good example is Canada. According to legal pluralists such as Ghislain Otis, professor and holder of the Canada Research Chair on Native Peoples and Legal Diversity, this is important. With the rise in the protection of "cultural and legal diversity," the human rights of indigenous societies are protected by state institutions regardless of the "individual choice of law" (Ubink, 2018a, p. 146). This is so because there is an overarching statute that subjects even indigenous laws to the Canadian Charter of Rights and Freedoms, which also promotes gender equality (Ubink, 2018a). The situation is similar in Nigeria and also applies to the Rukuba people in particular. All laws in Nigeria are subject to the provisions of the Constitution, which also promotes gender equality. Hence, infringements of the rights of a widow and child under statutory and customary law could be challenged in court. The main challenge therefore relates to a woman's access to courts for justice, which is determined by several factors.

The unique nature of customary law—that is, "unwritten, negotiable and relational" (in other words, flexible)—creates room for a renegotiation of structures and institutions that would enable the establishment of a more viable arrangement for participation of vulnerable persons for better access to justice (Ubink, 2018b, p. 931). For the Rukuba people, the traditional leadership and majority of the men interviewed expressed concern about the discriminatory practices of inheritance for women and children and thus appeared to be open to positively addressing these issues. Renegotiation of structures and institutions would provide a more viable path to access to justice for these vulnerable groups. The local chief expressed that

> the advocacy for testacy in favor of female children should continue to the level that would make parents reconsider the disadvantaged position of female children in Kiche land and do justice to the male children.

In other words, testacy under customary law should seek to give the widow and child more rights than they would ordinarily have in cases of intestacy under customary law. All of the women interviewed expressed a need to reform the applicable customary law to better cater for the widows and girl children. One expressed that it "would have been helpful to me if I was given land so I could be able to sustain myself and the children through farming." Therefore, inroads into addressing these challenges should be explored (Grant, 2006).

Where the willingness of leaders is in tune with the agitations of victims, the community where customary norms are determined by the majority should be more inclined to grant the speedy evolution of these customary norms for two reasons. First is the failure of reciprocal or consequential responsibilities to cater for the well-being of the widow and child tied to the landholding arrangement of the communities placing power and responsibility on the men. Hence, the customary norms for male primogeniture (first born) lose its legitimacy because if the limited customary rights of women to use land in terms of inheritance are discontinued, the primacy of proprietary rights of the men cannot therefore be sustained unless the obligations attached to them to cater for the widow and child are enforced. These proprietary rights have clear-cut obligations that are glaringly problematic. Second, with respect to the evolving realities of customary norms, there has been a move to a more individualized system of ownership in which property is acquired based on the individual rights of the persons, in their own names, and not tied to the community (Badejogbin, 2015). Should dispositions of such individualized acquisitions still be subject to male primogeniture that disadvantages the wife and child, especially considering that the wife most likely contributed to the cost of acquisition?

Customary norms are not "irreconcilable" with equality (Grant, 2006, p. 9). Since these norms are continuously evolving, it is vital that each inheritance situation is contextually examined to determine whether and to what extent it has imbibed the principles of equality with respect to women and children's rights to inheritance (Grant, 2006). The rules of living customary law are not rigid and accommodate contextualization of each inheritance situation. Therefore, where there are inheritance disputes and the matters are taken to court, the courts can acknowledge and rule in favor of these evolutions, based on credible evidence in the course of the process of ascertainment of applicable customary norms. Where necessary, the courts could carry out required development to bring the customary law in line with constitutional standards of equality—a view also supported by Justice Sandile Ngcobo, in *Bhe v. Khayelitsha* (Badejogbin, 2019).

CONCLUSION

The analysis in this chapter reveals that applicable laws that provide for the inheritance of the Rukuba widow and child under Nigeria's plural system, though elaborate, are not exhaustive. Where they fail, constitutional provisions on dignity, and against discrimination on the ground of equality, can and should be invoked. While the capacity to make adequate provision for widows and children under statutory testacy is guaranteed, it is still restricted in several ways due to provisions of the law. Some of these limitations contradict clear-cut constitutional provisions that guarantee the rights of women and children. With respect to statutory regulation of intestacy, the recommendation for Plateau State is to adopt better systems from other jurisdictions, such as Lagos State, with modifications that would improve the plight of the widow and child.

Ordinarily under customary law, the right to adequate provision for widows and children is not fully guaranteed except for the eldest male child. This is despite customary obligations by the broader family of the late husband and father to the widow and child of the deceased. Testacy under customary law should therefore seek to give the widow and child more rights than they would ordinarily have in cases of intestacy under customary law. Fortunately, the unique nature of living customary law creates space for a renegotiation of structures and institutions that would enable the establishment of a more feasible plan for participation and protection of vulnerable persons and grant them better access to justice.

NOTES

1. Generally, a will is an arrangement made by a person for the distribution of his/her estate after his/her demise in accordance with his express instructions.
2. Which is a state whereby a person dies without leaving a will to direct the distribution of his estate.
3. Statutory law applies where the deceased has a statutory marriage while customary law applies where the deceased has a customary marriage.
4. Made applicable to Nigeria through Nigerian legislation. The earliest piece of legislation with respect to this is the Ordinance No. 3 of 1863 which provided for the application of English law in the then Colony of Lagos and other subsidiary legislations establishing the various courts.
5. 1837 and its amendment in 1852.
6. No. 2 of 1988.
7. Cap. 2 1963 Laws of Northern Nigeria.
8. Probate registries of High Courts will not admit a will that does not conform to the formalities of the Wills Edict.
9. Section 2 Plateau State Wills Edict 1987.
10. Section 17(1) and (2)(a) of the 1999 Constitution of Nigeria.
11. Section 34(1) of the 1999 Constitution of Nigeria.
12. Section 43.
13. (1959) 4 FSC 280.
14. (1932) 1 WACA 215.
15. This is in line with the United Nations Study of the Problem of Discrimination against Indigenous Population (1987) which states that "marriages celebrated in accordance with indigenous rites and customs must be recognised as having full legal effect and as wholly equivalent to civil marriage ceremonies for purposes of registration."
16. Historical accounts reveal that marriage customs among the Rukuba people are exogamous, that is, characterized by marrying only outside the limits of a clan or tribe. Each village is also exogamous, and every girl from one social group must marry another social group signifying a unique system of preferential marriage.
17. See *Zaidan v. Mohsons* [1973] All N.L.R. 86 cited in Joy Ezielo "Laws and Practices Relating to Women's Inheritance Rights in Nigeria: An Overview." Available at https://silo.tips/download/laws-and-practices-relating-to-womens-inheritance-rights-in-nigeria-an-overview (accessed on 23/02/2021).
18. Section 2–4 No. 7 1988.
19. Section 43.
20. Repealed by Marriage Ordinance 18 of 1914.
21. Celebrating the naming ceremony of the child, payment of the child's school fees, paying the mother's maternity bill, and verbal and written affirmations are all forms of acknowledgment. Where the naming ceremony of a child born outside wedlock is celebrated in the father's family home, it is taken as an indication that he has accepted the paternity of the child.

22. 'Enventresamare' means a child conceived but yet to be born at the time of the demise of the father.

23. An example of customary adoption is seen in the case of *Jatua v. Bali* (2013) CCA (unreported) Appeal No. CCA/121m/2000. The subject of this case was about the inheritance rights of the adoptive child of the deceased. In line with the Berom customary law, a man who has no male child may adopt his brother's son to inherit his estate. The adopted son must however physically remain in the house of his adoptive father as a condition of the inheritance.

24. Constitution of the Federal Republic of Nigeria 1999. A child born outside wedlock may choose to institute an action either under the Fundamental Human Rights Enforcement Procedure Rules or other procedure by writ of summons in the High Court to enforce his/her rights to inherit from his/her parent.

25. See *Salubi v. Nwariaku* (2003) 7 NWLR, (Pt. 819) at P. 452 where the Supreme Court held that the two children of the deceased born outside wedlock are equally entitled—with the children born within wedlock—to the estate of the deceased.

26. Section 4(1) (a)–(c) Plateau State Wills Edict.

27. Sections 3(1), 4(1), and (4) ibid.

28. *Mojekwu v. Iwuchukwu* [2004] 11 N.W.L.R. 196.

29. From which appeal goes to the Supreme Court.

30. *Mojekwu v. Iwuchukwu* (1995) 9 NWLR part 419, 259.

31. (2013) LPELR-20389(SC).

32. Section 49 (5).

33. Laws of Northern Nigeria, 1963.

34. Section 2.

35. Section 3.

REFERENCES

Abayomi, K. (2004). *Wills: Law and practice*. Lagos: Mbeyi and Associates (Nig.) Ltd.

Abdulrazaq, O. O. (2002). Widowhood practices in Nigeria and support systems: Challenges to counselling for national integration. *The Counsellor, 19*(1), 125–133.

Adesanya, B. (2009). Marriage, divorce and succession: *The legal aspects*. Paper presented at a seminar marking the tenth anniversary of the Diocese of Lagos West on June 12, 2009. Retrieved from: https://www.refworld.org. Accessed March 16, 2021.

Ashen, K. A. (1990). *The noun phrase in languages in contact: The case of English and Rukuba: Implications for curriculum development* (Unpublished Master's Thesis). University of Jos, Nigeria.

Ajigboye, O. & Alabi T. (2015). *The protection of women's rights in Nigeria: An appraisal of judicial intervention on women and inheritance*. Retrieved from: https://www.researchgate.net/publication/287218117_THE_PROTECTION_OF_WOMEN'S_RIGHTS_IN_NIGERIA_AN_APPRAISAL_OF_JUDICIAL_INTERVENTION_ON_WOMEN_AND_INHERITANCE.

Ayodele, J. O. (2014). *Gender victimization: A study of widowhood practices among Ogu people of Lagos*. Retrieved from: http://www.uk.sagepub.com/aboutus/openaccess.htm.

Badejogbin, R E. (2019). The Conundrum of judicial notice as a means of ascertaining customary law in Nigerian and South African courts amidst the convergence of positivism and legal pluralism. *Potchefstroom Electronic Law Journal,* 22, 1–31. Retrieved from: https://doi.org/10.17159/1727-3781/2019/v22i0a7589.

Badejogbin, R. E. (2015). Interplay of the customary law of testacy and statutory regulation of intestacy with respect to the transfer of customary law rights in land in South Africa. *Southern African Development Commission Law Journal, 4* (1), 11–25.

Bennett, T. (2011). Legal pluralism and the family in South Africa: Lessons from customary law reform. *Emory International Law Review,* 25, 1029–1059.

Bennett, T. (2004). *Customary law in South Africa*. Cape Town: Juta & Co. Ltd.

Blench, R. M. (2004). Recent research on the Plateau languages of Central Nigeria. Retrieved from: http://www.rogerblench.info/Language/Niger-Congo/BC/. Accessed February 9, 2021.

Burton, D. (Ed.). 2000. *Research training for social scientists: A handbook for postgraduate researchers*. Thousand Oaks: Sage.

Commonwealth Secretariat. (2013). *Women's land rights handbook Nigeria*. Retrieved from: https://www.eldis.org/document/A68830.

Cooper, E. (2008). *Inheritance practices and the inter-generational transmission of poverty: A literature review and annotated bibliography*. London: Overseas Development Institute (ODI) and Chronic Poverty Research Centre (CPRC). Retrieved from: https://papers.ssrn.com/sol3/papers.cfm?abstract_id=1538942. Accessed February 16, 2021.

Cooper, E. (2010). *Inheritance and the intergenerational transmission of poverty in Africa: policy considerations. London: Overseas Development Institute (ODI) and Chronic Poverty Research* Centre (CPRC). Retrieved from: https://papers.ssrn.com/sol3/papers.cfm?abstract_id=1538942 Accessed February 16, 2021.

Cooper, E. (2011). *Women and inheritance in 5 sub-Saharan African countries: Opportunities and challenges for policy and practice change*. Retrieved from: https://www.files.ethz.ch/isn/128343/WP182%20Cooper.pdf. Accessed February 16, 2021.

Cotierrel, R. (2009). Ehrlich at the edge of empire: Centres and peripheries in legal Studies. In Hertogh, M. (Ed.) *Living law: Reconsidering Eugene Ehrlich* (pp. 75–94). Onati International Series in Law and Society. London: Oxford: Hart.

Dadem, Y. Y. (2012). *Property law practice in Nigeria*. (2nd ed). Jos: University Press Ltd.

De Vaus, D. A. (2002). *Surveys in social research*. (5th ed.). Australia. Routledge.

Egwuatu, O. A. (2014). *Protecting inheritance rights of the child*. Retrieved from: http://www.nigerianlawguru.com.

Emery, V. (2006). *Women's inheritance rights in Nigeria: Transformative practices' women's U N Report Network*. Retrieved from: http://www.wunrn.com/news/2006/02_19_06/021906_nigeria_womens.htm. Accessed April 10, 2021.

Erhlich, E. (2009). *Fundamental principles of the sociology of law*. New Brunswick: Transaction Publishers.

Experience of the Edo State chapter of the International Federation of Women Lawyers (FIDA) in South-South Zone, Nigeria Case Study No. 2: Engendering Legislative Issues (ELI) Project, December 2002. Retrieved from: http://pdf.usaid.gov/pdf_docs/Pnacu205.pdf Accessed February 24, 2021.

Ezeilo, J. (2000). *Laws and practices relating to women's' inheritance rights in Nigeria: An overview*. Retrieved from: www.muslimpersonallaw.co.za/inheritancedocs/lawandpractices%20in%2. Accessed March 20, 2021.

Ezejiofor, A. O. (2011). Patriarchy, marriage and the rights of widows in Nigeria. *Unizik Journal of Arts and Humanities, 12*(1), 139–157. http://dx.doi.org/10.4314/ujah.v12i1.9.

Frankfurt-Nachmias, C. & Nachmias, D. (1992). *Research methods in social sciences*. London: Edward Arnold.

Garner, B. A., & Black, H. C. (2009). *Black's law dictionary*. 9th ed. St. Paul, MN: West.

Gorman, G. E. & Clayton, P. (2005). *Qualitative research for the information professional: A practical handbook*. (2nd ed.). London: Facet Publishing.

Grant, E. (2006). Human rights, cultural diversity and customary law in South Africa: Human rights, cultural diversity and customary law in South Africa. *Journal of African Law, 50*(1), 2–23.

Griffiths, J. (1986). *What is legal pluralism? Journal of Legal Pluralism, 24,* 38–39.

Harvey, B. W. (1968). *The law and practice of Nigerian wills, probate and succession*. London: Sweet & Maxwell.

Himonga, C. (2005). The advancement of African women's rights in the first decade of democracy in South Africa: The reform of the customary law of marriage and succession. *Acta Juridica,* 82–107.

Himonga, C. (2013). *African customary law and children's rights: Intersections and domains in a new era children's rights in Africa: A legal perspective*. London: Routledge.

Himonga, C. & Diallo F. (2017). Decolonisation and teaching law in Africa with special reference to living customary law. *Potchefstroom Electronic Law Journal, 20*(1), 1–19. http://dx.doi.org/10.17159/1727-3781/2017/v20i0a3267.

Ige, R. A. (2015). Legal pluralism in Africa: Challenges, conflicts and adaptation in a global village. *Journal of Law, Policy and Globalization, 34*, 59–66.

Itua, P. O. (2012). Legitimacy, legitimation and succession in Nigeria: An appraisal of section 42(2) of the constitution of the Federal Republic of Nigeria 1999 as amended on the rights of inheritance. *Journal of Law and Conflict Resolution, 4*(3), 31–44.

Lawoyi, T. (2001). *UNICEF 2001: Children's and women's rights in Nigeria: A wake up call situation assessment and analysis. In chapter 3.3. Main causes of mortality and morbidity among children and women*. Retrieved from: https://www.researchgate.net/publication/260186830_UNICEF_2001_Children%27s_and_Women%27s_Rights_in_Nigeria_A_wake-up_Call_Situation_Assessment_and_Analysis_In_Chapter_33_Main_causes_of_Mortality_and_morbidity_among_children_and_women.

Menski, W. (2006). *Comparative law in a global context: The legal systems of Asia and Africa* (2 ed.). Cambridge: Cambridge University Press.
Merry, S. E. (1988). Legal pluralism. *Law and Society Review, 22*(5), 869–896.
Moore, S. F. (1978). *Law as process and anthropological approach.* London: Routledge & Kegan Paul.
Mtengeti-Migiro, R. (1991). Legal developments on women's rights to inherit land under customary law in Tanzania. *Verfassung Und Recht in Übersee/Law and Politics in Africa, Asia and Latin America, 24*(4), 362–371.
Muller, J. C. & Sangree, W. H. (1973). Irigwe and Rukuba marriage: A comparison. *The Canadian Journal of African Studies*, 27–57.
Muller, J. C. (1978). On bride wealth and meaning among the Rukuba, Plateau State, Nigeria. *Africa Journal of the International African Institute, 48*(2), 161–175. http://dx.doi.org/10.2307/1158606.
Ngassa, N. (2012). Women's inheritance rights in the north west and south west regions of Cameroon. Retrieved from: https://www.researchgate.net/publication/293204550_Women's_inheritance_rights_in_the_north_west_and_south_west_regions_of_Cameroon/citation/download.
Nhlapo, T. (1995). Cultural diversity, human rights and the family in contemporary Africa: Lessons from the South African constitutional debate. *International Journal of Law, Policy and the Family,* 9(2), 208–225. https://doi.org/10.1093/lawfam/9.2.208.
Nwabueze, R. N. (2010). Securing widows' sepulchral rights through the Nigerian constitution. *Harvard Human Rights Journal, 23*. Retrieved from: http://harvardhrj.com/wp-content/uploads/2010/10/141-156.pdf. Accessed February 21, 2021.
Nwogugu A I (2014) *Family law in Nigeria.* (3rd ed.). Ibadan: HEBN Publishers Plc.
Obi, S. N. C. (1962). Women's property and succession thereto in modern Igbo law (Eastern Nigeria). *Journal of African Law, 6* (1), 6–18.
Okanny, M. C. (2000). *Nigerian law of property.* Lagos: Fourth Dimension Publishing Co. Ltd.
Onyebuchi T. U. (1997). *Due process in Nigeria's administrative law system: History, current status and future*. Maryland: University Press of America.
Osamolu, S. A., Oduwole O. T. & Oba C. O. (2016). *Real property law and practice in Nigeria*. (2nd ed.). Abuja: Law Lords Publication.
Osman, F. (2019). *The administration of customary law estates post the enactment of the reform of customary law of succession act: A case study from rural Eastern Cape, South Africa.* (Unpublished PhD Thesis), Faculty of Law, Department of Private Law University of Cape Town.
Otitie, O. (n.d). *Nigeria's identifiable ethnic groups*. Retrieved from: https://onlinenigeria.com/tribes/tribes.php. Accessed February 21, 2021.
Richardson, A. M. (2008). Women's inheritance rights in Africa: The need to integrate cultural understanding and legal reform. *Human Rights Brief, 11*(2), 19–22.
Sagay, I. (2004). *Nigerian law of succession.* Zaria: Malthouse Press Limited.
Temple, O. (1922). *Notes on the tribes, provinces, emirates and states of the northern provinces of Nigeria*. Cape Town: Argus Printing and Publishing Co.
Widows as properties in a man. (2002). *The Guardian Newspaper*, p 1.

Ubink, J. (2018). Customary legal empowerment in Namibia and Ghana? Lessons about access, power and participation in non-state justice systems development and change. *Development and Change, 49*(4), 930–950. http://dx.doi.org/10.1111/dech.12415.

Ubink, J. (2018). Introduction: Legal pluralism in a globalized world. *U.C. Irvine Law Review, 8*(2), 141–146.

United Nations. (1987). Study of the problem of discrimination against indigenous population. Retrieved from: https://digitallibrary.un.org/record/139885?ln=en. Accessed March 20, 2021.

Waziri, F. (2007). *Critical analysis of discriminatory inheritance rights of the south eastern part of Nigeria.* (Unpublished LLM Master's Thesis). St Thomas University School of Law.

Woodman, G. (2011). Legal pluralism in Africa: The implications of state recognition of customary laws illustrated from the field of land law. *Acta Juridica, 35,* 35–50.

Yin, R. K. (2003). *Case study research: design and methods.* Applied social research methods series, 5. (3rd ed.). London: Sage.

Administration of (Real Estate) Law Plateau State.

Administration of Estate Law Lagos No. 16 1972.

1999 Constitution of the Federal Republic of Nigeria.

Marriage Act 25 of 1961.

Marriage Act Cap M6 Laws of the Federation of Nigeria 2004.

Ordinance No. 3 of 1863 which provided for the application of English law in the then Colony of Lagos and other subsidiary legislations establishing the various courts.

Plateau State married women and Property Edict No. 7, 1988.

Plateau State Wills Edict 1988.

Recognition of Customary Marriages Act 120 of 1998 for South Africa.

Reform of Customary Law of Succession and Regulation of Related Matters Act No. 11, 2009.

Wills Act 1852.

Wills (Amendment) Act 1837.

Bamgbose v Daniel. (1955). AC 107 all cited in Itse Sagay.

Jatua v. Bali (2013) CCA (unreported) Appeal No. CCA/121m/2000.

Jesco Manga Williams v Helen Otia & Chief Ikome Civil suit no. LM/16/97(unreported).

Johnson v. Maja. (1950/51). 13 WACA 290.

Lawal Osula v. Lawal Osula. (1995). 9 NWLR part 419, 259.

Mojekwu v. Ejikeme. (2000). 5 NWLR (Pt. 657) 402.

Mojekwu v. Iwuchukwu. (2004). 11 N.W.L.R. 196.

Mojekwu v. Mojekwu. (1997). 7 NWLR (Pt. 512) 283.

Nwosu v. Okeke. (2002). FWLR (part 95) 366.

re Adelaide Subulade Williams. (1941). 7 W.A.C.A. 156 cited in Itse Sagay.

Salubi v. Nwariaku. (2003). 7 NWLR, (Pt. 819) 452.

Uwaifo v. Uwaifo. (2013). LPELR-20389(SC).

(https://www.encyclopedia.com/humanities/encyclopedias-almanacs-transcripts-and-maps/rukuba)

Chapter 16

Transforming Traditional Justice through Gender Diversification

Comparing Two South African Communities

Sindiso Mnisi Weeks

INTRODUCTION

> *There are people chosen to come and listen to cases here and otherwise we don't come. And now they have women too. Before, anyone could come and listen and women could come but they could not answer; but now they can listen and answer, and share their views. This helps because if I, being a woman, come into a problem that leads to my appearing here; it may reach a point where I feel intimidated to raise it with only men and, even if I can see that they are oppressing me, I might not be able to say that they are oppressing me, but if there are women there, I, being a woman, gain strength to declare my problem.*

These were the telling words of a young woman who responded to my questions regarding the appearance, attendance, and participation of ordinary, unappointed community women in *libandla* (the village-level traditional council) in Mbuzini, Mpumalanga, South Africa. I initially asked her and another female community member in her company if they had ever attended the traditional court, to which she, the younger of the two, responded that they had not: "we don't come."

Following her pointed explanation above, I asked why having chosen women for libandla translated into them not attending, which they could presumably do. She responded that the people so selected were interested in attending—they were those "who liked listening to the cases" every Wednesday. I asked whether she heard about cases brought to or heard by the ward or village council, to which she responded that they rarely did—and added that they "do not pay attention." While we were having this conversation, her companion nodded, indicating her quiet agreement with these responses. Observing this, I asked who had selected the female councilors who were appointed to serve on libandla and whether she had been among those who had exercised this choice. Again, she said she had not been one of those who had made the selection but that, because the ward council called the community together in making this selection, it was tantamount to the community having chosen these female representatives.

This pattern of response was common in Mbuzini. When it came to giving reasons, on the one hand, women reported that they do not attend to law or wish (or feel the need) to come to the village council. They took a positive view, articulating that theirs was a win-win situation in that they felt adequately represented by their female representatives who they perceived as people who enjoy "coming and listening" to disputes. On the other hand, women justified their nonattendance on the grounds of structural limitations: particularly, not having time amid their obligations to labor at home and in the fields.

In either case, the result was the same: most ordinary women who were not elected to or selected for libandla did not attend or participate there except when they had to (for instance, due to a case being heard in which they were directly implicated). As implied by these women's responses and expressly divulged by a group of women with whom I spoke separately, local women were scared to attend and participate in libandla. Many were not even aware that they were permitted to attend council hearings. Being women, and following a lengthy history of women's exclusion from such hallowed spaces as the senior traditional leader's presence as in libandla at the village level, they thought they were only permitted to attend when there was a case pertaining to them. Even in such circumstances, it is common for women's participation in such spaces to be constrained.

That said, at least in Mbuzini, women are represented among council members who are formally appointed or elected. Since the Traditional Leadership and Governance Framework Act 41 of 2003 (TLGFA) was passed, some communities have already begun to diversify membership of their traditional courts based on the provisions of section 3(2)(b) that direct traditional councils to include one-third women unless an insufficient number of women are available for such purposes. However, there is compelling evidence—including from the Department of Cooperative Governance and Traditional Affairs itself—that elections have not taken place in many provinces. Similarly, the women's quota has not been satisfied in all traditional councils.

The Traditional Courts Bill (B1D-2017), which was still pending approval in the National Assembly in September 2021, remains controversial because of its denial of the right of rural people to voluntarily participate in or opt out of traditional courts' jurisdiction. This bill requires that the courts' composition be diversified to ensure that women are included among the community members who gather to *form* traditional courts and ensure that women have equal participation rights as contributors to, as well as parties before, these local customary forums. However, the bill does not provide specific guidance on how this mandate should be effected.

Through systematic comparison of ethnographic material on traditional courts at ward and village levels in two deep rural areas in Mpumalanga in the northeastern part of South Africa—where women regularly participate as appointed, nominated, or elected members of vernacular dispute-management forums—and KwaZulu-Natal on the east coast—where women do *not* regularly participate in these ways, this chapter explores the significance and impact that gender diversification can potentially have on the transformation of traditional justice. The discussion pays particular attention to the impact on women's and young people's equitable access to justice in and through vernacular forums transformed by such diversification. It considers women's "voice" (i.e., the agency by which women express their points of view and the rights they are granted to represent their needs) and, particularly, delivery of justice in and through women's participation in these forums.

This chapter is situated within a decolonial feminist theoretical approach (Lugones, 2010; Mohanty, 2003; Nyamu-Musembi, 2002a, 2002b; Oyěwùmí, 1997; Harrison, 2011; hooks, 1981, 2013). It engages with the impact of colonialism on institutions that have come to be dominated by a patriarchal identity and masculinist ideals. It also identifies women as agents in and around the institutions that shape their reality, whether passively or actively, as well as agents in their communities and their own lives (Abu-Lughod, 1990; Naples, 1992; Martin et al., 2007; Claassens & Ngubane, 2008; Disney, 2008, p. 33; Mansbridge, 2013; Mbilinyi, 2015).

This chapter primarily contributes to our understanding of "feminism as a *theory* [and is] aimed at sharpening the analysis . . . in order to better inform the strategies and tactics of the movement" (Disney, 2008, p. 45), geared toward improving the lives of women who are at the social and political margins. To this end, renowned feminist, Chandra Mohanty, urges us to ask a crucial question: "What kinds of feminist methodology and analytic strategy are useful in making power (and women's lives) visible in overtly nongendered, nonracialized discourses?" (Mohanty, 2003, p. 510). In other words, how do we make feminist methodologies and analysis more sensitive to and effective at advancing the sociopolitical struggles of *all* people, including "invisible" global majorities who are getting crushed under the weight of purportedly neutral systems characteristic of the contemporary global political economy?

The answer partly lies in making all women's stories more visible in the social discourses we develop. Mohanty succinctly explains the need for us to ground what is ultimately an exercise in "reimagination" and "reconstruction" (Lacey, 1996) of dominant discourses in the experiences of the *most* marginalized women:

> If we pay attention to and think from the space of some of the most disenfranchised communities of women in the world, we are most likely to envision a just and democratic society capable of treating all its citizens fairly. Conversely, if we begin our analysis from, and limit it to, the space of privileged communities, our visions of justice are more likely to be exclusionary because privilege nurtures blindness to those without the same privileges. (Mohanty, 2003, p. 510)

This chapter embraces Mohanty's argument fully and therefore centralizes remotely placed women in the deep rural areas of Mbuzini and Msinga in the narrative through which it contributes to feminist understandings of "voice" in the context of transforming access to and delivery of justice.

One claim that arises out of this methodological and analytical approach is to insist that, rather than ignore the actions of women positioned at the extreme margins as mere female agency, or reactive as opposed to proactive conduct, we should see acts performed by them that we would be tempted to write off as being (at least) microactivism (Marichal, 2013), and thus having transformative potential, if not transformative effects. This means analyzing and understanding not only the actions of the women who are positioned within the institutions that hold the power to decide disputes but also the actions of women who stay outside of them.

For context: Through policy, legislation, and force, South Africa's colonial and apartheid regimes precluded women from legal subjectivity (separately from their fathers and husbands), land ownership or administration in their own right, and participating in decision-making in what were then called tribes. There is a plethora of evidence of women's appeals to the state courts for relief and respite from the tightening yoke of male oppression under colonialism and apartheid (McClendon, 1995; Roberts, 2005). These studies reflect the important role that women's ability to exploit the ambiguities of marital status played under a fluid customary system in terms of which marriage is processual as opposed to a one-time formal event (Comaroff & Roberts, 1977; Griffiths, 1997).

In advocating for an actor-oriented perspective that focuses on women as agents in their local struggles for effective human rights protection, Nyamu-Musembi (2002b) compellingly helps us to see these strategies employed by women for what they are, and assess their value as feminist legal theorist, Lacey (1996), argues we should. Viewed through this lens, a woman in

Mbuzini who "takes her rights" by pursuing a maintenance claim against a wayward husband with whom she cohabits (G'sell, 2016) in the hope that it will *not* lead to her "sleeping on the street is arguably engaging in activism and thus evoking transformation" (Mnisi Weeks, 2011b). Could we go so far as to say that the decisions of the young woman who told me she does not attend libandla because she has no interest in disputes are just as important to understand as activism, in light of their (potentially) transformative effects? Over time, law and society scholars have come to regard various moves by ordinary actors—enduring, avoiding, sometimes violently resisting, ignoring, undermining, negotiating, challenging, capitulating, and so on—as relevant conduct (Ewick & Silbey, 1991, 1998; Merry, 1978; Sarat, 1990). This chapter looks at their connection with social change through women's voices and, more specifically, their relationship with the transformation of traditional justice through gender diversification.

LEGISLATIVE CONTEXT

It is important to understand the legislative and policy history of decision-making forums—and women's roles—in deeply rural areas like Mbuzini and Msinga. Section 11(3)(b) of the Black Administration Act 38 of 1927, as inserted by the Native Administration Amendment Act 21 of 1943, prescribed that

> a native woman who is a partner in a customary union and who is living with her husband, shall be deemed to be a minor and her husband shall be deemed to be her guardian.

This provision, which was repealed in the late twentieth century, has been described as having had the effect of making women perpetual minors who shifted from being minors under their fathers' authority to being minors under their husbands' authority. The greatest material effect of this was that women could no longer own or administer land. That is because they could no longer exercise decision-making authority, whether in their own right or on behalf of another. In fact, the legislation went on to express this explicitly when it stated in Section 3(1) that "the adult male members of the tribe" were the only ones who were allowed to participate in local decision-making. This distorted customary norms at the time (Chanock, 2001; Mamdani, 1996).

The Constitutional Court, in *Gumede (born Shange) v. President of the Republic of South Africa and Others* (CCT 50/08) [2008] ZACC 23; 2009 (3) BCLR 243 (CC); 2009 (3) SA 152 (CC) (December 8, 2008), summed the change up as follows:

> In our pre-colonial past. . . . Women, who had a great influence in the family, held a place of pride and respect within the family. Their influence was subtle although not lightly overridden. Their consent was indispensable to all crucial family decisions. Ownership of family property was never exclusive but resided in the collective and was meant to serve the familial good. (Para 18)

Yet, the court also observed in *Mayelane v. Ngwenyama and Another* (CCT 57/12) [2013] ZACC 14; 2013 (4) SA 415 (CC); 2013 (8) BCLR 918 (CC) (30 May 2013) that, while the colonial legislation's effect was significant in disturbing the delicate balance between the matriarchal and patriarchal elements of customary norms, it must be acknowledged that "even in idyllic pre-colonial communities, group interests were framed in favour of men and often to the grave disadvantage of women and children" (Para 71). Hence, the court emphasized that, while necessary to accord customary law the respect it deserves, it could not shy away from its obligation to ensure that living customary law (i.e., the vernacular forms of law grounded in tradition and yet evolved by communities in their day-to-day practice) develops in accordance with the normative framework of the Constitution, and thereby observe the vulnerability of women and ensure that their rights to equality are robustly protected.

The TLGFA professes the aspiration of shifting the balance back from the exclusion of women in customary decision-making bodies. Section 2 provides that:

(a) A traditional council may have no more than 30 members, depending on the needs of the traditional community concerned.
(b) At least a third of the members of a traditional council must be women.
(c) The members of a traditional council must comprise:
  (i) traditional leaders and members of the traditional community selected by the senior traditional leader concerned in terms of that community's customs, taking into account the need for overall compliance with paragraph (b); and
  (ii) other members of the traditional community who are democratically elected for a term of five years, and who must constitute 40% of the members of the traditional council.
(d) Where it has been proved that an insufficient number of women are available to participate in a traditional council, the Premier concerned may, in accordance with a procedure provided for in provincial legislation, determine a lower threshold for the 30 particular traditional councils than that required by paragraph (b).

It is with a view to realizing this aspiration that the Mbuzini traditional area started to include women in their traditional councils *and* courts at the turn of the century. Likewise, at the same time, Msinga began to include women in the traditional council (i.e., the legislative-administrative body) but *not* in the traditional courts. This is despite the fact that the elections envisioned in section 2(c)(ii) have either not happened or had serious problems in both provinces, as well as the others.

EMPIRICAL CONTEXT AND METHODOLOGY

Msinga is located in the eastern most coastal province of South Africa, KwaZulu-Natal—whose name combines the colonial descriptor, Natal, with the colonial representation of the primary reserve that was located in that colony, KwaZulu (the place of Shaka Zulu). Msinga, like the province as a whole, is predominantly populated by isiZulu speakers. It was chosen as the site for a postdoctoral study on how traditional courts operate because of the extent to which people there have maintained a traditional lifestyle. Mbuzini is in the north east of South Africa, in the province of Mpumalanga (which literally means, from whence the sun rises). Situated on the border with Mozambique and Swaziland, Mbuzini is predominantly populated by SiSwati speakers, yet its residents observe familial relations on all sides of the arbitrarily placed colonial border. It was the site of my doctoral research on women's rights to inheritance under customary law and was selected because of its accessibility based on my contacts and the local language being one I could speak.

As in other deep rural areas in South Africa, unemployment is high and poverty is rife in both Mbuzini and Msinga (Statistics South Africa, 2016, 2019, 2020). More than 72% of households in these areas are poor and depend on social grants as their primary mode of subsistence. In economic terms, Mpumalanga province fares better than KwaZulu-Natal; yet, given its distance from the primary income sources in the province (tourism in the Kruger National Park and a paper production industry run by Sappi), Mbuzini does not reap much of those benefits except through migrant labor. The two areas also are distinguished by Msinga's location as the "gun frontier" of South Africa, with the high levels of interpersonal violence that come with its history of firearms. In both areas, falling under the government-recognized authority of senior traditional leaders, people would describe themselves as *abantu* (isiZulu for very simple or ordinary people) or *sintfu* (SiSwati for people who observe a very traditional and unsophisticated way of life).

The qualitative data from Msinga were collected between October 2009 and June 2015, with the highest concentration of data collection completed between March 2011 and January 2012 in the form of daily recording of headmen's activities and day-to-day work; observing traditional dispute-management processes, such as hearings for disputes that headmen participated in managing; follow-up interviews with parties to the disputes and traditional authorities, including traditional council support staff; and focus groups with members of traditional councils and groups of local men and women.

During the latter period of research in Msinga, local fieldworkers and I recorded 183 instances of the informal process named *izikhalo* (cries/pleas), as contrasted with 71 formal case hearings across the six wards in two traditional communities (what were formerly referred to as "tribes") that were the sites of our research. This data was complemented by preliminary interviews and observations conducted from October 2009 to February 2011, and follow-up interviews, focus groups, and report-back sessions done between February 2012 and June 2015 (Mnisi Weeks, 2015a, 2016, 2018a). Material from Mbuzini was collected between February 2007 and January 2008, during which time I conducted ethnographic research using participant observation as my primary method (Mnisi, 2010; Mnisi Weeks, 2011a, 2015b). Permission to interview and write about study participants was obtained in accordance with the requirements of the Institutional Review Boards at the University of Oxford (for the Mbuzini study) and the University of Cape Town (for the Msinga study). Nonetheless, all names have been changed in order to protect the identities of the participants.

Some of what is revealed in the collected material are instances in which women living under traditional leadership in rural South Africa have felt they had little if any option but to stay married in order to hold onto marital property and other core elements of their material security (Mnisi Weeks, 2011b, 2013, 2018a, 2019). That set of findings is premised on an approach that one might describe as "feminism as an *analysis* of the oppression of women in the political, economic, social, cultural, and familial spheres" (Disney, 2008, p. 45). While drawing upon the same datasets, this chapter deviates somewhat from that approach. Other revelations that emerge from the data and have been featured in my previous works pertain to instances in which women have both implicitly and explicitly protested their circumstances and advocated for a different and more just outcome (Claassens & Mnisi, 2009; Mnisi Weeks, 2011b, 2015a, 2016, 2018a). In that vein, I have asked: "Could what appears simply to be rural women's acceptance or rejection of rights actually suggest important exercises of agency?" (Mnisi Weeks, 2011b, pp. 290–291). In this way, I have been with rural women employing an approach one might refer to as "feminism as a *movement*, based on this analysis, to end the oppression of women" (Disney, 2008, p. 45). This chapter seeks to explore the latter phenomenon in greater depth, finding that it is insufficient that scholars such as myself primarily point out women's vulnerabilities under patriarchal systems and then suggest possible solutions that often are out of realistic reach for women in those circumstances. To identify practical solutions, we must rather look at what women in those situations are already doing to advance their own liberation.

All of my prior work has been based on the notion that clear understanding of the local levers for change—particularly those determined and valued by the women at issue—is not merely optional but absolutely critical to any progress that can be made on women's emancipation. In making this sustained argument, I have often drawn on Lacey's work as she argues for securing the equal value of rights for "differently situated subjects" (Cornell, 1992; Lacey, 1996). Following, I attempt to describe how the contestation over accomplishing this expression of gender equality plays out in situ in two deeply rural villages and their traditional justice processes in South Africa.

MBUZINI

> *The men also agreed, and so did the women. The men know the law that is alive in libandla: the tribal law that if my child has taken you to be my daughter-in-law and I am unable to lobola you yet you have children, when your child is grown up and lobola'd, I don't consume these cows. They go to your parents' home to lobola you. This is an existing law; it's there and it doesn't change.*

These were the words of one of the female councilors in Mbuzini, Make Ng'khansela. She had just recounted a succession case to me in which the village-level council had ruled in favor of a female complainant. I followed up by asking if it was just the women of libandla who had stood up for the woman's rights under living customary law or if male councilors also had agreed that this was what the law required. Make Ng'khansela responded that the men and women of libandla were of one mind. She then explained the council's ruling using the words quoted before.

One might reasonably wonder what is meant by "being of one mind." Earlier in this chapter, I mentioned a woman who had "taken her rights" in hopes of *not* "sleeping in the street." This woman, LaSondlo, had come up in conversation in Mbuzini where I had met a group of middle-aged and older women and entered into an informal discussion with them about tensions between constitutional rights and their social context. This, after I had given up on conducting a formal interview with them on their understanding of constitutional rights because they told me they knew nothing about rights (*malungelo*) and law (*mtsetfo*).

While I was sitting with the women, they started discussing a local woman, LaSibindzi, sharing their shock at learning that she had called her husband dull-witted and yet continued to reside in "his" house. Their discussion then rapidly transitioned to how illogical it was that another woman, LaSondlo, was suing her husband for maintenance in the magistrate's court while the two of them still resided in the same home. These women lamented that the people who must have advised LaSondlo to pursue this path would probably turn around and laugh at her when her marriage was ruined by this action.

It was relative to this that the women had gone on to muse that, as one woman, LaMzambi, said, "If her husband bought her bread, soap, and built her a house then she was happy; what more should she want?" The women spoke, in turn, of people saying that it was their right to sue but that those people could really keep their rights, for "these rights ruin things for us." The suggestion was floated that "*Malungelo* are fine for young people like yourself." The oldest woman, LaNg'gogo, pointed at me as she spoke. But there was no agreement on this point as LaNakekela thought that rights are a problem even for young women because they make the young women think they can disrespect their husbands by saying it is their right. But then, "will your rights take care of you?" LaNakekela seemed to summarily ask the question of me. She then quickly added, "Take your rights then and sleep outside, on the street."

At first blush, this narrative might suggest a context in which the values are predominantly conservative. Indeed, Mbuzini is very traditional and thus quite conservative. Yet, if nothing else, these women's discussion of the merits of LaSondlo's actions demonstrates the internal contestation that is prevalent in even as traditional a context as Mbuzini. Returning to Make Ng'khansela's point then, describing all councilors in libandla as being of one mind would be inaccurate. However, it is accurate to say that internal tensions exist and the differences of opinion do not even break down simply along male/female lines. Indeed, echoing the women in the community like LaNg'gogo and LaNakekela, the women in libandla share many of the intuitions and beliefs that the men have. The women councilors' decisions also often reflect this shared value system.

Furthermore, some of the men's outlooks differ from one another and from those of some of the women. This fact was demonstrated in one of the first council meetings I sat in on when one Mr. Magagula disagreed with "the headman of the men" (*Ndvuna yemadvodza*) and accused the latter of making a statement that had sexist undertones. In this way, Mr. Magagula moved to defend the women while none of the women present at the council meeting spoke up on the matter. Certainly, Mr. Magagula's expressions in that meeting could be read as his performing rather than reflecting gender sensitivity—especially for my benefit as an external audience. That said, his orientation toward gender matters seemed to hold throughout my months of data collection in Mbuzini, thus leading me to believe that there was substance to it.

Members of the council would argue that the fact that councilors' opinions cannot be simply broken down along male/female lines is due to their impartiality. This point is particularly relevant considering the diversity of representation on the traditional council in Mbuzini, which is the legislative-administrative council constituted under Sections 2 and 28 of the TLGFA and yet also serves a judicial function when it hears cases at the level of the chief's court of appeal (*libandla lenkhosi*). The Mahlalela traditional community's leaders (i.e., *nkhosi*, who would previously have been referred to as chief, and *tindvuna*, or headmen) are exclusively male. Yet an overwhelming proportion (roughly 8 out of 14) of the councilors are women. That said, their numbers are counterbalanced by the additional number of members of the royal family (the remaining 16 members)—that is, brothers of *nkhosi*—and chief headman, who are all a permanent fixture of libandla and contribute in the council-as-court.

When it comes to operational dynamics, the women in libandla are often outspoken in their culturally prescribed, humble manner. As seen in the introduction, women outside of the council say that these women were elected to represent them or chosen to be part of libandla because they liked legal matters and wanted to participate in their hearing. This suggests their self-selection based on personality and preference.

Even though some of the female councilors are relatively young, the institution of libandla itself continues to be regarded—certainly, from the outside, but also, at least rhetorically, by those operating inside it—as being for the elderly who have gained sufficient knowledge, wisdom, and cachet. Though it is said that, like the women who participate in libandla, those young community members who go to listen or participate in the council proceedings also do so based on their self-selection, I did not see any attend in my time. The only exception was once, when government-employed community development workers attended out of what they described as curiosity or interest.

However, people are not necessarily pleased about these developments pertaining to the composition of the council. As one man told me:

> Things are changing, you know why? The old people who know . . . how a matter should be decided, matters that aren't for children, [are no longer there]. But now, young people go who are just attempting.

"Just attempting" meaning doing their best with little legitimate knowledge or experience in which to ground their efforts. This suggests that the gender and age diversification on libandla, and the greater representativity that is a consequence of it, has contributed to the institution's reduced credibility in the eyes of some community members. In other words, the sageness and authority that comes with age and experience continues to be attributed special value both by community members and by the councilors themselves, without equal appreciation for what women and young people bring to the institution.

Yet, this somehow did not translate into the women on the village council—or another council that I attended at the ward level—being cowed into silence. In fact, the female council members present at the Mgcozini ward council were also vocal and engaged in the hearing of cases alongside their male colleagues, even if the men did still largely take up more speaking time and hold a more prominent position, especially considering that the meeting was chaired by the ward headman. The degree to which the women on the council saw themselves as advocates varied. Nevertheless, if the speaker with whose words I opened this chapter is to be believed, the women's presence and refusal to be silent matters a great deal.

MSINGA

indoda iyinkinga ("a man is a problem")

So goes a local saying that is commonly deployed as both description and explanation of the challenges endemic to Msinga. In light thereof, women are expected to be understanding and forgiving when their husbands drink too much or stray in marriage. They are also to appreciate the benefits of polygynous marriage, such as its meaning that one's husband has declared his other love interests to one rather than having relationships with women who are unknown to his wife. While official polygamy rates in South Africa are down to 0.1% of the population, in Msinga, the rate is certainly higher.

Another sense in which this saying is employed is in the context of the disproportionate rates of male violence perpetrated against other men as well as women. In Msinga, when women are involved in violent disputes, it is usually as victims who often actually do not speak in the dispute-management process itself, even if they are invited and attend. As an example of this, in one matter, Nqabile was sexually assaulted by a group of five teenage boys, and her family discussed and decided whether charges would be filed or the matter against the young men would be discussed *isikhaya* (meaning between the families alone 'at home'). When we interviewed Nqabile, we learned that she had not been consulted in the decision-making process. She also said that she probably would have made a different decision and pressed charges rather than her family accepting monetary compensation. She was not given an opportunity for her voice to be heard on what would constitute justice in her case.

Prior to proceeding, it is vital to state three main things concerning the composition of the dispute-management forums in Msinga. The first is that, unlike in Mbuzini, the village-level traditional council recognized by Section

2 of the TLGFA did *not* carry out dispute management. Therefore, women did *not* participate ex officio in dispute management at that, or any, level of social organization within the community. The second is that the bulk of the forums making up the vernacular dispute-management system have a membership mainly comprised of ordinary members of the community: whether family, neighborhood, subward, or ward. This is qualified by the fact that forum membership is comprised of male residents in that jurisdictional sphere. Within that, we found that older men participate much more frequently than young men; and, in fact, unless young men are post-adolescence (which generally means married), they are not typically invited. The third is that, in each of the forums, there is a figure who chairs the proceedings. In some instances, this individual will hold more sway in the process of decision-making, but it is never the case that the decision in a dispute is solely made by any individual acting as judge.

The implication therefore is that older male family members of the patrilineage collectively dominate decisions at that level—though older females (such as the father's sisters) would play a role as well—with the patriarch or eldest male member of the extended family unit chairing the proceedings. Women are most likely to attend discussions at the neighborhood level; though they are not likely to speak up much (except as witnesses), they are welcome to attend. The person chairing the proceedings may be an informally elected chairman. We only saw this role held by a male community member.

The same applies at the subward level as at the neighborhood level yet with men being even more likely to attend and be vocal than women, including by playing the largest role of all as an informally elected chair of the proceedings or the headman's policeman (*iphoyisa lenduna*). At the level of the ward, women will typically only attend when invited to testify as witnesses in particular matters, not as regular observers or participants in forum discussions.

This ward-level dispute-management forum (*ibandla lenduna*) is named after the headman (*induna*) who serves as chair. Yet, he may sometimes bring in a close circle of men, who form a kind of mini-council of sorts, to accompany and think with him at mediations. He might also give these men's opinions greater weight in ordinary proceedings and these men may even be the primary questioners of parties and witnesses in those proceedings.

In Msinga, women featured in many of the disputes that we recorded for our study on traditional justice, though mostly as witnesses to what they had seen or heard from whom and/or said to whom. Their involvement in spreading information—or rumors—was what led to their being called to testify, in a handful of disputes, concerning a threat to kill someone or an actual attempt made on someone's life. This suggests a clear sense of ambiguity on the credibility of women's voices because, when male community members were asked whether women should become members of courts, it was women's reliability as witnesses that was given as a reason for their ongoing exclusion.

In less flattering language, this justification of their formal exclusion from the local dispute-management structures was described in terms of women's overinvolvement in spreading rumors or lies, being too often involved in "talk" (*izinkulumo*) or "talking too much" and not being as discerning as men but rather more child-like in their constitution and nature. Cited as further evidence was the fact that, as disputants, women were most commonly involved in nonviolent cases. In fact, they most often appeared in disputes over what had been said, such as accusations of slander and witchcraft. Otherwise, they might be the objects of contention in marriage disputes as in a case where a bride was called upon to return to her in-laws. Women's overwhelming association with speech acts like gossip that cause disputes was therefore the grounds on which their representation as members of vernacular forums was rejected.

Nonetheless, women found other ways in which to exercise more power in dispute-management forums within the confines of their social reality. In particular, women, in their capacity as mothers, featured heavily in the research findings. For instance, in family and neighbor conflicts, mothers very often participated as supports—in other words, as representatives and witnesses—appearing on behalf of or with their daughters (or sons) who, like daughters-in-law, often appeared as parties to the disputes.

For illustration, here is a dispute in which a mother represented her daughter, a young woman named Phikile, in a matter in which she was accused of stealing an older man's employment benefits using his government-issued identity number. The mother initiated the case against the older man, Dakiwe, on the grounds that he had come to the mother's yard and publicly shouted this insult against her daughter.

Phikile's case was one of a number of matters in which the fathers were absent from the picture, which was not the normative ideal in Msinga. That is, when people described the living customary law in Msinga, they always said that the father was the one who had to initiate a dispute in such a situation as this. Indeed, this proved to be true in several other cases that we recorded, in which the father was not physically present but was nonetheless a moral presence in the family's life and thus initiated the dispute by means of other family members (including the child's mother), who served as his agents.

One example of this is the case of Ntombi, who another young woman accused of no longer being a virgin. Ntombi attended every stage of the case as it went through multiple levels of review and appeal, even to the chief's council, with just her mother, grandmother, and sister. Yet, at every stage of the case's escalation (from the headman to the vigilante justice cooperative known as *isikebhe*), Ntombi described the impetus behind her family's pursuit of the case as her father's direction. Though Ntombi's mother exercised much less agency in the matter, by representing their daughters in their disputes in male-dominated forums, she and Phikile's mother were both leveraging the power they had available to them in their particular circumstances. Together and with other Msinga women, they gradually contributed to shifting the contours of traditional justice through gender diversification at a micro scale.

Even so, the further up one goes in the forum system as outlined before, the less authoritatively women get to participate. Thus, while the chief's council (*ibandla lenkosi*)—as a distinctly more formal space—welcomes the attendance and participation of members of the traditional community (*isizwe*) in its proceedings, few actually do so. People generally attend those proceedings only when they have cases being heard by the forum, or when they are accompanying or serving as witnesses on behalf of others whose cases are before the forum. Others who commonly attend are people in institutional roles—that is, members of the legislative-administrative council (which, as readers will recall, does not also automatically fulfill a judicial function) or lower level officials like headmen's policemen.

To illustrate, in one complex and lengthy case that I observed in *ibandla lenkosi*, *inkosi* remained silent through most of the proceedings. The primary party around whom this case turned was a woman named MaThembile, who had been shot at night by an anonymous assailant. The chief headman (*Ndunankulu*) and another one of the seven headmen in *isizwe* did the bulk of the questioning of parties and witnesses in this matter. Yet, one male member of the legislative-administrative council and an older man spoke from the floor in posing questions and sharing their opinions on what they described as "the truth of the matter."

Other people in attendance were predominantly men who somehow were associated with the other case that was to be heard that day; only a smattering of people attended out of interest alone. The headman's policeman responsible for MaThembile's subward was also in attendance and was questioned about the case's first hearing, which he had conducted; he seemed, at times, to be accused of giving the matter an improper hearing. No women asked questions; the only women who spoke did so as witnesses or disputants. This was a forum context in which women did not get to express as much voice and little gender diversification, and transformation of traditional justice through it, had occurred.

DISCUSSION

As seen in the narratives before, there are important comparative observations that can be made about the potential impact of gender diversification on the transformation of traditional justice based on the research in Mbuzini and Msinga. First, the separation of functions between the legislative-administrative council and court has led to significant impact in light of the quota suggested for traditional councils in the TLGFA. Second, there are meaningful convergences and divergences in men's and women's perspectives on what women have rights to and can lay claim to, given their social station. These views have implications for the extent to which such forum transformation through gender diversification is desired and supported in the context of the political economy of deeply rural areas.

Separation of Functions

A big distinction in the operation of traditional justice in the two communities described before is the separation of council (*bandla*) as a legislative-administrative body and court (*nkundla*) as a judicial body in Msinga as contrasted with Mbuzini. This shows itself in how the composition requirements for the TLGFA's legislative-administrative council have not been extended to vernacular dispute-management forums in Msinga. Of course, that is not the only factor at play in the differences between the transformation of traditional justice through gender diversification in these two locales. This is especially so in light of the difference in the ways and extent to which women have been incorporated into the forums in each place.

In Msinga, women have been incorporated to satisfy the one-third quota of members in the legislative-administrative councils, but these forums do not fulfill a judicial function. While women in one Msinga village definitely have made significant impact by securing access to land for unmarried women through their work as representatives on the legislative-administrative council (Mnisi Weeks, 2018; Cousins et al., 2011), this chapter focuses on the judicial sphere; I therefore will not elaborate on those legislative impacts here.

Vernacular dispute-management forums in Msinga are still predominantly male led and male dominated, though women are more welcome to participate and exercise that right more fully at the lowest levels of the structure. Women's contribution to the transformation of these forums, especially in the headman's and chief's courts, is therefore primarily limited to their roles as disputing parties or witnesses. For instance, by representing themselves and their daughters in disputes like Phikile's and Ntombi's, women are slowly shifting how they are perceived.

By contrast, in Mbuzini, by means of their participation in decision-making in cases they hear as members of these forums, women have now been involved in the transformation of traditional justice for a long time through their inclusion in the legislative-administrative councils, which also play a judicial role there. This is true both at the village level and the lower levels, such as the ward. If nothing else, they have shifted the impression that these forums are spaces not meant for women. However, while women's roles as members of the dispute-management forums in Mbuzini are significant, women's participation in informal roles is limited in ways that are comparable with Msinga. For instance, women in both places do not attend or participate in these forums unless they are explicitly charged with doing so; most women (and men) still see judicial forums as spaces that are largely not theirs. That said, the role that the female councilors have played in these councils-as-courts in Mbuzini, and the impact they have had on the lives of the women outside the forums, has not been straightforward as many of them continue to share patriarchal values and beliefs that dominate in their communities.

This complex position that women in Mbuzini occupy is best demonstrated by elaborating on a common concern in both Mbuzini and Msinga that has already been introduced: the contestation around the meaning of "rights." The disquiet surrounding changes in women's ordinary conduct and participation in local institutions has been expressed in focus groups that have been conducted by myself and others (Budlender et al., 2011; Cousins et al., 2011; Smith, 2015). In Msinga, men spoke of feeling that women had gotten the upper hand in the constitutional arrangement. Likewise, in Mbuzini, the feeling among men was largely the same and, hence, there was a raging debate about change expressed in terms of values and norms in the pushback against the imposition of constitutional rights for women and children and their potential implications for traditional justice.

One manifestation of this contestation is in how, in Msinga, sexual harassment (or unwelcome and intimate sexual remarks or physical advances made by men toward women) was not widely accepted as an offense warranting judicial proceedings. Men's concessions that some kinds of sexually oriented interactions—especially when linked with intimidation—were not ideal and may even be improper did not necessarily extend to outright condemnation. In their view, sexual harassment did not fall into that category of serious offenses. Hence, when it was reported (as it was rarely) by women, it was dealt with in accordance with how it was perceived: as trivial. After all, given that vernacular dispute-management forums are predominantly attended and contributed to by men, the next "problem man" (*indoda eyinkinga*), as the saying in Msinga goes, could be one of the men forming the forum.

Similarities and Differences over Rights in Socioeconomic Context

The divergence of opinion on how to view sexual harassment fits into a broader conversation about the place and impact of rights in local contexts. Ben Cousins, in his 2011 report on "The Living Law of Land in Msinga

District, KwaZulu-Natal," shared that, at a "report-back meeting with the Mthembu traditional council in 2008," while the senior traditional leader and councilors were reflecting on conservative ways in which to potentially address the problem of declining marriage rates, one councilor observed that 'the main obstacle to such an intervention would be government' which, this councilor explained, "protects people and gives them rights, in order to win their votes" (Cousins et al., 2011, p. 68). Another councilor then said:

> *We were happier before these rights came—we worked together in our homes. People used to be respectful, because of the powers of the Inkosi and the izinduna. Now, even prisoners and prostitutes have protection from government, whereas the Inkosi does not. The new laws are confusing us, they come with corruption.* (Cousins et al., 2011, p. 68; emphasis in the original)

In focus groups, I have likewise found that men—and, to some extent, women—saw laws, particularly the Constitution's impartation of rights to women and children, as having a profound impact on the ways in which they could and should regard and interact with these social groups, and vice versa.

The social role played by this perception of rights is then compounded by economic factors—especially severe poverty—impacting identity formation around care and financial support (Kingwill, 2008, 2011; Mbatha, 2002; Mnisi Weeks & Claassens, 2011; Rice, 2017). Of course, these views themselves often had contradictory impacts in terms of how they actually shaped interactions situationally, in day-to-day life. For instance, even for those members of the public who were interested in participating in *ibandla lenkosi*, in Msinga, a significant obstacle would be finances because, for most community members, getting there would necessitate travel over vast distances. This relates back to women's explaining their reluctance to attend and participate in vernacular dispute-management forums in terms of competing pressures that serve as barriers to gender diversification as a way to transform traditional justice.

To women in Msinga, participation in dispute management (especially at *ibandla lenkosi*) appeared to be a luxury. This, because of the physical demands of maintaining a home in the deep rural context where satisfying basic human needs is necessarily achieved by subsistence (thus, fetching water and firewood, cultivating crops, and rearing livestock) or by performing migrant labor. As noted before, these demands were named as a marked challenge and constraint by women in Mbuzini as well. In this sense, women's rights of participation were, in actuality, extremely limited when it came to *ibandla lenkosi*. Physical proximity as well as a more palpable social need to achieve peace and security in one's immediate surroundings made attendance more feasible in lower-level forums where, as noted before, women in fact participate more regularly and somewhat more fully. Even so, the lower-level forum leaders complained that people, particularly men, were "not attending meetings anymore."

As mentioned, the sentiments expressed on rights in Mbuzini were very similar to those in Msinga. As one middle-aged councilwoman in Mbuzini explained to me, "a person's right is *nhlonipho*." Ongoing discussion with the councilwoman, Make Lomdzala, and others, revealed that "right" (singular form: *lilungelo*) in their usage actually meant "duty." Thus, Make Lomdzala was not referring so much to what the person possessing *lilungelo* is entitled to (as in liberal conceptions of rights) but to what the person with *lilungelo* is constrained by and must therefore do: give respect. It is interesting to see how this local conception interacts—both clashes and melds—with the idea of individualized rights that prevail in the Constitution. As shown even in the discussion with LaNakekela before, the constitutional idea of rights as entitlements is often seen, even by women, as disconnected from women's local realities and thus a threat to their security.

It was clear that in Mbuzini, women's (constitutional) "rights" (plural form: *malungelo*) were viewed with some disapproval. In an official interview, the chief headman, Ndvunankulu, informed me that

> this law that exists concerning women's *malungelo*, we, as the kingship, as the indigenous, have observed that it is the same as concerning children's *malungelo*. From the start, women had *malungelo*, anyway, of course; a woman is respected, she has her station. But not this law that is said to be the constitutional law, that which says that a woman must have *lilungelo* to do whatever in the home.

Thus, key to this authority's objections was the translation of women's rights into roles in the household even as the language used to discredit the need for the articulation of women's rights in the Constitution was that women already had the rights they needed under custom—that is, "respect" (*nhlonipho*) according to "their station." This concern, as one elderly Mbuzini man concluded, "makes us say that these [constitutional] rights should stay and work in the cities and towns because when they come here the women misuse them to disrespect the menfolk."

When I interviewed the councilwoman, Make Ng'khansela, she echoed the fundamental objection to women's rights in the Constitution shifting expectations of men and women, as well as their respective social stations:

> If I'm living with a man, living in this home, I must know him that he's my husband, and even when he's at work, he's working for me and doing everything for me here at home. I mustn't say that I have *lilungelo* that my husband must now

> get up and wash the child's nappies [diapers] and cook and do everything. No, this is not a right—that's oppressing a person [the husband]. *Lilungelo* is that my husband must know that I eat here at home and what I want from him he does for me, as the mother of the home. This is the right that I must want. . . . Our rights, we women, are that our husbands maintain us and do for us whatever we want.

If one sets aside Make Ng'khansela's seemingly ironic addition of "do for us whatever we want," one finds that her words basically echo those of LaMzambi in so far as laying claim only to material provision as constitutive of women's rights and thus men's duty of care toward women (particularly emphasizing their roles as wives as did the BAA). Moreover, like Ndvunankulu who presumes to tell (all) local women what they need, she seeks to prescribe what they should want.

Yet, Make Ng'khansela's expectations also include the idea that husbands should do for women "whatever they want from them" is vital to note. This briefly intimates that the view of what women can and should claim that Make Ng'khansela herself holds is complicated. For instance, despite her rather traditional views on women's rights claims needing to conform to their station, she had also shared with me how she had successfully advocated for women's rights in terms of custom in libandla. The account she gave of her reasons for arriving at a pro-woman decision in that case demonstrates how it is that gender diversification can improve women's ability to access justice through vernacular forums.

Speaking on the regularity of inheritance-related disagreements and contests that come before the council, Make Ng'khansela expressed that

> the family might turn against you if your husband died and he had been working and earning money . . . you find that they do not want you to get the money; they ask if you and your husband were married, and how you got married out of the blue. . . . You can't be expected to stay in a marital home, not be *lobola*'d, give birth and finish and then when your child (whom you birthed) is *lobola*'d the people at her grandmother's house [the in-laws] enjoy the cows, even though they know that you haven't been *lobola*'d though you are living there. Why don't they take your child's cows and go *lobola* you?!

And so, that was the institutional decision in favor of which Make Ng'khansela had voted in that dispute. In sum, she empathized with the woman. Furthermore, she could relate to the complainant as she herself had experienced difficulty in securing the inheritance she and her children were due on her own husband's passing, though that was through her husband's employment benefits. This shows one mechanism by which women's membership on libandla matters for transforming traditional justice.

It is also worth noting that Make Ng'khansela's addition that husbands should "do for us whatever we want" is an interesting co-optation by the traditional authorities of the discourse that is often used to speak about what constitutional rights give people (especially young people and women). As one traditional leader once summarized to me what he took to be the public's conception: "it's my democratic right . . . to do whatever I want." Make Ng'khansela's addition therefore reveals that, ultimately, the contest in these rural communities is about what women *should* want in the context of what customary law (as interpreted and reinterpreted to bring it into conformity with the Constitution) gives them.

The concern from the perspective of traditional authorities was well summarized by *Ndvunankulu*:

> What grieves us most is this that when these laws are fashioned, they don't call and sit down with our senior traditional leaders to ask how we operate in these situations, how can we co-operate. . . . They sit on their own and create them, build them, then call our senior traditional leaders to say "now we have this." Then what do you find? Some of it causes us problems.

Ndvunankulu does not mention the fact that the women are also not included in discussions when developing laws, which causes (at least, some of) the women problems too. Yet the women find varied ways to navigate the remaining space. What do the authorities do as a reaction thereto? As Ndvunankulu put it, the community members seek to voice their opinions and appeal to the government to reconsider certain rules but, in the meantime, their solution is to continue with their practices: "[w]e just carry on with our laws, we don't stop." This is not that different to what some of the women do, too. Yet, as shown by some of the examples before, they are certainly not *all* simply compliant. The choices made by women are varied but some deliberately advance the cause of gender justice on their terms.

CONCLUSION

As seen, the contestation over rights is one shared element between the areas of Mbuzini and Msinga. It is integrally related to another commonality between these two areas: in particular, the impact of colonialism and apartheid in expanding and entrenching the patriarchal character of the local institutions. Thus, in both places, change with respect to this essential element of continuity between the past and the present of traditional justice in deeply rural South Africa is profoundly contested. This contestation is evident in both areas despite distinct variation in the natures and extent of women's opportunities to exercise agency in these distinct locales: whether as appointed, nominated, or elected members within the vernacular dispute-management forums or as ordinary members of the community who surround the institutions and periodically enter into these spaces in various capacities (both formal and informal).

In this chapter, I have shown that diversification of the gender composition of the vernacular dispute-management forums is a significant step toward transformation of traditional justice so as to achieve greater equality for women. However, I have also shown that the actual mechanics and impact of such diversification on ensuring women's and young people's equitable access to justice in and through transformed vernacular forums is complex and uneven. Nonetheless, there is clearly movement taking place—in a largely bottom-up sort of way—in the direction of giving women greater voice in these forums. That said, this objective is presently being achieved mostly at the lowest levels of social organization.

Finally, what does effective delivery of justice in and through women's participation in these forums looks like? This point continues to be contested by men with women (as well as men with other men, as seen in the Mbuzini traditional council) and by women among themselves (as seen in both Mbuzini and Msinga). Yet, it is clear that there is immense potential for effective delivery of justice to occur, and do so more often, if the composition of vernacular dispute-management forums were to become more diverse in terms of gender. Moreover, as the contestations discussed in this chapter take place—simultaneously, inside and outside of institutional spaces, and in mutually constitutive ways—women should be active and indispensable participants in defining what is true traditional justice and how it should be translated through the delivery of such justice by dispute-management forums in real life. Women's participation in these ways is not only just. It is an indisputable act of decolonialization.

REFERENCES

Abu-Lughod, L. (1990). The Romance of Resistance: Tracing Transformations of Power Through Bedouin Women. *American Ethnologist*, *17*(1), pp. 41–55.

Budlender, D., Mgweba, S., Motsepe, K., & Williams, L. (2011). *Women, Land and Customary Law*. Johannesburg, ZA: Community Agency for Social Enquiry (CASE).

Chanock, M. (2001). *The Making of South African Legal Culture 1902–1936: Fear, Favour and Prejudice*. Cambridge University Press.

Claassens, A., & Mnisi, S. (2009). Rural Women Redefining Land Rights in the Context of Living Customary Law. *South African Journal on Human Rights*, *25*(3), pp. 491–516.

Claassens, A., & Ngubane, S. (2008). Women, Land and Power: The Impact of the Communal Land Rights Act. In *Land, Power and Custom: Controversies Generated by South Africa's Communal Land Rights Act*. Cape Town: UCT Press; Athens, OH: Ohio University Press, pp. 154–183.

Comaroff, J. L., & Roberts, S. (1977). Marriage and Extra-Marital Sexuality – The Dialectics of Legal Change among the Kgatla. *Journal of African Law*, *21*(1), pp. 97–123.

Cornell, D. (1992). Gender, Sex, and Equivalent Rights. In J. Butler & J. W. Scott (Eds.), *Feminists Theorize the Political* (p. 280). Routledge.

Cousins, B., Alcock, R., Dladla, N., Hornby, D., Masondo, M., Mbatha, G., Mweli, M., & Alcock, C. (2011). *Imithetho yomhlaba yaseMsinga: The Living Law of Land in Msinga, KwaZulu-Natal*. Institute for Poverty, Land and Agrarian Studies.

Disney, J. L. (2008). *Women's Activism and Feminist Agency in Mozambique and Nicaragua*. Temple University Press.

Ewick, P., & Silbey, S. S. (1998). *The Common Place of Law: Stories from Everyday Life*. University of Chicago Press.

Griffiths, A. M. O. (1997). *In the Shadow of Marriage: Gender and Justice in an African Community*. University of Chicago Press.

G'sell, B. (2016). The "Maintenance" of Family: Mediating Relationships in the South African Maintenance Court. *Africa Today*, *62*(3), pp. 3–27.

Harrison, F. V. (2011). *Decolonizing Anthropology: Moving Further toward an Anthropology for Liberation*. American Anthropological Association.

hooks, bell. (1981). *Ain't I a Woman: Black Women and Feminism*. South End Press.

hooks, bell. (2013). *Writing Beyond Race: Living Theory and Practice*. Routledge.

Kingwill, R. (2008). Chapter 8 Custom-building Free Hold Title: The Impact of Family Values on Historical Ownership in the Eastern Cape. In A. Claassens & B. Cousins (Eds.), *Land, Power and Custom: Controversies Generated by South Africa's Communal Land Rights Act* (pp. 184–208). Juta.

Kingwill, R. (2011). Lost in Translation: Family Title in Fingo Village, Grahamstown, Eastern Cape. *Acta Juridica (Cape Town)*, *2011*, pp. 210–237.

Lacey, N. (1996). Normative Reconstruction in Socio-Legal Theory. *Social & Legal Studies*, *5*(2), pp. 131–158.

Lacey, N. (1998). *Unspeakable Subjects: Feminist Essays in Legal and Social Theory*. Hart Publishing.

Lugones, M. (2010). Toward a Decolonial Feminism. *Hypatia*, *25*(4), pp. 742–759.

Mamdani, M. (1996). *Citizen and Subject: Contemporary Africa and the Legacy of Late Colonialism*. Princeton University Press.

Mansbridge, J. (2013). Everyday Activism. In *The Wiley-Blackwell Encyclopedia of Social and Political Movements*. American Cancer Society.

Marichal, J. (2013). Political Facebook Groups: Micro-activism and the Digital Front Stage. *First Monday*, *18*(12), 1–7. doi:10.5210/fm.v18i12.4653.

Martin, D. G., Hanson, S., & Fontaine, D. (2007). What Counts as Activism?: The Role of Individuals in Creating Change. *Women's Studies Quarterly*, *35*(3/4), pp. 78–94. JSTOR.

Mbatha, L. (2002). Reforming the Customary Law of Succession. *South African Journal on Human Rights*, *18*, pp. 259.

McClendon, T. V. (1995). Tradition and Domestic Struggle in the Courtroom: Customary Law and the Control of Women in Segregation-Era Natal. *The International Journal of African Historical Studies*, *28*(3), pp. 527–561.

Merry, S. E. (1978). Going to Court: Strategies of Dispute Management in an American Urban Neighborhood. *Law & Society Review*, *13*, pp. 891.

Mnisi, S. (2010). The Interface between Living Customary Law(s) of Succession and South African State Law [PhD thesis, University of Oxford].

Mnisi, S., & Claassens, A. (2009). Rural Women Redefining Land Rights in the Context of Living Customary Law. *South African Journal on Human Rights*, *25*(3), pp. 491–516.

Mnisi Weeks, S. (2011a). Securing Women's Property Inheritance in the Context of Plurality: Negotiations of Law and Authority in Mbuzini Customary Courts and Beyond. *Acta Juridica (Cape Town)*, *2011*, pp. 140–173.

Mnisi Weeks, S. (2011b). "Take Your Rights Then and Sleep outside, on the Street": Rights, FORA, and the Significance of Rural South African Women's Choices. *Wisconsin International Law Journal*, *29*(2), pp. 288–314.

Mnisi Weeks, S. (2013). Women's Eviction in Msinga: The Uncertainties of Seeking Justice. *Acta Juridica (Cape Town)*, *2013*(1), pp. 118–142.

Mnisi Weeks, S. (2015a). Access to Justice?: Dispute Management Processes in Msinga, KwaZulu-Natal, South Africa. *New York Law School Law Review*, *60*(1), pp. 227–249.

Mnisi Weeks, S. (2015b). Customary Succession and the Development of Customary Law: The Bhe Legacy Part III: Reflections on Themes in Justice Langa's Judgments. *Acta Juridica (Cape Town)*, *2015*(1), pp. 215–255.

Mnisi Weeks, S. (2016). Women Seeking Justice at the Intersections Between Vernacular and State Laws and Courts in Rural KwaZulu-Natal, South Africa. In H. Klug & S. E. Merry (Eds.), *The New Legal Realism: Volume 2: Studying Law Globally* (pp. 113–142). Cambridge University Press.

Mnisi Weeks, S. (2018a). *Access to Justice and Human Security: Cultural Contradictions in Rural South Africa*. Routledge.

Mnisi Weeks, S. (2018b). Unintended Consequences in the Postcolonies: When Struggling South Africans Experience Rights Discourse as Disempowering. In R. Srikanth & E. H. Chowdhury (Eds.), *Interdisciplinary Approaches to Human Rights: History, Politics, Practice* (1st ed., pp. 111–128). Routledge.

Mnisi Weeks, S. (2019). The Violence of the Harmony Model: Common Narratives between Women and Lower-level Traditional Leaders. In M. Buthelezi & D. Skosana (Eds.), *Traditional Leaders in a Democracy: Resources, Respect and Resistance* (pp. 182–223). The Mapungubwe Institute for Strategic Reflection (MISTRA).

Mnisi Weeks, S., & Claassens, A. (2011). Tensions between Vernacular Values that Prioritise Basic Needs and State Versions of Customary Law that Contradict Them—We Love These Fields that Feed Us, But Not at the Expense of a Person Law and Poverty Special Edition. *Stellenbosch Law Review*, *22*(3), pp. 823–844.

Mohanty, C. T. (2003). "Under Western Eyes" Revisited: Feminist Solidarity through Anticapitalist Struggles. *Signs: Journal of Women in Culture and Society*, *28*(2), pp. 499–535.

Naples, N. A. (1992). Activist Mothering: Cross-Generational Continuity in the Community Work of Women from Low-Income Urban Neighborhoods. *Gender & Society*, *6*(3), pp. 441–463.

Oyěwùmí, O. (1997). *The Invention of Women: Making an African Sense of Western Gender Discourses*. University of Minnesota Press.

Rice, K. (2017). Rights and Responsibilities in Rural South Africa: Implications for Gender, Generation, and Personhood: Rights and Responsibilities in Rural South Africa. *Journal of the Royal Anthropological Institute*, *23*(1), pp. 28–41.

Roberts, R. L. (2005). *Litigants and Households: African Disputes and Colonial Courts in the French Soudan, 1895–1912*. Praeger Publishers.

Sarat, A. (1990). ". . . The Law is all Over": Power, Resistance and the Legal Consciousness of the Welfare Poor. *Yale Journal of Law & the Humanities*, *2*(2), pp. 343–379.

Smith, N. R. (2015). Rejecting Rights: Vigilantism and Violence in Post-apartheid South Africa. *African Affairs (London)*, *114*(456), pp. 341–360.

Smith, N. R. (2019). *Contradictions of Democracy: Vigilantism and Rights in Post-apartheid South Africa*. Oxford University Press.

Statistics South Africa. (2016). *Marginalised Groups Indicator Report, 2018* (No. 03-19-05 (2018)). http://www.statssa.gov.za/?page_id=1854.

Statistics South Africa. (2019). *Vulnerable Groups Indicator Report, 2017*. http://www.statssa.gov.za/?page_id=1854.

Statistics South Africa. (2020). *General Household Survey, 2018*. http://www.statssa.gov.za/?page_id=1854.

Conclusion and Recommendations

Chapter 17

Intersectionality, Access to Justice, and Women's Experiences

Policy Recommendations

J. Jarpa Dawuni and Stephen Muthoka Mutie

INTRODUCTION

Despite the plethora of domestic laws, constitutional provisions, and international treaties that guarantee women's rights as human rights, a majority of countries continue to falter in the enforcement of these legal instruments. As highlighted in the narrative by Judge Vera Duarte of Cape Verde, women judges have played significant roles in promoting women's rights and women's access to justice, as evidenced by her role in the passage of the Protocol to the African Charter on Human and Peoples' Rights on the Rights of Women in Africa (Maputo Protocol). The analysis of the Namibian context by Kennedy Kariseb brings to light what can happen when there is a judicial understanding, a gender-inclusive application of legal instruments, and a pro-gender stance by some judges in judicial interpretation. Though these two examples provide some comfort about the role judges in the courtroom have in pushing gender justice forward, more needs to be done to center the experiences of women and to address the challenges that limit their pathways as they seek justice whether as judges or as litigants.

The discharge of justice and marginalized groups' access to the courts in Africa have faced numerous challenges and have often been thwarted by a combination of institutional and cultural factors. African women continue to face different levels of marginalization in the justice system, whether as judges or litigants. This book has examined the impact of the interlocking vectors of oppression that symbolize the reality of women's experiences as they seek access to justice. Unfortunately, most justice systems have not been attentive to these overlapping layers while delivering justice to women. This chapter provides policy recommendations for easing women's access to the courts, whether as judges or litigants, that are based on these overlapping layers of oppression that inform African women's experiences. In addition, the chapter offers suggestions for gender-inclusive judging in Africa.

This book contends that an intersectional understanding of women's interlocking challenges is key to unlocking and dismantling the myriad obstacles that obstruct women's quest for justice as judges and litigants. The book generally acknowledges previous and ongoing efforts to address the complexities that disadvantage and discriminate against women in their pursuit of justice. However, as noted in chapter 1, it is also important to examine how these impeding intersecting complexities, especially within the African context, can be effectively addressed through the prism of a feminist decolonial framework. We argue that it is mainly within decolonial thinking that advocates for gender equity can address the interlocking power structures that thwart women's access to justice. The recommendations provided in this chapter seek to pluralize the avenues of justice systems and highlight the pathways to women's access to justice whether as actors or subjects of the courts. The chapter applies an intersectional and feminist decolonial lens in formulating recommendations that accommodate African realities and the multilayered disparities that block the pathways to women's access to justice.

Locating the recommendations within three central themes that cut across the 15 chapters in this book, the current chapter proposes specific recommendations to various stakeholders, including government agencies, civil society, international bodies, judiciaries, and funding agencies. The three identified central themes are as follows:

1. Women and access to the bench (the feminization of the judiciary),
2. Women and access to the courtroom (pathways to bolstering women's litigation in Africa),
3. Women and access to traditional justice (pluralistic legal systems and women litigants).

THEME ONE

WOMEN AND ACCESS TO THE BENCH: THE FEMINIZATION OF THE JUDICIARY

The first theme identified in this book is women accessing the bench, as actors within the law. The aspiration is that the feminization of the public space would equalize opportunities for women as agents for the delivery of justice. Feminization of the courts has been touted as a pathway to restorative justice

(Asadullah, 2021; Cunneen, 2002). The overall theme running through these chapters collectively call for institutional changes to address the barriers that prevent or limit women from gaining leadership roles in judiciaries. This book argues that the feminization of the judiciary is a necessary, but not a sufficient, condition for improving women's access to the bench. Additional institutional mechanisms are needed to provide gender-inclusive working conditions conducive to women's inclusivity as key justice providers.

Under Theme One, the case examples are drawn from the following countries: Kenya, South Africa, Malawi, Algeria, Cape Verde, Uganda, and Ethiopia. Collectively, these chapters examine women's experiences as judges in the courtroom and their individual and collective journeys, struggles, and contributions to justice delivery in their countries. Postcolonial nations continue to operate legal systems that are extensions of the colonial establishment, often securing the interests of the privileged—defined as those who have the economic and social mobility networks to access justice (Meng, 2020; Shomade, 2022). The colonial continuities of justice dispensation, combined with current challenges of gender inequity, greatly undermine the dawn of a new African reality in providing justice to marginalized groups. Undoubtedly, the feminization of the judiciary in Africa is a first step toward achieving gender equity in the courtroom. However, the feminization of the judiciary must be undertaken within a feminist intersectional framework that recognizes and explores how hierarchies of race, sexual orientation, class, and other identity categories define gender inequities. The intersection of sexual violence and racialized inequalities seeks to dismember women at the levels of class and gender (Harris, 2000). Feminizing the judiciary and creating a gender-sensitive institutional culture that involves women in the execution of state law and public administration must be prioritized at the national level. The feminization of institutional mechanisms creates space for women by offering opportunities, responsibilities, and power (Duarte et al., 2014, p. 30).

In chapter 2, "Status of Women Judges in Algeria: Achievements and Pathways for the Future," Samia Bourouba notes that feminizing the judiciary is a move toward gender equality. The chapter argues for affirmative action that secures women's career advancement in the judiciary as a key element of the feminization of the public space. The author highlights how Algerian women judges have successfully handled pressure from religious extremism and threats of political instability. Additionally, the author notes that women judges have broken the social barriers attached to the patriarchal views that question their competence. The chapter concludes that incorporating more women judges in the judiciary would be a step toward the delivery of better judgments.

In chapter 3, titled "Opening the Door for Women in the Cape Verdean Judiciary," Justice Vera Duarte narrates her personal experience as an actor on the bench. In recounting her journey as a trailblazer lawyer in her country, Duarte gives an overview of her journey and personifies the quest for a gender-conscious judiciary through her experience as a female jurist. Her narration shows how the feminization of the judiciary can happen if concerted efforts are put in place and shows that women can lead. Judge Duarte's life story exemplifies how women judges have accomplished crucial tasks in promoting women's rights, as evidenced by her role in the passage of the Protocol to the African Charter on Human and Peoples' Rights on the Rights of Women in Africa (Maputo Protocol). Indeed, women who are purveyors of justice play an instrumental role, one that needs more support to enhance the delivery of justice for all.

In chapter 4, "Women Judges in Ethiopia," Maame Efua Addadzi-Koom and Biruh Gage argue that invoking a feminized policy in the training and recruitment of judges is essential for bridging the gender gap between judges. Achieving gender parity in women's access to the bench would help promote the court's impartiality and legitimacy. Notwithstanding recent and ongoing efforts to recruit and train women judges, they are still underrepresented in numbers in Ethiopia and Egypt, due primarily to past marginalization.

In chapter 5, "Battle for Women in the Egyptian Judiciary: Reality, Laws, and Aspirations or a Dream Come True?," Omnia Taher Gadalla gives an overview of women's struggles to join the judiciary in Egypt. The chapter contends that even though feminist advocacy in the country began a century ago, there have been few gains for women in access to the judiciary. Lack of political will remains a massive obstacle for women trying to become judges in the male-dominated field. The author outlines as the main reason for this gender imparity Islam's religious doctrine, which hinders women from having more opportunities in the legal profession.

In chapter 6, "Making Gains for Women's Rights: Using Gender Quotas to Achieve Gender Equality in the Composition of the Supreme Court of Kenya," Annerita Murungi and Agnes Meroka-Mutua revisit the proposal to promote inclusivity of female judges by introducing of gender quotas, which they argue would be a necessary condition for the realization of women's rights in Kenya. With the goal of shaping the judiciary in a more gender-inclusive way, Kenya has made tremendous gains in promoting a work environment that offers opportunities for women to become judges. However, the symbolic representation of women judges has yet to be fully translated to the substantive representation of women's rights through gender-sensitive jurisprudence and the promotion of women's rights.

In chapter 7, "'Your Whole Life Is an Interview to Get to the Bench': Gender and Judicial Appointments in Malawi," Rachel Ellett examines how the pipeline of women's access to the judiciary remains narrow due to structural gender constraints inherent in the judiciary. The main concern in the Malawian case is that the persisting educational and legal professional barriers impede women seeking access to the bench. Malawi seems to have a massive deficit in the number of women serving in the judiciary, due to low pay, lifestyle incompatibility, and the politicization of the judiciary. To address gender parity, legal education in Malawi must be liberalized—freed from the tentacles of power structures that cripple women's representation in the judiciary. Similar to the situation in Zambia of women judges facing negative perceptions (Masengu, 2021), the case of Malawi points to the negative perceptions among some sectors of society and the legal fraternity, of women who attempt to join the bench. These perceptions and institutional barriers must be addressed, to create an even playing field for women judicial aspirants.

In chapter 8, "Gender Transformation of the Judiciary in South Africa," Justice Baratang Constance Mocumie argues that implementing structural policies to address gender transformation in the court system is of critical concern. The chapter discusses the intersectional nature of gender, race, and professional hierarchy in determining where women find themselves within the judiciary. The chapter highlights how age (seniority) and gender insensitivity at the bench can intersect to silence women judges. Mocumie argues that structural changes in the Constitution of the judiciary are imperative to effectively provide a balanced environment for women.

In chapter 9, "A Critical Assessment of the Status of Women Judicial Officers in Uganda," Josephine Ndagire notes that although women's numbers in leadership roles in law-related fields have increased tremendously, women still face leadership challenges in the judiciary. While the symbolic representation is impressive, women continue to struggle to access leadership positions within the court hierarchy. For example, only one woman has served as deputy chief justice, despite the high qualifications of women on the bench. The chapter explores the factors that influence both the recruitment and promotion of judicial officers and their appointment to leadership positions.

Policy Recommendations on Women and Access to the Bench

The following are the policy recommendations for feminizing the judiciary in Africa:

1. ***Support for women judges***:
   According to the analysis put forward in the 15 chapters in this book, women judges are strengthening the judiciary and helping to gain the public's trust. Support for women judges is needed because it will open opportunities for promoting an inclusive and more just rule of law. This

support should be given in the form of equal opportunities for employment and promotion and a gender-sensitive work environment, through trainings and opportunities and by changing institutional mechanisms and international and regional actors. In Algeria, support in the form of protection for the women judges is recommended. The author recommends that the Judicial Service Commission (JSC) support all women judges, especially those handling critical cases that tackle emerging global threats like religious extremism and terrorism, as such judges are likely to be intimidated. Security, welfare, and psychosocial support help enhance their delivery of justice.

In Uganda, support for women judges should start with the executive branch disengaging politics from the appointment process of judges. The fact that Uganda's current NRM government seems more comfortable with judicial officers who are openly supportive of the regime is, according to Ndagire—the author of the chapter on Uganda, worrying for Uganda and threatens the regional and continental justice system.

African countries should offer more opportunities for women in the judicial system. It is crucial to create induction forums that bring together social actors and legal experts to sensitize people to the harms of the discriminatory behavior often extended to women in their work environment. This entails dismantling the informal sexual power structure that belies the process of recruitment, appointment, and promotion by instituting a framework that encourages more women actors on the bench will help strengthen the representation of women in the delivery of justice.

2. ***Equal opportunities for employment and promotion***:

Another suggestion for addressing the issues of intersectional biases and discriminatory practices is the need for judicial training for judges to make them competitive for promotion and leadership positions. The judicial hierarchy presents a major challenge for most judges, since the appointment and promotion processes remain opaque.

The judiciary should develop a balanced employment policy by addressing intersecting constraints like ethnicity, class, and religion. Judicial employment should have a balanced representation that encompasses the face of the nation and gender equality. As captured by OECD (2016), "employment committees should draw a mainstream gender equality in designing, developing, implementing, and evaluating relevant public policies and budgets that guide public officials' hiring."

In addition, the law society organizations, in conjunction with law schools, should formulate internal policies that are gender sensitive, equal, progressive, and inclusive, to empower all legal practitioners and judicial officers at all levels of the judicial hierarchy on gendered practices. This will give women a better chance when competing against their male counterparts in the judicial fraternity. Lastly, courts of justice have a role to play in creating new opportunities and/or expanding existing opportunities for women. This applies internally to the operation of courts as arenas of justice, where women must have equal opportunity to be employed and equal opportunity to advance within the court hierarchy.

3. ***Trainings, recruitment, and opportunities for leadership***:

   Following the South African judicial experience, to enable a progressive approach to implementing women's rights it is imperative to introduce training programs on gender equality and empowerment for all judicial officers. The judicial training curriculum should be restructured to offer specialized training on gender and women's rights.

   Additionally, there should be engagement and consultation with NGOs and legal bodies to provide professional courses that equip female judges with adequate skills to better execute their mandate as legal officers. This initiative would increase their capacity in their pursuit of career progression and enhance their ability to compete equally with their male counterparts.

   Additionally, women judges' organizations should ensure that women are meaningfully represented on the bench. Some women judges' associations have taken active roles in building the capacity of female judicial officers (Institute for African Women in Law, 2022). These associations should organize from within by positioning their members for key positions and lobbying for gender parity in judicial leadership. I do recognize that judicial training is not a sufficient condition for being promoted within a court when institutional norms and practices remain masculinized and patriarchal. However, judicial awareness, gender sensitivity, and unconscious bias training should be provided not only to the women judges but also to their male colleagues. Collective judicial training on gender biases will not lessen the hurdles for women pursuing pathways to the bench, but could contribute to creating awareness among judges about the peculiar and gendered nature of the interlocking challenges women face in their pursuit of access to the courtroom, as a first step to accessing justice.

4. ***Gender-sensitive work environment***:

   Women also need support once they are on the bench; national judiciaries must offer support structures that help women judges balance family and professional lives. For example, the employing body (JSC) should design employment terms that are supportive and friendly to female judges. Additionally, the promotion of women should not be pegged to seniority since their numbers are smaller at the top level. Instead, performance appraisals should be based on competence, work ethics, and professionalism.

A gender-sensitive work environment is needed to facilitate women judges' work, with extra support staff for women judges in executing their mandate as judicial officers; this may include facilities like research support staff, high-performance electronic devices, gym facilities, and parental responsibility support for judges who are mothers.

5. ***Changing institutional mechanisms***:

   National legislation should seek to challenge institutionalization of courts as a continuity of hierarchical imperial structures. It is necessary to drift away from the judicialization of politics (Vallinder, 1994) so that courts become "more adjudication, less administration." Changes to current institutional processes must aim to build independent legal systems and make women equal partners in the justice delivery processes.

   African governments need to pass more technical laws of political inclusivity to create room for women to participate in nation-building. A majority of African countries rely on their colonial legal frameworks with exclusionary policies like cautionary rules that significantly affect the delivery of justice. Governments should initiate law reforms that involve all, including women, during public participation.

6. ***International and regional actors***:

   The African Union (AU) should lay out a framework of legislation and strategic resolutions that encourage all member states to abide by and implement gender equality in the Constitution of the JSC. Furthermore, in conjunction with laying out pro-African policies that seek to address the continent's contemporary realities, the AU should initiate more legal training, appointments, and empowerment programs to equip women judges with adequate skills and knowledge to enhance performance. This is in line with AU Gender Policy of 2009, which the AU has noted as: "transformational in that its outcomes aim to mitigate, if not eliminate, the major constraints hindering gender equality and women's empowerment, so that women and girls may participate fully in economic activities, political affairs, and social endeavours" (African Union, 2022).

   International organizations like the United Nations should offer women judges more opportunities and training in legal-related dockets to give women global exposure to compete at the highest levels of their profession. Additionally, the UN should monitor and ensure that all its member states adhere to gender inclusivity in the judiciary to enhance gender-sensitive decision-making processes.

THEME TWO

WOMEN AND ACCESS TO THE COURTROOM: PATHWAYS TO BOLSTERING GENDER-SENSITIVE LITIGATION IN AFRICA

The second theme details the pathways to bolstering gender-sensitive litigation as a strategy for promoting women's access to justice through the courts. This theme is discussed in the Nigeria, Ghana, Namibia, Egypt, and Rwanda chapters. Collectively, the chapters illustrate women's experiences in seeking justice as plaintiffs and defendants. As explained in chapter 1, women's access to the judiciary as subjects has been limited by overlapping and intersecting challenges. Gender-sensitive judicial processes that address the kinds of discrimination that block access to the courtroom for women actors must be developed, and where they exist, their implementation must be encouraged. Addressing racial injustice in a broader way means recognizing the work of communities in dealing with issues with inclusive civic engagement and creating stronger connections among residents, businesses, and nonprofit and government leaders (Christopher, 2021). Subsequently, applying feminist intersectional gender-sensitive remedies to environmental injustice, access to land and property, and inheritance rules would contribute to clearing the hurdles blocking women's access to justice (Wesley & Dewey, 2018).

The central focus of this theme is to evaluate how broadening avenues and pipelines for women's litigation simplify the nuanced definition of women as a social identity or category through the parameters of ethnicity, class, and social-economic status (McCall, 2005). Women's pathways to justice must be contextualized within specific spaces so that the intersecting barriers that hinder women's agency in their quest for justice are taken into account.

In chapter 10, "Women's Property Rights and Discriminatory Land Tenure Systems in Ghana: The Adjudicative Role of Courts," Michael Addaney assesses how, in their dispensation of justice, the courts strike a balance in safeguarding women's rights to property in Ghana when integrating customary laws into land governance. The author argues that customary laws governing land tenure and property rights in Ghana are discriminatory and do not comply with acceptable international standards and practices on women's property rights. In addition, the author finds that there is progress toward equity in ownership and women's access to property due to judicial efforts that have transformed customary practice. These efforts are a step in the right direction because they secure women's property rights and lay a firm foundation that helps women seeking legal redress have confidence in the courts.

In chapter 11, "The Making and Unmaking of Gender: Reflections on Questions of Gender and the Judiciary in Namibia," Kennedy Kariseb acknowledges the enactment of statutory laws to prevent gender-based violence and the role of the courts in developing gender-sensitive jurisprudence. The chapter also argues that Namibia's abolishment of the cautionary rule signals a progressive precedent in women's rights protection. Finally, the chapter concludes that the Namibian judiciary should strive to have a fertile gender-responsive legal framework, one that is moving toward raising the number of women in the legal sector.

In chapter 12, "Women and Environmental Justice Issues in Nigeria: An Evaluation," Eghosa Ekhator and Pedi Obani argue that expanding pathways to female litigation is critical for delivering environmental justice to women victims who need compensation for the multiple atrocities committed against them. Women are vital stakeholders greatly affected by the multidimensional challenge of maintaining an inhabitable environment. The chapter raises important concerns about the strategies to address the plight of the marginalized groups and the environmental sustainability in the Niger Delta. The intersection of gender and access to environmental justice forms the matrix of discrimination in the Nigerian case.

In chapter 13, "Contribution of the Judiciary to the Advancement and Protection of Women's Matrimonial and Inheritance Rights in Rwanda," Marie-Rose Turamwishimiye and Odette Uwineza trace the gains realized since the introduction of gender-neutral law no. 22/1999. Its adoption has led to more women's property rights, which is a great stride against gender-discriminatory customs and traditions. The chapter concludes that women now can claim matrimonial and property rights, an achievement that was not possible before the adoption of gender-neutral laws.

Policy Recommendations on Women and Access to the Courtroom: Bolstering Gender-Sensitive Litigation in Africa

1. ***Sensitization on women's rights***:

   While the 15 chapters in this book have shown the milestones African courts have reached to date, much remains undone. Sensitization about women's rights is still a challenge. It is important to create pro-women lobby organizations and legal groups that sensitize and raise women's awareness of the legal consultation services available to them in the courts and informal justice systems. These initiatives should provide civic education and pro bono legal services cognizant of gender equality and access to the courts. In addition, the law societies and civil societies should create avenues of cooperation dedicated to assisting women in need of legal representation in courts.

One such example given in this book comes from Addaney's chapter on Ghana, which explores women's access to land. It is important that women lawyers and women's rights groups are equipped to demand that existing laws on women's rights are implemented and interpreted in line with the acceptable international standards for the fulfillment and implementation of women's property rights. For example, Addaney argues that "Ghana should comply with acceptable international standards and practices regarding fulfilling and implementing women's property rights. The practical impact of the bill would be to first and foremost domesticate Ghana's international and regional legal obligations concerning women's property rights."

In the same breath and following Addaney's argument, it is vital that legislation on the property rights of spouses be implemented: a bill that guarantees the customary property rights for women. In this regard, this chapter recommends that governments and civil society create public awareness about women's rights, social cohesion, and the rights of women to own and access property regardless of ethnicity, class, and religion.

2. ***Funding opportunities for women's rights groups***:

   One step in the right direction would be to increase funding for women-centered legal groups to strengthen their efficiency in implementing their mandates. These legal organizations could in turn provide outreach services to women in rural and poor communities to increase awareness of women's rights. In addition to providing legal representation, women-centered legal groups should assist women offenders in their integration back into society through support programs that help them desist from crime. Meroka and Murungi's chapter on Kenya and Ekhator and Obani's chapter on Nigeria show how funding for women's rights groups can help change institutional norms and help provide pathways for women's access to the courtroom.

   Additionally, governments and international bodies should commit funds for research into the impact of gender relations on the delivery of justice in statutory courts and the traditional systems. This is the intention behind the three chapters in the third and final section of the book, which detail the impact of traditional legal systems on women's access to justice. Funding these women's rights organizations and groups lets them do more to help women get justice.

3. ***Establishing specialized courts***:

   Lawmakers, law societies, and gender rights groups should push for the creation of special courts dedicated to handling litigation that involves gender-based violence, inheritance, and women's property rights. Bringing together these stakeholders would facilitate the drawing up of contingency plans in case widening the channels of justice delivery to women fails. According to Open Government Partnership (OGP), specialized courts can provide greater access to justice and transparency for individuals with legal problems (OGP, 2019). Illustratively, Kariseb's exploration of the Namibian judiciary in chapter 11 concludes that "constitutional reforms that call for the protection of women, the complementary nature of statutory enactments, and the imposition of lengthy exemplary sentences in cases of domestic violence against women are indicators of progress." When women seek access to the courts as litigants, judiciaries are duty-bound to ensure that the interpretation of existing laws considers the gendered nature and construction of such laws in the first place. To that end creating specialized courts will ensure that access to the courts for women seeking justice remains accessible, cost effective, timely, and efficient.

4. ***Role of governments and gender-inclusive policymaking***:
   Respective governments should enact and enforce relevant laws that provide the framework for legal aid and legal counsel to women. This would benefit marginalized groups struggling to get legal representation in statutory courts. For instance, Ekhator and Obani argue that providing free legal representation for female litigants in the Niger Delta crisis would considerably reduce the barriers to justice. Moreover, if women have such special access to courts, the chance of environmental justice being delivered to women who have suffered atrocities due to the social-economic ripple effect of environmental degradation will increase exponentially.

   Ekhator and Obani's chapter recommends that the Nigerian government address environmental injustice since women stand to benefit from environmental governance in the Niger Delta. Promoting environmental justice increases the chances that sustainable growth and development, gender equality, and environmental sustainability will be realized.

   Women should be recognized and appreciated as key stakeholders in environmental preservation. They should be actively engaged in public participation openly and mutually, and their input should be appreciated. Furthermore, women victims of environmental injustices should be compensated.

THEME THREE

WOMEN AND ACCESS TO TRADITIONAL JUSTICE SYSTEMS: PLURALISTIC LEGAL SYSTEMS AND WOMEN-BASED LITIGATION IN AFRICA

The third theme examines the impact of pluralistic legal systems on women's access to justice and the courts. The discussion draws from the South

Africa, Nigeria, and Cameroon chapters. The central premise is that the diversification of justice delivery through plural approaches in both statutory courts and traditional justice systems helps widen the pathways of women's access to justice. In addition, this theme explores how the Traditional Leadership and Governance Framework Act (2003) recognizes traditional communities' councils and how gender diversity backs legal pluralism. Finally, these chapters explore, through a decolonial lens, the lingering effects of colonialization and patriarchal domination on women's access to traditional court systems.

In chapter 14, "Gender and Customary Justice among the Podoko of the Mandara Mountains of the Far North Region of Cameroon," Jeremie Diye pays attention to the role of women in the functionary elements of the traditional court system among the Podoko in northern Cameroon. The essential concern in the Cameroonian case is the gender-insensitive nature of laws and how such laws impact women. The chapter concludes by emphasizing the importance of a consolidated social framework that offers amicable settlements to the parties involved in a dispute. Further, customary justice should instill reconciliation and cohesiveness among the aggravated parties, rather than just sanctioning the offender. It is also important for the management of customary justice and to ensure fairer judgment for women litigants that women have full access and that gender-inclusive adjudicatory principles are followed in the traditional court sessions.

In chapter 15, "Juxtaposing the Efficacy of Testacy and Intestacy to Inheritance Rights for Rukuba Widows and Children under Nigeria's Plural Legal System," Rebecca Badejogbin and Vicki Lawal probe the limiting provisions under customary law for widows and children seeking to inherit property from their late husband and father, respectively. To tackle the gaps in the administration of justice in inheritance cases, the chapter advocates a dual approach to delivering justice to widows and children in scenarios where there are limited provisions in enforcing the constitutional rights of women and children.

In chapter 16, "Transforming Traditional Justice through Gender Diversification: Comparing Two South African Communities," Sindiso Mnisi Weeks argues that incorporating vernacular tribunals that are gender diversified will lay the ground for the transformation of traditional legal systems and, in the process, ensure equality for women. If the gender composition of traditional adjudicatory bodies is diversified, young people and women stand a better chance of fairer legal redress. Weeks concludes by indicating that a pluralistic justice system gives more alternatives to the majority of the people found in the lowest social strata—which are often inhabited by women.

Policy Recommendations for Pluralistic Legal Systems and Women-Centered Litigation in Africa

The following are the policy recommendations to address pluralistic legal systems and women-centered litigation in Africa:

1. ***Create bridges between customary and statutory adjudication systems***:
   Three of the chapters in the book discuss the utility of closing the gap between traditional and statutory justice systems. The two systems must cooperate and arrange mobile sessions of legal proceedings nearer to the women victims of injustices—specifically those whose litigation involves land—who lack access to relevant information and mobility to courts. The accessibility and affordability of legal representation will give women offenders and complainants a chance at access to justice. Governments should strengthen pluralistic legal systems to expand the corridors of justice to women litigants in the traditional court of justice by creating legal structures that foster women's inclusivity. Gender-inclusive adjudicatory processes can build the legal framework for expanding access to justice for women. Public awareness and policy directives must aim at formulating laws that recognize traditional courts as allies of the statutory courts. In addition, governments should offer to fund and organize seminars on gender equality to justice providers who operate in the most remote areas.

2. ***Reform and strengthen informal courts of justice to be centers of gender inclusivity***:
   As discussed in the first two themes, reform efforts must aim at reforming and strengthening of informal courts of justice to make them centers of gender inclusivity. These reforms should raise public awareness of the traditional justice system's importance and cultural significance. In addition, traditional courts' constitutions and modus operandi should be well documented and in line with the regulations set by the constitutional laws of a country.

   In the spirit of decolonization, this book recommends that African governments preserve customary justice approaches that consolidate peace and cohesion between the offender and complainant instead of heavily sanctioning the offender. Additionally, governments should address the lack of gender parity in traditional patriarchal settings and how they influence customary laws and norms. For example, a gender quota for appointing traditional judges should be put in place to promote and protect women's rights. In addition, more women should be inducted into the traditional court system to achieve gender equality in outcomes. The chances of fair judgment are likely to increase when there is gender equity in the court panels.

3. ***Role of development agencies***:
   Development agencies should recognize, regulate, and support indigenous ways of justice administration to instill confidence in people seeking their services. Strengthening these systems can help lift the burden off the statutory courts for cases that the traditional courts can handle. In addition, the two systems of justice delivery should reconcile and promote a consistent legal framework that recognizes the generational kinship system of administration to preserve the oral heritage of the people. Funding should be directed at the digitalization of traditional justice systems, proceedings, and outcomes, to provide a framework for evaluation and assessment over time.

4. ***Role of civil society organizations***:
   To promote women's access to the courts, women's rights organizations, civil society organizations, and public interest litigation lawyers must continue to work toward promoting gender sensitization in informal court/justice processes. Given that most citizens live in rural areas and have no access to the statutory courts, the informal justice systems are where most women access justice. The continuing complexities of access to justice for women in traditional settings are explored in detail by Diye in the case of Cameroon, Badejogbin and Lawal in Nigeria, and Weeks in South Africa. Most civil society organizations dealing with women's issues focus on socioeconomic rights, which are important in and of themselves. However, to move the needle forward on women's access to justice, women's rights organizations that focus on women's legal rights have to be encouraged, funded, and supported to act as important conduits for promoting women's access to justice in traditional justice settings by providing quasi-legal support and using arbitration and negotiation skills to help guide traditional leaders in their adjudication of cases.

5. ***Role of governments***:
   Diye's chapter on customary justice among the Podoko people of the Mandara Mountains in Cameroon recommends that governments offer traditional judges training opportunities by organizing conferences and training to broaden their expertise in handling emerging social disputes. Additionally, investments should be made to modernize the traditional courts' operations, by introducing record-keeping for reference. Proper documentation will also allow victims of injustice to have their verdicts enforced using recordings as proof of a verdict. Additionally, governments should determine what approaches and skills traditional court systems need in order to handle the evolving conflicts contemporary society is facing and equip the courts with those skills.

Research should be conducted on the impact of customary court systems and their effectiveness in administering justice. More research must be done on traditional justice systems, to document how they are constituted and how they operate. Their oral nature needs to be reconciled with modern justice mechanisms to prevent their extinction. Governments should prioritize the preservation of traditional justice through legislation that consolidates these systems' importance as social cohesion platforms that offer conciliation and reconciliation services to the people. Governments should revise or eradicate discriminatory laws that deny women litigants access to the customary justice system. Traditional courts should be managed to guarantee access for all people during the traditional tribunal proceedings of a case.

REFERENCES

African Union. (2022). AU strategy for gender equality and women's empowerment. https://au.int/en/articles/au-strategy-gender-equality-and-womens-empowerment.

Asadullah, M. (2021). Decolonization and restorative justice: A proposed theoretical framework. *Decolonization of Criminology and Justice*, *3*(1), 27–62. https://doi.org/10.24135/dcj.v3i1.25.

Christopher, G. C. (2021). Introduction—Healing through policy: Creating pathways to racial justice. *National Civic Review*, *110*(3), 6–10. https://www.jstor.org/stable/10.32543/naticivirevi.110.3.0006.

Cunneen, C. (2002). Restorative justice and the politics of decolonization. In E. G. M. Weitekamp & H.-J. Kerner (Eds.), *Restorative Justice: Theoretical Foundations* (pp. 32–49). Willan.

Duarte, M., Fernando, P., Gomes, C., & Oliveira, A. (2014). The feminization of the judiciary in Portugal: Dilemmas and paradoxes. *Utrecht Law Review, 10*(1), 29–43. http://doi.org/10.18352/ulr.255.

Harris, A. P. (2000). Gender, violence, race, and criminal justice. *Stanford Law Review*, *52*(4), 777–807. https://doi.org/10.2307/1229430.

Institute for African Women in Law. (2022). The Tanzania women judges association and the feminization of the judiciary. Available at https://www.africanwomeninlaw.com/_files/ugd/c889be_84e29efeed1b452e81a7a999f70712ca.pdf. Accessed April 22, 2022.

Masengu, T. (2021). One sauce for the goose, another for the gander: Zambian women judges and perceptions of illegitimacy. In J. Dawuni (Ed.), *Gender and Judging Across Africa* (pp. 209–230). Routledge.

McCall, L. (2005). The complexity of intersectionality. *Signs*, *30*(3), 1771–1800. https://doi.org/10.1086/426800.

Meng, M. (2020, October 19). Decolonizing law through restorative justice. *Harvard International Review*. https://hir.harvard.edu/decolonizing-law-through-restorative-justice/.

OECD. (2016, March 8). *2015 OECD Recommendation of the Council on Gender Equality in Public Life*. OECD Publishing. https://doi.org/10.1787/9789264252820-en.

Open Government Partnership. (2019). Justice policy series, part I: Access to justice. https://www.opengovpartnership.org/documents/justice-policy-series-part-i-access-to-justice/.

Shomade, S. (2022). *Colonial Legacies and the Rule of Law in Africa: Ghana, Kenya, Nigeria, South Africa, and Zimbabwe*. Routledge.

Vallinder, T. (1994). The judicialization of politics. A world-wide phenomenon: Introduction. *International Political Science Review/Revue Internationale de Science Politique*, *15*(2), 91–99. http://www.jstor.org/stable/1601557.

Wesely, J. K., & Dewey, S. C. (2018). Confronting gendered pathways to incarceration: Considerations for reentry programming. *Social Justice*, *45*(1 (151)), 57–82. https://www.jstor.org/stable/26677646.

Index

Page numbers in *italics* indicate figures, tables in the text, and references following "n" refer endnotes

1900 Buganda Agreement, 189
1900 Tooro Agreement, 189
1901 Ankole Agreement, 189
1960 Civil Code of Ethiopia, 72
1977 "Guide to Zone Courts," 67n1
1988 Family Law Decree, 287
1992 Constitution of Ghana, 223, 227, 228
1995 Beijing declaration, 95
2010 Constitution, 17
2019 SADC Gender Barometer, 139

Abdel-Rahim, Mohamed Hossam, 109
Abebrese v. Kaah case, 230
Abeokuta women in 1948, 264
Abrahamson, S.S., 120
Achebe, N., 313
ACHPR. *See* African Commission on Human and Peoples' Rights (ACHPR)
Addadzi-Koom, M.E., 5, 18, 271, 384
Addaney, Michael, 19
Addis Ababa City Courts, 75
Adjei v. Adjei case, 232
Administrative Prosecution Authority (APA), 99
African 2063 agenda, 111
African Charter on Human and Peoples' Rights, 269, 270
African Charter on Women's Rights, 65
African Commission on Human and Peoples' Rights (ACHPR), 59, 60, 63, 65, 226
African Commission on Human and Peoples' Rights v. Kenya, 276n4
African customary law, 326
African Union Agenda 2063, 95
Agnes Kahimbi Kashela v. Katima Mulilo Town Council and Others [2018] NASC 409, 251
Agyeman, J., 261
Ahikire, J., 266
Aketch, M., 126
Akpan v. Shell case, 267, 273
Akrofi, E.O., 231
Al-Ayoubi, Naima, 96, 112n1
Algeria, 13, 17; 1834 decree, 32; 1963 Constitution, 30, 31; 1976 Constitution, 31; 1989 Constitution, 31, 34; 1996 Constitution, 43; administrative tribunals, 32; appointment of female magistrates,

39; attorney general positions, 39; Black Decade, 41, 43; career development, 42; civil code, 31; The Constituent Assembly, 29; council of Muslim jurisprudence, 32; court structure and organization, 33–36, *35*; decolonization of justice, 33; Ecole Nationale d'Administration in 1965, 36, 40; formulation of Islam, 30, 31; future for female judge, 42; gender equity, 36, 37; gender parity, 38, 44; generation effect, 38; High Council of Magistracy, 34; Islamic courts, 32; judicial map, 33; judicial reshuffle, 39; *mahakmas*, 32; *medjles*, 32; Muslim population, 32; the National Assembly, 29; organic law 04-12 of 2004, 34; organic law 11-12 in 2011, 34; organic law 12-03 in 2012, 31, 32; Ottoman reign, 32; percentage of women judges in senior positions, 37, *38*; period of terrorism, 1990, 41, 43; professional responsibilities and family obligations, 41; promotion of female judges, 43; qualitative interviews, 40–42; rabbinical courts, 32; recruitment of judges, 36; Sharia law, 30, 31, 43; Sunni schools, 32; Tribunal of Conflict, 34; women's rights, 31

Algerian Constitution: 1963 Constitution, 30, 31; 1976 Constitution, 31; 1989 Constitution, 31, 34; 1996 Constitution, 43

Ali Aroni, Abida (Justice), 123

Alien Tort Claims Act (ATCA) 1789, 271

Allam, Shawki, 100

Almada, David Hopffer, 53

Al-Tallawy, Mervat, 108

Aly, N., 114n23

Amadiume, I., 266

Ambunda, L., 249

Amended Proclamation No. 684/2010, 79

Aminata Diantou Diane v. Mali (2018) ECW/CCJ/JUD/14/18, 275n1

Ammar, Amal (Judge), 109

anticategorical complexity, 6

Anti-Corruption Court, Uganda, 197

Anti-Discrimination Commission Law, 110

Anti-Homosexuality Act in 2014, 202

APDF and IHRDA v. the Republic of Mali, 270

Appellate Court, 75

appointment of women judges in Malawi: career paths, 153; formal appointment body and qualifications, 147–48; gender denigration, 152; higher-level judicial appointments, 152; historical context, 145–47; influence of chief justice, 149; judicial appointment bodies, 142; Malawi School Certificate Education examination, 147; percentage of women judges, 146, *146*; qualifications and promotion, 148–49; regionalism and judicial appointments, 150; salary and benefits, 152; "tap on the shoulder" phenomenon, 150; unreliable pipeline, 147; zero-sum game, 153

Apusigah, A.A., 220

Arab constitutions, 30

Arafat, Yasser, 58

Arthur v. Arthur case, 231

Article 2 of the 1971 Constitution, Egyptian judiciary, 11

Article 4 of the Federal Courts re-amendment Proclamation no. 454 of 2005, 72

Article 10 of proclamation no. 1234/2021, 75–76

Article 11 of the Amended Federal Judicial Administration Council Establishment Proclamation No. 684/2010, 74

Article 14 of the African Charter, 225
Article 17 of the UDHR (1948), 224
Article 18(3) of the African Charter, 225
Article 21 of the protocol, Ghana, 225
Article 22 of the Constitution, Ghana, 222–23, 228, 230
Article 27(8) of the Constitution, Kenya, 119, 128
Article 32 of Constitution, Uganda, 191
Article 34(5) of the 1995 Constitution, 72
Article 36(8) of the 1992 Constitution of Ghana, 216
Article 53 of the Constitution, Egyptian judiciary, 111
Article 128 of Constitution, Uganda, 193
Article 147(2) of Constitution, Uganda, 193
Article 166(3) of the Constitution, Kenya, 124, 129
Article 172(2) (b) of the Constitution, Kenya, 127, 128, 131
Article 267 of the 1992 Constitution, Ghana, 220
Article 295(1) of the 1992 Constitution, 233n1
Articles 142 and 144 of Constitution, Uganda, 193, 194
Ashenafi, Meaza, 69, 74, 85
Aura-Odhiambo, R., 123
Awumbilla, 232
Aziz, Dina Abdel, 109

Badejogbin, R.E., 8, 21, 393
Banda, Joyce, 146, 150–52
Banjul Charter, 59
Baraza, Nancy (Justice), 124
Barmes, L., 151
Batamuriza Zaïnabu v. Niyonzima Twalib (1987) case, 288
Benarbia, S., 114n21
Bensalah, Abdelkader, 39
Bindman, G., 119
Bishop, Maurice, 58
Black Decade, 41, 43
Black emancipation, 247
Bodo Community v. SPDC case, 267
Bohannan, P., 244
Bonthuys, E., 120
Bossa, Solomy Balungi (Justice), 195, 196, 198, 201, 202
Bourouba, Samia, 13, 17, 383
Bouteflika, A., 34, 39, 42, 45n4
Bowoto v. Chevron and *Wiwa v. Shell* case, 267
Brand, Fritz (Judge), 163
Bratton, K., 141
Brownhill, L.S., 265, 266
Building Bridges Initiative (BBI), 126
Buteera, Richard (Hon. Justice), 199

Canadian Charter of Rights and Freedoms, 344
"Can Judicial Independence Survive Transformation" lecture, 2009, 164
Cape Verdean judiciary: advocacy campaigns, 61; childcare and protection, 62; Citizenship Education curriculum, 61; civil and criminal trifles, 54; constitutional evolution, 55; Decree-Law 33/75 of October 16, 54; Decree-Law 58/81 of June 20, 1981, 56; Decree-Law 69/76 of July 3, 1976, 56; Decree-Law 71/76 of July 24, 1976, 57; Decree-Law 84/76 of September 25, 1976, 56; Family Code, 56–57; French Civil Code system, 53–54; gender composition of judiciary, 62; gender representation in public offices, 62, *62*; independence and legislative reform, 53–55; Indigenate Statute, 54; Law 9/3/86 of December 31, 1986, 57; Law on the State Political Organization (LOPE), 53; legal storytelling and historical analysis, 51; Movement for Democracy (MPD) in 1991, 54;

National Action Plan for Human Rights and Citizenship, 61; National Reconstruction, 53; "overseas provinces" of Angola, 53; *A Popular Justice in Cape Verde*, 54; Women's empowerment and parity, 66
cardinal principle, Ethiopia, 78
Cashgate scandal, 150
Castro, Fidel, 58
cautionary rule, 250, 251
Centre for Oil Pollution Watch v. Nigerian National Petroleum Corporation, 273
Chang, R.S., 6
Chanock, M., 326
Chanock's analysis of customary law, 327
Chitapi, R., 176
Citizenship Education curriculum, 61
City Courts, Ethiopia, 75
Civil Law system, 97
civil society organizations (CSOs), 267, 268, 271, 273
Clark, M.L., 168
Cohen, Mesaltob, 51
Colonel, Fatima (Judge), 59, 62
Colonial Charter of October 18, 1908, 287
colonial importation of legal systems, 14
colonialism, 220, 221
coloniality, 7
colonial racism, 8
Combating of Domestic Violence Act, 2003, 248
Combating of Rape Act, 2000, 248
Communal Land Reform Act 5 of 2002, 248, 251
community-based courts, 8
concept of "family," 294
Constitution of 2014, Tunisia, 14
Constitution of Kenya (CoK), 117
Constitution's impartation of rights to women and children, 370
continental legal system, Ethiopia, 72
Convention on the Elimination of All Forms of Discrimination Against Women (CEDAW), 249, 269
Convention on the Elimination of All Forms of Discrimination Against Women in Article 16(1)(h), 224–25
corporal punishment, 30
Cousins, Ben, 369
Cowan, R., 120
Cravos Revolution, 53
Crenshaw, Kimberlé, 5
critical mass theory, 70, 81–83
CSOs. *See* civil society organizations (CSOs)
Culp, J.M., 6
cultural relativism, 242
customary justice, 312, 313, 315–17, 320, 323, 324, 327, 328, 393
customary tenure, 192, 218, 220
Cyanzayire, Aloysie, 142

Dankwa, Vitor, 61
David Maraga, C.J., 126
Dawuni, J., 118, 121, 142, 143, 200
decolonial feminist theoretical approach, 21
deconstruction of race, 12
Decree-Law 33/75 of October 16, 54
Decree-Law 58/81 of June 20, 1981, 56
Decree-Law 69/76 of July 3, 1976, 56
Decree-Law 71/76 of July 24, 1976, 57
Decree-Law 84/76 of September 25, 1976, 56
Decree-law no. 42/1988 of October 27, 1988, 288
De Klerk, S., 249
Del Ponte, Carla, 43
demarginalizing the intersection of race and sex, 5
De Meijere, J., 220
Denning, Lord Thompson, 197
Department of Cooperative Governance and Traditional Affairs, 354
De Sousa Santos, B., 67n2
De Vos, P., 168

Dieng, Adama, 60
difference theories, 70, 71, 83, 84
Digest of old Ethiopian Judgments, 72
dispute-management forums, Msinga, 364–66, 368
Diye, J., 8
Diye, Jeremie, 393
Domestic Relations Bill, 191
Douglas, William O. (Justice), 204
dualist legal system, 234n4
dual judicial system, 74
Duarte, Vera (Justice), 18, 67n3, 383, 384; in Cape Verde judiciary and human rights institutions, 57–61; human rights activism, 64; personal journey to law, 51–53; Tchicaya Tam'si 2001 African Poetry Prize, 65; themes of violence against women, 65; women's rights in Cape Verde, 56–57
Dusabemariya Illuminata v. Sikubwabo Theodomir (1993) case, 288

ecofeminism, 262
Ecole Nationale d'Administration in 1965, 36, 40
Economic Community of West African States (ECOWAS) Community Court of Justice (ECCJ), 63, 269–71
Egyptian Feminist Union, 97
Egyptian judiciary: 1995 Beijing declaration, 95; Administrative Courts, 98; Administrative Prosecution Authority (APA), 99; Anti-Discrimination Commission Law, 110; Article 2 of the 1971 Constitution, 11; Article 53 of the Constitution, 111; Civil Law system, 97; courts and judicial structure, *98*, 98–99; Courts of Appeal, 97; Courts of Cassation, 97–98; Courts of First Instance, 97; discrimination, 96; Division Commission's report, 107; Egyptian Feminist Union, 97; Egyptian State Lawsuits Authority (ESLA), 99, 101; Egyptian women in, 99–104; gender-awareness campaign, 112; gender issues and rights, 111; *#HerHonorSettingTheBar*, 105–11, 114n18; host conferences and judicial exchange programs, 112; legal profession, 96; national and international legal rules, 104–5; Ottoman province, 97; Presidential Decree No. 356, 106; Public Prosecution, 98–99; State Council (Administrative Judiciary), 98; Supreme Constitutional Court (CSS), 99; tenacious feminine opposition, 96; unconstitutionality of Article 186-2, 107; Women's Empowerment National Strategy 2017, 108
Egyptian State Lawsuits Authority (ESLA), 99, 101
Ekhator, E.O., 19
Electoral Act of 2014, 248
Ellett, R., 13, 17, 384
El-Sisi, Abd El-Fattah, 110
Emmanuel, Dekane, 316
Enventresamare, 348n22
Environmental Rights Action, 268
equal, progressive, and empowering training of legal practitioners and judicial officers, 181
"equality is equity" principle, 230, 231, 232
Escobar-Lemmon, M., 142, 145
ethical relativism, 313, 314
Ethiopia, women judges: 1960 Civil Code of Ethiopia, 72; 1995 Constitution, 74, 88; Addis Ababa City Courts, 75; Amended Proclamation No. 684/2010, 79; Appellate Court, 75; Articles 11–15, 25, and 29 of the Federal Courts Proclamation No. 1234/2021, 76; biased societal perceptions, 86; cardinal principle, 78; change in workplace culture, 82; City

Courts, 75; civil and common law systems, 71; common law system, 72; continental legal system, 72; critical mass theory, 70, 81–83; Customary Courts, 74–75; difference theories, 70, 71, 83, 84; diverse and individual lived experiences, 88–89; documentary sources, 70; dual judicial system, 74; education policy, 81; family–work–social life balance, 85–86; fast-tracking system, 74; Federal Civil Servants Proclamation no. 1064/2017, 87; Federal Democratic Republic of Ethiopia (FDRE), 72, 78; Federal First Instance Court, 75, 80; Federal High Court, 75; Federal Supreme Court, 74, 75; "gender bias and few times harassment," 88; gender disparity, 80; gender distribution of judges, 76–78, *77*; gender-equitable judicial outcomes, 83; gender representation and diversity, 89–90; gender-sensitive judicial outcomes, 82; historical overview, 71–74; House of the Federation (HoF), 73; individual independence of judges, 78; intersectional identity, 87–88; Judicial Administration Council (JAC), 78, 79, 91n 2; judicial appointment process, 69; judicial legitimacy, 83; *Negarit Gazata*, 73; open-ended survey, 70; patriarchal rules and interpretations, 81; pluralism, 72; proclamations, 73; regulations and directives, 73; Religious Courts, 74; Sharia courts, 75; Social Courts, 75; State judicial power, 75; structure of Federal courts, 76, *76*; three-step appointment process for Regional (State) Court Judges, 78–80, *79*; trickle-up hypothesis, 77; unconscious bias, 87; work environment, 88; work ethics and societal perceptions, 84
Eunita Anyango Geko & Another v. Philip Obungu Orinda case, 2013, 123
European Christianity, 246
Évora, Teresa, female Judge of Instancia, 59
Ezielo, Joy, 347n17

Federal Civil Servants Proclamation no. 1064/2017, 87
Federal Democratic Republic of Ethiopia (FDRE), 72, 78
Federal First Instance Court, Ethiopia, 75
Federal High Court, Ethiopia, 75
Federal Sharia Court, 14
Federal Supreme Court, Ethiopia, 74, 75
Federation of Ogoni Women's Association, 264
Federation of Women Lawyers of Kenya (FIDA) & Others v. Attorney General & another case, *2011*, 127, 129
feminism as a *movement*, 360
feminist decoloniality, 7–9
feminist intersectional framework, 383
Fernandes, César, 53
Fetha Nagast, 71
Fineman, Martha, 244, 245
Fonseca, Jorge Carlos, 62
Fonseca, Lígia, 62
Fox, R., 140, 143
French Civil Code system, 53–54
French colonial administrators, 327
French courts, 32

Gadalla, Omnia Taher, 14, 384
Gage, B.G., 5, 18, 384
Gatera Johnson v. Kabarisa Teddy (2011) case, 295, 296
gender, definition, 241
gender-based realities, 9
gender-based violence (GBV), 246

gender diversification, 355
gender diversity, 21, 85, 90, 142, 161, 167, 175, 393
gendered insensitivity, 162, 179
Gender Equality Act (2014), 148
gender identity, 11
gender inequity, 383
gender justice, 8
gender-sensitive institutional culture, 383
gender transformation, South Africa judiciary: acting appointment guidelines, 182; acting appointments, 180; acting judicial appointments, 162; composition of JSC, 182; engagement and consultation with NGOs and legal bodies, 182; equal, progressive, and empowering training of legal practitioners and judicial officers, 181; equitable work allocation, 162; mentorship, 181; oppression and discrimination, 165; Section 174 of the Constitution (merit provision), 163–71; spirit, purport, and values, 180; women's challenges, 182–83; work allocation, 180–81
General Oil Limited v. Oduntan, 267
genesis of gender, 11
Ghana, women's right to property: 1992 Constitution of Ghana, 223, 227, 228; African Commission on Human and Peoples' Rights, 226; agricultural production, 222; ancestral property, 221; Article 14 of the African Charter, 225; Article 17 of the UDHR (1948), 224; Article 18(3) of the African Charter, 225; Article 21 of the protocol, 225; Article 22 of the Constitution, 222–23, 228, 230; Article 36(8) of the 1992 Constitution of Ghana, 216; Article 267 of the 1992 Constitution, 220; Article 295(1) of the 1992 Constitution, 233n1; colonialism, 220, 221; communal ownership, 221; customary law in land governance, 216, 217, 224–26; customary tenure, 220, 221; doctrine of "substantial contribution," 230; dualist legal system, 234n4; earned property, 221; "equality is equity" principle, 230, 231, 232; gender and kinship relations, 221, 222; human rights-based approach, 216; individualized ownership, 221; institutional arrangements, 219; international and regional treaties, 224; International Covenant on Civil and Political Rights (ICCPR), 224–26; International Covenant on Economic, Social and Cultural Rights (ICESCR), 224, 226; international development agendas, 218; jurisprudence and legislation, 232; Land Act of 2020 (Act 1036), 219, 227; land ownership, 218–21; Lands Commission, 216, 217; land tenure, 217–19, 222; Maputo Protocol, 226; matrilineal inheritance system, 222; Matrimonial Causes Act of 1971 (Act 367), 228, 230; patrilineal inheritance system, 222; Property Rights of Spouses Bill, 228; self-acquired property, 223; sociocultural norms, 218; statutory tenure systems, 219; substantial contribution, 230; Target 5A, 218; tenure insecurity, 217; tenure security, 217; Universal Declaration of Human Rights (UDHR), 224; women and gendered land tenure systems and legislation, 217
Ghana Shared Growth and Development Agenda II (2014–2017), 218
Gibson, Mavis (Judge), 253
Gilbert, J., 215
Gladys Mensah v. Stephen Mensah case, 231, 232
Gleeson (Chief Justice), 164

global feminist solidarity, 7
global women's emancipation movement, 64
Gluckman, Max, 244
Goliath, Patricia (DJP), 171, 173, 180, 184n4
Gomes, Maria das Dores, 61
Government of the Republic of Namibia v. LM and Others (SA-2012/49) [2014] NASC 19 (SC) (November 3, 2014)) case, 243
Green Belt Movement in 1977, 263
Grossman, N., 167
Gumede (born Shange) v. President of the Republic of South Africa and Others (CCT 50/08) [2008] ZACC 23; 2009 (3) BCLR 243 (CC); 2009 (3) SA 152 (CC) (December 8, 2008), 357

Habiyakare v. Gahongayire (2017) case, 292
Hammadi, 36
Henry, Nadia, 109
Her Honor Setting The Bar, 105–11, 114n18
Himonga, C., 7
House of the Federation (HoF), 73
Hugo, Victor, 52
Hunter, R., 12

Ige, Tokumbo, 60
Ikelegbe, A., 265
Indigenate Statute, 54
inheritance-related disagreements, 372
intercategorical complexity, 6
interlocking and overlapping challenges, 4, 382
Intermediate Court of Gasabo, 294
International Association of Women Judges, 2017, 151
International Commission of Jurists (ICJ), 59, 60
International Covenant on Civil and Political Rights (ICCPR), 224
International Covenant on Economic, Social and Cultural Rights (ICESCR), 224
International Federation of Women in Legal Careers, 60
intersecting challenges, 4
intersectionality: anticategorical complexity, 6; anti-essentialism, 6; beyond borders of U.S. Black feminist circles, 9; of Black feminist scholars, 5; in customary marriages, 7; definition, 5; ethnic identity, 7; global issues, 12; intercategorical complexity, 6; intracategorical complexity, 6; layered intersectionality, *10*, 10–11; in South African context, 6–8; U.S. feminist critical theory, 6
intestacy, definition, 333
intracategorical complexity, 6
Iyer, S., 142

Jatua v. Bali (2013) case, 348n23
Jensen, J., 144, 152
Jensen, W., 144
Johnson, R.E., 120
José Miguel Duarte Martins, 64
JSC Act, 1994, 128, 179, 185n21
Judicial Administration Council (JAC), 78, 79, 91n 2
judicial leadership, 15
Judicial Service Act (JSA), 127
Judicial Service Commission (JSC), 119, 125, 127–31, 142
Julius Rwabinumi v. Hope Bahimbisomwe, Civil Appeal No. 30 of 2009, 196
justice, definition, 311
Justice Vision 2000, 181

Kabaka (King) of Buganda, 189
Kadhi courts, 14
Kagwenyonga v. the sons of Rwubusisi (1956) case, 298

Kajeneza Beatrice v. Bigimba Akinyana Nadege (2018) case, 301
Kamatali, J.M., 143, 155
Kamau, W., 142, 144
Kang, A., 118, 121, 143, 200
Kariseb, Kennedy, 20, 381
Kashela, Agnes, 251
Katureebe, Bart (Justice), 201
Kenney, S.J., 124, 145, 197
Kenya's 2010 Constitution, 145
Kenya judiciary: alleged offense, 124; Article 27(8) of the Constitution, 119, 128; Article 166(3) of the Constitution, 124, 129; Article 172(2) (b) of the Constitution, 127, 128, 131; fail and explain approach, 130; female judges, role and limitations, 121–26; *FIDA* and *NGEC* cases, 129; gender composition, 119, 127, 129; gender equality, 117, 118, 122, 123, 126–30; gender quotas, 119–21; institutional norms and policies, 17; Judicial Service Commission (JSC), 119, 125, 127–31; principle of intersectionality, 129, 130; promulgation of Constitution of Kenya (CoK), 117; two-thirds gender rule, 117, 127, 128, 131
Kgomo (Judge), 179, 180
Khalil, A., 104
Khalil, Sanaa (Judge), 109
Kihan community, 338
Kikonyogo, Mukasa (Justice), 195
Kiobel v. Royal Dutch Petroleum Co., 271, 275n3
Kisaakye, Esther (Justice), 196, 203
Klibi, S., 14
Koome, Martha (Justice), 125, 126
Koranic law, 33
Kriegler, Johann (Judge), 164
Kuenyehia, A., 223

Lacey, N., 356, 361
Lady Justice Kalpana H. Rawal & 2 others v. Judicial Service Commission & 6 Others case, *2016*, 125
Land Act of 2020 (Act 1036), 219, 227
land ownership, 218; customary ownership, 219; split ownership, 219; state ownership, 219
land rights, 215
Lands Commission, 216, 217
land tenure, 217
Lawal, Vicki, 393
Lawal, Vicky, 8, 21
Lawless, J., 140, 143
Law no. 22/1999, 290
law no. 59/2008 Preventing and Punishing Gender-Based Violence (GBV Law), 294
Law on the State Political Organization (LOPE), 53
layered intersectionality, *10*, 10–11
Leeuw, M. (Judge president), 183n3
legal anthropology, 243
legal pluralism, 8
legal tradition, 16, *16*
Lima, Sofia, 62
Lindbekk, M., 14
Lisbon-based North-South Center of the Council of Europe, 60
LM & Others v. Government of the Republic of Namibia (I 1603/2008 I 3518/2008 I 3007/2008) [2012] NAHC 211 (July 30, 2012) case, 252
L.N.W. v. Attorney-General & 3 Others case, *2016*, 122
Local Authorities Act 23 of 1992, 251
Locke, John, 244
locus standi principle, 273
locus standi proof, 267
Lugayizi, Timothy (Justice), 196
Lugones, M., 7

Maathai, Wangari, 263
Machel, Samora, 58
Magna law, 55
mahakmas, 32
Mahomed, Ismail, 170
Maitum, Mary, 191

Malawi School Certificate Education examination, 147
Malawi's women lawyers: appointment process. *See* appointment of women judges in Malawi; Ellett's analysis of women judges, 17; formal selection mechanisms, 155; gendered dynamics, 140; hostile masculine environment, 143; insider-outsider collaboration, 143, 155; lives and biographies of judicial candidates, 145; proliferation and democratization of media, 145; recruitment processes, 145; selection mechanisms for judges, 141; seniority principle, 143; structural and sociocultural obstacles, 155; structural barriers, 154; structural obstacles, 139; transparent appointment systems, 141
Maliki rite, 32
Malleson, K., 143, 150, 151, 200
Mandela, Nelson, 60
Maphumulo, S., 186n34
Maputo Protocol, 60, 61, 148, 381, 384; Ghana, 226; Namibia judiciary, making and unmaking of gender, 249; Nigeria, women and environmental justice issues, 269, 270
Marilyn Muthoni Kamaru & 2 Others v. Attorney General & Another case, *2016*, 128
Married Persons Equality Act, 1996, 248
Martinek, W., 152
Marxist feminists, 13
Mary Sunday v. Federal Republic of Nigeria ECW/CCJ/JUD/11/18, 275n2
Mary Wanjuhi Muigai v. The Attorney General & Another case, *2015*, 123
Masengu, T., 142, 143, 145, 150, 151, 164, 167, 176
Matembe, Miria, 191
Matheka, Teresia (Justice), 123
matrilineal inheritance system, 222
Matrimonial Causes Act of 1971 (Act 367), 228, 230
In the Matter of JOO v. The Attorney General & 6 Others case, *2018*, 123
In the Matter of the Principle of Gender Representation in the National Assembly and the Senate case, 2012, 122, 128, 131
Maya, M., 167, 171
Mayelane v. Ngwenyama and Another (CCT 57/12) [2013] ZACC 14; 2013 (4) SA 415 (CC); 2013 (8) BCLR 918 (CC) (30 May 2013), 357
Mbabanjimana J. B. v. Ntaganzwa Charles (2017) case, 301
Mbendera (Justice), 151
Mbote, P.K., 126
Mbuzini: constitutional rights, 361, 371; ethnographic research, 360; female councilors, 361, 363, 369; gender sensitivity, 362; inheritance-related disagreements, 372; internal contestation, 362; maintenance claim, 357; sageness and authority, 363; unemployment, 359; village-level council, 361; women's roles in dispute-management forums, 369
McCall, L., 6
Medina, Raquel, 63
medjles, 32
Mends, T.M., 220
Mensah v. Mensah case, 230
Meroka-Mutua, A., 123, 384
Michelson, E., 142
microactivism, 356
Mjali, Nozuko (Judge), 179
Mlambo, Dunstan (Judge), 172
Mocumie, Baratang Constance, 5, 19
Mogoeng (Chief Justice), 165
Mohanty, Chandra, 355, 356
Mojekwu v. Ejikeme case, 269
Mojekwu v. Iwuchukwu case, 343
Mokgohloa, Fikile (DJP), 173

Monaghan, K., 119
Monteiro, António Mascarenhas, 60
Moore, E., 7
Morsy, Maya, 109
Movement for Democracy (MPD) in 1991, 54
Movement for the Survival of the Ogoni People (MOSOP), 264
Mpumalanga province, 359
Mrs Rwigema Josephine v. ECOBANK RWANDA SA (2013), 291
Msinga: dispute-management forums, 364–66, 368, 370, 374; ethnographic research, 360; *ibandla lenkosi*, participation in, 367, 370; interpersonal violence, 359; monetary compensation, 364; official polygamy rates, 364; postdoctoral study, 359; sexual harassment, 369; unemployment, 359; village-level traditional council, 364; women's overinvolvement in spreading rumors or lies, 366
Msosa, Anastasia, 146, 148
Mudug Region Peace Agreement, 266
Mugambe, Lydia (Justice), 196
Muhwezi, Jim (Maj. General), 197
Mujawamariya and others v. Bank of Kigali Ltd (2016) case, 291
Mukagasana Domitile v. Sarushi (2009) case, 299
Mukamuligo Alphonsine v. Rwabahashi François case, 298
Mukamusoni v. Buyitare (1985) case, 298, 299
Mukamusoni v. Mukagasana case, 299
Mukankusi Nadia v. Mbyayingabo Issa (2011) case, 294
Mukansanga v. Umutoni and Others (2014) case, 300
Mukansoro Monique (2015) case, 301
Mukarepubulika F. v. Hakizimana Viateur (2009) case, 293
Mukarugendo v. Munyaziboneye (1987) case, 288
Mukasa-Kikonyogo, Laeticia (Justice), 199
Mukula, Mike (Captain), 197
Munir, L., 265, 271, 274
Murungi, Annerita, 384
Museveni, Yoweri, 194
Muslim dominant countries, 14
Musoke, Elizabeth (Justice), 196
Mutoni Jackline v. Niwenshuti (2017) case, 295
Mutunga, Willy (chief justice), 122
Muwanga v. Kintu, High Court Divorce Appeal No. 135 of 1997, 196
Mwikya, K.K., 270
Mwilu, Philomena (Justice), 125
Mwondha, Faith (Justice), 197
Myburgh v. Commercial Bank of Namibia [2000] NR 255 (SC) (December 8, 2000) case, 243, 249

Naima Al-Ayoubi, 96
Namibia judiciary, making and unmaking of gender: Article 10, 247; Article 23(2) and (3), 247; Article 95(a) of the Constitution, 248; Article 100 of the Constitution, 252; assignment of roles and responsibilities, 249; Black women, 247; cardinal constitutional provisions, 250; cautionary rule, 250, 251; chilling effect, 254; colonialism, 242; Combating of Domestic Violence Act, 2003, 248; Combating of Rape Act, 2000, 248; common law rule, 249; Communal Land Reform Act 5 of 2002, 248, 251; Convention on the Elimination of All Forms of Discrimination Against Women (CEDAW), 249; cultural relativism, 242; doctrinal approach, 243; Electoral Act of 2014, 248; equal and inalienable rights, 247; equitably gendered, 242; feminist studies, 244; gender-based violence (GBV), 246, 250; gender-

responsive legislative framework, 20, 253; imperialism, 242; inherent dignity, 247; legal-anthropological approach, 243; legal interventions, 247; legal pluralism and cultural relativism, 20; legislative affirmative action, 248; Local Authorities Act 23 of 1992, 251; Maputo Protocol, 249; Married Persons Equality Act, 1996, 248; minor women, litigation purposes, 250; new judicial system, 253; political empowerment of women, 248; postindependence decisions, 243; sexual offense cases, 250; Social Security Act, 1994, 248; Sports Act of 2003, 248; Traditional Authorities Act of 2002, 248; violence against women (VAW), 244–46; vulnerability theory, 244–46
Nash, J.C., 9
National Action Plan for Human Rights and Citizenship, 61
National Association of Women Judges Uganda (NAWJU), 205, 206
The National Council for Women, 2017, 110
National Development Planning Commission of Ghana, 2015, 218
National Environment Act of 2019, 273
National Gender & Equality Commission & Another v. Judicial Service Commission & 2 Others case, *2017*, 128, 129
National Institute of Magistracy, 35
Native Administration Amendment Act 21 of 1943, 357
Ndagire, Josephine, 4, 13, 18
Ndulo, M., 324
Ndvunankulu, 371–73
Negarit Gazata, 73
Nenquimo, Nemonte, 274
neocolonial capitalist systems, 7
Ness Tengwe Slwandala violations: fines and repairs, 320–21; resolving and management, 320–23; summoning and banishment, 321–23
Neves, José Maria, 61
Ng'khansela, Make, 361, 362, 371–73
Ngcobo, Sandile (Justice), 346
Ngoepe, B.M., 164
Ngugi, Mumbi (Justice), 122
Nigeria, women and environmental justice issues: African Court on Human and Peoples' Rights, 274; civil society organizations (CSOs), 267, 268, 271, 273; doctrinal legal research, 260; ecofeminism, 262; environmental justice doctrine and movement, 261–63; gender-sensitive analysis, 260; litigation in domestic courts, 267–68; litigation in foreign jurisdictions, 271–72; litigation in subregional and regional courts, 268–71; Maputo Protocol, 269; monetary compensation of women, 273; nongovernmental organizations (NGOs), 273, 274; *Ogiek* case, 274; oil and gas pollution-related cases, 267; oil MNCs in Niger Delta, 263; oil pollution, Shell Oil Company, 263; Pearce Committee, 260; reform-oriented research, 260; socio-legal research, 260; state-sanctioned discriminatory practices, 272; United Nations Environment Programme 2011, 263; women-led protests, Niger Delta, 264–66
Njuba, Gertrude, 191
Non-Aligned Movement, 58
North-South Human Rights Award, 65
Nuno Miguel Duarte Martins, 64
Nyamu-Musembi, C., 8, 356
Nyiramutarama Ferdinand v. Kamanutsi Mathieu (2018) case, 294, 296
Nyirenda, Andrew (Justice), 148
Nyombayire Alexandre v. Nyiracumi Yolanda (2014) case, 292

O'Connor, Sandra Day, 59

O'Regan, K., 167
Obani, P., 19
The Observer in United Kingdom, 58
Ofei-Aboagye, 223
Ogiek case, 274
Ojigho, O., 270
Okafor, O.C., 267
Okoth-Ogendo, Hwo, 325
Olivier, B., 165
Ollenu (Justice), 229
Oloka-Onyango, J., 8, 226
organic law 12-03, 31, 32
Organic law no. 08/2005 of July 14, 2005, 287
Oshionebo, E., 264
Otis, Ghislain, 344
Otsuka, K., 221
Owinyi-Dollo, Alfonse (Hon. Justice), 199, 203
Oyěwùmí, O., 11, 266

Parity Bill, 63
patriarchal cultures, 15
patriarchal judicial system, 242
patrilineal inheritance system, 222
patrimonial rights of women in informal marriages: Article 17 of the 2003 Constitution of the Republic of Rwanda, 293; Article 20, paragraph 3 of law no. 27/2016, 293; Article 166 of law no. 32/2016, 293; concept of "family," 294; Intermediate Court of Gasabo, 294; law no. 59/2008 Preventing and Punishing Gender-Based Violence (GBV Law), 294; revolutionary judicial protection, 295–97
Pearce Committee, 260
Pires, Pedro, 58
Plateau State Wills Law, 342
Podgorny, M., 122
Podoko society, Mandara Mountains: absolutism, 314; adultery, 325, 326; African customary law, 326; *Blama*, 323; Chanock's analysis of customary law, 327; colonial administration, 328; crime perpetrators, 323; customary justice, 312, 315–16, 323, 327, 328; daily business, 312; ethical relativism, 313, 314; ethnic communities, 324; ethnic courts, 327; ethnicity, 330n5; feminist theory, 313; French colonial administrators, 327; indigenous land tenure systems, 312, 325; judicial actors, 316–18; land inheritance, 326; local law justice, 312; modern cultures, 312; modernization of traditional judicial structures, 327; multiculturalism, 314; neighborhood chiefs, 312, 314, 317, 318, 323, 324, 329n2; Ness Tengwe Slwandala violations, resolving and management, 320–23; oral sources, 314, 315; phallocratic community, 324, 325; queen's powers, 317; return or reimburse stolen goods, 323–24; social crimes, 318–19; theft, 319–20; traditional conflict resolution mechanisms, 328; witchcraft, 325; written sources, 314
policy recommendations for feminizing the judiciary: changing institutional mechanisms, 388; equal opportunities for employment and promotion, 386–87; gender-sensitive work environment, 387–88; international and regional actors, 388; support for women judges, 385–86; trainings, recruitment, and opportunities for leadership, 387
policy recommendations for pluralistic legal systems, 394–96
A Popular Justice in Cape Verde, 54
Principles and Guidelines on Economic, Social and Cultural Rights in the African Charter, 226
Problem of Discrimination against Indigenous Population (1987), 347n15

Property Rights of Spouses Bill, 228

Quartey v. Martey case, 229
Quartson v. Quartson case, 231, 232
Quaye, B.A., 231
Quisumbing, R.A., 221

racial politics, 12–13
Rackley, E., 166
Rateb, Aisha, 100, 113n4
Rawlings, Jerry, 58
RCA 0176/14/HC/KIG of February 27, 2015 case, 296
RCA00239/2016/HC/KIG of September 30, 2016 case, 296
RC/INCOST/SPEC 00002/2019/SC of December 4, 2019 case, 296
Rebbouh, Fettouma, 42
Re Estate of Francis Mwangi Mbaria (Deceased) case, 2018, 123
Religious Courts, Ethiopia, 74
repugnancy test, 190
right to land (property), 215, 218, 221
Rousseau, J.-J., 314
Rudahigwa, King Mutara, 298
Rukuba widows and children: Administration of Estate Laws, 344; BaCe, 336; Canadian Charter of Rights and Freedoms, 344; choice of marriage, 340–41; cultural and legal diversity protection, 344; cultural sensibilities, 334; customary law, 339–40, 345; customary practice, 337; discriminatory practices of inheritance, 345; farm work, 333; freedom of testamentary disposition, 342–43; historical sources, 336; illegitimate child, 341; Kihan community, 338; KuCe, 336; land control, 336; landholding rights of, 336; legal pluralism, 334, 335; legal scholarship, 335; legitimacy and legitimation, 341; nondisclosure interview, 337; proprietary rights, 345; research methods, 337; rules of living customary law, 346; Section 42(2) of the Constitution, 342; semi-structured interviews, 337; social realities, 334; statutory laws, 339; testacy and intestacy laws, 334, 338–40, 345
Rule of Law index 2020, 104
Rwanda: courts' protection of women's matrimonial rights after 1999, 290–93; courts' protection of women's matrimonial rights before 1999, 287–89; equality and nondiscrimination, 285; gender-neutral laws, 20; judicial protection of patrimonial rights of women in informal marriages, 293–97; judicial protection of women's inheritance rights, 298–302; matrimonial and inheritance rights, 20

Salim, Salim Ahmed, 60
Salubi v. Nwariaku (2003) case, 348n25
Santos, Leida, 62
Saudi Islamic *Sahwa* "awakening" movement, 113n7
Sebahutu Evariste v. Nikuze Primitive (1997) case, 289
Sebutinde, Julia (Justice), 195
Section 11(3)(b) of the Black Administration Act 38 of 1927, 357
Section 174 of the Constitution (merit provision), South Africa judiciary: academic qualifications, 165; appointment of judicial officers, 163; balanced decision-making process, 168; diversity/transformation provision, 163; ethnic/gender balance criterion, 164; Inclusive Interpretation of Section 174(1) and (2), 168–71; silk status, 163, 164; transformation/diversity clause, 166–68
Seignobos, Christian, 319
Sekitoleko, Victoria, 191
self-acquired property, 223

Selma, Belmihoub, 36
Semedo, Jaqueline, 62
separation of council *(bandla)*, 368
SERAC and CSER v. Nigeria case, 270
SERAP case judgment, 271
SERAP v. Federal Republic of Nigeria case, 270
Sharia courts, Ethiopia, 75
Sharia law, 30, 31, 43, 75
Shortell, C., 120, 142, 150
Sitati, Ruth (Justice), 123
Slotnick, E., 151
social construction of race, 12
Social Courts, Ethiopia, 75
Social Security Act, 1994, 248
socioeconomic standing, 13–14
Somalia, women judges, 14
Somani, A.A., 119
Sonneveld, N., 14
South Africa judiciary: acting appointments, 171–75, *174*; apartheid system, 15; balancing family life and judicial work, 178; dawn of democracy in 1994, 161; gender diversity, 161, 162, 167; gendered insensitivity, 179; gender equality, 118; gender transformation. *See* gender transformation, South Africa judiciary ; institutional racism, 15; inter alia gender equality, 161; judicial and legal profession, 161; legal narrative technique, 19; mentorship, 179–80; traditional gender participatory arrangements, 21; work allocation, 175–78
South African Chapter of the International Association of Women Judges (SAC-IAWJ), 172
Spill, R., 141
Sports Act of 2003, 248
spousal contribution to marital property, 196
The *State Party Reporting Guidelines for Economic, Social and Cultural Rights in the African Charter*, 226
state-sponsored traditional courts, 8
statutory tenure systems, 219
Steans, J., 242
Suba Customary Laws, 123
Sunni schools, 32
Sv. Katamba [1999] NASC 7 (SC) (December 7, 1999) case, 243, 251

Tahany El-Gebali (Judge), 102
Tamale, S., 8, 266
"tap on the shoulder" phenomenon, 150
Taskforce on Judicial Reforms, 2010, 126
Tebboune, Abdelmadjid, 44
tenure security, 217
testacy, definition, 333
Thabit, Munira, 97
Thornton, M., 163
three-step appointment process for Regional (State) Court Judges, 78, *79*
Tibatemwa-Ekirikubinza, Lillian (Justice), 195, 197, 203
tokenism, 122, 198
Traditional Authorities Act of 2002, 248
Traditional Courts Bill (B1D-2017), 354–55
Traditional Leadership and Governance Framework Act 41 of 2003 (TLGFA), 21, 354, 358, 363, 365, 368, 393
Tribunal of Conflict, 34
Tripoli program, 44
Tsekooko, Wilson (Hon. Justice), 201
Turner, T.E., 265, 266
"two-thirds" gender principle, 17

Uganda: 1900 Buganda Agreement, 189; affirmative action, 194; Anti-Corruption Court, 197; appointment processes, 193–94; Article 32 of Constitution, 191; Article 128 of Constitution, 193; Article 147(2) of Constitution, 193; Articles 142 and 144 of Constitution, 193, 194; Chief Magistrates Court, 192; Constitution

of Uganda 1995, 190; court structure, 192–93; Domestic Relations Bill, 191; emancipation process, 191; English legal system, features, 189; equality and gender parity clauses, 191; gender-sensitive approaches, 18; International Bar Association, 195; intersectional challenges, 13–14; judicial composition, 195; Judicial Officers Association, 201; Judicial Service Commission (JSC), 193, 194; Local Council Courts, 192; Northern Uganda Reconstruction Program, 203; Order-in-Council in 1902, 199; repugnancy test, 190; Uganda Constitutional Commission (UCC), 191; women-friendly policies, 190; women in public life, 190–92; women judges. *See* women judges, Uganda
Uganda Constitutional Commission (UCC), 191
Uganda Women's Network (UWONET), 205, 206
Ugochukwu, B., 267, 272
Unger, Nancy, 262
UN Habitat (2008), 215
United Nations Development Program (UNDP), 3
United Nations Environment Programme 2011, 263
Universal Declaration of Human Rights (UDHR), 224
UN Sustainable Development Goals (SDG's 2030), 95
U.S. feminist critical theory, 6
Usikpedo-Omoniye, C., 270
Uwera M. Louise v. Habyarimana Emanuel (2010) case, 292
Uwimana v. Sumbiri (1992) case, 288, 289
Uwiragiye Charles v. Uwamahoro Jeanine case, 296
Uzebu-Imarhiagbe, E., 15, 144

Valdini, M.E., 120, 142, 150
Vanderlinden, A.J., 72
violence against women (VAW), 244–46
vulnerability theory, 244–46

Waldron, J., 297
Washington Post in United States, 58
Washington Women's Network, 204
Whittal, J., 231
Wiwa v. Shell, 272
women judges, Uganda: "activist judges," 201–2; affirmative measures, 196, 206; Anti-Homosexuality Act in 2014, 202; 'cadre judges,' 200–201; cautionary rule in sexual offenses, 196; equal opportunities, 198; gender quotas, 206; gender-sensitive approach, 195; heads and deputies, 200; horizontal segregation, 199; independence and audacity, 197; internal selection processes, 204; judicial appointing bodies, 204; leadership positions, 198, 199, 206; maximalist approach, 202; National Association of Women Judges Uganda (NAWJU), 205, 206; "Performance Efficiency Audits," 201; policies and activism, 196; political affiliation, 199; recruitment and nomination process, 204; "sole women trail blazers," 200; spousal contribution to marital property, 196; tokenism, 198; Uganda Women's Network (UWONET), 205, 206; vertical segregation, 199; Washington Women's Network, 204
Women Lawyers Association of Malawi and the Women Judges Association of Malawi (WOJAM), 151
women-led protests, Niger Delta: Abeokuta women in 1948, 264; Federation of Ogoni Women's Association, 264; ground community protests, 265; memorandum of understanding (MOU), Ugborodo community, 265, 266; Movement for the Survival of the Ogoni People

(MOSOP), 264; Mudug Region Peace Agreement, 266; resource governance processes, 265
Women's Empowerment National Strategy 2017, 108
women's inheritance rights: exclusion of women from inheritance, 298; human rights-based approach, 298–99; insecurity of other rightful heirs, 301–2; law no. 22/199, 299, 300; law no. 27/2016, 300, 301; of surviving wife, 300–301
women's matrimonial rights after 1999: Articles 21–22 of law no. 22/199, 291; cancelation of mortgage contract, 291; community property structure, 290; joint management, 291; law no. 22/1999, 290–92; law no. 32/2016, 292; legal separation, 293; marriage annulment, 292, 293; matrimonial rights of spouses, 292; putative spouses, 293; sociocultural transformative tool, 291
women's matrimonial rights before 1999: 1988 Family Law Decree, 287; Colonial Charter of October 18, 1908, 287; Constitutions of 1962, 1978, and 1991, 287; Decree-law no. 42/1988 of October 27, 1988, 288; denial of women's matrimonial rights, 288–89; human rights-based approach, 289; Organic law no. 08/2005 of July 14, 2005, 287
women's right to property. *See* Ghana, women's right to property
Woodman, Gordon, 335
World Economic Forum, 2020, 104

Yaro, J.A., 234n3
Yeboah v. Yeboah case, 230

Zaidan v. Mohsons [1973], 347n17
Zeija, Flavian (Hon. Justice), 199
Zigha, Djamila, 39

About the Contributors

Maame Efua Addadzi-Koom is a lecturer of law at the Kwame Nkrumah University of Science and Technology, Kumasi, Ghana, where she teaches Constitutional Law, and Legal Writing and Study Skills. She is a PhD candidate at the University of Cape Town, South Africa. She is also the research and innovation lead at the Institute for African Women in Law (IAWL), Washington, DC, USA. Maame has been called to the Ghana Bar. She has published in the areas of International Law and International Human Rights; Constitutional Law; Women and the Law; and Law, Science, Technology, and Development.

Michael Addaney is an environmental social scientist whose expertise and current research interests are in the multifaceted and embedded relationships between humans and the environment, whether facilitated by institutions or by local organizations/communities, and the effects of this on public policy and planning processes and outcomes, particularly in relation to notions of rights, justice, and equity. More broadly, Michael's research interests include the social and human dimensions of global environmental change, environmental pollution and human health risks, and climate change interventions and socio-ecological systems in developing societies in Africa.

Rebecca Emiene Badejogbin is a lawyer and currently a director of Academics at the Nigerian Law School where she commenced her academic career in 2001. She holds an LLB and LLM from the University of Jos, Nigeria; an LLM (Research) from the University of Pretoria; and a PhD (Private Law) from the University of Cape Town, South Africa. Her research interests include court governance and judicial appointments at national and international courts, legal pluralism, and the legal profession/education and succession on which she has carried out extensive empirical and doctrinal research in Nigeria and South Africa and made presentations in national and international conferences and workshops. She has chaired and convened panels, and serves as an expert and trainer in her areas of research at regional and international forums. She currently sits on the board of an international organization that promotes justice education around the world. She has published in peer-reviewed journals and is the coauthor of *Law in Practice: Professional Responsibilities and Lawyering Skills in Nigeria.*

Samia Bourouba is a lecturer in International Law at the Faculty of Law Algiers University, associate professor at the Higher School of Magistracy and expert member of the Working Group on the Death Penalty, and Extrajudicial, Summary or Arbitrary Killings and enforced disappearances in Africa. She participated in several seminars and symposia, including the expert meeting on the draft protocol to the African charter on human and people's rights on the right to nationality and prevention and prohibition of statelessness, Tunis, April 8–10, 2015; the conference on "Global transformation toward gender equality and agenda 2030: A conversation about innovative approaches to break the cycle of violence against women," held in Mexico City, September 16–18, 2018. She is the author of many books and papers: Jurisprudence in the application of human rights standards in Arab courts, Algeria, Iraq, Jordan, Morocco, Palestine, RWI, 2012; Arab jurisprudence in the application of international conventions on the rights of women, Algeria, Iraq, Jordan, Lebanon, Morocco, Palestine, and Tunisia, RWI, 2016.

J. Jarpa Dawuni is an associate professor of Political Science at the Howard University. She is the founding director of the Howard University Center for Women, Gender and Global Leadership, and the founding director of the nonprofit Pan-African organization—the IAWL. She is the editor of *Gender, Judging and the Courts in Africa: Selected Cases* (Routledge, 2021), *International Courts and the African Woman Judge: Unveiled Narratives* (Routledge, 2018), and *Gender and the Judiciary in Africa: From Obscurity to Parity?* (Routledge, 2016).

Jeremie Diye is a Cameroonian by nationality. He is an associate professor in the Department of History at the University of Yaoundé I and the Department of Historical, Archaeological and Heritage Sciences at the University of Maroua. He is currently the chief of service for Education and Statistics at the University of Maroua. Prof Diye participates in international colloquia and is interested in issues related to intercommunity relations history, ethnicity, identity, conflicts, and peace building. Prof Diye authors several scientific papers, most recent of which are: Diye, J. (2021). "Boko Haram and the disruption of the agropastoral economy in the Mandara Mountains." In Revue Ivoirienne d'Histoire, no. 01, Vol. 36, pp. 195–214. Diye, J. and Nenkam, C. (2020). "Women and the culture of peace in the Mandara Mountains of the Far North and the Highlands of West Cameroon (XIXe-XXe siècles): cross-referenced views." In Lɔŋgbowu, Revue des Lettres, Langues et Sciences de l'Homme et de la Société, no. 010, Vol. 2, pp. 371–390. Diye J. et al (2021). "The use of kuley in resolving land disputes among the Mofu Cameroon." In Intégralité, Revue de développement holistique, vol 1, no. 3, Presses Universitaires de Mokolo (PUM), pp. 5–21.

Justice Vera Duarte, is a former justice of the Supreme Court of Cape Verde, a poet, and fiction writer. She graduated from the University of Lisbon, Portugal. She is a member of the Cape Verdean Academy of Writers, Academy of Science of Lisbon, among others. She is the recipient of several awards including an award for service from the president of the Republic ofCape Verde, the North Sud Human Rights award from the Council of Europa. Her poetry and novels include Amanhã Amadrugada, Arquipelago da Paixão, A Candidata Construindo a Utopia, APalavra e os Dias, A Matriarca uma estoria de mestiçagens, De risos e lagrimas, A Reinvenção do Mar, Cabo Verde um roteiro sentimental essay, Naranjas en el mar, Contos crepusculares, Desassossegos e Acalantos, A Venus, Crioula, Urdindo Palavras no Silencio dos Dias.

Eghosa O. Ekhator is a senior lecturer in law at the University of Derby, UK. He was previously a lecturer in law at the University of Chester. He holds a Master of Laws (LLM) and PhD in Law from the University of Hull. Eghosa has also been called to the Nigerian Bar as a barrister and solicitor of the Supreme Court of Nigeria. His main research areas include international environmental law, African international legal history, and natural resources governance. He has also published extensively on these research areas. Eghosa's academic papers have been cited by a plethora of organizations and international agencies, including the United Nations Refugee Agency and the Immigration and Refugee Board of Canada—"Responses to Information Requests (RIR) report (NGA106371.E) on Nigeria."

Rachel Ellett is a professor of Political Science at the Beloit College, where she is chair of the African Studies minor. Ellett has consulted for Freedom House on rule of law development in southern Africa. Ellett teaches courses in international and comparative politics, African studies, and women and politics. The author of *Pathways to Judicial Power in Transitional States* (Routledge, 2013) she studies comparative judicial politics, rule of law development, gender and judging, lawyers, and the state in sub-Saharan Africa.

She has published in *Comparative Politics*, *Journal of Law and Courts*, *Law and Social Inquiry*, *Journal of Political Science Education*, among others. She holds a PhD from the Northeastern University.

Omnia Taher Gadalla is an assistant lecturer at the Faculty of Law and Shari'a-Al-Azhar University (Commercial Law Department), founder of Her Honor Setting The Bar Initiative, and researcher at the Cambridge University. Holder of Master in Law from the Ain Shams University 2015 and Master in Law from the Al-Azhar University. Winner of Cambridge University Law Society Platinum Award 2022, Justitia Awards 2020, selected as Future Leader by the French Ministry of Foreign Affairs 2019, one of the top African Millennial by *PALM Magazine* in 2020, and one of the inspirational Egyptian women by the National Council of Women 2020. Former assistant lecturer at the AASMT—Egypt and former senior associate at Al-Feshawy & El-Shazly Law Firm, associate at Zulficar & Partners Law Firm, and others.

Biruh Gemeda Gage has over 10 years of professional experience practicing and studying law in Ethiopia. He specializes on trade law and policy issues, including Trade Competition, Consumers Protection, and International Trade Law with a focus on the AfCFTA agreement. Biruh is currently working as a trade policy adviser for GIZ, a German organization working in Ethiopia on behalf of the German Federal Ministry for Economic Cooperation and Development. Previously, Biruh served as a judge in the Administrative Court of the Federal Trade Competition and Consumers Protection Authority for five years. Prior to that, he worked as the coordinator—investigation and prosecution, consulted different organizations, participated in the drafting of various federal legislations, and gave trainings for stakeholders since 2012. Biruh has a Master's degree (LLM) in International Commercial and Trade Law from the University of Sussex and an LLB from the Hawassa University. He has also completed the coursework for an MA degree in Peace and Security Studies at the Institute for Peace and Security Studies, Addis Ababa University.

Kennedy Kariseb currently serves as a lecturer in the Department of Public and Procedural at the School of Law of the University of Namibia. He holds a doctorate in law from the University of Pretoria, South Africa. His research specialization and teaching focuses on international human rights and gender law.

Vicki Lawal is an associate professor of Library and Information Science at the University of Jos, Nigeria. Vicki Lawal holds a Masters degree in Law and Diplomacy from the University of Jos; a Master of Philosophy from the University of Cape Town, South Africa; and a PhD from the University of KwaZulu-Natal, South Africa. Among her areas of research interests are information literacy, human information behavior, information and communication technology, e-learning, legal education, and legal research and she has widely published in these areas.

Agnes Meroka-Mutua is a senior lecturer at the Faculty of Law, University of Nairobi. She is also a senior researcher at the Women's Economic Empowerment Hub, University of Nairobi. She holds a PhD in Law from the University of Warwick, School of Law. She is also the author of "A History without Women: The Emergence and Development of Subaltern Ideology on Land in Kenya." *Feminist Legal Studies*, DOI 10.1007/s10691-022-09488-4.

Baratang Constance Mocumie is a justice of the Supreme Court of Appeal, Republic of South Africa. She was nominated by the Chief Justice of the Republic of South Africa (the Republic) as The Hague Conference Primary Liaison Judge to represent the judiciary of the Republic on The Hague Convention matters and make submissions on behalf of the judiciary. She is a member of the Expert Group on Cross Border Family Law Agreements. She is a member and contributor (author of several chapters) of the Curriculum Development Committee of the South African Chapter of the International Association of Women Judges (SAC-IAWJ) responsible for developing the curriculum program for the SAC-IAWJ on topics, including Social Context, Ethics, Leadership, Family Law with special focus on Children's Hague Conventions (International Child Abduction, Child Support and Adoption); Trafficking in Persons (TIP). She is the former president and founding member of the SAC-IAWJ which represents judges and magistrates of the Republic on all matters on the transformation of the judiciary, including representation of the women judges in senior and leadership positions.

Annerita Murungi is an advocate of the High Court of Kenya. She is also a certified professional mediator—Accredited, Court Annexed Mediation (2018). She holds an LLB, an LLM, a Bachelor of Commerce (B-Com), and a Master of Business Administration—all from the University of Nairobi. She is currently the chief executive officer, HIV and AIDS Tribunal of Kenya. She is member of the Kenya Technical Working Group—HIV, TB, and Malaria. Annerita worked for the judiciary as an assistant administrator for over ten years, where she was first stationed at the High Court of Kenya, in Civil, Criminal, and Commercial Divisions, and then later at the Supreme Court of Kenya.

Stephen Muthoka Mutie (BEd First Class Honors, MA, PhD) is a feminist scholar, mentor, gender activist, and writer. He is a lecturer of Gender and Sexuality studies at the Kenyatta University, Kenya. Dr. Mutie has consulted for the IAWL on Women in Law and Leadership Project. He is a reviewer in the *East African Journal of Literary and Cultural Studies* (Taylor & Francis online) and a member of the IAWL Editorial Review Board. He is a member of the British Institute in East Africa and a double laureate (2018 and 2020/2021) of the Gender Institute of the Council for the Development of Social Science Research in Africa. Dr. Mutie has written and published on the intersection of politics, gender, and social media activism.

Josephine Ndagire is a lecturer in the Department of Public and Comparative Law at the School of Law, Makerere University and principal consultant, Grundstein Consult Ltd. Her expertise, research, and writing cover areas in criminal law, with a specific focus on the foundational and substantive principles in the Uganda context, international and transnational criminal law, human rights, as well as law and development. She was previously head of training at the International Nuremberg Principles Academy (Nuremberg, Germany), director Legal Services at the Foundation for Human Rights Initiative (Kampala, Uganda), senior researcher at the The Max Planck Institute for the Study of Crime, Security and Law (formerly the Max Planck Institute for Foreign and International Criminal Law) (Freiburg, Germany), and program officer for Africa at the IAWJ (Washington, DC, USA). Dr. Ndagire has published widely on criminal justice, gender, and human rights. She holds a doctorate in international legal studies from the Emory University (Georgia, USA) and a Master of Laws degree in international human rights law from the University of Notre Dame (Indiana, USA). She received her law degree from the Makerere University (Kampala, Uganda).

Pedi Obani is an associate professor in the School of Law, University of Bradford and a visiting research fellow in Water, Security, Policy, and Governance at the School of Politics and International Studies, University of Leeds. She is also an affiliate of the African Academy of Sciences and a senior fellow at the Edwin Clark University. Her research interests revolve around inclusive development and sustainability, especially the interactions between law and climate change, governance of water and other natural resources, and gender issues. In connection with this, she has authored several peer-reviewed publications; consulted for the public sector, NGOs, and international organizations; and received prestigious academic fellowships and research grants. Dr. Obani holds membership of professional associations, in addition to her active involvement in regional and international civil society networks. She sits on the Board of Directors of the Initiative for Equality and the Executive Council of the African Women Law Experts Network for the

IAWL. She is also a barrister and solicitor of the Supreme Court of Nigeria and was active in private law practice before starting her academic career.

Marie-Rose Turamwishimiye is a lecturer in the School of Law, University of Rwanda and serves as acting director of the Centre for Legal Aid and Mediation (CLAM) of the University of Rwanda. She holds a PhD in Public Law (Environmental Law) from the University of Cape Town, South Africa. She teaches Law of Persons (Family Law); International Labor Law; Legal Clinic; and Environmental, Energy, and Natural Resources Law. Her research interests include family law, domestic and international environmental law, biodiversity law, and international labor law. As director of CLAM, she provides direction and leadership of the center, coordinates legal aid provision activities, and coordinates students' supervision in the Module of Legal Clinic. She is the coauthor of "Implementing the Plant Treaty's multilateral system of access and benefit-sharing in Rwanda: Background analysis, recommendations and draft legal text for consideration, 2018, Bioversity International, Rome and Rwanda Agriculture Board, Kigali," available at https://www.bioversityinternational.org/fileadmin/user_upload/Implementing_Turamwishimiye_2018_new.pdf.

Odette Uwineza is an assistant lecturer at the School of Law, University of Rwanda and she is attached as supervisor of legal aid activities to the CLAM of the University of Rwanda. She holds an LLM in Private Law (Business Law) from the National University of Rwanda; Diploma in Legal Practice from the Institute for Legal Practice and Development (Nyanza Rwanda); Post Graduate Certificate in Teaching, Learning in Higher Institution from the College of Education/University of Rwanda; and practices as an advocate at the Rwanda Bar Association. She teaches family law, law of matrimonial regimes, liberalities and successions, law of insurance, and law of securities. She is the coauthor of "Rwandan family law, matrimonial regimes, family donations and successions." ISBN978-1-64786-260-2., 2020. She is the author of article "Consideration of the best interest of the child in divorce proceedings under Rwandan Family law: case law analysis" in *Rwanda Law Journal*, issue no. 2, November 2021.

Sindiso Mnisi Weeks is an associate professor of Public Policy of Excluded Populations, School for Global Inclusion and Social Development at the University of Massachusettes, Boston. She has has served as a senior researcher in the Centre for Law and Society at the University of Cape Town (UCT). In her role at UCT, she worked on the Rural Women's Action-Research program. This program combines research, advocacy, and policy work on women, property, and governing authority under customary law. She also taught African Customary Law as a senior lecturer in UCT's Department of Private Law. In 2013–2014, she was a resident scholar at the University of New Hampshire School of Law, where she held a fellowship for the completion of a book. Mnisi Weeks has published in academic and popular media on customary law, women's rights, cultural rights, governance, participatory democracy, dispute management, and the South African constitution. As a Rhodes Scholar at the University of Oxford, she researched the tensions between living customary law(s) and South African state law. Prior to Oxford, she clerked for the Deputy Chief Justice of the Constitutional Court of South Africa, Dikgang Moseneke. Her current work focuses on the pursuit of justice and human security in indigenous courts by poor women and men living in rural South Africa.

www.ingramcontent.com/pod-product-compliance
Ingram Content Group UK Ltd.
Pitfield, Milton Keynes, MK11 3LW, UK
UKHW041830031026
15587UKWH00002B/677

9 781793 632678